AF557794

THE *Assamese*

A PORTRAIT OF A COMMUNITY

SANGEETA BAROOAH PISHAROTY

ALEPH

ALEPH BOOK COMPANY
An independent publishing firm
promoted by *Rupa Publications India*

First published in India in 2023
by Aleph Book Company
7/16 Ansari Road, Daryaganj
New Delhi 110 002

ISBN: 978-93-91047-76-4

1 3 5 7 9 10 8 6 4 2

Printed in India.

THE
Assamese

To the late Mamoni Raisom Goswami who sowed in me the first seeds of curiosity for Assamese history and heritage....

MAHABAHU BRAHMAPUTRA

Where does spring come to its own?
By the banks of the Brahmaputra,
Isn't that so?

But have you wondered
What is the heritage
of the mighty Brahmaputra?

O Mahabahu Brahmaputra!
The abode of many a confluence.
For millennia,
It has illumined to mankind
The true import of assimilation.

The Baro Bhuyans arrived at its shores
From faraway Kannauj.
In that clan, on this land,
Sankardev was born.

From Persia came Azan Fakir,
Composed the melodious Jikir.
By its banks,
Dilvar from Delhi came too,
To draw the Hasti-Puthi here.
From the Land of Five Waters,
Appeared Guru Teg Bahadur,
To build a bridge of unity.
Sprouted many an example of union,
Mahabahu Brahmaputra.

Lachit fenced the enemy
At Saraighat itself.
Bound one and all,
In a veil of loyalty and patriotism,

Merging the lines of community,
Faith and tongue into one.

Son of the Kirata, Bishnu Rabha,
Enlivened the culture of the land,
Magnified the many facets
Of integration.

Swayed by the sweeps of River Padma,
Several reached the shores of Luit too.
O how many visitors
Have both the banks of Luit greeted!

Take some, give some,
Give and take,
To merge,
Open your arms, unite.
Open your hearts, give.
Tagore said so too.

It was here
that Jyotiprasad Agarwal had spread his light,
Botched the conspiracy
Of those who wouldn't merge!

Mahabahu Brahmaputra
O the abode of many a union,
For millennia,
The migrants continued to march to it.
Thus carving out a pilgrimage,
For assimilation.

From 'Mahabahu Brahmaputra', sung by Bhupen Hazarika*

*This is a loose translation of the popular Assamese song 'Mahabahu Brahmaputra' done by the author with help from Aruni Kashyap, a writer and translator from Assam and professor of creative writing at the University of Georgia, Athens, USA.

CONTENTS

FOREWORD

It has been my general experience that by and large, books in English released by national publishers on Northeast India have been few. This is even truer when it comes to the kind that puts a focused and firm lens on the history of the region, let alone linking it to its present. This vacuum is lately being addressed by publishers but more needs to be done, particularly by engaging and encouraging writers who have been experiencing this geo configuration and its people. Nothing like when people from the land tell their own stories.

There are certainly a few noteworthy works bringing out different dimensions of multiple communities and their sociopolitical and cultural lives in this part of the land. One such publication in recent times, very often referred to by the author of this book too, is the comprehensive history of the community penned by noted writer and former president of Asam Sahitya Sabha, Nagen Saikia, in Assamese which envelopes the source of the community, its multiple kingdoms, the diversity that enriches it while also throwing light on its cultural and material history. A portrait of the community in a language that can help non-Assamese readers to gather a perspective and understanding of the community, and thereby a swathe of the Northeast is definitely a welcome venture. The Assamese are undoubtedly the largest community of the region in terms of population.

Though there exists a well-received book, *The Assamese* by Audrey Cantile, since 1984, it is only an anthropological take on the community and, therefore, limited in its scope. The present portrait, however, attempts to cross that barrier and packs in a wide range of subjects to be able to draw an exhaustive pen picture of the community. The author deserves applause for putting in the effort; for weaving in quite a pile of information across myriad subjects that concern the community's past and present. The readers may expect to get an insider's narrative on the themes and their multi-directional trajectories by the author who was born and brought up in Assam.

The author aims at depicting the community to the outside world; it is a panoptic take, spanning from the possible birth of the state's name—Assam—to taking a peek at the constituents of the community, their rulers, their beliefs, food, weaves, jewellery, music, drama, dance, literature, and politics.

As stated by the author in the introduction, this book is not a definitive history of the community but it is certainly worth picking up if one is particularly looking for an ardent take on the Assamese and various hues of the community's life in a single book. To my mind, it is also timely as the section of youth in the state who are not acquainted with the community's history and related issues in the academic curriculum may get a holistic picture in this book. Additionally, the community's increasing diaspora, both within and outside the country, may like to bring this book to the notice of second generation Assamese youth to reconnect with the roots back home. During my presidentship at the Asam Sahitya Sabha, I made a sincere effort to set up a network of sorts to inspire and boost the popularization of Assamese language learning amongst the young ones residing outside the state and the country so as to speak and write the language, and develop a desire to know their community's history, folk tales, and literature.

It is appropriate to mention that putting together a book like this is no easy task; one cannot deny the possibilities of contentious issues cropping up here and there when you try to depict the life and living of a community, particularly so when it has a long historical journey over time and space, when you have a plethora of written commentary, inscriptions, and oral traditions enriching the community's arsenal. No such portrait is foolproof and beyond betterment; debates and discourses would definitely enrich it.

I am glad to extend this foreword to the book as this portrait can serve not just readers from outside the community but those from within too.

Dr Kuladhar Saikia
Guwahati
August 2023

INTRODUCTION

> 'Open your Mouth and let me check it myself.'
>
> When mother Yashoda demanded that of infant Krishna, he had to obey her.
>
> Peering inside his mouth, Yashoda gasped on seeing the entire universe in it: the stars and the planets, the hills and the dales, the land and the seas, all of yesterdays and tomorrows, the thoughts and sentiments of people in their home and hearth, the birds in the air, the animals in the bushes, the cows on the grass, the fruits hanging from the trees. Not a grain of gravel was missing. The immensity of the universe caught within the span of an infant's mouth was what captivated her.

As I wrote this book, this particular story that I had heard from my paternal grandmother in my childhood—retained somewhere in the web of my memory—kept returning to me. I thought of a universe that I was traversing, many parts of which I was oblivious to. Unearthing those parts became a journey, a learning, a joy, an overwhelming experience, and a challenge too.

In the course of writing this book, I asked myself: who am I when I say I am Assamese? What makes me Assamese? The language I speak, the culture I follow, my religion, or all of these things? What is my community's literature, food, and art like? Where lies the community's collective sense of piety and beliefs, the politics, its underbelly?

What is the wealth of collective heritage I carry in me; and also the baggage?

Who walked on the land by the Brahmaputra that I call home? Since when have we been here? Who were the royals of the community and where in our collective memories do they exist? And where are the memories of the common people, their daily lives, joys and sorrows? Do we find them in our literature, in people's conversations?

As a journalist, my method of enquiry into all these questions and more is primarily journalistic in this book. I have collated information through conversations with people, their lived experiences, which I have meshed with my own sense of growing up in Assamese society. I have also resorted to several books and research papers to drive home certain facts and arguments in the narrative.

While writing this book, I also sought to answer this question: what does an Assamese look like? Is there anything called an 'Axomiya look'? Does the physicality of a community lose its significance over time because it is bricked over by bouts of migration through the ages? Surely many a strain of human stock fused with each other by the Bor Luit, the Lauhitya, the Ti Lao, the Brahmaputra—call it what you may—to produce a set of people that populates a good stretch of Assam today.

So many questions and so many answers.

To my mind, the Assamese are a unique community within the Indian land mass simply because I can rarely spot any other which comprises both tribal and non-tribal subgroups with their respective microcultures strengthening the very fabric of the community. Politically, several smaller ethnic communities in Assam have gone on to assert their separate identity in due course of time; they have their own languages aside from speaking the lingua franca, Assamese. But culturally, the twain still binds all. The bond goes beyond the limits of language. Historically, too, they have fought the same enemies, celebrated the same festive occasions. After several centuries of co-living, no non-tribal Assamese aware of her culture can even think of locating a tribal person outside the pale of the larger community simply because the contribution of those smaller ethnic groups to the creation of the composite Assamese identity, their food, weaves, culture, sense of aesthetics, is immense and by now unbreakable. Even to the Assamese language, its word bank, the tribal influence is considerable.

The instances of such forging of the twain are all over. If the Bordoisila storm is Assamese, so is she a Bodo; if the dhuwa saang, the bamboo kitchen rack placed over the fireplace, is a non-tribal Assamese feature, so is it intrinsically tribal. If the red beads in the jewellery are non-tribal Assamese, so are they fundamentally tribal. Even in Sattriya, the Assamese classical dance, there are tinges of tribal dances. It is not for nothing the people who populated the banks of the Brahmaputra, tribal or non-tribal, came to be called khaar-khowa Axomiya (alkali-eating Assamese). If a dish prepared from the tender stalks of drumsticks is Assamese food, so is it utterly Adivasi (Tea Tribe). If poita bhaat is mainstream Assamese, so is it a prominent part of the food of the peasants of the East Bengal origin. These instances only go to show that sharing the land for a course of time leads to absorbing each other's culture, most times, unknowingly. Blending is necessary; it brings harmony, not hegemony.

Writing this book has also pushed me to step out of my comfort zone; to peer at what I didn't know, absorb it, and then reflect my learnings on to the pages before me. In the process, I became a student. No sooner had I started my research that the Covid-19 pandemic descended on us. Over a year went by. Libraries remained closed for most of this time. People were scared to meet people. Some conversations had to happen over the telephone or via e-mail. For a journalist to not be on the ground to gather inputs for her work was miserable. I felt utterly limited in my reach to write a tome of this sort. For a non-fiction work, the inability to access people and books, the freedom to travel at will became a huge handicap. Yet, the work must go on and so it did; the way it could.

The book is no way a complete story of the Assamese community, but a mere portrait of it. I can't even say that it is a complete portrait of how I see the community simply because I am so conscious of the fact that I have not delved deeper into many an aspect, good or bad, of the community; many a personality that I wished I could have given more space to. It would perhaps have then gone beyond its immediate brief too. Each chapter is worth a separate book anyway. Perhaps that is when a writer may be able to do justice to each topic the book has covered. In effect, each chapter is now just a gist of the complete story.

What came across during my research was also the framing of the community by the colonial masters as indolent because of their slow, content lifestyle. The Assamese lahe-lahe attitude began to be viewed akin to elehuwa or laziness; elaibadu or uselessness. Instead, it was a leisurely lifestyle tailored around the verdant nature the community was surrounded by; drawing from nature only what they needed. Dozens of Assamese sayings and idoms bear proof to a lifestyle hinged not on consumerism but on happiness with what one has in her backyard, the bari. Sadly, that colonial era construct gained weight after Independence when the community didn't quite show interest in competing with the rest of India in entrepreneurial ventures. For paucity of space, I couldn't accommodate a separate chapter on the lahe-lahe ethos of the community, which, to my mind, is no less than the Assamese version of the celebrated Japanese concept of ikigai.

At some places, I have used terms like Miya, Tea Tribe; it is only done with the aim of identifying a set of people with local terms and not to hurt any sentiments. Some archaic terms used for certain communities in colonial era may have been used in the narrative too only because they were unavoidable.

I have also used the Assamese velar fricative 'x' (xo) in some spellings to remind the reader that such a unique pronunciation is part of the community's rich linguistic history, even though we tend to often wipe it away with the English letter 's'. The pronunciation of 'xo' and 'so' are different in Assamese. I strongly feel that it is time this difference is acknowledged both within and outside the community while mentioning such Assamese words and names in English with 'xo' since it is proof of the language's uniqueness.

I have also taken the liberty of using the spelling Bhagawat to denote the Bhagawat of Sankardev based on the Assamese pronunciation, while referring to Bhagavad Purana and Bhagavad Gita with a 'd' as usually done elsewhere.

I am painfully aware of the fact that I have not been able to incorporate as many inputs I would have liked to from the state's tribal and other ethnic groups, which identify themselves as Assamese too, either linguistically or culturally; their histories, their tall leaders. A separate book on their contribution to Assam is urgently needed.

The rich culture of Assam's Barak Valley has been kept out of the pages simply because it is outside of the scope of the book.

Though I have tried to incorporate recent developments in most chapters, I have focused more on shining a light on the past rather than the present. Due to this I have been unable to include several contemporary names across various fields even though their work has made a difference to the community—my sincere apologies to them for this exclusion. I opted for this approach because I have become increasingly conscious that quite a few generations of Assamese, including mine, are today more cognizant of others' cultural mores and histories than that of their own. The education system in Assam in general has, over the decades, also facilitated this unlearning of what is our own. However, there is no denying that on the past stands the present, and so past must be in sight too. During my salad days in Delhi in the early 1990s, celebrated Assamese writer Indira Goswami (Mamoni Raisom Goswami), who used to teach at the University of Delhi then, had drilled this into my mind. She had frequently told me to talk to my non-Assamese friends in the capital city about Assam and Assamese history. Know your past, your culture to tell others about it; not from a point of hegemony but from the position of a person whose feet are on the ground, who is ready to appreciate better others' cultures and stories too, she would insist. Mamoni baidew had also often referred to the need to constantly keep the critical eye on one's own community in order to make it stronger than it is. Constructive criticism is something a community as a whole must be able to digest; self-introspection must be employed by any community that wants to grow with the times.

Here, I must also acknowledge that in 2019, noted Assam-based writer Mitra Phukan, had suggested to Pallavi Goswami, then of Aleph, that I might be able to deliver a portrait of the community. Mitra's confidence in me helped me carry on against many an odd that the pandemic threw at me during the writing of the book.

Heartfelt thanks must also be offered to all those domain experts who readily agreed to go through the draft of several chapters and offered their valuable suggestions and time to improve them. Thank you Naren Kalita, Moushumi Kandali, Bijit Barthakur, Areendom Borkataki, Sushanta Talukdar, Joi Barua, Ibsen Lal Baruah, Vandana Goswami, Rini Barman, Mallika Kandali, and Robhijita Gogoi, among several others. This book would not have been possible without all of you.

My deepest thanks to D'com Bhuyan, Sasanka Borua, Prasanta Bora, and Shankar Patowary for helping me find valuable and rare books and other materials which I couldn't have accessed otherwise due to the protracted lockdown. I also acknowledge my gratitude to Beda Dutta, Ajoy Pegu, and Jahnu Baruah from Majuli for facilitating conversations with several monastic heads of the Vaishnava Satras. Dhanmoni Das must be mentioned for ensuring that the pages of all the books that I wanted through the pandemic were delivered to me during the little window of access that I had to Gauhati University's library. Here, a word of acknowledgement must go to Akhil Ranjan Dutta for enabling access to the library. A thousand thanks to Kaustubh Deka of Dibrugarh University for always being ready to help out with anything I needed for the book.

My father Apurba Kumar Barooah needs a mention here for meticulously collecting for me any information on art and culture, politics and people that he thought might help my research during the very unusual times I was writing the book. Accessing his library which has a collection of many valuable old books also aided me greatly. My mother Punya Baruah's experience of growing up in an Assamese village in the 1950s and 1960s helped me understand certain cultural practices of the community better.

I thank each person who agreed to give me their definition of an Assamese for the book. In a state where politicians have been at the forefront of preaching what elements should define the community, it has been a contentious subject and yet, so many of them came forward with their opinion to be published in a book to save it for posterity. I deeply regret not being able to include a few more people's viewpoints in it simply because of the pandemic related travel restrictions. One such name is the noted Assamese and Karbi writer Rongbong Terang. By the time I finished the book, we also lost one such contributor to that segment—the noted writer and editor Homen Borgohain. I am glad that his valuable words to his community will remain alive through my book.

A word of sincere acknowledgment to writer and former Asam Sahitya Sabha president Kuladhar Saikia for agreeing to write a foreword to the book. I am so grateful for his kind words.

I am also thankful to several others who are not named here but went the extra mile whenever needed to help me find people and places during my multiple trips across Assam for this book amidst so many pandemic-related restrictions. Thank you Bapti for driving me through the state at short notice.

Thank you Mohit Beotra for not only providing a corner of quietude in your house while I went over the manuscript of the book unhindered but also for the moral support to steer through it.

Lastly, I must concede that I couldn't have been able to complete the book without my two pillars of support at home, my husband Mohan Pisharoty and daughter Omana. Since my daughter, and my niece Ahana Barooah Sahu, having grown up outside of Assam, have still not been able to pick up reading Assamese, I hope this book also helps them to discern their respective mothers' community, of which they too are a part. I also hope someday my two little nephews, Loi and Joi, and their generation also benefits from this book. Even though they live in Assam, their education, like several others from Assamese middle-class families today, is in English medium schools and is, therefore, largely limited in its understanding of Assamese language and history.

I present the book to its readers with a huge note of thanks to Kanika Praharaj for meticulously editing a very long narrative, and to Aleph for being generous enough to give me additional time to complete it. Any shortcoming in the book is only mine.

PROLOGUE

Aami Kun: Who Are We?

I carefully stepped on the lit glass floor of the high-rise that housed the Museum of Agriculture in Seoul, in the city's swish central district Jung-gu.

The floor was lit to attract visitors like me to a concrete platform dressed up as a wet field sprouting paddy on top of which stood a model of a farmer on the plough. I noted the bamboo hat with a wide rim placed on his head, so similar to the Assamese japi worn by our haluwa, farmers, in the field.

Tip-toeing over the glass floor covering the synthetic paddy field, I came across a makeshift hut with a thatched roof. On one corner of the hut stood a model of a woman using a tool that portrayed how Koreans in the olden times husked their rice. While one foot of the woman was shown pressing the grinder, the other foot was firmly on the ground; an arm rising to hold on to a rope hanging from the roof to keep balance while at work. What flashed before me was the childhood memory of my mother pounding rice on a similar instrument, a traditional Assamese rice grinder called dheki, at the onset of Rongali Bihu, the spring festival, to prepare til pitha, that cylindrical sweet filled with a mix made of black sesame and jaggery.

Dangling from an adjacent wall was a replica of the dola too, the traditional bamboo woven flat bowl used in households across Assam and the Northeast to clean rice before it's poured into a pot to boil. I noted the familiarity of surroundings and moved ahead, then spotted a specimen of another man at work, crafting what looked like a kaahor bati, a bell metal saucer, like the one many Assamese still use when eating the traditional snack jolpan.

Further on, the figure of another man was placed in what appeared to be a bazaar, peddling a kettle of fish, at once reminding me of a village haat back home.

Stepping out of the museum, I sat on a bench by the road. To my right was a flower bed covered with a circular bamboo lid that looked like a king-size Assamese bor japi. Using these japi like structures seemed to be the typical Korean method of protecting plants from the harsh winters.

I quickly recapped what I had just spotted at the museum. Wasn't that our dheki? The dola, the japi? So, the Koreans too used utensils made of bell metal, like the Ahom royals did in Assam?

Sitting on that bench in downtown Seoul on that windy afternoon, queries swirled my head.

Why such similarities? Is there a connection?

Aami kun? Who are we?

Where do the Assamese draw their roots from?

What encompasses our material culture? Whom all did we share it with—and also our physical features—from outside of India?

Which pages of Assam's history have been lost to the vagaries of time?

When I finally left that roadside bench, I seemed reassured that Assam is truly that Indian state where a tangible amalgamation between the extreme East—the South, Southeast, and East Asia—and the West, or say, Bengal onwards, had occurred. To understand Assam and Assamese culture, language, architecture, food, crafts, weaves, it becomes imperative then to look as much to its western border and the influences from mainland India as to its east because it is truly the gateway of India to South and East Asia.

Recognition of that reality that day had set me off on a journey of self discovery.

Poth Aru Pothik: Routes of Trade and Migration in Assam of Yore[1]

> K. P. Chattopadhya, in his book *Ancient Indian Cultural Contacts and Migration* mentioned the existence of a trade route between Korea and Iran that criss-crossed through China, Assam, North India, Pakistan, and Afghanistan. Another migratory route linked North India to Mongolia through China, which also passed by Assam. There have been traces of animal migration through these routes.
>
> Rajmohan Nath[2] has shown in his writings that there existed a route from Karnataka to the Brahmaputra Valley through Andhra Pradesh, Odisha, West Bengal, and North Bengal. Another path began in Karnataka and traversed through Maharashtra, Madhya Pradesh, Bihar, and Bengal and merged on to the other route near North Bengal. There was yet another passage that started in Tamil Nadu and touched this road in Andhra Pradesh. That route, in Madhya Pradesh, merged with a trading path that came all the way from Mongolia—navigating the Gobi Desert, Uzbekistan, Tazikistan, Kashmir, Punjab, Delhi, and Kannauj.

Yet another route carved out of Mongolia connected Uzbekistan through the Gobi Desert. The road swerved towards the Himalayas before reaching Tajikistan to open in Tibet. It extended to Assam through present-day Arunachal Pradesh. An arm of that road extended to Bhutan too. That road touched another international path which originated in Korea and snaked through China to emerge at Tibet, near Lhasa.

The road forked into two near Beijing; one section of it entered Assam through its north-eastern side. That path had begun in Guangzhou in South China, opened in Assam through Myanmar. A portion of the road also channelled in to Assam through Sadiya which borders today's Arunachal Pradesh. A section of the road passed by Mizoram and Manipur too. A road that came from Korea through China passed through Eastern Tibet to arrive at the Brahmaputra Valley through its south-eastern side.

These pathways that may have facilitated human migration highlight that movement of people to the Brahmaputra Valley of Assam may have occurred from Korea, Mongolia, China, Russia, Tibet, Thailand, Myanmar, Kashmir, Punjab, Delhi, Kannauj, other parts of Uttar Pradesh, Bihar, Bhutan, Sikkim, Nepal, Madhya Pradesh, East Maharashtra, Tamil Nadu, Karnataka, Andhra Pradesh, Odisha, and Bengal. A significant point to be added in this context is that when Bengal was still under the sea, people from a section of northern Gondwana, the dark-skinned Melid and the Vedic, may have stepped on to the Brahmaputra Valley from the East Sea from the southern front. The use of cowrie and the tradition till date—of tying cowrie and tiny snail shells around the neck of children for good luck—hint at a cultural practice of a sea-side civilization.

Where Do I Belong?

'Will you not want to share, ever your most intimate thoughts in your own language to the person you feel closest to? I mean, in Assamese?'

An elder cousin had tossed that question at me with all seriousness when I chose to marry outside of my community, to someone who didn't know Assamese, and would in all likelihood never speak it.

Her question was significant perhaps because I would live outside of Assam, like she had. Shouldn't Assamese, the language, then be the vehicle of my connection with my Assamese-ness?

For her, it was.

The Assamese language, for those whose mother tongue is Assamese, has been the pivot of their identity composition. Naturally then, I was raised in a milieu so Assamese that I only ever spoke my mother tongue at home and never experienced any major digression from the mainstream Assamese sociocultural life or the food habits. The khar, tenga, pitha, pitika variety formed the usual spread at the dining table.

I thought back to my past. I wore mekhela sador on my first day of college, like my mother did; broke into Bhupen Hazarika songs when joyous; harked back to his brother Jayanta's melancholy laced scores when pensive. My legs and arms moved almost unconsciously on catching a Bihu tune; hands folded in to a namaskar automatically on hearing a revered borgeet of the Vaishnava gurus Sankar–Madhav. The heart erupted with pride when the words of the cultural icon Bishnu Prasad Rava's song 'Nisola Ai Re, Aami Khati Axomiya' fall on my ears.

Munching black chickpeas and green gram with coconut slivers (praxad) collected by my mother from the neighbourhood naam-ghar during the holy month of Bhado, was the most natural thing to do on many an afternoon. During the community Durga Puja in my town, at the priest's nod, we would at once break into an ululation, the uruli. I also remember cycling down to a corner of my town with friends to the mazhaar, the mausoleum, of the unknown Sufi saint to place a candle and seek blessings a day before the school-leaving final examinations. A local ritual!

Many a cold night, I walked back home, content with noisy neighbours after watching Assamese Bhraymaman mobile theatre, dramatized under a huge tent pitched on a community-owned field, like most Assamese had done in the 1970s and 1980s. Ditto during the Bohagi Bidai, the musical adieu to Bohag, the season of spring beloved by every Assamese.

Would I then have to forego sharing with my life partner all those practices of a life lived in a small town Assam, just because I would never be able to relate them to him in my mother tongue, the language that had bound all those growing up experiences together?

What about the night before Bohag Bihu, always spent restively as we slept with Jetuka-coloured hands covered with cloth, conscious not to move an inch lest the wet paste left marks on the bed clothes? The morning after would pass by in deciding whose hands among the cousins had the brightest manifestation of the henna colours to be flaunted at the Bihu Xanmeelan. And those February days of Xaraswati Puja when teenage girls in Assam would relish their first taste of freedom, wearing adult clothes borrowed from their mothers' wardrobes! Every year, that day would end at the local photo studio to document the occasion in a group photograph with friends.

And, those memories of annual trips to my maternal grandmother's sprawling house in a village by River Dhansiri in Upper Assam to feast on Na-khuwa, the occasion to celebrate the arrival of the first harvest at the family bhoral, the granary!

Walking through my mother's xakoni bari, her kitchen garden, by the pukhuri, the pond at home bursting with fish; watching with alarm the high, reedy tamul (areca nut) trees around the house swaying perilously in the monsoon winds, the annual Bordoisila; the aroma of the seasonal xewali and bokul flowers speckled over the long pathway to home, even as the sky was filled with the red, pink, and yellow of Krishnasura, Radhasura, and Xunaru blooms; foraging through nearby fields with bortta, my father's elder brother, searching for herbs: manimuni, dhekia, bhedailota, brahmi, mosundari, maan dhonia—what about these lived experiences?

That day though, I didn't have much trouble answering my cousin with a no. However, often, in the last two decades, I have returned to her query. Essentially to dwell on what kind of an Assamese I am. Or have become. Or want to be perceived as? *Or, just be.*

Do I belong? Where do I belong? How much do I belong?

These questions, though, must be first asked of a broader locale because, unlike their western neighbour, the Assamese have always been home-bound. The alkaline-savouring, khaar-khowa Axomiya has never been traditionally known for going too far from the comfort of his home and hearth.

In pre-Independence India, quite a few batches of bright young men did hop on to Kolkata-bound steamers for higher studies, and further up to the United Kingdom, too, but only to return home at the end of their adventures. They went to Kolkata and beyond primarily because there was no scope for higher education in British-era Assam until the establishment of the Cotton College in Guwahati in 1901. That generation became a beacon of light for a community that had suddenly found itself at a massive disadvantage in a colonized circumstance—tied to mainland India for the first time as a mere arm of it, peripheral, with English and Bengali acting as markers of modernity and upward mobility, and as instruments of cultural domination too. The wisdom of a proud community that could successfully resist even the mighty Mughals—unlike in the rest of India—came to naught.

That generation of Kolkata-taught Axomiya young men sowed the first seeds of an educated middle class within the community, separate from the existing structure, the fount of which was the Ahom royals. That generation carved out a path for those at home on how to recover the fading Assamese pride and identity by hinging it on the Assamese language that was by then on the trail of being swallowed by the aggressive promotion of Bengali in Assam. The arrival of the printing press, sponsored by the Christian missionaries, came in handy to begin that fight.

Post-Independence, the trickle of bright young Assamese youth travelling for higher education—to Kolkata University, Vishwa Bharati, Banaras Hindu University, Allahabad University, and thereafter to the University of Delhi, and to the UK as well—remained a constant. Most continued to turn back home, though, after completing their studies. The Assamese diaspora has, therefore, remained relatively small.

It was only during the upheaval caused by the Assam Foreigners' Movement and the subsequent insurgency years (from the early 1980s to the 1990s) that the Assamese community saw a growing number of their youth travelling out of the state for education and employment. The trend was restricted among the fairly well-off at the time, though a bright youth or two from a lower middle-class Assamese family may also have made it by dint of their academic merit. In subsequent years, that tendency seeped into families which otherwise had few opportunities for social mobility in Assam. Many such families looked at enrolling their wards in short courses to wrest a quick 'diploma from Delhi' or Pune, Mumbai, or Bangalore, to be able to corner a mid-range job in those metros. The tendency to seek admission in paid-for engineering and MBBS seats in private institutions, mainly in Karnataka, had by then been noted widely across a socio-economic spectrum in Assamese society.

In the early 2000s, the trend of migrating to mainstream India has filtered further down to the most socially disadvantaged lot. Their land gobbled up by the recurring floods; their manual jobs affected by perennial bandhs or shut-downs by one angry group or the other; public educational institutions unable to give them a degree that can get them a job in a competitive arena, all these reasons have pushed out the youth from this section of the community, both tribal and non-tribal, to various metros in the mainland. Besides, the rampant corruption eating into the system of the state's public service further makes life miserable, particularly in the rural areas, which have anyway been facing the brunt of the draconian Armed Forces (Special Powers) Act for a long time. Under AFSPA, everyone is a suspect till proven innocent; young men are particularly vulnerable to suspicion. Weighed under such circumstances, the only option left to poor families, particularly young men in a family, is to flee the state in search of sustenance. In 2020, after the Centre's hasty announcement of a national lockdown in the wake of the Covid-19 pandemic, news about lakhs of migrant labourers from Assam stranded in other states only gave credence to the fact that Assam is today a veritable mine of unskilled migrant workers.

This brings me back to the question that my cousin had posed to me decades ago. It now often nudges me to also ask: what kind of Assamese are we producing? While the lot forming the labour class in posh cities outside of Assam are widely perceived as 'Assamese people' in their host states, how do they see themselves? Of course, it is more likely that the educated section among these migrants is able to afford to settle down permanently in these cities; this section is increasingly becoming comfortable within an English or Hindi speaking mileu, keeping their mother tongue in the background. It is the former kind of Assamese migrant who has strong ties with their land, often rushing back home as soon as they accumulate a trifling sum of cash. Their biggest complaint about staying out of their home state is their difficulty in getting used to the local cuisine and having to interact in a language other than their mother tongue, which is also why they are often seen living in ghettoized areas.

One wonders what effect this trend of reverse migration and its many shades have on the overall Assamese consciousness otherwise so palpable in the state. What stake will these categories of people eventually have in the overall construct of the Assamese identity, particularly when they stay outside of the state for a protracted period?

Social media has emerged as a vital tool of communication and seeped into all strata of Assamese society by now, but is it enough for an Assamese residing outside of the state during, say, the main festival Bihu, to post photos and videos wearing their festive mekhela sadors, dancing to a Bihu number, or feasting on traditional dishes either at home or with a few others at a small gathering? Will those permanently residing outside of the state continue to also have a say, or stake, in the overall priorities of the community back home? After all, many among them still count as an integral part of the larger Assamese community, its interests and well-being. Recently, while discussing a veteran Assamese/Northeastern thinker's ideas about the community's political future, a prominent citizen of Guwahati told me: 'He doesn't live in Assam, we do.' It triggered in me the cognizance, for the first time, that he was seeking a ready advantage over the other's opinion related to the welfare of the community and the state, simply because he physically lived in Assam.

I have faced the question too, but from within a patriarchal framework. What stake do you have in the community now? You married outside of it, frowned an elderly relative at me. It was his final defence against me during a conversation related to the political future of the Assamese community. In turn, he only helped me recognize that patriarchy—which exists in Assamese society more than we care to talk about—will allow only a man to belong to the community, no matter what. For a woman, society still has a claim over her personal choice; she must belong by the purity of her blood. Not by dint of her mind alone will her voice be deemed legitimate. Naturally then, Bhupen Hazarika never faced the question from the Assamese masses after marrying a Patel. Would Mamoni Raisom Goswami have to face this question had she written in a language other than Assamese? Prominent names aside, this must be a question negotiated by several Assamese women who have married outside of the community.

Let's set aside patriarchy for a moment. As an individual, where do I belong? Am I the kind of jajabor, the nomad that Bhupen Hazarika sang about in his inimitable number 'Moi Eti Jajabor' (I Am a Nomad)? Someone collating myriad experiences, the scent of life—from people, places—to exist on a wider plane and become a world citizen thus, and yet remain a khaar-khowa Axomiya? I would like to be in that space, rest there forever, like so many other women with a similar background may like it too. Why can't I be so, after all?

In the broader perspective, the question is germane to all within the Assamese community today because, as indicated above, there is a considerable section living outside of the state now, even settling down with partners from other states or countries, barely using the language like they did at home in their growing-up days back in Assam. Who knows, their progeny may end up not speaking the language at all! There are some prominent examples of it already. In the future, will this category of people form a substantial set of neo-Assamese? Assamese by dint of their parentage or by their surnames, but not entirely. Will they find difficulty in finding acceptance in the larger Assamese society that is primarily hinged on language? A community facing out-migration like never before will have to wrestle with the question, sooner than we think.

And then of course, a personal question shall no more remain so.

1

THOLUA–KHILONJIA–NA AXOMIYA: THE ASSAMESE

> Communities are people. They are not abstractions. They are not rhetoric. They are human beings.[1]

The revival of the Santa Cruz Museum of Art and History in California by its director, Nina Simon, led her to write *The Art of Relevance* in 2017, a ground-breaking prescriptive book on saving libraries, hinged on the 'needs, assets, and interests' of a community. The quote above, strangely, steered me to extract more meanings from them than just confining them to her immediate purpose—why or how to save a public library.

Like Simon's endeavour might have begun with a set of basic thoughts, suspended in the relevance of a community that she is trained to serve and value, I, being physically removed from the immediate ring of my community for nearly three decades at a stretch for a slew of reasons, too have mulled, from time to time, over questions around my community; its relevance in shaping one's identity, my identity, and thereby imparting a distinctiveness to the same, if any. Such thoughts kicked up a range of questions in my mind, like, who is an Assamese? Is there a pure Assamese? Khati Axomiya? If yes, what does a typical Assamese look like? I mean physically? Do I have that look?

Simon's words oddly prodded me, first, to look at the physiognomy of a community, more than anything else. What kind of human beings do we find populating the world in general, also, and who among them people Assam?

Aside from the basic corporal affinities—a pair of eyes and ears, legs and hands; a nose and a head; how do people from one community differ from another in the physical sense? Do these bodily variances speak of the identity of a community? What is the physical form of my community then, of a typical Assamese?

Biological taxonomy compartmentalizes the world population into three basic races: Caucasian (white), Mongoloid (Asian), and Negroid (black), aside from the later addition, Australoid. Who do the Assamese—located at a junction of Indian and East Asian civilisations—find their physical affinity with? Where lies their kinship?

Well, it is here that the story of the Assamese community becomes complex and layered, like a bloom which has a set of petals that are of not the same shape and size, colour and texture. Take my immediate family. My eyes are narrow and small, the cheekbones are high; so are my mother's. My sister and my brother's eyes are relatively bigger, cheekbones high. My nose, like my father's, is thin and sharp. Akin to my mother, my sister's nose is broad and thick. 'You look like your father and your sister, like your mother,' I have grown up hearing that remark from friends and neighbours, relatives. We, as a family, are owners of skin colours that stretch from boga (fair) to mitha-boronia (wheatish). If I can draw in my neighbour's daughter here too, she often complains that when she smiles, her pink gums against her wheatish complexion show more than they should and envies that mine don't. But I have only looked at my dull, curly hair and coveted her silky mop. In my neighbourhood itself, if I walk a few doors away from ours, there is a friend's family evenly divided in skin tones, from dhok dhok ke boga (very fair) to ketur kola (dark as night). Are they an anomaly? Their hair too differs, from Maggie curls to wavy. Are these differences a clue to the distinctiveness of my community?

In childhood, whenever my little sister would pass by my mother, she would remind her to pull her nose a few times; that is how it would grow sharper like your sister's, ma would repeat. Looking back, I can only laugh at her attempt to go against the genetic makeup of who we are, as a set of people. Incorporating all these variations, have we not become Axomiya, the Assamese, an amalgam of people under one broad umbrella?

The fact that there was an admixture of groups of people from diverse racial stocks settling down side by side in the Brahmaputra Valley over centuries and in course of time most of them metamorphosed into a formulation only reaffirms to me that there is no typical Assamese look. There cannot be. There are no archetypical Assamese eyes, like the Bengali eyes; there is no stock hair type in Assamese women like that of the crimped, wavy variety that most Malayali women flaunt. There is no set notion about what an Assamese man looks like as there is about a Punjabi man—strapping, well-built. From eyes—big to the tiniest; nose—sharpest to the most levelled, thinnest to the broadest; from dhok dhok ke boga to ketur kola skin tones; from curly hair to the glossiest silky head; from thin to the broadest lips; from high cheekbones to rounded cheeks; from thick, stocky bodies to lanky, tall beings, there are Assamese of every form. Sharp physical variations are found even within a single family.

How exactly do we define one's lineage? Journalist Tony Joseph's book *Early Indians*, which hinges on the latest DNA evidence as applied to the migration pattern of people in the subcontinent since pre-historic times, makes a case for the limitations of one's Y-chromosome or mtDNA in tracking one's lineage. Joseph highlights that the Y-chromosome doesn't say much about one's entire genetic make-up, but only who one's paternal or maternal ancestors are, a small fraction of the people one can rightfully call one's ancestors. The author nearly unnerves you when he says, 'Your mother's father, or your father's mother, or your father's mother's father, for example, are all left out in the cold if you go only by Y-chromosome or mtDNA lineages. If you go back ten generations, you will have 1024 people whom you can call your ancestors, but your mtDNA or Y-chromosome would have any connection with only ten of them. If you go back fifteen generations, the number of your ancestors goes up exponentially to 32,768, but your mtDNA or Y-chromosome would be connected to only fifteen of them!'[2] Since 'nations as we understand them today are no older than a few centuries, and we are all interconnected—genetically, culturally and historically—far more than we imagine',[3] it is possible for a person to have an ancestry from some place other than the country she now belongs to.

Joseph further argues that while mtDNA and Y-chromosome are helpful to comprehend population movement or histories of individuals or groups, the results may not be sufficient to have a full understanding of a person's or a population's entire genetic construct or its relationship to other populations. 'For that we need genome sequencing, which studies a person's entire genome, not just the Y-chromosome or the mtDNA.'[4]

Joseph's book places a greater focus on mainland India as compared to the Brahmaputra Valley and the Northeast, which being the gateway of the Indian subcontinent to South and East Asia, could perhaps have even greater genetic diversity in its population. Interestingly, a 2001 paper 'The Northeast Indian Passageway: A Barrier or Corridor for Human Migrations', based on a DNA study carried out by Oxford University on 173 persons belonging to four sets of tribal populations from Assam and Arunachal Pradesh, had found 'strong evidence for a genetic discontinuity between Northeast Indian groups and other Indian groups.'[5] The researchers had banked on Y-chromosome and mtDNa study and contended 'that the

Northeast Indian passageway acted as a geographical barrier rather than as a corridor for human migrations between the Indian subcontinent and East/Southeast Asia, at least within the past millennia and possibly for several tens of thousand years, as suggested by the overall distinctiveness of the Indian and East Asian Y chromosome and mtDNA gene pools.' The study said, 'Both north-eastern Indian Y chromosomes and mtDNAs consistently show strikingly high homogeneity among groups and strong affinities to East Asian groups. We detect virtually no Y-chromosome and mtDNA admixture between northeast and other Indian groups.' What is also striking about the study is the assertion that the 'Indo-European component among the Tibeto-Burman Y chromosomes is remarkably low (three per cent), given that although the study groups are primarily Tibeto-Burman speakers, they are also conversant with Indo-European speakers. This implies that the "Indo Europeanization" of northeast India, which is an ongoing process, is mainly a cultural process. This situation contrasts with southern India, where Indo-European speakers were integrated in non-Indo-European speech communities where Y-chromosome markers typical of Indo-European speakers have been detected in Dravidian-speaking tribal groups.'

The study is an eye-opener, but to my mind, the story is incomplete for not including what we now call 'the non-tribal' sections within the Assamese fold. To dwell further on the question: how much of tribal blood is there in the non-tribal Assamese? That could have opened a few more doors. Several tribal groups in Assam, over the last few centuries, have become non-tribals (such as the Sarania community) by entering the Hindu fold. The Koch community is said to be one of the biggest examples of this shift. Non-tribal Assamese groups, particularly the Kalita, have been placed by historians as those pre-Aryan Alpines, or Indo-Europeans who might have entered the Brahmaputra Valley by bypassing mainland India. How similar or different are they from the 'other Indian groups'? The Sutia (also termed Chutiya) community of Assam, who are of Mongoloid stock, have over the centuries intermingled with the Kalita and several don't quite have the pure Mongoloid look any more. Assam-based writer and medical doctor Satyakam Phukan has highlighted that the priestly class of the Sutia, the Deori, didn't intermingle with the Kalita and, therefore, have retained their Mongoloid features till date.[6]

MIGRATORY AND TRADE ROUTES

Nevertheless, to elaborate on the East Asian connection of Assamese tribals highlighted by the Oxford study, one will have to first glance at the physical layout of Assam. While the present state shares its border with two South Asian nations, Bhutan and Bangladesh, Assam, till a few decades ago, in independent India (through 1947 till 1987) technically shared borders with some other Asian countries too—with China (rather South Tibet through the North East Frontier Agency or Arunachal Pradesh) and the East Asian nation Myanmar (through the Lushai hills or Mizoram, and Naga hills or Nagaland and Patkai hills or Arunachal Pradesh). A peek at the warren of trade routes from and to olden Assam, paints a picture of the Brahmaputra Valley functioning, for centuries, not just as a part of the Asian trading axis but also as home to a cross-section of people, flowing in more from its eastern border than its western, linking it to mainland India through the narrow stretch of land that we call the Chicken's Neck. The excerpt from Nagen Saikia's book, quoted earlier, is further proof of the intermixing of peoples through these migratory routes.

Recognizing the diversity of people populating Assam since centuries, historian P. C. Choudhury had rightly termed ancient Assam 'a great anthropological museum' in his formidable book *History of Civilisation of Assam*, penned in 1959.[7] For the same reasons, ethnographer J. P. Mills had once remarked that Assam is situated in 'one of the great migration routes of mankind.'[8] Since, as of 2023, no well fleshed out scientific plan for archaeological excavations in and around the state has been rolled out on the ground, no human skeleton or cave has yet been dug out for historians to be able to pin down accurately whether there was any human habitation during or before the Palaeolithic age on that stretch of land. Dearth of such hard evidence or discovery of mere rudiments of an ancient material culture confines one to extant literary sources, oral histories, travelogues, a handful of archaeological findings, trade and migratory routes, philology, ethnography, etc. to air certain interpretations about how those times might have been and who might have inhabited olden Assam.

Even though Assam, as Pragjyotisa–Kamrup, had once stretched a considerable length of what we know as north-eastern India and parts of what is North Bengal and Bangladesh today, the newer geographies have certainly posed a challenge to tell the complete story of human migration to that part of the world. For instance, it can prompt the immediate question:

should one peek at the migration story of the Khasis or the Nagas, the Lushais and the Adis, Meiteis and the Tipperas, tribes residing in other north-eastern states too to look through the maze of human migration to olden Assam, or Pragjyotisa–Kamrup, now that the scope of the chapter is only about the journey of the people who comprise merely the larger Assamese community?

My contention is, since the past of no community is a recent construct, it is necessary then to also pull in to the narrative the migration story of certain other tribes/communities which had once been part of greater Assam, wherever it is relevant. Only through such a contiguous gaze can one paint the whole picture.

To do that, let's first take a peek at the trade routes that had coiled out of, and into, the valley abounded by the mighty Brahmaputra and its numerous tributaries snaking through different parts of the Northeast, facilitating human passage. These routes enabled a diverse set of people to arrive at the Brahmaputra Valley for centuries in continuum to eventually constitute from within them a community, the Assamese, which is, obviously then, so diverse in its physical features.

To draw a quick word atlas of such routes, I will have to fall back on Hiuen Tsang's account of his travel from Nalanda in the Magadha kingdom to Kamrup in 643 CE. He stepped on Kamrup after crossing a big river, which historians take to be the Karatoya as it was mentioned as the western border of Kamrup in old classical texts. The Chinese scholar's account is a testimony to the existence of a well-trodden path which might have been used not only by those who entered olden Assam from what is mainland India today to settle down but perhaps to carry out trade too. By his own admission, the Chinese scholar had passed by Campa (Bhagalpur), Kajangala (Rajmahal), and Pundravardhana (Rangpur) to land in Kamrup from Magadha.[9] Also, that in just two days, he could receive the letter of invitation at Nalanda from king Bhaskarvarman to visit Kamrup suggests the existence of a speedy channel of communication between Kamrup and Magadha then itself.[10]

Besides, the incident mentioned in Tsang's account about Bhaskarvarman hurrying to the banks of the Ganges near Kie-shu-ho-ki-lo (Kajurgira-Kaankjal, Rajmahal) to placate the upset Magadha king Harshavardhan for holding him back in Kamrup, also corroborates the presence of a swift means of communication with the mainland in those days.[11]

According to noted Assamese historian and folklorist Birinchi Kumar

Baruahh, such instances of communication between Magadha and Kamrup during the sixth century that one could pluck out of Hiuen Tsang's account only proved that 'there were regular routes to Kamarupa from Nalanda (in present-day Bihar) and Orissa....'[12]

About Assam's eastern routes (towards South and East Asia), one finds an interesting mention in the introduction to *The Life of Hiuen Tsang*, Samual Beal's English translation from 1884 of the Chinese traveller's account. The military allies, King Harshavardhan and King Bhaskarvarman, operated a sea trade route with China.[13] Significantly, when Hiuen Tsang expressed his willingness to return to China, Bhasakarvarman had replied, 'But I know not, if you prefer to go, by what route you propose to return; if you select the southern sea-route, then I will send official attendants to accompany you.'[14] As per Hiuen Tsang's account, Bhaskarvarman had a flotilla of 30,000 ships. Barua had not only held that up as a written proof of a sea link to China from Kamrup but also highlighted another nugget that Hiuen Tsang had recorded—the existence of a land route from Kamrup which had touched southwest China. The Chinese traveller had gathered from the people in Kamrup that southwest China (Ssee-chouan, Sichuan province) was about two months of arduous journey away. Additionally, that Bhaskarvarman had related to him that a Chinese song in praise of the victory of the second son of the Tang emperor Kao-tsou over rebel general Liu Wou-Cheou in 619 CE had gained considerable popularity among the people of Kamrup also indicates rather strongly 'the intimate intercourse that existed between China and Assam at the time'.[15]

Yet another confirmation about the existence of a well-trodden link between ancient China and ancient Assam comes from French Sinologist Paul Pelliot.[16] He had cited a route between China and Kamrup existing from at least the second century onwards quoting from the accounts of Chang Kien, the Chinese ambassador to Yu-Chi country (Taiwan); it only specifies the presence of perhaps not just a human migratory route to the Brahmaputra Valley but also of trade relations between eastern India and China through Upper Burma and Yunnan. In his report from 126 BCE, Chang Kien had referred to the amazement he felt in Bactria on finding silk and bamboo coming from the Chinese provinces of Yunnan and 'Szechuan'; he was later informed about the prosperous country of India across which 'the caravans carried these products from southern China to Afghanistan.'[17] While it has often been assumed that China's contact with India was only through the Gobi Desert and the west (mainland India), evidences like these indicate that neither the sea routes nor the Assam–Burma routes could be overlooked.

In the excerpt on p. xx, Nagen Saikia, quoting Rajmohan Nath, had also mentioned a route that traversed from Assam through Tibet to the Gobi Desert. It is only natural then to mention here that P. C. Bagchi's notable work, *India and China: A Thousand years of Cultural Relations*[18] too referred to a detailed itinerary preserved in the eighth-century Chinese work *Kia-tan* on how to reach Kamrup through Burma by crossing the Chindwin River all the way from Tonkin, the southern-most of the commercial centres of China.[19] There, Bagchi had underlined three routes that had existed between Pataliputra (near modern-day Patna) to China through Assam–Burma. While one was through the Patkai range to Upper Burma, another was through Manipur up to Chindwin. Yet another passage was through Arakan up to the Irrawaddy. All the three routes extended up to Kunming in China.

That Manipur and Eastern Bengal were channels of human movement could be understood from Arthur Phayre's *History of Burma*, written in 1883, where he states that the only contact the Gangetic plains of India had with the Tagaung region of Mandalay was through those regions.[20] Interestingly, Phayre had also noted, 'The oldest city said in Burmese chronicles to have been built by Indian princes is Tagaung, on the east bank of Upper Irawadi.'[21]

About the warren of old trade route and passages, P. C. Choudhury had summed up thus: 'At a subsequent time many routes were opened through Dihong, the Mishimi route, the Phungan pass (Hpungan pass on India–Myanmar border) leading to China, the route through Manipur to the Irrawaddy, and the Patkai passes to Bhamo (in Myanmar). To other routes through Hukawang valley (Myanmar) leading across the mountains from Myitkyana (a city on Myanmar) to Tipland near Margherita (in Assam) and Chaukan pass (Pangsau pass, India's easternmost point). The other routes lay through the passes of Donkin, Natu, and Jilap (in Myanmar). It was through these routes that the people from South-east Asia and China made their way into Assam.'[22]

John McCosh, calling the Patkai route the most important and easy one to step into Assam from Burma and China, had highlighted that it was through that route that the founder of the Ahom kingdom in Assam, Chaolung Sukapha, had entered the Brahmaputra Valley.[23] Also, in 1816, during the Burmese invasion of Assam, it was the same route that was utilized to filter in some 6,000 Burmese troops and 8,000 auxiliaries to occupy the Brahmaputra Valley. Scholars like Birinchi Kumar Baruah have referred to the Burmese administration settling villages or military settlement every 12 or 15 miles along the Patkai route, and that 'it was the business of the people to cut the jungles and to remove all other obstructions from the path'.[24] Mention must be made of G. Tucci too who in *The Sea and Land Travels of Buddhist Sadhu* in the sixteenth century,[25] had discussed monk Buddhagupta using a well-known land route from Guwahati all the way to Pagan in Burma.[26]

As stated earlier, Nagen Saikia, quoting from K. P. Chattopadhya's *Ancient Indian Cultural Contacts and Migration*, also underlined that there existed a trade route between Korea and Iran which criss-crossed through China, Assam, North India, Pakistan, and Afghanistan.[27] A migratory route that had linked Mongolia to China also passed by Assam. In 1260 CE, Minhaj-i-Siraj in *Tabaqat-i-Nasiri* referred to a route between Tibet and Assam through which horses were transported to Lakhnauti (Gauda, Bengal).[28] Among other routes, there was a track between Karnataka and the Brahmaputra Valley which traversed Andhra Pradesh, Odisha, West and North Bengal.[29]

Besides several such land routes passing by Assam, its land borders also had a number of duar (formal border gates for trade), some of which were functional till the early nineteenth century. It was through these duar that the Bhutanese and the Lhasa merchants had free-flowing commercial relations with Assam till the Burmese invasion in the early nineteenth century. Captain R. Boileau Pemberton's *Report on Bhootan* (Bhutan) had explained how trade between Lhasa and Assam was carried out in the olden times.[30] The route facilitated export of Assam silk, Assam rice, iron, lac, buffalo horns, pearl, etc. to China. Once the Burmese, and in quick succession the British, set foot in Assam to seize its territory, commercial transactions through those duar became highly regulated for fear of the powerful foreign invaders seeping into Tibet and Bhutan too. Even so, even in the twenty-first century it is not rare to come across Bhutanese women selling wares at the Tawang market in Arunachal Pradesh (a geographical arm of Assam till February 1987) after crossing over the peaceful international border. The present land route between Bhutan and Assam at Sandrup Jhonkar was a traditional trading point with Darrang. That, as late as March 1959, the present Tibetan Buddhist spiritual head, the Dalai Lama, could land up in Assam by one such route all the way from Lhasa only confirms the veracity of such well-trodden ancient paths still known to locals.

The Tai Ahoms of Mongoloid race advanced from Upper Burma towards the Brahmaputra Valley through the Patkai range. P. C. Choudhury has flagged four possible routes of human migration to the Brahmaputra Valley. 'First through the north or the mountain passes of Tibet, Nepal and Bhutan; second through the valley of Ganges and the Brahmaputra from India and the west; third by sea or the Bay of Bengal, passing through Bengal or Burma, and fourthly the Assam-Burma routes, one over the Patkai passes in the north-east, leading from the Lidu-Margherita road to China through Hukawang valley in Burma and the other through Manipur and Cachar in the south-east or south of Assam.'[31] That the routes through the mountain passes of Bhutan and Tibet had existed since ancient times had led him to deduce, 'It may be suggested that some racial elements, such as the Alpines and the Indo-Chinese (Tibeto-Burmans) made their way in small numbers into Assam through these passes in the north.'[32] Several scholars, though, have come to the conclusion that most of the Mongolian migrations to Assam had occurred through the north-eastern and southern routes of Assam through Burma. 'One wave of the Tibeto-Burmans came probably from the north, comprising the (tribes) Aka, Mishmi, Garo, Mikir, Kachari, etc., another from the south, the Lushai-Kukis and another of an earlier wave, the Kol-Mon-Annam, extending over parts of the area, now occupied by the Nagas. The Bodos are also believed to have come from the north, and it is possible that they got mixed up with the Mon-Khmer-Mundas in course of time.'[33]

In 1905, Sir Edward Gait in his monumental work, *A History of Assam*, had said that just like the Aryans had entered mainland India from the northwest 3,000 to 4,000 years ago, there was 'a similar influx of tribes of Mongolian origin' to Assam.[34] Just like the Aryans obliterated the Dravidians in the rest of India, Gait said the Mongolians too did the same in Assam (excluding the Surma valley) and North-East Bengal, 'while in the Surma valley and the rest of Bengal a mixture of races has taken place in which the recognizable Mongolian element diminishes towards the west and disappears altogether before Bihar is reached.'[35] Gait had marked the Kairbartta group among the Assamese as a Dravidian stock.

Eons ago, Pliny the Elder, the Roman author and naval commander of the early Roman Empire, had stated that the people of Ceylon knew the Seres, a set of people mentioned in *The Periplus of the Erythrean Sea.*[36]

Choudhury had placed that set of people in olden Assam: 'J. H. Hutton is perhaps right in assuming that some elements of the Nagas migrated from Southern India by sea and entered Assam through Burma.'[37] Besides the Indo-Chinese races, Oceanic elements, therefore, might have arrived in the land either by land or sea routes via Burma, or both. That southern India connection of the Nagas also perhaps justifies why several Naga tribes till date wear cowries. A section of people in present-day Assam also wear cowries for luck.

If one was to place people of diverse racial backgrounds that had come to settle by the Brahmaputra Valley and the mountain ranges in its vicinity in a timeline of sorts, those from the Austro-Asiatic stock have been typically put at the bottom, as the oldest inhabitants of the land. This is so because the Khasis are the only group in the Northeast today to speak a Mon-Khmer speech. The Khasis, who now populate primarily Meghalaya, are believed to have resided in and around the Kamakhya temple in Guwahati at some point in history and must have been pushed further into the hills with the arrival of a new batch of migrants. Looking at their use of stone celts and iron hoes, several scholars have concluded that the Khasis have close affinities with the Kol-Mon-Annam group of tribes.[38] P. R. T. Gurdon, in *The Khasis*, had come to the conclusion that they were connected to people who populated the Malaya Peninsula and Chotanagpur at the time of the Stone Age.[39] Some scholars also believe that even the Bodos of Assam may have been connected with the Ho-Munda-Mon-Khmer families; that some other tribes from the Austro-Asiatic fold, aside from the Khasis, might have migrated to Assam from the Pacific area, perhaps from the Philippines.[40] The cultures of head-hunting, erecting megaliths, fertility cults, having bachelor pads, etc., seen in several hill and plains tribes of greater Assam, are categorized as part of Austro-Asiatic culture.[41] According to P. C. Choudhury, it is possible that people from this fold were numerous at one time in olden Assam, and that an Austro-Asiatic strain may be found in many tribes in varying proportions. 'The Mon-Khmer speakers were followed by waves of the Tibeto-Burman, who entered Assam from various directions and at different periods of history.'[42]

Today, the plains tribes of Assam, be it the Karbi, the Bodo, the Rabha, the Tiwa, the Dimasa, or the Mising, are identified as people from Tibeto-Burman stock. However, rather than their physical features, these groups are more often classified based on their linguistic specialities.

In modern-day Assam, the people of the Bodo-Kachari fold encompass most tribes, making it likely that 'they were once a dominant people of the valley, and petty kingdoms, like those of the Kacharis and Chutias (Sutias), were established by them even before the intrusion of the Ahoms.'[43] That most river names in Assam start with the prefix 'di' or 'ti', the Bodo word for water, is widely considered a clue to their dominance in the area. Though the Ahoms ruled Assam for 610 years, their word for river, 'nam', occurs in only a few instances in the extreme eastern part of the state, for example, Namrup, Namtsik, and Namsang.[44]

Bodos are also said to be closely affiliated with the Kiratas or the Mlecchas mentioned in classical Sanskrit literature. The foundation of a kingdom in Pragjyotisa was said to have been by Mahiranga Danab. The Kiratas are associated with the Bhauma dynasty led by the great kings Narakasura and Bhagadatta. The description of Bhagadatta's army in the Mahabharata (slanted eyes, flat noses, yellowish skin tone) makes a case for the Kiratas being of Mongoloid origin.[45] Some had also argued that perhaps there was an initial wave of Tibeto-Burmans moving to Assam who were identified as the Kirata who later got mixed up with those from the Alpines after they spread themselves in eastern India and Assam.[46]

While scholars have hypothesized about where and by which possible routes the Tibeto-Burmans may have entered Assam, lack of any archaeological evidence on that front has kept the plausible entry route of the Alpines to the Brahmaputra Valley vague till date. Though the presence of certain Indo-European or pre-Vedic Aryan elements in modern Assamese language and Assamese culture has kept that part of the community's ethnographic history alive, not much detail is, however, known about that relic of the past. As mentioned above, several scholars have linked to this hidden past the origin of one of the largest non-tribal components of Assamese people: the Kalita.

From my understanding, there seems to be a general agreement among scholars that a set of Aryans might have stepped into India prior to the Vedic Aryans based on various cultural practices within the Indian fold, and that they might have entered through the northwest. Banking primarily on some unique features of the Assamese language, such as the existence of the velar fricative 'xo' which is present in Indo-European languages like German and Mexican, but not in any modern Indian languages, scholars in Assam have also concluded that there might have been a group of Alpines or pre-Aryans who too settled down in Assam at some point in time. Based on some exclusivities of the language, which is certainly older than the Ahoms who gave the present name Assam to the state, they suggest that a group of Alpines must have then arrived in Assam not from the western side, and the present language must have had their contribution too. Choudhury, banking on his deep study of the subject, had stated that an alternative route through the north and the Assam–Burma route could be possible for the Alpines to enter the Brahmaputra Valley.[47]

Quoting from an article in the *Journal of Royal Asiatic Society* in 1915 which had said that there were early Iranian–Magian settlements in eastern India, in regions like Videha (north Bihar), Magadha (South Bihar), and Pragjyotisa (Assam), and that the solar cult and the planetary worship in Pragjyotisa were linked to that settlement, and that its king Bhagadatta had the same Iranian–Magian origin, Choudhury had commented, 'It is possible, as shown by some early Brahmanical works, that even the rulers of Bimbisara-Saisunga dynasty and Janaka of Videha were not pure Aryans, but must have been Alpines, like those of the Bhauma dynasty of Assam. The epithets, asura and mleccha, of these rulers can be explained on the ground that they were neither pure Aryans nor Mongolians but Alpine-Iranians.'[48]

If this is true, then the Alpines must have settled much earlier in Assam than is usually believed. They could have been followed by a batch of Vedic Aryans who later incorporated some of their cultures into theirs. A relevant addition to the argument could be that while Vedic texts had called eastern India Anupadesa or the land of the Vratyas who were perhaps the Alpines or the pre-Vedic Aryans, N. N. Ghose, in *Aryan Trail in Iran and India*,[49] had tried tracing the Vratyas to the Magian–Iranians. 'The settlement of the Alpines in eastern India and Assam is supported not only by the presence of *bracycephalic leptorrhine* (shape of the head) features among the higher classes but also by the fact that in these areas the Austric and Dravidian speech were long superseded by the Aryan speech of the Alpines, who also introduced certain cultural traits, whose survivals may still be noticed in Assam.'[50]

While we come across words like Kaltis, Kakatiai, Colubae, and Koluta in ancient literature, including in *The Periplus,* which several scholars have tried to connect to the Kalita subgroup within the Assamese community, their origin is still shrouded in mystery. Linguist Banikanta Kakati in his book *Kolita Jatir Itibittya* (The History of the Kalita Community) had placed the Kalita people around Sadiya on the eastern tip of Assam, in Kalita Desa. He had based his claim on the genealogy of renowned Vaishnava seer Gopal Ata in the hagiography on saint Sankardev, *Katha Gurucharit.* Ata was admittedly from the Kalita Desa bordering south Tibet. The kingdom also finds mention in Edward Balfour's (in *Encyclopaedia Asiatica*) and R. G. Latham's accounts on that part of Asia. While there is also a general belief that they were Kshatriyas whose ancestors came from the west (mainland India), K. R. Medhi had refuted that suggestion though, and had instead called them non-Vedic Aryans who entered Assam, possibly from the northern side. Importantly, there are Kolitas in Odisha and Uttarakhand too. The surname can be found in countries like Poland, Russia, Belarus, Ukraine, and place names with Kalita in them can be found in Belarus, Estonia, Russia, Ukraine, and Iraq, as pointed out by Satyakam Phukan. In the United States, while 65 per cent of those with the Kalita surname are of Polish descent, only 35 per cent are Assamese.

Interestingly, there exists a theory of Kulalupta (concealment of caste) about the Kalita community in Assam. P. C. Choudhury had termed it an 'invention by some'[51] to place them within the fold of Kayasthas. 'The story is connected with the legend of Parasurama; in order to save themselves from whose wrath, the Kalitas are said to have concealed their Ksatriya caste. This may have a bearing on the Brahmanical reaction to Buddhism, which the Kalitas might have adopted at the time.'[52] The Kalita are also associated with the Buddhist Koliyas; it could be that they were Buddhists and later adopted Hinduism. That the Parashuram Kunda, now in Arunachal Pradesh, is situated close to the Sadiya tracts of Assam where the Kalita people were once said to have their kingdom, presents an interesting twist in the Kulalupta tale. There are several versions of the story of Parashuram washing his hands after killing his mother (in one instance leading to the birth of the Parashuram Kunda). Such stories exist in Kerala, too, where there are temples dedicated to Parashuram. This again lends credence to the idea that such legends were used to spread Brahmanical Hinduism in different parts of the country in the olden times. Gait also pointed out that the legend of Parashuram in Sanskrit literature was associated with renaming Ti-Lao, a non-Aryan name of the river, to Brahmaputra.[53] Choudhury had commented that the Kalita are more of an ethnic type rather than an Assamese caste.[54]

Yet another group, Koch, is also considered more of a tribe than a caste. Referring to the Hinduization of the Koch group among the Assamese, Gait had remarked, 'In the Brahmaputra Valley, Koch, formerly the name of a tribe, has become a caste which admits proselytes to Hinduism from the ranks of Kachari and other aboriginal tribes.'[55] About the Assamese

Bhuyan group, which Sankardev belonged to, Gait had said something similar, underlining that the surname had nothing to do with caste but 'is merely a Sanskrit equivalent of the Persian word, Zamindar'.[56] Later, however, some Bhuyans did settle down in the Koch kingdom after fleeing Bengal, the Bhuyans of middle Assam (Nagaon area) trace their ancestry to Santanu and Samanta, the two grandsons of Samudra, the minister of King Arimatta, who had ruled Kamrup after Bhagadatta, as per some accounts.

Assam also has a small Brahmin subgroup. At least since the beginning of the sixth century, there has been record of kings adopting the policy of setting up agraharas to settle Brahmins in Kamrup because of which it became a centre of Brahmanical learning. Hiuen Tsang, who visited Kamrup during that period, had said that Buddhism was not practised in the kingdom then and the place had numerous temples.[57] Narakasura too is said to have set up Brahmins from northern India during the rule of the Bhauma dynasty. In this way, though they were 'probably of Alpine origin, many rulers contributed to the Aryanisation of the valley and became responsible for the Hinduisation of the tribes.'[58]

Many Brahmins, particularly from Kannauj in northern India and later from Bengal, were settled in Assam by various kings over a period of time. The process of Aryanization set off by several rulers not only made some petty Tibeto-Burman chiefs embrace Hinduism, a change that filtered down to their subjects too, but the trend was also exported to neighbouring countries, like Burma and Southeast Asia.

Though today there are no representative groups within the Assamese tribal or non-tribal folds of Melanesian and Negrito stock, scholars like B. S. Guha have pointed out its existence akin to the Andamanese and Papuans in Brahmaputra Valley. Reverend A. Mills had claimed in 1928 that the inhabitants of the mountains of Assam were almost certainly Negritos, 'little dark men with curly hair.... Traditions speak vaguely of them and their curly hair still survives.'[59] Satyakam Phukan claimed, 'No segment of Assamese people from the most aristocratic of the so-called upper segments to the segments erroneously and conclusively dubbed as purely Mongoloid tribes, segments which refuse to identify themselves as "Assamese" on political considerations are biologically free from this strain. The Melanasio-Negritic phenotype shows up randomly and frequently in the physiognomy of all Assamese.'[60]

The arrival of so many people from different racial and linguistic stock over the centuries, and their gradual intermingling with each other, at times adapting to, and adopting too, not just each other's cultures but also religious practices, only makes Assam a melting pot of a diverse set of masses. Though Assam through centuries received Austro-Asiatics, Alpines, Vedic Aryans, it is, however, the Tibeto-Burmans who have remained predominant. Today, if you look at the linguistic wealth of the state, Assamese is the only Indo-Aryan language and the rest of the bunch is of Tibeto-Burman stock.

After coming in contact with Muslim invaders in the thirteenth century, not just a Mech king but his subjects too converted to Islam, giving birth to the denomination of Assamese Muslims. In the seventeenth century, parts of Goalpara came under Mughal rule. During the same time period, Sufi saint Ajaan Fakir converted many to Islam in Upper Assam.

The miniscule Assamese Sikh community in middle Assam trace their ancestry to the soldiers sent by Maharaja Ranjit Singh of Punjab to fight by the side of the dethroned Ahom king Chandrakanta Singha to defeat the Burmese invaders in the early nineteenth century. Several Assamese Muslims are also descendants of the defeated army of Mughal soldiers who settled down in the state and adopted local cultures, discarding their language and culture or merging them with the local practices.

During the British colonial period, more migrants arrived on the land from the western side. While the Marwari traders trod in all the way from Rajputana to augment the colonial economy by engaging in trade, so did the Bengali Hindus and Muslims from East Bengal to take up government jobs and as agriculturalists, respectively. A large span of Adivasis, now locally termed as the Tea Tribe, also became part of Assam, drawn from Odisha and elsewhere when the tea gardens were set up by the colonial administration. In due course of time, several people from Nepali subgroups entered the state too, some after Independence. Several within this lot—barring a majority of the Marwaris, the Hindu Bengalis, and Nepalis—adopted Assamese as their official language in Census reports, merging their own into it, almost. While in the last few decades, several ethnic groups, particularly the tribes, may have begun asserting their indigenous cultures and speech, according to me, it is primarily done keeping political considerations in mind. Culturally, the term 'Assamese' is still relevant to all—tribals and non-tribals. Importantly, the tribal, the pre-Aryan, and Vedic Aryan cultural imports have intermingled in Assam to such an extent that it is no more easy to segregate one from the other. The umbilical chord exists, and is visible at various times while one explores what constitutes the Assamese community.

It is the physical diversity within the wider Assamese community that also speaks of this distinctiveness. This phenomenon of assimilation makes Assam not just a miniature India with people of diverse racial stocks populating but it also makes the wider Assamese community somewhat unique. Nowhere in the present atlas of India does one locate a set of people who come under one umbrella, culturally at least, not only with their religious diversities—Hindus, Muslims, Sikhs, Buddhists, Christians—as Assamese, but with their tribal and non-tribal cultures and religions too. Herein lies the strength of the larger community.

And herein lies, perhaps, the essence of being a true blue Khati Axomiya. And my identity too.

2

PRAGJYOTISA–KAMRUP, ASHAM–AXOM–ASSAM: WHAT'S IN A NAME?

'So you are Assam-i?'

'What is that?' I quipped.

'Someone who is from Assam; like Bengal–Bengali, Gujarat–Gujarati,' replied my landlady.

'No, I am Assamese, like Sikkim–Sikkimese? Assam-i in my language means somebody accused of a crime.'

My riposte kicked up considerable mirth; and the matter was sorted for good. From Assami with an 'i', I became an Assamese to her.

Looking back at that conversation with my simple-mannered landlady in a South Delhi colony some twenty years ago, I feel that I had perhaps helped her grasp the point that in our country there also reside people who don't identify themselves only with the suffix 'i' attached to the states they belong to. That some sets of people may be categorized with the suffix 'ese' or 'ite' in English but may have their vernacular terms too to label themselves, just as the Assamese call themselves Axomiya (Asamiya) too.

Axomiya is a direct import of the Assamese word 'Axom', meaning Assam, the state. I didn't tread far enough that day to explicate further on the matter but history is witness to the fact that the same land may have had several different names in the past, and thereby some of the antecedents of a certain group of people may have labelled themselves by an altogether different name. Then, of course, there were names given to them by others too.

Today's Assam is Axom for the Axomiya community. The anglicized spelling of Assam speaks of the state's British colonial past, which also makes the people 'Assamese' in English language. Similarly, the name Axom (or Oxom) also envelops the medieval past of the community, making them Axomiya. And, if you go further back in history, more names of the present state of Assam will pop up; say, Pragjyotisa and Kamrup.

Both Pragjyotisa and Kamrup retain within their names their contribution to the antiquity of the land, and of the identity of the people who once populated them.

AXOM FROM AHOM? ASHAM TO ASSAM?

Nowadays, there is little doubt among historians of Assam that the source of the Assamese name Axom, to mean the state Assam, has everything to do with the Ahoms, those 9,000 people who began walking behind a dejected prince Sukapha when he left Mungmau, a Shan principality in Upper Burma, in 1215 CE, after his brother had ascended the throne. For thirteen years, Sukapha, advised by a pack of nine noblemen, wandered in the region; crossing the Patkai pass before setting foot on the Brahmaputra Valley in 1228 CE. Two elephants and 300 horses comprised his possessions from home. In addition, he had with him the prized heirloom to claim his Shan lineage—the revered Somdeo idol.[1] According to Sir Edward Gait, the Somdeo idol was still in possession of the last Ahom ruler Purandar Singha when he took refuge in Bengal in 1819 to escape the Burmese attack on Assam but 'was sold in Calcutta by a nephew of Purandar Singha when in financial difficulties'.[2]

Gait, in *A History of Assam*, provides a comprehensive account of the origin of the name of the state.

> Many attempts have been made to trace the origin of the word *Assam*. Muhammadan historians wrote *Asham*, and in the early dates of British rule it was spelt with only one *s (Asam)*. According to some, the word is derived from *Asama* in the sense of 'uneven', as distinguished from *Samatata*, or the level plains of East Bengal. This, however, seems unlikely. The term nowhere occurs prior to the Ahom occupation, and in the *Bansabali* (biography) of Koch kings, it (*Asama*) is applied to the Ahoms rather than to the country which they occupied. There is, I think, no doubt that the word is derived from the present designation of the Ahoms.[3]

Gait also highlighted that among the Ahoms themselves, it was believed that the word Assam was derived from Asama, 'in the sense of "unequalled" or "peerless".'[4] The term was given to them by the local tribes during Sukapha's invasion of Assam 'in token of their admiration of the way in which the Ahom king first conquered and then conciliated them.'

Though the word Asama is a Sanskrit derivative, which Gait sensed would not have been well-known to a Mongolian tribe, he still felt that this theory was sound. As the Ahoms call themselves 'Tai', meaning glorious 'and of this *Asama* is a fair Assamese equivalent'.[5] Proffering more examples of such possibilities, he had highlighted that the 'Burmese called Assam, *Athan* or *Weithali*; to the Chinese it was known as *Weisali*, and to the Manipuris, as *Tekau*. Van Den Broucke and other early European geographers called the country west of the (river) Bar Nadi, *Koch Hajo* and that to the east of it, *Koch Asam*.'[6]

The earliest reference to the state in a European language can be traced to 1590, as stated in the dictionary Hobson-Jobson: 'The dominions of the rajah of *Asham* join to Kamroop; he is a very powerful prince, lives in a great state, and when he dies, his principal attendants, both male and female, are voluntarily buried alive with his corpse.'[7]

Historian B. Bhattacharya however 'points out that the Vajrayana sect and the Bodhisattvas are called *asama* in the *Sadhanamala* and so the name of the country may be associated with them.'[8] The Buddhist influence in the area during the early period of Assam is noteworthy; the same land could have had a different name then. 'A distant association of *Asama* with Saumara (pitha) of the Puranas and the Tantras cannot also be ruled out.'[9] He also highlighted the use of the word 'Asam' in *Qazim* (by Persian historian Mirza Muhammad Kazim, the author of *Alamgirnamah*) and in *Padshah-nama*, the biography of Mughal emperor Shah Jahan written by Muhammad Warris, and 'Asem' by the seventeenth-century French traveller Tavernier in his book *Travels in India*.[10]

Some historians also link the origin of the word Asam to the Bodos, one of the oldest communities from the Tibeto-Burman stock to settle in Assam, by associating it with the expression 'ha-com', meaning lowland in their language. If this is true, then the name Asam or Acham or Asham must be much older than the Ahoms. However, in 2013, over a century after Gait posited his explanation for the possible origin of the name of the state, Nagen Saikia in *The History of Assamese People* argued that the construction of the present name of the land, Axom (or Oxom), was the fount of the construct Ahom—the community whose rulers led the Brahmaputra Valley for over 600 years in a row, the longest in Indian history. 'Between 1228 AD and 1523 AD, the Ahom kingdom stretched from the shores of Rivers Dikhou and Dihing to the Patkai and the border of the Naga hills. During that time, the nation ruled by the Ahoms was referred to as *Axom* by the others.'[11]

Saikia also underlined that the name Axom in the written form could be seen for the first time in Sankardev's adaptation of the Bhagawat carried out in the sixteenth century, where he replaced the names of the communities mentioned in the original Bhagavad Purana with local groups to make it more relevant to the people of the region. The saint wrote thus: 'Kirata Kachari Khasi Garo Miri/ Javana Kanka Guwal/ Axam Muluka Rajaka Turuka /Kubasa Mlecha Chandal'.[12]

Not Sankardev alone but his prime disciple Madhabdev too had used the name Axom to define a community, the Ahoms, not the nation they ruled. In the Vaishnavite verses in praise of Lord Krishna, Nam-ghosa, Madhabdev wrote: 'Hari na me Nahike Niyom Adhikari/Ram buli tore Miri Axom Kachari.' (O lord...you are called Ram by the Axom and the Kacharis.)[13]

Saikia had pointed out that though in the sixteenth century, Sankar-Madhab had used Axom to mean the Ahoms, in the seventeenth century, one finds the mention of the name Aaxam in Sankardev's contemporary Daityari Thakur's *Charita Puthi*. 'Aaxam Rajya' was also used to describe the Ahom kingdom. The same word is also used in the chronicle on Vaishnava saints, *Gurucharit*, said to be written by Daityari Thakur's father Ramcharan Thakur. But in the eighteenth century, in Suryakhadi Daivagna's *Darrang Rajbanshabali*, the word Axom is found wherever a reference is made to the Ahoms, the community. In some other old Assamese annals, the word Asama too could be spotted, leading Saikia to conclude that while usage of Axom was prevalent in the fifteenth to sixteenth centuries, the word Aaxam or Asama might have crept into the vocabulary later. As to how Aaxam or Asama might have slipped into usage, the *Datiyaliya Buranji*, considered an important source for information on the neighbouring states of the Ahoms, contains references to both terms.

In the *Kamrup Buranji*, an account of ancient Kamrup and the recurring conflicts of the Moghuls with Assam and Cooch Behar till 1682 CE, though the term Axom was used to describe the Ahoms, Asama was mentioned whenever the Ahoms were referred to by others. Looking at such variations in history, Saikia raised a pertinent point:

> If we speak in support of the usage of the term *Axom*, it can be deduced that in Magadhi Prakrit or Aprabhansha, or if we accept the existence of Kamrupi Prakrit, one can trace the birth of the velar fricative sounds—*talupia xo, modoniya xo* and *dontiya xo*. These sounds do not exist in any other modern Indian language. However, the springing out of the word *Hindu* from *Sindhu* indicates that the pre-Vedic Aryan languages had used *ha* to denote *sa*. Therefore, people

> outside of Kamrup might have also used the pronunciation *sa* instead of *dontiya xo* and that is how the term *Axom* gained the coinage of *Asam* or *Aasam*. On the other hand, those from the Tibeto-Burman lineage couldn't have pronounced *xo* and, therefore, took the next sound *ho*. If you look at it from such a perspective, you get to see that it is from *Axom* that the term *Ah-om* or *Aa-hom* was born.[14]

Saikia also emphasized, 'It is for sure that before the Ahoms arrived in the Brahmaputra Valley there was no nation called Axom or Assam or its inhabitants called Axomiya or Assamese. Therefore, both the words, *Axom* and *Axomiya* were the contribution of the Ahoms.'[15]

Noted linguist Suniti Kumar Chatterji had, however, claimed that the word Axom (with dontiya xo) was born of the term Ahom which might have come from the word Rhwam which is how the Burmese referred to a section of Shan people who had migrated to their land from South China. Sukapha's caravan had entered Assam from Upper Burma in the thirteenth century. Chatterji had also underlined that the term Rhwam is still used in Burma. In Assam, because of the Burmese influence, the word Shan could have become Shyam, Hiyam, Huwam, and Rhwam gradually. Saikia had refuted the argument thus: how could the word Axom or Asama get born of the word Ahom, when 'ho' is oft-seen replacing 'xo' in daily speech in Assam even in modern times, but never otherwise. Hence, there is a greater likelihood that the word Ahom was born of Axom than vice versa.[16]

Assam's first trained linguist Banikanta Kakati, who happened to be a student of Chatterji, has however, given prominence to the term Acham, by which the local tribes—the Borahi, Kachari, Moran, Sutia, Nora, and others—addressed the Ahoms. According to him, the word came from the Tai word Cham which means 'to be defeated' and since they were never defeated, the Assamese prefix 'a' was added to mean the undefeated. He had stated that Gait's reference to the word Asam 'may be a later day Sankritisation of some earlier form, like *Acham*'.[17]

US-based writer Rajen Barua, in a detailed article in the July 2009 edition of the popular Assamese magazine *Prantik*, also contradicted Chatterji's contention on the ground that he didn't lend any importance to the other communities contemporary to the Ahoms using the terms Axom, Asama, or Acham to denote them; and that no medieval text shows them being termed Ahom.[18] Barua, who has done extensive study on the etymology of the words Assam, Oxom (Axom), and Acham, referred to a UK-based Shan writer Sao Noan Oo who stated that Asam is a much older term, and all the three terms—Shan, Siam (Syam), and Asam—were derived from the word Sian which defines the Tai group of mountainous people who originally drifted from the Yunnan province of China to the Shan state in Burma in the sixth century. Barua also suggested that the term Acham or Asama had turned into Axom (pronounced Oxom in Assamese language) once the words began to be written down. The dontiya xo was first used to spell Asam or Asama by Sankardev. By using dontiya xo, he made sure that the word would have to be pronounced as Axom when one read it and not as Asama. 'It could be that the words were first taken from the Farsi or Hindi script, or it could be that in the earlier period the syllable dontiya xo was used in Assamese script to also mean prothom so (the soft s sound, as in Asama or Asam). We have such examples in Assamese language till date, say, the word bix (using talupiya xo) to mean the word bees (the number twenty in English) in the language. Same with baix (pronounced bais in Assamese meaning the number twenty-two in English), roxkora and roxogulla to mean the sweets roskora and rosogulla.'[19]

After Asyam, Asam, or Asama became Axom, the word had undergone a gradual sound variation to formulate the term Ahom, Barua argued, because the Tai people couldn't pronounce the dontiya xo and instead opted for the similar sounding syllable ho. The term Assam is, thus, not simply a British contribution but has its origin in the state itself. This may also be the reason why the British administration initially pronounced it as Asam, and had perhaps added an extra s to the word in order to emphasize the local pronunciation.

Rajen Barua had written the *Prantik* article to oppose the then Assam government's resolution to alter the state's name on the argument that the present spelling was a British legacy while the actual name of the state was Asom (Oxom or Axom). The government's resolution taken in 2006 was based on the suggestion of Chandra Prasad Saikia, the former president of Asam Sahitya Sabha. According to Barua, doing so would mean 'refusing to acknowledge the antiquity of the word *Asam* or *Asama* which is much older than *Axom*, *Asom* or *Oxom*. Also, by now, there are several brands with the name *Assam* that have gained national and international repute, such as Assam silk, Assam oil, Assam tea which would be lost forever if the term *Assam* is taken away from the state.'[20] He had also reminded readers that in 1905, during the division of Bengal, 'there was a threat to the term *Assam*. There was a possibility of combining Assam and Bengal to turn the area into a North East Province by the British. During that time, both the Europeans and Assamese had submitted memoranda to the British administration to not snatch the name *Assam* from the region. ... The name *Assam* or *Asam* has been used to mean our state for 800 years.'[21]

Though the likes of Barua had opposed the resolution, many of the powerful Assamese language lobbyists of the time came out in support of the proposal. However, the decision was eventually not implemented.

Pragjyotisa, Kamrup–Kamakhya

As mentioned earlier, in the drift of Assam's ancient names—Pragjyotisa and Kamrup-Kamakhya—one can also find remnants of not just what the region was but also of the people that must have inhabited the area.

Unlike Acham, Asama, Axom, the names of Pragjyotisa and Kamrup, and Kamakhya, exist in the epigraphs and ancient literary sources respectively, starting with perhaps the first century CE, during the reign of kings Narakasura and Bhagadatta, considered the first Kirata or Mleccha rulers of Pragjyotisa–Kamrup to establish an Aryan civilization in the region. Scholars like Choudhury state that since the word Pragjyotisa stood for both the city and the country, it was hard to establish its origin. However, he felt the name appeared to be a Sankritization of some non-Aryan formation. Banikanta Kakati too gave an explanation that rested on its non-Aryan origin using an Austric phrase: Pagar juh (jo)-tic, meaning a region of extensive hills.[22]

Offering another explanation, R. M. Nath in *The Background of Assamese Culture*[23] had stated that a set of people called Chao Theius of China had come towards India, and began to be known as Zuthis. They occupied three key centres. The branch that landed up in today's Assam began to be called Prag Zuthis which was subsequently altered into Pragjyotisa.

The furthest back one can go within Indian classical writings while looking for the word Pragjyotisa is *Sankhayana Grhyasamgraha*, or the *Grihya-sutra* by Sankhayana which mentions it as a sacred country associated with the solar cult. One finds it in the Ramayana too, through a reference to the foundation of the kingdom, peopled by Mlecchas, ruled by an Aryan king Amurtaraja, one of the four sons of king Kusa.[24] Later texts like Mahabharata, Harivansha, Vishnu Purana, and Brahmanda Purana, also mention Pragjyotisa, but not Kamrup, which leads scholars to state that the term Kamrup used for the same land could have been a later development. In Kalika Purana, Brahma is said to have made the first calculation of the stars at Pragjyotisa, making it a city equal to that of Indra (Indraprastha).

In fact, 'Prag means former or eastern and Jyotisa a star, astrology, shining. Pragjyotispura may be taken to mean the city of eastern astrology.'[25] Yet, this may only be an indication of 'the early importance of the place on astrology and astronomy'[26] which is confirmed by a number of Assamese manuscripts, dealing with these subjects. Markendeya Purana, said to be written in about 250 CE, makes reference to the predominance of the solar cult in Pragjyotisa. The presence of the Naba-graha Temple (temple of nine planets) on a hill top in Guwahati known as Narakasur Pahar, the Surjya Pahar (sun hill) in Goalpara, the continued obsession of common Assamese folk to consult astrologers periodically and wear a number of stones on their person to placate various planets, the presence of the Assamese subgroup Ganak, distribution of fish among relatives when the horoscope of a newborn is written—these can only be called remains of rituals practised on that land at some point in history. Choudhury had connected the solar cult in Pragjyotisa to the arrival of the non-Vedic Aryans in the land, combining it with the practice of fire worship during the Assamese festival Magh Bihu as 'relics of a vanishing Austric and Alpine-Iranian culture in ancient Assam'.[27] The words Kamrup and Kamakhya are similarly believed to be of Austric or Alpine origin and are often seen together in classical texts. Banikanta Kakati, while agreeing to its Austric link, has argued that the word denoted the birth of a new cult of Austric divinity since the name Kamrup was always followed by Kamakhya.

Interestingly, two other stories are related to Kamrup-Kamakhya. One is in a *Gopatha Brahmana* text delineating the story of the rebirth of the lord of love, Kamdev, by Shiva after he was burnt by him in rage. Kamdev was assigned by the gods to bring back Shiva to his normal state after the demise of his consort, Sati (Goddess Durga). The return of the rupa (rebirth) of Kamdev by Shiva is said to have bestowed the name Kamrupa to the region. Another story alluding to the origin of Kamakhya is also a Shiva–Sati episode. As per Kalika Purana, a text written in Kamrup between the seventh and eleventh centuries, the genitals of Sati were said to have fallen upon Kamakhya as Shiva lugged her body around. Choudhury had linked both the stories to the Austric-Alpine culture prevalent in the region prior to the advent of Aryan culture. Kamdev's revival or rebirth can only be explained in the light of the prevalence of the cult of magic and sorcery associated with the Austric-Alpine culture; so also the story of Sati's Yoni falling on Kamakhya. According to the historian, the latter could also be 'explained on the basis of a pre-Aryan cult of the Phallus, receiving new orientation with the introduction of Aryan culture'.[28]

It is also to be mentioned that in the Buddhist texts such as the *Caryas*, in *Hara-Gauri Samvada*, and in Islamic sources like the *Tabaqat-i-Nasiri* and *Riyaz-us-Salatin*, the word Kamrup is not found, but Kamru or Kamrud is mentioned. Hiuen Tsang had called it Kamolup in 640 CE. In the Tang dynasty classic *Tang-shu*, the word used for Kamrup is Kamopo and Komelu. In classical Sanskrit literature, such as the works of Kalidasa, the name Kamrup occurs side by side with Pragjyotisa.

Referring to another description in the Kalika Purana, Saikia thought that the place may have taken its name from the time when the goddess came to Kamakhya covertly to meet Shiva (another name of Durga is Kama). According to linguists, the root of the word Kama as mentioned in Kalika Purana, lies in non-Aryan words like Kamoi, Kamyot, Kumoi, etc. Some say that Kamrup drew its name from a god named Kamru, who was also not from the Aryan fold.

Kalika Purana has another tale about the birth of Kamrup. Soon after Naraka of Mithila took over as the king of Pragjyotisa and was placed in charge of Goddess Kamakhya, the land changed its name to Kamrup.[29]

Location and Stretch of Pragjyotisa–Kamrup

While there is no doubt in the minds of the majority of Assamese people that Pragjyotisa–Kamrup is ancient Assam, by the river Lauhitya (the Brahmaputra), the abode of Goddess Kamakhya, this idea is still contentious among some historians. R. C. Majumdar, for instance,[30] had claimed that Pragjyotisa was not in present-day Assam but in Odisha. He also argued that there was a Pragjyotisa in the northwest of India based on an inscription of a little-known Shahi ruler from Gilgit named Patoladeva who claimed that his lineage was from the Bhauma dynasty, a name historians in general associate with the Pragjyotisa kings Naraka and Bhagadatta. On that basis, Majumdar had concluded that there was a Pragjyotisa kingdom in that part of the world and the name Pragjyotisa and the dynasty, Bhauma, may have later shifted to present-day Assam from their initial location. Bengali scholar Benu Madhab Barua had placed Pragjyotisa in eastern Punjab. While countering these arguments with a number of reasons, P. C. Choudhury had underscored a valuable point: that there is no evidence of the existence of Kamrup–Kamakhya anywhere except Assam. Saikia too pointed out that the ancient traces of Pragjyotispur still remain in Assam.[31] In the

Mahabharata, during the ritual of Asvamedha, one finds the mention of Bhima's campaign in the Lauhitya region in the east.[32] Choudhury added further reinforcement to support this:

> That Kamrupa always implied Assam or at least a part of Assam, is proved by the extant literature of the period. The close association of Pragjyotisa with the Lauhitya and Kamarupa-Kamakhya in both epigraphs and literature points to their existence in the same region from the dawn of history. The *Arthashastra* (by Kautilya), referring to various places of Kamarupa in connection with its industrial products, confirms its location in Assam. We have examined other literary sources, beginning with the Epics, the Brhatsamhita, the Raghuvamsa and the early Puranas and the Tantras which indicate the ancient kingdom of Pragjyotisa-Kamarupa lay to the east of Lauhitya.[33]

In the local grants of kings, the name Kamrup does not appear; only Pragjyotisa and Pragjyotisadhipati can be found. The first mention of Kamrup can be found in the fourth century, in the Allahabad Pillar inscription of Samudragupta. Thereafter, it is found in several other grants. Lauhitya too finds mention in contemporary epigraphs. That the later inscriptions had mentioned Kamrup and that only one, the Bhagalpur grant of Narayanapala, mentioned Pragjyotisa, further lends credence to the contention of scholars like Kanak Lal Barua that the name Kamrup had a medieval origin while Pragjyotisa was the ancient term. Several scholars have also pointed at the first important European classical work, the *Periplus of the Erythrean Sea*, to suggest that ancient Assam was known to its writers. Scholars like Choudhury deduced that Chryse might have comprised parts of southwest Assam, southeast Bengal, and Burma and could have extended till the Philippines. 'Chryse may have stood for a vast area, which included also parts of Assam and Bengal.'[34]

As late as the fifth century BCE, Brhatsamhita mentions that the confluence of the Ganga and the Brahmaputra formed the East Sea, which meant that at a time when Pragjyotisa was a thriving country, a major part of southeast Bengal was still under the Lauhitya Sea and the Bengal Delta was just starting to form. Till the Epic age (Later Vedic Age), places like Mymensingh and three-fourths of modern Bengal (east Bengal) were under the Lauhitya Sea and this was where the Brahmaputra emptied after taking a southern course bending around the Garo hills.[35]

Banking on a number of such classical accounts to show the antiquity of Pragjyotisa, Choudhury argued, 'It appears from the accounts of both *The*

Periplus and Ptolemy's geography that their authors knew something of the geography and peoples of Assam and that during the first–second century AD if not earlier, the land was known as Thina or Seres and extended from the extreme Sadiya region to southeast Bengal.' Archaeological findings have shown that the ancient city stood where the present city of Guwahati does. Pragjyotisa enveloped 'the area from Dispur to Jatia-Narakasurgaon and beyond to the west, lying to the south of Kalapahar (a neighbourhood in present-day Guwahati), surrounded by hills on all sides and marked by royal establishments including fortresses. The capital was no doubt at times extended beyond the Brahmaputra.'[36]

A later Sanskrit work, *Hara-Gauri Samvada*, divided Kamrup into four segments: Saumarpeeth, Swarnapeeth, Kampeeth, and Ratnapeeth. If one draws an imaginary map of the then Kamrup based on the text, it would look like this: Saumarpeeth spanning the northern and southern parts of the Brahmaputra stretching between Dikrong or Dikorai River and Bhoroli; Bhoroli till river Barnadi constituting Swarnapeeth; Kampeeth spanning the land between rivers Barnadi and Sankosh and from Sankosh onwards till river Karatoya embracing Ratnapeeth.[37]

As per later texts like Vishnu Purana and the Tantras, the Pragjyotisa kingdom might have stretched till river Karatoya in the west, and at times beyond the river too, and also included Manipur, the Jaintia hills, Cachar, parts of Mymensingh, Sylhet, Rangpur, and portions of Bhutan and Nepal.[38] In the first century CE, the kingdom may have 'extended up to the gulf of the Meghna, probably up to Noakhali and Chittagong coasts.'[39]

While in 643 CE Hiuen Tsang wrote that the entire kingdom was over 2,600 kilometres in radius, *Tang-shu* mentions crossing over a large river named Ka-lo-tu to reach Kamrup, which may be the Karatoya. Kanak Lal Barua, in his notable work *Early History of Kamrup*, stated that Pragjyotisa appeared to be larger than most of the kingdoms mentioned in the Epics or early literature. The boundary up to the Karatoya remained intact until the Pala line of kings ruled Pragjyotisa–Kamrup, the beginning of the second quarter of the thirteenth century.

As Nagen Saikia accurately pointed out in his book, no social unit, community, or state can frame its history within a short spell of time. Brick by brick, over widths and lengths of time, does the past of a community build itself, and then provide clues to the present. Various names and boundaries of Assam in various epochs of history only prove that it was the same for the Assamese too.

3

AXUR–DANAB–MLECHHA, ROJA–MOHAROJA–SWARGADEO: THE RULERS OF ASSAM

A flight of over 200 steps surrounded by flower beds and hedges takes you to the tip of Agnigarh, a hillock in Assam's Tezpur city. Assamese romantic songs play in the backdrop, likely to remind visitors of the popular local belief that it is here that the most fabled Assamese love story unfolded.

The hillock, overlooking a vast swathe of the waters of the Brahmaputra, has been the sanctuary of the community's collective memory of the famed legend of Princess Usha, who is believed to have rebelled at some point in Assamese history against her father, Baan Roja, the king of the ancient city of Sonitpur (present-day Tezpur). The rebellion was due to the king's refusal to permit Usha to marry Aniruddha, the handsome grandson of Lord Krishna.

According to popular lore, Usha had seen Aniruddha in a dream and had since fallen in love with him. Vehemently opposed to her choice, Baan Roja imprisoned his beloved daughter in Agnigarh, hoping she would change her mind. During Usha's confinement, her confidante and artist Chandralekha who was by her side, drew a sketch of Aniruddha based on the princess's description of her lover. That moment of love and longing is depicted on a stone slab placed at the peak of Agnigarh by the government of Assam during a beautification drive in the 1990s. The addition of music to the historical site is also to their credit.

Stories like that of Usha and Aniruddha have a special significance in Assamese history, considering the lack of archaeological evidence. This has compelled historians through the decades to seek their historicity in oral accounts, classical texts, lores, beliefs, and remnants of certain social and cultural practices. By that yardstick, Usha's confinement at Agnigarh by Baan Roja can be seen as more than a fable. It is also a Vedic tale to legitimize the Aryan civilization by showing how it vanquishes the 'other'—the asura, the danab, the demon—punishing it for its non-conformity, and thereby bringing under its sway not just a strip of land but also spreading its culture and practices among the people that are conquered; in this case through love.

Though the forging of the ties with a set of people of non-Aryan roots is shown through the tale by establishing a romantic relationship between Usha and the grandson of Krishna, the incarnation of the Vedic god Vishnu, this is followed by Lord Krishna annihilating the father, the asura, the danab, the non-conformist. Since at least four Assamese kings, identified in classical texts and legends as asura, were vanquished by Krishna or Vishnu, a bit of foregrounding of the Aryan–non-Aryan contact, clashes, and subjugation in ancient Assam is necessary here to get a grip on the early history of the region.

Baan Roja or Baanasura was one of the four annihilated asura kings. Baan was the eldest son of King Bali of Sonitpur and succeeded his father to the throne. It is noteworthy that King Hiranyakachipu, killed by Lord Vishnu's Narasimha (half-lion) incarnation for not accepting Vedic Hinduism as followed by his son Prahlad, was an ancestor of Baan Roja. In *Early History of Kamarupa*, Kanak Lal Barua had shown Hiranyakachipu's son Prahlad as the great grandfather of Baanasura.[1]

Present-day Tezpur, or the land of blood (Tez), is the ancient city of Sonitpur, the capital of Baan Roja. Though remnants of old structures can be found in several parts of Tezpur, there is still a dearth of serious efforts by concerned authorities such as the Archeological Survey of India (ASI) to conduct more excavations and field studies in and around the city to put an approximate time stamp on Baan Roja's reign. However, in 1948, R. M. Nath, in *The Background of Assamese Culture*, placed Baan Roja's rule in around 1900 BCE, stating that the king had established his monarchy in the present Dinajpur district of West Bengal with Sonitpur in present-day Assam as the capital by the banks of Lohit, the Brahmaputra. Baan Roja had formed the kingdom by capturing the principalities of two ethnic tribes of Assam belonging to the Tibeto-Burman stock: the Bodos (in the Kapili Valley, in modern-day middle Assam) and the Dimasas (in parts of present-day Arunachal Pradesh).[2] According to British historian Edward Gait, Baan Roja's fort could have been where the Tezpur courthouse stood in the early nineteenth century. 'Numerous carved stones and frescoes are still to be seen in the locality, but they seem to have belonged to temples rather than to a palace. About a mile to the west is an old silted-up tank (*pukhuri*) which is ascribed to his time, and another tank in the same neighbourhood still bears the name of Kumbhanda, his prime minister.'[3]

Bhalukpung, the city that Baan Roja's grandson Bhaluk had built, still exists as a town by River Kameng along the southern reaches of the

Himalayas in Arunachal Pradesh, thus indicating the extent of the ancient kingdom at least till that frontier. As of 1905 the old fortifications of that city were 'still visible' and the Aka (Hrusso) tribe of Arunachal claimed Bhaluk as their ancestor, suggesting that they were 'the remains of a people who once ruled in the plains and were driven into the hills by some more powerful tribe.'[4]

Though leftovers of history in the form of 'carved stones and frescoes' are certainly a sign of a kingdom that had once thrived, not much else is known. As per inferences from classical texts and their understanding by early historians on Assam, just as Baan Roja met his end at the hands of Lord Krishna so also did King Naraka or Narakasura, who is considered the first great king of Pragjyotispur, the founder of the Bhauma dynasty.

BHAUMA DYNASTY

The early kings of Pragjyotisa–Kamrup are largely considered to be of danab and asura lineage by Assamese historians based on prevalent legends and classical texts and on the existence of certain physical traces till date, such as the Narakasur village and Narakasur hill, in and around Guwahati. Early British historians like Gait had mentioned Mahiranga Danab as the first known king of Kamrup who was succeeded by a line of kings: Hatakasur, Sambarasur, Ratnasur, and Ghatakasur. 'No details are given regarding these rulers but their appellations *danab* and *asur* suggest that they were non-Aryans.'[5] Mahiranga Danab had his capital in Mairanka, which 'suggests an Aryanisation of some Austric formation with "ong" meaning water.'[6] 'The probable historical character of the chief seems to be indicated by the existence of a hill, Mairanka-parbat in Beltola near modern Gauhati (Guwahati); but how and when the kingdom was established are not known.'[7]

It is possible that the name Mairang was Sanskritized into Mairanga. As per Kanak Lal Barua, 'It is clearly a Bodo name and the people of this race who then inhabited the country were called Kiratas and Mlechhas as they were Mongolian immigrants.'[8] Choudhury, though, had maintained that the Kiratas had probably a trace of Alpine blood 'because the foundation of the Kirata rule book took place at a time when the Alpines may have already settled in eastern India.'[9]

As per Kalika Purana and *Yogini Tantra*, the classical Sanskrit texts written in medieval Kamrup, the curtain on the Mahiranga Danab's line of rule came down with the killing of Ghatakasur by Narakasura with the help of Krishna, thus enabling a new line of rulers in ancient Assam under the Bhauma dynasty. Nath's book, a fascinating take on the history of Assam, presented an interesting tale about how Narakasura came about instituting a kingdom in Pragjyotisa. 'Siradhwaja Janaka, the king of Mithila who by giving the daughter (Sita) in marriage to Ramchandra (of Ayodhya), was in a way responsible for crushing the influence of the *asuras*, brought up an orphan *asura* boy in his family and gave him education along with the royal princes. The boy is said to have been left at a crematorium immediately after his birth by his parents probably due to some illicit background, and Janaka picked him up from that uncomfortable environment.'[10]

A young Naraka began to outshine the princes, instilling a fear in King Janaka and the queen about him usurping the throne someday. On sensing their feelings, a dejected Naraka, accompanied by friends and followers, left the kingdom on the pretence of bathing in the Ganga and marched eastwards to reach the shores of the Brahmaputra. The then king of Pragjyotisa was Ghatakasura whose subjects, as per Nath, were Kirata 'of yellowish complexion, short stature, flat nose, round face and shaven heads and fond of drink and raw meat—very likely Austrics and Bodos.'[11] Ghatakasura, by then, had lost his kingly valour and soon met a crushing defeat at the hands of a valiant Naraka. 'The king was killed, some of his subjects fled eastwards to the sea shore, while others who survived the massacre submitted to the invaders.'[12] The young asura king, conditioned in Aryan culture, adopted a royal name Nara-ka, presumably imitating his godfather Jana-ka, both meaning the protector of men. Ghatakasura's capital Prag-Zuh-This was retained as Pragjyotispur.

In the classical texts however, Naraka's claim of descent is shown to be from Bhumi, the Mother Earth, and her divine union with Vedic Aryan god Vishnu in the form of a boar (Varaha) to birth him. Thus was born the name of his dynasty, Bhauma. 'The mythological union of the earth with the boar is explained as a stage of geological evolution when the earth had just emerged out of water and was in a clayey state so that all the creatures on her were besmeared with clay like a boar soaked in mud; and the people claiming their origin from this mythological union, in other words, claimed themselves to be the first human race on the face of the earth.'[13]

On ascending the throne, Naraka maintained friendly terms with Mithila. If you go by the classical texts, he had, true to his training, begun propagating Aryan culture in Pragjyotisa by settling down Brahmins from

Mithila (Kannauj) and gradually effaced the Austric and Tibeto-Burman cultures, sometimes by annihilation and sometimes by assimilation. 'The Austric Ka-Mei-Kha and the Bodo U-Mei-Ludai were gradually assimilated to the Hindu pantheon and became goddess Kamakhya and Siva Umananda (The Umananda temple till day is located in the midst of the Brahmaputra close to Guwahati city).'[14] Aryan culture hence swept through ancient Assam.

By Nath's account, Naraka's Bhauma dynasty ruled Pragjyotisa for several generations, enabling the spread of Hinduism in the region. 'But this also gave an impetus to the *asuras* living in other parts of India. Many of them flocked to the kingdom ruled by a king of their race, and others who could not move, owed theoretical allegiance to the Naraka and sent him contributions from their respective areas.'[15] Nath claimed that the asuras populating the western, north-western and the northern parts of India considered themselves subjects of Naraka and each chief considered him to be his deputy.

P. C. Choudhury, however, posited a different theory regarding the asura origin of Naraka. The eminent historian felt that the association of the kingdom of Videha with that of Pragjyotisa during Naraka's time in the classical texts was significant because Videha 'also very likely formed part of the Alpine-Iranian culture of eastern India.'[16] Since the army of Naraka's successor Bhagadatta is described in Mahabharata as having Mongoloid features, there is a possibility that Narakasura's lineage could be traced from the Bodos, one of the oldest tribes of Tibeto-Burman stock to settle down in the Brahmaputra Valley. Choudhury had, however, disputed this on the ground that the Tibeto-Burmans could hardly establish themselves in the form of a kingdom in their early period in the Brahmaputra Valley. 'The evidence of such a domination and rule, as indicated by the survival of the remnants of their language and culture in the names of places and rivers is to be attributed to a later period, just prior to coming of the Ahoms.'[17] The rule of the Kiratas, the first of whom was Mahiranga Danab, was certainly in the early period of Assamese history, he had supposed that 'it didn't amount to more than the foundation of a small principality; while the dynasty of Naraka that followed it can reasonably be called the first political dynasty in Assam.'[18]

While Barua had suggested that both Naraka and Janaka had Dravidian roots and concluded that there probably was a Dravidian kingdom ruling Kamrup during the period of Mahabharata as the phallus was an idol of worship in Pragjyotisa, Choudhury countered this: 'The worship of the phallus in the temple of Kamakhya may be associated with some pre-Aryan Austric culture, developed later on into the cult of Sakti, and this does not prove the Dravidian origin of Naraka.'[19] Since Barua himself had stated that the earliest Aryan colonists in Assam were the Kalitas, 'the kings of the Naraka line were probably Aryan Kalitas. Whatever may have been the actual origin of Naraka and his descendants, there is no doubt that the Brahmanas extolled them as Aryan Ksatriyas and made them perform the various caste ceremonies, usually observed by Ksatriyas.'[20] Therefore, 'it is reasonable to hold that, as the Kalitas were the Alpines with an admixture of Aryan blood, Naraka had the same origin.'[21] To my mind, what needs to also be taken into account is that in neighbouring Bhutan populated by people of Tibeto-Mongoloid stock, the phallus is the principal item of worship till date. Interestingly, Chimi Lhakhang, the seat of a fertility ritual with the phallus as the deity at Punakha, is a chorten, a Buddhist monastery. The association of the Kalitas of Assam with the Buddhist Koliyas, as mentioned in Chapter 1, becomes most interesting if this custom in Buddhist Bhutan is taken into consideration. Naraka 'may have been called [an asura in the classical Hindu texts] by the compilers of the Puranas because of his inclinations towards Buddhism.'[22] Though when exactly Buddhism swept through the Brahmaputra Valley has not yet been established, that it did is beyond doubt. Not for nothing did the Burmese and the Chinese called olden Assam Wessali, meaning Vaishali, an ancient city associated with Lord Buddha. Vaishali, in present-day Bihar, is also the birthplace of Lord Mahavira and there exists a temple to Lord Mahavira at Surya Pahar in Goalpara, alongside multiple stupas of varying sizes which are estimated to belong to the eighth and ninth centuries.

Sanskrit texts have uniformly given prominence to Narakasura's Aryan and Kshatriya 'birth' from Bhumi—fathered by Vishnu in the incarnation of a boar—and his subsequent upbringing in Videha through a string of legends, and that he was established as a king of Kamrup by Lord Krishna himself—a Yadava prince, and an incarnation of Vishnu—can be understood as a constant endeavour to undermine if not wipe out altogether his non-Aryan blood, but only to disclose later that he or one of his successors had resumed worshipping the linga (phallus), or a symbol of Shiva, like Baan Roja had. This only highlights that till that period, Shiva most likely was outside the Hindu pantheon. The Mahabhairav temple, said to have been built by Baan Roja which is still functional in Tezpur, is a Shiva temple with a linga. Baan Roja is widely believed in Assamese society to be one of the most ardent followers of Shiva. It leaves one wondering whether following Shiva, not Vishnu, in the early Vedic era led the lord himself in the incarnation of Krishna to eliminate both the asura kings Baanasura and Narakasura. Like Prahlad was installed as the king after his father's annihilation, Bhagadatta was installed as the king after the last Naraka was crushed by Krishna.

As to why Narakasura went back to his asura way of life: Baan Roja might have warned Naraka of the 'grave danger of giving a free hand in all matters of the state to the Deva party.'[23] Taking Baan Roja's advice to heart, Naraka returned the Kamakhya temple to the Austrics and set up 'an *asura* institution named Parasuram Kunda at the source of the Lohit river.'[24] When some Brahmins brought a sage from the family of Vasistha muni they were not allowed to enter Kamakhya; this was considered a huge insult to the Brahmins residing in the area. Protests ensued in Pragjyotisa, pushing Naraka to imprison many. 'Sri Krishna, the king of Dwarka, the leader of the Deva party at the time, came with a strong army and after a very stiff fight killed Naraka and disbanded his army. Naraka's treasury was looted, his trained elephants were presented to the king of Delhi, his jewelled umbrella was taken away and Naraka's son Bhagadatta was installed on the throne as a vassal and ally of the Devas denuded of the hereditary title of his family.'[25] However, as per Chinese traveller Hiuen Tsang's account from the seventh century, the later Kamrup king Bhaskarvarman, who too claimed his lineage from Naraka, had gifted an ornate umbrella to his contemporary, the Magadha king Harsha, calling it a family heirloom. This invalidates Nath's claim, at least as far as the umbrella is concerned.

On the north bank of present-day Guwahati stands the temple of Asvakranta, meaning 'ascended by horses'.[26] As per local belief, it was there that Krishna stopped by when he came to subjugate Pragjyotisa. 'A number of small holes in the rock near the river are pointed out as the footprints of his (Krishna's) horses.'[27] 'The story of Krishna's invasion may perhaps be taken to indicate an expedition by some ancient Aryan chief. We have already seen that as far back as 105 AD, an Indian king named Samuda was reigning in Upper Burma, while in 322 AD, a prince of Cambod in north-west India set up a kingdom in Siam; it is, therefore, by no means improbable that other adventures found their way, at a still earlier period, to Northern Bengal and Assam.'[28]

In all, the Bhauma dynasty had nineteen kings after the first Naraka. Bhagadatta, his successor, is presumed to be a contemporary of the Pandavas and the Kauravas of Mahabharata as he is mentioned to have fought in the Kurukshetra War as an ally of the Kauravas. The Drona Parva of Mahabharat speaks of Bhagadatta's exploits and bravery, how he saved Duryodhana from the clutches of Bhima in the battlefield, and how Arjuna succeeded in stopping him only after eight days of intense fighting—he was no petty character in the epic. In the Udyoga Parva of Mahabharata, Bhagadatta is described as an equal to Arjuna. Prior to the Kurukshetra War, Bhagadatta had come under the sway of Jarasandha, who was described in Adi Purana as an asura in his previous birth.[29] A powerful king, Jarasandha, ruled over a number of Aryan and non-Aryan kings in northern India and was invincible. Krishna, Bhima, and Arjuna had to surreptitiously enter the city in disguise to eliminate Jarasandha to ensure that Yudhisthira could be the emperor. After the Kauravas had lost the Kurukshetra War and Bhagadatta his life, probably along with a son, the kingdom must have come under the political sway of the Pandavas and subsequently under Magadha after Bhagadatta's immediate successors.

In Kalika Purana, we find reference to the four sons of Naraka: Bhagadatta, Mahasira, Madhavan, and Sumali. Since some records had named a Vajradatta as Bhagadatta's successor, it could mean none of the last Naraka's remaining sons ascended the throne. *Harshacharita*, the biography of emperor Harshavardhan written by his court poet Banabhatta, had mentioned Pushpadatta and Vajradatta as Bhagadatta's successors. While the grants of the later Pala kings mentioned Vajradatta as Bhagadatta's brother, both the Dubi and Nidhanpur grants of later Kamrup king Bhaskarvarman referred to Vajradatta as Bhagadatta's son.

It is not clear who ascended the throne after Vajradatta. The thirteenth-century texts like *Hara-Gauri Samvada* penned in Kamrup had stated that the Pala line of kings began their rule after Vajradatta and continued to rule for at least seventeen generations. The last kings of this line were Subahu and Suparua. 'Subahu became an ascetic and went to the Himalayas, and was succeeded by his son Suparua, who was afterwards killed by his ministers.'[30] No clear account, mythological or otherwise, could be found for a protracted period as to what immediately ensued after this act of regicide. The political history of the wider Assamese community during the early historical era is fraught with ambiguity at multiple places, making it difficult to establish any kind of chronology. However, Gait still concluded that the numerous references to the Bhauma kings Narakasura and Bhagadatta in ancient literature 'as well as from the remarkable way in which their memory has been preserved by the people of Assam down to the present day, that Narak and Bhagadatta were real and exceptionally powerful kings and probably included in their dominions the greater part of modern Assam and of Bengal east of the Karatoya.'[31] 'It is wrong to infer that Pragjyotisa alone continued to flourish throughout the (early) period' as there is historical evidence that hints towards the existence of kingdoms in places like Davaka, Kadali, Manipur, Hidimba, and Tripura 'though subsequently these may have been absorbed by the larger kingdom of Kamarupa.'[32] It could be reasonably concluded that during an early period in Assam's history, Bodo or Mongoloid chiefs had set up their principalities after Naraka and his successors, when the central kingdom of Pragjyotisa began to disintegrate. As per Nath, around the sixth century, several Austric, Tibeto-Burman, and Aryan principalities may have sprouted up in several parts of ancient Assam. Since the Kiratas comprised the majority of the population, this could be the reason why Assam was described as Cilata in the Nagarjuni Kunda inscription of Deccan in the second century CE.[33] It was also during this political interlude that Vajrayana Buddhism had crept into olden Assam. In the western part of Assam, the Dhekeri state (now Lower Assam), which is believed to have been influenced by Buddhism too, had sprung up encompassing the contiguous Goalpara and Kamrup areas.

VARMAN DYNASTY (350–654 CE) AND KUMAR BHASKARVARMAN (594–650 CE)

The Varman reign in Pragjyotisa–Kamrup had begun with Pushyavarman. Copper plates from the era of Bhaskarvarman, undoubtedly the most renowned king from the dynasty, had helped historians of Assam to gather the genealogy of at least thirteen kings from that lineage, spanning their reign in ancient Assam at least till the middle of the seventh century. Based on epigraphical studies, it has been argued that the Varman dynasty might have risen to power in the first century CE, but there is still ambiguity about when and how Pushyavarman, the first king, ascended to the throne. There is also disagreement among historians about whether Pushyavarman was a contemporary of the powerful Magadha king, Samudragupta (350–75 CE). By the fourth century CE, the Guptas had risen to eminence in Magadha. Pushyavarman's likely concurrent rule with Samudragupta's reign had come to the attention of researchers primarily because it is in the Allahabad Pillar inscription of the Gupta emperor that Kamrup finds its first historical mention. But the name of its king is not cited, therefore the ambiguity. The inscription recorded that frontier kingdoms like Nepal, Kamrup, Davaka (a kingdom in middle Assam), and Kartipura were 'pratyanta nripati' or under the sway of the Gupta empire. Though there is no epigraphic evidence to support this, historians like Kanak Lal Barua were of the opinion that Subahu, a king from the Naraka dynasty who had supposedly challenged Samudragupta's suzerainty by keeping in captivity the horse meant for the latter's Ashwamedha yagna, was none other than Pushyavarman. In that case, it would not only make him a contemporary of Samudragupta but also a vassal as he might have had met a crushing defeat at the hands of the Magadha king after interrupting the free movement of the horse. Accepting that Subahu was Pushyavarman would also explain the story about him performing obeisance to the Gupta emperor as mentioned in the Allahabad epigraph.

R. M. Nath, however, placed Pushyavarman's reign in around 350 CE when he ruled over a small kingdom in central India (near Pushkarna). He might have ruled Kamrup as a representative of Samudragupta by adopting the Naraka lineage after driving away the king of Kamrup to Davaka. 'Who this Pushyavarman was, and how he traced his pedigree is not known, but a tradition is current among the Hajongs, a Bodo tribe of Assam, that Pushyavarman's original name was Pradangshu and he was a son of a fugitive of Malava area who fled for her life to Kamarupa when her husband and father-in-law were killed in a battle with the Satavahanas. This tradition, when connected with the Varman kings mentioned in the Susunia rock inscription of Bankura (Bengal) and in the Mehrauli pillar inscription of Delhi makes irresistible suggestion that Pushyavarman belonged originally to central India.'[34] When Samudragupta took control of Bengal, Pushyavarman might have aided him, resulting in his accession to the throne in Kamrup, either by marrying locally, or just by adopting the Naraka lineage. Choudhury saw no basis for truth in that conclusion simply because nowhere did one find mention of Samudragupta invading Kamrup. Due to absence of historical evidence, he also rejected the idea of Kamrup coming under the sway of the Guptas. Rather, he highlighted that since Pushyavarman had declared himself Maharajadhiraja (king of kings), it only indicated his independent status and that after a long spell of insignificance he might have been able to elevate Kamrup to some prominence in the political sphere of ancient India. According to noted historian Surya Kumar Bhuyan, Kalidasa's reference to Raghuvamsa of

Raghu crossing over river Lauhtiya (Brahmaputra) causing the defeat of a Kamrup ruler was at the hands of the son of Samudragupta, the equally accomplished emperor Vikramaditya or Chandragupta II (380–415 CE).[35] It is worthwhile then to mention that Nath had written about Samudravarman coming to the aid of Chandragupta II when he had faced rebellion from the Khasa tribe after the death of his father, Samudragupta. Though the Davaka king, presumably of Tibeto-Burman origin, had sided with that tribe, he had to soon dispatch an emissary to the Chinese king for help but his effort was in vain. It must have been during this time that Davaka began to see its downfall and Samudravarman adopted the Maharajadhiraja title.[36] In history books though, Davaka is shown to have united with Kamrup only between 420 and 440 CE during the reign of Kalyanavarman, the grandson of Samudravarman.[37]

Historians like N. N. Vasu placed Pushyavarman between 275 and 300 CE and assumed that it was his grandson, Balavarman, who was a vassal of Samudragupta. One finds a name, Balavarman, mentioned in the Allahabad epigraph. There is also mention of Balavarman hosting the swayamvar of his daughter Amritprabha who chose the prince of Kashmir Meghavahana as her groom.

About the Gupta-era association with Kamrup, what is to be noted is that the ASI had dated the doorway found at the Da Parbatiya site in Tezpur not later than the sixth century and significantly, had found traces of art from the Gupta period on its carvings. It only indicates the existence of some influence of the Gupta empire in Assam during that period. The Gupta empire lasted till the middle of the sixth century. (The Umachala rock inscription from the fifth century, located on the north-eastern slope of the Nilachal hill in Kamakhya, provides the earliest historical record discovered so far in Assam about the establishment of a temple in the Brahmaputra Valley.)[38]

During the Varman rule, the kingdom of Kamrup was extended to Bengal by taking advantage of the weaker hold of the Guptas on it by then. That development might have occurred during the reign of Skandagupta (445–67 CE).[39] Mahendravarman who ruled between 450–85 ce was said to have extended the boundary.[40] 'The importance of [Mahendravarman's] political career can be gauged from the performance of his two Asvamedha sacrifices…he was the first Kamarupa king to perform the Asvamedha sacrifices, indicating his independent status and political influence over his neighbours.'[41] Based on the Nidhanpur epigraph, it can be said that the boundary of Kamrup had stretched to include territories in Pundravardhana (in present-day Bangladesh as well as the present Dinajpur district of West Bengal) to the west of Trisrota (Teesta) between 545–50 CE when King Bhutivarman was on the throne. The decline in the Gupta empire's hold over Bengal must have made this conquest possible. It also meant that Sylhet was under the sway of the later Varman dynasty of Kamrup. Nidhanpur and Doobi copper plates contain references to grants of huge tracts of land made to Brahmins in Sylhet and North Bengal at this time.[42] 'Bhutivarman's victories not only made him master of North Bengal, and the outlying regions of Samatata, Tripura, Sylhet, Cachar, Davaka, including greater portions of modern Assam in the east, but also laid the foundation of the future greatness of Bhaskara.'[43]

After Bhutivarman, four other kings occupied the throne at Kamrup before Bhaskarvarman, one of the most illustrious monarchs of eastern India, came to power. The reign of Bhaskarvarman led to a new dawn in Kamrup's political history. His rule also has sufficient epigraphic evidence to support it, not just in the form of grants of copper plates but also via Chinese records, the Nalanda seal clays, and the *Harshacharita*. As per Assamese chronicle *Kamarupar-Puravrtta*, he ascended the throne in about 594 CE, after a short rule by his deceased brother Suprastisthitavarman. He assumed the title of Kumar perhaps because he became a king early in life, or maybe he remained celibate, a bachelor all his life. Significantly, Bhaskarvarman began the Kamrupa era probably just after his coronation which was also implemented in Karnasuvarna (Gaur or Bengal) after he occupied the area by chasing away its king Sasanka. 'It is, however, strange that this local era was discarded in favour of either Gupta or Saka era in the epigraphs, but survived in some circles for over 600 years.'[44]

Bhaskar was a contemporary of emperor Harshavardhan (590–647 CE), who ruled over North India with his capital at Kannauj; the latter's eastern territory touched Kamrup. It is likely that developing friendly relations between the two had become the need of the hour. Bhaskar, having already endured two attacks in close succession from Gaur king Mahasenagupta, and losing to him not only slivers of his territory but presumably his brother as well, had the burning urge in him to strike back at the kingdom (which had by then passed on to Sasanka) and thereby secure the borders of Kamrup. Harshavardhan, too, found it necessary to go after Sasanka. By then, Sasanka had killed his brother-in-law Grahavarman and also his brother Rajyavardhana, captured his sister and occupied Kannauj.

Harshacharita expounds on the alliance between Bhaskar and Harsha in detail. As per records, though the two kings were known to each other from earlier, their war coalition against Sasanka was ensured by Bhaskar's emissary Hamsavega, who visited Harsha's court with an assortment of exquisite gifts representative of his land and the people. The alliance was sealed and the duo succeeded in chasing away Sasanka not only from Kannauj but from Gaur as well. While Kannauj fell back to Magadha rule, Gaur became a part of Kamrup. Their alliance was significant because without Bhaskar's assault on Gaur from the eastern frontiers, Harshavardhan could not have been able to wrest back Kannauj from the north. Together, they rose to take on two of the most prominent powers then—the Guptas and their ally Sasanka.[45]

A triumphant Bhaskar issued the Nidhanpur copper inscription from his military camp at Gaur. Since Pundravardhana was already annexed to Kamrup during Bhutivarman's time, Bhaskar added Karnasuvarna (Gaur) too to it. There are several differing accounts about how and when Bhaskar had occupied these regions including that Karnasuvarna was annexed only after Sasanka's death, but such theories hold no water. Among other pieces of evidence, the Nalanda clay seal of Bhaskar supplied historical materials to indicate that the boundary of Kamrup had perhaps touched a region beyond Bengal. Both Harsha and Bhaskar left their seals at Nalanda to commemorate their visit. It could well be that Bhaskar had extended his territory till Nalanda by then.[46]

According to the annals of Assamese history, Bhaskar had heard about the genius of Chinese scholar Hiuen Tsang from a Kamrup Brahmin who lost a religious argument to the visitor at Nalanda and left the centre of learning completely impressed by his knowledge. On arriving in Kamrup, he related his experience to the king. Soon, Bhaskar attempted to send out an invitation to Hiuen Tsang to visit Kamrup through Silabhadra, the administrator of Nalanda, a native of Sylhet. When Silabhadra refused his request twice, he wrote a stern letter to him, threatening even 'to trample to the very dust that monastery of Nalanda.'[47]

'He could not have sent such a strong letter, had Nalanda not been within the sphere of his influence.'[48] The epithet 'king of eastern India' used in Chinese sources to describe Bhaskar is also noteworthy. It could well be true that his kingdom enveloped not only Assam but a large segment of Bengal and some parts of Bihar too, or at least the Nalanda belt. Hiuen Tsang was asked by Bhaskar if he would like to use the sea route to return to his home in China; this also indicates the physical extent of his kingdom. It could well be the delta of the Ganges and Brahmaputra opening to the Bay of Bengal. That the Chinese pilgrim crossed a large river to reach Kamrup, which scholars identify as Karatoya, also gives details about the physical map of the kingdom. Besides this, Hiuen Tsang also referred to a land route to the Szechuan region of China from Kamrup which suggests that the Kamrup borders had touched China on one side during Bhaskar's reign.

Bhaskarvarman is mentioned for the last time in the story of Wang-hiuen-ti's raid on Tirhut in about 648 CE. He had kidnapped Harshavardhan's minister Arjun who had usurped the throne after the king's death and brought under his control 580 walled towns. Wang-hieun-ti had taken Arjun to China. 'It may be concluded...that Bhaskarvarman lived until at least 650 AD.'[49]

SALASTHAMBHA OR MLECHHA DYNASTY (655–1000 CE) AND SRI HARSHA OR HARSHADEVA (730–50 CE)

Due to the availability of little to no evidence, there cannot be any accurate answers as to who immediately occupied the throne in Pragjyotisa/ Kamrup after Bhaskarvarman. A further cause of confusion is that he is taken to be a bachelor by historians and is said to have no heirs. There is, however, a general consensus that Bhaskar may have been succeeded by an Avantivarman, supposedly from his immediate family, but the throne was usurped by Salasthambha, believed to be from non-Aryan (Mlechha) stock, based on whose name this period of Assamese history is referred to as the Salasthambha or Mlechha dynastic reign. Taking advantage of the ensuing chaos after Bhaskar's demise in Bengal, where he had remained for the last part of his life, Salasthambha fomented a revolt and usurped the throne back in Kamrup.

Choudhury suggested that Salasthambha (r. 650–75 CE) may have been a relative of Bhaskarvarman or belonged to at least a parallel branch of the family of the Varmans, and, therefore, didn't overthrow the line or the dynasty of Bhaskarvarman but sprang up to the throne from within. Gait, however, branded Salasthambha as 'a great chief of the Mlechhas',[50] who was followed by kings Vigraha, Stambha, Palaka Stambha, Vijaya Stambha, and others of the same race ending with Shri Harsha. 'From the names of these Mlechha kings it may be concluded that they, like so many of their successors, were converted to Hinduism as soon as they became worthy of notice of the local Brahmin priest.'[51] Nath too posited that Salasthambha was put up as a leader by the orthodox Brahmins around Tezpur as they were vehemently opposed to Bhaskarvarman's growing proclivity towards Buddhism.

Under Salasthambha, the capital city was shifted from Kamrup to Tezpur and a new name, Hattokeshvarpur, was accorded to it in reverence to the deity of his supporters, Hattopeswar; the city later began to be called Harrupeswara. One finds mention of the vassals of Karnasuvarna (Bengal) and Samatata (East Bengal) increasingly displaying the propensity to rebel against the Kamrup king during this period, implying there was political upheaval in Kamrup at this time. It is also worth noting that the Tripura king had by then declared independence by bringing Cachar and the eastern part of Sylhet under him. It was probably shortly after the Salasthambha king Kumara's reign that Kamrup's control over Pundravardhana and further west was lost.

Kumara was succeeded by Sri Harsha or Harshadeva or Harshavarman (r. 725–50 CE) who took ancient Assam to yet another peak after the illustrious reign of Bhaskarvarman. The primary reason for such a claim was that Sri Harsha, perhaps for the first time, had extended the kingdom of Kamrup by incorporating Odra (Odisha), Gauda (Gaur), Kalinga (Ganjam), and Koshala (North Bihar). This theory is bolstered by Nepalese king Jayadeva II's epigraph where Sri Harshadeva was described as a descendant of Bhagadatta and as Gaudodradi Kalinga Koshala Pati. King Harsha's daughter Rajyamati was given in marriage to Jayadeva II.[52]

As per historian R. D. Banerji, Harshadeva had controlled Bengal for a long time which enabled him to pass through that stretch of land to conquer the contiguous segments of Odra, Kalinga, Kosala, and other areas. If such a claim of conquest is true, even if for a short while, Kamrup must have reached the pinnacle of its glory by the eight century CE. Ancient Kamrup 'included lands from Sadiya in the east to Ayodhya in the west, and from the Himalayas in the north as far as the Bay of Bengal and Orissa in the south-west. It included, therefore, Assam, Gauda, a great part of Orissa, portions of Magadha and a northern part of Madras State, including South Koshala. This conquest must have been completed before Yasovarman's invasion of Gauda and Magadha.'[53] As per S. K. Ayengar and Barua, it was Kamrup king Harshadeva who was defeated by Kannauj king Yasovarman who took over Gaur.

While Gait had concluded that the curtains came down on the Salasthambha dynasty with the killing of Harshadeva or Sri Harsha, Barua had tried drawing historians' attentions to the Tezpur grant of Vanamala, the grandson of later king Pralambha, which had called Salasthambha and Sri Harsha his father's ancestors. In a stray plate of later king Harjaravarman, there is a mention about Sri Harsha being succeeded by his son Balavarman II. 'With Sri Harsha's death, the empire which Bhaskarvarman acquired and which he largely extended also fell to pieces. Practically, the whole of Gauda passed out of the hands of the Kamarupa kings. Only a small stretch of the country in northern Bengal appears to have been retained in Kamarupa for we find that Vanamala, who ruled in the ninth century, granted lands within this area.'[54]

Scanning through the various histories of Assam, it can be safely said that five rulers ascended to the throne after Pralambha. All these kings had their capital at Harrupeswara. The Borgaon grant of the later king Ratnapala mentioned the fall of the Salasthambha dynasty after the reign of Tyagasimha, though when this exactly happened is debatable. While Barua had positioned Tyagasimha's rule between 970 and 985 CE, according to Choudhury his rule ended much earlier in 910 CE.

PALA DYNASTY (985–1130 CE) AND RATNAPALA

This new line of Assamese kings also claimed to be progenies of Naraka, thus reinstating this particular king's importance in ancient Assamese political history. On observing the extended line of rulers claiming the same legacy in olden Assam with such uniformity, what becomes apparent is that whether they were direct blood relations of Naraka-Bhagadatta or not must have become less significant over time than the allure of upholding the kirata or asura element in them.

Going by epigraphic evidence, the Pala dynasty of Assam had eight kings, beginning with Brahmapala and ending with Jayapala. As per the Bargaon grant of his son Ratnapala, Brahmapala was picked from among the Salasthambha brood after the last king, Tyagasimha, died without an heir. What is to be also noted is that in the Assamese chronicle *Hara-Gauri Samvada*, there is the mention of one Jitari, a Kshatriya, who came from a Dravida country along with a clutch of Brahmins and Kayasthas from Kannauj and Gaur to claim the throne after Tyagasimha's demise. Giving credence to this, Choudhury had remarked, 'It is possible that he came from the Nalanda region or Orissa, and was the descendant of the royal princes established by Bhaskara or Harshadeva, or from the region of North Bengal, which may have been ruled by a royal prince established by Vanamala.'[55] *Hara-Gauri Samvada* and the Bargaon grant had apparently claimed eight kings in that line. The kings mentioned in the Assamese chronicle following Jitari also had the surname Pala, and the last king's name was Ramachanda. 'The identification of Brahmapala with Jitari, therefore, appears almost certain,' Choudhury postulated.[56] Nath, however, linked Jitari to the Kamata king Arimatta in a much later period.

Choudhury had placed the rule of Brahmapala between 990 and 1100 CE. So far, two copper plates—Bargaon and Sualkuchi—from Ratnapala's reign have been discovered. As per his grandson Indrapala's epigraph, Ratnapala was a mighty king and 'crusher of his enemies....'[57] Ratnapala's capital, the impregnable Durjaya, was presumably set up on the north bank of the Brahmaputra opposite Pragjyotisa and was a prosperous settlement with merchants, learned men, religious preceptors, and poets alike making it their abode at the behest of the king. In the Bargaon grant, there is also a mention of Ratnapala coming in hostile contact with the kings of Gurjara, Gaur, Kerala, and Deccan.

Ratnapala's son was Purandarapala but according to epigraphic evidence it was his grandson Indrapala who rose to the throne. The Gauhati grant of Indrapala refers to the marriage of Purandarapala to a descendant from 'the royal races of the extreme kingdoms conquered by the victorious arms of the Jamadagni's son (Parashurama).'[58] The extreme kingdoms are 'probably...the ancient Kundina or Bhismaka, as given in the Vishnu Purana and the existence of which is shown by the ruins of forts and temples. The reference is significant as it shows that Ratnapala's kingdom may have touched the north-eastern frontiers of modern Assam.'[59] The Palas continued to rule from Durjaya after Ratnapala's death. It is possible that the name of a town in present-day Assam, Hojai, was born out of Dujai, a corrupt form of Durjaya.

As per Indrapala's grants, he too donned the grant moniker of Paramesvara Paramabhattaka Maharajadhiraja. From this rather ostentatious title, one may infer that he did not cede any territory during his reign. That Indrapala had embarked on an invasion and vanquished the powerful king of Vanga (Bengal), Kalyana Chandra, who had gained military fame by defeating the king of Gaur, is evident from the Gachtal inscription of Gopala. 'By this brilliant conquest, Indrapala extended the frontiers of his kingdom in the west to include a major portion of modern Bengal. Another important event of his reign is his marriage alliance with the Rastrakutas which was but his diplomatic triumph over his political rivals of Gauda and Vanga.'[60]

Indrapala was succeeded by his son Gopala, as evident from the grants of Dharmapala, his grandson. The grants also prove that the lineage of the Pala kings ended with Dharmapala. His rule was followed by a period when Kamrup was in decline, which was taken advantage of by the neighbouring Bengal king. Rampala, the then king of Bengal, is said to have sent a large army to invade Kamrup under his general Mayan. Mayan succeeded in his endeavour and set up Mayangarh (today Mayang). When a vassal by the name Tingyadeva revolted during Kumarapala's reign in Bengal, he was killed by a Vaidyadeva who subsequently declared independence. He gradually extended his rule over a major part or whole of Kamrup, precipitating the end of the Palas altogether in olden Assam. Though there are a few kings who are known to have ruled Kamrup after Vaidyadeva, there is no historical corroboration to state for sure who succeeded him. The closest we can get is the mention of a king, Vallabhadeva (1107 CE), in the Tezpur plates, who belonged to a line of kings who traced their lineage from 'Bhaskar'. This Bhaskar could well be the deceased Varman king Bhaskarvarman.[61]

FIRST INVASIONS INTO KAMRUP

Though it is not clear who succeeded Vallabhadeva, during the first Muslim invasion of Kamrup in 1205–1206 CE, Prithu ruled Kamrup as per the *Tabaqat-i-Nasiri* by Minhaj. According to the Kanai Varasi rock epigraph of North Gauhati, Bartu was the ruler at this time. According to British civil servant Sir Thomas Wolseley Haig's interpretation, the Kamrup king who not only crushed the army of Baktiar Khilji which had launched itself from Bengal, but also Giaduddin Iwaz in 1226 CE, was Bartu. He was eventually overthrown by Nasiruddin, Iltutmish's son, in 1228 CE. The North Gauhati inscription also mentioned the first date of Muslim attack on Kamrup on the thirteenth of Sott or the Hindu month of Caitra in the Saka era 1127, while the Nagaon inscription placed the second invasion in the Saka era 1149, meaning 1227 CE.

In order to decipher who Bartu or Prithu was, P. C. Choudhury looked at the Nagaon inscription which recorded that King Visvasundaradeva had ordered a Canakakanta to repair the damage done by the Mlechhas (as it referred to the Muslim army) to the temple of Shiva. 'Visvasundaradeva was probably the real name of Bartu or Prithu, as mentioned by Minhaj; he may have been the son or successor of Vallabhadeva.'[62] British revenue official from Bengal Province E. G. Grazier, in the *Report on the District of Rungpur*, highlighted that local traditions spoke of Prithu as a great king of Kamrup who also erected high fortifications in the present-day Jalpaiguri area of Bengal. It could well be to ward off any further Muslim incursion. The Shiva temple damaged by the invaders may have been situated in Jalpaiguri as per the *Yogini Tantra*. 'So, Prithu, Jalpesvara and Visvasundaradeva may probably stand for the same ruler, who after the repulse of two invasions of Bakhtiyar and Ghiasuddin Iwaz, was finally overthrown by Nasiuddin.'[63]

The subsequent Muslim invasion of Kamrup was helmed by Ikhtiyaruddin Yuzbak in about 1256–57 CE. 'At this time, immigration of Muhammadans began slowly into this part of the country and in 1312 AD, the Moor traveller Ibn Batuta, the ambassador of the emperor of Delhi to China, on his way through Assam, met a Mohammadan sage, Shah Jelal, on a hillock, to the west of the Garo hills—near present Mahendragarh, surrounded by a large number of disciples.'[64] Shah Jelal went on to become a celebrated Sufi saint in Bengal whose name is often linked to the conquest of Sylhet and the spread of Islam in that region.

Yuzbak's steady march towards Kamrup was curtailed by a Kamrup king named Sandhya as per the Vaishnava text *Gurucharit*. Due to the continued assault by rulers from Bengal on present-day North Guwahati, and with the Kacharis increasingly being pushed towards Guwahati due to the advent of the Ahoms, Sandhya moved the capital further west to Kamata. That move gave rise to a separate line of eight Kamata kings, and eight other rulers, possibly of another stock, from around 1250 CE to 1498 CE. This paradigm shift was momentous because the Vedic Hinduism largely patronized by the Kamrup and Tezpur kings since ancient times began to progressively lose splendour, giving rise to a cluster of non-Aryan principalities within medieval Assam. A number of principalities—of the Ahoms, Sutiyas, Kacharis, and Khasi–Jaintia zones, among others—began to thrive on the eastern and southern side of the Brahmaputra Valley, which together would subsequently go on to swing the axis of Assam's political past till the time the Koch kingdom raised its head in the west in the sixteenth century to challenge these forces.

KAMATA KINGS AND NILAMBAR

The name of the kingdom—Kamata—is believed to have been derived from Kamada, Kama, or Kanta, all names of Goddess Kamakhya, mentioned in the Kalika Purana. The goddess worshipped in the capital cities of Harrupeswara (Tezpur) and Durjaya (North Guwahati)—as Kameswar Maha Gauri or Maha Gauri Kameswar—was said to have been transported to the new capital by the Kamata kings, subsequently acquiring names like Kamteswar, Kamteswari, Kanteswar, and Kanteswari. King Sandhya might have shifted his capital after defeating Tugril Khan in 1255 CE. The Kamata kingdom included the Goalpara, Barpeta, and Kamrup districts of modern Assam besides a segment of northern Bengal and parts of Mymensingh to the east of the Brahmaputra as it flowed through that district at the time. Around the time the king transferred the capital to Kamata, the founder of the Ahom dynasty, Chaolung Sukapha, had more or less entrenched himself firmly in Charaideo in Upper Assam. The hostilities between the Ahoms and the Kamata kings began towards the end of the thirteenth century. To guarantee peace between the two kingdoms, it was probably Kamata king Pratapadhvaj (1305–25 CE) who gave his sister Rajani (who some say was his daughter) in marriage to the third Ahom king Sukhangpha (1293–1332 CE). Rajani's son Chao Pulai was appointed Saring Roja, a deputy to the Ahom king, but he later rebelled and sought help from his maternal family, the Kamata kings, to grab power. The then Kamata king, presumably Durlabhnarayan (1330–50 CE), brought his forces to Saring in 1340 CE. Tensions were defused at the behest of the Ahoms. Durlabhnarayan was a significant Kamata king during whose reign poets like Hema Saraswati, Kaviratna Saraswati, and Haribor Bipra contributed a number of splendid works to classical Assamese literature. As per the annals of the Ahom rulers, the Kamata kingdom became embroiled in a conflict with the Ahom kingdom yet again towards the end of the fourteenth century. However, at that time, the Muslim invaders from Bengal approached the Kamata boundary again, leading the king to seek military help from the Ahoms; the combined forces chased away the enemy.

A number of other kings ruled the Kamata region but there is no established chronology for who ruled when. Besides Dharmanarayan, K. L. Barua placed eight other kings—Indranarayan, Arimatta, Sukaranka, Sutaranka, Mriganka, and then Niladhaj, Chakradhaj, and Nilambar—between 1350 and 1498 CE. The last three kings were probably from the

Khan or Khen dynasty. Historians had placed the Khen dynasty in the second quarter of the fifteenth century, after the demise of the Kamata king Mriganka. If this holds true, then the first Khen king was Niladhvaj who must have occupied the throne in around 1440 CE. 'He was succeeded by his son Chakradhvaj, who might have been the king who had faced the general of Sultan Barbak (Ghiasuddin Barbak Shah) and routed him near Sankosh river.'[65] His son Nilambar is said to have wrested a part of North Bengal most likely from Barbak.

There is little evidence to support the idea that Husain Shah, the Sultan of Gaur (Bengal), succeeded in capturing Kamata, though Edward Gait suggests that he did so in 1498 CE. Since this invasion was not recorded in detail by Shah's chroniclers, there exists little information on the Muslim rule in that part of Kamrup. It is, however, known that on reaching Bengal in 1502 CE, Shah had minted coins to commemorate his victory as the 'conqueror of Kamru Kamata'. He also left behind his son Daniel at Hajo as the governor and celebrated his success by erecting a madrassa at Malda, the inscription of which corresponded to 1501–1502 CE. It was also during this time that the masjid at Hajo, Poa Mecca, was constructed.[66]

Like Gait, Barua too ended the second Kamata line with King Nilambar. A litany of petty chiefs ruled after the retreat of the Muslim rulers from Bengal. 'This state of affairs continued for a few years and then the Koches under Biswa Singha made themselves masters of the country west of the Bar Nadi.'[67] The petty chiefs could either be Bodo chiefs, or the Bhuyans who were pushed into Kamata from Bengal due to Muslim incursions. As per Barua, Husain Shah's army could have been chased away by Nilambar with the active participation of the Bhuyan chiefs, several of whom had, by then, consolidated power by taking advantage of a gradually weakening Kamata kingdom. Several chiefs from among the Bhuyans who had settled there also adopted the Khan surname to add a sheen of nobility to their names. One of the Bhuyan chiefs who had submitted to Husain Shah after the escape of Nilambar was Ghosal Khan. A relative of Vaishnava saint Sankardev, who belonged to the Bhuyan clan, was named Buda Khan and yet another Ketai Khan. Husain Shah's chief minister was a Kayastha named Purandar Khan. Together, they might have come to be known as chiefs of the Khan or Khen dynasty of Kamata. After the loss of Muhammadan hold in that region, the Bhuyans returned to their old glory and the Muslims who had settled down there came under their control. R. M. Nath, however, has differentiated between Khan and Khen as added to the surnames in the Kamata region. While the Bhuyan chiefs had adopted the surname Khan to reconcile with their new rulers, the Khens were of Bodo race who had seized control of the Kamata kingdom. He also considered Nilambar a Bodo, and not a Bhuyan, who had hired several Brahmins at his court. As to why these kings didn't find much mention in Assamese chronicles, Barua wrote, 'It is true that Niladhaj and his successors were not mentioned either in the *Gurucharit* or in any of the local contemporary writings now extant in Assam valley. Perhaps these kings did not exercise any real authority over the eastern part of Kamarupa where the Bhuyans (another set of them) were ruling and that accounts for the absence of any mention of them in Assamese chronicles.'[68] To go by his chronology, Kamata continued to be the capital of the kingdom till the first quarter of the sixteenth century.

BARO BHUYAN AND SANKARDEV'S ANCESTOR CHANDIBAR

Though the Bhuyans were said to have been settled in middle Assam by the Kamata kings, they initially trickled into medieval Assam from next-door Bengal to escape persecution by their Muhammadan invaders. They had earlier fled Bihar to also escape Muslim rulers. Clearly, their surname Bhuyan had associated them with the landlordship, just like the Persian word zamindar. On settling down in western Assam with the blessings of the successive Kamata kings, they were handed over the same occupation. 'Probably, since the transfer of the capital to Kamatapur, the actual government of eastern Kamarupa, as far as the Subansiri in the north and the Kapili in the south, was in the hands of petty Bhuyan chiefs who were nominally feudatories of the kings of Kamata or Kamarupa but who were actually independent chiefs.'[69] While these chiefs were independent, they would often join forces to repel a common enemy. They behaved like feudal lords till the king was strong and in due course turned into petty rulers.

The notion of Baro Bhuyan (Twelve Bhuyan) in Assamese history is associated with this clan. The Bhuyan clan is said to have stemmed from seven families of Kayasthas and seven Brahmin families, settled by Kamata king Durlabhnarayan under the leadership of Chandibar in about 1330 CE. If this number is correct, by common sense, they should have been soddho (fourteen), not baro (twelve), Bhuyan. As per *Gurucharit*, the seven Kayastha families included an ancestor of Sankardev.

Unable to decipher the meaning behind Baro Bhuyan, which is attached to this group of people not just in Assam but in Bengal too, Gait had compared it to the Muhammadan term Panch Pir where different saints were counted by different people as five holy ones. His analogy was: 'It seems to have been the practice in this part of India for kings to appoint twelve advisors and governors. Nar Narayan (Koch king of Assam) and twelve ministers of the state; twelve chiefs of *Dolois* administered the hilly portion of the raja of Jaintia's Dominions, and there were twelve State Councillors in Nepal. The number may thus have become connected in the minds of people and with all dignitaries ranking next to a Raja, and so have come to be said in a purely conventional sense.'[70]

There are two popular narratives about the origin of the Bhuyans in Assam. The Bhuyans of eastern Assam had claimed their descent from Santanu and Samanta, grandsons of Samudra, a minister in Kamata king Arimatta's court. Samanta had apparently seized the Kamata throne by expelling Arimatta's son Ratna Singh. Samudra was succeeded by son Manohar who married Ratna Singh's daughter Lakhimi. Santanu and Samanta were their offsprings. There is a belief that while Santanu became a Vaishnava, Samanta became a Sakta worshipper, leading the two families to separate. While Santanu and his family settled in Rampur area of Nagaon in present-day middle Assam, Samanta remained in Lakhimpur area in the present Upper Assam. Sankardev, born in Borduwa area of Nagaon is said to be Santanu's descendant, though *Gurucharit* had stuck to the origin of the Bhuyans as settlers from Bengal. With increased Muslim invasions on western Assam, the Bhuyans seemed to have taken a lead in defending the borders, and established themselves as powerful chiefs before the rise of the Koch king Biswa Singha in the west towards the beginning of the sixteenth century. It was due to the Koch king's battering on them that had led several Bhuyans to move towards the eastern part of the Brahmaputra, to the Ahom kingdom.

KOCH KINGDOM—NARANARAYAN AND SILARAI

Biswa Singha, the founder of the Koch kingdom, is undoubtedly one of the most fascinating characters in Assamese history. Though there is little historical material on him compared to his two illustrious sons—Naranarayan and Silarai—sieving through available sources, one can surmise that his was, nonetheless, a story of naked resolve, of tenacity to dream big and make it happen.

Biswa Singha's birth name was Bisa. His father, Haria Mech or Haria Mandal, was the headman of a group of twelve Koch families within the Kamata region.[71] From the surname of his father, Mech, and the fact that he was a headman of a group of Koch families, one can infer that Bisa had tribal roots. However, there exists a legend that suggests that he was originally of Kshatriya origin but all Baro Bhuyan families had to conceal their true identity and hide in the jungle as Mech, and marry women from the Mech community because of the fear of Parashuram who had vowed to eliminate all Kshatriyas. Most likely invented by Brahmins around him, one can surmise this was an attempt to place him in the caste structure of Vedic Hindusim based on the notion that all powerful kings must have a Kshatriya origin. To possibly ascribe divinity to the king, another narrative was circulated to show that Bisa was the son of Shiva. 'He was named Bisu as he was born on the Bihu day (Visuva Sankranti).'[72] In the sixteenth century text *Behula Upakhyan* by noted litterateur from western Kamrup, Durgabar Kayastha, Bisa was named the lord of the Kamata of Kamateswar.

Bisa's great political and military successes are worth noting. When Husain Shah had invaded Kamatapur, resulting in Nilambar fleeing from his kingdom, Bisa was a young man. The Bhuyan chiefs were quick to ingratiate themselves to the new administration and thereby retained their feudatory powers over the region. Haria Mandal had come in conflict with one such Bhuyan in Phulguri area because of which he was taken captive, and released later only after paying tribute to the Bhuyan chief. His son, having watched all this unfold, had resolved to take revenge, not only on that particular chief but also on all such landed gentry. He went about subjugating them meticulously. By and by, Bisa conquered the entire southern portion of Kamrup till Guwahati. Thereafter, he turned his attention towards the north bank of the river and eventually succeeded in crushing all such petty chiefs, who either lost their lives to his sword or fled to the Ahom kingdom. That cleared his way to install the Koch kingdom and announce himself as the new king of Kamatapur, around 1515 CE—thus bringing the curtain down on about three decades of chaos in that region caused by Husain Shah's army. Bisa soon carried out a census of his subjects, organized his army by hiring military officers under various grades, say, Thakuria (more than twenty men), Saikia (more than 100 men), Hazari (more than 1,000 men), Umra (more than 3,000 men), and Nawab (more than 60,000 men).[73] The terms Hazari, Umra, and Nawab show Islamic influence on the region. Bisa, or Biswa Singha, also moved his capital from

Chikangram (in present-day Kokrajhar district of Assam) to futher west, to Koch Bihar (present Cooch Behar in West Bengal) where he erected a fine city to suit his new-found stature. With Brahmins as his advisers, he not only rebuilt the Kamateswar and Kamakhya temples demolished by the Muhammadan invaders and revived worship in these shrines but also brought in more Brahmins from Kannauj, Benaras, and other centres of Vedic learning from northern India to settle down in the Koch kingdom. Additionally, the influence of the Brahmins over him can also be observed in his decision to send his sons Malla Deva and Sukladhvaj—he had eighteen sons from various wives—for higher studies to Benaras.[74]

The king soon embarked on an expedition to militarily engage with the eastern forces, the Ahoms. Though the Koch chronicles state that he had invaded the Ahom kingdom but had to withdraw due to difficulties in ensuring military supplies, the Ahom Buranjis merely mention that he paid a friendly visit to king Suhungmung in 1537. During Biswa Singha's reign, in 1532 CE, the Muslim invaders repeated an attack on Assam but it was on Ahom territory.[75]

In about seven years' time in 1540 CE, Biswa Singha passed away after contracting smallpox while his two eldest sons were still in Benaras. His third son, Nara Singha, taking advantage of the absence of the heir-apparent Malla Deva, installed himself on the throne. Rushing back from Benaras, the brothers challenged Nara Singha which forced him to abscond to Morang on the outskirts of Koch Behar. Since the local chief refused to hand him over, Malla Deva and his brother launched an attack on that territory, and defeated the chief, pushing Nara to escape further, first to Nepal, then to Kashmir before finally slipping into nearby Bhutan. Apparently, he never returned to the kingdom but may have become a ruler in Bhutan.

With Nara Singha gone forever, Malla Deva rose to the throne by assuming the name Naranarayan. He kept his brother Sukladhaj by his side, as his commander-in-chief. Together, they took the Koch kingdom to the pinnacle of glory. Sukladhaj, for his swift movements in war, was nicknamed Silarai or Chilarai, as the celebrated general in Assamese history who could supposedly fly like a kite in the sky.

Under Silarai's command, the Koch army subsequently subjugated the Kacharis, the Jaintia kings, the Manipuri king, and possibly the Tippera king as well as the Sylheti king. The Koches also met the Ahom army on the battlefield thrice. Around 1546 CE, an expedition under Silarai had reached the Ahom country, resulting in a battle at Koliabar where the Ahoms were routed. During the course of that attack, an impressive, 350-mile-long road was constructed by the Koch king from his capital Koch Behar till Narayanpur in Upper Assam, which is in the present Lakhimpur district. Since the work was carried out under the supervision of Gosai Kamal, one of the king's brothers, the road, completed in 1567 CE, was popularly called Gosai Kamal road; parts of it still exist. The Koches also erected a fort at Lakhimpur, named the area around it Narayanpur, which is known by that name till date. While a strong resistance from the Ahoms forced the Koch army to retreat to safety, in 1562, yet another offensive was launched on the Ahoms under Silarai. This time, the Koch army stepped into the Ahom capital city Garhgaon, near today's Sivasagar town. 'Some months later, the Ahom raja sued for terms, and peace was concluded on the following conditions, viz, the acknowledgement of the Koch suzerainty, the delivery of a number of sons of the chief nobles as hostages, and the payment of an indemnity, consisting of sixty elephants, sixty pieces of cloth and a quantity of gold and silver.'[76] The next skirmish between the Ahoms and the Koches occurred a decade and a half later during which the Ahoms were defeated once again, leading them to submit to the Koches.

Silarai's army is also said to have turned towards the Padshah of Bengal. 'There is very little authentic information about the war, but according to the chronicles of Koch kings, [Naranarayan] was the aggressor. His army under [Silarai] was defeated, and [he] was taken prisoner. The Muhammadans ascended the Brahmaputra as far as Tezpur, but they made no attempt to take permanent possession of the country, and returned to Bengal after demolishing the temples at Kamakhya, Hajo and other places.'[77] The general who led the blitz on medieval Assam in about 1564 CE for the Bengal Padshah, Sulaiman Kararani (1563–72 CE) was Kala Pahar, part of contemporary Guwahati as the name of a locality. Kala Pahar is also said to have demolished the Jagannath temple at Puri in Orissa in 1568 CE.[78] The accounts of the aggressors, though, don't mention taking Silarai as a prisoner. The invading Muslim army had to retreat because of an incursion in Orissa. After the invaders had left, Naranarayan reconstructed the Kamakhya temple. It is said that he was under the influence of bad stars at the time and, therefore, a stone slab placed at the temple mentioned that it was repaired under the supervision of his brother Silarai. Two statues—one of the king and the other of Silarai—were also installed at the premises. Lakhs of animals were sacrified at the temple during its re-inauguration event.[79]

About two years later, when following the Bengal Padshah's passing away his son Daud ascended to the throne of Gaur, Mughal emperor Akbar developed an interest in annexing Gaur. Naranarayan joined hands with the Mughals to crush Daud, as revenge for the defeat he had sustained. In 1576 CE, the Mughals routed Daud's army with the help of Silarai who opened yet another war front with the Padshah of Gaur from Kamrup. However, the military cooperation between the Koches and the Mughals finds no mention in the Mughal-era records, unlike Assamese chronicles of the time. In *Ain-i-Akbari* though, there is a mention about Naranarayan sending an envoy with presents, including fifty-four elephants, to Akbar's court in 1578 CE. The text had said that the Koch king was powerful and had under his command 1,000 horses and 1 lakh foot soldiers. 'Chilarai (Silarai), thereafter, became an able ally of the Mughals. In 1583 AD, he appears to have cooperated with the Mughals in the fight with Masum Kabuli on the banks of the Ganges. Here, he contracted small-pox and died.'[80]

Silarai's demise was the beginning of the end of the Koches. Though Naranarayan, the king, was still on the throne, it was his beloved brother who had carried out all the military conquests and contributed to the glory of the Koch kingdom. After Silarai's demise, his son Raghu Deb rebelled against his uncle. From *Akabarnama*, it comes across that Naranarayan lived the life of an ascetic and didn't marry till late in life. He had married at the behest of his brother, and fathered a son. This must have triggered a fear in Raghu Deb about not being the natural heir to the throne any more.[81] Not willing to fight his nephew, Naranarayan chose to split the kingdom into two. While he kept the part west to Sankosh River to himself, he handed over the eastern tract of the river to Silarai's son. Gait had noted that in 1581 CE, the Muslim chroniclers clearly named the two parts of Koch kingdom as Koch Behar and Koch Hajo. Naranarayan died a dejected man around 1584 after reigning over the kingdom for half a century. The division of the kingdom sounded the death knell for the Koches. Gradually, fratricidal fights between Raghu Deb and Naranarayan's son Lakshmi Narayan began to develop and in due course the Mughals and the Ahoms stepped in to claim their territories. The local chiefs yet again took on more power sensing the weakening of the kingdom. Several mini principalities mushroomed in Kamrup. Taking advantage of the division in the family, Afghan ruler Isa Khan, having lost his terriroties to Shahbaz Khan, engaged with Raghu Deb in a war hoping to form a new kingdom. Though Raghu Deb succeeded in occupying a fort in Mymensingh in present-day Bangladesh, he couldn't hold it for long against Isa Khan's forces and had to flee. 'Following up his victory Isa Khan took from the Koches the whole country as far as the Rangamati in the Goalpara district.'[82] Raghu Deb died in about 1603 CE. His eldest son Parikshit occupied the throne, and moved his capital to North Gauhati. In the years after this, both the Koch branches sought the help of the Ahoms to crush each other but the Ahoms were busy fighting the Kacharis. To defeat the other, Lakshmi Narayan sought the protection of the Mughal emperor and became his vassal. *Akbarnama* recorded that Lakshmi Narayan also gave his daughter in marriage to Mughal governor of Bengal Raja Man Singh in 1597. Man Singh would later come to invade the Ahom country, unsuccessfully. In 1612 CE, Lakshmi Narayan travelled to Dacca to plead the Nawab, Shekh Alauddin Fathpuri Ismal Khan, to intervene in the fratricidal fight. The result was the invasion of Koch Hajo. After a month or so of intense combat, the garrison at the Dhubri fort fell; Parikshit was taken to Dacca and thereafter dispatched to Delhi to the Mughal emperor. As per local accounts, Jahangir agreed to restore him to his kingdom after getting an undertaking from him where he agree to pay a sum of ₹4 lakh to the Mughals. However, Parikshit fell sick on his return home and died on the way. His kingdom was then annexed to the Delhi empire with headquarters at Hajo. Parikshit's brother, Bali Narayan, had, by then, fled to the Ahom kingdom. Several chiefs from within the Koch unsuccessfully rose to fight the Mughals. After a while though, with the help of the Ahom forces, they were all chased away from Hajo and Bali Narayan was installed as the king as a raja of Darrang with the name Dharma Narayan. The new king then aided by the Ahoms went on to attack parts of Kamrup held by the Mughals but achieved no great success. It was only when Shah Jahan rebelled against his father that the Mughals became a bit disorganized which helped to restrict them around Hajo. Hajo slipped away from the Mughals in 1635, leading the Ahoms to grab the whole country west of Bar Nadi. The Ahoms placed Dharma Narayan's son Sundar Narayan on the throne under the supervision of a Barphukan, an Ahom viceroy. That king made Mangaldoi his capital. This ended the independence of the eastern Koch king who became a subordinate of the Ahoms after this. The western Koch kings continued to rule as vassals of the Mughals with Koch Behar as their capital. Post-Partition, Koch Behar became part of West Bengal while some fringes remained in Assam.

NARANARAYAN AND NILACHAL ARCHITECTURE

Aside from military accomplishments, Naranarayan's rule is also known for the propagation of art and culture, and for a unique style of architecture, termed 'Nilachal' by P. C. Sarma in his insightful book *Architecture of Assam* in 1988.[83] That the sanctuary offered by the Koch king to Sankardev proved to be a life saver for the saint is etched in Assamese public memory, but that he also encouraged a distinctive style of architecture which was later adopted by Ahom king Rudra Singha is not often noted, even though leftovers of that style of construction straddles present-day Assam and North Bengal.

Nilachal architecture is essentially a temple style which can notably be spotted in the Kamakhya temple on the Nilachal hills, restored by Naranarayan (1540–87). The style of this temple is unique because of its bulbous polygonal dome inspired by Islamic architecture. Such a dome can be spotted at the entrance of the revered Haigrib Madhav temple in Hajo too which was also renovated during Naranarayan's reign. The Nilachal style most likely also includes the turtle-shaped thick roof since it too made its appearance in the temple at Kamakhya after its restoration. A similar style of roofing was also done on the later Ahom two-storey Rang Ghar.

On the roof of Rang Ghar stand miniature replicas of the three Dols or temples constructed during Rudra Singha's tenure in Sivasagar sporting the Nilachal style dome: the Devi Dol, Shiva Dol, and Joi Dol. As to how such a Koch style of architecture was adopted in the Ahom country may be understood from the fact that Rudra Singha had hired the services of an architect from the Koch country, Ghanashyam Khanikar, to build those Dols and his palace Kareng Ghar. The concrete dome used in the Ahom temples was used in the tombs or maidam of the later Ahom kings too, before the structures were covered with earth and made to look like mini Egyptian pyramids. Such an architectural practice wherein there was a shift to concrete from the earlier practice of making maidams with bamboo and wood, began during Rudra Singha's reign.[84] The use of the dome could well be because Ahom rulers were also considered Swargadeo, kings of the heavens. The largest of the maidams built in that style at the first capital of the Ahoms, Charaideo, is believed to be that of Rudra Singha's while the first one with a concrete dome is said to be of his father Gadadhar Singha.

It needs highlighting that the entombing of the Ahom kings is a unique feature of Assamese historical edifices. Some tombs were enormous enough to accommodate not just the king's corpse but also his brigade of private help and, at times, the king's favourite elephant, all buried alive akin to that of the Egyptian pharaohs.

P. C. Sarma, highlighting the role played by Ahom king Rudra Singha in promoting Nilachal architecture in Upper Assam, wrote, 'His (Rudra Singha) successors simply reaped the benefit of what he had projected. His adoption of the "Nilachala type" in the construction of Jai Dol paved the way for the popularity of this form in Assam.'[85] A notable feature of these Ahom-era Dol, also found in the Kamakhya temple, is the sunken cellar in the sanctum sanctorum, a few feet below the plinth level of the main temple.[86]

'While the Islamic influence was prominent in a few temple architectures of his (Rudra Singha's) time, the indigenous *do-chala* type was given much more importance. A peculiar plan adopted in his time was the apsidal shape similar to the caityas.'[87] Sarma called the Fakuwa Dol built during his period 'the greatest of the innovations' of that era as it was 'the only type in Assam which does not maintain any link with the Indo-Aryan style which had dominated the architectural developments of the state.'[88] He found its architecture similar to some structures in Burma and Java too. 'Even the expression "dol" so popularly used to denote an Ahom (era) temple is found to have come from a Pagan race of Malay.'[89]

There exists yet another unique structure in Sivasagar called Ghanashyamor Ghar (Ghanashyam's residence). While some say it was built during Rudra Singha's third son Rajeshwar Singha's era for his grandson—it is also referred to as Naati Gosain Dol—others claim that it was built during Rudra Singha's time for the architect brought from the Koch country, Ghanshyam Khanikar, a Muslim by birth named Samuddin. The structure stands out not only for the turtle-back roof but for its unique terracotta exterior, the kind spotted in the later Kachari constructions in Khaspur in today's Barak Valley. Khaspur was granted to the Kacharis through marriage relations with the Koches and most likely those structures too were built by architects brought from the Koch country. The Khaspur palace of the Dimasa Kacharis, built in the nineteenth century, which stands today in a dilapidated state about twenty kilometres from Silchar town, also has the turtle-back roof.

Notably, Ghanshyam, after the completion of the palace of Rudra Singha, was put to death. The story goes that the king, on finding the architect Ghanshyam leaving the Ahom country with a drawing of the palace, suspected him of conspiring against him.

A clear difference in the use of building material from the earlier Ahom era architecture is noted when one looks at the Rudra Singha-era edifices. While the early Ahom edifices were of only wood and bamboo, the later ones had bricks. The practice of using wood and bamboo as the primary material for construction continued in Assamese society, though, till the British colonizers introduced to the state a new style of architecture, popularly known as Assam type houses. The style, even though it is essentially concrete, makes ample use of wood, bamboo, and a local reed called Ekora, thus fabricating a unique model of architecture by marrying indigenous Assamese practices with European aesthetics. The Assam type houses were seen by the British as an answer to dwell safely in the earthquake-prone zone.

However, on observing the ruins in the former Dimasa Kachari capital Dimapur (in present-day Nagaland), it may be deduced that it must have been the Kacharis who had the knowledge of using bricks for construction in the Brahmaputra Valley prior to the Ahoms.

In today's Cooch Behar in West Bengal, several secular and religious structures also exist with a Nilachal-style turtle back roof and dome-like structures. Even though later Koch king Nripendra Narayan had built his palace in 1887 inspired by the Buckingham Palace (European style), it also featured a similar dome.

KACHARI KINGDOM

The Kachari kingdom in medieval Assam had enveloped a considerable swathe of areas, from Dimapur in present-day Nagaland to Cachar in modern Assam, over a span of a few centuries. Since there are no written annals of the Kachari kings, historians have principally banked on the buranji of their contemporary, the Ahoms, to pluck out a sense of their sway and scope of supremacy in medieval Assam. Nevertheless, sifting through the pages of the Ahoms' written history, Gait had concluded, 'In the thirteenth century, it would seem that the Kachari kingdom extended along the south bank of the Brahmapurtra, from the (rivers) Dikhu (Dikhou) to the Kallang (Kolong), or beyond, and included also the valley of the (river) Dhansiri and the tract which now forms the North Cachar sub-division.'[90] There is also a theory that some of these parts in Barak Valley were included in the Tippera kingdom which the Kachari king inherited through marriage about 300 years ago.[91]

Though Gait doesn't talk about how the Kachari kingdom came into being, R. M. Nath had placed its birth in the 'chaotic period'[92] of the thirteenth century where 'innumerable chieftainships'[93] had mushroomed when each chief posed 'as an independent king over his area all along the country from the south of Sadiya up to the north of Nowgong along the eastern belt.'[94] He linked the origin of the Kachari kingdom to the Barahi principality which, owing to recurring pressure from the Ahoms, had to give up Charaideo in present-day Sivasagar district and move to the southern part of Darrang. Nath had credited the formation of Barhampur as the capital by the Kallang River to a minister, Virochana, of the Barahi king of Darrang. Virochana had fallen out with the king and moved his capital to Barhampur, in present-day Nagaon; the place still exists. Virochana's son, Vikramaditya-pha (pha seems to be a suffix drawn from the Ahom kings) is said to have shifted his capital further northeast to the slopes of the Mikir (Karbi) hills and named it Sonapur. A golden image of Durga was installed in the capital from which Sonapur derived its name. The place exists on the outskirts of Guwahati and still has its old name.[95]

While several Bodo chieftains joined forces with Naga chiefs to resist the rise of Vikramaditya-pha, he succeeded in neutralizing his detractors and thereafter shifted his capital near the Naga hills, to the banks of the Doyang River, and later to that of the Dhansiri. 'The first of these cities were called Kacho-mari, i.e. the city established for crushing the kings of the foothill kingdoms. The second city was established after all the turbulent chiefs were subdued; and after installing a stone image of Vishnu, the lord of Lakshmi, the goddess of wealth, the city was named Lakshmidrapur, the city of the goddess of wealth.'[96] In due course, Lakshmidrapur became better-known as Dimapur. The new name stemmed from the name by which the Kacharis were known: the Dimasa. 'In the Brahmaputra Valley, the Kacharis call themselves *Bodo* or *Bodo fisa* (sons of the Bodo). In the North Cachar Hills, they call themselves Dimasa, a corruption of *Dima fisa* or sons of the great river. They were known to the Ahoms as *Timasa*, clearly a corruption of *Dimasa*, so that this name must have been in use when they were in the Dhansiri valley.'[97]

While most historians of Assam agree that the origin of the word Kachari is difficult to trace, Gait had a theory. According to the Limbu legend of creation explicated by British enthnographer Sir Herbert Hope Risley in *Tribes and Castes of Bengal*, one of the two progenitors of humankind settled down in the Khachar country, which is also the name given by the Nepalese to the tract at the foot of the hills between the Brahmaputra and Kosi rivers. This progenitor became the father of the Koch, Mech, and Dhimal tribes. 'Khachar was an early home of the Mech or the headquarters of a powerful Mech dynasty, the members of the tribe in Assam may well have been called *Khacharis* or *Kacharis*; the omission of the aspirate is common…in words borrowed from Bengali or Assamese. The word *Khachar* is derived from a Sanksrit word meaning a bordering region.'[98] Gait had also categorically stated that the name of the present Assam district Cachar might have got its name directly from its principal tribe. In terms of language, while Gait had stated that the Kacharis were closely allied to the Koch community and also to the Sutiyas, the Lalungs (Tiwa), and the Morans of the Brahmaputra Valley, Sidney Engle, in his authoritative book published in 1911, *The Kacharis*, had often switched the words Kachari and Sutiyas with each other and had seldom used the term Dimasa, though today, we identify the Kachari kingdom primarily with the Dimasa tribe of Assam, and slot the Sutiya kingdom separately. In fact, Engle had tried to suggest that these communities had a common origin, including the Garos and the Barahis, and referred to them as Kacharis of different regions of olden Assam. Engle had noted that the Hindu influence among the Kacharis only became visible after moving to Khaspur, as did Gait, too, commenting on the ruins at Dimapur that 'the Kacharis were free from all Hindu influences'.[99] Nath, however, had written that the Barahi culture 'with the background of Hindu culture reigned supreme (in Dimapur), gods and goddesses of the Hindu pantheon were installed and worshipped in different parts of the empire.'[100] The kingdom flourished for three generations through kings Mahamani-pha (1460–70 CE), Mani-pha (1471–1485 CE), and Lado-pha (1485–1502 CE). As per Gait, two wars had broken out in 1526 between the Ahoms and the Kacharis; while the Kacharis were victorious in the first one, the Ahoms won the second. 'Hostilities were renewed in 1531, and a collision occurred in the south of what is now the Golaghat subdivision, in which the Kacharis were defeated and Detcha, the brother of their king, was slain.'[101] Five years after the Ahoms slayed the Kachari king, his relative Detsung rose in revolt against the Ahoms who once again defeated the Kacharis and occupied Dimapur. It was after this rout that the Kacharis left Dimapur and the Dhansiri Valley forever to move further south to institute their new capital at Maibong, by river Mahur, which flows by the present Dima Hasao district of Assam.

In Maibong, they faced another enemy—the Koch—under the valiant general Silarai. As per the Bansabali (family history) of the Darrang Rajas, the Kachari king lost to the Koch army in the middle of the sixteenth century. 'There is a small colony of people in the Cachar district known as Dehans. These are reputed to be descendants of Koches who accompanied Chilarai (Silarai)'s army and remained in the country. They enjoyed special privileges in the days of the Kachari rule, and their chief, or Senapati, was allowed to enter the king's courtyard in his palanquin.'[102]

The Ahom–Kachari skirmishes began to wane in the seventeenth century as for about four decades in that period, the Ahoms were engaged in war with waves of incoming Muslim invaders. Later Kachari king Tamradhvaj, a contemporary of Ahom king Rudra Singha, declared independence from the Ahoms, leading them to invade the Kachari kingdom in 1706 CE. The Ahoms could easily occupy Maibong; they destroyed the fort and left for their own country. Soon after this, Tamradhvaj passed away. His nine-year-old son was put on the throne with Ahom officials as advisers.[103] Much later, during the Moamoria uprising in the Ahom kingdom, then Kachari king Krishna Chandra offered protection to the rebels, resulting in another war with the Ahoms between 1803 and 1805 CE in which the Kacharis were routed. After Krishna Chandra's death in 1813 CE, his brother Gobinda Chandra occupied the throne. A subsequent invasion of the Manipuri king was the beginning of the end of the Kacharis, leading the British to ultimately take over the area in November 1838.

SUTIYA KINGDOM AND OTHER PRINCIPALITIES

The Sutiya kingdom was founded by someone named Birpal around 1194 CE by organizing fellow villagers from as many as sixty settlements along the hill tracts by River Subansiri. He soon adopted Hinduism, introduced it to his clansmen and a temple to Kuvera, the god of wealth, was built here since they lived by the Subansiri, the river that gave gold to the diggers.

R. M. Nath described Birpal as the general of a former Sutiya kingdom in the Jaintia hills. He had called the Sutiya community 'a section of Bodo'[104] who initially lived near the Swat Lake located in the east of the Manas Lake close to Bhutan before migrating in the middle of the seventh century CE during the Varman dynasty rule to the plains along the course of Subansiri River in the present North Lakhimpur sub-division. According to the historian, they were initially called Swatias by the residents of Kamrup which in course of time became Sootea/Chutiya/Sutiya. The Swatias comprised of four clans; all of them populated the frontier areas of Subansiri under the headship of twelve chiefs. Birpal was able to organize the villagers by taking advantage of the fall of the Pala kingdom. In course of time, some Pala chiefs were subdued; their kingdoms annexed to the principality. The capital city was named Ratnapur and, therefore, the king's name became Ratnadhvaj. As per the *Deodhai Buranji*, the Ahom chronicles, and W. B. Brown's *Deori-Chutiya Grammar*, there were ten kings who ruled the Sutiya kingdom, starting with Ratnadhvaj Pala and ending with Niti Pala. The third king Vikramadhvaj Pala, whom Nath placed between 1360 and 1390 CE, invaded the Kalita kingdom and brought it within his kingdom. But the win was short-lived as the Kalitas fought back. Finally, the Ahoms got involved and annexed the Kalita kingdom in 1512 CE, but they had to fight the Sutiyas till 1523 CE to annex the Sutiya territory. The Sutiya army apparently included the 120 wives of the last king, Nitya Pal, who were also soldiers. To escape the ignominy of defeat at the hands of the Ahoms under King Suhunmung, Nitya Pal and his main queen Sadhini killed themselves by jumping off the Chandangiri hills into a deep gorge.[105] The five-year-old Sutiya prince, Sadhak, was deported to Kabirali near Mangaldoi.

Apart from the major dynasties, Assam had several smaller principalities which also held sway over some expanses of land. History books indicated that those principalities could have cropped up largely due to the dwindling power of the Pala dynasty. One such offshoot was the Barahi kingdom. 'When the Pala dynasty was ousted, an enterprising young man of the Barahi race—Babru-Vahana by name—organized a big following of the Barahis and the Bodos and established an independent kingdom with his headquarters at Ghuguramukh, somewhere to the north-west of Dibrugarh.'[106] Gradually, they set up their seat of power at Charaideo, the name taken from the image of a bird god they had placed there. The first Ahom king snatched Charaideo from them, thus pushing the Barahi kings to the north bank of the Brahmaputra; they settled on the eastern part of Darrang by naming their capital Barhampur. In the seventeenth century, Pratap Singha attacked the Barahi kingdom too and seized its territory.

Yet another kingdom that rose from the ashes of the Pala dynasty is the Kalita kingdom. Several historians have theorized that a Kalita desa or a Kalita kingdom existed around Sadiya and spread towards Tibet. According to R. M. Nath, they thrived here after the Pala line of kings lost power.

He suggested a multitude of probable origins for the Kalitas: a set of Alpine Aryans entering Assam before the Vedic Aryans; people related to the Kolutus, the founder of the Kullu kingdom of Kashmir in the fourth century; they drew their name from the Tamil words for stone (kallu) and stone mason (kal-taton) connecting the community to artisans brought from the Deccan by the Pala kings to build temples and who settled in that part of the country. 'The mason, the carpenter, the iron and copper-smith, the potter and the cobbler—all fall under the same category of Kalitas. …A man in the lower grade of the society has a tendency to be classed as a Kalita, and the proselytising system marks the Kalita as the highest grade caste second only to the Kayasthas.'[107] This argument was also applied to hypothesize that the Kalita kingdom around Sadiya was the result of mobilization of these temple builders as they were the wealthiest and most powerful during the fall of the Pala dynasty. Nath's supposition was that they might have come under a leader who entered into a matrimonial alliance with the third Pala king Purandarapala and established the Kalita kingdom around 1132 CE in the north-eastern part of the country.[108] They founded their capital in Bishmaknagar, apparently in memory of the city by that name in Berar in the Mahabharata and connected themselves with the legend of Bishmak's daughter Rukmini's marriage to Lord Krishna.

With further consolidation of their territory, they moved their capital to Sodhoyapur on the north bank of the Brahmaputra and the town set up opposite the river was named Sodhoyaghat. Sodhoyapur later became Sadiya and Sodhoyaghat turned into Soikhowaghat. The kingdom had extended to the west up to river Subhansiri and included the north of modern Lakhimpur besides a portion of the river island Majuli. Nath's annals tell us that Majuli, those days, was called by a Bodo name Habung (or Haband), meaning a vast land. That kingdom was called Habung and was likely under Kalita rule. Nath had highlighted that Ibn Batuta, during his travels to China through Assam, had paid a visit to Habung and presented a glorious account of the place and its flourishing bazaars and art.

Though it is difficult to trace the exact geneaology of the Kalita kings, in Nath's account, we can find names like Suvali, Padmanarayan, Mohendranarayan, Premnarayan, Joynarayan, Kesavanarayan, and Ramchandra (r. 1375 CE). The weakening of the Kalita kingdom began with Ramchandra's rule. In 1512 CE, the Ahom king Suhungmung invaded the Kalita kingdom and annexed it.

Then, there were the Garo, Karbi, and Pator chiefs too who rule over some tracts of land but eventually came under the sway of the Ahoms. The Moran–Motoks of Upper Assam too had founded a principality around Dibrugarh (there is still a town there by the name of Moran) after the Bhauma Pala dynasty had collapsed.[109] For this kingdom too, not much is known about the exact genealogy of their kings. 'The Morans were very likely a remnant of the ancient Austric Moria clan intermixed with the Bodos. They were really the Mei-Morias (mei, mi-men, people) and were later on known as Maya-Morias or Moa-Morias.'[110] The Ahoms, on settling at Charaideo in 1253 CE, subjugated the Morans. After defeating Morans and Barahis, Sukapha 'wisely adopted conciliatory measures, and by treating them as equals and encouraging inter-marriage, he welded them all into one nation.'[111] However, in the eighteenth century, the Moran community revolted against the Ahoms in what is today known as the Moamoria rebellion. The rebellion substantially weakened the Ahom kingdom and hastened its downfall.

THE AHOMS, CHAOLUNG SUKAPHA, AND KING SUHUNGMUNG

The foundation of the Ahom kingdom in Assam which traversed a span of more than six centuries was laid by Chaolung Sukapha, a prince hailing from the Tai/Shan race from a territory set in Upper Burma. Like all other dynasties, the Ahoms also claimed that their kings were of divine origin. According to the *Deodhai Buranji*, god Lengdon commanded his son Thenkham to descend from the heavens to establish a kingdom on earth. A hesitant Thenkham instead passed on the duty to his sons, Khunglung and Khunlai. Lengdon presented the grandsons the family idol, Somdeo (life- and strength-giving god); Hengdang, a magical sword; two drums to invoke the gods for divine aid if necessary; and four roosters to forecast the omens. Khunglung was to be the king and Khunlai his chief councillor. They descended on earth in 568 CE on Mungrimungram, an uninhabited strip of land. On arrival, they realized that they had left behind the roosters. One aide was sent back to fetch them from the heavens and was rewarded the kingdom of China for accomplishing the task; the blessed Hengdang was handed over to him too.[112] Khunglung and Khunlai, thereafter, raised their kingdom in Mungrimungram. However, an ambitious Khunlai soon usurped the throne, forcing Khunglung to proceed further west with the Somdeo. He founded a new kingdom in Mungkhummungjao. The youngest of his seven sons, Khunchu, ascended the throne after his demise while the rest were made tributary kings of other principalities. The eldest of the sons who was handed over the Mungkhang principality, inherited the family heirloom, the Somdeo. Yet another son was made the king of Ava (Burma). The Burmese rulers always called the Ahom princes their 'brother kings'.

After seventy long years of rule, Khunglung's brother Khunlai's lineage was passed on to his son Tyaoaijeptyatpha. This is said to be the start of the Aijepa era, which is still prevalent among the Burmese and the Naras.[113] Tyaoaijeptyatpha, however, died childless, and the throne was filled by one of the sons of the Khunglung and Khunchu lineage. After him, the kingdom was divided between his two sons. While Mungrimungram was allocated to one, Maulung went to the other. That line of lineage also became extinct for want of a male heir after about 333 years of rule. Yet another of Khunglung and Khunchu's decendants was installed on the throne. One of that descendant's grandsons was Sukapha, the founder of the Ahom kingdom in Assam.

Sukapha, on finding himself in conflict with his stepbrother, left the city in 1215 CE with a swarm of followers and the Somdeo idol in tow; climbed over the Patkai range and stepped onto the Brahmaputra Valley. Interestingly, akin to all kingdoms in Assam which had accepted Vedic Hinduism, the Brahmins who converted the Ahom kings much later to the religion, spun a slightly different tale around the kings' divinity. 'It is said that Vasistha Muni had a hermitage on a hill east of Saumarpith. Indra held high revels there, and was one day seen by the Muni sporting with (wife) Sachi in his flower garden. In his wrath, the Muni cursed Indra, and condemned him to have intercourse with a low caste woman. This happened; a woman, who proved to be an incarnation of Bidyadhari, begot a son who was highly favoured by Indra. He had many children, of whom Khunglung and Khunglai were the eldest, and ruled in Mungrigmungram.'[114] The rest of this narrative matches that of the *Deodhai Buranji*. The *Deodhai Buranji* provides a full account of the route Sukapha and his followers took to reach Assam. That the Ahoms under Sukapha entered the Brahmaputra Valley much before the other Shan tribes of Assam is borne by the fact that they were not Buddhists. 'The Khamtis, Phakhals, Aitonias, Turungs and Khamjangs are all Shan tribes who have, at different times, moved along the same route from the cradle of their race; but the Ahoms were the only ones who did so before the conversion of its inhabitants to Buddhism. The other Shan tribes of Assam are all Buddhists, which shows that they migrated at a later date. The Turungs, in fact, did not reach the plains of

Assam until the beginning of the nineteenth century.'[115] However, there are competing theories here as well. R. M. Nath attributed the suffix 'pha' to all Shan kings (adopted by Ahoms too) to a distortion of Buddhism. 'The influence of Lord Buddha reached them only in a distorted form—Fvat, Fia, till he became Fa or Pha and was honoured by the use of the term as an epithet after the king's name.'[116] This hypothesis could well have a grain of truth in it as till date any relic associated with Buddha in countries like Laos has the term 'pha' or 'phra'. For instance, the Phra Bang Buddha is the most revered Buddha image in that country. Tam Pha in Laos is also known as Buddha cave and estimated to be over 450 years old.

Nath had also affiliated the Tai or Shans to the Mongoloid tribes—Chaos—from the western fringes of China who succeeded in overthrowing the Tsang dynasty in 112 BCE. These tribes constantly fought amongst themselves, pushing one segment among them to move to the southeast, to set up the Tai kingdom after subjugating the Mon-Khmers. The Burmese had called it the Shan or Sham kingdom. This lot came in contact with the Buddhist and Hindu faiths, and came to be known as the Siam or the Thai people. The conservative group, which remained in the hilly area of China, continued to pray to Somdeo and Al-Phra-Loung (Mother-goddess-lustre).[117] They, however, absorbed elements not only from Tsang culture but also from the Egyptians with whom they had trade relations. This was why the Ahoms buried their kings and nobles in maidam. Nath also linked the Ahom kings' practice of writing their histories in the form of buranji as an adoption of Tsang customs.

Between 1215 and 1228 CE, Chao-Ka-Pha or Sukapha had to face the Nagas, Barahis, and Morans. While he took conciliatory measures to include the Morans and Barahis to formulate a nation after bringing them under his sway, he perpetrated extraordinary brutalities on the Nagas. Having taken control of these portions of land, Sukapha reached Tipam (near present-day Dibrugarh in Upper Assam) and by 1236 CE, he arrived at Abhaypur, pitched his tent there for some years. Owing to the difficulties posed by the recurrent floods, Sukapha, in 1240 CE, sailed down the Brahmaputra to settle in Habung (Majuli) which too flooded, thus necessitating him to leave after two years of stay. He and his contingent continued to move down the Brahmaputra till he pitched tent by the river Dikhou. By 1246 CE, he moved to Simaluguri and in 1253 CE, deserted it to settle down at Charaideo where a capital city was built. The king appointed two higher officials to aid him in administering the new kingdom—the Bargohain and the Buragohain. After bringing the Barahi and the Moran territories under the Ahom kingdom, Sukapha breathed his last, in 1228 CE.

He was succeeded by his son Suteupha (r. 1268–81 CE). It was during his reign that a skirmish with the Kacharis occurred, leading the latter to vacate the country west of the Dikhou River. In 1281 CE, after the king passed way, his son Subinpha ascended the throne and ruled till 1293 CE. The king was succeeded by son Sukhangpha who led the Ahom kingdom till 1332 CE. This was a period of some stability and the population of Ahoms, perhaps due to greater migration from their original home and also owing to marriage with members of local tribes, swelled in number. 'The result was succession of wars which eventually made them masters of the whole of the Brahmaputra Valley. It is said that they first tried their strength not against their immediate neighbours, the Chutiyas and Kacharis, but against the Raja of Kamata.'[118] After a long-drawn out battle, peace eventually was established between the Kamata and Ahom kings leading to a matrimonial alliance. After the king's demise, his eldest son Sukhrangpha took over and ruled till 1364 CE. Sukrangpha was succeeded by his brother Stupha, who engaged in several conflicts with the Sutiyas and eventually lost his life at their hands. For about four years, the kingdom was administered by the Ahom top officials Bargohain and Buragohain, before the third brother, Tyaokhamti, was put on the throne in 1380 CE and given the name Sukhangpha. He remained in power till 1389 CE, and also avenged his brother's death by defeating the Sutiyas. The king, however, had to face a rebellion from the nobles for failing to stop the palace intrigues of his first queen which turned ugly, causing the king's assassination.

Once again, for about eight years, there was no heir to the Ahom throne. By chance, a man named Thao Cheoken, found out that king Sukhangpha had a son who was being raised in Habung by a Brahmin. The child's mother, when pregnant, was ordered to be executed by the chief queen who took advantage of the king's absence from the palace due to the Sutiya expedition. She was apparently allowed to flee by her executors. The young man, Sudangpha, all of fifteen when he was discovered, was soon installed as the king by the Buragohain in 1397 CE. Because he was raised by a Brahmin, he began to be called Bamuniya Roja (Brahmin prince). 'His accession marks the first stage in the growth of Brahmanical influence amongst the Ahoms.'[119] He learned the ropes of administration fast and succeeded in entering into a treaty with the Tipam chiefs in 1401 CE, agreeing that Patkai would be the boundary between the two countries.

By the side of the Nongnyang lake, near the existing town of Margherita in Upper Assam, their agreement was carved on a rock, an oath of unity was sworn, and a fowl was sacrificed to seal the deal. 'The word *Patkai* is said to be derived from this incident. The full name was Pat-kai-seng-kau which means "cut-fowl-oath-sworn". The former name of the pass was dai-kau-rang or "the junction of nine peaks".'[120]

The Ahom king, during the rest of his rule, ensured complete subjugation of the Tipam, Khamjang, and Aiton tribes. The Bamuniya Roja was succeeded by his son Sujangpha. His great grandson, King Suhenpha was assassinated in 1493 CE by men from the Tairungban clan, leading his son Supimpha to ascend the throne. He too was assassinated for challenging the Buragohain who was suspected to be complicit in his father's murder. The king's son Suhungmung, also called the Dihingia Roja, thereafter, took the throne and ruled till 1539 CE. He was called Dihingia Roja because of his capital Bokota by the river Dihing. It was during his reign that Habung was annexed to the Ahom kingdom.

Suhungmung's reign would remain an important epoch in Assam's history for not only consolidating the Ahom monarchy by including the Sutiya and the Kachari kingdoms but also for routing at least three 'Muhammadan' invasions. Additionally, his reign is also noted for the ascent of Brahmanical power within the Ahom kingdom, and of Vaishnavism under Sankardev.

It was during his reign that new posts like Sadiya Khowa Gohain (to administer the Sutiya territory), Barpatra Gohain (an administrative post), and Marangi Khowa Gohain (to administer the Kachari kingdom in the Dhansiri valley) were created. The Muslim invaders who engaged in a battle with the Ahoms for the first time attacked in Suhungmung's era (in 1529 CE). Though chased away, they returned to raid the Brahmaputra Valley under commander Turbak by April 1532 CE. The king's son Suklen was defeated, pushing the Ahom army to retreat. The attacking army subsequently reached Koliabar in today's middle Assam but had to halt there for months together because of the rains. Since naval combat was the forte of the Ahoms, they successfully directed the invaders towards the waters to engage in a naval battle near Duimunislia in March 1533. The invaders were eventually chased away till river Karatoya. Husain Shah, who came with the reinforcements, was captured and killed. A messenger was dispatched to the king of Gaur with presents to inform him of the defeat; the messenger is said to have returned home with a princess for the Ahom king. 'It would thus appear that this invasion was the work, not of the nominal king of Bengal but of some local Muhammadan chief or freelance, of whom, at this period, there were many in the outlying parts of the province.'[121] The use of firearms by the Ahoms was also recorded at the close of this battle. 'Up to this time their weapons had consisted of swords, spears, and bows and arrows.'[122]

After an action-packed rule of forty-two years, Suhungmung was assassinated, apparently at the behest of his son Suklen with whom his relations had strained. Thereafter, his son Suklengmung shifted his capital from Charaideo to Garhgaon, around present-day Sivasagar town, and is, therefore, known as Gargoya Roja. It was during his rule that the Koch had also occupied Garhgaon and constructed a road till Narayanpur, as mentioned earlier in the chapter. The Ahom king, though, eventually succeeded in retrieving his lost territory from the Koch. The highway Naga Ali, which still exists, was laid from the Ahom country till the Naga hills during this era. Sukhengmung would also be remembered for being the first Ahom ruler to mint coins.

Suklengmung's son, Sukampha rose to the throne in 1552 CE and was better known as Khura Roja or the lame king as he had a limp due to a foot injury during an elephant hunting expedition shortly after ascending the throne. In his reign, the Ahoms once again confronted the Koches in the battlefield but met defeat. Interestingly, one of the demands of the Koches on the Ahoms was handing over sixty pieces of cloth, which indicated that the Ahom country was perhaps known for its exquisite silk, the Muga. Soon though, the Koch defeat against the Padshah of Bengal reversed the situation, prompting King Naranarayan to extend a hand of friendship to the Ahoms. 'It is said that a number of Koch artisans accompanied the Ahom hostages on their return to their own country. Amongst them were potters skilled in the art of making images of Durga and other Hindu deities.'[123] During his rule, Sukampha successfully countered the Sutiya rebellion against the Tipam king, a vassal of the Ahoms, defeated the Dhekeri king of Lower Assam, and the territory of the Bhela Roja (presumed to be a Bhuyan chief) annexed to the Ahom kingdom. The death of Sukampha can be called an end of an era in Ahom history because till then the Ahoms had tried to expand their territory in order to entrench themselves as the principal rulers of the Brahmaputra Valley. The period from the thirteenth to sixteenth centuries can consequently be termed as one of consolidation of Ahom power and establishing power relations with the neighbours.

Sukampha was followed by King Susengpha or Pratap Singha, till 1603 CE. Due to his father's long rule, he rose to the throne late in life, thus earning the sobriquet of Burha Roja (the old king). 'He was also known as Buddha Svarga Narayan, on account of his great wisdom, and as Pratap Singha because of the great deeds done during his reign.'[124] Interestingly, from this king onwards, along with their Ahom titles, rulers also began to have Hindu names given to them.

Pratap Singha's period too witnessed an attack, this time by the Mughals, under Said Hakim, an imperial officer, who came with more than 10,000 horses and foot soldiers besides 400 large barges. They were accompanied by a zamindar's son from Dhaka who was opposed to Koch king Parikshit and by Akhek Gohain, an Ahom military official banished by the king for his carelessness in battle which led to the death of several Ahoms at the hands of the Kacharis. The invaders were routed and some of the captured top Mughal officials were said to have been sacrificed at the Kamakhya temple.[125] This defeat led to the deposition of Qasim Khan from the office of the governor of Bengal.[126] Yet another similar conflict took place in which the Ahom kings seized Pandu, forcing the enemy to retreat to Hajo. In all, there were at least five confrontations between the Ahom army and the Mughal invaders during Pratap Singha's term. He finally took possession of Hajo which had been under Muslim rule for some time.

Pratap Singha died in 1641 CE after thirty-seven years of an eventful regal career. It was during his tenure that the first census of people was conducted in the Ahom country. He also created two administrative posts: Barbarua and Barphukan. The king's maternal uncle Momai Tamuli became the first Barbarua, who reorganized Assamese villages to make them self-dependent. Pratap Singha was also an astute elephant hunter and was referred to as Gajapati, ruler of elephants. He organized several elephant races called Khedda too, and renamed the town of Jamurguri to Gajpur to commemmorate an event.

Palace intrigues to control the throne surged after the powerful king's death. His youngest son who tried to usurp the throne was put to death. His two other sons, Surampha and Sutyinpha, ascended the throne one after the other. Surampha, who died of poisoning, is known in Assamese history as Bhoga Roja (the deposed king) while his brother Sutyinpha was called Noriya Roja (the unhealthy king) because of his perennially ill health. Sutyinpha was followed by son Sutamla who adopted the Hindu name Jayadhvaj Singha and ruled the Ahom kingdom till 1663 CE. During his time too the Mughals invaded the Ahom country, resulting in him fleeing to Gargaon; he is also referred in Assamese as the Bhogonia Roja (the runaway king). This tradition of granting sobriquets to various Ahom kings is noteworthy, perhaps done not only to distinguish one from the other but also to not take their actual names out of respect. The Ahom kings were anyway addressed by all others as Swargadeo, or the lords of the heavens.

As mentioned earlier in the chapter, taking advantage of the Mughal emperor Shah Jahan's ill health, Koch king Pran Narayan attempted to seize Goalpara in present-day Lower Assam. Keeping the Delhi developments in mind, Jayadhvaj Singha too assembled a strong army and wrested Gauhati from the Mughals. The Ahom army marched against the Koches too, defeated them and, thereafter, drove them across the Sankosh River, thus capturing the entire Brahmaputra Valley for the first time.

When Mir Jumla became the governor of Bengal, Jayadhvaj Singha, dispatched a messenger to him to inform him that he had taken control of the entire valley only to chase away the Koches and was prepared to hand it over to any officer whom the governor might send for the purpose.[127] Accordingly, Rashid Khan was dispatched, which led the Ahoms to abandon Dhubri. But they suspected that something big was afoot. Their suspicion turned out to be true as Mir Jumla soon occupied Koch Behar and in January 1662, embarked on an invasion of the Ahom kingdom too. Accompanied by Rashid Khan, a large Mughal force under Mir Jumla pitched tents opposite the Ahom fort at Jogighopa. The army comprised of several Europeans, most of whom were Portuguese. Soon the Jogighopa fort was seized. By the time the king could send his troops to Pandu and Srighat, it was too late. By February, Gauhati had been recaptured. Mir Jumla, thereafter, marched towards Gargaon, the Ahom capital. As the march progressed, the Darrang Roja, a vassal of the Ahoms, submitted to him; so did the Dimarua Roja. In due time, the Simalgarh fort fell to the Mughals. Mir Jumla continued his march and arrived at Kaliabor. Several Ahom nobles reached out to him with letters of peace from Jayadhvaj Singha but to no avail. The Ahoms retreated to Lakhaugarh, at the confluence of the Brahmaputra and the Dihing rivers. It was then Jayadhvaj Singha resolved to fight back; a thousand boats were readied. Meanwhile, Mir Jumla occupied Gargaon. He is also said to have opened a mint at Gargaon to make coins in the name of the Delhi emperor. Various villages were occupied by the invading army. However, by then the rains had set in, posing a huge challenge to the Mughal army as they struggled to sustain their outposts. Channels to negotiate peace with the Ahoms had to be opened. Ahom chronicles narrate that they fell through as the terms were unacceptable to the Ahoms. To aggravate things for the Mughal army, an epidemic had also ravaged its Mathurapur camp, needing quick movement of the troops from there. Taking advantage, the Ahoms attacked Gargaon and occupied half the city. 'The Muhammadans were reduced to severe straits. They were exposed to constant attacks both by day and by night. The only food generally obtainable was coarse rice and limes. Salt was sold at thirty rupees per seer, butter at fourteen rupees a seer, and opium at sixteen rupees a tola. Fever and dysentery became terribly prevalent, and a detachment which numbered fifteen hundred men at the beginning of the war was reduced to five hundred. Many horses and draught cattle also died. To add to his troubles, Mir Jumlah heard that Pran Narayan had returned and driven out the garrison he had left in Koch Behar. The troops, commanders and common soldiers alike, had become utterly dispirited, and they thought only of returning to their own homes.'[128]

With the cessation of the rains by September, the Mughal army recovered some morale. Fresh supplies of food began to arrive by October from Bengal too. The Ahom king and his nobles once again shifted to Namrup. Ahom military officials like the Baduli Phukan, thereafter, moved over to the Mughal side. Phukan submitted a plan to hunt down the Ahom king.[129] However, due to the famine in Bengal, food supplies to the army couldn't be sustained. Additionally, Mir Jumla fell seriously sick. These circumstances forced the Mughal general to negotiate with the Ahoms once again. As per the agreement, Jayadhvaj Singha was to send loads of gold and silver, several elephants, six sons of his chief nobles as hostages, and all the family members of Baduli Phukan who had been taken as prisoners. Additionally, the country west of the Barali River on the north bank of the Brahmaputra and of river Kolong on the south was to be ceded to the Delhi emperor, aside from giving in marriage the king's daughter to Aurangzeb's son Altamash. The treaty was concluded on 9 January 1663, leading the Mughal army to return to Bengal, taking with them the sons of the Ahom nobles, the princess—said to be only nine-years-old then—along with a Tipam princess to give her company. The Ahom princess' grave now lies in Dhaka's Lal Bagh.

A sick Mir Jumla could travel to Dhaka only by palanquin, and died on the way on 30 March 1663. His grave is in Meghalaya's Garo hills.

A few months later, Jayadhvaj Singha too passed away, a dejected man. Since he had no sons, the Saring Roja was placed on the throne, as Supungmung or Chakradhvaj Singha who ruled till 1669. He too was at loggerheads with the invaders from Bengal which created the ground eventually for the Battle of Saraighat in 1671, a decisive war that virtually ended the Mughal incursions into medieval Assam.

In 1667, Saiad Firuz Khan, who had taken control as the thanedar of Gauhati after Rashid Khan, wrote a stern letter to Chakradhvaj Singha demanding payment of the balance indemnity as per the treaty signed with Mir Jumla. Only after all the clauses of that treaty were fulfilled would the hostages to Dhaka be released. Incensed by the letter, Chakradhvaj Singha decided to fight the Mughals. In August 1667, after making sacrifices to the rain god Indra, a large army was packed off to Gauhati to raid it under the generalship of Lachit Barphukan, the youngest son of Momai Tamuly Barbarua. The Ahoms marched on, first taking over the Mughal outposts at Kajali on the south bank of the Brahmaputra, and Bansabari on the north, capturing a number of cannons and horses, and soldiers as prisoners. After about two months, Gauhati and Pandu were netted. A fresh batch of warships arrived from Bengal by November, but the Mughals were unable to recoup their losses. The frontier zone of Agiathuthi fell, pushing the Mughals to recede further to the Manas riverside. A rock inscription dated 1667 CE near Mani Karneswar temple in Kamrup said it was written 'after the defeat and death of Sana and Said Firuz.'[130] An old cannon at Silghat has an inscription in Sanskrit stating that Chakradhvaj Singha, having defeated the Mughals in 1667 CE, obtained that weapon. Yet another inscription was found etched on a Mughal cannon in Dikom saying the same. 'This cannon is peculiarly interesting, as it also has an inscription in Persian, reciting that it was placed in charge of Saiad Ahmad al Husain for the purpose of conquering Assam in 1074 Hijri (1663 CE).'[131] Thus Gauhati was conquered by the Ahoms.

A year later, another skirmish with the Mughals was successfully warded off. When news of the loss of Gauhati reached Emperor Aurangzeb, he picked Raja Ram Singh to avenge the defeat. He was accompanied by Rashid Khan, the former Gauhati thanedar. A huge army comprising 18,000 cavalry, 30,000 infantry, and 1,500 archers set out from Koch Behar. They reached Rangamati by February 1669. The Ahoms were not ready for another war, and sent emissaries to Ram Singh to enquire why they were invading the country. They were told that they had violated the border decided by Mir Jumla. By the time the Ahoms received a reply, Lachit Barphukan had had ample time to prepare for war—he replied that the king would rather fight than give an inch of the motherland. The battle began. Ram Singh's army was routed successfully. He first sought a one-on-one battle with Chakradhvaj Singha but on being refused, asked for peace altogether. The Ahoms were also war weary by then and agreed. However, soon after that, the Ahom king died of edema.

His brother and Saringia Roja, Sunyatpha or Maju Gohain, ascended the throne under the Hindu name Udayaditya Singha. Meanwhile, Ram Singh, on receiving reinforcements from Bengal, regained his confidence and marched forward. In 1671 CE, the Battle of Saraighat began. The Mughals were defeated by Lachit's army not only on land but in a decisive naval battle on the Brahmaputra with the aid of several able deputies including Bagh Hazarika, an expert on naval warfare. By March 1671, Ram Singh, sapped by recurrent losses to the Ahoms, retreated, first to the Haran river and then to Rangamati. The Mughals didn't show any signs of renewing the battle and there was finally some peace between the two countries. Strong fortification was built around Gauhati and Kamrup was thus seized back from the Mughals and annexed to the Ahom country. By that time, the Ahoms were capable of making their own cannons. 'There is one at Gauhati, near the house of the Deputy Commissioner, which bears an inscription to the effect that it was made under the orders of the Sola Dhara Barua in the reign of this king, in the year 1594 Sak, which corresponds to 1672 AD.'[132]

Soon after winning the final battle, Lachit Barphukan passed away on the way to Gargaon, near present-day Jorhat. His maidam bears an inscription testifying to this. He was replaced by his brother Laluk Nimati Phukan as the Barphukan.

By 1673 CE, yet another protracted round of palace intrigues ensued. From 1670 CE onwards, for about eleven years, the Ahom throne saw as many as seven kings in quick succession and none met with a natural death. Ahom kings became mere putty in the hands of top Ahom officials. This was also the period when the Ahom general Laluk Xula Barphukan invited Aurangzeb's son Azamtara to seize Gauhati, which he succeeded to do with ample insider help. Azamtara's wife, the Ahom princess Ramani Gabharu, who had been given in marriage to him as per his agreement with Mir Jumla, famously wrote a letter in Persian to her maternal uncle Laluk Xula not to do so. The subsequent chain of intrigues also took the life of a child king, Lora Roja or Sulikpha (1681–91 CE) who was placed on the throne as a puppet king by Laluk Xula and given the latter's five-year-old daughter in marriage as his chief consort. While Laluk Xula, as the regent, ensured that all other possible threats to the throne were neutralized, he wasn't able to find the biggest threat, Godapani, the son of Gobar, a disbanded prince from an ancillary royal stock who could stake claim to the Ahom throne. Godapani lived a life of disguise in a Naga village and couldn't be traced but his wife Joymoti, said to be pregnant with a child, was thereafter bound to a tree and physically tortured till she died. Their two sons were also hidden in a Naga village.

TUNGKHUNGIA DYNASTY AND GODAPANI

Godapani eventually killed Lora Roja, while Barphukan was stabbed to death by a servant as he slept. He rose to the Ahom throne as Gadadhar Singha or Supatpha in 1681 CE. Since he drew his lineage from his father Gobar, a prince of the Tungkhang stock, he and the rulers who followed him, till the reign of the last Ahom king Purandar Singha, are considered a part of the Tungkhungia dynasty, encompassing 145 years.

A semblance of order returned to the Ahom kingdom for some decades after Gadadhar Singha rose to power. He wrested back western Assam from the Mughals in July 1682, thus reinstating the original western boundary of Assam.[133] During his reign, Laluk Xula's brother Bhatdhara had travelled to Dhaka hoping to receive support in their endeavour to take over the Brahmaputra Valley, however, he didn't recieve much support.

RUDRA SINGHA AND NEW AHOM ARCHITECTURE

After Gadadhar Singha passed away in 1696 CE, his son Rudra Singha or Sukrungpha, ascended the throne. 'The son was more statesman-like than his father…he aimed at elevating his kingdom to the rank of a first rate power in India.'[134] Unlike his father, Rudra Singha was liberal towards the Vaishnava monks and set up an efficient administration. As mentioned above, some of the prominent Ahom edifices that stand today around the erstwhile capital Gargaon and Sivasagar were built during his time. He brought artisans under the headship of the architect, Ghanshyam, from the Koch country to construct his palace, the Kareng Ghar. One gets an impression of the exquisiteness of the Kareng Ghar, replete with wooden art, from the glorious account presented by the Persian historian Shihabuddin Talish who had accompanied Mughal general Mir Jumla during his Gargaon expedition in the seventeenth century. However, the Kareng Ghar underwent multiple changes during the time of Rudra Singha's heirs.

Rudra Singha's time also saw the Ahoms capturing Maibong from the Kacharis; they had to rescue the king from the Jaintias and made him a vassal of the Ahom king in the process. Truly the last big king of the Ahom royalty, Rudra Singha had also prepared to attack Bengal by joining forces with his vassals, the Kacharis and the Jaintias, and take advantage of the weakening of the Mughal kingdom after the death of Aurangzeb. The king had sent several kotoky, messengers, as hermits to different parts of India to survey the terrain, the customs, etc. while planning to take on the Mughals. The kotoky had returned home with the message that various kings would offer their help to the Ahom ruler to seize power in Delhi because of the multiple indignities that they had suffered under the Mughals. 'Rudra Singha mobilised at Gauhati an army of 4,00,000 and he planned to enter into Mughal territories in November 1714. When preparations were on foot for the march of the expedition, Rudra Singh suddenly died at Gauhati in September 1714.'[135]

The eldest of the king's five sons, Siva Singha or Sutangpha, became the next Ahom king. His reign was noteworthy for the complete subjugation of the monarcy to Sakta Brahmanism, brought over from Nadiya by Krishnaram Bhattacharrya who had taken control of the Kamakhya temple. On the Brahmin's prediction that he would die soon if he remained the king, he made his queen Phuleswari assume the name Pramateswari (after Goddess Durga) to rule the kingdom as his regent. Phuleshwari was a dance girl but he made her his Borkuwori, chief consort. Interestingly, the king outlived Phuleswari Kuwori and later married her sister Deopadi and made her the Bar Roja with the name Ambika.[136] Several dol or temples were built in the Ahom kingdom during his reign including the temples Siba (Shiva) Dol and Joi Dol that stand in the present-day Sivasagar district. Also constructed were the tanks Gaurisagar and Sivasagar. He conducted a land survey too. 'The register, or pera kagaz, based on this survey of Kamrup, was still extant at the time of the British conquest. It contained a list of all occupied lands, except homestead, with their areas, and particulars of all rent-free estates.'[137] It was in this period that the Ahom dynasty began showing chinks in its armour, leading to its imminent doom in some years to come. Extreme exploitation of the peasants by the royalty and insults borne by the Vaishnava followers, particularly by the Moamorias at the instigation of the Nadiya Brahmins, precipitated their fall.

After Siba Singha's death, the nobles put the next in line, Pramatta Singha or Sunenpha on the throne. Rang Ghar, the one of a kind amphitheatre in Sivasagar district, was constructed during his reign. He also built the Sukreswar and Rudreswar temples in Guwahati; the Kamakhya temple at Silghat near Nagaon, among others; and a temple in North Gauhati where Rudra Singha had breathed his last.

Pramatta Singha was followed by Rudra Singha's third son Rajeshwar Singha or Surampha. Rajeshwar Singha helped the Manipur King Jai Singh retrieve his throne from the Burmese in 1768 CE, leading him to give his daughter, Kuranganayani, in marriage to the Ahom king. 'A number of Manipuris who accompanied her were settled near the mouth of the Desoi at Magaluhar or the "Manipuri market".'[138]

The end of the recurring Mughal invasions, overall peace and internal order, and the rise of Sakta Hindusim among the Ahom royalty somewhat restricting their food habits and exercise of martial abilities, gradually took away the will and aptitude of the Ahoms to engage in warfare. When the king asked some of the nobles to proceed to Manipur to fight the Burmese on his behalf, several backed out citing bad health. 'The warlike spirit which animated their ancestors had almost wholly evaporated, and, for the first time, we find high officers refusing to go on active service. The people were already priest-ridden, and sectarian disputes had begun to strangle their patriotic aspirations. The Moamaria Gosain was brooding over his wrongs, and was secretly spreading disaffection amongst his disciples.'[139] Rajeshwar Singha had become a disciple of Krishnaram Bhattacharrya too, also known in Assam as Parbatiya Gosain, or Nati Gohain. Unlike previous Ahom kings who were typically entombed in a maidam at Charaideo or some other place in Upper Assam, Rajeshwar Singha was said to have been cremated on the banks of the Brahmaputra, and only his ashes were interred at Charaideo, perhaps due to the extreme influence of the Nadia Brahmins on royal affairs. Though the king's body was buried as per Ahom customs, his shraddha ceremony was conducted as per Brahmanical rites.[140]

After his demise, Rudra Singha's youngest son Lakshmi Singha or Suneyopha, was installed on the throne instead of Rajeshwar Singha's eldest son. Apparently, Parbatiya Gosain, upset at the new king bringing another Brahmin from Bengal, the first of the Na-Gosains, refused to bless him. Lakshmi Singha, having risen to power at age fifty-three, left the affairs of the kingdom to his Barbarua who had a role in installing him as the king. It was the arrogance of that Barbarua which finally pushed the Moran–Motok community to rise in rebellion against the Ahoms in end 1769. They took control of power at Rangpur and made the Ahom king a prisoner at the Joysagar temple. The son of the Moran chief Ramakant took over while his two other sons were made the subsidiary kings of Tipam and Saring. Coins were minted in Ramakant's name. Ragha, who led the rebellion in 1769 against the Ahom rule, became the powerful Barbarua. By April 1770 though, the Ahom king was freed; Ragha's house was surrounded and he was killed with help from the Manipuri princess Kuranganayani. While Ramakant evaded the Ahoms for a while, his father, the Moamaria Gosain who was the head of the Vaishnava monastery, was put to death. Ramakant was eventually caught and killed too.

Though Lakshmi Singha was re-installed at the throne, the beginning of the end of the Ahom kingdom had begun in earnest by then. After him, his son Jubaraj, or Gaurinath Singha, was declared the king under the Ahom name Suhitpangpha. The Moamarias attempted to reignite their fight at this time. They aimed at occupying the Ahom capital Rangpur. The new Ahom king panicked and sought military aid from the Kacharis, Jaintias, and Manipuris and eventually had to run to Gauhati for safety. The rebels took possession of the Ahom capital once again, and burnt down the palace and pillaged the neighbouring villages. Common people suffered immensely during the skirmishes; several escaped to neighbouring countries and other parts of present-day Assam. Because most of the rebels were peasants, the cultivation of rice suffered, which also triggered a famine. 'The price of rice went up to one rupee per lime pot. One mango cost one rupee. A bundle of arum used to be sold for one rupee or one rupee eight annas. The sufferings of the people thus knew no bounds.'[141]

While the Kachari and the Jaintia kings refused to get involved, the Manipuri king offered help to the Ahom king but it was of no use. Gaurinath Singha finally had to beg the British for help who were well entrenched in Bengal by then. In September 1792, Captain Welsh with six companies of sixty sepoys each was dispatched from Calcutta to Goalpara (Bengal had come under the British in 1765) for an enquiry into the matter. On reaching Goalpara, he realized the gravity of the matter, wrote to Governor General Lord Cornawallis about the ground reality, and at once set out towards Upper Assam to save the Ahom kingdom. He soon received more reinforcements from Calcutta and carried out the expedition into Upper

Assam in January 1794. The city of Rangpur was retrieved from the rebels. The Ahom king pleaded with Welsh to remain put for some time. The British official waited for about a month for the Moamarias to submit to them but they didn't, leading Welsh to proceed towards their headquarters at Baghmara. Before he could reach the destination, however, the expedition was called back by the new governor general, Sir John Shore.

After Welsh's departure, as the Moamorias readied themselves for confrontation once again, the king's atrocities against them resumed too. For the first time in the history of the region, a standing army was put together by the Ahom king that was modelled on the British army. They were given a uniform, armed with flint-lock guns brought from Calcutta, and were trained by two of Welsh's native officers who accepted the job after being bribed.[142]

Taking advantage of the turbulence, the Khamti tribe took control of Sadiya on the eastern tip of Assam in 1794. In less than eighteen months after Welsh's departure, a dejected Gaurinath Singha died from a bout of dysentery. Notably, it was during the reign of Gaurinath that half anna silver coins were minted for the first time; he was forced to do so as he ran out of cowries.

Gaurinath was succeeded by Kamleswar Singha or Suklingpha who ruled till 1810. During his reign, a furtive attempt was made by the rajas of Koch Behar and Bijni through two brothers, Har Datta and Bir Datta, to recover Kamrup from the Ahoms. They raised an army comprising Kacharis and Punjabi and Hindustani refugees and declared themselves independent. Nearly the whole of North Kamrup was captured. The Bargohain too raised some Hindustanis aside from borrowing some local men from the chieftains of Beltola and Dimarua and succeeded in warding off the encroaching army. The Kacharis, along with Moamorias, had begun to launch fresh attacks on the Ahom kingdom. Several Moamorias had taken shelter in the Kachari country by then. The Moamorias had unsuccessfully reached out to the Burmese for military help too.

After the king's demise, yet another new king rose to the throne: Chandrakanta Singha or Sudhinpha. The king's close friend Satram, sensing the hold of Purnananda Burhagohain, the prime minister, on the day to day administration of the kingdom, plotted to eliminate him. He filled the ears of the king against him, and also of the Ahom viceroy, Badan Barphukan. Badan's daughter who was married to a son of the prime minister, was roped in too. On finding out about the plot, Burhagohain, stationed in Guwahati, punished all the conspirators in June 1814. Thereafter, in September 1815, he sent a message to Badan to clear all doubts. Badan panicked and fled the country, apparently with his daughter, for Calcutta. He pleaded the governor general for military support to take on Burhagohain but received no help. Badan then made similar pleas to the Burmese king Bodawpaya (1782–1819). The Burmese king was somewhat related to Badan since he had an Assamese consort from Badan Barphukan's immediate family. The consort, Rangili Mepaya, played an important part in ensuring that Badan got the king's attention.[143] Ultimately, in March 1817, a large Burmese contingent marched towards Assam, which was joined by the chieftains of the Hukong Valley, Mungkong, and Manipur. The Ahom fought a battle with the Burmese at Ghiladhari unsuccessfully. The Burhagohain who led the expedition died, which some say was by suicide. His death at this critical moment meant that the Ahom army crumbled in front of the foe. Soon the Burmese occupied Jorhat, then the Ahom capital. On regaining powers with the help of the Burmese, in April 1817, Badan Barphukan installed Chandrakanta on the throne but executed all the regal decisions himself. 'The king had no alternative but to acquiesce in Badanchandra's proposal. Friendly overtures were also made to Chandrakanta from the Burmese camp. Chandrakanta had sent Hemo or Bhamo Aideu, sister of Jogeswar Singha (his brother) as a present to the Burmese harem and the Burmans peacefully retired to their kingdom.'[144]

Soon intrigues ensued at the palace, resulting in the murder of Badan Barphukan. Ruchinath Burhagohain took control of the situation, planted Brajanath Gohain, the great-grandson of Rajeshwar Singha, on the throne, forcing Chandrakanta to flee to Rangpur. Brajanath, however, couldn't remain the king as his body had mutilation marks from a previous attack, a disqualifier as per Ahom rules to ascend the throne. Brajanath's son Purandar Singha was, thereafter, placed as the king in 1818. When Chandrakanta was finally captured, his right ear was slit to make sure he could never become king again.

LAST OF THE AHOM ROYALS AND BURMESE RULE

The Ahom line ended barely one year into the rule of Purandar Singha. Supporters of the slain Badan Barphukan sought assistance from the Burmese once again and a fresh force was dispatched which reached Assam in February 1819. By that time, Burmese king Bodawpaya had died; he was succeeded by his grandson Bagyidaw. The *Tungkhungia Buranji* notes that when it came to the Burmese king's decisions on Assam, the opinion of the two Assamese women in the king's harem were granted significance. The story of how Rangili Mepaya reached the Burmese king's harem is a tale of how women were frequently used as tokens to buy peace. Rangili was presented by Prime Minister Purnanda Borgohain to Singhphou leader Bichanong along with a number of slaves and attendants to dissuade him from aiding the Moamorias to rebel against the Ahom king. The Singhphou chief, in turn, passed her off in 1797 to the Burmese king to reinforce his ties with the monarch. She, however, succeeded in winning the king's attention. Some years later she was joined by Hemo Aideo in the harem. On hearing about the fall of Chandrakanta Singha and the death of the Barphukan, the two Assamese consorts of the Burmese king prodded him to dispatch the army under the headship of Aliungmingi. The Ahoms were easily decimated by the invading army; King Purnananda escaped to Gauhati. Chandrakanta, waiting for his turn to grab power, joined hands with the Burmese, and was installed as the king though the real powers were vested with the Burmese general. The invading army killed Purandar Singha's Barbarua and Burhagohain, and went up to Gauhati in search of him too. But by then Purandar had fled into British territory pleading for the urgent interference of the Europeans. The Burmese army killed several Ahom nobles, pushing Chandrakanta to think up a plan to throw out the invaders. However, by then, the new Burmese king had developed an ambition to take control of Assam and thereafter other parts of India. On learning of Chandrakanta's strategies, fresh reinforcements were sent from Burma, leading Chandrakanta to bolt to Bengal. Thereafter, the Burmese installed Hemo Aideu's brother Jogeswar Singha as the king. Meanwhile, both Purandar Singha and Chandrakanta Singha tried in their own ways to arrange an army with the help of the British and others to snatch back their lost kingdom. Chandrakanta is said to have succeeded in bringing to Assam a small army of Sikh fighters from Maharaja Ranjit Singh but his plan proved ineffective. The small Assamese Sikh community, settled in middle Assam, claim their ancestry in the state from those troops.

By 1821, the Burmese consolidated their power in Manipur too. In January 1824, they crossed the Cachar frontier, forcing the British to respond. They were completely routed by the British. The Burmese had already been intruding on the Chittagong front, in the British territory. It dawned on the British high officials then that both the frontiers needed protection from the marauding Burmese army.

By the time the British saw the reason to go after the Burmese, they had been in Assam for about three years. During that period, 'thirty thousand Assamese had been taken away as slaves' and the invaders had 'destroyed more than half of the population, which had already been thinned by their intestine commotions and repeated civil wars.'[145] Those who survived had been so oppressed by the continued wars that several had given up cultivation and lived on jungle roots and plants. 'Famine and pestilence carried off thousands that escaped the sword and captivity.'[146] The Brahmins and Ahom nobles had fled to Goalpara, as had thousands of commoners. After the Burmese had left the land, the first two groups could return home 'but the poor refugees did not and their descandants still form a large proportion of the inhabitants of the eastern part of Goalpara.'[147]

Jishnu Barua, former Assam chief secretary whose maternal grandfather was Nagendra Narayan Singha, the grandson of Purnanda Singha's brother Radhanath Singha, recalled hearing from his mother a story about her elders throwing a number of family heirlooms into a pond adjacent to the house before fleeing the Burmese. 'After the Burmese were driven out, there was an attempt to fish them out but one elder in the family saw a bad dream which forced them to stop the work. For a long time, when the water would move because of the wind, they could hear the clanking of the utensils but that has stopped now, most likely because those things must have gone further down into the mud after so many decades,' Barua had related to me.[148]

BRITISH TAKEOVER AND YANDABO TREATY

The two-year-long First Anglo-Burmese War began in 1824, causing the decimation of the Burmese and their sway over Assam in 1826. The victory was sealed with the ratification of the Yandabo treaty. None of the two Ahom kings were made party to the treaty. As per the agreement, not only Assam but the frontier state of Arakan (Rakhine) too was wrested from the Burmese essentially to shield the Chittagong frontier.

After a hiatus of eight years, in early 1833, Purandar Singha was once again made the king of Upper Assam by the British, excluding Sadiya and the Matak country. It was originally the idea of Captain Welsh which was executed in April 1833 by his successor T. C. Robertson.[149] Purandar Singha was asked to pay an annual tribute of ₹50,000 to the British. *Tungkhungia Buranji* states that Purandar Singha made the first payments in earnest but after three years he began to falter.[150] Captain Jenkins, who took over from Robertson as the Commissioner of Assam, blamed this on corruption and misrule. In October 1838, he was removed from his post with a pension of Rs. 1000 and his territories placed directly under British dominion. He continued to live in the last Ahom capital Jorhat, where he was buried under a maidam in 1846. The place around his maidam is still called Roja Maidam or the king's burial ground.

In 1847, his son, Kameshwar Singha, was allowed by the British administration to use the title Roja. He too passed away in 1852, leaving behind three widows. His maidam is located next to his father in Jorhat town. His son Kandapeswar was granted the title of Saring Roja in 1848. However, since he actively pushed for reinstatement of the Ahom king on the throne during the Sepoy Mutiny, he was packed off to Alipur jail on the charge of conspiring against the British, and his close aide and Ahom noble Maniram Dewan was hanged to death. The king was later released and kept on a pension. His two sons died before the father.[151]

'Not much is known of the Purandar Singha family any more,' Jishnu Barua told me. 'Descendants of the Rajeshwar Singha family have been the *moujadar* (land revenue collectors) of some areas of Jorhat for decades now.' Though some descendants of the Rajeshwar Singha clan to which the last king Punanada Singha belonged are traceable, only one branch of the family has two male heirs, the rest are all women. According to Barua, 'In the next twenty years or so, there would be no male heir in the Nagendra Singha and his brother Dandeswar Singha's stock.'

Perhaps it is late to even dwell on the fate that the last of the Ahom royals are set to meet for history had sealed their doom way back in 1838 when the curtain had lifted on British colonization. The British rule would go on for nearly a century at the seat of the Ahoms' power—the Brahmaputra Valley.

4

'SILY SIKEN' AND THE 'X' FACTOR: THE HISTORY OF ASSAMESE LANGUAGE

On a summer day in 1973, then Assam chief minister Sarat Chandra Sinha visited our tiny town. The occasion had nothing to do with my birth later that evening but it turned out that it had everything to do with the name I would be known by.

Sinha, known to my family, was in Golaghat town of Upper Assam to inaugurate a music school donated by my grandmother in memory of her husband Maheswar Barooah. Since I too happened to be born later that evening, he named me Sangeeta, constructed around the 'Sangeet' School he inaugurated. Since then, I have a recurrent problem at hand which I am sure he too had; something akin to the issue that Satyakams, the Sangamitras, the Sanjoys of Assam have or, for that matter, any Assamese whose first name starts with or contains the English alphabet 's'. The problem is associated also with those who carry the Assamese surnames Das, Saikia, Sarma, Sarania, Sabhapandit, Sonowal, etc.

Such categories of Assamese forenames and surnames have an inbuilt 'X' factor. The consequence of this is that such name-holders pronounce their names in two dissimilar ways across two languages.

For those outside Assam, I am S-angeeta (pronounced the way 's' is in English), while being X-ongita for Assamese speakers in keeping with its guttural pronunciation in the vernacular.

This peculiar X pronunciation exists in Assamese because the three commonly used xo alphabets in the language have no correspondent pronunciation in English or Hindi. By the same logic, in transliteration from English to Assamese, the word Assam itself becomes Axom or Oxom when spoken/written in the Assamese language/script.

Since the Mongoloid and Tibeto-Burman stock of languages spoken in Assam also don't have the pronunciation xo in them, those who speak such languages by birth often replace it with the nearest pronunciation: ho. Thus, my name may sound like Ho-ngeeta (same as 'h' in English) in Assam too.

In phonological terminology, the x or xo is the voiceless guttural velar fricative, arguably a feature that makes Assamese the most distinct amongst the languages spoken in eastern India, or in any Modern Indo-Aryan (MIA) language. Such a pronunciation cannot be found in Sanskrit, or the Magadhi Prakrit from which Assamese is considered to have sprung, along with its sister languages Bengali and Odia.

Turning a finer lens on this particular pronunciation, represented by three alphabets—talupiya xo (শ), modoniya xo (ষ), and dontiya xo (স) in written Assamese—is, therefore, essential here to better comprehend the origin of the language, and its antiquity. To get a better idea of the language, one would also have to draw in the similarities in pronunciation of certain consonants between Assamese and some Indo-European languages. Assamese has, anyway, been termed the easternmost of the Indo-European languages by linguists.

The story goes that after examining Aryan languages like Sanskrit and Persian vis-à-vis the European languages, say, Greek and Celtic, etc., linguists worldwide had arrived at the conclusion that there was a mother language of all of these tongues which they termed Indo-European or Indo-German. Out of that language emerged seven more tongues: Celtic, Teutonic, Lithu-Slav, Latin, Greek, Iranian, and Sanskrit. Most scholars have also opined that Central Asia was the cradle of the Aryans, though some locate their origin in Southern Russia.[1]

Anyhow, with the migration of people from that stretch of land in batches, the language carried by them began to change, simply because a language is never static. Aryan migrants are, therefore, typically divided into two linguistic groups based on those changes that they might have absorbed during their relocation to different corners of the world.[2]

Those who replaced the sound sh (श) with ka (क), such as in Greek, Latin, and Celtic and Teutonic languages, are believed to have migrated towards the west.[3] Those who did the opposite, replacing ka with sh, are believed to have settled in India, Persia, Afghanistan, etc. and thereby became the Indians of Aryan origin, Iranians, Albanians, Tracians, and Slavs. An oft-cited example of this change in pronunciation is the Sanskrit word shatam (meaning hundred in English) which is centum in Latin. And it is here that the story of the Assamese language (and also Bengali to an extent) becomes interesting. Assamese linguist Debananda Bharali had pointed out in his 1912 book *Axomiya Bhaxar Moulik Bisar* (The Basic Tenets of Assamese Language) that certain Assamese words follow the norms noted in the first language group, meaning Latin, Greek, etc. For instance, the Sanskrit shyam becomes kaam (kaam sorai, a bird) in Assamese; the Sanskrit word dansha becomes Daak, as in snake bite (xape dake) in Assamese. The Greeks call it dankam. This discovery had led Bharali to argue, 'Such examples in Assamese language could only indicate that even before those who spoke the "centum" language, such as the Greeks, had left their original land, a group of people may have gone out, that was during the Indo-German language period itself, and might have entered the eastern frontiers of India. And, some within that lot are still holding on to their original pronunciation.'[4]

Bharali, a self-taught linguist, offered a number of such words in Assamese in that book, aside from also arguing that 'k' in European languages became 'p' in Sanskrit but didn't do so in Assamese. For example, pongu (lame) in Sanskrit is kunga in Assamese; purva (the easterly winds) is kuruwa in Assamese.[5]

There are examples in Assamese which flout yet another norm, that of the Sanskrit 'd' becoming 'j' in Greek. The Sanskrit word for the Assamese jah is dah. Even Assamese words like 'boga' (the colour white, baga in Bengali) have no similarities with Sanskrit but rather with old Slavonic 'bondo'. Also the word 'botor' (weather) in Assamese is 'wetter' in German; 'selek' (lick in Assamese) is similar to the Icelandic 'sleikja' and German 'schlecken'; the word 'suka' (sharp in Assamese) is similar to Old Slavonic 'socha'. The word 'uruli', meaning ululation, contains the Latin equivalent ululo, meaning to howl, and olu-luzo (howl) in Greek. The Assamese word axuro (asura in Sanskrit) is ahura in Zend Avesta, meaning god.[6]

A curious word in Assamese is also jui (fire). One doesn't find it in any MIA; the common equivalents are agni, aagun, aag, anga, aangar, etc.[7] In neighbouring Bengal, it is agun. A parallel to jui can, however, be found in 'joy' and 'jwe' in the Bhatri dialect of Odia and in the Bhuliya dialect of eastern Hindi respectively. Both these areas are in the south of the Vindyas.[8] Jui can, however, be compared to the Sanskrit word dyui or dyuti.[9] Even if one takes that into account, it would be difficult to pin down which among these words—jui or dyui—came first though. 'Most likely, the two words were used by two sets of Aryan settlers. Though *dyui* or *dyuti* is rarely used for *agni* but the word exists in the dictionary.'[10]

The talupia xo, modoniya xo, and dantiya xo exist in Bengali too but they are all pronounced 'sa', unlike in Assamese. Such voiceless velar fricatives do exist among Indo-European languages. The International Phonetics Association (IPA) has compartmentalized such voiceless velar fricatives into eight parts. Examples of them can be found in distinctive pronunciations of words like loch (Scottish), Me-xi-co (Mexican), Bach (German), Gogh (Dutch), yech (English), genre (French), Michael (Hebrew), techni (Greek), tiho (Bulgarian), khami (Urdu), deoch (Irish), heungjeong (Korean), aakha (Nepali), etc. This feature in Assamese hints at the antiquity of the language, and its independent historical trajectory which Chinese traveller Hiuen Tsang might have been able to pin down in the seventh century itself. 'He probably referred to the individuality of the Kamarupa (early Assamese) language when he spoke of it as "slightly differing" from mid-India,' pointed out Bani Kanta Kakati[11] in his book, the result of a monumental post-doctoral work at the Calcutta University, the first such published attempt by a formally trained linguist from Assam. Kakati's senior and noted Bengali linguist and the writer of *The Origin and Development of the Bengali Language*, Suniti Kumar Chatterji, too had remarked, 'The change of initial, inter-vocal and final "s" to the guttural aspirant (x) in Assamese is something remarkable and is paralleled by what we see in Sinhalese and Kashmiri. This is also noticeable in Iranian, Hellenic and Celtic.'[12]

While in the nineteenth century, IPA decided to denote the voiceless velar fricative in various global languages with the letter x, in Assam the Asam Sahitya Sabha, the highest literary body of the state, chose to stick to s, and registered its name officially using s instead of x. When asked about this, former Sabha president Nagen Saikia had responded to me with the argument that it was to avoid what happened to the global pronunciation of a nation's name like Mexico. 'The Mexicans pronounce the *x* as our *xo* when they refer to their country and their people, Mexicans. But the whole world cannot, and, therefore, do not pronounce it that way. So, it would remain for the world Meksi-co and Meksi-can.'[13] By that logic, he said Assam would become Aksham, not Axom. Calling the IPA categorization mainly for scholars and for scholarly work, not for common people's use, he continued, 'Scholarly pronunciations should not be imposed to corrupt the name of Axom into Aksham.'

The argument seemed well meaning, though a tad weak to me. Even if the world pronounces Mexi-co as Meksi-co, it acknowledges the real pronunciation used by the native speakers, which establishes to one and all that the Mexican language is indeed unique. The same could have perhaps been achieved then by using Axom instead of Asom. Nevertheless, both the state-run Gauhati and Dibrugarh universities today follow the rule set by the Sabha when it comes to using the Assamese sound xo in English.

Assamese linguists, since the early twentieth century, have uniformly linked the probable root of xo with the Indo-European and Indo-Iranian languages, with some underlining it as a veritable clue to the entry of a batch of Aryans into the Assam plains through a route distinct from what was noted in most parts of India. The standard Indian belief has been that the Aryans entered the country through Afghanistan. Those who settled in Persia became Zoroastrian, and the ones that arrived in Afghanistan and India became Hindus. As per the usual theory, they, thereafter, pushed to the periphery the early inhabitants—the Kolarians and Dravidians—and occupied the central region, introducing their language to the land where they settled down. It is possible that several such groups among the Aryans had their own distinctive dialects but over time, certain languages from amongst them gained more prominence and ascendency due to advancement in, say, literary work, distinction in trade, religious practices, powerful rulers, etc. and eventually outmoded the others.

In 1914, E. J. Rapson in *Ancient India, The Earliest Times to the First Century AD*, had stated, 'In India, such a standard or literary language appears first in the hymns of the Rig-Veda, the most ancient of which probably date from a period at least 1200 years before the Christian era.'[14] Linguists, based on their philological particularities, have categorized Indo-Aryan languages of India into three parts: the midland tongue, the intermediate, and the outer languages.[15] According to yet another noted Assamese self-taught philologist Kaliram Medhi, while the midland languages encompass the western Hindi of the Gangetic Doab and the eastern part of Punjab (the stretch where hymns in the Rig Veda were composed), the intermediate fold included Gujarati, Nepali, central Punjabi, Marwari, and the eastern Hindi of Oudh and the country to its south. The outer band of languages included Assamese, Bengali, Odia, Bihari, North Kashmiri, Western Punjabi, Sindhi, and Marathi. British-era scholars added one more category on the grounds that the Aryan migration to India had taken place in two bouts. Both migrations are said to have started from the west (mainland India). Assamese language scholars have, however, expressed the opinion about the possibility of a group entering the Assam plains from a different route. 'A wave of Aryan immigration over the Himalayan passes across Tibet or through the eastern gorge from western China into Assam is not merely a fanciful idea.'[16] Such scholars have long suggested such a possibility due to the presence of Vaishnavism in ancient Kamrup, the origin of which is traced to the Visanins of the Rig Veda, and also the commonly practised fire rituals during the Bihu festival. 'The peculiar Assamese pronunciation of sibilants which may be connected with that of the Perso-Aryans and Greeks, some grammatical peculiarities of Assamese which are to be found only in the Vedas and Zend-Avesta and several other characteristics of the Assamese' which 'indicate a state of Aryan civilisation in Assam which date back to the pre-Vedic time.'[17]

In due course of time, several Prakrit or vernacular dialects emerged, most of which collided with the language used in the Brahmanas and the Sutras, the literary works of the Vedic-era post Rig Veda, to give birth to Sanskrit. From at least the seventh century BCE to about the fourth century CE, there rose a clump of literature also in Pali, the language of Buddhism and Jainism. The early Jain texts were also in Prakrit. Here, it is vital to mention that the oldest Prakrit grammarian Vararuci, in the first century BCE, categorized Prakrit into four varieties in *Prakrit Prakasa*: Prakrit proper, Sauraseni, Magadhi, and Paisaci. Later Prakrit scholar Hemchandra created two additional categories: Culika-Paisaci and Aprabhramsa. The Aprabhramsa has been defined by linguists as the speech of the aborigines that got mixed with the Prakrit varieties, thus reflecting in them both Vedic and pre-Vedic languages like Pali.[18]

Historians like Kakati and Chatterji considered Assamese to be an offshoot of the Magadhi Prakrit, the language spoken in Magadha in present-day North Bihar. However, this, to my mind, is a hegemonic gaze, based on the notion that all civilizational milestones must have flown into Northeast India only from the mainland and never vice versa. History is proof that the ancient Kamrup kings had ruled over a wide swathe of North Bengal and probably North Bihar too, and Assamese had classical literature dating from much earlier than several MIA languages. Therefore, weightage must be given to various later-day scholars too who suggest the possible existence of a Kamrupi Prakrit that spread to North Bengal and thereby also contributed to the modern Bengali language. 'There must be some influence of the Magadhi Prakrit in Assamese language but there is no truth to what several scholars had claimed its sole origin to be from it or from eastern Magadhi Aprabhramba.'[19]

Scholars who question the theory that Assamese was derived from Magadhi Prakrit bank on not only what Huein Tsang had stated in the seventh century but also the ancient copper epigraphs which, in spite of being written in Sanskrit, had their peculiarities in morphology.[20] Bharali had also highlighted the occurrence of the Naraka phenomenon in the history of ancient Kamrup to drive home the point that there was a separate batch of pre-Vedic Aryans who had settled in Assam. While in the Mahabharata, Naraka is referred to as a king of Pragjyotisa, in Ramayana, Naraka is described as king of a country or a city state located in the western part of India. Bharali had contended that the author of the Ramayana, being from the west, obviously had no clue about such a practice (of keeping the Naraka title) in the east, which is likely where the author of Mahabharata was from. 'The conclusion necessarily follows that a race of Non-Vedic Aryans who came to settle in India being unable to enter the midland which had been occupied either by the Vedic Aryan or some other powerful race, divided themselves into two parties, one migrating down the Indus as far as Sindh and the other party marching eastward along the foot of the Himalayas till they reached and settled in Kamarupa. It was these Non-Vedic Asura-Aryans who carried with them the traditions of the legendary Naraka and Bana both to Sindh and to Kamarupa and localised these traditions in the respective countries of their adoption.'[21] This is also perhaps the reason why certain linguistic affinities are found between Assamese speakers and those in the northwest and west of India in modern time. As per classical texts, the ties of Kamrup with Mithila were established only during king Naraka's period. But there existed a group of pre-Vedic Aryans in Kamrup who differed from the Vedic Aryans and were termed asuras by the latter. The early texts also classify Naraka as an asura. 'The location of the affinities the linguists have noted in Assamese with the Pisaci and Sauraseni Prakit only indicates that they were prior to the arrival of the Vedic migrants in the land. In other words, those affinities had arrived in the Brahmaputra Valley before Christ. That some of the words in (modern) Assamese have similarities with those in (modern) Gujarati and Marathi is not a sudden development but only historical.'[22]

Those non Vedic Aryans later naturally mingled with the batches of Vedic Aryans arriving from the west, primarily the Brahmins, leading to the gradual intermingling of the existing Kamrupi Prakrit with the language of the new arrivals, Sanskrit. This could be the reason why several Assamese words in use today are derived from Sanskrit. The migrants came to Assam from North India and Bengal where Sanskrit was the language of culture and literature. This migration from the western border continued as several people fled to Assam from mainland India to escape the waves of invaders encroaching from the north.

Add to this give and take the Mongoloid non-Aryan group of languages already present in the state through various bouts of migration of people from the east. 'The present Assamese language is made up of the following elements: 1) The primary Prakrit of the non-Vedic Aryans; 2) The Sanskrit of the Vedic Aryans; 3) The Indian Prakrits of the middle age; 4) The contribution made by the modern languages of Northern India which consists generally of new "tatmasas" and words of Arabic origin; 5) Some words from the surrounding Non-Aryan races who also gave an analytical character more to this than to other Indian languages.'[23]

Today, the Assamese spoken in eastern Assam is the standard Assamese but within the state itself, there are broadly three categories of spoken Assamese. While the one spoken in eastern Assam till Sadiya is commonly called the Sivasagar dialect, the second consists of the bunch of dialects with minor differences heard across Kamrup district. The third bunch is spoken in and around Goalpara, contiguous to North Bengal. The Goalpara dialects have the admixture of the Koch Rajbonshi dialect since Goalpara was a part of the Koch kingdom that had encompassed western Assam and present-day Cooch Bihar in North Bengal. The dialects of Kamrup district differ only in phonetics; there are hardly any morphological dissimilarities or differences in vocabulary. 'The differences, however, between Eastern and Western Assamese are wide and range over the whole field of phonology, morphology, and not frequently vocabulary.'[24]

North Bengal became 'the meeting ground' of Kamrupi and Magadhi Prakrits.[25] It is significant that Hiuen Tsang had mentioned the difference between the language spoken in Kamrup and the language of middle India in the seventh century but didn't refer to any variance in language in any part of Bengal. This may mean that separate languages had not evolved in Bengal then.

Nagen Saikia, noting that the Chinese traveller had said in the seventh century that the Buddhists in Kamrup had to practice their religion in secret, linked Tsang's statement to the beginning of the Vajrayana sect of Buddhism which, in due course of time, became an important religious segment of Kamrup and seeped into parts of Bengal too. 'The Dohas written by the Vajrayani Siddhacharyas were the first Assamese written examples. Several of such Siddhacharyas were from Kamrup, say, Sarahpa, Luipa or Minanath. Though Bengali, Oriya and Maitheli languages also claim their origin from the 86 Buddhist Dohas and other texts by the Siddhacharyas, from the linguistic and grammatical viewpoint though, the language of those texts comes closest to modern Assamese.'[26] According to Kakati, too, 'Certain phonological and morphological peculiarities registered in the Baudhha Dohas have come down in an unbroken continuity through early to modern Assamese.'[27] While Suniti Kumar Chatterji had claimed in his book that the language of *Krishna Kirtan* preserved the early Bengali formations, Kakati had pointed out its similarities more with modern Assamese than modern Bengali. For instance, '*Krishna Kirtan* places the negative particle *na* before the conjugated verbal roots as in Assamese and it is assimilated to the initial vowel of the conjugated root. Assamese have kept up the idiom but modern Bengali places the negative particle after the conjugated root.'[28]

AFFINITIES WITH PICHASI LANGUAGES

As mentioned above, a significant feature of the Assamese language is its close affinity with the Kaffir and Pichasi languages. A section of such speakers had migrated to parts of Maharashtra and Goa too, the reason why Assamese has certain affinities with, say, the Kudali dialect of Ratnagiri. Some common examples from this meeting of twains would be, the Assamese word jun (moon). It means the same in Pichasi languages like Kashmiri, Kauthali, and the Pahari dialects of Himachal Pradesh and Khas Kura (Nepali). Though the word jun is used in middle India too, it means time; in Dutch, the word for jun means sun.[29]

Another common word is aai, mother in Assamese, which is not commonly found in MIA languages but can be found in the Pichasi languages. There are two separate words (kokai and bhai) to address an elder brother and a younger one in Assamese. In Bengali, even if it has a word, dada, to denote the elder of two brothers, the most commonly used versions are borobhai (elder brother) and chotobhai (younger brother). An equivalent of kokai (elder brother) can be found in the Pichasi dialect Silasi (kaku). Another common word between Assamese and certain Pichasi languages is khel, meaning a guild, group, or sub-tribe. In Dadri, khel means a group. In most Pichasi dialects, the word used for legs is khur; in Assamese too, khura is commonly used for the legs of inanimate objects such as tables. Modern Assamese has two words for legs—bhori, like in Bengali and theng, which seems like a non-Aryan contribution to the Assamese dictionary.

According to Bharali, bhori could well be a later entry, after the pre-Vedic Aryans came in touch with the Vedic group whose language was Sanskrit (bhor in Sanskrit means weight).[30]

Another rare word in MIA languages that exists in Assamese vocabulary is mekuri, cat. Even though no language groups around Assam or elsewhere in India use that word, there exists a word meku in the Ainu language of Japan for cats. The Ainu language, now mostly spoken in the northern Hokkaido region of Japan, is one of the endangered aboriginal languages of the world. Its origin is different from that of the Japanese language and predates the arrival of the primary ancestors of Japanese people. Bharali, through his research, had shown that much before the Sanskritized Aryans had left their land for India, a set of people from that region might have entered eastern India. And some among that group might have migrated further east.[31]

DIFFERENCE WITH MODERN BENGALI LANGUAGE

The scholarly deliberations on the origin of Assamese language within the community began in the nineteenth century as a resistance to the imposition of Bengali on the Assamese people by the British colonial administration, and the simultaneous assertion of the Bengali intelligentsia in Calcutta that Assamese was an offshoot of their language. The linguistic assertion stemmed from the Bengali cultural and literary renaissance that occurred in that era after Bengal was freed from centuries of imposition of Persian. This theory was, however, refuted by multiple scholars and historians. Nevertheless, this notion has persisted all through the history of linguistic study into the languages of Assam and can be found even in J. M. McCosh's writings on Assamese, written about eight years after Assam was usurped by the British. M'Cosh, an assistant surgeon in the General Hospital in Calcutta, was dispatched to Assam. Aside from conducting his medical duty, he admittedly took 'a good deal of interest in the Statistics of Assam generally during a residence of more than two years of [his] leisure hours towards their investigation'.[32] The result was the *Report on Topography of Assam* published in 1837. In that report, M'Cosh, while referring to the Ahoms 'managing the state with great skill and moderation', also noted its downfall in these words: 'About 1665 AD the reigning Rajah Chukum (likely Ahom king Supungmung) became converted to Hindooism; and their original god Chung fell into neglect; the nation soon after adopted the language of Bengal and the ancient Ahom language became obsolete and extinct.'[33]

Though M'Cosh's report was more about a general overview on the people and the topography of Assam and the then existing trading routes with Bhutan, China, Bengal, etc., his observation on the language was nevertheless a telling portrait of the times. M'Cosh looked at Ahom kings' adoption of the Assamese language which had been spoken by a large number of the subjects much before the Ahoms themselves had arrived in the Brahmaputra Valley, only as a 'language of Bengal'. From this one can surmise that the colonizers during that time must have looked at Assamese language only within those margins. This tendency during the early colonial era had, however, caused immense harm to the wider understanding and study of the foliation of Assamese and its literature for nearly four decades, before it was re-established as an official language in Assam in the late nineteenth century.

Since the early books like those of Bharali and Kakati on the origins of Assamese were written in that environment, they laid particular stress on the dissimilarities between the two languages and their antiquity. Kakati had dedicated five pages of his introduction to the book on the 'agreements and differences' between Assamese and Bengali languages. He had pointed out words like pani (water in Assamese) which are found commonly in dialects of Bihari and Eastern Hindi but not in Bengali (jal).

Significantly, Assamese vocabulary doesn't have the stressed ch sound, only a soft s, and this is why many native speakers tend to pronounce words like chilly chicken as sily siken. Or, say, the Hindi word chachi, aunt, as sasi. 'Assamese and Bengali have contrasting systems of accentuation. Assamese follows the pan Indian system of penultimate stress and Bengali has an initial stress.'[34] Also, 'Assamese devised from the earliest times a symbol (wabbo ৱ) for the *w* glide. Bengali has no distinct symbol; it has only a spelling device to denote the glide sound.'[35] While Assamese has a complete set of negative conjugations with the negative particle na (ন) placed before the verbal root, Bengali has no negative conjugation.

Taking into account the fact that a) modern Assamese language is closely linked to the Buddhist dohas and the chariapadas which are believed to have been written from the eighth century onwards, b) some of the people writing those dohas and chariapadas were from Kamrup, and c) the *Krishna Kirtan* was written in the later half of the fourteenth century, the Assamese language certainly has an older antiquity than modern Bengali. Anyway, it is already settled that Hema Saraswati, the court poet of Kamata king Durlabhnarayan, can be considered the earliest Assamese writer. Saraswati was the author of *Prahlada Carita*, most likely written in the second half of the fourteenth century. Celebrated poets Harihar Bipra and Kabiratna Saraswati were in the court of Durlabhnarayan's son Indranarayan. There also lived Rudra Kandali whose *Drona Parva* is an important pre-Neo-Vaishnavite work. Before Sankardev began writing his impressive oeuvre in the fifteenth–sixteenth centuries, his mentor Madhav Kandali had translated and adapted the Ramayana into classical Assamese in the early fifteenth century. This is the oldest Ramayana written in a Modern Indo-Aryan language. 'In all these writers, the Assamese idiom seems to have been fully individualised. The language bears certain archaisms which are remarkably free from the writings of Sankar Deva and his school.'[36]

NON-ARYAN CONTRIBUTIONS TO ASSAMESE

Akin to other groups settled in Assam, the Non-Aryan or the Tibeto-Burman and Austric groups too had contributed to Assamese language extensively. Such an occurrence is only natural considering people from these language groups have lived together for centuries with the primary speakers of Assamese, and had been using the language to interact with other linguistic groups. Nagen Saikia had called the intermixing and cultural give and take between the Aryan and the non-Aryan linguistic groups (Mongoloid) co-residing in Assam one of the most vital chapters of the history of Assamese people.[37] When asked about the contribution of the tribal languages of Assam to Assamese vocabulary, writer and professor of Assamese literature at Gauhati University, Upen Rabha Hakasam, had an interesting response. 'It is very difficult to quantify it but perhaps to get an honest answer, it would be pertinent to ask the question the other way round. We should ask, how many words in Assamese vocabulary are not from the tribal languages.'[38]

Though there is a general notion among some that the Assamese language doesn't have 'tribal' words, looking at a rich list that Kakati, way back in the 1940s, had put together from the Tibeto-Burman language groups (Bodo Kachari), the Ahoms, and the Austric stock, demonstrates Hakasam's point. Several place and river names prevalent till date are of Bodo and Austric origin. Ahoms, though more open to absorbing the local linguistic strains than imposing theirs, have also made their contributions to the language, say, with words like dunga (puddle), thunga (packet), kareng (palace), buranji (history), jaan (shallow canal), jenga (uneasy situation), jeka (damp), kai (used as a suffix to a proper noun to show seniority as in kokai, or kai, meaning elder), etc. The Ahom influence also abounds in place and river names in present Assam, say Namrup and Namdang.[39]

Drawing loan words from other spoken languages in Assam made the scope of Assamese language considerably broad. The language, for a long period, could therefore, serve as the lingua franca of not just what is Assam today but also through a wide stretch of the Northeast. The Nagamese and Arunachali Assamese are its offshoots, necessitated by a need to have a common tongue for various socio-linguistic groups to communicate with each other. Assamese became the link language between the pre-Aryan, Vedic Aryan, and non-Aryan groups that called Assam their home, and thereby helped create a cultural and social cohesion of sorts. Today, though, that cohesion is considerably brutalized and credit for that must go to not only the hegemonic conduct spotted among several primary speakers of Assamese language for a protracted period—ignoring the need for equal development and preservation of the rich bouquet of other dialects/languages of the state—but also to the growing politicization of language in general within the ethnic groups. Language has become a weapon of assertion of an exclusive political identity across social groups in Assam though, culturally, the appeal of the Assamese language still exists.

ASSAMESE SCRIPT

Let me begin the story of the Assamese script with an incident from early 2021. A Delhi-based Bengali friend who had never been to Assam, reacted to a photograph I had uploaded on social media which had a plaque with Assamese writing on it, as thus: 'Bengali script'.

That reaction only came as a reminder to me that my well-meaning friend would not be alone in confusing the Assamese script with that of Bengali as the latter has been far more visible in mainland India and also often been projected, not only by a section of Bengali speakers but by others too, as the sole representative of the whole of eastern India. The long struggle by the likes of Satyakam Phukan to get the Assamese script recognized in Unicode as separate from Bengali only highlights the deeper roots and wide reach of an assumption that hinges on colonial-era linguistic hegemony.

As mentioned earlier, the early twentieth century 'renaissance' in Bengali literature nearly overshadowed other eastern Indian languages. Assamese and Odia language speakers could successfully counter that strident drive for submission to Bengali but smaller languages like Sylheti, which even while having a separate script couldn't rise against the tide, and ended up eventually as a 'dialect' of Bengali.

My friend's impromptu reaction to the Assamese script did nudge me to think of Bengali historian R. D. Banerji, the author of *The Origin of Bengali Script*, who took an inscription from Kamakhya near Guwahati from 1744 to claim it as an example of 'modern Bengali inscription' and had found in it the final development of Bengali script.[40] Assamese linguist Upendra Nath Goswami, commenting on Banerji's need to depend on that inscription from Kamrup to state that claim, had cited renowned Assamese poet and literary critic Dimbeswar Neog's remark in that regard, 'The so-called Bengali script and Maithili alphabet are really one and the same with the old Kamarupa script from which Bengali and Maithili have separated and started independent careers.'[41]

The modern Assamese script differs from the modern Bengali script only in two letters: the ro and the wabbo. While the Bengali script has no wabbo ৱ, its ro (র) is different from the Assamese ro (ৰ). Though Bengali linguists have often claimed that the modern Bengali script emerged as a fully developed distinct script perhaps from the tenth century onwards, several experts have also acknowledged that the ro used in modern Assamese script appeared in several inscriptions scattered across Bengal in the sixteenth, seventeenth, and eighteenth centuries.[42] Goswami particularly highlighted Mitali Chatterji's paper 'Development of "r" in the Bengali Script as found in Inscription', to underline that the ro was written with a dot inside the letter ba (ব) in several inscriptions beginning 1545 CE. 'In her own words, "during the period of the 17th to 18th century, inscriptions bearing 'ro' (of the present-day Assamese) were very common". On the other hand, the modern Oriya and Maithili scripts have embraced a good number of the ancient, medieval and modern Assamese letters.'[43]

While most Assamese scholars and linguists have claimed that the Assamese script grew out of the Kutila variation of the Gupta script of eastern India, Goswami, significantly, had pointed out that while the Kutila variation had been in existence from sixth to the ninth century CE, Assam had possessed stone inscriptions beginning from the fifth century onwards. While the Umachal rock inscription of Surendravarman in the fifth century is one, another epigraph of an earlier period is the Nagajari-Khanikargaon stone inscription. The Nagajari inscription was the only one from ancient Assam to maintain the distinction between the bo (ৱ) and bho (ভ) in the language. The Nilachal epigraph of Kamakhya in 1565 also preserves the letters ro and bho as we find in the modern Assamese script. Historian P. C. Choudhury had pointed out that the Kanaivarasi rock inscription at North Gauhati, dating back to 1127 saka, had a few specimens of Assamese characters which are used in the present form. He too had considered the Kamrupi script as 'the parent speech of eastern India including North Bengal, Mithila, Videha, Orissa, Nepal and Tibet.'[44] He underlined two other vital points. First, not a single old manuscript is found written in Devanagiri though the language used is Sanskrit. 'The early evolution of the Assamese script perhaps explains for its universal use in producing both the Sanskrit and Assamese manuscripts.'[45] Secondly, the modern Tibetan characters seem similar to the Assamese letters 'which is possible because of the common origin'.[46]

Though we find traces of tribal languages of Assam in the modern Assamese language, there is no evidence yet of the use of any Mongolian or Mon-Khmer Khasi scripts.[47]

Scholars like Goswami had categorized the development of the Assamese script into three periods: the ancient Assamese script or the Kamrupi script from the fifth to thirteenth centuries; from the fourteenth century to the middle of the nineteenth century, just before the publication of the first Assamese newspaper *Orunudoi*; and the modern script, from 1846 onwards, when the paper began to be published by American missionaries, till contemporary times.[48]

The medieval script, which was used to pen manuscripts, is also classified into three kinds: the Gargaya, Bamuniya, and Kaitheli or Lahkari. Noted cultural historian Maheswar Neog mentions that the most commonly used script those days was the Gargaya akhar (letters) and possibly named so because it was emanating from the principal centre of culture, the Ahom capital Garhgaon, in present-day Upper Assam. The Sanskrit scholars used the Bamuniya script while the writer class, the Kayasthas, used the Kaitheli or the Lahkari script. In other words, while in Upper Assam, the Gargaya style ruled, in Lower Assam, the Kaitheli did, though the difference between these scripts in terms of letter formation was not stark.[49]

With the arrival of the printing press, the Christian missionaries displayed an interest to print books in local languages. In Assam too, the development was noticed, and the first Assamese book, printed at a press in Srirampur (on the Bengal–Assam border presently) was a translation of the Holy Bible. The translation, titled Dharmapustak, was done by Atmaram Sharma in 1813. The letters were modelled after the Assamese manuscripts, though certain letters were of the Kaitheli style of Assamese manuscripts.[50]

After the Assamese Bible came the first Assamese grammar book, also printed at the Srirampur press by Assam-based missionary Miles Bronson in 1839. He included the letter bho in it and also followed the writing tradition of Assamese manuscripts. At the time of publishing *Orunudoi*, the Assamese ro case for printing was brought from Srirampur and after much insistence by linguist Hemchandra Barua, the bho case too was fetched. Barua went on to write the first Assamese etymological dictionary *Hemkosh* which was posthumously published in 1900 under the supervision of Captain P. R. Gordon. Prior to this, in 1837, Bronson published the first Assamese dictionary at the Baptist Mission Press in Sivasagar. Assamese scholars unanimously give the credit for Assamese printed books to Christian missionaries and also to *Orunudoi* for standardizing the modern Assamese script. Thus culminated a journey that began in the fifth century with stone inscriptions, and then moved to copper plates, to handwritten manuscripts, and finally to the bound books produced by the imported printing press in the British era.

5

PUJA–PATOL, NAAM–PROXONGO: ASSAMESE FOLK AND RELIGIOUS BELIEFS

A few minutes' walk from the sandy banks of the Dikhou River takes you to the mausoleum of Ajaan Pir, the resting place of a saint who was believed to have reached that stretch of land in Upper Assam after travelling all the way from Iran in the seventeenth century. Though he spread Islam in that belt of Assam, he is better known within the Assamese community for his unique musical contributions, the Jikir and the Jaari, hinged on devotion to the almighty and about spreading religious amity between Hindus and Muslims in the area.

The present white and black marble encasing of the mausoleum, located in Sivasagar district, makes it impossible to guess what must have been its original look. Hundreds of ribbons are tied to the iron railings that mark the four corners of the mausoleum. A young man at the site, Jahid Rahman, told me that he belonged to the family of the Khadim who has traditionally been its caretaker. On being asked whether the people residing around the Pir's mausoleum are Muslims too, he replies, 'We usually don't look at ourselves as Hindus and Muslims here; we have visitors from both the religions. In this village, you will find mostly Assamese from the Das community.'

This chance remark by that young man is, however, a testament to the myriad beliefs and practices that have been long prevalent in Assam. These sociocultural principles that tend to blur the firm boundaries of religion in the daily lives of the Assamese are also a reminder of a fundamentally tolerant and liberal foundation of the community, perched on an adopt-and-adapt approach. I have hardly come across an Assamese person who dithers to visit a religious place of some other community. The Assamese, by nature, are essentially superstitious and don't mind discarding their rigidities to usher in a new practice to attract an extra blessing. Quite effortlessly, an Assamese Brahmin will, therefore, step inside a dargah to light a candle prior to an important event in her life, or offer a Xorai (traditional offerings) at a Vaishnava naam-ghar during Bhado, the birth month of saint Sankardev. Similarly, a woman from a Vaishnava household would happily visit a Shiva temple every Monday to pour some milk on the lingam to ensure a long life for her husband. Each subgroup, tribal or non-tribal, within the larger Assamese fold, may have their particular folk and religious customs, but what unites them all culturally are the three Bihus that knock at every door thrice a year: Rongali or Bohag Bihu, Kati or Kongali Bihu, and Magh or Bhugali Bihu. The reason is the same—a collective coming together to bring in blessings. It must be noted though that the plains tribes of Assam have different names to mark these occasions, while the non-tribal Assamese call them Bihu.

SATYANARAYAN PUJA

Before delving into the principal folk festival Bihu, let's bring in another common ritual in Assamese Hindu households held principally to seek blessings for a wish fulfilment, say a marriage, a business deal, a career move, or a child's examination. It is the Satyanarayan Puja, often performed on a full moon night, or on any other day convenient to the host. Interestingly, noted Assamese author Nirmal Prabha Bordoloi, in *Axomor Loka-Sanskriti* (Assamese Folk Culture), had located the plausible origin of this puja in a ritual prevalent among the Muslim community of Goalpara in Lower Assam. '[The] Satyanarayan Puja that...spread across Assam seemed to have entered the state much later. Since Muslims of Goalpara have a ritual to offer prayers to *Satya pir* (Saint of Truth), some proffer that this custom of praying to Satyanarayan (Supreme Being of Truth) in Assamese households had sprung out of it.'[1] Bordoloi's mention does tally with what noted Bengali linguist and historian Sukumar Sen had written in *History of Bengali Literature* on the birth of Satyanarayan Puja in parts of Bengal. 'The traditional stories of the local Muslim ("pir") were woven with romantic tales to form a new type of religious poetry in West and North Bengal and were responsible for the emergence of a new deity called Satyanarayan (i.e. Haq the Narayana—Haq in Arabic means truth) by the Hindus, and Satya Pir (Haq the Pir) by the Muslims. The writers of such poems (Satyapir Panchali) were mostly Hindus. The earliest traditions regarding the Muslim Pirs of Bengal are recorded in *Sekasubhodaya* (circa 1550) written in hybrid language which is as much Sanskrit as Bengali. It contains stories of the spiritual powers of Sheikh Jalaluddin who, as the book says, came to Bengal during the reign of (king) Laksmansen.'[2]

Sheikh Jalaluddin was identified in the book as Satya Pir, a Sufi saint from Baghdad whose disciple was the grandfather of the famous seer

Nizamuddin of Delhi. Jalaluddin had camped in Delhi before moving to Bengal. The Satya Pir tradition exists in parts of Odisha too, and also among a faction of Buddhists in Bangladesh, thus indicating strongly that the puja was an influence on Assam from its western border. Anyhow, today, while in some Assamese Brahmin households the story of the greatness of Satyanarayan is read after invoking Vishnu, thereby equating him to the lord himself, in several non-Brahmin houses, particularly in Upper Assam, there is a ritual of reciting Vaishnava devotional songs (naam) after reading out the Chalisa.[3]

AJAAN FAKIR

If what is explained in Sen's book holds any truth, it provides an explanation for a possibly different origin of pir Ajaan Fakir in Assam too. There is an established belief in Assam that Ajaan Fakir was a Sufi saint by the name of Shah Milan who also hailed from Baghdad like Satya Pir. The couplets of Satya Pir were composed by Hindus who knew the local languages, which leads one to wonder how could Ajaan Fakir string together such soulful Jikir and Jaari in chaste Assamese having come from a distant land? According to noted Assamese botanist and folklorist Padmeswar Gogoi, Ajaan Fakir could have been from Assam itself and might have come in contact with a renowned Sufi saint from Baghdad and thereby adopted the mystical form of Islam, and propagated the religion to seek God through songs and poetry, shunning materialism. Gogoi has no historical evidence to substantiate his argument but highlights that Ajaan Fakir had established his ashram by the Dikhou in the Ahom kingdom, which might not have been an easy task to achieve for a foreigner at a time when their entry into the Ahom country was highly restricted. He also told me about the practice of 'fakir culture' among the lower strata of society in olden Assam in which songs were sung in praise of an unseen force while dining on meat and wine.[4]

Ibn Batuta, in his account on his visit to China traversing through western Assam in 1312 CE, mentions spotting the noted Sufi saint from Baghdad, Shah Jalal, on a hillock to the west of the Garo hills (in present Mahendragarh) surrounded by a posse of disciples. This posse, however, couldn't have included Ajaan Fakir as a mureed for he is considered to have lived and preached in seventeenth century Assam, based on a Jikir he is believed to have composed about himself.[5] Could he then have come in contact with some other Baghdadi saint passing by Assam during this time? In the absence of historical proof, one can only resort to guessing. Still, Ibn Batuta's statement is significant since it indicates that Islamic proselytization in Assam might have begun before the emergence of Ajaan Fakir.

The Jikir he is believed to have composed about himself had cited his name as Shah Milan, and his year of coming to Assam as 1145 Hajiri, which would roughly be in the seventeenth century. However, writer Syed Ikram Husain, in a 1940 article on Ajaan Fakir in *Bahi*, had underlined that there was no consensus about when and from where he arrived in Assam. In this article, we also find a fascinating sliver of information about a popular belief in Upper Assam associated with Ajaan Fakir. There has been a saying across Assam that the only river which flows 'backwards' (ujai jai) in the state is Dikhou. Husain's article refers to a story wherein the Ahom king Shiva Singha, on being misinformed that Ajaan Fakir was a Mughal spy, ordered that the fakir's eyes be gouged out. His eyes were then thrown into Dikhou, near which the fakir had pitched his tents alongside those of his followers. No sooner did his eyes fall on the river that its waters began to move backwards, leading the king to accept his folly and recognize the fakir's divinity. The king, thereafter, sanctioned a piece of land to Ajaan Fakir by the river on Haraguri Sapori (in the present Sivasagar district) where his mausoleum lies today. This land grant is mentioned in the Jikir he is believed to have written. As per Husain, Ajaan Fakir began preaching Islam only after that episode; prior to this he was only a minstrel. Even today, across Assam, Ajaan Fakir is revered more as a poet-musician who advocated for amity between Hindus and Muslims than an Islamic preacher, which is why believers of both faiths visit his mausoleum.

RELIGIOUS TOLERANCE

The strength of the long-practised religious tolerance in wider Assamese society lies in the lived experience of a people with diverse roots living as neighbours over the centuries which must have helped evolve a system of give and take, thereby melding, knowingly or unknowingly, multiple strains to formulate a composite culture that we know today as Assamese culture in general. For instance, in several Assamese Muslim families, particularly in western Assam, women continued to wear sindoor (the red vermillion mark) on the parting of their hair till a generation ago. Till date, it is common to find Assamese Muslim women, and also Bengali Muslim women of Bangladesh, wearing bindi on the forehead like a Hindu woman, not common among their counterparts in mainland India. For the absence of religious rigidity in the society, it is also not rare to hear an Assamese Muslim calling the place where he keeps his Quran his guxai ghar (prayer room), like his Assamese Hindu neighbour does. Muslim historians who accompanied the invaders had noted that the followers of Islam in Kamrup differed from their counterparts elsewhere. Birinchi Kumar Baruah has also written about the openness among certain Kamrup kings towards different faiths.[6] For instance, King Dharmapala paid respects to both Shiva and Vishnu in his epigraph; Vallabhadeva invoked Bhagavata Vasudeva and Lambodara. The Guakuchi grant of Indrapala is one such example. So is Kalika Purana. Though the text was devoted to the worship of Devi, according to Barua, it eulogized the worship of Shiva, Vishnu, and other gods too. A wide gamut of pujas, rituals, and xobah (occasions) that are today a part of the extended Assamese Hindu culture undoubtedly have roots that lie outside its pale. This can be seen in the worship of nature, in attributing a soul to all animate or inanimate things, to the natural phenomena, to a belief in supernatural powers that stir the physical world. It is here that the Assamese tribal and non-tribal cultures fuse, the reason why the religio-cultural traditions of Assam are somewhat different from the standard Vedic Hindu practices. P. C. Choudhury has rightly pointed out that before the introduction of Aryadharma and Brahmanical faith in Assam, the foundation for the evolution of various cults was laid by non-Aryans—the Austric, Alpine, and Tibeto-Burman elements. 'It was natural that Brahmanism, more appropriately, Aryanism, had to be modified to a great extent by these cults, and, by a process of absorption, had to incorporate into its fold not only a number of non-Aryan deities, but also, to introduce various local myths and rituals. Even after the spread of Hinduism, the non-Aryan cults continued to survive in some form with the result that in revered temples like Hajo or Kamakhya, we find a meeting place of Aryan and non-Aryan faiths.'[7]

SHIVA AND DEVI: THE GOD AND GODDESS OF FERTILITY

The primacy of Shiva, and Devi or Ma, in Assamese religio-cultural ethos, both tribal and non-tribal, can be traced to a number of folk practices and beliefs still prevalent. For instance, on the onset of spring, the Assamese new year, the eldest in the family in a traditional household would pen the Sanskrit mantra 'Deva deva mahadeva, nilagriba jatadhara, baato bristi harang deva mahadeva namas tu te' on the leaves of Nahor (Indian chestnut) trees. These leaves would then be rolled and strategically hidden in the corners of the house to protect it from natural calamities, particularly from the Bordoisila, the annual rush of rain and heavy winds that marks the onset of the monsoons. The Sanskrit mantra evoking Shiva could be a later addition to the custom. The deity, however, is an obvious choice as he was the chief mountain god and worshipped in various forms by the non-Aryans and the pre-Aryans in Assam as their protector.

The word Bordoisila is Assamese adaptation of the Bodo word Bardoisikla and comes from a story of the annual return of the goddess of nature to her mother. There exists a folk tale about two sisters, Bordoisila and Xorudoisila, visiting their maternal home from their marital abode for the Bihu in spring. They rush in, breaking trees, flooding the fields, causing thunder. A mere mortal can only wait and watch the movement of these fiery daughters of nature, sending out a silent prayer to Shiva for protection. Shiva is the male counterpart of ma, the Devi, the goddess, the female force of nature.

To appease her and slow down the speeding Bordoilisa, people would traditionally keep a small mirror and a comb for the goodess in their courtyards. This practice too is a contribution of the non-Aryan elements within the larger society where forces of nature are prayed to.

Generally, Shiva and Parvati in the Hindu belief signify conjugal bliss, the consort complimenting the lord. In Assam, one senses the coming together of two forces as the communion of two opposite powers of nature conjugating to administer the material universe. Not for nothing is Mount Kailash the abode of Shiva; he is the mountain god, the Pashupati. Devi or ma in Assam, or mata in the North Indian heights, the revered goddess, is also the deity of the mountains. To comprehend better the primacy of these dual forces in Assam, certain primordial practices and beliefs extant in Assamese religio-cultural life must be taken into cognizance, particularly within the tribal fold's cult of fertility.

In neighbouring Bhutan, there exists a popular monastery, Chimi Lhakhang, in the Punakha province, known as the Fertility Temple. If you take into account the fact that across Bhutan the phallus is a sign of worship and that the country borders Assam where Shiva (linga or phallus) worship in multiple forms is still practised within various ethnic groups, it gives us an indication that there might have been a male fertility cult across the contiguous region of Assam and Bhutan before Buddhism swept through the region. P. C. Choudhury had noted, 'The cult (of fertility) is to be associated with the pre-Aryan element; even the word *linga* has been attributed to an Austric origin. Phallic worship definitely formed part of the religious life of the non-Aryans and Aryans in Assam.'[8] Could it be that in Kamrup, at some point in history, certain things turned towards developing a female fertility cult too, precipitating the birth of Saktism and Tantrism?

N. N. Bhattacharyya had equated the female fertility cult to the primacy of women in matriarchal tribal social systems. 'Clan life in which the mother is the head of the group is likely to lift the Mother Goddess into a supreme position.'[9] By now, several scholars have concluded that the word Kamakhya is an adaptation of the Khasi word ke-mei-kha. 'Ke-Mei-Kha is the primordial Female Principle, the eternal mother who is the source and spring of creation and all created beings.'[10] Aside from the matriarchal Khasis and Garos, among the Bodo–Kachari tribes of Assam too, Kamakhya is Kham-Maika which suggests the old Mother, worshipped alongside a form of Shiva called Bathouborai. Khasi writer Hamlet Bareh Nyapkynta has also stated that Pragjyotisa was a derivative of the Khasi pagar juhatich. 'Maibong (former capital of the Dimasas of Assam) is also a Khasi word. The Aryan speaking races of the plains drove away the Austric speakers in the hill region but Aryanised some of their cults which included that of the Mother Goddess Ka-Mei-Kha, the Ai Gosani or Yoni Devi.'[11]

Till date, the Rabha tribe of Assam perform Kamakhya pujas. The one held by Rabhas at Kamakhyaguri in Alipurduar in West Bengal, near the Assam border, is a huge occasion. Another of community's pujas, Bayakhothan, at Phulbari in Meghalaya, is also a Mother Goddess ritual. The Dimasas too had built a Sakta temple in Maibong. The Tiwa tribe of Assam evoke Bauli, who is equated with Parvati. 'Among the Karbis, Mother Goddess Haimu is the goddess of vegetation and fertility. The fertilising rains are her tears caused by her unfulfilled love with a mortal being on earth.'[12] The tribe also worships Bachinja, the goddess of energy or Sakti.

Choudhury had also underlined that belief in Sakti cosmic energy personified as feminine—is one of the oldest faiths in India and that names of the Devi, like Durga, Kali, and Uma, can be found in Vedic literature.[13] 'But it is almost certain that Saktism had a non-Vedic origin and Uma or Kali was probably a female mountain apparition, which was later on identified with the wife of Rudra, or brought into line with the Brahmanic thoughts. Even Rudra is called Girisa (Mountain god). The names like Uma and Durga of the Vedic literature can hardly be identified with Devi or Sakti of the Sakta faith. But with the development of the faith, these names of the goddess, whether Hindu or Buddhist in origin, came to be taken as manifestations of the same female principle of Devi, like her consort Rudra, Siva or Mahadeva, known under various names.'[14] This is most likely the basis for the revered Ugratara temple in Guwahati with Tara as a manifestation of Devi though she is also a Buddhist goddess. Kamakhya too has a Tara temple attached to it. Certain Devi Than or holy abodes of the Mother Goddess across Assam have also been cited by scholars as places where the primitive tribal Mother Goddesses were worshipped in symbols but were later converted into Hindu temples where images of Durga or Kali were installed.[15]

Saktism and Tantrism in the Hindu faith are widely believed to have been birthed in Kamrup–Kamakhya. Noted cultural historian of Assam, Maheswar Neog, has stated that there is enough basis to believe that the Hindu Tantrism practised in Assam sprung out of the religious beliefs and practices of tribal communities in the area which was later influenced by Buddhist Tantrism too. Neog had particularly referred to the similarities between Hindu Tantrik practices and that of Vajrayana Buddhist worship, practised in Kamrup and Kamakhya.[16]

King Narakasura is bestowed the credit of instituting Sakti worship in Kamrup–Kamakhya. Interestingly, though later kings would uniformly claim their origin from Naraka, none of the earlier epigraphs had any avowal of devotion to the Mother Goddess or Kamakhya but to Shiva. This could be a sign of the prevalence of Shaivite beliefs in Assam then.[17] Saktism received state patronage during the later part of Ahom rule in medieval Assam, and also during the reign of Koch king Naranarayan. In spite of the existence of Kamakhya, an important Hindu peeth, only 2 per cent of the Hindu population had marked themselves as Sakta worshippers in the 1901 census of Assam.[18] This could well be due to the spread of Neo-Vaishnavism. People those days seem to have found themselves at odds with the Western classification of their religious beliefs. For example, in the introduction to the 1921 Madras Census, the census commissioner had remarked, 'The chief hindrance to the obtaining of accurate returns is the fact that the terms used to classify the religions are unfamiliar to the people of the country, and do not really suggest what is really meant in common parlance by religion. The worst instances are the terms "Hindu" and "Animist". No Indian is familiar with the term Hindu as applied to his religion. If asked what his religion is, he usually replies the name of the sect (e.g. Saivite), to which he belongs....'[19]

At this juncture, it is vital to also highlight the presence of certain revered godly forces in Assamese folk and oral culture, like that of the burha guxain, dighol thengia, and isto devota. A little digging reveals that they are considered ethereal forms of Shiva by the common people, thus prodding you to wonder if those versions were also the earlier names and forms of this mountain god across the region before he was identified as Rudra in Vedic literature. Mention must be made here of the deity Langa among the Rabhas which is equated with Mahadev or Shiva, and this is true for their primary deity, Rishi Deo, as well.

In the Bathou Puja among the Bodo–Kacharis, the Supreme Being is Sri Brai or Shib Bwrai, worshipped as the regulator of the five elements of nature: air, water, earth, fire, and ether. The sijou (euphorbia) plant is the physical manifestation of the deity. Like dighol thengia, isto devota, and burha guxain, Sri Brai is also invisible; his presence can only be felt. The Bodo practice of planting a Sijou in the family courtyard in reverence to Sri Brai is akin to worshipping the tulsi (holy basil) as the sacred plant under which Lord Krishna resides among the Assamese Hindu fold. It is under the tulsi that an earthen lamp is lit in Assamese households on the night of Kati Bihu, when the paddy is in the field and the granary is nearly empty. Is this ritual a later entry into Assamese society due to the growing significance of Vishnu in their religious beliefs? Like in Bodo households, it is common to find a tulsi plant in the courtyard of a non-tribal Assamese. Such a practice can be noted in some other South Asian countries too, say, in Thailand, influenced by Buddhism; this could well be the outcome of the religion meeting animism. The ancient Thai belief in the female spirit Phi Nang Ta-Khian is associated with the practice of tying colourful ribbons around a big tree, a feature quite common in the Devi temples of Assam. The Thai belief that a young man passing by a big tree could be consumed by it has a parallel among the Misings of Assam who believe that devils may reside in a gigantic tree. The Vaishnava text *Katha Gurucharit* states that 'a good number of *yakh* (Yaksha) who lived at the outskirts of a marshy land near Barpeta (in Lower Assam) were forced to abandon the place due to constant congregational prayers conducted by (Vaishnava guru) Madhabdeva.'[20] Ahom king Pratap Singha (1603–41) was apparently frequently possessed by evil spirits and, therefore, was reluctant to ascend the throne. He had attempted to appease Mahadeva (Shiva) by constructing a temple (Shiva Dol in Sivasagar) to rid himself of the spirit. There also exists a folk culture in Assam, *mongol-suwa,* or forecasting one's future wherein soothsayers do so by drawing lines and circles on the ground. 'The Ahom foretellers used fowl legs in calculating the future.'[21] In *Dakor Boson*, a book of advice believed to have been written in the seventh century, and popular in rural parts of the state even today, there exist multiple adages aimed at bringing good luck to the self and warding off bad omens. Additionally, the now extant practice of black magic in the village of Mayong in middle Assam, suggests its acceptance in the society of that region.

WORSHIPPING STONES

In the family temples of Assamese Brahmins, there is the presence of the Xalegram, or the Shiva linga in stone. Some of them are centuries old. The practice of worshipping Xalegram in Assamese Brahmin households is a manifestation of the Xil Puja which constitutes worshipping certain forms of stones.[22] The stones in the shape of a linga or a yoni have been in the sanctum sanctorum of several revered Hindu temples in Assam, indicating the practice of worshipping the natural forms of the celestial powers before the iconography of gods became popular.

MULTIPLE WAYS OF WORSHIPPING DEVI

Just as there are many manifestations of Shiva in folk and non-Aryan practices in Assam, this is true of Devi too. In Kesaikhati or Tamreswari temple in Sadiya, a revered site mainly for the Sutiya community of Tibeto-Burman lineage, there existed the practice of human sacrifice till some centuries ago, like that of the Kamakhya. The Devi is in the form of a yoni carved in stone. Around Goalpara, the Byagheswari Puja is conducted under a Bel tree where animal sacrifices are carried out to protect the devotee from calamities. This has a parallel to the Dobur Puja of the Mising community. Then there is the practice of Kumari Puja or worshipping virgins, as the Devi. While Assamese Brahmins typically perform it during the annual Durga Puja, there is a practice among non-Brahmins of feeding a group of young girls if a family takes a pledge to do so any time of the year after its members are cured of an outbreak of chickenpox or some other such disease. Aai-Xobah or Xitola Puja is also popular—the Devi is worshipped to please Aai (mother in Assamese) in order to prevent one from falling victim to the dual killers of smallpox and chickenpox which could be fatal earlier. 'The worship of goddess Sitala (small pox) by the Hindus suggests the tribal practice of worshipping deities of illness.'[23] Another example of this is the practice of revering Moirabi and Khusumbia among the Rabhas where pigeons are offered to the deity to cure a person of any disease or abnormality. Several such Xobah in Upper and Lower Assam continue among the caste Hindus, primarily performed by women, say, for easy childbirth and at times by unmarried women to find spouses, such as the Bon Durgar Puja or Xubusoni Puja. There is also a folk practice to worship the apessari (apsara, female celestial being) by women. Like isto devota, there is a female version of the household deity too: ghar deuti.[24] 'Much like the tribes, an Assamese household (non-tribal) is put under a period of uncleanliness during childbirth, death of an inmate and the menstruation of a woman when certain rules are followed by the individuals or the family concerned.'[25] While menstruating women are asked to leave Mising tribal villages before the Dobur Puja is conducted, women in caste Hindu households are also not allowed to work or touch anyone during their monthly period. There is also a tradition, albeit dying now, of gifting an Assamese bride a single bed on her wedding for use during menstruation.

Over the centuries, several tribal male and female forms have been equalled with gods of the Hindu pantheon due to the growing influence of Vedic Hinduism. This phenomenon is exemplified in the two female goddesses among the Rabhas, Rungtuk and Basek. Since they are considered daughters of Rishi Deo, who in turn is equal to Shiva, these goddesses are believed by many Hindu Rabhas now to be a tribal version of Lakshmi and Saraswati.[26] This is also true of the Hindu god Kuber. One of my family heirlooms is an aged wooden box called Kuberor bakos which is taken out of safekeeping every Lakshmi Puja for worship alongside the goddess. Kuber was the lord of wealth of the Kinnars, an asura, a yaksha, chief of evil spirits in *Atharvaveda* who was much later elevated to the position of a god in the Puranas. Perhaps due to the spread of Vedic Hindusim Kuber lost his primacy in several households in olden Assam which had embraced the religion but the original god never left the family rituals.

TOTEM WORSHIP

Like in several South and East Asian countries, in Assam too totem worship is prevalent. In the state's Goalpara area, a bamboo pole is used as a totem in Madan Puja or Bah Puja. This ritual has similarities with the Bhatheli Puja or Sori (some say Suanri) in parts of Kamrup where essentially two poles are stuck to the ground, as male and female versions, to be wedded to each other. The bamboo pole with a flag is worshipped as the god Madar or Midar in Goalpara while men dance around it singing about the benefits of bamboo. Both Hindus and Muslims take part in it. In Bhatheli, two small bamboo plants are grown on the spot too. A perfect example of totem worship among the larger Assamese community is, however, the Jambili Athon of the Karbi tribe. A wooden pole with arms speaks of the tribe's idea behind life and death, its social foundations, and religious practices. Just as the symbol of the phallus, also made of wood, is placed in every household for good luck in Bhutan, so is the Jambili Athon. It is even woven on garments.[27]

The Bhatheli Puja is also a manifestation of the fertility cult, like the Hudum Puja in Goalpara and Bhekulir Biya (marriage of frogs) and Dheki pota (ceremony to erect husking paddle) in various parts of the state.[28]

MANAXA PUJA

Yet another unique ritual among a section of Assamese Hindus is the Manaxa/Maroi Puja which is performed to appease the goddess of serpents, particularly in Kamrup and Goalpara. Some call it Bix-hori Puja too.[29] The popular legend of Beula and Lokhindor that eulogizes Goddess Manaxa exists in Bengali and Assamese Hindu societies. The snake is also a symbol of Shiva, a common reptile in an Assamese backyard whose venomous bite can be fatal.

SOLAR CULT

Religious rituals hinged on local beliefs echo the idea that the Assamese have traditionally viewed their daily lives as a blessing from nature and that their existence can be perpetuated so long as the natural order is not violated. A primordial belief suggests that there are forces beyond the human hand and, therefore, such forces must be appeased. One can locate here the solar cult, and the general proclivity among the Assamese to believe in astrology and palm reading too.

That Pragjyotisa became the land of the solar cult was perhaps only natural with Assam being the land of the rising sun. The place where the sun is spotted first in India is in Dong village in Arunachal Pradesh, once a part of greater Assam. In Markandaya Purana, Assam is referred to as Udayachala, the land of the rising sun. The scripture also mentions that there stood a sun temple in Pragjyotisa–Kamrup. 'The same reference is found in the Brhatsamhita, based on the geography of the Parasara Tantra of the first century AD. The evidence proves that Pragjyotisa-Kamarupa attained celebrity in sun-worship from early times.'[30]

That the cult was once in vogue in Assam is borne by the presence of a clutch of relics at Surjja Pahar, Da Parbatiya, Sukreswar temple, among others. Noted historian R. D. Banerji had noticed 'a beautiful figure of the deity in a panel from the ruins at Tezpur, and on the basis of other remains of the area, he rightly concluded that a gigantic Suryya temple existed there.'[31] Till date, there is a folk practice of offering obeisance to the Sun God if someone can't look up to its strong rays. 'To cure oneself from such a disability, prayers are offered to Xurjya Debota (the sun god) with fresh cow milk and a red Hibiscus flower.'[32] The sacred fire too holds importance in Assamese society—if someone touches the fire with one's feet they have to seek its forgiveness. Since Brahma is the symbol of the rising sun, that the mother river of Assam is called Brahmaputra or the son of Brahma, may also have some connection with the solar cult. 'The solar cults and fire worship in Assam later on came to be divested of their original meaning, and were no longer associated with the Visnu cult. In some form or the other, sun worship may be noticed even today not only in the harvesting rites of the tribes, but also among the people of the plains, particularly in their national festival "Bihu", associated both with the fire cult and harvesting rites.'[33]

BIHU RITUALS

Fire worship in Bihu rituals is quite prominent. If in Kati Bihu, there is a custom of the women of the family lighting an akax bonti, a clay lamp lit by the paddy field at dusk as an offering to nature to deliver a good harvest, on the morning after the Magh Bihu feast, the head of the family is to light the meji, the bonfire, while praying for their wellbeing. Traces of the fertility cult can be found in several other Bihu rituals. 'First, they (Bihu rituals) embody a kind of synthesis of the Aryan and non-Aryan cultures. Secondly, the Bihu festivals include both pre-harvesting and post-harvesting ceremonies. Thirdly, they may rightly be looked as festivals of fertility magic,' remarked Birendra Datta in *A Handbook of Folklore Material of North-East India.*[34] Datta, who had co-written the book with writers Nabin Chandra Sarma and Prabin Chandra Das, also emphasized the existence of several customs based on the fertility cult in agricultural practices in various world cultures. 'Belief goes that such kinds of customs have magical actions upon the promotion of the fertility of Mother Earth.'[35] In Bihu too, particularly the one celebrated in spring, unmarried women have the social sanction to go out without an escort and make merry and possibly run away with a beau to set up her family, which is a reason why Bihu was branded vulgar by Assamese caste Hindus in the beginning. Most upper-caste Assamese Hindus would not allow their girls to learn the Bihu dance. None of the old Assamese texts elaborate on the Bihu rituals. 'Most likely a report left on it by a Muslim traveller in the seventh century was the first. He compared it to Navroz and stated that men and women get together to dance to celebrate the arrival of the new year in Assam.'[36] It is possible that the festival gained popularity under Ahom rule but when the rulers came under the influence of the orthodox Brahmins imported from Bengal, particularly in the nineteenth century, the festival lost its royal patronage. Assamese caste Hindu writers from the colonial era like Holiram Dhekial Phukan, who was highly influenced by upper-class Hindu Bengali culture, had also termed Bihu songs and dances vulgar.[37] 'The fun part was, what writers like Dhekial Phukan had termed to be the unrefined and depraved elements in Bihu were actually its primary elements. In other words, in ancient India, there were rituals like sacrifice and puja for the betterment of harvest but in Assam, there were vibrant dances and songs between men and women. The motive behind both the exercises was the same.'[38]

Another important aspect of Rongali/Bohag Bihu every April are the rituals surrounding the primary animal that helps out the farmer in the fields: the cow (goru). The first day of Bohag Bihu is, therefore, Goru Bihu. The rituals were, however, never carried out the way Vedic Hindusim did by deifying the domestic animal as gaumata. In Assam, it has remained a useful animal in an agrarian society which must be looked after. (In Assamese lingo, a loveable fool is also called a goru.) The ritual around the cow is common across traditional tribal and non-tribal Assamese households. It is on Goru Bihu that the rope (pogha) to tie the animal at the cowshed is changed with a new one. The cows are herded to the riverside for a ceremonial bath with a paste of turmeric and black gram. Then they are dusted with the local vines, dighloti and makhiloti, to protect them from mosquitoes as the bug season begins around that time of the year.[39] Among the Bodos, there is also a tradition of praying to Guhali Madai, a god that they believe resides on the cowshed.[40]

Like the Misings remember the dead in their agricultural festival Ali-Ai-Ligang, so do the Rabhas in Bihu. Highlighting the tribal influence on Bihu, Choudhury wrote, 'The stoppage of field work on certain days by the tribes compares well with the same Hindu restrictions on days like *ekadasi* or the *samkranti*. In fact, most of the tribal agricultural rites lay at the foundation of the Assamese Hindu harvesting festival Bihu....'[41]

The Husori, or a collection of Bihu dancers, call on each household for an annual blessing in keeping with the community's ardent desire to attract good luck and fortune. Seeking blessings, also from the elders, is an important component of Bihu rituals aside from community bonding.

CASTE

Epigraphic confirmation about several kings periodically settling Brahmins in Kamrup through land grants strongly indicates that Assamese society, since a long time, must have had certain elements of the Vedic caste system in their socio-religious life. At least, the division between Brahmins and non-Brahmins, or Brahmins and Sudras, had occurred. While the Nidhanpur grant of King Bhaskarvarman spoke of 're-establishing the institutions of classes and orders, which had for a long time past become confused',[42] Birinchi Kumar Baruah had pointed out that the Gauhati grant of King Indrapala had mentioned, that since the time of King Prithu, 'the laws of the four Asramas and of the four Varnas were observed in their proper divisions.'[43] Barua, though, had underlined, 'It should, however, be noted that *varna* (colour) had by this time lost its original significance and become synonymous with *jati*, the system which laid emphasis on birth and heredity. Consequently, the original division of the people into four *varnas* had been submerged and numerous new castes and sub-castes had been evolved, mainly by the development of different arts, crafts, and professions.'[44]

A significant feature, akin to mainland India, is the presence of gotra among Assamese Brahmins to help trace their legacy from a certain sage.

While there were originally eight gotra, the number, subsequently, exploded to several hundreds. The Nidhanpur grant mentioned fifty-six gotra. The surnames granted to the Brahmans in the epigraphs were typically Deva, Sarman, and Svamin. 'Their names generally end in Bhatta, Dama, Deva, Dhara, Dasa, Datta, Ghosa, Kara, Kunda, Mitra, Naga, Namdi, Palita, Sena, Soma, and so forth. It is, however, not possible to say whether these name-endings were real hereditary family names. Many of them are still used as surnames by the Kayasthas of Assam and Bengal; but it is interesting to note that they are not in use among Brahmanas now.'[45]

While from the inscriptions, one can gather only the presence of Brahmins, and at times non-Brahmin castes like Kayastha and Karana, it is through the jati system that one can better discern the complexities of the social construct in Kamrup.[46] 'Epigraphs, beginning with the sixth century AD, mention Kayasthas, Karanas, Lekhakas, Daivajans (Ganaka) and others; but most of them, if not all, were officers and professional classes rather than castes.'[47] However, the epigraphs of the Kamrup kings didn't establish with certainty that Kayastha was used in the sense of caste and, therefore, one has no way of pinning down exactly when Kayastha began to be used in Assam as a caste name. It can be assumed that they may have had Alpine blood and they were connected with the Nagar Brahmins too as the Nidhanpur grant had showed that the donees included Kayasthas and Nagar Brahmins with surnames like Datta, Soma, Nandi, etc. '[The] Kayasthas might have made their way into Assam at an early period, and some of the Kayastha families of Bengal are the descendants of those from Kamrupa. In Assam, they are now given a position next to the Brahmanas, and constitute the main priestly class of our society, unlike those of other parts of India.'[48] Then there is the sizeable Kalita community in Assam who are also considered Kshatriyas and upper castes. That some inscriptions refer to Kairbartas also gives one the basis to believe that they perhaps had played some role of prominence in olden Assam. The Tezpur rock inscription mentions a Kaibarta in charge of collecting state toll on the rivers.[49]

A vital component of the Assamese caste story is also that several tribes began denoting themselves as castes after their Aryanization. 'The most important of them are the Rabhas, Kacharis, Meches, Koches and the like. The Hindu priests have been responsible for making them *saraniya* (i.e. they have been accepted as Sudras) according to Hindu rites, and all of them were included within one class (Sudras). This process has been going on for a long time past, with the result that there has been an increase in the members of the Hindu fold.'[50] The Assamese subgroup, Sutiya, was originally a tribe.

Because of a liberal outlook of the Hindu social system at play in Assam, it may be deduced that 'probably no caste or class, including that of the Brahmanas followed their caste rules in strict accordance with the *sastras*. The higher classes didn't look down upon the degraded ones, as they did in other parts of India, and were not so strict in the observance of the rules relating to food and profession.'[51] There has also been the practice of Brahmins marrying into lower castes in Assam. 'Bariya is a peculiar caste to Assam formed of the off-spring of Brahmana and Ganaka widows and their descendants.'[52]

For this character of Assamese society, P. C. Choudhury had credited the Vaishnava reformation in Assam in the fifteen–sixteen centuries and the more than six centuries of the reign of the Ahoms, who for a long period were out of the Hindu fold. This accommodative nature might have also helped the later Ahoms to further dilute the caste system by launching a structure of granting surnames principally based on one's profession. This structure couldn't altogether wipe away the caste system but could loosen the rigidities to a large extent for a Brahmin and a non-Brahmin to become, say, a Baruah, Phukan, or a Rajkhowa, For instance, Baruah, Phukan, or Rajkhowa would be officers of various ranks in the Paik system followed by the Ahom army. A Paik is an adult Assamese male called on to serve the irregular army of the Ahoms when required.

However, to fully comprehend the subtle play of caste and class in Assamese society, it is also vital to note the privilege enjoyed by certain social groups, particularly among caste Hindus, till date, over the tribal population, say, in the field of higher education, government jobs, or better social mobility. Although a large swathe of the tribal population were brought into the Hindu fold in an exhibition of religious liberalism, the wider community couldn't quite succeed in breaking the caste and class privilege beyond a point for the socio-economic emancipation of all. In modern times though, one notes a growing awareness about the existence of inequity in Assamese society in both tribal and non-tribal groups, particularly among the younger generation.

While there has been the practice of endogamy, particularly among the Assamese upper castes, for a long time, some other groups, like the Ahoms, Sutiyas, Koch, also the Kalitas to an extent, practice exogamy too. Traditionally, if an upper-caste Hindu person married someone from a lower caste, or say, a tribal outside of the Hindu fold or someone from a Tea

Tribe, there was every possibility of the family cutting all ties with them. However, in the last few decades, inter-caste marriage between Assamese upper castes and members of tribes is frequently noticed and has become less of a social taboo.

BUDDHIST INFLUENCES

Since ancient Assam was principally allied to Kamrup–Kamakhya, an abode of the Sakti cult, several historians argue that Buddhism, therefore, might not have spread its deep roots there. Most had based that conclusion also on the Chinese Buddhist scholar Hiuen Tsang's account from the seventh century that Kamrup had many deva temples while neighbouring Magadha was a Buddhist centre. Additionally, most early Buddhist texts and Ashoka's inscriptions don't mention Kamrup. However, later chroniclers have altered that position based on a line in Hiuen Tsang's account that suggests that Buddhists in Kamrup were following their religion in secret.[53] Did they have to do so because the royal patronage shifted to worshipping Hindu gods and goddesses? Bhaskarvarman, the then king, is widely believed to be a Shaivite.[54] Still, the account had mentioned that he had substantial knowledge about Buddhism and displayed an interest in the religion to Tsang. Where did he draw his knowledge from? That he was not averse to the religion is clear from the fact that he had invited the Chinese Buddhist scholar to visit Kamrup. Some scholars in Assam also assume that his forefathers might have been Buddhists too.[55]

A glance at certain local religio-cultural practices provide clues to what Buddhism was like in the society of the times. Even the edifice of Neo-Vaishnavism constructed by Sankardev in the medieval era smacks of Buddhist practices and material culture. The Tibetan historian Taranath, in his *History of Buddhism*, had stated that Buddhist teacher Dhitika had converted people from sun worship to Buddhism in Kamrup.[56] L. W. Shakespeare had also concluded that the religion prevailed in the land even before the introduction of Hinduism and that many Hindu temples were constructed on Buddhist sites.[57] There still exists an exclusive door at the revered Haigrib–Madhab Vishnu temple in Hajo for Tibetan and Bhutanese monks to pay a visit for an annual prayer. According to P. C. Choudhury, 'It is likely that some relics of the Buddha were carried to Assam and enshrined in a place near Gauhati, probably at Kamakhya where a relic casket of stone has been found and which almost certainly contained some ashes of the Buddha, over which a *stupa* or *chaitya* was raised, or at Hajo.'[58] This is similar to the tooth temple in faraway Kandy in Sri Lanka where a Buddha relic is preserved.

Significantly, the four-armed figure at Haigrib Madhab temple, identified by Hindus as Vishnu's incarnation Madhab, has a Buddhist mantra inscribed on it. Padma Sambhava, a saint in the seventh century CE, probably died at Hajo, and the shrine was built over his ashes. 'This is supported by the mystic syllable, *mane padme hum, mani* standing for the Buddha, and *padme* for Padmasambhava. The sanctity of the place is also borne out by the fact that some monastery of Tibet is believed to have been built with clods of earth from Hajo.'[59] While Tsang saw little evidence of Buddhism being practised in Kamrup in the sixth century, in the twelfth-century *Rajatarangini*, there is a reference to Amritprabha, the daughter of a Kamrup king, who brings with her a Tibetan Buddhist guru, Stunpa, to Kashmir after her marriage to the king. Stunpa is said to have built a monastery in Kashmir.[60] C. N. K. Aiyar, in *Sankaracharya – His Life and Times* also mentioned the revered Brahman seer visiting Kamrup in 900 CE during the Salasthambha rule to defeat the Buddhist scholar Abhinavagupta. P. C. Choudhury had, however, contested the notion that Shankaracharya had wiped away Buddhism from India altogether. 'Kamarupa, we know, became a stronghold of later Buddhism and this happened at a time when no sharp distinction remained between Brahmanical and Buddhist gods. In the Tantrik-Buddhist days, Kamarupa was one of the most important *pithas* in eastern India and the faith was patronised by the Pala rulers of Assam.'[61]

Aside from existing ruins of temples and icons that suggest the prevalence of Buddhism not only in Hajo but in sites like Sujjya Pahar in Goalpara, Tezpur, Kamakhya, etc., there are other pointers to substantiate the prevalence of Buddhism in Assam too. Saumadeep Datta's book on Buddhism and Buddhist culture in Assam, *Asomot Buddha Dharma aru Boudha Sanskriti*, is extremely helpful in this aspect. Highlighting a local belief that the area around Haigrib–Madhab temple was known as Kusinagar at some point in history, Datta had drawn readers' attention to some village names in the three Lower Assam districts of Nalbari, Barpeta, and Kamrup. These villages till date use the suffix 'kuchi' in their names, say, Betkuchi, Ketukuchi, Kalakuchi, Sualkuchi, etc. These western Assam villages are not too distant from Magadha, Pataliputra, Kalinga, Vaishali, etc. which were important centres of Buddhism. Emperor Ashoka had set up 80,000 villages by sending out people to different places with the ashes of Buddha. Datta's assumption was that these villages could be among them. 'The word *Kuchi* has a Buddhist cultural overtone. Since Gautam Buddha had passed away in Kushinagar, whenever the Buddhist believers migrated to another place and set up a new village, they must have added the suffix *Kusi* to the names. *Kusi* might have undergone some change in these areas to become *Kuchi*.'[62] Since Hajo is not far from these areas either, Datta saw this as a sign that there existed a wider area in western Assam where Buddhism might have been in practice, much before it was brought by certain Tibeto-Burman groups to the Brahmaputra Valley from Upper Burma. This is especially believable since these areas are contiguous to Cooch Bihar (Koch Behar), and that Behar is commonly used to mean a Buddhist site.

Datta, through his deep research, not only presented Buddhist links to several folk beliefs and practices across Assam, including that of worshipping the serpent goddess Manaxa, and that several communities looked at Buddha as Shiva, but also highlighted that Ganesha was also a Mahayana Buddhist deity. Banking on the recent discovery of three stone epigraphs in Tibetan script in Mayang, located close to Guwahati, he had argued that there had been so many Ganesha statues littered around it because of the prevalence of Buddhism in that area.

'When Gautam Buddha was in his mother Maya Devi's womb, she dreamt of elephants, the reason why Buddhists had placed idols of elephants in various places. People of Assam don't see this connection at once due to their lack of adequate knowledge about Buddhism; that Ganesha is a Mayayana Buddhist deity and that the Buddhists have a religious connection to the animal.'[63] The Rumtek monastery in Sikkim, an important Mahayana Buddhist centre, also has Ganesha idols. Stone Ganesha idols are present in Kamakhya too, among so many other old temples of Assam. It is worth mentioning here that Ganesha is found on the murals of the Alchi monastery in Ladakh which is believed to be in existence from tenth century onwards. The monastery particularly reveres Avalokitesvara which signifies a compassionate Buddha. In Angkor Wat of Cambodia too, Ganesha idols are found. That city was built in the early twelfth century by Khmer king Jayavarman VII who was a devotee of the Avalokiteswara version of the Buddha in Mahayana sect. Ganesha idols can be seen in some Mahayana monasteries of Thailand too. In Japan too, Ganesha finds expression through the local god Kangiten.

While most gamusas of Assam's tribal communities are colourful, that only the one used by Assamese in general is white with red flowers may also be due to Buddhist influence. That most religious places in Assam have a big banyan tree is reminiscent of a Buddhist site; Buddha, for about hundred years after his salvation, was worshipped only through a tree as a symbol where he had attained nirvana.

Noted writer Leela Gogoi in his book on Assam's culture (*Axomor Xangaskriti*) highlighted that though Ahoms are widely believed to have entered the Brahmaputra Valley before Buddhism had swept through Upper Burma, several of their customs are similar to Buddhist traditions such as the Phuralong Puja or a ritual that forbids animal sacrifice and the use of Buddhist chants in the Ahom marriage ceremony called Chokolong. Datta's book also expounded on several Kamrupi Buddhist scholars, thus holding up the argument that the Buddhist Charyapadas are, therefore, a vital source of Assam's early social life. Since the language used in the Charyapadas was for common people, Buddhism could easily seep into those social brackets. Several top linguists, including Banikanta Kakati, had stated that the language used in Charyapada has several similarities with Assamese. Additionally, Datta had pointed out that the *Dakor Boson*, the aphorisms of the wise man Dak who is believed to have lived in Assam's Barpeta in the fifth–sixth centuries, resembles the language of Charyapadas. 'According to local beliefs in Assam, *Dakor Boson*, the aphorisms, were born in Lahidonga village of Barpeta. According to Ashutosh Bhattacharyya (the author of *Folklore of Bengal*), Dak was the surname of the Buddhist tantriks. In other words, it was through Dak's words that Buddhism was spread among common people.'[64]

The most prominent remnants of Buddhist practices can be spotted in Sankardev's Neo-Vaishnavism. While scholars have pointed out that Sankardev most likely plucked some features of the indigenous Shamanistic form of dance, the Uja-pali of Lower Assam, to create the Sattriya dance, Datta tried to place the original form itself in Buddhist traditions. Additionally, the monasteries set up by the Guru's followers after his demise to house Vaishnava devotees match the structure of the Buddhist monasteries. Most naam-ghars in Assam commonly have the lion, a Buddhist image, at its entrance as a guardian. It is not uncommon to find in the Vaishnava monasteries of Majuli the tradition of keeping an earthen lamp lit continuously, some for over 100 years in continuity; this is a practice also in the Buddhist monasteries. It is rather interesting that though Sankardev had criticized Tantrik Buddhist practices, his faith ended up adopting the monastic structure among other features from Buddhism. These monasteries, set up by his followers after the Guru's demise were perhaps to also persuade the Tantrik Buddhists of the times to join his Ek Sarana Nama Dharma. Datta had anyway claimed that most Assamese Muslims might have been from the lower caste (Sudras) who had converted to Islam from Buddhism, as they could have been looked down upon by the upper-caste Brahmanical structure of the times and not given due space within it.[65] About the popularity of Tantrik Buddhism, Datta had argued that keeping in sight Buddha's cardinal principles of non-violence and the singular stress on the morality of a believer, the crudeness, if any, in Tantrik Buddhism prevalent in Assam, might have sneaked in from Sakta–Shaivite and Kirata religious practices, such as the sacrificial rituals.[66]

What is noteworthy among the Assamese is also the importance granted to the sacred sound drawn from the bell metal, such as the sounds emanating from the bells of a Hindu temple or the cymbals used at a Buddhist monastery or a Neo-Vaishnavite shrine.

NEO-VAISHNAVISM AND SANKARDEV

While there is a common notion about the spread and embrace of Vaishnavism in Assam only since Sankardev's period in the fifteenth–sixteenth centuries, there exists enough historical evidence to deduce that worshipping Vishnu as a Vedic god was in practice in the land since ancient times.[67] It is vital to note anyway that the Bhakti cult that had emanated from devotion to Krishna in medieval India was different from Vishnu puja stemming from the Vedas. Vishnu finds mention for the first time in the Rig Veda but he was only a minor god then. Also, Vaishnavism as a faith didn't find any mention before the Mahabharata. Vaishnavism set roots in Assam at a time when the solar cult and Brahmanical culture had made considerable progress.[68] 'In the *Mahabharata*, Visnu is called Pragjyotisa jyestha. The *Kalika Purana* describes in detail about the worship of Visnu-Vasudeva with rituals and mentions as many as five incarnations of the deity as being worshipped in different places of Assam.'[69]

The first historical instance of Vishnu worship in ancient Assam can be traced to 554 CE, as seen in the Badaganga rock inscription of King Bhutivarman.[70] After Bhutivarman, Vaishnavism might have plummeted to a subordinate position for a few centuries till it regained royal patronage during the reign of Dharmapala in the thirteenth century. Ruins of several Vishnu temples across Assam since the seventh century onwards exist as reminders of the prevalence of the faith in Kamrup.[71]

About the factors leading to the rise of Sankardev's Neo-Vaishnavism, Choudhury had stated, 'With the extinction of the Pala rule in Assam during the 12th century AD and while the Tantric-Buddhist system became strong, there was a period of chaos in the land, marked by revolting rites, until these were temporarily suppressed by the Vaishnava reformers.'[72] Referring to Vajrayana Buddhism, noted historian Kanak Lal Barua, in 1933, had said, 'The excesses which were indulged in the name of religion under this system are too revolting to be enumerated.'[73] Barua had mentioned a Ratikhoa or Purandharia sect of Assam, the traces of which could be seen during his time too.[74] In 1920, M. C. Goswami, in the first report of the research group Kamrup Anusandhan Samiti, stated that the Ratikhoa sect was founded by Gopal, a contemporary of Sankardev, but it could well be drawn from a splinter cult of Buddhism of a degraded form.[75] Choudhury had called it 'remarkable' that several Tantrik-Buddhist rites had crept into Sankardev's Neo-Vaishnavism too and that his preachings were fundamentally based on those of Buddhists of the earlier period.[76] In effect, Choudhury had pointed out that Sankardev's dharma was aimed at ushering in an easy-to-follow religious order among common people by discarding some existing norms and embracing some others. That his preachings had extensive appeal for people from different social sets only underpins the fact that religious beliefs are never static and a person, at least during those times, was quite open to the idea of adopting a better spiritual experience.

Apart from the 'chaos' that Choudhury had referred to in the religious space then, the political landscape of Assam too was disorderly. There was no one kingdom, and no one set of rules. While some parts were with the Sutiyas and the Kacharis, some others were under the Ahoms, and Kamata and later Koch kings. Sankardev's new faith gradually helped cement a bond between people residing in various principalities and provided the basis to eventually carve out a fresh cultural and spiritual, identity.

Sankardev brought Neo-Vaishnavism to the Assamese society during the Bhakti movement which had taken over large swathes of northern India. The saint had brought the cult to Assam much before Chaitanya did so in Bengal. He had met Chaitanya (1485–1533 CE) in Puri only at the fag end of his life, during his second pilgrimage to mainland India with 127 followers.[77] Barua had placed that meeting in about 1530, when Sankardev might have been eighty-one years old. On that journey, he is said to have met the granddaughter of Kabir too.[78] Aside from the fact that Sankardev was older than Chaitanya, Barua had also refuted some Bengali historians that he was a disciple of Chaitanya on the grounds that he never promoted dualism but the creed of monism of a special kind.[79]

While most saints of the Bhakti movement had concentrated primarily on the religious and devotional aspects in their sayings in the search of the supreme self, Sankardev, went much beyond it, equally becoming a preacher of a new dharma in medieval Assam and also a painter, a performing artist, and a writer to provide early Assamese society the required reinforcements to effect a 'renaissance' of sorts to institute itself as a community. As linguist Banikanta Kakati had said in *Mother Goddess Kamakhya*, 'Sankardeva had given Assam life, letters and a state. Rules have come and gone and their kingdoms perished in the dust, but Sankardeva's state endures and broad in the general heart of men his power survives.'[80] He ushered in a sociocultural renaissance which helped the Assamese community flower like never before. His cultural gifts to the community have been highlighted elsewhere in the book.

A major difference between Sankardev's cult and that of other major Bhakti scholars was also his emphasis on monism; he kept out the cult of Radha from his preachings and evoked only Krishna.

A quick run through Sankardev's family background shows that he had hailed from the Shaivite fold. The story goes that he was born after his father Kusumbar prayed to Shiva for a son. He was, therefore, named Shankarbar. His parents passed away in his childhood, leaving him under the care of his grandmother Kherxuti Aai. At the age of twelve, he joined the local Sanskrit tol (school for tutelage) run by the noted scholar of the times Mahendra Kandali.[81] Swadesh Ranjan Ghosh, in his essay on Sankardev wrote thus, 'We are not sure about the course of studies in the "tols" in those days and about the duration. But it is pretty certain that in about six to seven years, Sankardeva came out a finished scholar in the usual Sanksrit lore, not excluding the Vedas and the Upanishads, and including the Ramayana and the Mahabharata, the puranas, tantras, Kalapa grammar and literature (kavya) in general. He could make fine poems now, and easy narrative. *Harishanra-Upakhyan* is ascribed by his biographers to his days in school.'[82]

Sankardev soon married and settled down for a domestic life. His wife passed away after the marriage of his daughter. 'Shankar, who had always religious leanings, now felt inclined to renounce the world and devote himself to religious exercises.'[83] In 1491, he set out on a pilgrimage to what is mainland India now and probably visited several temples of north and south India, in the company of seventeen men including Mahendra Kandali.[84] Gaya, Vrindaban, Puri, Dwarka, Kashi, Ayodhya, Prayag, etc. are some of the places his biographers had mentioned as part of his itinerary where he had theological deliberations with Neo-Vaishnavite scholars. Twelve years later, he returned home, remarried, and didn't renounce the world. Instead, he instituted the Ek Sarana Nama Dharma where he promoted devotion to one Supreme Being, Lord Krishna, suggesting that it was even more appropriate than pursuing renunciation or mukti from mortal existence. Stressing on chanting to express devotion, he moulded the practice of naam-proxoingo (singing in praise of the lord) by composing easy cantos. He asked the devotees to take only the lord's name to evoke him while clapping in rhythm on common ground—the naam-ghar. He, thereby, promoted Naam Bhakti which, according to him, would bestow on a devotee xahaj ananda (simple joy) and eternal bliss.[85] The saint rejected worshipping minor gods and goddesses in practice in Assam then and also the sacrificing of animals; he simplified the structure of imparting religion thus opening a door to the common folks untutored in Sanskrit slokas to seek the Supreme Self. The holy book, Bhagavad Purana, which he had adapted in Assamese and included names of local tribes and communities, was the sole article to be placed on the monikut (sanctum sanctorum) as a sign of devotion. Avoiding Sanskrit, the language of Vedic scriptures and scholars, he crafted Brajawali, an admixture of early Assamese and Maithili, thus making sure, like in Buddhism, that his teachings spread through a medium that common men could relate to. Knowing well that food can also be a way into people's heart, he enticed the man on the street to step inside the naam-ghar by offering them a praxad of green gram and black chickpeas.

'Because of this liberal view, a large number of people belonging to the tribal and backward classes (including Muslims) embraced Vaishnavism and the rigour of the caste distinction was considerably reduced. Therefore, Sankardeva's contribution to the integration of Assam is a glorious chapter in the cultural history of Assam.'[86] However, some later scholars in Assam do point out that even though Sankardev's religion was egalitarian and inclusive in nature, it was not completely free of the notions of 'pure' and 'impure' birth (yoni).[87]

During Ahom rule, Sankardev, after returning from his first pilgrimage in 1439 CE[88], set up a monastery at Batodroba; completed his adaptation of Bhagawat in early Assamese language sitting under a Xilikha tree which still exists at the site. According to common credence, Sakta Brahmins of the times were alarmed at the growing pull of his faith on common people and filled the ears of Dihingia Roja Suhungmung (1497–1539) against him, prompting Sankardev to seek shelter first in the Kamata kingdom, and subsequently under the Koch king Naranarayan in present-day Cooch Behar. Because of his extraordinary talents and religious knowledge, Sankardev also began to be called Mahapurux and his cult Mahapuruxia.

Sankardev spent his last years in the Koch kingdom. The Shamrai monastery in Goalpara town, part of erstwhile Koch kingdom, claims to have the asthi (ashes) of Sankardev. During my visit to the monastery in 2018, I was shown the asthi by its chief bhokot. However, it is well recorded that Sankardev passed away in Madhupur monastery in Cooch Behar. Years after Sankardev's demise, in the seventeenth century, his religion achieved the status of a national religion throughout Kamrup and the Upper Assam districts. 'It was not the national adoption of the faith but the religious organisations called Satras which no doubt sapped, to some extent, the authority of the Ahom kings of the eighteenth century.'[89]

Gradually, the faith forked into two: the Mahapuruxia cult through his disciple Madhabdev's leadership around the Barpeta monastery, and the Bamunia cult through the disciple Damodardeb in Majuli island. The kings granted these monasteries huge tracts of land which, in turn, were leased out to local peasants, mostly from the tribal communities, in lieu of a portion of the harvest. The system ensured food security of the monks while they engaged in religio-cultural activities.

These centuries-old socio-religious structures continue to exist in Assam as sentinels of the vestiges of the times that once were, albeit without much of the old glory and sway they had over the wider Assamese society.

6

TI–LAO–AANOI–ABUNG–BULUNG BUTUR, LAUHITYA–LUIT–BRAHMAPUTRA: THE RED RIVER IN ASSAMESE LIFE

From the vantage point of the Bhupen Hazarika Setu—India's longest bridge—the waters of the Lohit look like ribbons snaking through blotches of sand that typically rise from the river bed with the receding rainwaters post monsoon. A little away stood the Dibru Saikhowa National Park, bounded by the river. That utterly brilliant natural spectacle stretches out as if touching the horizon.

Lohit is a confluence of two other rivers flowing from Arunachal Pradesh in the immediate neighbourhood: Dihang and Dibang. The coming together of the three rivers carves out a massive swathe of floodplains off Sadiya, Assam's easternmost town. A little after that picturesque point, Lohit flows as Luit or the Brahmaputra, the mother river that not only pumps in water to a warren of tributaries orbiting Assam, thus becoming the lifeline of Assamese rural existence, but also the reason for its sorrow and pride; love and despair. The river fills the substratum of Assamese culture and has been the hub of luit poriya or riverine civilization that has bricked itself by its banks.

If it was on the Brahmaputra that the Ahoms fought a decisive battle against the Mughals, it was also through the river that the British entered Assam to chase away the Burmese in 1826, leading to its colonization. Academic Arup Jyoti Saikia had rightly noted in his one-of-a-kind biography on the river, 'Assam's colonization was facilitated by the Brahmaputra, the same river that had provided leverage to Assam's military in earlier centuries.'[1] In the colonial era, the British built the Northbrook Gate on Guwahati's Sukreswar Ghat to commemorate the first visit of a viceroy (Lord Northbrook) to Northeast India. It was there in 1874 that his ship anchored and wherefrom he stepped on Assam's soil.

There is no denying that Brahmaputra has a deep connect with Assam's history and the civilizational construct of the greater Assamese community. It is by the Luit that batches of people from multiple races came from the eastern and western directions to settle down and be known as Axomiya.

Not for nothing then that Bhupen Hazarika's song 'Mahabahu Brahmaputra' labelled the river as a metaphor for mahamilonor tirtha, the hub of a grand assimilation of people. The popular number had fleshed out through music the basic construct of the Assamese identity spun around the river.

The legendary musician's brother Jayanta Hazarika's memorable Assamese song 'Luitor Boliya Baan' (The Mad Floodwaters of the Brahmaputra) also perfectly encapsulates the community's discernment of the river. It is the unquiet, untamed, impulsive nature of the Brahmaputra that makes it volatile and an object of both awe and anger in Assamese minds. In the song, Jayanta Hazarika begs the river to not touch the standing paddy nurtured by the peasant with love; to not be the vulture (xogun) that sits on people's roofs and heralds death. The song also reminds the river that it is its waters that the people depend on for survival, and also draw strength from to fight for their existence. The Hazarika brothers hailed from Sadiya, not far from where the Brahmaputra enters Assam discarding its Tibetan name, Yarlung Tsangpo, and the Arunachali name Siang. Once a bustling town, Sadiya had lost a huge chunk of its landmass to the river after it had changed course due to the massive earthquake in 1950. In Hazarika's popular song on the river, 'Bistrino Parore', the balladeer had placed the Brahmaputra not only as the witness to what was happening to the people who lived by its banks but also prodded it to be their voice, as they are the voiceless. This particular Hazarika song might have been inspired by Paul Robeson's famous score 'Ol' Man River', but the Assamese balladeer had sung over a hundred songs around the Brahmaputra and its link rivers, thus richly deserving of the sobriquet, the Bard of the Brahmaputra.

These iconic Assamese songs only underline that the river is all pervading in Assamese life and never quite leaves the sociocultural consciousness and conditioning of the people. Innumerable Bihu songs with allusions to Luit form the bedrock of Assamese folk music. Birinchi Kumar Baruah, in his article in 1966 on the portrayal of daily life in Bihu songs, had pointed out common references to the river in Bihu songs, say, with words and phrases like 'Luitor paar' (the shores of Luit), 'kohua bon' (the reeds that grow by its banks), 'rupali bali' (its silvery sands), 'Luitor sapori' (the sand bars), the water animals like 'xihu' and 'ghorial', 'sirip sirip kori kapur dhui asilu siri Luitoloi sai' (washing clothes looking at the river), the dhol.[2] Assamese cultural icon Jyoti Prasad Agarwalla's evergreen number written in pre-independent India—'Luitore pani jabi o boi' (Flow, the waters of Luit)—is an ode to the Brahmaputra and a plea to the river to carry, wherever it traverses, tales of bravery of Assamese people including the Ahom queen Joymoti's sacrifice for her motherland.

The river is also addressed by various other names over the centuries. Nahendra Padun, Assamese writer and academic from the Mising tribe, had once pointed out to me, 'In the Mising folk form Oi-Nitom, we find reference to not only Brahmaputra but its tributaries too but their reference is by different names. Say, Brahmaputra is called Ah-Noi-Abung. The Lohit is De-lu. Subansiri is Obonori; Dihing is Diying; Jia Bhoroli is Burili.'[3] The Bodos call the river Burlung Butur. Historians and linguists have already established the analogy that the name Luit might have stemmed from an Austric formation Ti-Lao. The Mishimis from whose ancestral land flows the Dibang which meets Dihang to join Lohit near Sadiya, call the Brahmaputra Tellu. P. C. Choudhury had underlined that the name of the Brahmaputra, 'the Lauhitya of literature, the Tsangpo of the Tibeto-Burmans, or the Lohit (Luit) of the Assamese popular literature, appears to have its origin in an Austric formation like *Lao-tu*, '*tu*' meaning water; similarly the Karatoya, called *Kalotu* in Chinese records, may be derived from an Austric word. The *Kalika Purana* (Chapter 82) gives the mythological origin of the name of the Brahmaputra.'[4] Linguist Banikanta Kakati too had mentioned that Ti-Lao was used to refer to the Brahmaputra in Ahom annals, deducing that the name might have been popular when they had entered the Brahmaputra Valley in the thirteenth century.[5] Choudhury had also noted, 'It was in the valley of the Brahmaputra that a high civilisation was evolved, for the development of which the Aryan and non-Aryan elements had their part to play.'[6]

A glimpse of the daily negotiation of the common people with the river can be found in Bhupen Hazarika's soulful singing: '*Luitor saporit kore naowaiya balit bhate randhi khai.*' Who is this unknown boatman preparing his meal on the sands of the Luit? It magnifies the image of the river in a common man's daily life, as a channel of transport and communication to the rest of the world. It is the Brahmaputra that connected the people of Assam with mainland India, especially in terms of trade, long before the railways did in the colonial era. Arupjyoti Saikia had called the boats on the river a symbol of the human conquest of the Brahmaputra.[7] With a mesh of tributaries of the Brahmaputra snaking through Assam, and rains splashing the state for a good part of the year, and barely a highway or two careening through the land until well into the nineteenth century, the Assamese conducted local economy through the river ways.[8] In saint

Sankardev's life too, we often come across boat journeys on the river, highlighting it as a major means of communication in medieval Assam. Goalpara in Western Assam was the gateway to the state's trade with Bengal and mainland India for a long time. While the high silt content in the Brahmaputra waters favoured the canoes more than big barges, in the monsoons it gets severely restrictive for any type of boat to navigate the force of the river. Highlighting the trouble of the Nadiyals (boatmen or people living by the river), Saikia had stated, 'Nadiyals had to both depend on the current of the river and fight against the current. Their boats were propelled by oars or paddles, and often they pushed along the shore with long poles. When wind was unfavourable, more people had to push the boats from the banks while the boatmen punted.'[9] Over time, the Nadiyals developed their own techniques to create channels on the Brahmaputra to add sail to the boats. It is common to come across bamboo fences strategically placed on the Brahmaputra to help a boat or a ferry sail faster against the current on the Majuli route. Thanks to the river, Assamese also witnessed a glimpse of modernity enveloping the rest of the world with the arrival of the steamer ship. It enabled not only the colonial economy to pick up but the first batch of English educated youth to reach Kolkata and pursue higher studies.

Over the centuries, the river has also created countless sandbars, locally called sapori (also char in Lower Assam). These sandbars became the designated space for goru-mohor khuti (sheds for cows and buffaloes) of nearby villagers, and also additional common property for farming vegetables that need soft soil. Even today, while crossing the Brahmaputra from the Nimati Ghat in Jorhat to Majuli Island, one spots sapori being used in the traditional way. The dunes are created by the silt from the river.

It is important to note that though the river is central to Assamese life it has never been venerated as an idol for worship, like the Ganga is. The Brahmaputra is placed in classical texts as the son of Brahma, the only 'male' river in Bharat and never worshipped. 'Strong undercurrents all along the river were possibly a powerful deterrent to the river being regarded as a holy site.'[10] No wonder then that when the Assam government tailored a festival around the river in 2017, like that of the Holy Ganga, it generated considerable public ire. The festival dates were close to Bohag Bihu in April, the most important festival for the Assamese and a time when the Luit typically becomes a metaphor of the community's traditional life in the folk songs that waft through the air. Such a cold reaction to a festival around a river which otherwise is an integral part of their collective ethos can give a peek into how the Brahmaputra has been imagined and related to by the community for centuries. No surprise then, a paean to the festival eulogizing the Brahmaputra by Assamese heartthrob Papon didn't cut much ice with the public either, while two years later, an eulogy to Majuli, the island dependent on the mood of the river, belted out by a lesser known singer Nilutpal Bora, topped the charts. Bora's song 'Majuli' asked the listener a question that is in the heart of every person who dwells by the Brahmaputra: *Barixare gohuli thakibone eibeli nodikhoni mone mone xui?* (On this monsoon night, will the unquiet river quietly sleep?)

The annual devastation that it wreaks on the riverine people snatches away lives and land, leaving scores in grief, landless and penurious, so much so that there has been a perennial demand by local political players and student activist groups to declare Assam floods as a national disaster. Calling it so would not only help get the necessary attention from the mainland but also the required funds and policies to tackle it once and for all. Often the gripe is that there has been a dearth of a political will at the Centre to bring about an end to the annual floods. That emotion was evoked by Narendra Modi when he campaigned in Assam during the 2014 parliamentary elections.[11] Not that former prime ministers before him never made such electoral promises. Morarji Desai, in 1978, had also delivered a fiery speech in Assam, promising to harness the hydro power of the Brahmaputra if his Janata-led government was voted to power.[12] His was a challenge to the Nehruvian India which had promoted hydro-electric power as a new engine of development for the country but kept the Brahmaputra out of it.

Saikia's book on the Brahmaputra, however, gives a front row view of how the river was envisaged as a 'commodity' during British colonization and thereafter as the 'nation's river' in post-Independent India with multiple steps taken to essentially tame its recurrent floods with little success. Even before the British took control of Assam, European explorers had invested a good deal of time charting out the course of the Brahmaputra from its origin in Tibet. In 1715, Ippolito Desideri, a Jesuit priest from Pistoria of northern Tuscany, was the first to report that Tsangpo and Brahmaputra were the same rivers.[13] Till the middle of the eighteenth century, there existed confusion about whether Tsangpo joined the Irrawaddy or the Brahmaputra.[14] After the formal takeover of the province, in 1872, Major James Rennell, the surveyor general of East India Company, for the first time showed in *Memories of a Map of Hindoostan*, the first map of India, the source of Brahmaputra as Tsangpo.[15] Ranjita Biswas, in her coffee table book *Brahmaputra and the Assam Valley*, offered an explanation on how the colonizers had tried to ascertain the source of the river, 'The British government sent many explorers as they wanted to open trade routes with Tibet but success was limited. In 1825, Captain Philip Burton went up the Brahmaputra by boat and found the water divided into three different directions—on the east the Lohit, to the north Dihang and Dibang.'[16] Locals were trained to survey the land; some had to sneak into Tibet disguised as monks as Tibet wouldn't allow foreigners. 'Among the real-life accounts of these adventurers, which read like film scripts, stands out the name of Kinthup, a Sikkimese, unsung hero who spent four years in Tibet since 1879. He was perhaps the first to connect Siang with the Brahmaputra. But his supervisor, H. J. Harman, had left India by the time he returned and his feat remained buried in official reports.'[17]

Rennell's findings shaped the tone and spirit of future understanding of the river.'[18] The official control over the river during the British period came with a focus on restoring the bunds so that revenue could be extracted from agriculture. 'The Assamese officer Anandaram Dhekial Phukan, posted in the district of Nagaon, as a junior official, repeatedly expressed concern about the damage caused by the floodwaters of the Brahmaputra. He had no doubt that floods were inimical to the agriculture; they destroyed crops and as a result the government incurred losses.'[19] The result was the demand for restoring the ancient river bunds which found support from the tea planters as they could then grow tea in the low-lying areas. In 1893, the British administration conducted a detailed survey leading to restoration of the old embankments and the construction of some new ones.

While the policy to embank the river continued, in the early twentieth century, the colonial administration began exploring the hydro-electric power of not just the Brahmaputra but of all rivers across India. The first push to harness the hydro power of the Assam's rivers came in 1905; in 1910, an extensive survey was conducted on various rivers of India. However, the idea was not taken forward after the surveys.

Post-Independence, there was a proposal to dam a few rivers in Assam with the idea of controlling the annual floods. Towards the end of 1947, a survey was conducted to construct a dam near Pasighat in present-day Arunachal Pradesh. However, the government move was restrained by the devastating earthquake of 1950. In 1974, the Assam government began rethinking the idea of erecting a dam to control the floods and carried out surveys on Dihang and Subansiri, but nothing much happened. A number of regulatory bodies were periodically created to generate ideas to bridle the river from the mid-1950s onwards. In 1954, the Brahmaputra River Commission was formulated, followed by Assam Flood Control Board in 1963 after the devastating 1962 floods. In July 1970, the Board was taken over by Brahmaputra Flood Control Board and the Centre resorting to surveys to build dams on Dihang and Subansiri to control the floods. In 1980, Parliament passed the Brahmaputra Board Act. 'The task of owning a river by the Indian government, long desired by Assam's political class, was thus completed. Mandated to look after the Brahmaputra, the board was established in 1982 with a techno-official team containing twenty-one members.'[20] In 1983, the Board charted a road map suggesting that multipurpose dams be placed on the Subansiri and the Dihang, but progress slowed down as substantial central funding was required. 'Assam desperately awaited the benevolence of the federal government. The Board too, facing popular denunciation and financial irregularities, had to fight a protracted battle to safeguard its image as the guardian of the river.'[21] Years later, in 2009, though work began on the Subansiri dam, it was halted in 2011 due to local protests. In mid-2019, the National Green Tribunal gave a go-ahead to the mega dam, setting aside the petition of the anti-dam organizations of Assam that had questioned the environment clearance report that had favoured the building of the dam. This legal clearance to the mega dam in an earthquake prone zone also came at a time when China was seemingly already constructing a dam upstream.

Alongside the idea to dam the Brahmaputra to control the floods, there has also been a parallel narrative, both in popular imagination and in the government circles, about 'dredging' the river, essentially to excavate the silts from the river bed to deepen its depth further so that it can hold the monsoonal waters. Assam government, in 1966 and 1974, did embark on this experiment. 'The dredging carried out during 1974–5, however, saw mixed results, at best...the scheme was put to rest after a few months of experimentation.'[22] Yet decades later, on the closing ceremony of the Namami Brahmaputra festival in 2017, central surface transport and shipping minister Nitin Gadkari announced that the Centre would dredge Brahmaputra and the silt collected would be paved into a 'Brahmaputra Highway' along its banks at an estimated cost of ₹40,000 crores.[23] He said the Bangladesh government had agreed to India's proposal to dredge the river course from Sadiya till the Chittagong port and the river link would be extended to Haldia port of West Bengal too at a sum of ₹250 crore. Once completed, it would become the 'economic corridor' between Assam, West Bengal, and Bangladesh, a part of India's Act East Policy.[24] However, as per an Assam government statement in the assembly in March 2020, in 2017 an expert committee led by former Gauhati University professor Dulal Goswami rejected dredging as a viable option to control floods and erosion by the Brahmaputra.[25] In February 2021, Gadkari told Parliament that the Centre didn't have any proposal to build a highway along the river's banks.[26]

Meanwhile, the Centre has moved the narrative towards reviving the old waterways on the Brahmaputra and linking it to Bangladesh to stimulate bilateral trade. In November 2019, the government also dispatched for the first time a containerized cargo on the Inland Water Transport route from the Haldia port to Pandu port in Assam. In the early nineteenth century, the Pandu port, and thereby the Brahmaputra, played a vital role in the success of the tea industry in Assam. Till the Assam–Bengal railway became operational in 1904, it was only by the river that tea, timber, jute, rubber, etc. were dispatched out of Assam.[27] By the end of the twentieth century, long distance steamer services were stopped, thus bringing the curtains down on an important symbol of colonialism, and of early modernity touching Assamese life.

Much time has flowed since, as have the waters of the Brahmaputra. The river continues to bring to its shores hope and sorrow like it has always done even as new sets of governments come forward with newer plans to tame its waters. The turbulent red river lingers on, through new songs and new literature in Assamese and other tribal languages of the state. It inspires and unnerves yet another generation of Axomiya and also evokes raw sentiments in them every year when the floods sink a large swatch of the land.

7

KHAAR–KHORISA, LAI–LOPHA, MAAS–KASO, HAAH–PARO: ASSAMESE CUISINE

'Whose daughter is this one?'

A grey-haired man serving khisiri, the quintessential Indian gruel, to a crowd of devotees at the revered Nabagraha temple in Guwahati, asked.

It was in response to my query whether he also had khisiri without the meat.

On someone uttering my father's name, the man called out an aide. Few dollops of 'vegetarian' khisiri (khichdi) soon landed on the banana leaf in front of me. 'Nirami-x khisiri is prepared in small quantity, only for Bamun widows and devotees with high blood pressure,' the aide said curtly.

The Assamese Brahmin (Bamun) widows traditionally abstain not only from non-vegetarian food but also vegetarian fare traditionally considered tamasik (food that raises body heat). I was in none of the categories he named but was still glad to have got a few ladles of the vegetarian khisiri.

Typically, khisiri in Assam is served as a special praxad, blessed hand-out, to believers gathered at a temple. Though the Assamese are believed to have been introduced to khisiri after coming in contact with the Muslim invaders in the medieval era,[1] one is not sure when the dish crept into the Hindu temples to be served as praxad to the devotees. Anyway, often, a call on whether the khisiri should be vegetarian or otherwise at some temples in Assam is taken depending on what is offered by the devotees to the goddess that day. At Guwahati's Ugra Tara temple, fish curry over steamed rice is regularly served as praxad since devotees offer fish to the deity.

That night at the Kali Puja in the Nabagraha Temple in Guwahati, a sizeable group of goats, ducks, and pigeons were sacrificed to the goddess in quick succession to the deafening sounds of bell metal chimes and uruli, the ululating sound made by women in eastern India in commemoration of the deity worshipped or to usher in good fortune. I had joined the congregation on the condition that my extended family would neither force me to watch the horrific sight nor to eat the khisiri prepared with the meat of the sacrificed animals. As a child, I had once locked eyes with the head of a freshly beheaded goat placed before the goddess at a Kali temple. The picture of brutality committed on that hapless animal by my kind left an indelible stamp on my nascent self and I began avoiding the meat of ritually sacrificed goats since.

In my family temple though, a long da, a machete, wrapped in a piece of old yellowed cloth, had been a perennial presence. People would regularly come home to borrow it for use in temples nearby. My father had once told me that there would regularly be animal sacrifices at our Shiva temple in praise of his consort Durga till his mother intervened. 'Since then we have followed the ritual symbolically by sacrificing a kumura (ash gourd) to the goddess but the da has remained in the temple.'

Even as I was re-circulating those thoughts in my head, a woman sitting next to me at the dining hall of the Nabagraha temple whispered into my ears, 'Are you a vegetarian?'

No, just avoid mutton.

She seemed relieved at my answer, and repeated that an Assamese can never be a complete vegetarian. 'Unless one is a Bamun widow or a Keoliya Bhokot (celibate Assamese Vaishnava monks too avoid tamasik food).' Pointing at a piece of meat on the leaf in front of her, she added, 'Eating this is our culture, age-old practice.'

That woman proffering me a quick primer on non-vegetarian fare as the core of Assamese food habits was not far from the truth though. Leave aside temple food, no special Assamese lunch or dinner can be imagined without throwing in at least one non-vegetarian dish into the menu.

The significance of eating non-vegetarian food for the Assamese can perhaps also be gauged from the list of animals endorsed for sacrifice in Shakta Hinduism practised in Pragjyotishpur/Kamrup. The list mentioned in the revered texts written in Pragjyotishpur/Kamrup—Kalika Purana (eleventh–twelfth centuries) and *Yogini Tantra* (sixteenth–seventeenth centuries)—is exhaustive. Not far from the Nabagraha temple in Guwahati, at the Kamakhya temple atop the Nilachal hills, a major Shakta Hindu peeth, buffaloes are a common sacrificial offering to the goddess even today. In *Axomiya Manuhor Itihaax*, a treatise of sort on the community, noted writer Nagen Saikia had pointed out that the list of animals certified for sacrifice in Kalika Purana and *Yogini Tantra* were noticeably different from that of the rest of Hindu India.[2] These old texts are often referred to in order to better comprehend the food habits of the early inhabitants of Kamrup. Saikia had noted that the sacrificial meat is consumed by Brahmins too in Assam as praxad.

Yogini Tantra not only mentions that shunning of non-vegetarian food was not a requirement but also that celibacy (brahmacharya) was not a requisite in Kamrup, thus emphasizing the presence of an altogether different socio-religious cultural order in that swathe of land. The existing food habits of people since the ancient times is the reason why even Assamese Brahmins consume not just sacrificial meat but other non-vegetarian food too, just as those in North and South India do not because they had not been meat eaters since the Vedic era. Sarbeswar Rajguru, in *Medieval Assamese Society (1228–1826)* had underlined the point on the intersectional and overlying tribal influences on the non-tribal Assamese food habit, 'The predominance of the non-Aryan inhabitants and their inclusion in the Hindu fold may rightly be inferred as one of the strongest factors for which not only caste system but also the dietary system had to be made more liberal.'[3]

Assamese food cultures, therefore, were woven around multiple bouts of migration of people and their assimilation into each other's cultures over the centuries. This makes Assamese cuisine somewhat exclusive. Just like Assamese cuisine has several dissimilarities with Bengali and North and South Indian fare, it is not akin to other South Asian food either. 'It means that when the Satvik food from Mithila blended with the Tamasik food of the Kiratas of Assam, the process led to the crafting of a unique food culture of assimilation.'[4] The Assamese traditional spread, like other aspects of the community's material culture, is, therefore, a testimony to its mixed ancestry located in the South Asian migratory route through which there was a continuous ebb and flow of people to the land for long stretches of time. Naturally then, Assamese food is also the story of the community's collective memory, way of being, and its response to the natural and cultural landscape it has inherited.

Inspite of Hinduism, Vaishnavism, and Christianity sweeping through the hills and dales of Assam in varying degrees, certain things remain constant. For instance, though Brahmins in Odisha, Bihar, and West Bengal are meat-eaters too, they are not quite known to put duck, deer, or pigeon meat on their plate, like the Brahmins of Assam do. *Yogini Tantra* had recommended duck, pigeons, tortoises, and wild boars for consumption besides the flesh of goats, deer, antelope, rhinoceroses, and iguanas.[5] Today, if I have to name two Assamese meat delicacies across the tribal and non-tribal social groups that make up the larger community, they have to be pigeon meat cooked with banana flower or raw papaya; and duck meat cooked with gourd or khorisa (bamboo shoots). In my childhood, I had seen several Brahmin families in Upper Assam keeping out deer meat in the open overnight on a khorahi (a bamboo woven basket, a ubiquity in Assamese kitchen) for it to become a tad tart before it was prepared for lunch the next day. Sour deer meat is a delicacy. Here, it needs a mention that the Dubi copper inscription of a grant issued by the Assamese king Bhaskarvarman (600–50 CE) had spoken of snaring a deer.[6] Now though, with stricter animal conservation rules in place in Assam, deer meat is no more sold in its bazaars. The prevalence of consuming tortoise meat has also dwindled over time for similar reasons.

Another common meat Assamese caste Hindu families relish in the Brahmaputra Valley is the flesh of a range of birds, say, dauk (white breasted waterhen), xarali (lesser whistling duck), dorik (a type of waterhen), haitha (green pigeon), porghuma (imperial pigeon), raaj hah (swan), and bota (quail). Among Assamese Muslims though, pigeon meat is less popular than that of the duck prepared with an ample dose of wild pepper.

Highlighting the practice of sacrificing animals to gods and goddesses in olden Assam, Saikia had also stated, 'Sacrificing animals to commemorate the gods and goddesses is traced to pre-history when people gathered food as hunters. In order to satisfy nature's forces that they thought had enabled them to hunt better, people offered animals to their deities before partaking them as meat.'[7] Some day-to-day customs across Assam are reminiscent of this. To cite an example from my home itself, if a sizeable fish is caught from the pukhuri (pond) attached to the house, it is first offered at the family temple before it is cooked; almost in the fashion of a praxad.

The ritual at a non-tribal household in Upper Assam seems not too disparate from that of a tribal household in my neighbouring district. Moushumi Bordoloi Hazarika in her book on the Tiwa people that reside in the Karbi Anglong district mentions that the hill tribe is particularly fond of meat and rears domestic animals for a continuous supply, but the animals have to be raised only as a utsorga (offering) to the debota (deity).[8] Hazarika states that there are still several hill Tiwas who refrain from consuming the meat of an animal not raised as an offering to the deity. Folk singer Tarun Chandra Rabha, taking part in a discussion on tribal influence in Assamese food habits organized by Guwahati-based web magazine *Nezine* on 9 January 2021, had also highlighted a similar practice within his ethnic community that comes under the wider Assamese umbrella.[9] To my mind, such social practices in a society that has traditionally lived in close proximity to the forests, not only points towards showing gratitude to nature for providing a sumptuous meal and accepting it as blessed food, but perhaps helps curb unbridled hunting.

INFLUENCE OF HINDUISM AND VAISHNAVISM IN ASSAMESE MEAT-EATING HABIT

A vital fragment of Assamese food story will go missing though if it is mentioneed that there also existed, till recently, a rather rigid practice of engaging a randhoni, a cook, by a household strictly from one's ethnic group within the community. This was particularly applicable at a caste Hindu household where no tribal would be hired to work in the kitchen. There was also a common practice once of employing only deuri bilonia within some sections of Assamese society. Deuri bilonia, or the priestly class of the Assamese Deuri ethnic tribe, was specially assigned the task of distributing food at a public gathering.[10] Often a bilonia (server) would wrap the traditional kerchief, the gamusa, around his face so that nothing falls from his mouth into the banana leaf laid on the ground on which food would be traditionally served to guests. Such a practice exists among the Brahmins of Manipur too.

Such segregated practices of cooking and serving food traditionally within the Assamese community only confirm that certain groups had once closely guarded their exclusive food habits.. It then underlines the fact that when a person from a certain Assamese social group speaks of the community's cuisine, there is every likelihood of a certain dish being cooked in a certain way by one or the other, and therefore, they may not be not representative of the entire community. Additionally, some Assamese may avoid eating a certain variety of fish or meat too even while it is enjoyed by the wider community. The story will be half-told if it is not also located within the proliferation of Hinduism in Pragjyotishpur/Kamrup, and thereafter in the propagation of Neo-Vaishnavism in the fifteenth–sixteenth centuries which considerably influenced the food habits of the people of Assam. Those who underwent formal initiation into Sankardev's Ek Sarana Nama Dharma had to shun pork. The embracing of the new religion largely changed the meat-eating habits of a section of tribal communities too including those identified as Xarania (Sarania, or those who take formal initiation).

Here, it needs a mention that there is a reference of devotees eating deer and tortoise meat in some Vaishnava texts. The *Kumar Haran Kavya* of poet Ananta Kandali (1540–80), a contemporary of Sankardev, also gives a peek into Assamese food habits of the times. In this work, he described the elaborate meal that Chitralekha prepared for Aniruddha, Krishna's grandson whom she lured from Dwarka to marry her friend Usha, the daughter of Kirata king Banasura (explained earlier in the book). Kandali cited seasoning deer meat with asafoetida for a dish, preparing a curry named tala with pigeon meat, yet another curry of tortoise meat with a pulse called barkal, also a dish of boar meat with plantain besides whipping up a ghonto with fish head, and roasting illish and kandhuli fish on a spit.[11]

The fact that Assamese Neo-Vaishnavite monks are supposed to stay away from meat may be linked to Sankardev's open rebellion against the rigid Brahmanical rituals too, particularly of animal sacrifice, that had been practised since the time the Ahom king Suhungmung converted to Hinduism (in 1497). Most Vaishnava monks eat fish though. As indicated earlier in the chapter, Keoliya Bhokot are, however, strict vegetarians and consider even tamasik food like onions, garlic, and masoor (red split lentil) as non-vegetarian fare. Assamese Vaishnavite believers are meat eaters too, though they avoid pork and beef, just like Assamese Brahmins who are part of the Shaiva and Sakta cults.

Sankardev and his principal disciple Madhabdev were non-vegetarians. 'It is narrated in the medieval biographies that Sankardev used to select sites of his residence keeping in mind the availability of fish, fire-woods and foodstuff. Even the celibates living a cloistered life did not deprive themselves from non-vegetarian diets.'[12] I have come across some monks in the monasteries of Majuli who are regular fish eaters and don't deny it to the child monks either. It was, therefore, rather odd to spot a board in 2020 at the revered Batodroba monastery in Sankardev's birthplace Borduwa, where he had preached the religion initially, advising devotees to reject non-vegetarian food.

Shunning pork by some social groups initiated into Hinduism and Vaishnavism in Assam at various points in history is primarily to do with notions of 'impurity'. Such a rule had to be strictly adhered to. It is worth a mention here that when Hinduism began to blow into the Mlechha (non-Aryan) and Kirata (asura) kingdom of Pragjyotishpur, two food habits of those who embraced the Hindu fold—eating pork and drinking alcohol—became an 'impure' practice and, therefore, was forbidden. Narakasur, the first Aryan king of Pragjyotishpur who was of Kirata origin, was not only dethroned but was believed to have been beheaded by Lord Krishna for returning to the Kirata behaviour which included drinking and merry-making too.[13] To proffer an extant example of such notions of 'impurity' in Assamese mainstream social milieu, the Biswanath unit of the Srimanta Sankardev Sangha, the state's largest religious organization with over 30 lakh members, had made national news in 2019 for throwing out a member because his son had started a commercial piggery unit. The member, Balendra Nath, told a national newspaper then that he feared that the ban could possibly lead to a social boycott of his family.[14]

Interestingly though, even after the later Ahom kings had adopted Hinduism, it is not easy to come across any indication of the royals abstaining from pork for religious reasons. Till date, the Ahoms, one of the largest Assamese subgroups, have remained a consumer of pork. It is also the primary meat of those from the Bodo–Kachari stock. Still, for reasons of 'impurity', not just the Kalitas and Kayasthas, the Assamese Brahmins too have traditionally stayed away from consuming pork. They also abstain from eating crab meat, though it is commonly eaten among several tribal ethnic groups in Assam.

Another meat that, till recently, was a taboo in an Assamese non-tribal household for its 'unclean' nature was the chicken. In several households, if chicken had to be consumed, it needed a separate kitchen. In the 1970s–80s, some Assamese caste Hindus in Upper Assam would take the liberty of consuming it by calling it Ram sorai.[15] The bird had been somewhat legitimized by affixing the term 'Ram', and therefore, acceptable as food! Adopting chicken among Assamese caste Hindus happened also because of the broiler farms that mushroomed across small towns from the early 1990s onwards. Those units were run by Assamese caste Hindus too. The notion that the birds were raised under 'cleaner' conditions in those farms perhaps diminished the existing taboo against 'impurity' among several such groups. The spike in the number of roadside dhabas run by Hindi-speaking settlers which had begun rustling up delicious chicken curries and tandoori chicken to primarily cater to truckers from North India, also contributed to its local popularity to an extent.

The country chicken variety has, however, been a common meat among most tribal groups, the Adivasis (Tea Tribes), and also Muslims, both of Assamese fold and of East Bengal origin. Shabnam Bora, granddaughter of Moidul Islam Bora, former Asam Sahitya Sabha president and the state's first doctorate degree holder, recalled for me learning from her grandmother how to prepare a country chicken dish with jati lau, a local gourd variety.[16]

These days, chicken korma and pulao is a common combination during the annual Eid feasting at an Assamese Muslim household, including Shabnam's. She, however, added, 'My grandmother used to prepare pulao but also say that the practice of making it was adopted from people who came to Upper Assam to work in the tea gardens. My family never cooked biryani though; they didn't know how to. These days, many Assamese Muslim families make chicken rezala during Eid but that is also a later addition.'

The Rai and Limbu groups among the Nepalis/Gorkhas of Assam have a rather interesting country chicken dish called Wachipa, particularly cooked during a puja to remember their ancestors.[17]

The general ground rule about consuming different kinds of meat in Assamese society is also hinged on reasons of health. The religious rigidity against consuming a certain variety of fish or meat can be relinquished easily for medicinal purpose. For instance, fish from the dark-skinned variety—magur, kawoi, kusia, xol—are ushered in to a Brahmin, Kalita, or a Kayastha kitchen if required to tame anaemia in a family member or to help a woman regain strength after childbirth. Yet another instance of this is a rare practice of consuming the flesh of the one-horned rhino, or of eating gharial.[18]

However, beef continues to be strictly avoided by Assamese Brahmins, Kalitas, and Kayasthas for religious reasons, though certain other communities in the state consume beef without restriction. Shabnam particularly referred to a beef dish cooked with bamboo shoots in Assamese Muslim households in Upper Assam. Writer Sanjay Kumar Tanti who belongs to the Tea Tribe/ Adivasi, recollected a childhood memory of some sections of his community in greater Darrang district consuming beef. 'I saw this among some groups between late 1960s and the 1970s, though beef is a no-no among some other sects of my community due to the influence of Vaishnavism.'[19] P. C. Choudhury had pointedly mentioned that it is not unlikely that the practice of beef eating even among Aryans in ancient India was probably common, adding, 'But the absence of any definite reference in Assam does not help us to come to a definite conclusion about the prevalence of the practice among the Assamese Hindus as well.'[20]

Some ethnic groups in Assam have also traditionally consumed buffalo meat. A copper plate of King Vallabhadeva's era refers to buffalo hunting.[21] Non-Brahmin Nepali residents of Assam, of Newari stock, also consume buffalo meat.[22]

DRINKING

The introduction of the concepts of 'purity' and 'impurity' by Hinduism and Vaishnavism to larger Assamese society substantially influenced not just people's extant food habits but also the consumption of alcohol. This, even while we find in written annals Bhaskarvarman's court poet Bana mention that the king had dispatched to Magadha king Harshavardhan 'cups of ullaka, diffusing a fragrance of sweet wine.'[23] Choudhury too points out, 'The *Kalika Purana* refers to modaka, pistaka, and payasa along with madhu. The "mahdumada" of the Bargaon grant (the second plate) was perhaps a kind of preparation of honey. *Yogini Tantra* mentions wine in connection with the worship of (goddess) Kameswari.'[24]

Still, Assamese caste Hindus, in general, stay away from local brews. Saikia had underlined that several ethnic communities in Assam who have their own rice-based alcoholic brews, had also taken a rather meticulous approach towards the habit after adopting Hinduism.[25] For instance, the Ahom rice brew xaajpani has been made respectable by making it mandatory in some rituals and thereby restricting its use only for special occasions. Some others, to add even more decorum to it, began calling it karon (a good reason). 'Xaajpani began to be prepared after a bath, wearing a pair of clean clothes and thereafter was placed at the prayer room. It also began to be used in the indigenous customs that crept into the Hindu dharma.'[26] A section of such Hindus also pour xaajpani into a bowl and share a sip each from it to enhance its stature as a praxad, according to it the status of being 'pure'.

Though the question of 'impurity' bridled this practice to a large extent, a dispassionate look at the procedure adopted to distil the wide range of brews by the tribes should make one appreciate not just the technique applied but also the ingredients meticulously gathered from amidst nature to prepare the concoctions. For instance, in the book *Mising Sanskriti*, Jawahar Jyoti Kuli gives a detailed account of how the tribe's brew, pong aapong, is prepared in about ten to twelve days.[27] Same is true of other brews: jou (Bodo), ju (Tiwa), judima (Dimasa), laupani (Rabha), halong (Karbi), suje (Deuri), and xaajpani (Ahoms and Sutiyas), etc. There is also a potent variety called photika, and I dare say it is a clear distilled drink akin to the Russian vodka in taste and refinement. The Tea Tribe enjoys ruhi, though there exists a greater affinity within the community, so also among people of Nepali origin, to have sulai mod, a rice and jaggery based drink. Tanti points out that during the colonial period, distilleries to produce the alcoholic beverage were set up (in Numaligarh, Tezpur, etc.) by the British close to the tea gardens. A supply of the drink was channelled to the labourers as a means of weekend entertainment and thereby an avenue to earn revenue.

The Gorkhas of Assam have two rice-based brews: ningaar, a rather potent concoction with a smoky flavour, and jaar, a lighter version. Though the Muslims of East Bengal origin don't have a particular brew to call their own, they have the practice of consuming a fermented rice preparation, pasoi, which if eaten in large quantities can be intoxicating.

Even though drinking is a taboo among the Assamese caste Hindus, a special drink, ghuta, is prepared during the annual Shiva puja in several Assamese households and temples by mixing into milk powdered hemp, sugar, powdered cloves, cinnamon, cardamom, and seeds of the dhatura plant; it is drunk in small quantities as praxad. These practices may well be non-Aryan imports to the Hindu fold since in Vaishnavism drinking is a complete no-no.

TEA

Drinking ronga saah (red tea), prepared without the addition of milk, is a common practice across Assam, a British colonial gift to the community. Tea trees had grown wild in Assam's jungles, particularly in the upcountry, prior to the British experimenting with tea cultivation in an organized fashion in the state. The local variety of the plant was used to develop the industry in the colonial era. Prior to it though, there was a practice of tea leaves brewed as a hot beverage among some ethnic groups. The Singhphos, till date, drink such a tea called falap. Drinking tea with milk is a fairly new phenomenon in Assamese society. One unique style of drinking milk tea in Assam is by adding bay leaves to the boiling water.

FOOD HEGEMONY

Drawing a parallel between the food habits of the people of Assam and Southeast Asians with whom several ethnic communities of the state have common cultures and ancestries, Saikia had reiterated, 'The entire South East Asia is non-vegetarian. If you glance at the tribes that reside on the hills and dales on all four corners of Assam, it is not too difficult to note that there has never been strict rules about what flesh can be or can't be eaten. There has been no cultural or social taboo to eating any flesh that the body can digest, or can be prepared as palatable. In some communities, it is noted that no flesh, apart from that of human being, have been considered unworthy of consumption. It is worth noting that the list of food in China includes almost everything and sets aside only human flesh.'[28]

Saikia's comparison of the food habits of the people of olden Assam with China which we should better understand as the rice-based civilization of the Yangste Valley—one of the oldest in the world—is striking, particularly when juxtaposed with a common perception of northeastern food choices in mainland India as being uncivilized. This dominant tendency at times pushes a section of caste Hindu Assamese also to proffer the habit of consuming certain kinds of meat in the state as only a 'tribal' practice. It needs noting that this undercurrent in mainstream India's thought process against northeastern food habits reared its head during the Covid-19 pandemic. North-easterners were discriminated against in several states because they were suspected to be 'Chinese' due to facial similarities but particularly because 'they eat everything'.[29] Such a notion was hinged on the theory circulating then across the country that the killer virus had sprung out of a Chinese wet market where the flesh of wild animals was sold.[30] The pandemic had only firmed up the existing notions in the mainland towards 'non-Indian' food habits.

A decade ago, as part of an Indian media entourage to Hong Kong for a promotional food tour, I had come face-to-face with ideas related to 'what we Indians don't eat' at every turn. One evening, when I told the Hong Kong Chinese official accompanying us to a dinner about food habits that some 'Indians' (from the Northeast) also have, like consuming duck and pigeon, dog and mongoose, tortoise and snail, deer and buffalo, rats, and ant eggs and silkworms, he was a bit surprised. Thankfully, it dawned on my fellow travellers from Delhi that Indian mainstream food hegemony has scant consciousness towards the micro food cultures that fall outside of the mainland.

Unfortunately, for too long, eastern food habits in India have been equated to only Bengali cuisine, leaving out a wide gamut of diverse cuisines that can only enrich the country's food experience and history. While there has been a modest amount of interest in Assamese and other Northeastern cuisines, India is yet to see a broad-based food atlas that celebrates its multiplicity by inducting not just certain non-vegetarian dishes as 'Indian' too but also methods of cooking and food preservation, including the widely eaten fermented foods in the Northeastern belt.

Quite often, while introducing Assamese food to the outside world, certain words are commonly employed, even by a section from within the Assamese community, say, 'less spicy', 'bland', 'plain', 'simple'. To my mind, that approach must also be viewed as a submissive response to the operative hegemony of taste and what is widely acceptable as Indian food. Discussing such manifestations of food hegemony, American food writer Phyche Williams-Forson had once said that talking about food 'lends credence to the notion that food is always about more than what it seems.'[31]

Indian food, worldwide, is portrayed through mass media as 'spicy'. To my mind, therefore, whenever there is minimum or no use of spice in a dish, the general tendency seems to be to dismiss such dishes as 'basic', essentially to indicate a dish deficient in something. Even the Assamese, particularly those on the higher side of the social hierarchy, usually the non-tribals, tend to stereotype the food of the state's ethnic communities also as 'plain' or 'bland'. The approach is the same and hinges on the denial of the cultural underpinnings that make up the complete story.

History has shown that such tendencies lead to corrupting the general attitude towards a particular community or social group's food culture and culinary memory. Food studies scholar Zilkia Janer in her 2012 paper on Assamese cuisine 'Assamese Food and Politics of Taste' has dealt with this flawed approach rather impressively. 'Food talk and judgement are part of the larger process, not only of identity construction but also of the creation of cultural hierarchies, which are used in the legitimisation of unequal power relationships.'[32] Just because techniques like smoking and fermenting have been practised by many in Assam for centuries doesn't make them simple. 'On the contrary, today, fewer and fewer people know how to control the processes of fermentation and smoking in a way that is safe and enhances flavour, and we depend instead on additives and preservatives (for instance, soda bicarbonate is used by several households in Assam instead of Kola Khaar, extracted from banana peels) that require no skill to use but do not deliver the same complexity of flavour.'[33]

Proffering a prescription to Indian food writers on how to approach Assamese cuisine, Janer had stated, 'Just like Japanese cuisine introduced the world to the taste they call "umami", food connoisseurs would be delighted to learn about the Khaar (alkaline) taste.'

Rightfully, the taste of khaar should be called one of the prime markers of Assamese cuisine. No discussion on the food of the wider Assamese community is comprehensive enough without a mention of khaar, an alkaline concoction made from the peel, burnt or sun-dried, of a ripe banana of a local variety called bhim kol. The blackened peel is soaked in water to draw out a limpid brown liquid. This extract is used to prepare a wide selection of dishes. Since a preparation made of khaar is consumed at the start of a meal, it highlights the role that such a dish plays in lining the stomach with alkali, considered beneficial for digestion.

The story of khaar in Assamese cuisine is also linked to paucity of salt in the past, signified by a popular Assamese saying, 'Lunn daan xunn daan-or xomaan' (Donating salt is akin to donating gold to someone). French traveller J. B. Tavernier who passed through the Brahmaputra Valley in the seventeenth century had written in his book *Travels in India* of the extraction of salt from plantain leaves to also prepare a bleach-like mixture of ashes in which silk was boiled to make it as white as snow.[34] Muslim invaders of Assam, in their annals, also mentioned khaar.[35]

These days though, with easy access to kitchen salt, Assamese cooks use the condiment even in khaar-based dishes. The traditional use of khaar among the caste Hindus and Assamese Muslims of Upper Assam only in vegetarian dishes continues while Assamese in Lower Assam use it in their fish dishes too. Vegetarian khaar is generally prepared with banana stem, cucumber, raw papaya, pumpkin, or long gourd. The one made from the leftover maah praxad (black chickpeas and green grams), a typical offering at Vaishnava naamghars and in many temples, is the most common though. Since the use of khaar is absent in Bengal, this arguably makes khaar an Assamese food speciality. Not for nothing then is a true-blue Assamese often denoted as a khaar-khowa axomiya (alkaline-eating Assamese).

All ethnic groups in Assam use khaar. A signature dish of the Rabha tribe is a snail curry made with black gram and pitha guri (rice powder) in which khaar is a key ingredient. Writer Upen Rabha Hakasam had once described to me how he would go about preparing the snail curry at home. 'Unlike me, my wife is a Paati Rabha (Rabhas who speak Assamese language as their mother tongue instead of the Rabha dialect) but loves the snail curry the community traditionally eat. I am the designated cook at home for this curry as I have grown up eating it. In some Rabha families, particularly those from the hills, there has been a practice of taking out the hard casing of the snail after the curry is made, to wash and save them for one more use as they don't commonly find snails in the hills.' Snails are abundantly found on the grasslands of Assam. Bodos, too, have a scrumptious snail curry.

Another prevalent Rabha dish made with sidol (dry fish) needs a sprinkling of khaar too. While Rabhas call khaar kharsi, for the Bodos, it is kharwi. The Karbi ethnic tribe, considered one of the first sets of people to have arrived in the Brahmaputra Valley, also use khaar as an essential ingredient in both vegetarian and non-vegetarian preparations; they call it kangmoi. Aside from vegetarian preparations with khaar, Karbis make kangmoi with dry fish, dried venison, and pork too.[36] The Misings and Tiwas, the two major plains tribes in the Brahmaputra Valley, also use khaar in their vegetarian and non-vegetarian preparations. The Dimasa tribe are khaar eaters too. The widespread dominance of khaar in tribal food is a strong indication that it must be their contribution to mainstream Assamese cuisine.

Assamese Muslims too relish khaar. However, the Muslims of East Bengal origin and the Adivasi/Tea Tribe, the two communities that had settled in Assam during the British colonial period, traditionally don't use khaar in their cooking.

While the peel of the podgy bhim banana variety is used to extract khaar, the fruit itself, filled with seeds, is an ideal accompaniment to the traditional snack jolpan, which typically also comprises of curd, jaggery, and beaten/puffed rice. Mashed bhim kol is a traditional baby food in Assam too.

In Assamese cultural and food history, the role of not just bhim but other kinds of banana is substantial, so also of kol gos (banana plant) and kol paat (banana leaves). The banana plant is considered a propitious presence—in wedding songs and ceremonies, various pujas, Dewali (Deepawali) decorations, and Bihu compositions—and is the reason why almost every traditional Assamese household has bananas growing in the backyard. Never have I come across such an assortment of bananas (both in size and taste) at a fruit seller's other than in Assam. Though the widely available jahaji variety is a relatively newer entry into people's food habits and is also found across the country, some of the bananas endemic to the state are the senisompa, malbhog, athiya, monuhor, bogi monuhor, tulasi monuhor, ramkol, and keteki malbhog. In *Dakor Boson*, the oft-cited book of instructive verses on life, there is a detailed explanation on how to judiciously grow 360 banana plants in one's yard, hinting at the important role plantain plays in daily Assamese life.[37] The ubiquity of this fruit in Assamese society has also led to its large-scale farming, leading Assam to have the largest market for bananas in Asia today, found at Darrangiri in Goalpara district.

Most parts of the plantain tree are consumed in Assam. The kaas/pura kol (raw banana) is either fried as an accompaniment to the main meal, or boiled and mashed to make cutlets to snack on as part of the abelir sah (evening tea). The banana flower (kol dil), and posola, the tender part of the banana stem, are a favourite across communities in Assam. Pigeon meat cooked with banana flower is an Assamese delicacy. The Tai Phake community prepares a delicious banana flower soup. Some plains tribes make a delectable pitika from smoked or boiled banana flower. Assamese mostly eat posola either lightly fried in mustard oil (at times with red chickpeas) or by adding khaar into it. A dessert, ghul, prepared from mashed monuhor/malbhug varieties with a generous dash of camphor—served as praxad during the Satyanarayan Puja—is a one-of-a-kind dish.

TENGA AND TITA: TART AND BITTER

If khaar or alkaline food is a speciality of Assamese cuisine, so is tenga or acidic food and tita, the bitters.

If khaar is eaten first while consuming a traditional meal, a tenga curry is eaten at the end, purportedly to avoid acidity affecting digestion. The easily available wide assortment of lemons is a prime souring agent in Assamese cuisine. Nowhere else will you spot such diversity in lemons in India except in the Northeast. While kaji lemon is available throughout the year, the winter variety, guul nemu, bursting with a unique aroma, is the most prized one. There is also the elasi nemu (smells like cardamom) and jora nemu (also has a distinctive flavour). It goes without saying that a dash of any of these lemons at once enhances the flavour of a plain dal or a curry besides adding acidity to the meal.

The Assamese signature dish masor tenga is an acidic preparation—cooked either with lemon or other commonly used souring agents, say, ou-tenga (elephant apple), three varieties of thekera (similar to kokum), omora (a sour fruit), tengamora (rosella), or jolphai (Indian olive). The vegetarian version of this signature tenga dish substitutes the fish with fried lentil dumplings. A common lentil preparation also uses the sour rosella leaves; each leaf meticulously tied into a knot and plonked into a bubbling bowl of masoor dal. While having the dal mixed with rice, the knotted leaves are typically sucked to extract the remaining sourness from them, like the pieces of elephant apple put in a curry/dal are chewed for the same effect. Tengamora, a fruit, is also a common source of acidity in Assamese cuisine.

Various historical texts and accounts have underlined the particular penchant in the Assamese for sour food. Some of the tenga recipes mentioned in *Katha Gurucharit* are small whole fish cooked with suka (sorrel leaves), and fish with elephant apple. Padma Purana by the seventeenth-century poet Narayandeva, spoke of xol, a local fish variety, cooked with tangy jujubes (bogori). *Dakor Boson* mentions a recipe for cooking slightly aged borali fish with tamarind; also a curry made of fish like kos, bos, and sitol with lemon.

Assamese cuisine includes a selection of tita or bitter preparations too. Several households have the practice of biting into steamed rice roundels mashed with deep-fried sweet neem leaves to prevent chickenpox and to build up immunity against other illnesses. A popular winter herb is Babori, essentially a bitter. *Katha Gurucharit* mentions a Babori recipe made with the small fish variety, moa maas.[38] The Tea Tribe prepare a tasty fried dish with the bitter sojina flowers which have been adopted by other social groups too.[39]

Black sesame (til), used widely in tribal and non-tribal kitchens, is also bitter. Besides using a roasted paste to prepare a delicious meat curry, ground black sesame seeds are also mixed with jaggery to prepare the rice-based Assamese signature sweet, til pitha; also tilor laru (laru is a popular form of the laddu, also made with grated coconut). Chinese traveller Hiuen Tsang had noted the abundance of jackfruits and coconuts in Kamrup in the seventh century.[40]

Quite commonly, Assamese also bite into the bitter xilikha (terminalia chebula). Also, on the morning of Mahalaya that ushers in the annual Durga Puja, Assamese Brahmins eat some bitter flowers of the Arjun tree for good health.

There are also bitter curries made with dried xewali (Jasmine) flowers; some sprinkle khaar on this before tucking in. Some others drink a bitter tea made of xewali flowers to enhance immunity. Yet another flower that the Assamese savour is that of pumpkin which is generally eaten as a fritter with a coating of moong dal paste, and the taste is nowhere near tita.

The narzi oma curry of the Bodo community is also a bitter cooked with dried jute leaves.

XAAK AND JOLOKIA: GREENS AND CHILLIES

The presence of a wide assortment of herbs and greens in Assamese cuisine is noteworthy. The most common herb across the communities is the fiddle-headed fern, dhekia, a popular choice to prepare masor tenga. A fried version of the fern with mua aloo, a local variety of baby potatoes, is a must-try.

In *Dakor Boson*, there is an instruction to cook fish with another common green, purulia or puroi xaak (spinach).[41] A spinach-based peppery curry made with rou fish is common across Assamese households. *Katha Gurucharit* mentions a similar recipe made with the local kawoi fish.[42]

Several tribal communities also have their own selection of herbs and greens that grow in the wild. While the hill Tiwas would commonly have herbs like samsuri, jogali, lai milur, lai sadap, murjing, the Misings, like other tribes of Tibeto-Burman origin, are particularly fond of the nephafu (*Clerodendrum colebrookianum*) and mejenga (*Zanthxylum oxphyllum*) leaves. Every October–November, brahmi xaak is cooked in several Assamese households. A popular herb among the Adivasis is the spiny dhaan xaak, named so as they are typically found amidst the rice stalks (dhaan) on the fields every June–July.[43]

Some other common greens found in the bazaars of Assam are matikaturi, kosu (taro leaves), bhedailota, manimuni, matikaturi, and mosundari. There is a practice of making a dish, xan miholi, with 101 varieties of greens every Magh Bihu. Traditionally, these herbs were collected through foraging which also helped pass the knowledge about identifying edible herbs to the next generation. The practice, though, is fast dying in Assamese society as a wide assortment of greens is easily available in the umpteen daily and weekly bazaars across Assam. Often, these bazaars are also where people from the surrounding hills, even from neighbouring states like Nagaland, Meghalaya, or Arunachal Pradesh, come trickling down with their fresh farm produce. In earlier times, the common mode of exchange in these bazaars was the barter system. Junbil Mela, the annual bazaar of the Tiwas held not far from Guwahati every winter, is a reminder of the tribe's cultural memory of exchanging produce with other social groups.

Three of the commonly consumed winter greens in Assamese households are lai (rai), lofa (Chinese mellow), and suka. Lai cooked with pork and lofa with fish are popular combinations. A common leaf on the Assamese plate is also sojina (moringa); its tender stems are fried too. According to noted botanist and Assamese folk tradition researcher Padmeswar Gogoi, the Assamese learnt to eat sojina from the tea garden community. 'The practice, to my mind, is not older than eighty-ninety years. Sojina trees were grown inside the tea gardens from where the leaves and the tender stems began to gradually come to the nearby bazaars.'[44]

The Assamese also have a penchant for eating seeds (guti) of the bitter gourd, pumpkin, and jackfruit, either deep-fried or boiled and mashed as a pitika. In Lower Assam, there is a delightful curry prepared with ground pumpkin seeds.

The particular use of a wide variety of fresh chillies, available throughout the year, is also a part of the Assamese food story. Freshly plucked green chillies split into two are habitually dropped into a bubbling hot curry. In neighbouring Bhutan, because of the harsh winter, chillies are often sun-dried during summer for winter, a practice not followed in Assam as there is sufficient supply of jolokia (chillies) round the year. Still, certain tribes dry chillies on the dhua saang, the ubiquitous bamboo rack erected over a traditional kitchen furnace, for later use.

A common practice of preserving chillies of all varieties in Assam is in pickled form or as a chilli oil as a taste enhancer. Few drops of mustard oil infused with the searing sharpness of the bhot jolokia, the world's hottest chilli that grow abundantly in Assam; or that of the tiny hot varieties kon and mem jolokia will be enough to lift the taste of the common gruel poita bhaat.

PITIKA

Assamese cuisine also has an extensive range of pitika, essentially a mash, both vegetarian and non-vegetarian, served as a side dish. Common vegetarian mashes are made of roasted potatoes (also squashed with boiled eggs), and local vegetables like kon bilahi (baby tomatoes), jolphai (olives), bhaat kerela (a gourd variety), etc. The Dimasas prepare a delicious pitika with the roots of the chameleon plant and fermented small fish. Steamed small fish pitika is rather popular. A pitika of roasted black sesame mixed with smoked brinjal and garlic is to die for. The Tai Phake community which had migrated to Assam from the Hukong Valley of Myanmar in the eighteenth century, also prepare a delicious peanut pitika, a reminder of its roots in China's Yunnan province.

FISH

Like in other parts of the world, food habits of the Assamese have also been shaped by what has been commonly available in their skies, water bodies, and forests. Naturally then, a wide selection of maas (fish), misa maas (shrimp), and kekura–kusia (crabs and eels) found in the umpteen brooks and streams of the state is also a staple non-vegetarian food across the region. In no other state except in neighbouring Bengal does one notice such a strong influence of fish in not one's food habits alone but in the cultural life too. Fish is mentioned in Vaishnava sayings, Assamese wedding songs, Bihu and other folk songs, in idioms and phrases, in place names, as an antidote to seasonal and other ailments. If a child suffers from worms, feeding a fistful of rice soaked in the pith of a carp is often prescribed in rural areas.[45] A certain fish is fed to children to stop bedwetting.

No Magh Bihu feast is complete without a fish curry and the throng of customers at Guwahati's Ujaan Bazaar fish market by the Brahmaputra every Magh Bihu morning is a testimony to that thriving culture. In a wedding, the groom's family carries a sizeable fish to the bride's house. Half a century ago, the bride was to clean and cut the fish in front of the guests to exhibit her kitchen skills.

Assamese also have a ritual to distribute fish among relatives and friends if a baby boy is born; sweets for a baby girl. That a fish is distributed on the birth of a son may be read as a reflection of the patriarchy in Assamese society. Surja Das, in his informative book on Assam's fishing culture, while referring to the custom had also highlighted that distribution of fish is done particularly on the day the horoscope of the newborn is written.[46] Das noted fifteen traditional ways of catching fish practised by the community.

To ensure continuous supply of fish, certain ground rules have been followed traditionally. The eggs of the puthi, a preferred variety among small fish, must not be consumed during March as that would affect its spawning cycle. So also the borali fish during July. To ensure that no one breaks the rules, certain social taboos have also been tied to them—there is a common saying in villages that those who eat egg-laden puthi in March will be hit by lightning and die.[47]

Although an entire community (Koibarta) has traditionally been associated with fishing as a profession in Assam, it is not uncommon for other Assamese subgroups including Brahmins to venture into water bodies with fishing nets. For a special feast on Magh Bihu every January, village youth enter nearby rivers to practise community fishing. Author-academic Nahendra Padun in *Axomiya Xonoskritiloi Jonojatio Borongoni* (Tribal Contribution to Assamese Culture) mentions the age-old ritual as a tribal influence in mainstream Assamese society.[48]

BAMBOO AS FOOD

Baah (bamboo) is yet another speciality, not just in Assamese cuisine alone but in cuisines across the Northeast. Bamboo shoot is a popular ingredient across Asian cuisines. That bamboo shoot (khorisa) is not quite the part of cuisines from West Bengal onwards shows that this ingredient is a unique contribution to Indian food culture. Assamese communities residing in Lower Assam also use less of Khorisa in their daily food than that of Upper Assam underlining the fact that the prevalence of bamboo shoot in food habits has traditionally been more of an upcountry custom.

The strong influence of bamboo in Assamese cuisine is spotted mainly in the use of khorisa or gaaj tenga. Baah gaaj plucked from the foot of the bamboo bushes is spread across the knolls and vales of Assam, and is a common item in the state's bazaars. Bamboo shoot is used to prepare some utterly delicious fish, pork, duck, and country chicken dishes by both tribes and non-tribes. In many Assamese households, there will invariably be a row of glass bottles filled with grated bamboo shoots pickled with mustard oil and chillies put out to mature in the sun. A spoonful of pickled bamboo shoots from one such bottle is sufficient to spice up an otherwise plain steamed rice–dal combination.

Khorisa in Assam typically comes in two types: dry and wet. While the wet variety is used in pickles and in curries like poka khorisa, the dried version (xukan khorisa) is eaten either fried or sprinkled on vegetarian and non-vegetarian preparations to boost flavour.

RICE

A food that all Assamese can't do without is rice; served at lunch and dinner and eaten as breakfast in some form or the other, this is the reason why some Assamese are self-declared bhotua (ardent rice eaters). The community's rice-based food culture only highlights that since ancient times, rice farming—akin to several Asian groups—has been its mainstay. A proof of their protracted engagement with rice is in the long list of varieties that are endemic to Assam. In *Yogini Tantra*, as many as twenty rice varieties have been named for use at a funeral ritual. Nagen Saikia has named 215 rice varieties grown in the state in his book on the community to comment, 'This list only gives a hint of Assamese people's connection with rice not just as food but also of the mind and culture.'[49] The nature's blessed hand on Assam is palpable when you notice how the bau dhan (boro dhan) variety grows on its waters. This variety is particularly popular among the residents of Majuli, an island resplendent with water bodies and also swamped by the annual floods. Small balls of mud (batolu guti) are meticulously made, and into these the grains of bau dhan are inserted and put out in the sun for drying. They are then strategically thrown into waterlogged areas. In some time, they shoot out of the water and within months the tops are laden with grains. This variety is harvested in boats. The Mising community which predominately resides in Majuli are the primary cultivators of bau dhan. This variety is an ideal option for a set of people that has to face the brunt of the yearly floods.

Another unique variety of rice in Assam is kumol/buka saul. It is a boon to the flood-affected too as this variety doesn't require a pot on fire to prepare it; just some hours of soaking in water will do. Floods or not, kumol saul is a popular Assamese breakfast, combined with milk/curd and slivers of jaggery or in a savoury avatar with onions, ginger, chillies, and mustard oil.

In a year, the Assamese practice three kinds of rice farming: Aahu, Xali/Sali, and Bau. That the Assamese cultivate rice both in water (pani kheti) and in the shallows (baam kheti) is indicative of its topography. All the varieties that grow in summer and are ready for harvest from October onwards are called Sali Dhan Kheti. It is this harvest that is secured in the granary by early winter (from October onwards) that let's the community pick two occasions to feast on the fresh harvests: first as Na Khuwa (a feast prepared with the newly harvested rice) and then during the Magh or Bhogali Bihu (in January).

The one of a kind Assamese rice varieties like the aromatic joha and the sticky bora are Sali crops. Once the Sali crop is safe in the granary, farmers get busy with Bau Kheti, when the dry or semi wet field is ploughed before rice saplings are planted. The harvest is ready by June–July.

In *Dakor Boson*, there is an instruction on the right measurement of water to be used for cooking rice: 'Saul diba jotek-tekek, Pani diba tini tetek' (Whatever is the amount of rice, add three more ounces of water to it).[50] A few tribes in Assam also prepare rice by steaming it over a pot of hot water.

A common by-product of rice is pitha guri or rice powder, used not only to prepare a wide array of pitha or rice cakes/pancakes but also sprinkled into curries to make them thicker. Earlier, the rice powder was pounded at home on a traditional foot-held grinder, the dheki; now it is commonly available in the market.

The variety in pitha in Assamese cuisine is extensive. Aside from the ones specially made to celebrate Bihu, like the til pitha and ghila pitha, there are several other kinds, such as, tel pitha, meni pitha, xutuli pitha, sunga pitha, bhaat pitha, and tekeli pitha. Several of these varieties are also consumed as snacks and as part of breakfast. In Assamese Muslim households, the xutuli pitha, also called the saneki pitha, is eaten often as breakfast either with milk and jaggery/sugar, or as a savoury dish with a portion of seasonal greens or a scrambled egg on the side. 'While porotha is now a common breakfast in an Assamese Muslim household, it crept into our food habits much later as flour was not so easily available earlier in Assam. We also eat now an egg pulao made of the local aromatic rice variety Joha as a breaker. An egg is broken into the steamed rice when very hot, mixed well and put under the lid for some time to help the egg get scrambled. But during my grandmother's time, the standard breakfast was the jolpan eaten in any Assamese Hindu household,' related Shabnam Bora.

The popular Assamese snack, jolpan, is rice-based and served with milk/ curd and jaggery/sugar. It is typically a combination of any of the following: sira (flattened rice), muri (puffed rice), aakhoi (a puff rice variety), hurum (a thinner variety of puffed rice), pitha guri (rice powder), xandoh guri (a rice powder variety). Some tribes also have jolpan with black sticky rice or the sticky bora white rice variety with sugar sprinkled on top.

The Assamese Muslims with origins in East Bengal and the Tea Tribes too eat pitha. The Bengali-origin Muslims have a bhapa or bhaha pitha, which is steamed and eaten at breakfast mostly during winter. Goalpara-based Hussain Ahmad Madani, hailing from a Muslim family of East Bengal origin, added, 'We have the tradition of inviting the sons-in-law home during the mango and jackfruit seasons. Alongside serving chiti pitha to them, the fruits are mixed with milk and paired with rice.'[51] As a child, Madani remembers eating a rice powder halwa with jaggery at home.

Among the Tea Tribe, there is a tradition of frying tel-pitha on the morning of the community's Tushu Puja that coincides with Magh Bihu.

The Gorkhas of Assam prepare Kharu Pitha, which is but a local adaptation of the popular Nepali dish Sel Roti that resembles a bangle (kharu). While the sweet version is used for rituals, the savoury one is oft-eaten with a black sesame chutney.

As highlighted by Shabnam, the use of wheat flour and the making of rotis is a fairly new phenomenon in Assamese kitchens. Tanti had mentioned to me that Adivasis learnt to make use of aata only when it became a part of the monthly ration of the tea garden workers in the late 1960s. 'In my family, wheat flour began to come only around 1969 when there was a scarcity of rice in Assam, and its effect was felt in the Darrang area where we resided then. Because my mother didn't quite know how to make it edible, she created a batter with it like we do with rice powder to make pitha. We had a Bihari settlement nearby from whom she eventually learnt how to roll a roti from the wheat flour.' This food memory can be linked to the scarcity of rice felt across India prior to the Green Revolution. In Assam too, the rice, then typically dispersed through the public distribution system, failed to meet the monthly demand, thus allowing not only wheat flour but rice varieties grown elsewhere in the country to enter Assamese food habits. The Marwari traders in Assam, also predominantly flour consumers, became the prime suppliers of the new food item. These traders since the British era have also introduced to the Assamese community new vegetable varieties, like the large-sized tomatoes, onions, and potatoes.

Two types of rice powders are in common use: pitha guri and xandoh guri. While pitha guri is essentially a ground rice variety made from wet or semi-wet rice soaked in water for a few hours, xandoh guri is the ground dry rice, habitually eaten with curd and milk as a snack or breakfast. Assamese also make mithoi (sweets) from rice powder. While poka mithoi is made from the lahi (thin) variety of rice, and is used in Vaishnava rituals, kesa mithoi, prepared from the wet ground lahi rice, is used in ai xobah, a local ritual performed by women to bring good fortune to a family, and also in a puberty-related ritual. Korai guri laru is yet another popular rice powder based Assamese sweet. In Lower Assam though, korai guri also means rice roasted with black gram and black chickpeas, consumed commonly during Magh Bihu.

A common rice-based dessert in Assamese households is paramana or payax, also served as praxad in temples. While refined sugar is the common sweetener these days, the prevailing use of jaggery in Assamese jolpan suggests that it must have satisfied people's sweet palate before refined sugar, in tandem with honey. Hiuen Tsang's account of Kamrup in 640 CE spoke of King Bhaskarvarman dispatching pots of jaggery to Magadha king Harshavardhan as a royal gift.[52] *Katha Gurucharit* mentions the processing of sugar by boiling.[53] Interestingly, the Vaishnava text had also mentioned that Sankardev, on his return from his first pilgrimage in what is mainland India now, brought grains of sugar with him. His disciple Jayanta rubbed it on smoked 'baat' fish but didn't quite enjoy the taste. Sankardev then instructed him to mix the sugar with milk.[54]

A noteworthy feature of Assamese cuisine (generally true of the cuisine of eastern India) is also the use of whole spices and condiments. Therefore, in Assamese cuisine, like that of Bengali food in the neighbourhood, one notes the common use of pass-phoron (tempering a dish with five whole species including fenugreek and fennel seeds). *Yogini Tantra* mentions another spice commonly used in Kamrup: joni (lovage seeds.)[55] In general though, instead of banking much on spices, the cook makes an ardent go at retaining the freshness and natural flavour of the vegetables she uses in her preparation. Rules about using only certain vegetables in certain preparations to derive a particular taste and aroma are, therefore, sacrosanct. For instance, in *masor tenga* (sour fish curry), the gourd used is only the jati lau and never the oval white variety, the jali kumura, because only the jati/pani lau can infuse the required zest to complement the sourness of the curry. That the Bargaon grant of Kamrup king Ratnapala (908–940 CE) refers to large tracts of land with clusters of gourds only confirms the age-old proclivity of the Assamese towards that vegetable.[56]

Talking about combinations, there are some typical recipes, say, mutton cooked with raw papaya that have become embedded in Bihu songs and folk tales. Saikia has pointed out the allusion to jaluk–jolokia (pepper and chillies) in Bihu songs; also the common folk sayings about food combinations: kosure mosure (taro with masoor dal), kopou koldile (pigeons with banana flowers), dorike bengenai (waterhen with aubergines), xole mule (a dark-skinned fish variety with radish), haahe baahe (duck with bamboo shoots).[57]

AROMA AS AN INGREDIENT

With ample use of fresh vegetables and a variety of rice, a significant feature of Assamese cuisine is also in making adequate use of the natural aromas of food to not only make a preparation palatable but also appealing to one's senses. One such unique aroma is the joha flavour, found not just in some rice varieties but also in a gourd and a bhul (of the cucumber family). There is also a civet in Assam that produces that aroma and is therefore called joha-mal.

Assam's varieties of lemon also have distinct aromas, as do the leaves of mezenga (a spiny shrub), maan dhania (the Burmese cilantro), and elephant apple. Just cooking a dish with these naturally aromatic food items fills the Assamese kitchen with a one-of-a-kind scent that works as an appetizer, and also evokes the sense of having been satiated by one's meal.

Another unique feature of Assamese food culture is the use of curry leaves, locally called noroxingxo. This aspect of Assamese cuisine, present in both tribal and non-tribal households, needs a special mention simply because the general tendency in mainstream India is to treat curry leaves as part of only South Indian cuisines. In Assamese cuisine, the wet paste of noroxingxo leaves is used to prepare a flavourful curry, with lentil dumplings, and also with fish, particularly the dark-skinned kinds. Pork and country chicken curries are made with the paste too. The Karbis prepare a dish of curry leaves with dry fish. The leaf is also popular among the Bodo Kacharis.

The common medium of cooking in Assamese cuisine is mustard oil. Mustard seeds have grown in Assam for a long period of time and the oil from the seeds have been used in cooking for a while. In everyday cooking though, frying food, including fish that is added to curries, is not so common as is evidence by how a variety of greens, khaar, and pitika are still prepared—by adding a dash of mustard oil only at the fag end, essentially to enhance the aroma of the dish.

Still, use of mustard paste in cooking exists in both tribal and non-tribal food practices. Kharoli is a fermented paste of black mustard consumed as a taste enhancer. The Assamese also have kahudi, similar to kasundi in Bengali cuisine. *Dakor Boson* mentions a Senga and Sengeli fish dish with kahudi.

The Karbis have traditionally used black sesame as oil, in a paste form. Black sesame and black gram (mati maah or khesari) have been conventionally associated with the food habits of all social groups in Assam. In rural Assam, the preferred lentil till date is black gram.

Karbis also follow an oil-free cooking method called karnu pakrengsoi during which salt and crushed garlic cloves are first stirred dry over heat before the addition of fresh herbs; this method imparts a unique flavour to a dish.[58]

METHODS OF COOKING

Across Assamese households, roasting or pura is a method of traditional cooking. A popular way of eating the finger-sized fish varieties, also chunk-sized pork, among the wider Assamese community is to pass a sleek bamboo stick (khorika) through them, and barbecue them on charcoal or over a wood fire.

Steaming food, both vegetarian and non-vegetarian, is also an old practice in Assam. All Assamese subgroups steam rice. Archaeological evidence found by researchers from Gauhati University in 2018 near Dudhnoi proved that the practice of pitha preparation by using the traditional steaming method goes as far back as 3000 years.[59]

A selection of rice-based preparations like sunga pitha, sunga soul, tupula bhaat, and fish and meat are prepared in bamboo hollows placed in fire. Besides being used as a cooking vessel, bamboo hollows are also used as storage jars in traditional Assamese kitchens. In several bazaars of Assam, curd is still sold in bamboo hollows. That king Bhaskarvarman had sent mango sap to Harsha Vardhan in bamboo pipes only speaks of their age-old use in Assamese society.[60]

The popular Assamese tekeli pitha is steamed by putting the uncooked pitha tightly wrapped in muslin on the spout of a tea kettle filled with water. The steam rising from the boiling water readies it for consumption.

Assamese traditional cooking has also seen the use of leaves for steaming. The Misings cook rice in small parcels wrapped in banana leaves which infuses an excellent earthy aroma into the steamed grains. The rice used is often the khamti lahi variety to further enhance its taste. A popular Assamese dish is patot diya mua maas—freshly caught small fish wrapped in banana leaves and roasted on a wood fire. The smoked fish are then given a coating of mustard oil, chopped ginger, onions, chillies, and Burmese cilantro. Chopped dhekia leaves, and poppy seed paste, are also smoked by some using this method. In Assamese Muslim households, small fish mixed with turmeric powder, salt, and chillies, wrapped tightly in a banana leaf, are dropped into a pot of boiling rice. 'By the time the rice is cooked, the fish is ready too,' said Shabnam Bora.

The banana leaf is also used to roast meat, mainly by the tribes. There is also the culture of using other leaves to roast or steam food, mainly rice, such as in tupula bhaat made by enfolding rice in tokou and tora leaves by the Singhpho and Tai Phake ethnic groups in Upper Assam.

DRIED FOOD

Easy availability of food from one's surroundings has ensured that in Assamese food culture, there is little requirement on drying food items. Only a few things are preserved for later use such as the yellowed gul and kaji lemons soaked in salt and the seasonal jasmine flowers, dried and stored to be added to khaar.

While non-tribes have the practice of storing only vegetarian food, including bamboo shoots, in fermented or dried forms, the tribes do dry and ferment small fish and meat for later use. Rabhas, Bodos, Misings, Tiwas, Dimasas, Ahoms, and Sutiyas have the habit of savouring dry fish. The Mising dry fish namsing is a delicacy. The Bodos also have a fermented small fish dish, napham; the Tiwas have naflang. Rabhas also have a similar dish called nichaow. The East Bengal origin Muslim community also dries fish and uses it to prepare a tasty chutney with garlic and chillies. The only time the community dries beef, their primary meat, on the rack above the kitchen furnace is just after Bakrid when there is plenty of meat in most households. Assamese Muslims too dry beef in a similiar fashion.

ANT EGGS AND FROGS

Some social groups in Assam, particularly the Ahoms, have the habit of consuming ant eggs (tupp), especially of the red variety called amroli porua. Tai-Ahom culture expert Girin Phukon had pointed out to me that unlike today where various forms of protein were easily available to a community, people in olden times had to discover sources of food for good health from their surroundings itself.[61] The habit of consuming amroli tupp can be traced to this need. The eggs are available only between February and April. People also eat meleng, the little winged creatures that come out by breaking the eggs. Tupp is also eaten by other ethnic groups, particularly the Rabhas.

Ahoms also consume silkworm (leta/polu). Several Ahom families in rural areas raise silkworms at home for food. Silkworm is eaten by the plains tribes too.

Ahoms also eat frogs that are large-sized (bor bhekuli/paat beng). Phukon particularly recalled an experience from his youth of lighting a bamboo torch every night during February–March and following the village elders into the rice fields to catch frogs.

GROWING POPULARITY OF ASSAMESE FOOD

In the early 2000s, if you had asked an Assam-based Assamese where would one get Axomiya food, the answer invariably would have been a question instead—where else if not at home?

This may not remain true forever though. Post the 2010s or so, not just in the big city of Guwahati but across Assam, a slew of budget restaurants and roadside eateries have popped up to dish out food, primarily in a North Indian thali format, from different Assamese ethnic groups. The trend must be located within the agency developed lately in local communities to not only derive pride from their respective micro food cultures but also to monetize their unique food cultures by taking advantage of an emergent openness among all ethnic groups within Assam to try out each other's food. That there has been a spike in tourist footfall in Assam has also created opportunities for such small businesses to thrive. The combined outcome of this is an ever-expanding number of eateries along the highways and in the towns with boards that say Mising Kitchen, Rabha Kitchen, Tiwa Kitchen, Dimasa Kitchen, Bodo Kitchen, Khamti Kitchen, etc. This trend is complementary to the fine dining restaurant chains that offer Assamese food, like at Paradise, Khorika, etc. in urban areas like Guwahati. The Paradise group, a pioneer in wedding catering in Upper Assam, was also among the first to open a restaurant, Jakoi, specializing in Assamese cuisine, in New Delhi over a decade ago. At the Khorika outlet in Guwahati's Silpukhuri, a photograph capturing a pivotal moment in the trajectory of the growing popularity of Assamese cuisine even outside the state is hung prominently. Khorika owner and chef Atul Lahkar is seen posing with Gordon Ramsay, the celebrated British chef and TV host, who had travelled to Assam in 2009 to feature him rustling up an Assamese dish for his popular food and travel show *Gordon's Great Escape*. Lahkar is admittedly a self-taught chef who developed an interest in Assamese cooking and invested time and effort required to make Khorika stand out before displaying his expertise at Delicacy, another popular Assamese restaurant in Guwahati. In an interview to *Guwahati-Plus* magazine in 2017, he spoke of his multiple visits to villages across Assam to gather a collection of recipes of 400 traditional dishes.[62] The name of his restaurant, Khorika, was derived from the traditional practice of roasting finger-length whole fish and pork slivers on bamboo sticks. Lahkar shall be remembered for promoting this cooking method particularly among urban folks.

Over the years, with an increasing number of Assamese migrating to mainstream India primarily for work, the willingness to showcase their food has led a handful of exclusive restaurants to pop up in metros like Delhi, Bangalore, and Mumbai. This is aside from regular Assamese food pop-ups which have gone on to create a niche clientele for their hosts. Snehalata Saikia, who started her pop-up in South Delhi in 2015, told me, 'I just planned to host a group showcasing our food to remove certain misconceptions about our cuisine; they just loved it.'[63] Since then, she hasn't looked back. While visiting Assam, she makes sure to drop by Assamese tribal villages to acquire different traditional cooking techniques, including how to prepare their brews to serve her guests in Delhi.

The most challenging part for Sneha and all others who organize such pop-ups in cities across India is to ensure the steady flow of authentic ingredients since an organized supply chain outside of Assam is hard to set up. Small attempts have been made to fill that gap lately with the advent of online shopping such as through the shop, www.juhaal.com, in Delhi.

ARECA NUT

Perhaps it would only be appropriate to end a chapter on Assamese food with a reference to the areca nut, since any sumptuous meal in an Assamese household typically ends with chewing tamul. Aside from the salience of tamul in Assamese cultural life, chewing a piece of a freshly cut nut in a foil of a gaan paan leaf after a heavy meal works as much as a digestive as a neutralizer of the multiple food flavours left in the mouth from various dishes. In Kalika Purana, women in Kamrup are particularly mentioned to have a penchant for the nut. In the seventeenth century, Shihab-al-Din Talish, in *Fathiyah-i-Ibriyah*, also refers to the tamul chewing practice in Pragjyotishpur. In modern times, in every Assamese household, a visitor is traditionally welcomed with a bota (a bell metal tray) of tamul and paan leaves.[64]

In my ancestral home in Upper Assam, akin to several others, a small portion of land is dug every year to carve out a pit where the long leaves of areca nut trees are carefully laid before ripe orangey nuts plucked from the trees around the house are dropped into the pit and covered, first with more leaves and then topped with soil. They are pulled out of the ground only after some months to procure gela/burha tamul, a delicacy. Interestingly, the process of fermenting tamul in Assam is similar to preparing hundred-year-old eggs in Chinese cuisine. The nuts, like the eggs, turn deep brown from fermenting and acquire an earthy taste. Interestingly, just as the eggs are called 'hundred-year-old' in China, the fermented tamul in Assamese are also referred to in terms of age—burha, or 'ripe old'.

The practice of chewing tamul exists in several other societies across India. However, one may say that it is not so deeply entwined in the daily life of these communities as it is in Assam. No Assamese traditional home with a backyard is without an areca nut tree. Some such backyards have paan vines too. It is a common saying in Assam that the paan vines, particularly the prized gaan variety, don't grow in every household since they need constant care.

In my household, not everyone is allowed to touch the gaan vines, a traditional rule. My mother had once explained it thus: 'An Assamese handles a gaan paan vine with care and also gratitude, as only it can give a mouthful of bliss.' Her explanation had only reiterated the overriding concept in traditional Assamese society of taking every edible element from nature as a blessing.

Praxad.

8

KAAH–PITOL, DA–KUTHAR, DOLA–KHORAHI: ASSAMESE CRAFTS

The clock has barely struck eight but the clang of hammer meeting metal is already sounding out through the Tamul Supa locality of Sarthebari town in Lower Assam.

Sarthebari, in Barpeta district, has been the locus of the Assamese bell metal industry for centuries. Over 2,000 artisans work every day at kilns in the fashion of a cottage industry, to carve out cymbals of varying sizes for use in the Vaishnava monasteries of the state and also as a musical accompaniment in the Bihu and Sattriya dances, aside from producing an array of utensils for everyday use in Assamese households.

Amidst the sounds of metal hitting metal stands the modest house of two artisan brothers, Maheswar and Tapan Neog. Since 1989, the middle-aged Neog brothers have charted out a new course with bell metal in Sarthebari, which is the reason why I knocked at their door first when I got there.

The trend among the Sarthebari Kohar (bell metal artisan) community to produce only utensils has been a constant for a long while. The Neog brothers chose to also craft furniture and art and decor items using the medium for creative gratification as artisans and to revive the old glory of the industry. 'It is widely believed that the bell metal gifts that the great Assamese king Bhaskarvarman gave to Chinese traveller Hiuen Tsang during his visit to Kamrup in the seventh century were crafted in our area. But somehow, we ended up restricting our art only to making utensils for day-to-day use. We want to revive that glory,' Tapan Neog told me when I met them in 2020.[1] Maheswar elaborated, 'We take pride that Sarthebari, since the time of our ancestors, has been the hub of kaah (bell metal) and pitol (brass) ware of Assam but when it comes to showcasing our craft to others, we have nothing much to show except the cymbals and the utensils we make; not the intricate hator kaam (expertise of the hand). But we are essentially artisans. As self-respecting artisans, that was the driving force for us to do something beyond the usual. If today, I would have made only utensils like the others, you wouldn't have come looking for us from Delhi; that's our prize as artisans.'

In the olden times, the bell metal craft was once practised in some upper and middle Assam pockets too, like Raha, Karanga, and Titabor.[2] The Vaishnava text *Katha Gurucharit* had mentioned the prevalence of the practice in the Koch kingdom in western Assam. 'Chilarai (Silarai), the brother of the Koch king Naranarayan, once offered a pair of *chappals* (slippers) made of bell-metal to Sankardeva while the latter paid a visit to the Koch Behar state.'[3] Older texts written in Assam like the Kalika Purana not only speak of the use of bell metal utensils in Assamese society but also jewellery made from it, like, bangles.[4]

While younger brother Tapan concentrates on making things that need minute detailing, such as bell metal clocks, portraits of Assamese cultural icons (and Bollywood heroes and singers on demand), replicas of the one-horned rhino of Assam and the Kamakhya temple, etc., the elder one trains his interest on making bigger articles: four poster beds, dining tables, ornate jars, and jewellery boxes. 'All the designs in bell metal are from our own perseverance; not copied from anywhere,' Maheswar emphasized to me. While smaller pieces of the craft go off the rack fast, the same is not true of the bigger items, particularly the furniture. 'It took me more than two years to finish the bell metal bed; I invested ₹25 lakhs on it, not knowing whether I would get a buyer for it. It weighs about 1,200 kilograms,' Maheswar said. For some years now, he has been using the bed himself to turn it into the colour of engaar kola, dark as ashes. 'A polished piece has the new look but I want to give it an aged look; that's more invaluable.'

About 3 kilometres from Maheswar's house stands Assam Samabai Kohar Sangha Limited, an eighty-eight-year-old cooperative body with which about 150 of the over 300 artisan units that function across the town are affiliated. The outfit, thereby, facilitates employment for at least 10,000 people in and around that area.

At one corner of the Sangha's premises is a cabinet showcasing a row of the prized utility items crafted by its member units. Since they are not made by the artisans any more, they stand only as a reminder of Assam's rich material culture. Manoj Kumar Bhuyan, the Sangha secretary, pointed at a fading black and white photograph of a long-deceased town resident hanging on a wall and said, 'That is Kuhiram Das…he singularly contributed to the economic emancipation of the local Kohar artisan community way back in 1933.' Das was not an artisan but a studious young man from the town who held the pride of place as the first honours graduate of the state in the British era. Bhuyan related that being an educated young man, he understood more than the unlettered artisans of his town that they would die of hunger if something was not done to draw them out of the repressive control of the mohajans, the local traders. The traders, the majority of whom were from the Assamese community, would pocket all the profit from the wares while a measly sum would be handed over to the artisans for their work. 'Das helped bring a revolution of sorts in Sarthebari by mobilizing the artisans to set up this cooperative society,' related Bhuyan, who belongs to a family that has traditionally dealt in the craft.[5]

On Kuhiram Das's call, about 2,000 artisans joined hands to promote and practice the craft without the intervention of intermediaries. With no liquid cash at hand, each donated at least a kilo of bhoga kaah, broken pieces of bell metal that is required to craft new pieces, to the cooperative society as the initial capital to be distributed to the artisans to make their wares which the Sangha would then sell through an outlet in Sarthebari. 'Each of the 2,000 artisan families has since got shares in the co-operative society; some got only one share, some more than one, depending on how many kilos of bhoga kaah they had donated at that time. In all, we have five thousand shares,' Bhuyan said, recollecting the history of the artisans' body that gave the Assamese craft a new lease of life in the colonial era.

The practice of distributing broken bell metal to the member artisans continues in modern times too. Artisans deposit items of typical use in Assamese society with the Sangha—daily-use utensils, cymbals required in Vaishnava prayer halls, and bells in temples. In lieu of their deposits, they are paid a remuneration pre-decided by the Kohar Sanstha, the primary body of the local artisans. Bhuyan said the surge in the industry over the years has led the units to double in and around Sarthebari but the new ones function independent of the Sangha. 'Even though we don't mind expanding the Sangha to include them in the fold, our inability to procure adequate quantity of raw material has come in the way,' he said.

Each unit needs at least 30 kilograms of bell metal sheets per day. 'We are struggling to supply metal sheets regularly even to our member units.' Though the co-operative society accepts broken bell metal pieces from the clientele (hawkers also pick up such pieces door to door across Assam to sell to the Sangha), the primary source of the metal is through traders from outside the state. 'We buy the readymade bell metal scrap which is 70 per cent copper and 30 per cent tin. We hear that the metal is brought to India from old broken edifices from Pakistan, Afghanistan, etc. We, however, procure them from traders from Delhi, Moradabad, Kolkata, etc. There is a scrap collection centre at Guwahati's Fancy Bazaar also,' Bhuyan related.

While Assamese writers like Sarbeswar Rajguru state that the bell metal workers of Sarthebari once had the know-how to blend copper with tin (taam and raang in Assamese) to make kaah (bell metal),[6] Satyendranath Sarma suggests that the metal in its finished form was obtained from the well-known annual bazaar held at Chauna where traders of Assam, Tibet, Bhutan, and China frequently exchanged commodities.[7] There could well be a grain of truth about the latter theory considering bell metal, since ancient times, has been the favoured tableware of societies east of Assam's border, particularly for the royals in countries like Korea. Ancient Assam's trade route with Korea could also be the procurement route for the raw material.

Called bangjja, the Korean bell metal utensils were particularly used for the royal cuisine Surasang. The royals used the metal, prepared with 78 per cent copper and 22 per cent tin, chiefly because of its self-sterilizing quality. This is the reason why this form of bronze ware could have also gained wider popularity, and might have led Korea or/and China to export the metal to neighbouring countries. That the Ahom royals in Assam had principally used bell metal tableware also could be because of that particular feature of the metal. The bangjja utensils are said to have originally entered Korea through trade relations with China. Interestingly, the bangjja tableware is also hand forged by beating the metal, like it is done in Sarthebari. Till the advent of Japanese colonial rule, utensils made of bangjja were popular in Korean homes.

In modern Assam, the demand for kaahor bason, bell metal utensils, has seen a spurt after the 2010s. Before this, an Assamese family bought bell metal utensils typically only to gift them to their daughter on her wedding, or if needed at the prayer hall or to serve areca nut to a guest. This is shifting, however—more and more households have set aside their stainless steel and melamine dinner plates and bowls in favour of eating on bell metal plates just as their ancestors did. A growing cultural consciousness within the community is responsible for this change in lifestyle. Additionally, with a spike in restaurants in towns and cities and highway eateries serving Assamese food in a traditional style, the use of the metal has increased.

The recent spike in demand has facilitated the cooperative society at Sarthebari to expand its market by granting franchise to as many as fifteen outlets across Assam till 2020. In my town in Upper Assam, till the early

2000s, the only way to procure bell metal utensils from Sarthebari was to wait for a kohar to come to our door with the wares set on a bhaar, a traditional bamboo carrier. Post 2020 though, an outlet has opened up in the local bazaar, set up with the help of the Sangha.

The increased demand has, however, begun affecting the quality of the craft, rued Dinabandhu Deka, the president of the cooperative society and a practising Kohar. 'Earlier, Kohars would compete with each other on how best to make a piece; today though, the competition is over quantity, leading the quality to suffer. This is happening also because a Kohar who makes sub-standard ware, say of 10 kg bell metal in a month, would be paid more by us than another who would take good care to craft each piece and in the process could produce only, say, 6 kg within that time.' Much as he would like to rein in such practices, Deka said it is not in the office bearers' hands as the consensus among the artisans at the annual general meeting is the sole deciding factor behind resolutions like, whether to pay a Kohar by the kilo, or only after a quality check of the finished good. 'We can't reject a piece even though it is affecting the quality of our craft.' About ₹1.5 crore are annually paid as remuneration to the member artisans, Bhuyan added.

Artisans like Maheswar Neog who have shares in the co-operative society, though, finds its role in promoting the craft restrictive because it doesn't provide a market for their products. 'In the hurry to make money, most artisans don't show any inclination to mass produce the old intricate designs even in utensils. Many such designs are, therefore, becoming history; that particular know-how will be lost soon.' Sangha officials Bhuyan and Deka agreed that at least a limited edition of old designs must be brought back to the market but added, 'The artisans who take such decisions at the annual meeting would have to come forward for it.'

Amidst such worries are also concerns of the artisans about the absence of modern advancement in the craft. Though since 2014, the Sangha has been running a rolling mill to press the scrap to create bell metal sheets of varied sizes, it is not enough to meet the monthly requirement. 'Each day, the machine presses about 2,000 kilograms of bell metal sheets and yet it is not enough for the existing member artisans,' said Deka. Next to the rolling machine is a traditional kiln hinged on bamboo poles and plastered with mud to burn each sheet with wood to solidify it. Every month, the bill for wood is upwards of ₹80,000. 'We take out the entire expense only from our sales,' Deka emphasized. In 2013–14, though the

Assam government had sanctioned the cooperative society a sum of ₹5 crore for modernization and allied use, only ₹2 crore from it had been utilized by the time of this interview. 'This is because we used the money to buy scrap but failed to get proper receipts from the traders who anyway never give us any such documents. Since the state government still wants us to furnish original receipts, the rest of ₹3 crore is sitting only in our annual balance sheets but we are not able to use it for betterment of the artisans,' related Bhuyan. A growing worry among the office bearers is also the need to procure a Goods and Sales Tax (GST) number for the cooperative society. Additionally, a number of memoranda have been submitted to the Assam government to install a museum of bell metal ware at Sarthebari and to make a move towards getting geographical indication (GI) for the hand-made craft. 'The government is quiet thus far. Our products, mainly the cymbals, are regularly exported to Asian nations including China but we have no way to claim that they are products of Assam and can't be duplicated. Already, our designs are being duplicated in Moradabad and sold in Assam as bell metal products,' Bhuyan rued.

BRASS, COPPER, AND IRON WARE

In Sarthebari, while some artisans, mainly from the Kalita community, also make wares from pitol (brass), the craft is more prominent within the Moria fold of the Assamese Muslim community residing around that area. *The Gazetteer of Bengal and North-East India* states, 'The industry in Assam Valley is largely in the hands of Morias, a class of degraded Muhammadans, who are said to be the descendants of prisoners captured by the Ahoms when Turbak was defeated in 1532.'[8] Those soldiers were essentially brass makers.[9] Some locals claim that the term Moria by which the captive soldiers began to be known in their new home was due to their act of continuous hammering (moriua in Assamese) on the metal.

Though brass ware began to gain importance after the arrival of the Moria community in the sixteenth century, the discovery of a few brass Buddha statues from the ninth to tenth centuries in Assam demonstrates that the practice must have predated them. '[The] names of musical instruments like bells (*ghonta*), *mohori*, *kali*, etc. mentioned in pre-Sankardev texts in Assam suggested that they might have been made of brass. We can, therefore, safely say that the arrival of the Morias, who were essentially brass craftsmen by profession, gave a stimulus to the craft in Assam, and, prior to them, the pieces made were done in pre-set casing, unlike how the Morias began to do—by setting up *kamaar-xaal* (kilns).'[10]

Like brass, there is evidence of copper usage in ancient Assam. The copper epigraphs of several early kings are proof of this. One can tread as far back as Bhaskarvarman's era in the seventh century to get an idea about the use of copper through the inscriptions written on the metal. In the tenth century, King Tyagasimha had minted copper coins. Saikia had pointed out that in the later period, the shed over a small edifice placed between the podium of the Kamakhya temple and its sacrificial area was made of copper. This was also true of the roof of the Somdev temple in today's Sivasagar and the original roof of the Tamreshwar Devi temple in Sadiya.[11] There is also a reference in the *Darrang Rajbanshavali* annals about Koch king Naranarayan donating utensils made of bell metal, gold, silver, and copper to the Kamakhya temple.[12] The presence of copper utensils in the temples and Assamese houses only suggest that they have had their utility in both ritualistic and domestic life.[13]

Aside from articles made from these metals, the common use of certain iron tools in Assamese rural life—the kotari (knife) and da (bill-hook), kuthar (axe) and khonti (sickle), bothi (chopper used with a foot) and kur (shovel), also kerahi (heavy bottomed pan)—underscore that the art of blacksmithing has been known to the community for a protracted period.[14] A distinct guild or khel of blacksmiths, called Kamar in Assamese, had existed during the Ahom period. 'The Kalitas formed the bulk of the blacksmiths in Assam, known as Kamar-Kalita.'[15] They not only produced household and agricultural implements but a section of them also manufactured war gear, like swords (*hengdang*), spears, arrow heads, guns, matchlocks, cannons, etc. 'There was another guild called Lo-Saliya who smelted iron from the clay comprising iron oxides found on the slopes of Tiruparbat and in the Kacharighat area of the present Golaghat district.'[16] According to Ahom noble Maniram Dewan, there were about seventy lo-sals/mines in the Tiruparbat area. Those involved in mining iron were known as Tiruwals. Like the Sonowals knew how to sieve gold dust from the river waters, Tiruwals knew to locate ferruginous soil in an iron mine and only did that; they were not blacksmiths. Iron ore was also scattered across the Koch kingdom, and in parts of Dibrugarh, Sibasagar, in the Karbi hills, and also the Naga and the Khasi hills. *The Gazetteer of Bengal and North-East India* had called smelting of iron ore a 'considerable industry'[17] before the arrival of the British. 'The chronicles of Muhammadan invasions frequently refer to the large numbers of cannon possessed by the enemy, and these guns, some of them of great weight and size, are found scattered over the Assam Valley at the present day. (Francis) Buchanan-Hamilton, writing at the beginning of the last century, makes mention of a valuable iron-mine south of Jorhat, and the remains of iron workings are to be seen all over the Khasi hills,' its authors had noted in the early twentieth century.[18] Mughal general Mir Jumla, during his return to Dhaka, is said to have taken away with him as many as 8,788 guns including cannons. The practice of cannon making began in the sixteenth century during King Suhungmung's era. As many as 3,000 blacksmiths worked at that time. The practice continued till the eighteenth century. Those who operated such weaponry were called Hiloidhari Baruah. A section of blacksmiths in Assam were called Dheker Garha Kamar and were experts in sculpting dheker or the crooked supports for palanquins.[19]

The arrival of the British in the early nineteenth century, precipitated the end of frequent wars in Assam and caused the gradual decline of the iron industry which was principally hinged on manufacturing artillery. Only small amounts of iron smelting continued to meet the domestic and agricultural needs.[20]

IVORY AND WOOD CRAFT

Among several exquisite artefacts at the museum of the Auniati Monastery in Majuli is a mat woven from strips of ivory. The museum, though, hasn't put a date on the creation of that gorgeous piece. However, it is well known that most of the precious articles that Vaishnava monasteries possess today were gifts from the Ahom royals; ivory is still owned by several other Majuli monasteries. At Dakhinpat Monastery, centuries-old ivory works have long been placed on either side of the Mother Goddess placed inside its storehouse. The presence of ivory in these institutions is only an indication of Assam being the land of elephants. 'The biography of the pilgrim (Hiuen Tsang) states that (king) Bhaskara went to meet (king) Harsha with a huge number of elephants.'[21] Magadha king Harsha was gifted 'rings of hippopotamus ivory, encrusted with rows of huge pearls from the brows of elephants.'[22]

The art of ivory carving was pursued by a set of khanikars (artisans) during the Ahom rule but it saw a gradual decline after the British takeover of the state. The kings had valued the art immensely and the artisans had to pursue it compulsorily. In 1989, Satyendranath Sarma wrote, 'The art of ivory carving, though once practiced by a few Muslim families at Jorhat sub-division, has ceased to exist now. It is still being cultivated at Barpeta where figurines of deities, chariot, comb, throne (*simhasana*) etc. are carved adroitly.'[23] Some Assamese households still have combs made of ivory.

Aside from ivory and elephant tusk, the horns of the one-horned rhinos and buffaloes were also used to craft musical instruments. The Assamese wind instrument pepa, without which a Bihu song is incomplete, is moulded from a buffalo horn. Combs used in Assamese houses were once commonly made of buffalo horns. *Yogini Tantra* spoke of the use of utensils made of rhino horns especially during death ceremonies. Gunabhiram Barua, in *Assam Buranji*, highlighted the fact that Ahom kings exported rhino horns to neighbouring countries and that the royalty and commoners alike wore rings made of it.[24]

Deer and buffalo horns were also common decorative pieces not just in olden Assam but across the Northeast. Wooden replicas of the hunted animals were carved to which the horns were fixed to be put up in one's home as a sign of bravery. A common wooden item was also a dish on a stand, the ronga xorai, so called because they were painted red with hengul (vermillion). The dish came both with a cover and without it. It was used to make offerings to guests of honour, and in modern Assam there is a common saying related to this: Tuk akou ronga xorai di matibo lagibo neki? (Do I have to invite you home with a ronga xorai?) Essentially, the epithet means, don't be pesky.

Yet another important wooden article in an Assamese house is the bor pira, a stool that stands on beautifully sculpted short legs which is customarily used during special occasions. Several old houses in Assam also have the mogor or gharial carved on wooden doors and door-lintels. '[The] wooden palace of (Ahom king) Jayadhvaja Singha, so highly praised by Shahbuddin Tallish, the Muslim historian (who accompanied Mughal general Mir Jumla during his invasion of Assam in the seventeenth century) was the creation of Assamese artisans. They also painted their products with different colours, mainly with *hengul* (vermillon) and *haital* (yellow arsenic).'[25]

BOAT-MAKING

A giant wooden sculpture of Garuda, preserved at the Auniati Monastery and a replica of a wooden canoe depicting the Nauka Jatra, Sankardev's voyage on a boat with his disciples to mainland India in search of religious knowledge, also highlights the exquisiteness of the wood craft that has been practised in Assam for a long time. The craft of boat or canoe-making has been long associated with daily life in Assam. In 1870, Samuel E. Peal, in his monograph *The Canoes of Assam*, had identified the use of four types of boats in the state: soosia nao, a small dugout canoe that carries five-six persons and is used to transport goods in small quantities; khel nao or boats used for sport; maar nao or two or more canoes tied together to be able to carry more goods for use of traders; and hoolong, a one-sitter canoe.[26] Arup Jyoti Saikia, in *The Unquiet River*, has noted some other types of boats too which were recorded during the Ahom era: chora nao, mayurpankhi, paltora nao, and pansai or dinga. All such boats were crafted from local wood. The hoolong canoes were made of hoolong trees, known for not just their sturdy texture but also for the ability of the wood to remain free of mites. Then there were hilchora nao, magarchora nao—war boats with cannons mounted on the prows.[27] The craft of boat-making and the astuteness of the artisans was not only the prime driver of Assam's trade and commerce with Bengal and North India but was also at the centre of Assam kings' acumen in naval warfare, not in the Ahom era alone but prior to it too. 'The Aphasad stone inscription of Adityasena (660–675 CE) in Bihar refers to sixth-century naval battle on the Brahmaputra between the Kamarupa king and later Gupta emperor. The Nidhanpur copper plates refer to the seventh century Kamarupa king Bhaskarvarman's splendid ships. The Chinese pilgrim Hiuen Tsang gives the number of Bhaskarvarman's ships at 30,000. The rulers of Kamarupa placed great faith on their navy, regarding it as an indispensible weapon of defence and offence.'[28] During the Ahom period, there were special officials—Nao Saliya Phukan and Nao Boisa Phukan—who oversaw the work of the boat-making guild to ensure the steady supply of boats for royal use and warfare. Rangpur, Majuli, Garhgaon, and Dergaon were where these guilds were active, employing about 6,000 to 7,000 people.

In the middle of the nineteenth century, rampant use of local trees for boat-making led to shortage. In the colonial era, taxes were levied on boat construction, which pushed away a large chunk of people from the craft. The arrival of steamers on the Brahmaputra also contributed to the gradual decline of traditional boat-making.[29] In modern times, the craftsmanship is visible only in Majuli. Local artisans constructing a traditional canoe by hollowing out an ejaar tree, or repairing a wooden ferry with a new set of khil beside the Brahmaputra, is a fascinating sight. Khil, larger than iron nails, are the traditional locks used to attach two pieces of wood. Yet another iron tool commonly used in boat-making is bais, a thinner version of a kur, the traditional cutter-cum-shovel. In December 2020, I had spotted a team of Salmora-based artisans led by a fellow villager, Uttam Somua, building a boat with ejaar trees for the use of the state government. They would need four months of work to finish the barge for it to be able to cart people and machines weighing 700 quintals on the Brahmaputra. 'We have about 300 such artisans in Salmora but the village is shrinking because of the annual erosion of the land by the flood waters of the Brahmaputra. The craft is also getting affected because of the declining use of boats with the construction of more and more concrete bridges over the river,' Uttam had rued then.[30] His team was also the envy of fellow villagers as that boat was the only new barge to be made in Majuli between 2020–2021. 'Orders for new boats are fewer than before. We artisans mostly engage in repair work of the old ones,' he told me.

In 2018, days after the country's longest rail-cum-road bridge, Bogibeel, was inaugurated, I had met a pair of dejected boatmen with their barges parked just under the bridge, wondering what would they do for a living as the regular passengers to cross the river from Dibrugarh in the south bank to Dhemaji in the north bank had dried up. 'Even if we want to sell the vessel and get into another profession, we can't do it easily because there is hardly any buyer for them. Though the ferries are plying on the Majuli river route, we don't know till when they will be the sole means of communication; every other day we hear about construction of a concrete bridge there too,' a boatman told me.

CANE AND BAMBOO CRAFT

Like wood, cane and bamboo too have been common mediums of artistry in Assam; both to create materials of daily use and for decor. A marker of Assamese identity, the red japi, needs bamboo. An Assamese kitchen is incomplete without a range of pasi, khorahi, and dola (oval and flat baskets). Bisoni (hand-held fan) made of bamboo is a common article in a rural home even today. Husked rice is traditionally stored in a dun, a life-size bamboo container. An array of hand-held fishing apparatus is fashioned out of bamboo too. Several weaving tools use bamboo as the base material. Bamboo strips are used to create decorative fences and windows in Assamese houses. Bamboo is a common element in several musical instruments. Bamboo utensils are in everyday use. In 2019, an Assamese youth hit the local news by crafting bamboo water bottles.[31] Though cane is primarily used for furniture in Assam, it is not unusual to find a range of cane baskets, mats, etc. A stopover at a cane or bamboo outlet by a highway in Assam can be an eye opener regarding the proficiency of the rural craftsmen and the array of goods that they produce from these two commonly found plants.

SHOLA, MASK, TERRACOTTA CRAFTS, AND POTTERY

There are several other Assamese crafts that require the use of raw material from the bounty of nature across the state, such as the clay and terracotta toys of Goalpara; the art of weaving sitalpati or cool mat from the reeds that grow in the marshes of Lower Assam; the Shola art prepared from the pith of a fibrous reed that grows by rivers; the drama masks of Majuli made with clay and bamboo. In my childhood, we had hawkers coming home from Barpeta, Dhubri, and Goalpara in Lower Assam all the way to Upper Assam to sell terracotta toys in bamboo baskets. Birendranath Dutta in *Folk Toys of Assam* had classified such toys into three categories: baked in the sun; fired in a furnace; and painted toys.[32] The art practised in western Assam is similar to that of the contiguous North Bengal. 'The toy-makers of these places, belonging mainly to the Hira community, have been producing pottery as well as toys and some other earthen articles of general utility like Dunari and incense-burner.'[33]

Excavations carried out in the Ambari area of Guwahati in the 1960s uncovered evidence of the excellence in pottery-making in olden Assam. Shards of a number of glazed, rouletted, and kaolin pottery were discovered from the pits. Aside from items of daily use, excavators also found bits of clay idols too.[34] 'According to some experts, certain pieces of broken clay idols and pots, hardened with fire, were perhaps as old as first or second centuries, or could be even older.'[35] That pieces made of clay were in ample use can be understood from how even today they are in wide circulation, not just for daily use in households but also in the temples and Vaishnava prayer halls. An example of clay articles can also be the one-of-a-kind Assamese musical instrument Gogona which requires a piece of carefully carved dry clay to produce a unique sound that accompanies Bihu songs. In the Ahom period, like all other professions, there were separate guilds for pottery making too. There were five categories of potters in the state: 'attached to the king's household; to the estates of the nobles; to the Vaishnava satras; to the temples and those allotted to make wares for the public.'[36] Known as Kumar, the profession could be taken up by any caste, though the Kalitas and Hiras were majorly seen to have followed it. Those who used their hands to make pottery, mainly the Hiras, were once looked down upon but never those who used the wheel. As much as this offers a peek into the prevalence of the caste system in medieval Assamese society, it also brings us to the point that in Assam, pottery has been made in two ways: with and without the wheel. Certainly, the former is older than the one dependent on the invention of the wheel. In Majuli, handmade pottery is still in practice and in early 2021, I had watched in amazement a clutch of men in the island's Salmora village placing pots and bowls in a layered heap in a round kiln called poghali. They then carefully enveloped the lot into a round casing by smudging wet clay over them before starting a gentle fire underneath to slowly harden the wares they had prepared. I watched that sight with the consciousness that it was perhaps a repeat of the first lessons of how a civilization had learnt to make pottery after the invention of fire.

Nagen Saikia, citing noted Assamese folklorist Pradip Chaliha, had mentioned that Assamese community had crafted pottery by following essentially three procedures. One, by making a dry muddle of hay and putting around it layers of soft clay to formulate a shape and then burning it so that the hay turned into ashes and in the process the clay ware hardened. Two, by weaving a particular shape with bamboo strips and then filling it with soft clay to form a pot and burning it thereafter so the bamboo disintegrates into ashes. This process is similar to mask-making in Majuli, though the artisans don't burn the mask after layering soft clay over the bamboo outline. The third method is by using the potter's wheel, which certainly is a younger process than the other two.[37]

In Majuli, modern potters are usually women, while the men dig out the required soft clay (lodha mati) for them from the Brahmaputra after its water recedes. Even today, once the articles are hardened at the kiln, the men load the pieces onto the boats parked on the Brahmaputra that flows by the three potter villages of Majuli, like they used to do traditionally. In the olden times, these potter-cum-traders (locally called mudoi) would set sail on the river to deliver them in lieu of other goods from different parts of the state. Though most of the merchandise nowadays is sold in exchange of hard cash, there still exists the age-old system of the Kumar community of Majuli swapping their newly made pots and bowls for rice from their Mising neighbours who farm, unlike the Kumars.[38]

As stated earlier, the Assamese masks are made by layering clay onto a bamboo frame made to look like a skull. The art of Assamese mask-making is concomitant to the Neo-Vaishnavite culture that Sankardev had disseminated across the state in the late fifteenth and early sixteenth centuries. The plays or Bhaona that the revered sociocultural reformer wrote are analogous to the morality plays of Europe, which thrived around the same time. The characters in a Bhaona are augmented on the stage through masks. Though Assam has the culture of carving out masks from wood too, the ones used in a Bhaona are made of bamboo and clay. Noted Assamese mask maker from Majuli, Hem Chandra Goswami, had told me in an interview for *The Wire* in 2017 that bamboo and clay may well have been used to make the masks lighter to wear during a performance by actors.[39] With close affinity between the Vaishnava Satras and the Buddhist monasteries, there is ample reason to also consider the art of story-telling through masks as another Buddhist influence on Sankari culture. Mask dance is a common Buddhist monastic norm.

Goswami, a Sahitya Akademi Awardee, underlined the use of sharp and very strong lines on the characters drawn on the masks as one of its unique features. 'Also, they differ from many other forms of masks because of the materials used to make them. We primarily use bamboo and cane, no Plaster of Paris is used—only local mud. The colours used to draw on the masks are made of leaves, seeds and flowers and also stones.'[40] Essentially, there are three types of Vaishnavite masks. One is the mukh mukha or face mask, which requires an appropriate costume to create a complete get-up. Then there is the lotokori mukha or masks which also covers a part of the actor's body. The third type is the big mask, bor or cho mukha which cloaks the entire body. Goswami has made some impressive bor mukha, specially that of the mythological characters like Garuda and Kalia Nag. Though masks are made in other monasteries of Majuli too, the Samaguri Satra to which Goswami belongs, has arguably made an indelible mark on the study and promotion of the medieval-era craft. For instance, Goswami, since 1984, has not only been running a mask-making school, Sukumar Kala Peeth, from his residence to teach students, but has also supplemented the craft immensely by thinking up a new type of mask, one whose lips can be made to move when delivering dialogue on stage. 'Though top organisations like Lalit Kala Akademi are yet to acknowledge it, I am very proud of thinking up an indigenous way of doing it without using any spring, etc. It is done by clever use of bamboo in the jaw area,' he had told me.[41] Among several places, his masks were displayed at the Victoria and Albert Museum in London in 2016.

Many of the masks placed on the racks at a front room of his modest house in Majuli, which is also his work area, not only tell the journey of this immensely talented man but also that it has been fraught with continuous struggle to keep alive the craft, both due to lack of state patronage and natural calamities like the annual floods. In 2011, when I had visited him a few months after the floods had receded, he showed me a photograph of him taken as he desperately tried to save some of his masks from being swept away by the waters from inside that room.[42]

Yet, Goswami has trudged on. At the time of writing, he had also begun to use the particular bamboo weave used in mask-making to create life-size human and animal sculptures including replicas of Bihu dancers. Though using this broad weave of the bamboo for artistic purposes other than mask-making is novel, it is, however, commonly seen across Assam, particularly in the rural areas of the state where hawkers bring pigs and hens in baskets made of that weave to the weekly bazaars. Interestingly, the same broad weave in bamboo baskets is also widely spotted in South and East Asian countries, particularly in Vietnam, thus underlining, yet again, that the continuity of the land has also influenced each other's crafts, both for daily use and for artistic purposes.

9

ERI–MUGA–PAAT–KOPAHI–KERU MONI: ASSAMESE WEAVE AND JEWELLERY

Nani Gopal Devagoswami directs his heir apparent, the deka guxain, to bolt the door to his boha, the hall in which he meets visitors at the Vaishnava monastery.[1]

Devagoswami, the monastic head of the revered Dakhinpat Satra, one of the four key Vaishnava monasteries located in Majuli amidst the Brahmaputra, is keen to show me in private the outcome of a one-of-a-kind initiative he has led since 2018. In mid-2019, that initiative offended the largest Vaishnava body of Assam, the Asom Satra Mahasabha, which threatened to file a legal case to stall it.[2]

Xoru Goxain, Goswami's heir, dutifully shuts the door, opens a steel almirah standing in the corner of the hall, and carefully brings out something covered in a thick fabric before unrolling it on the floor.

What lies in front of me is an exquisite piece of textile with a blue base. A number of religious motifs have been woven into it with the thread of the one-of-a-kind silk native to Assam, the Muga. The exclusivity of that piece of fine fabric is in a first-ever initiative in the state—undertaken at the behest of that over 300-year-old monastery led by Goswami—to recreate a piece of a sacred Assamese weave, the Brindabani Bastra.

The Brindabani Bastra has a rather strong emotional connection with a wide swathe of Assamese community as it was created at the behest of the revered saint Sankardev in the sixteenth century, the usherer of a Vaishnavite renaissance hinged on egalitarian values.

This particular piece at Dakhinpat Monastery—15 feet in width and 180 feet in length—is the first of the six segments of equal size set to be woven by a clutch of fifteen weavers from Lower Assam, to replicate the exquisite work undertaken by a set of Assamese weavers from that particular area under the supervision of Sankardev over 400 years ago.

BRINDABANI BASTRA AND A SCHOOL OF SACRED WEAVE

The original piece, believed to be 120 cubits long and 160 cubits broad, was put together by the weavers of Tantikuchi in Barpeta area of Lower Assam. It featured Krishna Leela, or scenes of significance from Krishna's childhood, a period in the life of the Lord that Sankardev's Neo-Vaishnavite faith particularly extols. The popular story goes that Sankardev was once asked by his royal patrons, Koch king Naranarayan and his brother Silarai, to narrate to them the story of Krishna's childhood in Brindaban (Vrindavan) amidst the cows and cowherds. Impressed by the account, the duo asked if the saint could retell it visually too. An astute artist, Sankardev is said to have drawn the scenes for the royals. Thereafter, he also accepted the challenge from them to weave each scene into a tapestry, which eventually led to not only the creation of a length of exquisite Muga silk textiles with a play of colours but most likely also gave birth to a school of sacred Vaishnava textile art in medieval Assam which used the intricate lampa weaving technique.

On Sankardev undertaking the task of replicating the scenes in textile with help from local weavers, the Koch king circulated a royal charter granting the saint the administration of Patbausi which included Tantikuchi. Thus, Sankardev became its Bor Bhuyan (chief administrator) and could pass orders to the resident weavers with royal patronage. The saint is widely believed to have zeroed in on a clasp of twelve weavers to accomplish the feat with craftsman Gopal Ata in the lead.

Using threads supplied by the royalty in red, blue, green, white, yellow, and the golden Muga, the team assembled a gorgeous tapestry in about half a year's time. Beginning with Krishna's birth in captivity, the scenes in the scroll ended with him vanquishing his maternal uncle Kansh (Kanxa Bodh). In all, there were twenty-seven scenes, woven on the loom, picked from Bhagavad Purana, the holy book that is typically placed on the monikut, the altar, at a kirtan-ghar/naam-ghar, the Vaishnava prayer hall. Two other important design features from that sacred textile were the use of verses in classical Assamese to describe the scenes from *Kalio Damana*, a play penned by Sankardev to narrate the tale of little Krishna crushing the serpent-demon Kaliya, and the depiction of Vishnu's incarnations. In keeping with the tale from Krishna's birthplace Brindaban (Vrindavan), the name of the cloth, the Bastra, was called Brindabani.

Sankardev, who resided in Patbausi then, set up a monastery where he visualized the scenes for the weavers and how they could be illustrated on textile. Twelve strips of woven textile of equal size were born of that effort. The story goes that Sankardev had to seek the help of three dozen people to cart the bundles to Patbausi Satra from the karkhana, the weaving shed. Thereafter, the bunch was loaded on to a boat to reach the royal palace at Koch Behar.

General Silarai and King Naranarayan were over the moon to see the Lord's story recounted in delicate weave. They offered to hand over to Sankardev the administration of the Barpeta principality as a present which he declined, though his grandson Ram Rai later took charge of it. A belief among a wide section of people in Assam has been that after the scrolls were formally presented to the king, they were preserved at Madhupur Satra in Koch Behar, the last abode of Sankardev (the Satra is in present-day West Bengal). The scroll seems to have vanished from the monastery one fine day though. What ensued is an interesting story of trade, preservation, loot, and discovery spanning several centuries and three countries before parts of the scroll could be traced, all thanks to a British journalist.

Back in 1904, Perceval Landon, a journalist associated with *The Times*, donated to the British Museum in London about nine and a half inches of a splendidly woven work with silk borders. Landon had accompanied the British expedition to Tibet under Sir Francis Younghusband in 1903–1904 to establish trade with Lhasa, and had brought that tapestry home.

The Assamese community had long concluded that the Brindabani Bastra was a lost artefact. And for about eighty-five years, the piece donated by Landon remained identified in the Museum's catalogue as 'Tibetan Silk Lampas' simply because he had sourced it from that region. In 1992, a British art scholar, Rosemary Crill, then associated with the Victoria and Albert Museum in London as a senior curator, which also possesses a similar piece with lampa weave, identified it, in addition to some other similar pieces preserved at the British Museum and elsewhere in Europe and the United States, as belonging to the legacy of the most precious Assamese weaving tradition, the Brindabani Bastra. That year, Crill put together a well-received exhibition titled 'Fabric of India', in which she also included the piece of Brindabani Bastra from the museum's collection, raising eyebrows in faraway Assam.

As per T. Richard Burton, the head of the South Asian department at the British Museum, the panel of Brindabani Bastra—presently preserved as a wall hanging at the Museum—was traced to the Gobshi Temple near Gyantse in Tibet. It probably ended up there through a trading route between medieval Assam and the neighbouring country, or through Bhutan with which the Koch country had shared its border.[3]

While curators like Burton have supposed that the pieces might have reached the Tibetan monastery separately, not as woven originally, they were stitched there, by adding broad silk borders in the style of a tankha and put up in the monastery. The present display at the museum has those silk borders. Burton had reasoned that the pieces could be immaculately preserved at the monastery for centuries perhaps because smoke from butter lamps and incense protected it from moths.[4]

The lampa weave used by the Assamese weavers on those pieces meant they used two warp systems with two or more wefts to produce the highly lavish texture of the textiles. Burton, who visited Majuli in 2016 chasing the story behind the textile preserved at the British Museum and went back to London to curate an exhibition titled 'Krishna in the Garden of Assam', documented in a short video that the technique is still being used by Assamese weavers even in cotton textiles, say, in weaving a gamusa; the method is commonly termed in Assamese as bhul bosa. Burton's Assam visit was significant as he could successfully link the motifs and writings on the museum pieces and the lived traditions in Majuli and the prevalent Sankari culture in the northeastern state. The clay masks made in Majuli, till date, of various characters to dramatize the Ankiya Nat (plays) of Sankardev, are readied as per the description of the saint in his writings, and their look matches those of the motifs woven in the museum pieces and the text knitted into the pieces in classical Assamese. That visit to Majuli had helped Burton contextualize the cloth at the British Museum with a lived culture and help revive for posterity a significant chapter of Assamese weaving traditions that was believed to have been lost.

Interestingly, Burton has stated that the British Museum piece dates back to around 1680. If the dating is correct, that piece can't be the original one woven during Sankardev's lifetime; he is believed to have passed away in 1568.

What then also comes across is that following the path laid by the great saint, there may have been successive endeavours to weave such sacred textiles in Vaishnava tradition, and a new school of devotional textile art using the lampa weave must have been prevalent in medieval Assam, something akin to the tankha art in Buddhist monasteries. Quite a few similarities can be drawn between Buddhism and the Neo-Vaishnavism of Sankardev anyway.

That there could have been such a prevalent practice even after the passing of the saint perhaps justifies the reason why there are several such pieces of

Brindabani Bastra, which the western scholars date to the seventeenth century. A point to note is, as per Crill, not all of them match in texture with each other.[5] Such pieces are well preserved in the Guimet Museum in Paris, the Chepstow Museum in Wales, the Victoria and Albert Museum in London, the Los Angeles Country Museum of Art, and the Philadelphia Museum of Art in the United States. According to noted Sankari studies scholar Sanjiv Borkakoty, there is a high possibility of the existence of a school of sacred weave that Sankardev's venture had given birth to in Kamrup. 'To my mind, the British scholars are correct; the pieces available at the London Museum or at the Victoria and Albert Museum are not the original ones; they were the later products that weavers trained by Sankardev had woven.'[6] As to how such sacred weaves might have reached Tibet, Borkakoty said, 'There is nothing to be surprised at; Assam and Tibet had trade relations for long and one of the items for commerce was textile.'[7]

Significantly, in the catalogue for the 1992 exhibition titled 'Vrindavani Vastra – Figured Silks from Assam', Crill had written on the Assamese tapestry, that those scrolls depicting scenes from Krishna's childhood tracing back to Assam might have been the precursor to what the Assamese community presently calls the guxain kapur or the cloth with religious and floral motifs with words of the Lord in Assamese script to be used at the altar or thapona cover of a Vaishnava monastery. 'It is thus likely that those in use today or in the recent past represent the much simplified tail-end of the design tradition, in which the complex registers of small, finely-drawn figures have been abandoned in favour of fewer, large-scale motifs. The design elements may also have lost their original identity.'[8]

In 2017, yet another significant event took place around the Brindabani Bastra in the UK. The event was at the Chepstow Museum in Wales. Titled 'Hidden in the Lining – Krishna in the Garden of Assam: Inside an Eighteenth-Century Banyan', it was a study highlighting an important connection that the nine-metre-long piece at the British Museum had with the lining of a luxurious gown preserved at the Chepstow Museum. The gown was a Banyan, a European unisex morning or night robe from the seventeenth–eighteenth century, said to be inspired by the Japanese kimono. Banyan was part of elite fashion which had seeped into high society colonial India too as a house gown worn by men and women.

Burton and Crill were among the speakers at the 2017 event. By then, the exhibition curated by Burton at the British Museum had placed the eighteenth century Banyan coat from the Chepstow Museum alongside the

Brindabani Bastra wall hanging to underline that the lining of that coat might have been cut from the same piece as that of the wall hanging.[9] The coat's lining also has the classical Assamese texts typically used in the Bastra. It is most likely that the lining was much older than the garment stitched in the eighteenth century, the experts suggested.

The museum curator Anne Rainsbury mentioned that the piece had reached them from the Cobb family who had owned the Caldicot Castle. Joseph Cobb's wife had links to the East India Company. 'Therefore, it is possible that this is where the Assamese lining was sourced,' she underlined.[10] Susan North, senior curator of Fashion at the Victoria and Albert Museum, highlighting the eastern roots of the Banyan at that event, emphasized on that kind of garment representing 'exoticism'.[11] Visual records specialist at the UK National Archives, Olivia Gecseg also rightly pointed out, 'Susan's explanation points us to the answer of the broader question of why a sacred textile is lining a banyan; that is, that the owner had no idea of the cloth's meaning. At the time of the banyan's production, probably sent to a tailor to be made up, the cloth had been detached from its cultural roots, thereby left open for appropriation into Western fashion.'[12]

A point of curiosity among that group of Western curators was: what was a scroll considered sacred in the Hindu context doing at a Buddhist monastery in Tibet? To my mind, the answer may perhaps be found if it is placed vis-à-vis the centuries-old practice of Bhutanese Buddhist monks visiting the Haigrib Madhab temple in Lower Assam. While the Hindus of Assam worship the idol at the temple rebuilt by Koch king Naranarayan as a reincarnation of Vishnu, the Buddhist monks continue to pray there as the burial ground of Buddha which some also believe to be that of the revered Buddhist monk Padmmasambhava. Such a belief exists in Tibet too, as highlighted elsewhere in the book. Vishnu, whose incarnation Krishna was depicted in the Assamese scrolls, was not so much outside of their devotional pale.

Ever since the news spread in Assam about Crill's discovery, there has been a steady demand from within the community on subsequent state governments to pressurize the Indian government to employ diplomatic channels to bring the prized artefact home. In mid-2020, Kanaksen Deka, well-known Assamese editor-commentator and a strong voice behind that popular demand, had told me about penning a letter to Prime Minister Narendra Modi during his first term with a suggestion that it be displayed at the podium of the United Nations where prized artefacts from several member countries are exhibited to represent their culture. 'There are none from India at the moment. Can his government not use diplomatic channels to display some bit of what I saw at the Victoria and Albert Museum in London at the UN podium as a proud insignia of India? Unfortunately, I didn't get any response from him,' Deka told me.[13]

In 2013, some unsuccessful private efforts were initiated to fetch the drape back home, temporarily, for a display. In mid-2019, the Sarbananda Sonowal-led Assam government said its cultural department was making efforts to move on those lines but no progress had been noted till mid-2023. It is here then the initiative taken by the monastic head of Dakhinpat Satra of Majuli becomes significant. The first of the splendidly woven piece that he had shown to me that winter day in 2020 behind closed doors was a replica of all the incarnations of Vishnu as depicted in *Gurucharit*, which was woven also as a part of the Brindabani Bastra. A group of fifteen weavers from the Lower Assam town of Sualkuchi, the present hub of Assam's weaving industry, had impressively shaped each motif with a palette of basic colours used in the original with a Muga and Eri base in a specially designed loom created by a young entrepreneur from Sivasagar in Upper Assam. Goswami told me a sum of ₹18 lakh was spent to ready that piece of textile.

The initiative to imitate the sacred cloth was formally flagged off in July 2019 at an event at the monastery; a committee of eminent citizens of the state led by the monastic head of Dakhinpat was formed to take the project forward. According to Mon Rajguru, the joint chief secretary of the committee then, the initiative had the backing of ten other Vaishnava monasteries.[14] The entire process was to be accomplished in about eighteen months costing around ₹60 lakh which was to be secured through public donation. The weaves were to be then displayed at the Kalakshetra in Guwahati. However, at the time of the writing of this book, the first piece had not yet reached its final destination due to the court case filed by Asom Satra Mahasabha to stall the project altogether. The argument given by Mahasabha president Jitendra Nath to media was, 'Making a copy of the Vastra would reduce the sanctity of the original and we will not accept it.'[15] Nath seemed to be oblivious to the existing museum pieces dating to the post-Sankardev era which signals towards the high possibility of a school of sacred weave that the singular effort of the saint might have triggered in medieval Assam. The effort by Dakhinpat may well lead to the revival of that lost heritage. In March 2021, noted Assamese actor Pranjal Saikia, executive president of the committee then, told me in Guwahati that soon after the state assembly elections wrapped up in the beginning of May that year, the committee would push for the display of the first replicated piece at the Kalakshetra. Though Saikia sounded hopeful about bringing around the Mahasabha members on the issue, till date there is no sign of any such tapestry at the Kalakshetra.[16]

As pointed out by Crill, the guxain kapur of many sizes in white and red continue to adorn the sanctum of the Vaishnava prayer halls. In other Hindu temples across Assam, there is also the use of another sacred cloth, the Sandrataap, in the same hues.

The tradition of sacred weave exists among Assam's tribal population too. In the Bodh Vihar at Upper Assam's Nam Phake village populated by the Tai Phake tribe, a living example of it can be sighted. Dozens of woven sacred wall hangings called tong-khowan, hang inside the premises in a riot of colours. The tribe also weaves a decorative cloth, Phachanglong, used for the initiation ceremony Charman to declare someone a monk besides weaving a handkerchief, pha-chet, offered to a man when he becomes a monk. There is yet another sacred weave of the tribe, Chankandra, comprising seven squares with religious significance commonly used in the community's annual festival Poi-kithing. 'It is the tradition that on the day before the festival, the womenfolk of the village assemble either in the (Buddha) Vihar compound or in the village headman's house and weave this symbolic cloth in the course of a single night. The cloth is offered at the Vihar in the early morning of the festival day,' highlights Labanya Mazumdar in *Textile Traditions of Assam: An Empirical Study*.[17] There is also a unisex garment in that community, pha-mai, essentially a shoulder cloth used by the adults when entering a Bodh Vihar.[18] That the villagers believe that it is the best gift that they can offer to Buddha also indicates that weaving is a skill that the community has long considered to be among its best abilities.

A mention may also be made here of a piece from the Assamese weaving traditions, the Anakata, which also has ceremonial use. The strands of the yarns at both ends of the piece, after it is woven, remain uncut and therefore its name Anakata (uncut). On completion, it is taken out of the loom by loosening the knots. Anakata is used in weddings, funerals, first pregnancies, the head tonsure ceremony of a child, sacred thread ceremony of a Brahmin boy, etc. 'Anakata is woven only in the months of Kati, Puh and Sott and the weavers avoid weaving it on a Tuesday and a Sunday,' highlights writer Nagen Saikia. The practice of slipping out a woven fabric from the reed of the loom exists only in Assam.[19]

GAMUSA, ERPOB, ARONAI, POHO, PAJAR....

A piece of weave closely related to the guxain kapur in Assam is the Assamese trademark red and white gamusa. In the absence of a sacred weave, gamusa is a standby as it is also a cloth offered to someone as a mark of respect. It is also a symbol of love, at times woven by a woman for her beau, to particularly wear as a headgear or around the waist or the neck including during the annual spring festival Rongali Bihu to usher in the Assamese New Year.

Gamusa is also worn in other colours; Assamese Koch-Rajbonshis wore a bright green and yellow gamusa. The equivalent of the multi-hued gamusa is prevalent among all tribes of Assam. Say, the fali of the Bodo-Kacharis; rikong and poho of the Karbis; risa rimai of the Dimasas; aronai of the Bodos; pajar of the Rabhas; and the dumer and erpob of the Mising tribe. Mising girls use dumer also as a wrap around their chest.[20] The Deori boche has close similarities to the red and white gamusa.

Since the late 1990s-early 2000s, the traditional pride attached to wearing these scarves has become interlinked with the assertion of each social group's ethnic political identity. Today, no cultural or political meeting in Assam is complete without the use of the gamusa. 'Gamocha (Gamusa) of suitable size is now hoisted as a ceremonial flag during community Bihu celebrations in the plains of Assam. These indicate the increasing use of Gamocha as an item of ethnic cultural identity in the case of plains Assamese. The place of golaban (Arnai) among the Bodo Kacharis and Fali among the Rabhas are comparable to that of Gamocha in plains Assamese culture. These textile items, though used as mere comforters, have increasingly acquired distinct cultural connotations among the groups.'[21] In 2013, an effort to weave a silk Gamusa by twelve weavers from Jorhat in Upper Assam—interspersed with motifs of Majuli, the one-horned rhino, and imminent personalities of the community like Bhupen Hazarika—made it to the Guinness World Records as the longest handmade scarf in the world, a moment of immense pride for the community.

The wider Assamese community also has a tradition of weaving kerchiefs. One such kerchief, the hasoti, said to be the result of the influence of the Bhuyan social group within the Assamese community, is generally the last piece to come off a loom. Its traditional use has been to wrap cut pieces of areca nut and betel vines to be carried on a trip. The traditional handkerchief of the Rabhas, the fali, is yet another example, woven with care by women who add their choicest traditional designs, and gift it to someone as a token of life-long friendship, love, and respect.[22]

WAR WEAVES

The wider Assamese community also have traditional weaves predominantly meant for war time use, mostly worn by men as a talisman to return home victorious. In this category of weaves is a particular type of gamusa called the tongali, and the kavach kapur. Tongali is traditionally given by a mother/wife to the son/husband before the latter ventures out for war. 'It was believed that this piece of cloth, where every thread is charged with potent love of a mother or a wife, would protect the son or the husband from dangers in the battlefield.'[23] According to author Sarbeswar Rajguru, the custom of tying a Tongali by the women on the men heading to war had crept into Ahom society from the Bhuyans. The Ahoms, he notes, borrowed yet another piece of clothing, Bachowal, a waist cloth, from the Bhuyans. In the Assamese weaving traditions, the kavach kapur is also offered by the wife to her husband as a protective armour against death in a battlefield. A wife would weave that piece the night before her husband went to battle.

That such textiles were a part of the weaving heritage of the tribes too only points at a rich culture of war weaves that had thrived across bor Axom or the wider Assamese community. Among the Bodo–Kacharis, men heading to a battle used the loin cloth fali with a round floral motif called derhachar-agar (derha means success). The Dimasas too had the belief that wearing a particular weave would help them return victorious from war. Khadom, the war shield, was made of cotton and padded with stitches running over it.[24]

Among some Assamese, there exists a theory surrounding a motif, mokordoma phul, rung around a belief that those who wear an attire with the design, or carry a kerchief with that weave, will win any battle in the court room.

MOTIFS, DYES, AND LOOMS

Not just in Assam, but across the Northeast, each social group has a particular motif/set of motifs that are used in their looms as a marker of their distinctiveness. However, since the inspiration for the designs were often drawn from one's surroundings, certain commonalities of shape and subjects exist across the board. This is why it can be safely said that the typical designs that one spots in Assam's weaves have local flora and fauna besides being geometric and structural. In the floral variety, there are the classic gos (tree or plant), the lota (creeper), ful (flower), and paat (leaves) motifs besides use of local flowers like bokul, nahor, champa, podum, gulap, gutimala, babori, etc. 'Aou-phul (flower of Dillenia indica) is found to occupy a vital place in the textile design of Assam, especially in the textiles of Bodo-Kacharis, Deoris, Karbis and plains Assamese. It is named Thagir-bibar, Chapa-eba, Plim-plum and Aou-phul by the Bodo-Kacharis, Deoris, Karbis and plains Assamese respectively.'[25]

Flowers in geometric forms, called buta, is a common medium to fill up the mid-section of a traditional sador/mekhela, or to accentuate their borders. Lotus and rose are, however, traditionally not used in a lower garment as these motifs are also woven in the sacred fabric (guxain kapur). Local herbs like the dhekia and tengeci, and fruits like pomegranate, pineapple, bitter gourd, etc. and a design from betel leaf (paan-kota) are common weaving motifs.[26] The adaptions from the natural settings of the state into the textile traditions by the weavers only highlights that their primary sources of inspiration were always their immediate surroundings.

Yet another design that is often spotted in Assamese textile, particularly in silk, is the kolka (paisley), probably borrowed from the Gomcheng and Kingkhap silks imported from China during the later Ahom rule.[27]

Among animal motifs, the oft-found designs in Assamese textile are that of butterfly, fish, duck, swan, elephant, peacock, tiger, also rhino lately in a motif featuring the tiger, deer, and the rhino, collectively called Kaziranga design after Assam's famous national park. The butterfly motif is a particular presence across tribal and non-tribal textiles of Assam; so is the lion. In tribal motifs, designs in the shape of horse, deer, pug marks of a cat, etc. are common. 'The human figure in a highly stylized form used singly or as a man riding a horse or an elephant appears frequently in the textiles of the Bodo-Kacharis, Rabhas and Karbis.'[28]

Geometric designs run through both tribal and non-tribal weaves. The Mising gha-yamik is a diamond-shaped geometric design central to the community's weaving traditions. A geometric design representing the eye is present in tribal and non-tribal weaving traditions of Assam. Pharao magon (pigeon's eye) and daoral mokhrep (peacock's eye) are examples of such design found among the Bodo–Kacharis. 'The same design is known among the Karbis as Poho-amang, denoting an eye. It is called Guna-phutuki by the plains Assamese. The term literally means "gold dots". Another design having a diamond within a diamond with a dot in the centre is named Daotho gogo by the Bodo-Kacharis. It symbolises the pattern made by feathers in the neck of a dove.'[29]

The geometric designs also include river currents and its course (Dharphul, Nadirpak, Chikadara par) and hills, besides the weavers replicating the traditional Assamese ornaments like the gaam-kharu and the golpata.[30] Kania-phul, woven with colourful threads, is an interesting theme regularly found in the traditional black Mising mekhela sador with colourful weaves, the play of hues inspired by sparkling stars on a dark night sky.

A common form of textile ornamentation, kech, also called dobua, was probably adopted from tribal designs done on loin loom. Interestingly, among the tribes, some designs have drawn their names from either those weavers who revived them or had created them. For instance, the geometrical design Ramdial kothali eba among the Deoris, had been named so after the cloth traders of Ramdia area of Kamrup (rural) district who used to bring Muga yarn to the Deori villages. So is the popular Bandhuram agar among the Bodo-Kacharis named after a weaver who revived the traditional weave. There are also weaves named after a person, say the Daoki agar, Bireswari eba, etc.[31]

There are also structural designs frequently found in Assamese textiles, mostly in non-tribal weaves, both in cotton and silk, say, the xorai, japi, saki (lamp), ghoti (pot), dhupdani (incense stand), Bhagawat (the holy book). The typical thai-phake weave can be identified from the marked plain lines criss-crossing horizontally and vertically, creating a set of checks and stripes.

Among Assamese weavers across social groups, there is typically a custom of preserving traditional designs for the next generation. The tribes often do so through a collection of old scraps of cloth which serves as a design catalogue of sorts.[32] Among the plains Assamese, the motifs were drawn on banana and palm leaves before paper took over. A common method of preserving the designs for a long period of time in Assamese society is also through ghai or kathi saneki wherein designs woven with coarse yarn and thin bamboo sticks are inserted through the weaves to preserve the steps taken by a weaver to arrive at the motif.[33] However, such traditions are gradually disappearing with the advent of computers, particularly in Sualkuchi where jacquard machines with pre-fitted design cards are attached to the traditional looms these days.

Like weaving in Assam has largely been practised by people of all castes and tribes, so is the case with the dyeing of yarns. Dyes have typically been prepared with things drawn from nature, like in any other culture engaged in weaving. Assamese weavers, since olden times, have extracted the colour red from the roots of achugach (*Morinda augustifolia*), chopped into bits and boiled in water along with the bark of the local leteku fruit and the leaves of bhoomlati plant (*Symplocos spicata*). Lac too was used to colour the yarn red. 'Dying of Eri silk in lac dye was very common, especially among the Karbis till very recent years. Leaves of an indigenous plant Tamchir were boiled in the dye solution as mordant.'[34] Similarly, the jackfruit tree, turmeric, and jorot shrub were used to derive the yellow hue; stalks and leaves of rum plant for indigo; the bark of xilikha (*Terminalia chebula*), jamun, amla (Indian gooseberry) for the colour black; the root of the madar tree for reddish-orange; xewali flowers for orange too, etc. were some of the common plant sources used to colour the yarn. However, like in any weaving tradition, the easy availability of factory dyed yarn has slowly steered the traditional techniques out of practice.

When it comes to looms in Assam, the traditional ones are essentially divided into hills and plains kinds. The hill tribes uniformly use the loin loom while the plains people use the throw shuttle variety. In commercial ventures, say, in Sualkuchi, the fly-shuttle looms are in vogue. In Upper Assam, however, weavers generally believe that the throw-shuttle ones produce more durable fabric.[35]

The advantage of a loin loom is that it comes without a permanent frame and, therefore, has greater portability with the convenience to erect and dismantle it at will. Mazumdar appropriately underlines, 'The compact texture of the cloth woven in a loin loom and its intricate designs are the most important factors for which the loin-loom has still not lost its popularity.'[36] The loom is kept steady by tying a belt around the weaver's waist while in a sitting position. Like the loin loom, the material used to construct a throw shuttle loom and also the range of accessories used for weaving, are bamboo and wood, resources most easily procurable for rural folks.

In 2014, an entrepreneur in the state's Sivasagar district brought out a new programmed machine, Maina Automatic, to use which the weaver must be in a standing position.[37]

PAAT SILK AND SUALKUCHI

An important silk in Assamese weaving traditions is Paat. The silk is an absolute must for a wedding trousseau. An Assamese bride, particularly a non-tribal, is wedded in a Paat mekhela sador, traditionally in white and gold which is gradually being replaced by a choice of sunny colours. Since the silkworm (*Bombyx mori*) from which the yarn is produced feeds on mulberry trees, Paat is also called mulberry silk. 'The Mulberry silk industry in Assam is pretty ancient. The climatic condition of Assam is favourable for mulberry culture.'[38] Lately though, the Paat silk produced in the rural belts of Assam is insufficient to meet the high demand for mekhela sador in the local market; the breast cloth riha required in weddings (called augron in Lower Assam); shirts, dhotis, and gamusa worn in ceremonies, etc., leading the weavers to procure the yarn more and more from Karnataka. Even the guna, the golden thread used to weave the motifs in Paat mekhela sador, is imported from Surat and Varanasi these days. For some decades now, this has been the new normal at Sualkuchi village in Lower Assam, the epicentre of the Assamese Paat industry.

Located about 35 kilometres from Guwahati, Sualkuchi has over 17,000 looms that are predominantly engaged in weaving Paat silk, though other Assamese silks and cotton weaves are created here too. Several stories abound in Assam about the possible birth of this iconic weavers' cluster. While some claim that a clasp of weavers from Tantikuchi area in Barpeta were shifted to Sualkuchi around the eleventh century, some others say that fifty weaver families were settled there during Ahom king Pratap Singha's reign in mid-seventeenth century to produce silk for export to the Mughal kingdom.[39] During the reign of that Ahom king, Assamese weaving tradition, pushed to become self-reliant, had received a massive boost. The king's prime minister Momai Tamuli Barbaruah had ordered women across the kingdom to engage in weaving; their daily produce was monitored. Mazumdar points out that while no caste bias in weaving and silk rearing is observed in Assam—perhaps because of interventions like the one carried out during Pratap Singha's reign—yet the mulberry silk culture was originally practised by a caste known as Jugi or Katoni. 'However, that caste-based specialisation has almost disappeared now-a-days.'[40]

In Majumdar's descriptive book, what one comes across is a mantra (hymn) used by silkworm rearers. 'According to this, Lord Shiva gave a species of silkworm to a man of (the) Kachari tribe (of Assam). Based on this, it can be said that the art of sericulture and weaving was introduced into Assam by the Kacharis, when part of Assam was ruled by them during the pre-Ahom period. But very little is known about the handloom weaving prior to Ahom rule.'[41] Even today, the majority of professional weavers that one comes across in Sualkuchi are of Bodo–Kachari origin.

At Sualkuchi, the rich history of Assamese weaving is remembered in the present, with the gateway to the town announcing the famous words spoken by Mahatma Gandhi during his visit to Assam in 1946: 'Assamese women weave dreams on their looms.' The arterial road that passes through the town is lined with showrooms that sell the two-piece traditional ensemble, the silk mekhela sador, in vibrant colours straight from the weavers.

When I last visited Sualkuchi, it was two months after the Covid-19 induced national lockdown had been lifted by the government. The weavers and the silk traders were, perhaps for the first time, in the same space complaining about lack of cash at hand to stay put in the business. Bipul Saharia who runs a home-based cottage 'factory' with fifty looms in Sualkuchi told me about spotting weavers begging on the streets during the lockdown seeking monetary help from fellow residents. 'There was no sale then; the shops were shut; most mahajan (traders and storeowners) were not forthcoming in helping the weavers. Several weavers from the size of factories like mine had to be thrown out of job, they came to the streets overnight; I had never seen such a sight in Sualkuchi.'[42]

Saharia is one among several in Sulakuchi to cater to high-end boutiques in Guwahati but also supplies mekhela sador to a few showrooms in Sualkuchi. He called his factory 'kheti' (farming land). 'We have nothing else in Sualkuchi, this is our kheti; if this gets affected, not just factory owners like us and the weavers but the showroom suppliers too will be affected. The entire supply chain can be affected in no time; the lockdown had proved it.'[43] His 'kheti', like several other such home-based weaving establishments across Sualkuchi, is typically dependent on weavers from the Bodo, Rabha, and Mising communities. The front yard of his house, like so many others across Sualkuchi, is lined with modest living quarters to house the resident weavers; a cook is hired to prepare food for the weavers. Each weaver is assigned a loom; they begin weaving at 9 a.m. and end the day at 5 p.m. with an hour-long lunch break in between. 'They go home only during festivals,' said forty-year-old Saharia, who too came to Sualkuchi in his childhood to learn weaving and never returned to his home in Mangaldoi area of Darrang district.

For each woven set, a weaver engaged at a high-end factory in Sualkuchi earns a payment upwards of ₹4,000; it usually takes about a week's time to produce an outfit. Factory owners like Saharia purchase the silk threads in bulk directly from suppliers in Karnataka, Varanasi, and Surat. 'The Guna ranges from ₹200 to ₹2500; the better its quality, the more lasting the piece,' added Saharia. A front room of his house stocks the finished sets. 'I try not to make the same piece; it helps to keep the price high with a sense of exclusivity of colour combination and design.' This is a common trick followed by several weavers in Sualkuchi.

True to his words, each set of sador mekhela at his factory costs upwards of ₹15,000. 'There is profit in the business provided we don't face competition from fake goods that are increasingly flooding the market in Assam from Varanasi and elsewhere,' he said.

Saharia recalled for me that in 2013, Sualkuchi had erupted in violence with weavers and smaller factory owners clashing with state police during a protest opposing the sale of mekhela sador made in Varanasi, passed off as Assamese Paat sets woven in Sualkuchi. Such a strong reaction from those dependent on the weaving industry was because several stores in Sualkuchi itself had begun stocking such Varanasi-produced wares to reap greater profits. Mrigen Kalita, a fourth-generation weaver of Sualkuchi, had then told *Indian Express*, 'Once the market is flooded with duplicate Assam silk, where will we go? This is a traditional industry that provides livelihood to about 25,000 people in Sualkuchi and to over 50,000 people across the state. We will all simply get wiped out.'[44] Naren Barman, a small-time trader in the town, pointed out to me that the weavers are worried also because the Varanasi-made sets not only have the Assamese traditional motifs, making it very difficult for customers to differentiate the original from the fake, but are also using online platforms like Amazon to sell their wares.[45] Only if a customer places an order for a set at a Sualkuchi factory with personalized colour combination and motifs can they ensure that they have bought original Sualkuchi silk, he said.

Barman, for the last five years, has been supplying such sets to boutiques and 'direct from Sualkuchi' shops in Upper Assam 'to ensure that buyers pick the original stuff'.

Two months after that three-day March 2013 protest at Sualkuchi, a non-profit named Sualkuchi Tanti Silpi Unnayan Samiti, was formed to combat the prevalence of cheap imitations woven using power looms set up outside the state. In September 2013, the Samiti applied for an official trademark for products produced in Sualkuchi. With support from Silk Mark Organisation of India, a testing lab was set up in 2015 at Sualkuchi. In 2016, the trademark earned the seal of approval from the central government and yet it took over two years for it to be officially inaugurated. The Samiti, in the interim, conducted surveys to collate the number of looms, their types and the products they create in Sualkuchi that could be granted the Silk Mark tag; the process began from June 2018. Kalita and fellow members are fighting for a Geographical Identification (GI) tag for the Assamese bridal paator sador mekhela. 'If we achieve that, Sualkuchi will live on,' Kalita had told the newspaper then.[46]

MUGA SILK

Some distance away from the market in Sualkuchi is the Naktadol area where lies the home-based weaving establishment of Punnu Mahajan. He is a veteran loom owner in the town, particularly known for weaving Muga silk only.

Muga is a silk exclusive to Assam, the priciest of the three silk varieties traditionally used in Assamese weave, the other two being Paat and Eri. The Muga silkworm (*Antheraea assamensis*) is reared mainly in Upper Assam, though some areas in Lower Assam too rear them, mainly on the Sualu trees. In Upper Assam, the common tree used for the rearing of the worm is the som tree. Once, the Mariani area in Jorhat district was the principal producer of Muga cocoons. The cocoon typically develops a colour depending on the leaves of the host tree that the silkworm munches on—from golden yellow to a faint brown. For instance, if the silkworm feeds on mejankari leaves, it will produce the fine golden yellow Muga silk, one of the varieties most prized by the Ahom royalties. A glossy white yarn is produced from the silkworms that feed on the pan-chapa leaves. The mejankari and chapa varieties were considered the luxury silks and could only be worn by the royals during the Ahom rule.

In 2007, after a protracted battle, the Muga silk of Assam bagged the GI tag but it took another seven years to get an exclusive logo to be issued to the producers to put on the products to highlight their origin. When asked about the delay, Punnu Mahajan seemed resigned to the slow approach of the authorities to also help factory owners like him find a national and international market even after their products had bagged a coveted GI tag. 'Officials keep coming to my factory; sometimes from the local authorities, sometimes from the state's cultural department but except for the promise, we have not received anything so far,' said the seventy-year-old in 2022.[47]

A kilogram of Muga thread costs upwards of ₹20,000, thus making a set of Muga sador mekhela an expensive buy and yet, in every Assamese wedding, gifting the bride at least one such set is customary—thus indicating the existence of a sizeable market within the state itself. 'An authentic piece with elaborate design can set you back by ₹40,000,' Punnu Mahajan told me.

For some years now, a major constraint for people like him has been to find enough thread to keep the looms busy all year round. When I first visited him towards the end of 2020, half of them were not operational. 'We are waiting for thread; its supply has also been affected by the Covid-19 lockdown.' While the Muga worm is reared only in certain districts, mainly in Upper Assam, he felt the government can create more such rearing clusters and ready a blueprint, linking the supply of threads to factories like the one he runs and a ready market. Those in the Muga business at Sualkuchi are on the same page with Punnu Mahajan on the matter. 'We as factory owners are keeping the tradition alive; our products, say, from readying the design onwards, are only handmade but the government is failing to give us an adequate market to retail them with the required respect for a handmade product. We only have the domestic market so far and with scarce supply of the thread, we can't give the authentic product at a low price. No wonder then, you will find several weavers mixing Tassar silk with the Muga thread sometimes to lower the price of a mekhela sador set or at times selling Tassar as Muga too to some unsuspecting customers. Ultimately, it harms a product that we as a community, for generations, have been proud of and fought hard to get the GI,' Punnu Mahajan rued.

True to his claim, on the verandah of his house, his employee and a local artist, Haren Das, was busy drawing a pattern on tracing paper. 'In the age of creating designs on computer, I still follow the old method,' Das told me with a trace of pride. 'Not that we are opposed to modernity but I am scared of my designs getting stolen if I draw on a computer. If that happens, what will be the exclusivity of our factory?'[48]

ERI SILK

Yet another silk that is central to Assamese weaving traditions, particularly among the tribes, is the Eri. Mazumdar calls this coarse durable yarn the silk of the poor. Pointing at an Assamese proverb to strengthen her argument, she writes, 'The status for Eri clothes in the folk life of Assam can be gauged from an old Assamese proverb, "Doir pani, Erir kani", which implies that while curd (doi) cools, the Eri clothes (kani) warms up a person.'[49] The silk has iso-thermic qualities, meaning it will feel cool in summer and warm in winter. That Eri-culture is widely practised by the tribes also indicates that the precious Eri sador or Eri shawl of the Assamese community may likely be a tribal input to the shared textile heritage of the larger Assamese society.

Once, the Karbi villages of Assam were the largest producers of Eri cocoons. Today, even though the price of a kilo of Eri silk yarn is at least ₹5,000 in the local market, most villagers engaged in Eri-culture in the Karbi Anglong district don't get to make that money as they tend to sell the cocoons at a nominal rate to wholesale traders. Thus, not only are they gradually losing their traditional skill of spinning the yarn from the ripe cocoon but are also not able to pocket the exact profit from such farming.

The cocoons to produce the silk are collected without taking the life of the worm, which is why Eri is also called Ahimsa silk. Since the silkworm feeds on Era gos (castor oil plant), it is called Eri. It is reared in some other parts of the Northeast and in other states too. It is also called Endi or Erandi (Erandi too means castor). Since the worm leaves the cocoon, one side of it—unlike the Muga and the Paat cocoons—is open, and the silk doesn't become an unbroken strand. 'Hence the Eri silk is spun, not reeled.'[50]

Most of the Mising tribe's traditional woven clothings—the ege (the lower part of a female garment that falls till the ankle, traditionally black); the ribi-gacheng featuring a design called yapapacha (also worn by men as a turban or dhoti); the gero, a shawl worn over the ege by a married woman; or the mibu-galuk sleeveless jacket (worn by men); dumer or jinrek (a girdle tied around a mibi-galuk to complete the traditional Mising man's outfit)—are woven either with cotton harvested at home or with Eri. The Mising attire was aptly documented in Bhupen Hazarika's popular song 'Bulu O'Mising Dekati' (O the young Mising man). The song, highlighting the traditional black ege worn by women, had compared it to smearing darkness (endhar xanili) on the skirt. Today, however, like most traditional wear of tribes and plains Assamese, ege too is worn in other colours.

The Mising Eri sador or tapum-gachar, a unisex winter shawl, is also woven from hand-spun Eri. Eri shawl is a highly prized garment in Assamese society. A piece lasts a lifetime.

The Mising tribe is also known to grow cotton which is then spun by hand to produce the thread for weaving. These days though, the culture has more or less disappeared as weavers can easily procure readymade thread from the bazaar. The dying practice has, however, affected one of the most prized woven materials of the Mising community: the gadoo or the miri jim. A ribbed rug intricately woven by ginning and spinning cotton picked from one's backyard, it takes months to finish a piece. Home-spun cotton, painstakingly collected by the older Mising women are thrust through each woven rib of the rug. 'It is a pious hope of every Mising mother to be able to provide a gadoo to all the children when they get married.'[51] During the research for this book, Majuli resident Ajoy Doley, explained to me how times were changing. 'It is no more possible to grow cotton in such a large quantity. Most Misings in Majuli have lost land to the Brahmaputra. So, cotton is increasingly being replaced by plastic which is pushed through the woven ribs of a gadoo to make it warm in our villages.'[52]

Among the Rabhas, be it their riphan (also called lemphata), which is worn as a mekhela by a woman; or the kambung (the sador); or the women's headgear (traditionally worn only in black and maroon)' the angcha, khore, or the pajal worn by men; or the shawls alan or anay (worn by women), the base material is either cotton or Eri. Like the Misings, the Rabhas too make a quilt, nenthanen, using fine strips of old cloth.[53]

The Karbis, Dimasas, Tiwas, and the Bodos too use Eri and cotton more than Muga or Paat silk. The Karbi woven blanket rinjitho is made of handspun Eri. Pini, the Karbi female lower garment; pekok, the cloth worn over it, pecheleng, the ceremonial cloth; piba, the cloth used by married women to tie their babies around the waist, etc. come mostly in cotton or Eri. The woven traditional bag of the Karbis, jambeli, was made of Eri. Though not much in use now it was 'an important textile item of the Karbis'.[54] 'Besides the cotton and Eri, use of Muga and Paat (mulberry) silk for weaving Pekok (among the Karbis) is also marked in recent years particularly in the commercial production centres.'[55]

A typical Bodo–Kachari male dress, gangrachi, a lower body garment worn very much like a dhoti, is made of cotton too; so is the loin cloth fali or the tribe's neckwear aronai. The same is true for what the women wear, the elegant dokhona, and the woven stole, jomgra, worn over a dokhona. They typically use the Eri shawl too, the chimachi, made of cotton.

Kasong, the female lower garment of the Tiwa plains tribe; an elaborately woven upper garment for women, the phaskai; the men's jacket thagla; the neckwear phaga—all come either woven in cotton or in Eri. A special cloth among the Tiwas is re-chokdo, made of Eri and used by men in ceremonies. Till some years ago, it was considered a lost part of the community's heritage. A Tiwa weaver, Lashti Mithi, took up the challenge to weave it from her childhood memory on being prodded by an Assam-based photo-historian Samir Choudhury. Yet another piece of weave that has nearly gone out of common use is the riphan chakkey of the Rabhas, an exquisite female garment made of cotton.

The Dimasas too wear an Eri shawl, rhithap. Most of their woven clothing come in either cotton or Eri including the women's wrapper rigu; risha, a common lower garment worn like a dhoti by men; rijamphan, the traditional female attire; the ramai or the rijamphan beren, wrapped around the chest for special occasions like weddings, and also put on married women before they are cremated; and the ceremonial rijhamphai gufu (required during birth and death rituals). One of the most exquisite pieces of woven material among the Dimasas is the multicoloured rikhu, an extremely time consuming and complex weave which showcases the rich weaving heritage of the Dimasas.

The Deori plains tribes too are no different when it comes to the use of yarn for their weaves. Interestingly, the traditional women's lower garment of the Deoris, the igu, when worn around the waist is pleated on one side, in the same manner as the non-tribal Assamese do with their mekhela. Like the non-tribal Assamese, the Deori elderly women use khania or seleng over the igu. 'It is pertinent to mention that Khania-kapur and Bar Kapur are typical textiles of the Upper Assam region. These are not commonly woven in Lower Assam homes,' emphasizes Mazumdar, which indicates that these may have been Deori contributions to the non-tribal Assamese weaves.[56] The similarity between the Deori and non-tribal Assamese wear can also be seen in the traditional colours of their clothing: red and white. The Deori boche, used by men, has close similarities with that of the Assamese red and white gamusa.

ROYAL INTERVENTION

While for male members of the tribes, the common lower garment is a wraparound that doesn't go below the knee, among the non-tribal Assamese, the common counterpart is the dhoti or suria, typically woven in white with a thin border. Assamese Muslims usually wear a woven lungi in the form of a sarong but some also wear dhoti. The dhoti is colourful when it comes to groups like the Koch Rajbonshis. With the colonial influence encompassing Dimasa for some centuries now, there is rarely an Assamese man today though who has not begun wearing trousers—Assamese men began wearing trousers (ijar) from the late seventeenth century onwards. The Thengal Kacharis under the later Ahom rule particularly began to be called so because they wore the lower outfit with theng (legs) or trousers.

In the early eighteenth century, during the reign of Ahom king Rudra Singha, certain new dresses and accessories crept into Assamese society through royal clothing, particularly among men. For instance, there arose the trend of wearing a stitched upper garment, the sula. Though among the tribes, the female lower garment is still unstitched, the mekhela worn by non-tribal Assamese woman is a stitched garment today, a practice that stemmed from the royal households too at a later date.

During Rudra Singha's reign, the Ahom ministers were also handed over outfits that matched those of the Mughals: the pag, jama, and ijar.[57] The king himself wore them and the practice continued to be followed by the Ahom royalties since his time. His ministers had initially returned those outfits saying that they won't wear outfits worn by foreigners. 'The king had to send again the country-made dresses to the ministers.'[58] The initial resistance to wearing clothes brought from outside was recorded in the sixteenth century too. Koch king Naranarayan had presented to the Ahom king a few pieces of sari which were returned as the Ahom women wore only mekhela sador and riha then.

Before the Mughal-style pag and paguri crept into Ahom attire in the seventeenth century, kings wore a very simple turban called phachau. The trend of wearing the pag caught on later; bridegrooms too adopted it. 'The Sutradhar (narrator) of the Bhaona (Vaishnava devotional plays) performances and the members of the band of singers and players of instruments (accompanying the performances), called the Gayan-bayan, put on this Jama, in some parts of Assam.'[59] The Ahom soldiers also began wearing the tupi (cap) later. Soldiers wrapped their body either with a Muga or an Eri woven cloth called gati too. After coming in contact with the East India Company in the early nineteenth century, Ahoms introduced trousers as a uniform for their army. The informal army was organized as a formal one by introducing the uniform; each solider was also given a bag. The tradition of wearing leather shoes—paijar—also began in Assamese society towards the later part of Ahom rule. The shoes were made by

Bengali shoemakers and initially worn only by the kings. The Brahmins and the Mahantas were allowed to wear khorom or their wooden sandals only at home. The commoners mostly went about barefoot.

The old trade relations between Assam and Tibet, Bhutan, and China also ensured that not just certain silk varieties but also textile for winter was imported regularly, principally for royal use like the Banat from Bhutan or the Thanga, used for sitting on the floor. The variety of silk imported from those countries included the Gom-cheng, a fine Chinese silk used by the Ahom royals to make an upper garment. This exquisite silk with a black base had floral designs like on the body of a snake called gom, giving it its name. There were other such silks in use, such as the Pamari and the Lahari; also Toss (Tassar). But the Gom-cheng, and also the Kingkhap silk mentioned earlier in the chapter, were the most popular among the Ahom royals. 'The word Kingkhap is said to have derived from the Chinese word *Kumkhwab* meaning "less sleep". The irritation caused by gold and silver threads while wearing Kingkhap could indeed impair sleep. The root of the term could also lie in the anxieties the wearer had due to fear of losing such precious cloth.'[60]

With the advent of the British and the fall of the Ahom kingdom in the early nineteenth century, the supply of Kingkhap and Gom-cheng dried up but the Assamese community's longing for the textile has remained.

ASSAMESE JEWELLERY

On the arterial Gopinath Bordoloi Road in Guwahati stands Zangphai. A billboard displaying models decked in Assamese jewellery announces to passers-by the wares that Zangphai retails. Even on a winter evening, customers can be seen striding through the glass push-door of the showroom.

Inside, the owner, Lakhimi Baruah Bhuyan, is at her busiest. Aided by a group of saleswomen, Baruah explains to each client what a specific cut of the ornament is called in Assamese and how best to pair it with a particular tint of a mekhela sador ensemble. Among the customers is a bride-to-be; she can't seem to zero in on any of the readymade sets on display. 'Choose the bits that you like from among these designs and I will put them together for you in a few days' time,' assures Baruah. Soon the design is locked and a date fixed for delivery.

Baruah, flaunting a pair of traditional Assamese Thuriya earrings with sparkling black stones—a Zangphai product—turns to me to comment,

'Some young women sometimes want slightly different touches within the traditional designs these days. Axomiya gohona (Assamese jewellery) has so many motifs; various combinations are possible.'[61]

Baruah should know. Her father, late Pranab Baruah, a well-known Assamese oil artist, had worked among the xunar (goldsmiths) of Rontholi village near his home town Nagaon in middle Assam. He had also tweaked the traditional designs to suit the individuality of women, including his daughter. Lakhimi Baruah not only wore those designs with mekhela sador during her growing-up days but also inculcated her father's sense of aesthetics to begin mixing and matching certain smaller pieces with modern outfits. That was in the late 1980s.

'I stood out then. Because, thirty-five or forty years ago, Assamese women preferred Bengali jewellery more than Axomiya gohona. In the weddings, a family would typically gift the bride an Axomiya gohona set just for the sake of tradition, but that's it.'

In the early 1990s, Baruah took her penchant for Axomiya gohona one step further to open a showroom attached to her residence in Guwahati; Zangphai became the first retail outlet for Assamese jewellery in the state, certainly a novelty as till then customers needed to visit a jeweller's village to place an order, and wait for months to get a finished product.

ARRIVAL OF BENGALI JEWELLERS DURING THE COLONIAL ERA

The absence of pride in wearing Axomiya gohona could well be the fallout of a colonized community having found itself in a peculiar predicament in the beginning of the nineteenth century. The Burmese invasion and their subsequent plunder prior to the British takeover of Assam had turned the life of common Assamese upside down. People had to also endure the turbulent two years of the First Anglo-Burmese War (1824–26). Though the English chased away the Burmese from Assam, what followed was nearly seven years of political ambiguity, followed by five more years of rule by the Ahom king Purandar Singha as the vassal of the British before Assam was permanently annexed to the Bengal Province in 1838. The weight of those decades of political uncertainty fractured the prevailing order in Assamese society beyond repair. The Ahom royals who promoted Assamese jewellery were no more in a position to do so. The years of war must have also snapped the supply chain of materials, like the precious stones that by then had gained considerable centrality in Axomiya gohona. All of a sudden, the nucleus of the state's economy under colonial rule also shifted to Calcutta; a new set of merchant class emerged with the arrival of the Marwaris from the West. The state was suddenly consigned to the fringe of a new geographical map. The fledgling industry must have found itself orphaned.

In 1905, British civil service officer F. C Henniker carried out a reconnaissance to check the commercial potential of Axomiya gohona, and published *The Gold and Silver Wares of Assam – A Monograph.* In it he noted: 'Assamese jewellery is by no means without merit.'[62] What he was wary of, though, was the fact that only 'a relatively few jewellers' were associated with the craft. It essentially meant lack of manpower to turn it into a trade on a large scale. The jewellery was never kept ready, and was made only on order. Prior to him, William Robinson, in his classic *Descriptive Account of Assam*, had stated that 'there is scarcely a river (in Assam) that does not yield more or less of this precious metal (gold).'[63] Henniker, however, stated that the yield of gold 'was always very small and the industry has practically died out.'[64]

Published in 1909, *The Gazetteer of Bengal and North East India*, was rather economical in praise of Assamese jewellery but noted that the 'artistic necklaces of gold filigree work are produced at Barpeta, and the enamelled lockets and ear ornaments of Jorhat are not unpleasing.'[65]

The subsequent move of the British administration not to patronize the local craft overlapped with Bengali jewellers spreading themselves across the Brahmaputra Valley. The Marwaris became the new gold suppliers from Calcutta.

The loss of British interest in Assamese jewellery might have also gradually instilled a sense of inferiority within the small gentry that existed among the native population. Additionally, penetration of the Bengali culture as more 'civilized' than the native culture, particularly in the fairly well-to-do Assamese non-tribal society in the early British period, could well have played a role in the growing patronage given to Bengali jewellery instead of Axomiya gohona. Gradually, there arose notions of Assamese jewellery's lack of shine and durability; they were considered to not be as long-lasting as Bengali jewellery.

In the process, what was missed, though, was the core feature of Assamese jewellery—its slight dulling with age. That dull look clashed with the mainland Indian understanding of gleaming, 'pure' gold. An inferiority complex developed within the colonized Assamese community about their gohona and continued to grip the larger consciousness much after Independence.

The exquisiteness of Assamese jewellery lies in the way it is arranged. It makes use of lah, lac, a softer substance, in good measure, to frame a piece before gold is added, unlike in Bengali jewellery. Lah was one of the major products that the foothill dwellers of Assam traded with the plains people before the arrival of the British. Produced by a tiny scale insect, it is not to be confused with lacquer.[66] Twenty-four carat gold manually placed on lac creates a soft, delicate piece of Axomiya gohona. Because of the use of lac, the pieces tend to be malleable at times, and can run the risk of chipping off with rough or constant use. In contrast, Bengali jewellery is firmer and can be worn on a daily basis. Some Assamese jewellery also has mina kora, delicate enamelled work, and prominently uses stones like bakhor (precious red stones), puwal moni (coral beads), panna (emerald), which means they need careful handling lest a stone or a precious bead falls off.

CHANGE OF MINDSET

In the late 1990s through the early 2000s, jewellery showrooms like Zangphai run by modern, educated women from well-known Assamese families played a role in making traditional jewellery enticing. A relationship of reliance also developed with customers with after-sales service in the showroom itself. 'Customers began to feel if anything goes wrong they can easily get it fixed; there is no need to go to the villages looking for a jeweller,' Lakhimi Baruah told me. The advent of Assamese cable television in that era also helped give a push to the wares. Additionally, to keep prices low, she eschewed using the 24 carat fare—the mainstay of the jewellers in Jorhat district of Upper Assam—and brought in more of silver jewellery dipped in gold (xun pani sotiua), created in the Barpeta jeweller cluster of Lower Assam, and gold plated silver wear (kesa xun), created in Rontholi village in Nagaon. 'I wanted to convey to customers then that tradition has an appeal of its own. You don't need to think of owning just one Assamese gold set in your lifetime because it is costly; buy as many as you want in silver base.'

Today, the revolution that Zangphai started in Guwahati three decades ago has tipped the scales, to a large extent, in favour of a dying cottage industry. A proof of it is not found only in a row of Assamese jewellery showrooms in and around Zangphai in Guwahati and elsewhere in the state but also in more and more Assamese women flaunting traditional jewellery in weddings and other social and cultural occasions. 'We have to preserve our culture but at the same time we are also an industry; more showrooms mean more work for our craftsmen; a large number of people will be employed because they now have a ready market,' Baruah emphasizes.

With time though, some old ornaments worn in Assamese society have disappeared; even the Zangphai on which Baruah had named her showroom. A traditional ear adornment, the front part of Zangphai is a round-shaped bokul flower with a melange of colourful stones placed on the petals, with a thick, stalk-like rear. In the olden times, it used to be worn by both men and women. One can spot a real pair of Zangphai Keru on display at the State Museum in Guwahati.

The Misings wore Zangphai in the form of Biri, a typical Assamese unisex jewellery design which has a voluminous body with two tapered ends. Though generally the inside of a Biri is filled with lac, the Mising chieftains used to fill it up with Jangphai, a luminous gum or amber extracted from fossilized trees. Jangphai is believed to have been easily available in the Mishimi hills of today's Arunachal Pradesh bordering Assam's Sadiya district on its eastern tip, towards the Indo-Tibet border. The earrings, Jangphai Kerus, are not too dissimilar from another Assamese earring, the Thuriya, which too traditionally had a thick cylindrical stem that needed to be passed through the ear hole. In my childhood, I have seen Thuriya worn only by the oldest women in rural areas, both tribal and non-tribal. Henniker's monograph, a valuable document on jewellery clusters in Assam and Sylhet divisions of British India in the early twentieth century, notes as many as seven types of Keru and Thuriya made only by the artisans of Jorhat district. He described Jangphai, as 'amber mounted with gold', a pair even then priced in the range of '₹24 to ₹120'.[67] He also mentions several other types of Thuriya made in Assam at the time including the practice amongst the Jorhat jewellers of crafting Karshipi Mina-kora Thuriya, 'embossed gold with blue, green or red and white enamel'; Nejpata Thuriya, 'set with stones on the portion behind the ear and sometimes at the back in which case they are (then) called Talpata Thuriya'; and the Sach (Xachh) variety, 'plain Thuriyas with stones only in the front.'[68]

The Thuriya that Lakhimi Baruah wears with black stones is the Xachh variety but is now better called Pes-diya Thuriya, as it has undergone an improvisation. Instead of a cylindrical single piece, a Thuriya these days is a two-piece ensemble customised to pass through the smaller ear holes of modern-day women.

In *Axomiya Manuhor Itihaax*, Nagen Saikia mentions that the thick-stemmed Jangphai Keru was once worn by common women.[69] If you glance at the traditional jewellery of the South and East Asian countries located beyond Assam, say, Myanmar, Tibet, Bhutan, etc., and the large holes in the ear lobes of local women, it only confirms this theory. Saikia also points at the strong influence of the ethnic groups of Assam in mainstream Assamese jewellery and particularly the use of red beads in a fashion similar to what women and men among the tribes that populate the region wear traditionally. 'You don't notice use of red beads in Bengali jewellery. Then, the designs like that of the Biri, Gejera, Keru and Thuriya have no similarity with that of North Indian or South Indian jewellery. Even though there is a practice of wearing thick jewellery among the tribes of Odisha, Bihar and Madhya Pradesh, they are not similar to these designs.'[70]

Among the wider Assamese community, the Tiwa ethnic group still wears the mainstream Assamese gohona designs, such as the Gal-pata, Bena, and Dhul-biri till date. They have their own names for the Gal-pata (Kolponda), which is made of strings with red, blue, or white small beads; the style could well be their gift to Axomiya gohona.[71] The male Tiwas, mainly the chieftains, also wore Mota-Moni with the red beads interspersed with beads made of gold. The Mota-Moni is now considered a mainstream Assamese design. The performers of the Assamese dance, Uja-Pali Nritya, also wore Mota-Moni.[72] The Tiwas also wear an earring with a name that sounds similar to Thuriya—the Khoriya. They also traditionally wore Kundal, another piece of typical Assamese male ornament. However, there were no jewellers among the hill Tiwas, and their oldest ornaments were those that they had brought with them from their earlier abode, the Khasi hills, now in Meghalaya.[73]

That the Bodo and Rabha women, like Assamese non-tribal women, wore the thick, five-layered Chandrahaar (moon-shaped necklace) only tempts me to say that the ornament being made also as a necklace in the Goalpara belt, which has a sizeable population from both the communities till date, could well be due to a demand in these communities. According to Henniker's monograph, the Chandrahaar that was made by the jeweller clusters in then Silchar, Hailakhandi, Karimganj, Dhubri, Barpeta, and Jorhat, which are in Assam, and also in the Habibganj area of Sylhet district, were worn only as a waist band, but the kinds made in Goalpara were also worn as a necklace.[74] Taking note of these admixtures, Saikia makes this significant observation: 'In the Brahmaputra Valley, a new form of jewellery birthed itself from an assimilation of mainland Indian and South-East Asian civilisation and cultures.'[75] The remark only echoes the unique position of Assam as the place of assimilation and integration of multiple sociocultural strands drawn from these two civilizations which is reflected in every aspect of Assamese material culture.

VARIETY AND MOTIFS IN ASSAMESE ORNAMENTS

Traditionally, aside from a range of Keru and Thuriya, Assamese jewellery also included ear adornments like Kaanphul, Koria, and Makori.[76] In *Medieval Assamese Society*, Sarbeswar Rajguru mentions Kanthasa and Karnaphul too besides adding, 'On the top of the ear, the women put on an ornament called Chai-Khale or Chaki-sala.'[77] Kaanphul were meant for young girls soon after their ear lobes were pierced as the hole would be small initially. In traditional Assamese society, the ear holes were made large by inserting a thin stick made of bamboo (khorika) or by a short dried stem (xukaan thari) chiselled out of a banana trunk. These sticks would be used to widen the hole after greasing the lobes with mustard oil.[78] The ear holes needed to be expanded to be able to wear the thick-stemmed Thuriya or Keru. In the past, Assamese men, particularly the royalty, like in several communities across India, also pierced their ears; they too wore Keru, as well as Kundal, another ear ornament. Karna-bhushan, Makara-kundal, Hangsa-kundal, Loka-paro, Karna-bala, Long-keru, etc. were some ear ornaments flaunted by the Ahom male royals. Besides arm bands and rings, men also wore a range of neck ornaments. 'The rings worn by the king and his ministers had a particular shape and significance. The kings mainly wore Bakhorua rings. The ministers too. (Ahom prime minister) Purnananda Borgohain dying by suicide after licking the diamond ring on his hand has been kept alive in Assamese loka-geet (folk songs).'[79]

While on their wrists men wore Gaam Kharu, in both gold and silver, some Assamese royals also turned the imperial stamp (muhor) into rings.[80] Henniker called this style of ring Chamchow and found the expertise to make these rings only among the artisans in Jorhat area.[81] Henniker also states that the Gaam Kharu was made by jewellers in the area from Kamrup onwards till Upper Assam which suggests that Mising community, whose artisans are credited for that particular piece of Axomiya gohona, were absent in Lower Assam at the time. Barpeta and Dhubri jewellers, however, also made a similar wrist ornament, Muthi Kharu, though it is difficult to say since when.

Saikia's significant book points out that while there is a sizeable range of jewellery for men, the exquisiteness of the craft was practised essentially to accentuate the beauty of a woman. The women's range, naturally, is exhaustive then. On the head, an aristocratic woman could wear a three-part Siti-pati or Xir-pota (xir in Assamese means the parting of the forehead) in gold and silver. The lotkon (front part) that typically falls on the forehead would be studded with red bakhor while the two other parts would be attached to either side of the head to make an inverted half-moon shape. Henniker mentioned that the jewellers in Jorhat and Lakhimpur called the ornament Kopali (Kopal means forehead in Assamese).[82] P. C. Choudhury in the *History of Civilisation of Assam* called the ornament 'Lalatika', as it is referred to in the Kalika Purana, 'worn on the forehead just below the hair by married women.'[83]

Axomiya gohona has a large selection of neckwear for women: Golpota (choker), Haar (necklace), Xaatxori, Bena, Dug dugi, Jun biri, Dhul biri, Thoria biri, Parosokua biri, Lota bakhorua biri, Mogormuri biri, Gejera, Thupa moni, Sipaat moni, Xilikha moni, Phuti moni, Chandrahaar, and Xun Puwalmoni or Mala moni, among others. Saikia, while describing how each piece differs from the other in design, also underlines, 'It must be observed that the necklaces of Assamese women don't fall below their chest. They are made keeping that in mind. Also, there is time and occasion to wear particular pieces.'[84] Assamese jewellery also has waist ornaments for women, like the Korodhoni, Kokali, and Ghagor.

The names given to particular rings, bangles, and necklaces are either due to their shape or for the motifs used in the designs. That the sense of aesthetics in Assamese jewellers has traditionally been stirred by nature is evidenced in the motifs. 'For example, the Jon-biri means an ornament made in the shape of the crescent moon; Silikha-Madali is an ornament made in the shape of the Silikha (Xilikha) fruit; Kathal-Kuhia Madali is an ornament made in the shape of the bud of the jack fruit tree; Jangphai-Keru is an earring made of amber; Jethi-Neguria-angothi is a ring made in the shape of the tail of a house lizard, etc.'[85]

Similarly, a Biri shaped like a dhul (local drum) is called Dhul-biri; Magar-muri Biri looks like the head of a crocodile; Babori phulia angothi is a ring that has been styled on the local herb Babori. Bakhorua Biri is called so because it uses red stones; in the traditional choker—Golpata—the flowers made in gold imitate the shape of either the xewali or gutimali flower. A Bena is moulded to look like a crescent moon. The Dug-dugi is styled after the leaf of a banyan tree. The hawk is a motif in the Xen-pota ring. So is the commonly used country boat in Gejera. Even the Chandrahaar is made with small motifs reflecting the crescent moon. The Paro-Sokua Biri or a Horin-Sokua Biri are shaped like the eyes of a pigeon, common in Assam, and that of a deer, respectively. If a lota, vine, is carved on the Biri, it becomes a Lota Biri. The beads in Sipaat moni look like the local fruit Kordoi. Lokaparo is a design made in the shape of a pair of pigeons. The Dhaan-sira design is a replica of a set of grains in a paddy plant. Podum-kolia and Maas-bokolia rings are inspired by a lotus in bloom, and the scales of a fish, respectively. Saikia has pointed out that the two flower motifs found in Axomiya gohona are the commonly grown bokul and podum. Even the process of manufacturing the gohona has traditionally made use of local elements like the bamboo, tengesi xaak, thekera tenga, jawan stone, and a bristle made of hog hair.

Ornaments like hair pins shaped like butterflies are commonly found among the traditional ornaments of the Karbi tribe and confirm that their jewellery motifs too have been drawn from nature. The top part of the Bodo ear ornament Khumani Khera (a Keru) also uses the common flower podum as a motif. The Bodos have a pair of traditional earrings shaped like a wooden sandal (Khorom Pula). A significant motif that had crept into Assamese jewellery in the 1980s—the period of students' agitation against undocumented foreigners in Assam—is the traditional headgear Japi, a representation of Assamese ethnic distinctiveness. Japi is a cultural article of a Bihu stage; the folk dance has been a custodian of Axomiya gohona for a long span of time. The get-up of a Bihu dancer is incomplete without Assamese ornaments.

The adornment for the feet in Assamese jewellery includes Kharu, Pa-jup, and Ujaanti—all crafted in silver. That they are traditionally made using silver could be because there were restrictions on wearing gold ornaments below the waist in olden Assam and silver above the neck, as mentioned in Kalika Purana.[86] Describing the ankle pieces used traditionally, Saikia writes, 'Though Assamese women have no history of wearing toe rings, one does find references to a toe ornament Ujaanti at some places. Apparently, this ornament, if worn, could save the wearer from certain diseases.'[87] Though it is rare to find Assamese women wearing nose rings, the practice had crept in from mainland India but began to wear off in later times.

HISTORICAL TRAJECTORY OF ASSAMESE JEWELLERY

There exist two Ahom-era surnames among the Assamese—the Xun-uwal (Sonowal) and the Rupuwal—their names essentially signify that they were gold and silver diggers respectively. The Sonowals, residing by the rivers Subansiri and Sankosh (Swarna-Kosh), were proficient in sieving gold dust from the waters. While the Subansiri drifts in from the Tibetan plateau, Sankosh flows into Assam from Bhutan; both empty into the Brahmaputra in Upper Assam, where one finds clusters of the Sonowal community till date. Rupuwals either were silver diggers or dealt with the metal during the Ahom era. Saikia underlines that the existence of these two surnames only point at the common use and abundance of gold and silver in the region. He refers to William Robinson's *A Descriptive Account of Assam* and W. W. Hunter's *Statistical Account of Assam* to note the availability of silver locally, and also to Kanak Lal Barua's allusion to Bhattasvamin, referring to existence of silver in Goalpara.[88] Interestingly, if you look at Henniker's monograph, jewellers in the Assam region are said to procure gold from the Keya, or the Marwari community, during the colonial period. This indicates a huge shift in the pattern of procuring the basic raw material in a colonized land. Till date, it is the 'Khans' from Rajasthan who settled in British Assam that supply the Assamese jewellers the enamel (mina) and the plastic (semi-precious) stones which are now a replacement for the precious stones once imported from Burma and other Asian nations.

Nevertheless, the gold dusting trade of the Sonowal community suggests that old Assam had a repository of that yellow metal. While Saikia takes recourse to Kautilya's description of Pragjyotishpur/Kamarupa as Xubarna-kunda (Swarnakunda) in *Arthasashtra* to state that it was indeed a thin strip of land where the precious metal could be found easily, Birinchi Kumar Baruahh, in *A Cultural History of Assam,* lists an array of forty ornaments that were worn in the region as cited in Kalika Purana.[89] That Hiuen Tsang spoke about Kamrup king Kumar Bhaskarvarman (600–50 CE) donning an ornamental tiara while attending a religious convocation held in Kannauj also suggests that the craft was being practised in ancient Assam as well. To these written sources, Assam-based independent journalist Rini Barman adds the medieval text *Katha Gurucharit* from the Vaishnava era, and Madhav Kandali's Ramayana as being 'mostly categorical in nature about (Assamese) jewellery—listing of ornament items, and where they were worn, for instance.'[90]

Saikia mentions that the range of ornaments in Assamese jewellery widened during the Ahom rule. 'One finds mention of the practice of wearing gold ornaments with Bakhor among the Tai-Ahom when they resided in North Burma and prior to that, in the Yunnan province of China.'[91] Rini Barman also tells me, 'Among the traditional jewellery craftsmen of Jorhat, there is a visible similarity with Mughal enamelling styles, and this is not just in ornaments but also in other objects like tamul pota too. Many believe it was the Ahom kingdom's trade relations that ushered in this style influence.' She adds, however, 'The manufacturing equipment used locally by the craftsmen in Jorhat is unique and that has a lasting impact on the final piece.'

The Ahom kingdom's trade relations with Burma also helped in the procurement of precious stones like ruby and emerald to heighten the beauty of a piece. Henniker also mentions Ahom king Rudra Singha importing goldsmiths from Benares to learn 'how to manufacture better sorts of gold and silver ornaments'.[92] 'It appears the raja selected certain Kalitas to learn and to do the work, hence Sonaris formerly were Kalitas only.'[93] Later though, people from other communities—Keot, Koch, Kaibartta—joined the profession. With the gradual expansion of the Ahom kingdom, enveloping the Kachari, Sutiya, Koch, and several other smaller principalities, various local jewellery practices must have merged to form a single entity to become Axomiya olonkaar or Axomiya gohona as we know it today.

SILVER

What also needs highlighting here is that though there is evidence of wearing gold ornaments in popular folk songs among the tribes, like the 'Bagurumba' that mentions 'sonali jinjiri' (golden chain in Bodo), the standard medium for jewellery for the commoners of all ethnic groups was silver, brass, copper, and wood. The majority of the ornaments that Assam's ethnic communites have traditionally worn, including the Gaam Kharu (Tiwas call it Kham-Kharu) worn by the Mising chieftains, are made with silver, and with colourful beads. Rabha community's Hasa necklace comes in silver. Their Chandrahaar is also silver, so are the Haat-Baju and Kata-Baju, the armlets. The most distinct piece of necklace that Karbi women wear, Lek, is made using silver (men only wear gold Lek). Karbi Anglong-based academic Kache Teronpi highlights in an article, 'Karbi women are usually not allowed to wear gold ornaments; only their men are. Since women wear more ornaments than men, silver is abundantly used.'[94]

Wearing silver coins as ornaments was also quite popular among certain ethnic communites. Saikia mentions commoners making rings of brass (taam) as it looked almost like gold. Karbi priests, however, wear rings only made of copper.

There is a wedding tradition called jurun where a groom is customarily expected to gift gold jewellery to the bride. Hence it is not traditionally binding on the bride's family to ready a mandatory set of gohona for their daughter, unlike in most parts of India. Therefore, in rural areas particularly, it is not rare to find a family borrowing a gold set from a relative for the bride to wear on the day of jurun, until she is gifted her own set by the groom's mother.

CHALLENGES IN THE TRADITIONAL HOTSPOTS

Over the centuries, the Ahom-era jewellery clusters in Assam have shrunk considerably, so much so that there are now only three such distinct areas/villages—one each in Upper, Middle, and Lower Assam. Each has its exclusivity; each closely guards their skill.

Today though, the long-existing reluctance to pass on the skill to those outside the family/clan has proved to be a bane to the survival of the jewellers and their craft, particularly in the Jorhat district of Upper Assam. Some amount of realization seems to have seeped into the small community when you note attempts to train the younger generation of Jorhat jewellers by senior practioners like Pratap Bordoloi and Lakhinath Bordoloi. Still, the lure of a better occupation looms, especially because unlike in the other clusters, youth in Sonarigaon cluster of Jorhat are educated.

Since this cluster only deal with 24-carat gold jewellery, there is an additional challenge—they get an order for an expensive set every day. The Assamese middle class prefers the gold-plated variety. Jeweller Naba Bordoloi from Sonarigaon tells me he has been catering primarily to a clientele that the family has traditionally dealt with. His clientele is small which means he does not get a well-paying order often.[95]

In Naba's village, there are only about ten active artisans while some others who have learnt the craft have not gone on to practice it as a full time occupation. The dwindling scope of the craft in Sonarigaon also means some of the unique features of this particular jewellery tradition are perhaps on the brink of extinction. Rini Barman pointed out to me some special features of the method of jewellery making practised in Sonarigaon: 'For instance, the *lah* (lac) to fill the frame; the *paat-xun* (gold leaf) to embed the stones; and a unique stone called *Kosoti Khil* to test the purity of gold.' Quoting from the observation of the former director of Land Records H. Z. Darrah in *Notes on Some Industries of Assam* (1896) that the enamelling tools were 'peculiar' to the Jorhat artisans, Henniker had mentioned the use of hola (xola), ghor and khon by the Jorhat artisans.[96] Darrah had also noted the use of Jawon, 'like a heavy sandstone in appearance', which would be pounded into powder and mixed with hot lac to create a compound which would be pressed onto the end of a bamboo piece to to smoothen the surface of the gold.[97] Naba says while the hammer can be easily procured from the market these days, he has to make some other tools needed in the craft himself.

The Barpeta and Rongtholi clusters are certainly better off than Sonarigaon, particularly in terms of human resource. Barpeta has about 155 craftsmen, mostly youth. The entire Rontholi village in Nagaon has practising artisans.

Barman says not broadening the categorization of Assamese jewellery enough is also a challenge to the craft. 'The current categorisation is from a dominant lens. We only look at metal work as "legitimate"...or capable enough to be representative culturally. Hence, many don't realize the erroneous but very popular categorization of Assamese jewelley into a) pure gold (practised in Sonarigaon); gold-plated on silver (practised in Rontholi); and 3) gold-washed or polished (practised in Barpeta).' There is a need for more accommodative categories based on designs, say, folk, nature-based, royal collections which include different kingdoms, etc.,' she says.

Appropriate training for young hands is also the call of the hour. Lakhimi Baruah shares a concern, 'The young generation tend to not learn the art fully. A piece is made following a set of stages. Anyone can pick up the skill of gold leafing or adding stones to a piece but the real work is in framing, how to put the lac first. There are still only a few craftsmen who can skilfully do the framing work.'

One other challenge that the industry is navigating through currently is the stiff competition not only from the branded corporate-backed jewellery lines increasingly opening shop in Guwahati and elsewhere but also the flooding of the market with duplicate ornaments manufactured outside Assam using a low-quality metal and sold as Axomiya gohona at a much cheaper rate. No wonder then that there is a growing demand within the industry for GI status to be given to Axomiya gohona.

10

GADYA–PADYA–SUTIGOLPO: MODERN ASSAMESE LITERATURE

A piece of literature stands out as extraordinary not for a distinctive style of narration alone but also for its ability to tell a riveting story. For me, a memorable book is so also because it has a remarkable protagonist.

Historically, more often than not, such a literary character has usually been a man. To expound on the span of Assamese literature beyond the typical, let me begin by recalling two formidable fictional women in modern Assamese literature who have the same name: Menoka. The first is from Homen Borgohain's eighth novella *Matsyagandha* published in 1987, and the second is her namesake in Bhabendranath Saikia's novel *Antareep* and *Agnisnaan*, the film he made in 1985 based on it about which I elaborate about in the chapter on Assamese cinema.

In my understanding, Saikia and Borgohain were two of the most intrepid minds to have filled the Assamese creative space in the latter half of the twentieth century. Like any good writer should, the duo could at once pin down a reader's interest with their crisp characterization, sharp dialogues, and gripping plot. Set in two different realities in a similar timeline, both versions of Menoka were striking enough to leave an indelible mark on readers for a long time to come.

Saikia's Menoka was the wife of an upper-caste, rich Assamese landowner who, in the nineteenth century world of the book, stepped out of her comfort zone to challenge patriarchy and demanded gender and sexual rights at par with her husband. Borgohain's Menoka was an unlettered lower-caste orphan from around the same era who, on growing up, generated within her the wherewithal to contest the set norms of society in the only way that she could and turned the tables on her oppressors. The use of two female protagonists by Saikia (1932–2003) and Borgohain (1932–2021) to expose the ugly underbelly of a community the writers belonged to and which they cared for exceedingly, was a rarity in Assamese literature. This is why I chose to begin a chapter on the subject with a focus on their writings.

In Borgohain's *Matsyagandha,* published in 1987 (first as a series in *Xiralu* magazine edited by noted Assamese poet Nabakanta Barua), Menoka is placed in an imaginary village Goroimari on the banks of river Mohghuli; it is a Kaivartta village, meaning, populated by people from a lower caste once derogatorily termed Dom. Borgohain had said several times that Menoka's character and the overall plot of that novel were drawn from his childhood memory of growing up in a village by a river in Assam's Dhakuakhana area of Lakhimpur district in the 1930s where the ugly reality of caste played out in his immediate surroundings. His story was set somewhere in the latter part of the nineteenth century when caste distinctions were at a peak in Assamese society, permeating down to promotion of practices like untouchability and segregated living. The author astutely wove into the storyline the everyday miseries of being born into a low-caste family, leading even a strong-willed woman like Menoka to seek momentary bliss through her addiction to opium, a common occurrence in Assam in that era.

Not just Menoka, most other female characters of Borgohain's fictions were astutely characterized to reflect the lives of women with a variety of lived experiences. His first novel *Subala*, penned in 1963, had created a ripple not only for the protagonist he had picked—a sex worker—but also the rectitude with which he represented her life. He later said in his first autobiography *Atmanusandhan* ('Self Introspection', 1988), that the idea of the novel was born after seeing abject poverty at Chaygaon on the outskirts of Guwahati when he was posted there as a government official during 1958–61.[1] It was the first Assamese novel to be written on a sex worker. Noted literary critic and Borgohain's contemporary Hiren Gohain had rightly called the novel 'a poem of anger and pity'.[2] Another notable literary work of Borgohain was *Pita Putra*, a novel for which he had bagged the Sahitya Akademi Award in 1978. It stunningly captured the impact of India's Independence on two generations. Another significant novel by him is *Astarag* which encaptulates the existential crisis a man goes through as he ages. Borgohain's *Ismail Sekhor Xondhanot* held up life lived in a makeship camp of the so-called 'illegal immigrants' from across the border with Bangladesh. His two other notable literary contributions to modern Assamese literature would be *Xisur Hahi* (hinged on abject poverty) and *Hati Aru Gorokhia* (a pen picture of Assamese ruralscape).

In all, the celebrated author known for his descriptive style, wrote twelve short novels, the last being *Edinor Diary* (Diary of a Day) in 2003. He was also a prolific short story writer and wrote at least four autobiographies, several incisive articles on a range of subjects including politics, besides publishing a poetry collection, *Haimanti*, in 1987. Anindita Kar, in her obituary on Borgohain, written with inputs from Bijit Borthakur, had underlined that the author was often referred to as 'batabrikkha' in Assam, a revered banyan tree that sustained an entire ecosystem of readers, writers, and literary enthusiasts.[3]

Till the end, Borgohain followed a strict regime when it came to writing and reading. In 2017, at age eighty-five, he told me in an interview for *The Wire*, 'I write two hours and read for two hours every day.'[4] That was aside from editing an Assamese daily (*Niyomia Barta*) then; hosting a TV talk show (*Kotha-Barta*), editing a health magazine (*Swasthya*) published by Guwahati Neurological Research Centre, and running a charitable organization, Karunadhara, for the disabled. Like several regional language authors, Borgohain also couldn't make a living only by writing books which came in the way of fulfilling his dream of penning a long novel. He had told me, 'My Sahitya Akademi Award winning novel *Pita Putra* ran into 370 pages. I had a dream of writing a novel longer or of equivalent length, and in fact, declared such an intention at the end of *Pita Putra*. But being forced to give a lot of time to journalism due to livelihood reasons, that dream remained unfulfilled.' He was attracted to the form of short novels after reading Thomas Mann's *Death in Venice* and Adalbert Stifter's *Brigata* in his youth. 'They had made a profound impression on my mind and I had a strong conviction that for a part-time writer such as me, such short novels or novellas would be the proper mode,' he said.

Though he found his final calling in prose, Borgohain had begun writing with poetry and contributed some significant poems to Assamese literature. At thirteen, he was overjoyed to see his poem 'Rani Gaidalu' (on the Naga freedom fighter) published in the well-known Assamese magazine of the times, *Banhi*.[5] Some other poems by him were also published in *Ramdhenu*, the celebrated Assamese magazine, before his interest shifted towards prose. Edited by Birendra Kumar Bhattacharyya (1924–97), *Ramdhenu* had published the best of new Assamese writings then, leading many to term the period from 1950 onwards—when the magazine had begun publishing—as *Ramdhenu* jug or the era of *Ramdhenu*. It was *Ramdhenu* which clearly established Borgohain as a writer of significance.

RAMDHENU ERA

Ramdhenu became the springboard for the success of almost all top of the line Assamese writers from mid-twentieth century onwards. This period is also commonly termed the golden era of Assamese modern writing, not merely for the amount of literary work that the popular magazine could produce but also for the variety of eclectic subjects covered, genres represented, and literary techniques employed by the contributors. For instance, during that era, Borgohain, in his novel *Kusshilava* (1970), had used a new narrative technique wherein he divided each part of the novel (except for the last part) with names of individual characters that he then introduced to the reader. In 1971, Borgohain also published a novel *Puwar Purabi Sandhyar Bibhas*, jointly written with noted Assamese writer Nirupama (Tamuly) Borgohain who was also his wife, making it the only jointly written Assamese novel of note thus far.[6]

Ramdhenu presented to its readers elements of social realism through the creative work of a wide galaxy of gifted poets and writers. Some such names would be Navakanta Barua, Birinchi Kumar Bhattacharyya, Saurav Kumar Chaliha, Syed Abdul Malik, Bhabendranath Saikia, Hiren Gohain, Lakhinandan Borah, Nirupama Borgohain, Nilamani Phookan, Chandraprasad Saikia, Indira Goswami, Hiren Bhattacharya, Mahim Bora, Nirmal Prabha Bordoloi, Padma Barkataki, Jogesh Das, Rohini Kumar Kakati, Medini Choudhury, Padma Borkotoky, Bireswar Barua, Saidul Islam, Atulananda Goswami, Nirod Chaudhuri, Nagen Saikia, Nilima Sarma, Imran Shah, Anima Dutta, Mahendra Barthakur, Prabina Saikia, Rudraprasad Kakati, Govinda Prasad Sarma, Kumud Goswami, Pranabjyoti Deka, Hare Krishna Deka, Dipali Dutta, and Alimunissa Piyar, among several others. In 1979, the magazine's editor, Birendra Kumar Bhattacharyya was conferred the Jnanpith Award for his celebrated novel on the Indian Independence movement, *Mritunjoy* (Immortal). The coveted prize was the first in Assamese literature. Considered a classic of Assamese literature, the novel deals with the derailment of a military train during the Quit India Movement by a set of non-violent followers of Mahatma Gandhi. Bhattacharyya had also given Assamese readers another masterpiece, *Iyarungam* (1960), for which he was conferred the Sahitya Akademi Award. *Iyarungam* had incisively delineated the struggle of the Nagas, then living in a district of Assam, to gain independence from India. His deft handling of a sensitive political subject from the Northeast remains a significant milestone in Assamese literature. Two other noted novels of Bhattacharyya were *Rajpothe Ringiai*, which embraces Assam's socialist movement, and *Pratipad*, based on the labour movement in Assam's Digboi oil refinery in pre-independent India. His short story collection, *Kolong Ajio Boi*, was notable too for capturing in the literary world how a part of a living river (Kolong in today's middle Assam) was put to death to control the floods in the British era.

To my mind, another of Bhattacharyya's notable novels is *Munichunir Pohar* (1976) that bore witness to the viciousness of the Emergency. Bhattacharya's prose, often presented against the backdrop of a historical event, was graphic. He frequently introduced his characters to readers with a detailed sketch including their physical traits while inserting them into the plot. Bhattacharyya's contribution to Assamese literature was not just through an oeuvre of formidable novels but, as seen through his work at *Ramdhenu*, was also in encouraging talented Assamese writers and poets to write and help fortify its roots. Prominent Assamese literary critic Areendom Borkataki had commented thus on Bhattacharyya successfully steering *Ramdhenu* and fashioning a remarkable era in Assamese literature, 'Though Bhattacharyya was himself a great writer then but as the editor of *Ramdhenu*, he promoted others which helped bring a new wave of writing in Assamese literature. That is what a great editor could do, something that we miss now, a reason why we can't call the work published in any other literary magazine thereafter to have ushered in a new era in our literature.'[7] I also remember one more observation of Borkataki from that conversation on Assamese literature in 2021. 'Though *Ramdhenu* began in the 1950s, Assamese literature is still continuing in that praxis of modern writing. It is yet to firmly break that trend and bring newer components to make it truly post-modern. There have been impressive sporadic individual efforts on that count but they are yet to take the shape of a new wave of sorts to define Assamese literature as an era different from the *Ramdhenu* era.'

A powerful individual effort to roll out a truly post-modern Assamese novel, though, was made by the novelist-poet, late Ajit Barua (1926–2015). His *Ekhon Premor Upanyax* (A Novel on Love), an autobiographical take following the French Nouveau Roman and Avant Garde styles of the mid-twentieth century, was published in 1993. Bijit Barthakur, in a podcast on Assamese literature some years ago, had rightly noted that the poet's only novel 'was an aberration in Assamese literature'. Barthakur, who had an audience with the author after reading his compelling novel, related, 'It was a rare example of self-mockery of a bachelor seen in Indian literature, a great read.' The dream-like sequences in that Assamese novel reminded some readers of ace Russian filmmaker Andrei Tarkovsky's movies.

Here, it is only appropriate to also highlight for the readers that a distinctive feature of Assamese literature is categorizing different waves of writing after literary magazines, like *Jonaki* jug, *Banhi* jug, *Avahan* jug, *Jayanti* jug, and *Ramdhenu* jug. The trend underscores the fact that Assamese literary magazines had played a significant role in setting the drift in modern Assamese writing. The rise of *Ramdhenu* as a magazine, therefore, needs a bit of discussion here. The precursor to that magazine was another magazine, *Rang Ghar*, edited by a venerated Assamese writer Birinchi Kumar Baruahh in 1948. Top names of the Assamese literary and cultural landscape of the times contributed to it. From Kamala Kanta Bhattacharya to Jyoti Prasad Agarwalla Devkant Barooah to Navakanta Barua, Upen Lekharu, Maheswar Neog, and Ratnakanta Borkakoti to Mahim Bora, several literary stars of the times frequently wrote for *Rang Ghar*. It was in that magazine that Agarwalla's popular children's poem 'Bhoot Puwali' (Baby Imp) was first published. 'Ami Duwar Mukoli Koru' (Let Us Open the Door), the well-known poem by Devkant Barooah was first published in *Rang Ghar* too.

Rang Ghar was shut after two years to be started anew, in April 1950, as *Ramdhenu* (Rainbow)—a monthly literary magazine. After six months, in September 1950, distinguished Assamese writer Maheswar Neog took over its editorship from the founding editor Indra Kamal Bezbarua. A year later, the baton was passed on to yet another literary luminary, Kirti Nath Hazarika, from whom Birinchi Kumar Bhattacharyya took over in April 1952 and continued as the illustrious editor till May 1963.

In 1967, with the death of its founder Indra Kamal Bezbaroa, the magazine ceased to exist. Though four years later, an effort was made to revive it by Radhika Mohan Bhagawati, it shut shop again after a two-year run. In 1995, Nilakamal Bezbarua from Jorhat did try to resuscitate the proud legacy of the magazine once more but he too gave up in mid-1996.[8] Still, for two decades in a row, under six editors, the magazine moulded the trajectory of Assamese modern writing with aplomb. As I write this chapter, two of the luminaries from the *Ramdhenu* era had fallen victim to the Covid-19 pandemic—Homen Borgohain and Lakshminandan Bora, both eighty-nine. Like Borgohain, Bora too was the president of the prestigious Asam Sahitya Sabha, the genesis of which I shall discuss later in the chapter. A writer of several significant novels, an autobiography (first published in a serialized form in *Prantik* magazine edited by Bhabendranath Saikia), plays and short stories, Bora's debut as a writer also happened through the pages of *Ramdhenu*, in 1954 with a short story, 'Bhaona'. His noted novel *Patal Bhairavi* (1986) won him the Sahitya Akademi Award. His first novel, *Ganga Silonir Pakhi*, considered his magnum opus, was turned into a moving film by Padum Baruah in 1976. Bora's political novel *Akou Saraighat* (1980) reflected in good measure his nationalist sentiments; his overt political stand resulted in him getting arrested in 1981 under the National Security Act. In an obituary on Bora in Assamese daily *Niyomia Barta*, Assam observer and political commentator Mayur Bora had also highlighted his deep study on Sankardev and the import of that subject into his novels. 'Dr. Bora, by creating *Jaheki Nahike Upam*, a significant novel on the life of Sankardev, had strengthened the silo of Assamese literature. He had written some more novels on similar lines, *Xehi Gunonidhi* (1997) and *Goti Moti Bhokoti* (2005), also *Xehi Xavyaxasi* (2014), based on the life and works of Pitambar Deva Goswami, the maverick head of the Garamur Vaishnava monastery of Majuli.'[9]

Some other top novels by the writers of the *Ramdhenu* era were Navakanta Barua's *Kokadeutar Haar* which bagged him the Sahitya Akademi Award in 1975; Mahim Bora's *Putala Ghar* (1973), and *Edhani Mahir Hahi* which fetched him the Sahitya Akademi Award in 2001; Medini Choudhury's (1928–2003) Sahitya Akademi winning novel *Bipanna Samay* (Endangered Hours, 1999), *Ananya Prantar* (on local influences in Assamese language, 1976), and *Pherengadao* (on Assamese literary luminary Bishnu Prasad Rava, 1993); *Taat Nodi Nasil* (There Was No River There), etc.

Literary critic Bhaben Barua, highlighting a significant moment in Assamese literature, had named another Ramdhenu-era writer Bina Barua's post-war novel *Jibonor Batot* (1944) as 'the finest creation in the whole range of Assamese literature'.[10] Bina Barua was the pseudonym of writer Birinchi Kumar Baruah. Bhaben Barua, in his valuable essay on the birth of an Indian novel for the *Assam Quarterly* in 1967–70, had placed that book 'along with a very few other Indian novels' in 'that category in which embodiment of reality becomes a revelation of its inner tendencies; the weight of the tradition it bears and pull of the future it registers.'[11] In the next two and a half decades, *Jibonor Batot* set a trend in Assamese novel writing to portray rural issues, particularly describing to the reader rampant urbanization bearing down on pastoral life. Some such novels were Dinanath Sarma's *Nadai* (1956), Syed Abdul Malik's *Surumukhir Sapna* (1960), Birendra Kumar Bhattacharyya's *Aii* (1960), Lakhinandan Bora's *Ganga Silonir Pakhi* (1963), Homen Borgohain's *Pita Putra* (1975), and Debendra Nath Acharya's *Anya Yug anya Purus* (1970).[12] *Jibanor Batot* would, therefore, remain a milestone in Assamese literature for carving out the coming of age of the genre of Assamese novel and also for the ensuing literary criticism.

Both Bhaben Barua and Hiren Gohain came to prominence as Assamese literary critics after *Jibanor Batot*.

Yet another ground-breaking novel by Birinchi Kumar Baruahh was *Seuji Pator Kahini*. Published in 1959, it was also written under a pseudonym, Rasna Barua. The novel described the lives of the Adivasis/Tea Tribe in Assam's tea gardens, a subject not often covered in the mainstream then.[13]

Syed Abdul Malik (1919–2000), another literary stalwart in Assamese writing, too was part of the *Ramdhenu* era, even though he had started writing before the magazine was reborn as so. Sailen Bharali, in his essay on Assamese literature in *Modern Indian Literature, An Anthology: Surveys and Poems*, had accurately stated that Malik 'has to his credit the largest number of novels with characters drawn from almost all sections of society.'[14] Although Malik's approach to literature was essentially romantic, he also 'brought to light certain socio-economic problems in a number of novels, the best of which is perhaps *Surujmukhir Sapna* which envelops life in a Muslim village on the banks of river Dhansiri.'[15] That novel had painted for readers 'a graphic picture of the village and the struggles undergone by the villagers to earn a living.'[16] Malik's yet another marvellous novel *Oghori Aatmar Kahini* had fetched him the Sahitya Akademi Award in 1972.

In mid-2020, following attacks on Malik's writings in general by a section of right-wing Assamese, Dhurjjati Sarma from the Department of Modern Indian Languages at the Gauhati University had highlighted a pertinent point in regard to the author's approach towards the revered Assamese saint Sankardev in his biographical novel *Dhanya Nara Tanu Bhal* (1987). 'What makes the novel stand out amongst the rest is its depiction of an Assamese cultural space continually subjected to numerous social and political upheavals of the time coupled with the revolutionary impulse of the Bhakti Movement cutting across religious and sectarian boundaries. And upon this wide terrain of a social–cultural geography extending from Dhuwahat, near Narayanpur, to Cooch Behar that Malik has mapped in the life-journey of Sankardeva.'[17] In that novel, Malik also wove in the spread of Islam in Assam as a parallel manifestation which Sarma had interestingly analysed as 'an authorial intervention that has often been glossed over or considered extraneous by critics in their evaluation of the novel,' thus underlining the inherent danger that 'given the circumstances (the rise of Hindutva politics in Assam), one may even accuse him of appropriating the narrative space for the propagation of his personal faith.'[18]

Aside from his celebrated poem, *Moi Axomiya* (I am Assamese), Malik has enriched Assamese literature with as many as sixty-seven novels, and also over 2,000 short stories, thus leaving his indelible mark on the literary sphere.[19]

Some writers and poets from the *Ramdhenu* era also tried their hand at incorporating into their narrative the Brajabuli dialect used by Sankardev. Malik and Nabakanta Barua, though, were the prominent examples of that trend. Malik, in both *Dhanya Nara Tonu Bhal* (1987) and *Prem Amritara Nadi* (1999), had sprinkled bits of the dialect born of the Vaishnava revivalist movement of the fifteenth–sixteenth centuries in Assam. Prior to Malik and Lakshminandan Bora's biographical writings on Sankardev and his disciple Madhabdev, Medini Choudhury also wrote a novel, *Banduka Behar* (1976), inserting the Brajabuli dialect in places. Together, they ushered in the genre of biographical novels into Assamese literature in the second half of the twentieth century.

To talk about the presence of historical novels in Assamese, one must hold up Devendranath Acharya's *Jangam*, a salient contribution in the 1970s not just to Assamese literature but to Indian literature in general. It was a moving tale of the exodus of ordinary people on foot from Burma to Northeast India in the midst of World War II. Thousands had lost their lives on the way to the forces of nature during that journey. Referring to an English translation of the book by Amit R. Baishya published in 2019, celebrated writer Amitav Ghosh had stated, 'To the best of my knowledge it is the only Indian novel devoted entirely to this sadly-neglected episode in modern Indian history; it is a document of inestimable value.'[20] Baishya, in his translator's note to the book, had aptly noted, 'The tempest that was the Second World War cut right through the heart of Assam nearly four decades ago. But hardly any signs of this massive calamity that faced humankind has registered in our literature.'[21] Acharya had been posthumously conferred the Sahitya Akademi Award for the novel in 1984.

ORUNUDOI ERA

Ramdhenu had begun publishing its editions in 1950, barely three years after Independence and after Bengali-majority Sylhet had once and for all been separated from colonial-era Assam due to Partition. Thus, that period was at the cusp of a beginning when the Assamese community was breathing easy, setting aside their over-a-century-old apprehension about losing their language to Bengali in their homeland. Since Sylhet was appended to Assam

Province in the colonial era, Bengali speakers had outnumbered Assamese speakers, thus creating this insecurity in Assamese speakers. The root of that fear was in the imposition of Bengali language on Assamese for nearly four decades (1836–73) which came as a rude shock to a community which till then had not suffered imposition of a foreign language on it. Since the Ahoms never imposed their language on the ruled, the linguistic history of Assam till the early nineteenth century was unlike that of Bengal. Islamic rulers made Persian the court language in Bengal, a practice the British continued. Persian was replaced by Bengali as a court language only in the early nineteenth century. Alongside, the colonizers imposed Bengali on the newly acquired territory of Assam too. The effect of the domination of Bengali on the Assamese during the colonial era didn't restrict itself only to the use of the language in official records but also trickled down to the level of primary school education. Gradually, Bengali became the language of the 'cultured' and the 'educated'. Since the Bengalis of Kolkata, mostly Hindus, were exposed to English language from the long rule of British in Bengal, they were also preferred by British officials over the native population of Assam when it came to filling government jobs for a protracted period of time. It took decades for the Assamese, even after the rise of a newly educated Kolkata-returned middle-class, to break that glass ceiling. Areendam Borkataki had rightly stated, 'Overall, Bengali in the colonial period had a similar status in Assam as English is today among the middle-class Assamese.'

Since English education can be the passport to social mobility and better opportunities today, many parents prefer not to send their wards to an Assamese-medium school; so was the case with Bengali in colonial Assam. Being well-versed in Bengali opened the door to securing government jobs, thus pushing more and more Assamese middle-class families to send their sons to Kolkata for higher education in Bengali and also English.

However, this promotion of the Bengali language became so chauvinistic in nature that it also tried to swallow a much older language like Assamese on the pretence that it was a mere dialect of Bengali and would soon merge with Bengali. Articles supporting such a theory were published in many Bengali journals of the nineteenth century. In Bengali journals like *Mrinmoyee*, Laxminath Bezbaroa wrote counters to this notion and even had arguments on the subject with Rabindranath Tagore in Bengali periodicals *Bharati* and *Punya*. He continued to 'strongly criticise the grabbing tendencies of a section of the Bengali intelligentsia' in his Assamese magazine *Banhi*.[22] Such developments further inspired the likes of Bezbaroa to push further for the development of Assamese literature. By then though, the first batch of Kolkata-educated Assamese had begun writing in Bengali. An instance would be Holiram Dhekial Phukan's *History of Assam* in Bangla (1829). The Kolkata-educated Assamese who became the new elite of the community not only adopted Bengali but also began looking down on the Assamese language, an indicator of the loss of self-confidence in their own heritage due to imposition of Bengali on the community. Alongside writing in Bengali, several Kolkata-educated bright Assamese youth also married into prominent Bengali families. Lakhminath Bezbaroa, considered the father of modern Assamese literature, also married into the Tagore household. Noted Assamese writer Chandradhar Barua, speaking at a memorial function on prominent Assamese leader and advocate Tarun Ram Phukan at Jorhat in 1939, related how Phukan had once told him about Tagore approaching him to marry his daughter while he was practising as a barrister in Kolkata after returning from London.[23] Such episodes only indicate the times that were. It is then rather interesting that the Bengali linguistic chauvinism supported by Tagore eventually found its opposition from a son-in-law from within the Tagore household; Lakhminath Bezbaroa was married to Pragyasundari Devi, daughter of Debendranath Tagore.

While Bezbaroa and his ilk played a big role in strengthening modern Assamese literature, it is worthwhile to also acknowledge the role of the American Baptist Mission in promoting the Assamese language and the first writings in that medium. That intervention was well-represented in Trailokya Bhattacharjya's first historical novel *Sanchipator Puthi*. Much before Assamese was officially recognized in Assam, the Christian missionaries had set the boat sailing by bringing out the first Assamese newspaper, *Orunudoi* (1846–80). It gave a much-needed platform to early Assamese writers like Anandaram Dhekial Phukan and Hemchandra Barua to publish their work. By then, Phukan had submitted a memorandum to the British authorities to make Assamese the medium of instruction in the state. His action was proof of the fact that the first generation of Modern Assamese intellectuals had to make 'the case that they were a distinct people with a distinct language and culture'.[24]

Christian missionaries were pushing for the local language on the conviction that their proselytization mission would succeed in the state only if done through the vernacular. Nevertheless, it helped the cause of protecting the Assamese language from being swallowed by Bengali. Nagen Saikia, in *Background of Modern Assamese Literature,* had also underlined that prior to the coming of the missionaries to Assam, the earnest zeal of William Carry led to the translation of the Bible into Assamese by Atmaram Sarma, a resident of Koliabor in Nagaon district; it was published by the Serampore Mission. 'Dr. Banikanta Kakati (eminent Assamese linguist), therefore, is of the opinion that the modern period of Assamese begins with the publication of *The Bible* in Assamese prose by the Missionaries in 1819. But this beginning was a lone effort and it was not followed by other work till the coming of the British power and the American Baptist Missionaries into Assam.'[25] Thereafter, several other religious books and hymns were translated into Assamese from Serampore and were circulated among people in Assam. 'In 1836, James Rae (a missionary from Serampore Mission) travelled to Upper Assam and distributed the Assamese tract, *The Boorie and Deka*, which was in great demand.'[26] Reverend Brown who published *Orunudoi*, published a religious book, *Khristar Vivaran Aru Subhavarta*, in 1854 and wrote the story of Saint Joseph with the title *Josephar Kahini* aside from publishing a book on the life of Christ. 'He was also credited with the publication and preparation of eleven school books to meet the immediate demand of the newly opened missionary schools (in Assam).'[27]

In *Orunudoi*, Brown ran a translated series of John Bunyan's *Pilgrim's Progress* as *Jatrikar Jatra* in 1851 which was also later published as a book. Saikia had stated that Brown's translation of the novel 'paved the way for writing novels in Assamese language'.[28]

In 1840, Brown's wife Eliza Brown wrote *Gananar Katha* (a book on basic arithmetic), *Bhugulor Bibaran* (on geography), and a children's storybook. Brown also began collecting old Assamese manuscripts for preservation. In 1840, Reverend Cutter's wife H. B. Cutter compiled a book on the vocabulary and phrases of Assamese language, making it the second book on the language published by the missionaries.

Between 1844–45, Brown also published *Assam Buranji* by Kashinath Tamuli Phukan; *Sutia Buranji* and *Kitbat Manjari* of Bakul Kayastha.[29]

Reverend Miles Bronson, who took over the post from Brown, immersed himself fully into the mission of restoring Assamese as the medium of instruction in Assam. In 1867, Bronson put together the first Assamese dictionary. Reverend A. K. Gurney, on arrival in Assam in 1874—the year Assamese was restored as an official language in Assam—picked up the language to pen books and wrote several along with his wife Mary F. L. Gurney. In 1877, while his wife translated Hannah Catherine Mullens' Bengali novel *Phulmani O Karunar Bibaran* into Assamese, Gurney published

Assamese novelette *Kaminikanta* from the American Baptist Mission Press which had begun functioning from Sivasagar by then. In 1877 itself, he brought out yet another Assamese novelette, *Elokeshy Beshyar Bishaye*, written by M. E. Leslie. In 1878, he published a booklet titled *Kanibeheruar Bisaye* and then *Ruthar Bibaran* (1880) and *Josephar Bibaran* (1881). Gurney also translated the Old Testament from Hebrew to Assamese. Though such publications were primarily religious literature aimed at propagating Christianity among locals, Saikia underlined that it was still a remarkable effort and contributed to the arrival of modern Assamese fiction.

Several other Assamese titles were published thereafter. Anandaram Dhekial Phukan, in his booklet *A Few Remarks on Assamese Language*, had supplied a full list of Assamese books published by the missionaries. Among them were also books by Nidhiram Keot writing as Nidhi Levi Farewell, the first Assamese convert to Christianity; one of the books was an Assamese translation by him of the Indian Penal Code in 1865 titled the *Bharatiya Dandabidhi Ain*. *Orunudoi* also introduced Assamese readers to the subject of science. Saikia, summing up its contribution to modern Assamese language and literature, said that publication of stories and novels, dramas and dialogues, autobiographies and travelogues, etc. brought new life to Assamese literature. 'No doubt, the stories were related to Christianity but the characters and events had their bases in facts in which the readers found whiff of reality rather than anything from the world of myths and fancies.'[30]

Saikia was on the mark. The first Assamese drama, *Ram-Navami*, written by Gunabhiram Barua (1834–94), was serialized in *Orunudoi* in 1858. The newspaper also printed biographical notes on public figures like Benjamin Franklin and Martin Luther, somewhat related to the biographical literature that would be published in the Assamese language later. *Orunudoi* also published book reviews; Anandaram Dhekial Phukan's *Asamiya Lorar Mitra* was reviewed on its pages. Various secular themes were also offered space in the monthly. Interestingly, in *Orunudoi*, several writers published their work either under pseudonyms or by placing a distinctive sign at the end.

Gradually, several Assamese newspapers and periodicals began to come up such as *Asam Bandhu*, *Assam Bilasini*, *Mau*, *Assam News*, and *Asam Tara*. The newspapers and the periodicals that followed *Orunudoi* played a vital role in the development of prose in a standardized Assamese language.[31]

Meanwhile, the continuous demand on the British administration to reinstate Assamese as the official language of the Brahmaputra Valley bore fruit in 1874. It was also the time when Sylhet was cut out of Bengal Province to append to Assam under a commissioner with Shillong as its capital. The anxiety about the domination of the Bengali language among the educated Assamese, therefore, didn't evaporate entirely even with the restoration of Assamese language in schools, courts, etc. in the Valley. Moreover, Bengali continued to be taught in the schools for a protracted period due to a dearth of sufficient school books in Assamese language. Anandaram Dhekial Phukan's book *Asamiya Lorar Mitra* was the only available textbook then. After his passing in 1859, Gunabhiram Barua edited the book to keep it in circulation. To encourage book writing in Assamese, the commissioner of Assam had to announce a monetary reward. A committee was set up to select entries for the competition. Ten sets of books were selected, of which Hemchandra Barua's *Adipath* won and was awarded a prize of ₹50.[32] Several other textbooks published soon after by Barua and other Assamese writers helped tide over the crisis. However, with Bengali officials continuing to rule the rank and file of Assam's officialdom, the language continued to dominate the corridors of power, thus the insecurity of the Assamese about their language losing its primacy in their own land continued to linger. With the British dividing Bengal on religious lines in 1905, thereby knitting Assam and East Bengal with Dhaka as the capital also aggravated matters. Though after about six years, both sides of Bengal were reunited, Bengali-speaking Sylhet continued to remain with Assam under a chief commissioner. Like the Assamese were upset at that decision, so were the Bengalis of Sylhet for they had been kept away from the rest of Bengal. The Bengali Hindus had submitted a memorandum to the British masters seeking reunification of Sylhet with greater Bengal but to no avail. So, till Partition, the see-saw of power struggle between the two linguistic communities remained unremitting.[33]

ASAM BANDHU

Towards the end of the nineteenth century, a small educated Assamese middle-class emerged to compete for jobs in Assam with the educated Bengalis. The Assamese intelligentsia during that period was led by Hemchandra Barua (1872–1928) and Gunabhiram Barua (1834–94) who, through their writings, also tried marrying Western values with Assamese traditional mores, prompting the creation of work like *Bahire Rong Chang Bhitore Kowa Bhaturi* (1876) and *Kaniyar Kirtan* (1861). Both Hemchandra and Gunabhiram Barua were also influenced by the Brahmo Samaj of Raja Ram

Mohan Roy which had questioned Hindu orthodoxy. In 1900, Hemchandra Barua brought out *Hemkosh*, the first Assamese etymological dictionary. He not only gave the Assamese language 'a scientific modern grammar for its healthy development, but also its first etymological dictionary' with 'as many as 22,346 words to stand on'.[34] Some years later, Barua went on to write the first sonnet in Assamese, 'Pritomor Sithi' (The Beloved's Letter), published in the Assamese magazine *Jonaki*. Decades later, in *Ramdhenu*, Devkant Barooah evoked similar romanticism in yet another landmark poem in Assamese literature, *Xagor Dekhisa?* (Have You Seen The Ocean?). Saikia had accurately noted that the writings of Hemchandra Barua, Gunabhiram Barua, and some of their contemporaries 'paved the way for an age of reason in the literature as well as in the society in Assam in the mid-19th century.'[35] 'Therefore, though the span of this era was shorter in comparison to the *Orunudoi* era, it proved to be the most important one in the history of modern Assamese language.'[36] Following the footsteps of *Orunudoi*, Gunabhiram Barua started the monthly *Asam Bandhu* (1885–86), which added new life to modern Assamese literature. During its short run the magazine managed to produce an array of powerful writers: Hemchandra Goswami, Ratneswar Mahanta, Bholanath Das, Lambodar Bora, and Satyanath Bora, among others. A major theme for writers during the *Asam Bandhu* era was to produce works based on old Assamese literature. Prior to this, Haribilas Agarwala (1842–1916) had printed Sankardev's *Kirtan Ghosa* (1876) and also the *Bhagavad* books I–III, X, and XI and other noted Vaishnava texts, like *Gunamala*, *Bhakti Ratnavali*, and *Gurucharit*, besides several other mythological and religious books. Agarwala's contemporary Madhab Chandra Bordoloi (1846–1907) was the first to publish the modern Assamese version of Madhav Kandali's Ramayana. Kaliram Barua brought out the *Gita Govinda* of Rama Saraswati in Assamese, among other books.

Gradually, several other newspapers sprung up in Assamese. Two years after *Asam Bandhu* shut down, the next batch of Assamese intelligentsia sprouted through yet another literary journal, *Jonaki*. Remarkably, it began in Kolkata, by drawing inspiration from the Bengali literary 'renaissance', the very movement that resulted in the dismissal of Assamese as a dialect of Bengali.

JONAKI, BANHI, AVAHAN, JAYANTI ERA

The first sparks of an Assamese literary 'rennaissance' flew at a tea party in Kolkata held on 25 August 1888, at Boarding House No. 67 on Mirzapur

Street. It was attended by a motley group of Assamese students. By the time their tea cups were empty, an organization named *Asamiya Bhasar Unnati Sadhini Sabha* had been formed. It was essentially an outfit to help push the growth of the Assamese language and literature. This group would reorganize itself after *Asamiya Satrar Sahitya Sabha*—founded at the behest of Ganga Govinda Phukan in 1872 in Kolkata—became defunct in 1885. Phukan, along with Manickchandra Barua, Jagannath Barua, Devicharan Barua, and some others, then students in Kolkata, had revived an existing organization of Assamese people there by renaming it as *Asamiya Bhasar Unnati Sadhini Sabha*. That Sabha in Kolkata is considered the first such move for the promotion of the Assamese language and literature after *Asam Desh Hitoisini Sabha*, established by one Priyalal Barua along with some others in Sivasagar, Assam, in December 1855. The Sivasagar Sabha was backed by the American Baptist Mission. Though not much is known about the fate of that outfit, it can be inferred from the backing it received from the missionaries that the religious body had then played a role in consolidating public opinion among the linguistically conscious and educated Assamese to organize themselves for the restoration of their language in Assam.

In that Mirzapur Street tea party in 1888, the attendees resolved to have a literary organ too, named *Jonaki*, thereby emphasizing bringing a ray of moonlight (jonak) to the backward land of Assam by helping expand the reach and oeuvre of Assamese language and literature. Writer Chandrakumar Agarwalla, also an uncle of Jyotiprasad Agarwalla, became the owner/editor of *Jonaki*, aided by Lakshminath Bezbaroa and Hemchandra Goswami. This was the trimurti, trio, of modern Assamese literature.

The first edition of *Jonaki* was published on 9 February 1889. Perhaps keeping in mind the sensitivities of the times, the editor in that issue of the magazine categorically stated that it would not involve itself in politics but with literature, science, and society and would also publish criticism without personal prejudice besides taking special care for the promotion and study of the language. After about four years, *Jonaki*'s editions began to be published irregularly, but it picked up pace again in the sixth year. While eminent writer and historian Kanak Lal Barua edited the magazine in the fifth year, in its sixth year, Ramakanta Barkakati became its editor and succeeded in publishing the monthly regularly. By the time the magazine reached its sixth year, several students who were part of the early days of the Sabha, returned home after finishing their academic term in Kolkata. By then though, *Jonaki* had contributed substantially to the promotion and expansion of Assamese literature. In 1901, though an attempt was made to publish *Jonaki* from Guwahati with Satyanath Bora as its editor, in about three years's time, it shut shop for good.

Interestingly, another Assamese literary magazine had begun publishing simultaneously with *Jonaki* from Kolkata, purely because of intellectual disagreement among the students over the publication of a criticism on an article '*Deka-Gabharu*' (Young Men and Women), written by two Sabha members. That magazine was named *Bijuli* (Thunder) and started by the Assamese Students Literary Club in 1813 with Nilakantha Barua as its editor. Writers Padmanath Gohain Baruah and Krishnaprasad Duara took up the role of editor in the future. Writer Benudhar Rajkhowa was also a force behind that magazine. In 1893, it, however, ceased publication.

In the early years of that Assamese literary movement started from Kolkata, *Jonaki* led the way by echoing the notions of romanticism reflected in the Western writings then, and also in writings in Bengali. 'Though *Jonaki* ceased to function in 1903 forever, yet its spirit remained vibrant in Assamese literature till the fourth decade of the 20th century. Assamese periodicals published during that time could not come out of the spell of ideals created by *Jonaki*.'[37] That *Bijuli* couldn't weaken the Kolkata group's endeavour was perhaps because the trio behind *Jonaki* were much senior to the ones behind *Bijuli* both in age and experience.[38] Gunabhiram Barua, however, did promote *Bijuli* by publishing a range of his writings in the monthly. Writers Anandachandra Agarwala, Lambodar Bora, Ratneswar Mahanta, etc. were also *Bijuli* contributors. Padmanath Gohain Baruah wrote several articles about village heads called gaonbura in *Bijuli*, a precursor to his famous play *Gaonbura*.

In 1875, after taking up a schoolteacher's job at a government school in Kohima, then part of Assam, Gohain Baruah penned his autobiography *Mur Suwarani*, a riveting read not just for its evocative nature but also in holding for posterity the times that were and the arduous means of communication that had existed in the Northeast in the early part of the twentieth century. There, he went on to make one of the most noteworthy contributions to Assamese literature by forming Asam Sahitya Sabha. The Sabha, which became a central body of Assamese language and literature in due course, helped shape a reading public within the wider community. The office of the Kohima Sahitya Sabha, known as Lal Ghar for the red painted on its exterior walls, still stands in that city.

By successfully re-establishing the Sabha after his return from Kohima in

Upper Assam, he filled a need increasingly felt by the linguistically conscious to have an exclusive and all-encompassing platform for the promotion of their language and its literature. The first session of the Sabha was held in Sivasagar in 1917 where Gohain Baruah became its president and Sarat Chandra Goswami the secretary. The second president of the Sabha was Chandradhar Barua, a resident of Jorhat, where the literary body had its headquarters before shifting base to Guwahati. The Sabha held its session biennially across different urban and semi-urban parts of Assam to kick up enthusiasm among the masses about reading books, listening to new and established writers, and thereby promote the language. The practice has continued till date. The Sabha also has a publication unit and has printed over 5,000 titles.

Alongside the Sabha working with such literary objectives in the early part of the twentieth century, *Jonaki* was taking romanticism further into Assamese literature, criss-crossing the genres of poetry, essay, belle letters, farce, short story, novel, book reviews, riddles, and students' columns. Since Bezbaroa had led the *Jonaki* era or the first phase of modern Assamese literature (1890–1940), Maheswar Neog had termed the *Jonaki* era as the Age of Bezbaroa or Bezbaruar jug. However, the first bells of romanticism through *Jonaki* were rung by Chandraprasad Agarwala with his poem 'Bon-Kuwari'. Agarwala went on to publish a number of significant Assamese poems in the magazine including 'Tejimola', the first symbolic modern poem in Assamese. Bezbaroa's poem 'Dhanbar Aru Ratani', along with 'Tejimola', laid the path for the creation of literary ballads in Assamese. The genre could be seen in Ananda Chandra Agarwalla's 'Panesai' too. During this time, Chandraprasad Agarwalla's brother Anandachandra Agarwalla came to be referred as Bhangoni Kunwor among Assamese readers for translating English poems into Assamese.

Aside from the likes of Bezbaroa and Hemchandra Goswami, then young Kolkata-based Assamese poets like Chandradhar Barua, Benudhar Rajkhowa, Anandchandra Agarwala, Kanak Lal Barua, and Kamalakanta Bhattacharyya, also showcased their linguistic prowess on the pages of *Jonaki*. Three of *Jonaki*'s major contributions to modern Assamese literature were satirical writings, farces, and short stories. Bezbaroa's extraordinary satirical writings under the pen-name Kripabar Barua were published in *Jonaki*. Kripabar was presented as an alter ego of Bezbaroa, like Pickwick was to Charles Dickens. Nagen Saikia's observation on Kripabar and the intent of the author in creating it can help appreciate the character better.

> His character is in the grand line of Sir Roger De Coverly of Addisson alongside Mr Pickwick of Dickens, to be followed in an Indian literature by *Kamalakanta* of Bankimchandra. Of course, a living character of his mess-mate whose physique and nature provoked Bezbaroa to imagine the character also cannot be ignored. The comic essay on *Barbaroah's Photograph* accompanied by a drawing of the pot-bellied man, and the satirical sonnet on Kripabar Barua shows that he belonged to a world of nonsense rather than that of any sense. He is never conceived as a clown by himself, but there is something clownish about him—an amiable rogue in the sense similar to Shakespearean Fools who represents the mocking conscience-keeper.[39]

Kripabar was massively popular among Assamese readers then, and has continued to be an immortal creation of Bezbaroa. The character was later kept alive by the author through *Banhi*, a literary magazine he went on to publish from Kolkata after *Jonaki* had shut shop.

Bezbaroa's talents also shone with *Litikai*, a farcical drama. The play, along with Kripabar's character, established Bezbaroa as an ace humourist, earning him the sobriquet of Raxaraj or the king of humour. Bezbaroa was also the first to write a modern Assamese short story in *Jonaki* titled 'Konya', which helped lift the curtain on a new genre that would go on to reinforce Assamese literature like none had done. Significantly, thanks to his effort to import the youngest genre of Western literature to Assam at an early stage, the history of Assamese short story is one of the oldest in Indian literature. Interestingly, Bezbaroa could push the edges of the genre also due to his ability to draw inputs from Assamese folktales. His *Burhi Aiyr Xadhu* (Grandmother's Tale), a collection of thirty short stories, is testament to this. 'He is by all means the progenitor of this new genre with a great future in it. And to be so, he owed no debt to any Indian literature.'[40] It is for these remarkable contributions that Bezbaroa is termed the father of modern Assamese literature. Noted Bengali linguist Suniti Kumar Chatterji had once written that 'there should be a study of Lakshminath in the background of the modern 19th century Renaissance of Indian literature and Indian thought.'[41]

Bezbaroa also wrote a novel *Padmakumari*, termed the first historical novel in Assamese. It was the only novel to be serialized in *Jonaki*. In *Bijuli* though, Padmanath Gohain Baruah did serialize two of his novels including *Bhanumati* (1890). Later writers like Trailokya Bhattacharjya (1939–2014) and Debendranath Acharya (1937–81), the genre of the novel in Assamese literature was perfected by Rajani Kanta Bordoloi (1867–1939) with *Mirijiyori* (1895). Another of Bordoloi's great novels was *Manomati* (1900), a poignant tale about the life of a woman during the Burmese invasion of Assam in the early nineteenth century.

Though the practice of reviewing books had started with *Orunudoi*, it was in *Jonaki* that an Assamese book began to be critically looked at for its literary merit. Even though *Jonaki* contributors were Kolkata based, the subjects they discussed were principally from Assam's bucolic life. Though that literary movement in Assamese language was stirred by Bengal's literary movement in the nineteenth century, it is vital to recognize here that the entire exercise also pivoted on shaping Assamese nationalism and identity based on the distinctiveness of the language from Bengali. Therefore, the journey of modern Assamese literature is also closely linked to shaping the Assamese sub-nationalist identity which is why Assamese identity is hinged on language, though culture is also an integral aspect of it.

The year *Jonaki*'s production shifted to Guwahati (1901) was also the year Assam and the Northeast got its first centre of higher education, Cotton College, in Guwahati. Assamese students were no longer compelled to sail to Kolkata for college education. However, the public demand for a university in Assam since 1917 remained unfulfilled till Gauhati University was finally opened in 1948. Noted Sanskrit scholar and former president of Asam Sahitya Sabha, Krishna Kanta Handique, became the first vice chancellor of the university. All the colleges of the Northeast remained affiliated to that university for a long period till the North Eastern Hill University (NEHU), a central government entity, opened its doors in Shillong in 1973. This only underlines the struggle that an average student from the region had to endure in comparison to several other parts of the country to access higher education since the colonial era, which also indirectly cast its shadow on the growth of modern literature in the northeastern languages.

As indicated earlier, after *Jonaki* ceased publishing from Kolkata in 1901, Bezbaroa started *Banhi* from the city. Through *Banhi*, he continued the journey of romanticism in Assamese literature started by *Jonaki*, and offered a much-needed literary universe to a set of newer writers, like Surya Kumar Bhuyan, Nalinibala Devi, Jyotiprasad Agarwala, Tarun Ram Phukan, Ghanashyam Sharma, and Dandinath Kalita, among others. 'O Mur Apunar Dex' a song by Bezbaroa which went on to become the state anthem of

Assam, was published in *Banhi*. The magazine published Assamese cultural icon Bishnu Prasad Rava's songs too, as well as Assamese translations of poems by English writers like Percy Shelley and Lord Byron.

The periodical also published travelogues. Chandradhar Barua's *Bilatot Bhumuki*, a series of travel writings from his visits to London by ship to attend the Round Table Conference in 1930 as a representative of India (the only one from greater Assam), is an interesting read not only for its vivid portrayal of the places seen but also as a documentation of parts of Europe as they were in that era. Significantly, it was in *Banhi* that Bezbaroa also began writing on Sankardev, which makes him the first to begin studying the work of Sankardev. Much later, noted Assamese critic Hiren Gohain presented a perceptive take on Sankardev in the book *Asamiya Jatiya Jibonot Mahapurusia Parampara* (1987) for which he was awarded the Sahitya Akademi Award. While Gohain's book was a critical take on Sankardev's mahapurusia dharma, Bezbaroa's approach on the revered saint in *Banhi* was more adulatory, most likely written with the aim of reminding lay Assamese readers to take pride in their literary and egalitarian religious heritage.

After his demise in 1938 in Kolkata, the magazine continued to be published till 1965 from Assam, edited by his nephews Madhab Chandra Bezborua and Amiya Kumar Das.

Thereafter, a new wave of writings by an altogether fresh set of authors sprung up in Assamese literature, once again brought to the public through a literary magazine—*Avahan*. Started in 1929 with litterateur Dinanath Sarma as it editor, *Avahan* ran till 1942. It became the vehicle for the promotion of short stories penned by the likes of Nagendra Narayan Chaoudhary, Mohichandra Bora, Lakhmidhar Sarma, Holiram Deka, Bina Barua (also Rasna Barua; both are pseudonyms of Birinchi Kumar Bhattacharyya as mentioned above); Birinchi Kumar Baruahh; Trailokyanath Goswami, Roma Das, Krishna Bhuyan, among others. In *Modern Indian Literature, An Anthology: Surveys and Poems,* Sailen Bharali had adequately summed up why *Avahan* became a different era in the trajectory of modern Assamese literature, 'With the exception of Nagendra Narayan Chaudhury, Bina Barua and Trilokyanath Goswami who were primarily concerned with giving a realistic picture of rural life, the others drew their material from the urban society. Birinchi Kumar Baruahh also wrote a few urban-based stories. Lakshmidhar Sarma, a committed writer with a revolutionary outlook, deals with the man-woman relationship from the biological as well as the social point of view. Depicting characters free from the inhibition of traditions, Holiram

Deka touches on contemporary life, particularly of the middle class in its varied moods, and presents it in a lively prose. A moving narrative spiced with subtle humour and satire characterises his stories.'[42] While each writer was different in their approach and selection of subject matters, collectively though, they explored newer vistas which were missing during the *Jonaki* era. Also, unlike *Jonaki*, *Avahan* published political articles, hence creating a pool of new writers and commentators in that genre too.

Still, the influence of Bezbaroa on Assamese literature was strong even in the 1930s. After his death, some other stalwarts of romanticism, like poets Devkant Barooah (1914–96) and Ganesh Chandra Gogoi (1907–38), were entrenched in the genre, ensuring that the sway of romanticism over Assamese literature continued. No wonder then, even promising young poets of the times, like Dhirendra Chandra Dutta (1920–72) and Prasanalal Choudhury (1902–86), were also penning verses reminiscent of Wordsworth, Keats, Browning, etc.[43] But the world was changing fast with the start of World War II. Soon, its influence on the pages of *Avahan* began to surface. 'The rays of the changing times were clearly seen in the poems and thinking of Dhirendra Chandra Dutta. He was a humanist. But his humanism was not like that of the famous poet Chandra Kumar Agarwalla. He was influenced by Kazi Nazrul Islam of Bengal. He could see the result of the class struggle in the society. So his poetic mind was gradually attracted to the real problems of the society. Thus, instead of romantic allusion, he drew the real pictures of the society,' noted academic Maheshwar Kalita.[44] Kalita had also noted that similar poetry was being written by Prasannalal Choudhury in the 1930s. Dutta and Choudhury were influenced by Marxist ideology.

It was also the era when Bezbaroa, his contemporaries and proponents of romanticism passed away, including Kamalakanta Bhattacharyya (in 1936), Chandra Kumar Agarwalla (1938), Ananda Chandra Agarwalla (1939) and Ganesh Gogoi (1938), enabling the entry of new genres of writing in *Avahan*. Perhaps due to such strong and protracted influence of the romantics, the shades of October Revolution (1917) that had cast its shadow on Indian writers didn't quite touch Assamese literature then and could be seen developing only from the 1930s onwards.

In 1942, even as the Quit India Movement swept through India, *Avahan* ceased production. By then, the greater Assam region was engulfed by World War II. The confrontation between the British and the Japanese Army was both on the ground and on air in greater Assam, triggering panic and confusion in common people. 'The situation forced the publishers of magazines to shut down their printing presses. As a result, the famous romantic...*Avahan* age came to an end.'[45] A rich period of regional literature had to meet its sunset due to the war, a rare occurrence in the Indian literary landscape. The void was filled, albeit for only a short period, by yet another literary magazine of the time, *Jayanti*. Between 1943 and 1946, it succeeded in adding new work to the oeuvre of Assamese literature before shutting shop also because of the War. By then, the War had triggered a famine in Assam (1944–45).

The short *Jayanti* era is widely categorized in Assamese literature as the progressive movement. The magazine's editor was the well-known romantic poet of the times, Raghunath Chaudhary. Chaudhary had started the magazine in 1938 but was able to get the readers' attention only after *Avahan*'s closure. After Chaudhary ceased editing it in 1942, young writers Kamal Narayan Dev and Chakreswar Bhattacharyya began co-editing *Jayanti*. Though the duo focused on progressive literature spanning critical essays, short stories, etc. in *Jayanti*, Sailen Bharali observed that progressive themes were more evident in poetry than in any other form of literature.[46] Significant work like Prasannalal Choudhury's 'Nanglalar Geet' was published in *Jayanti*. Among the most distinguished poets from the *Jayanti* era was Bhabananda Datta (1919–59) whose 'Rajpath', published in the first issue of *Jayanti*, used a strikingly new technique and theme. To that period also belonged noted poet and politician Hem Barua (1915–77) and Amulya Barua (1922–46) besides Dev and Chakreswar Bhattacharyya. They were also influenced by Marxist ideology. Kalita, in his book *Navakanta Barua and Sitakant Mahapatra: A Comparative Study*, had put other young poets of the times—Navakanta Barua, Keshav Mahanta, Birendra Kumar Bhattacharyya, and others—also in the *Jayanti* era. Consciousness about the changing realities of the country, Assam and its people had led this young brigade to pick subjects far removed from those from the previous era of romanticism. 'As a result, we have some famous progressive poems by Amulya Barua—*Endharar Hahakar* (Clamour of Darkness), *Kayala* (coal), *Kukur* (Dog), *Beshya* (Prostitute), etc.'[47] After *Jayanti* closed down in 1946, another magazine, *Posuwa*, also contributed to progressive writing in Assamese literature.

Navakanta Barua, one of Assam's eminent poets, had begun his trajectory as a poet during his college days in the 1940s. He too began his literary career by writing romantic poems, like his elder brother Devkant Barooah. Having come in contact with the progressives, he composed poems like 'Prarthana' (Prayer), published in *Jayanti*, portraying disbelief in God. Influenced by T.

S. Eliot, Barua, though, soon changed tack, and published yet another poem in *Jayanti*—'Amar Pritihivi' which echoed romanticism. In all, Barua came out with at least eight collections of poems, of which his first, *Hey Aranya Hey Mahanagar* (O' Woods O' City), published in 1951, created a sensation in Assamese literary circles, thus establishing him as a poet to watch. That collection, with sixteen poems written between 1945 and 1951 mostly in Kolkata where he was a student, was noteworthy for its historical features, a speciality of his poems. The title poem was dedicated to Russian poet Vladimir Mayakovsky (1893–1930). In the collection Navakanta brought alive the dark alleys of Kolkata, drawing a detailed backdrop of life in that city upset by preparations to face World War II. It was within this backdrop that he became a part of the Progressive Writers' Movement that had set off in Assam in the early 1940s. However, as mentioned, Navakanta changed his approach soon. 'Like other poets of the 1940s, Navakanta came to know that the rise of capitalist forces intensifies the class differences. But he did not believe in class struggle. This was the difference between the progressive poets of the 1940s and Navakanta Barua. Navakanta believed that one day the capitalist and the exploited classes will create a new *Ramayana*. Like Ratnakara becoming Valmiki, the exploiting, aristocratic class will have to change their mind and contribute for the development of the society.'[48] It is due to the effort of poets like Navakanta Barua that Assamese poetry acquired a distinctive nature in the 1950s through the 1960s, drawing inspiration not only from Eliot and other English poets of the 1930s but also French symbolists. It helped strengthen Assamese literature well into the post-Independence period, into the *Ramdhenu* era. Though Barua is generally known for his poems, he received the Sahitya Akademi Award for a novel.

Some of the other noted poets who drew from the new romantics and the symbolists were Jnanpith winner Nilamani Phookan, Bireswar Barua, Hirendranath Datta, Ajit Barua, Nirmal Prabha Bordoloi, Harekrishna Deka, Dinesh Chandra Goswami, and Bhaben Barua. 'Ajit Barua, Nilamani Phookan, Bhaben Barua and Hiren Datta were known for their individuality, economy of expression, and the symbolic suggestiveness of style,' noted Bharali.[49] Nilamani Phookan, through his poetry collections like *Surjya Henu Nami aahe Ei Nodiyedi* (The Sun Is Said to Descend from This River, 1963), offered to Assamese poetry a new poetic sensibility.

Simultaneously, there emerged another set of poets moved by the need for economic justice, humanism, and social equality, like Hem Barua, Syed

Abdul Malik, Keshab Mahanta, Ram Gogoi, and Hiren Bhattacharya. 'A set of promising poets joined them in the seventies. They include Rabindra Sarkar (born in 1945) and Samir Tanti (born in 1956). Hiren Bhattacharya is perhaps the most popular poet of the group,' noted Bharali.[50] Citing two of Hiren Bhattacharya's important poetry collections noted for their lyricism—*Mur Desh Mur Premar Kabita* (Poems of My Country and My Love, 1972) and *Bibhinna Dinar Kabita* (Poems of Different Days, 1971)—Bharali remarked, 'It is in his poetry that progressive social ideas appear in the most distilled form.'[51] Homen Borgohain's selection of poems and poets spanning a century, *Exo Bosoror Axamiya Kobita*, is a precious peep into the trajectory of poetry in Assamese literature. Some other noted names of poets of the times were Gyan Pujari, Rafikul Hussain, Kabin Phukan, and Sananta Tanti.

Poetry aside, in the *Ramdhenu* era, the genre of short stories also got further impetus from fresh writers contributing to it with newer subjects. Among the shining stars was Surendra Nath Medhi (1930–2011), better known in Assamese society by the pseudonym Saurabh Kumar Chaliha. He brought to Assamese literature the Sahitya Akademi Award in 1974 for his short story collection *Gulam*. Chaliha, who taught statistics at Gauhati University, was the son of noted writer, linguist and the third president of Asam Sahitya Sabha, Kaliram Medhi. Though he is considered a writer from the *Ramdhenu* era, Chaliha's recognition as a short story writer of note began with *Banhi* and *Jayanti*. While 'Era', 'Karl Marx', 'Censor', 'Bihu Dhanatantrar Saat', etc. were published in *Banhi*, the likes of 'Deenbabu', 'Tinilakh Bonua', and 'Rivhan' were seen in *Jayanti*.[52] However, his sensational short story was 'Oxantro Electron' which bagged him the first prize at the short story competition for students at Cotton College in 1950. 'Like his other short stories, *Osanto Electron* was also unusual. It didn't have a well bloomed narrative structure. Unlike other stories, there was no one main character but multiple characters at play; their mental workings become the mainstay of the narrative,' stated Prahald Kumar Baruah in his detailed work on the genre *Asomiya Suti Galpar Adhyana*.[53] That short story held up for readers the post-World War II society where people became increasingly money-minded, unscrupulous. Arup Kumar Dutta, in his foreword to the English translation of Chaliha's 'Oxantro Electron' (The Restless Electron) by Jiban Goswami, stated, 'Chaliha's forte is the piling of details after minute details of the background within which the story is placed.'[54] Chaliha's forte lay in drawing the reader into the gradually developing urban scape, which is portrayed splendidly in yet another short story, 'Bina Kutir', through a clash of two generations. His 'Bhraman Biroti' is particularly notable for putting a Freudian lens on life philosophy.[55] Many had found Kafka in his stories.[56]

The modernist approach of Chaliha's short stories was further carried forward in their own way by writers like Pranab Jyoti Deka (in 'Bewaris Laas'), Apurba Sarma (in 'Bandhur Pathot Keijonman Dekamanuh' to 'Baghe Tapur Rati'), Harekrishna Deka (in 'Bandiyar'), Devabrata Das (in 'Arpitar Erati') and Manoj Kumar Goswami (in 'Samiran Barua Ahi Ase').

A writer contemporary to Chaliha who had an equally modernist approach was Rebatimohan Duttachoudhury, in the pseudonym Silabhadra. He rose to prominence with his first short story collection *Bastab* (Reality) published in 1964 in the magazine *Assam Batori*, then edited by Chandraprasad Saikia. A prolific writer, in the next twenty years, he wrote twenty-two short story collections, seven novels, and several essays. Though he belonged to the *Ramdhenu* era, he remained one of the rare noted Assamese writers to have begun writing in another magazine first.

Though the magazine ceased production in 1959, the *Ramdhenu* era that had begun in Assamese literature soon after Independence has, in a way, continued largely due to the general absence of postmodern subjects in Assamese literature. 'Though the 1961 Chinese aggression had hit hard the common man both in Assam and Arunachal Pradesh (then attached to Assam), we didn't see it surfacing in our literature of the 1960s to the 1970s as a trend. The same thing happened during Assam agitation and insurgency in the 1980s and the 1990s, with some rare exceptions. Only the human rights violation part from the insurgency era was picked by most writers but several other aspects of the movement hardly got reflected in our literature as a new wave of writing. So, the *Ramdhenu* era has practically continued,' critic Areendom Borkataki had told me.

Though since the 1980s, some popular literary magazines have been published, particularly *Prakash*, *Goriyoshi*, *Xatsori*, and *Prantik*, they have not been able to firmly make space for themselves in Assamese literature. Noted literary critic Ananda Barmudoi had observed that the Assamese short story trajectory 'exhibits a double tendency which is somewhat contradictory: on the one hand, the new-age writers manifest a desire to extend the glorious tradition of the *Ramdhenu* and *Awahan (Avahan)* era, and on the other, there is conscious effort to resist the impact of the previous tradition.'[57] He said, 'It has resulted in the evolving of a creative praxis that entails series of experiments in the art of narration. Absence of a central theme and a non-committal authorial stance invest contemporary short story writing with signs of modernity, which were hardly seen before.'[58] Speaking in the context of short stories, noted poet, critic, and short story writer Harekrishna Deka, though, had written that the *Ramdhenu* era had technically ended as writers of that period focused on the nature of reality in the modern era while the present short story writers are concentrating on the form of the narrative.[59]

Deka had also served as the director general of police in Assam aside from being a noted writer. Interestingly, this trend is seen quite prominent in Assamese literature. Two other writers who also served as DGPs in Assam Police were Jnananada Sarma Pathak and Kuladhar Saikia. Saikia, aside from being the president of Asam Sahitya Sabha, also bagged the Sahitya Akademi Award in 2015 for his short story collection *Akashar Chhabi Aru Ananya Galpa.*

Two noted Assamese writers who also need a mention in this chapter are late Umakanta Sarma, and Dhrubajyoti Bora, much younger than Sarma. Some of Sarma's notable works include the novel *Ejak Manuh Ekhan Aranya*, and *Bharanda Pakhir Jaak*, hinged on the Bodo ethnic conflict. Sarma began as a playwright, then moved on to writing short stories and later to novel writing. Dhrubajyoti Bora has rolled out impressive literary work too, from travelogues to historical novels to short stories. Some of his notable work are the *Luha* (1985), *Bhuk* (1987), *Jatrik Aru Ananya* (1994), *Kalantarar Gadya* trilogy (1997–2003), etc. In 2009, he was bestowed the Sahitya Akademi Award for his novel *Kala Ratnakar.*

Between 2016 and 2019, a group of young writers and poets affiliated to Char Chapori Sahitya Parishad of Assam had attempted a postmodern trend within Assamese literature pivoted on the state's migration issue and the alleged mistreatment of the Assamese Muslims of Bengali origin (often called Miya locally) by the mainstream Assamese communities. The writers had termed it Miya poetry. Though the Parishad president Hafiz Ahmed had told me in an interview for *The Wire* in 2019 that most Miya poetry was written in Assamese and only a few in their dialects, those verses, nevertheless, kicked up a controversy in the state with the poets being targeted by the local media, by right-wing politicians, and also by a wide section of the public.[60] Almost all the poets and writers involved were Muslims with Bengali origins, and at the time the National Register of Citizens (NRC) in Assam was being updated, which somewhat contributed to the sharp reaction they faced.

However, a section of Assamese writers, including noted public intellectual Hiren Gohain, had also opposed their choice on the grounds that the dialects in which some of the poems were written are considered a part of Bengali, and therefore, they could not be part of Assamese literature. Nevertheless, Ahmed, in his interview with me, had tried piecing for me a continuity, albeit sporadic, of writings on the sufferings of the migrant Miya community in Assam in Assamese literature since the 1930s. He had counted an Assamese poem written by Maulana Bande Ali in 1939 on the travails of the *Char-ua Mussalman* or the Muslims residing on the sand bars (char) of the Brahmaputra as the fount of the trend in Assamese literature; he was later corrected by Homen Borgohain that it was noted poet Atul Chandra Hazarika who wrote that poem in pseudonym. 'Whether he was Atul Chandra Hazarika or Maulana Bande Ali, Miyah poetry owes its origin to him,' Borgohain had said. Ahmed also counted in this genre a collection of idioms and phrases prevalent in the sand bars of Assam written by M. Illimuddin Dewan in the 1960s and pointed out to me that after the Nellie massacre of 1983, Khabir Ahmed wrote a poem 'Binito Nibedon' (I Beg to State) in Assamese with words like 'I am a settler, a hated Miya'. 'After Khabir Ahmed, people like us have been writing. I have published two books of poetry in Assamese,' he added. One of his poems is 'I Am a Miya', an Assamese poem now highly controversial in Assam, based on a poem by Palestinian poet Mahmoud Darwish. Upset at being attacked for writing that poem, he had retorted, 'I want to ask those who have questioned me about the poem, is my love for Assam, Assamese language, and literature any less than theirs?'

ASSAMESE WOMEN WRITERS

A number of women writers have also contributed substantially to the literary world of Assam. We find mention of Padmavati Devi Phukanani (1853–1927), daughter of Anandaram Dhekial Phukan, whose *Sudharma's Upakhyan* (Sudharma's Tale) penned in 1884 was the second Assamese novel. Thanks to her visionary father who had also batted for women's education, she became one of the first Assamese women to have been formally educated. She later wrote a book for students, *Hitahadhika*. As a feminist writer too, her contributions are noteworthy. Widowed at thirty-two, she penned articles on the travails of a widow in *Bidhoba* and on the social status of women in *Samajat Tirutar Sthan*.

Gunabhiram Barua's daughter Swarnalata Baruah (1871–1932) penned *Aarhi Tirota* (Model Woman) besides contributing to *Asam Bandhu* and *Bijuli*. Barua's wife Bishnupriya Devi also wrote a story book, *Niti Katha*. Dharmeswari Devi Baruani (1892–1960), influenced by romanticism, composed poems like *Phulor Sorai* way back in 1929. Jamuneswari Khatoniyar (1899–1924), in her short life, not only left a collection of Assamese poems (*Arun* in 1919) but had also organized the Juroni Sabha, a religious and literary gathering at her house every evening.

Perhaps the most well-known of women poets in Assam from the *Jonaki* era was Nalinibala Devi (1889–1977). Her *Sandhyar Sur* was noteworthy as was her autobiography *Eri Aha Dinbur* (The Days Gone By). She became the first woman president of Asam Sahitya Sabha in 1954, to be followed by Nirmal Prabha Bordoloi only in 1991. That in the 105-year-old history of the foremost literary body in Assam, only two women have risen to the position of president thus far hints at the intrinsic patriarchy in Assamese society. This is particularly deplorable when one takes into account the trajectory of Assamese women writers starting from the likes of Padma Priya who was one of the earliest poets in Indian vernacular literature.

Much later, in the *Avahan* era, Chandraprava Saikiani raised many an eyebrow by writing her short story 'Daibagyar Duhita' (The Brahmin's Daughter). A tale of a child widow, her story had given Assamese literature yet another Menoka who chose to not remain silent in the face of patriarchal practices. Saikiani herself became an unwed mother. Her stories in *Banhi* and *Avahan* in the 1920s, like 'Devi' (in *Banhi*, 1921), 'Akul Pathik', and 'Daibagyar Duhita' (in the first issue of *Avahan*, 1929) had 'carved out a space for women as writers and women as the radical subject of delineation in literature'.[61] Noted Assamese feminist writer Aparna Mahanta in *Journey of Assamese Women (1836–1937)* remarked, 'If Chandraprava Saikiani had concentrated on writing, she would have become an important short story writer but her energies were diverted to her social and political activities.'[62] Hemjyoti Medhi, in her essay in *Communities of Women in Assam*, had showed that the way Saikiani led her life was in itself a powerful message to the society of her times. 'The dynamics of sexual morality, caste and class construct acquired new significance when Chandraprabha Saikiani assumed leadership of the provincial AMS (Asam Mahila Samiti) as the founding secretary. Saikiani belonged to the *Sut* caste and was a mother outside of marriage. She unapologetically carried her toddler son in most of her socio-political engagements, whether as a volunteer in the Indian National Congress in Pandu in 1926 or as an AMS secretary during the Golaghat AMS conference in 1929.'[63] The first women's journal in Assamese, *Ghar Jeuti*, began in 1928 and ran till 1932.

Medhi, highlighting how various women tried organizing themselves during that period, had pointed out that the Agarwallas (the family of Jyoti Prasad Agarwalla) of Tezpur provided space in their house Poki to women to start a sipini bhoral (weavers' store) and reporting the activities of the local mahila samiti in their weekly *Asamiya* (started in 1918). Several magazines of the times had also facilitated community mobilization.[64]

Post-Independence, in the *Ramdhenu* era, a galaxy of women writers began penning short stories, novels, and poetry. Nirupama Borgohain, Sneha Devi, Kamalini Borbora, Nilima Sarma, Anima Dutta, Prabina Saikia, and Indira Goswami (Mamoni Roisom Goswami) were among the top names to attract readers' attention. Nirupama Borgohain's short story *Anthropologir Saponar Pisot*, though written in her college days, is still talked about in Assam's literary circles as a great piece of literature. In 1996, she bagged the Sahitya Akademi Award for her novel *Abhijatri*.

Celebrated author Indira Goswami (1942–2011) followed the course of Assamese women writers offering a peep into the inner world of women through their work through a succession of extraordinary novels. Goswami truly became the one who could cross the threshold of Assamese literature to become a national literary figure. A huge amount of research has been conducted around her characters particularly in the discourse of feminist writing, be it Giribala in *Datal Hatir Uye Khuwa Hawda* (1988) or Houdamini from *Nila Kantha Braja* (1976), Damayanti in *Sanksar*, or even the depiction of her own life in her marvellous autobiography *Adhalekha Dastabej* (Unfinished Autobiography). Her novels have also been translated into multiple national and international languages.

Goswami, through her writings, also brought to Assamese literature characters and plots from the rest of India. Her novel *Mamore Dhora Taruwal* (written in 1980 for which she was conferred the Sahitya Akademi Award in 1982) showcased the plight of construction workers at a building site in 1960s Madhya Pradesh. In *Nilakantha Braja*, she presented the utter poverty and sexual exploitation of the widows of Vrindavan. Having witnessed the 1983 anti-Sikh riots of Delhi, she wrote the poignant novel *Tej Aru Dhulire Dusharit Pristha*. An expert on Ramayana literature, her *Dosorothor Khoj* is worth a read. Her novel *Chinnamastar Manuhto* is based on the ritual of animal sacrifice practised at the Kamakhya Temple in Guwahati; she remained a vegetarian all her adult life in protest against that ritual.

Goswami's literary genius also pivoted around short stories and poems. In 2000, she was conferred the Jnanpith, making her the second Assamese writer to be given that prestigious award.

After formidable writers like Goswami entered another set of distinguished Assamese writers, like Arupa Patangia Kalita, Tilottama Misra, Manorama Das Medhi, Anuradha Sarma Pujari, Karabi Deka Hazarika, Rita Chowdhury, and Moushumi Kandali. The list is only getting longer. Rita Chowdhury's powerful novel *Deo Langkhui*, with a plot based on a Tiwa tribe in Assam, won her the Sahitya Akademi Award in 2008. Her *Makam* (2010) was a groundbreaking work, depicting the travails of people of Chinese origin in Assam, worsened due to the Chinese aggression.

To my mind, one of the strongest voices today not only within the arena of Assamese literature but also in Indian vernacular literature is Arupa Patangia Kalita. Reading her novel *Felanee* can be an extraordinary experience for a reader. *Felane*e, focused on Assam's conflict-torn society between 1983 and 1998, was her seventh novel; each of her novels is worthy of one's time. In an interview with Aruni Kashyap in 2008, Patangia had related that she usually picks subjects related to women because she is a woman herself. 'If I were a black woman, I would have written about black women. It is as simple as that. In this uneven society that I belong to, I always feel I have a lot to say about women, as a woman.'[65]

Patangia is also a powerful short story writer. In 'Bir Daimalur Xadhu' (The Tale of Brave Daimalu), 'the myths and legends of the hoary past come alive as the old man, visited by the narrator, unfolds the accounts of the genesis of the Bodos.' Aditi Chowdhury, commenting on the short story, wrote, 'The tale becomes a kind of a parable for the rampant violence and unwarranted killings ravaging the community in recent years. The entire story is not about Daimalu alone. The narrator simultaneously chronicles the history of the Bodo community traversing many time zones.'[66] In the short stories 'Ashrulipi' (Written in Tears) and in 'Podulit Duta Bokul Gosere Niva Bou' (Niva and Her House with Two Bakul Plants), Patangia who has so fittingly located the conflict situation in Assam as the backdrop to tell her stories, accentuates the point that 'conflict situations lead to gendered experience where women face psychological trauma, physical violence, sexual harassment more than men'.[67]

Tilottama Misra must be acknowledged for her brilliant contributions as well, like *Swarnalata*, a historical and biographical novel circling around three women in the mid-ninteenth century Assam; *Lauhitya Sindhu*, a novel on life around the Brahmaputra; and *Ka Meikhar Ghar*, based on the Assamese society in Shillong when it was a part of Assam and inter-community relations in a Khasi-dominated city. Her book, *Literature And Society in Assam: A Study of Assamese Rennassiance 1826-1926*, published in 2011, is a dazzling contribution to the oeuvre of non-fiction from Assam that encapsulates Assamese literature from the nineteenth century to the early twentieth century.

Another powerful voice in the realm of contemporary Assamese short story is Moushumi Kandali. Writer and journalist Ratna Bharali Talukdar told me in June 2021, 'Short story is one of the strongest genres of Assamese literature because a lot of good writers have over the decades contributed to it which includes a number of women. However, after Saurab Chaliha's celebrated oeuvre encompassing a wide diversity of subjects and their unusual treatment, I would have to come straight to Moushumi Kandali's work even though she had begun writing in that genre only since the 1990s.'[68] Across Kandali's writings, one can spot diverse thematic concerns—from modernity to identity dynamics, gender, intra-personal relations, and significantly, the complexities of life against the backdrop of the sociocultural ethos of various tribes of Assam. In 2013, in an interview for *The Hindu*, Kandali, a winner of Yuva Purashkar of Bharatiya Bhasha Parishad (2005), told me that she derived that consciousness about the tribal life of Assam from her upbringing in Karbi Anglong where her father was posted.[69] Hiren Gohain had once written about her, 'In Moushumi Kandali's short stories, there is a proclivity to highlight the significance of even a minor event. It is as if the feelings that surface in that intellectual journey becomes an instance of T. S. Eliot's unified sensibility.'[70]

Kandali was first noticed in 1993 on the pages of *Prantik* magazine for her short story 'Junakot Dhekia' (Ferns in the Moonlight). Since then, she has only broken barriers in that genre. Her 'Tritiottor Galpa' (Tale of Thirdness) dexterously brings to readers the subject of the third gender and the raw sensitivities associated with it.

In due course of time, a number of formidable young women have popped up on the literary horizon, thus promising a bright future for the genre. Nandita Devi, Purobi Bormudoi (Sahitya Akademi Awardee in 2007 for her novel *Swadhinata)*, Monika Devi, Manikuntala Bhattacharyya, Jamuna Sarma Choudhury, Anamika Borah, Bipasha Borah, Rashmirekha

Bora, Bonti Senchowa, Parthana Saikia, Gitali Bora, Juri Borah Borgohain, Juri Baruah, etc. have been stirring the literary scene. Mention must be made here of Nandita Devi's one-of-a-kind novel *Bangal Bohu Dur* (2019), which deals with the life of Brahmin priests from Kamrup who had once regularly travelled to Bengal for rituals and would not return home for long periods of time.

Translation work by Assamese women writers got a fillip in 2021 with Pori Hiloidhari bagging the Sahitya Akademi prize for translating from English to Assamese *The Legends of Pensam* by noted writer Arunachali writer Mamang Dai. Two noted women literary critics are Aparna Mahanta and Malini Goswami. Mahanta is currently the editor of *Ghar Jeuti*, the first Assamese women's journal that was published in the 1920s, and was revived in the 2000s. Two of the noted names from the 1920s–30s who were the original editors of *Ghar Jeuti* were Kanaklata Chaliha and Kamalalaya Kakati.

Ever conscious of what is engulfing the present times, this crop of women writers are already bringing to Assamese literature the realities of the devastating effect of the Covid-19 pandemic too. Ratna Bharali Talukdar's short story 'Hengulia Tuponir Bate Pari Diya Soku Haal' is a moving take on the real-life toils of a migrant who ends up burning hundreds of bodies of Covid victims at a Guwahati crematorium. Bharali's 'Kiling Songkrat' is yet another story inspired by the real-life tragedy of the rape of a young Karbi girl, and draws a parallel with a popular Karbi folklore to present for readers the degradation of human beings in today's world.

11

XUR–TAAL, NAAS–GAAN: ASSAMESE MUSIC AND DANCE

Have you ever had a madeleine de Proust moment for sound?

Sound, or song, that awakens a childhood memory or two?

While approaching this chapter on Assamese music, certain distinct moments from my childhood in Assam came alive for me, particularly in relation to three songs. The first among them was a Bhupen Hazarika rendition of the sixteenth century Vaishnava saint Madhabdev's adulatory composition on little Krishna: 'Tejore Kamalapati Porobhato Nindo'. These words would roughly translate to English as, 'Quit your slumber O Kamalapati; wake up, it is dawn.'

The inimitable Hazarika, through his slow and deep delivery of the devotional song, gave to my nascent self a curiosity about a set of words that I didn't quite grasp fully then. Yet, I could profoundly connect with those words through the semantics of music.

The second song that evoked a remembrance of childhood in me was:

Saheb Jai Aagote
Hoi Saheb Hoi
Bhokot Jai Pasote
Hoi Saheb Hoi

This is also a Hazarika song, sung with Mohammad Rafi and composed by decorated Assamese writer Syed Abdul Malik.[1] The words in English would mean: the Sahib leads, is followed by his cohorts; yes, they do, yes they do.

The composition is a Jikir, a form of devotional music sung in a group crafted by the seventeenth century Sufi saint Ajaan Fakir. I didn't quite understand the words of this number either in my childhood but felt particularly attracted to it because of its playfulness and the listener's ability to sway to it in simple joy just by the clapping of hands. It was the Assamese version of a qawwali, aired often by the Guwahati and Dibrugarh stations of the All India Radio (AIR), the only way for many in the state to listen to recorded music from 1950s to the 1980s.

The third song that peeped through the recesses of my mind was a Bihu number that I don't get to hear any more, and can recall only four short lines of. It went somewhat like this:

Niru Niru Niru Mai
Niru Aaji Ghorot Nai
Niru Goisil Brahmapoutrar Paroloi
Xute Nile Utuai

In English, those Assamese words would mean 'O Niru, Niru, where is she? Not at home today; she had gone to the banks of the Brahmaputra; its current washed her away.'

The tragedy of the event—the reality of life led by a riverine community—didn't quite hit me then; I only sang it as a frisky song set to Bihu tune, meant only for springtime joy. I don't even remember who had sung that Bihu score.

Now, decades later, on reflecting, I derive a strange sense of gratification for having instinctively kept in my mind's bank three songs from my early life that have turned out to be from three genres of Assamese music; each unique in its own way; each underlining the eclectic expanse of the community's sense of descant and ardour towards piety, syncretism, and nature and its rubrics.

BORGEET

The song mentioned first—'Tejore Kamalapati'—is a Borgeet, meaning 'great song' in English. In Assamese, anything special or large has the prefix bor, a reason why the largest cloth is called bor kapur; the commander of the Ahom army bor phukan, and so on.[2] It is no surprise then that the songs composed by the most revered saint of the community, Sankardev, and his principal disciple, Madhabdev, in late fifteenth and sixteenth centuries in devotion to little Krishna—the form that their 'Ek Sarana Nama Dharma' extols—are also called Borgeet.

Borgeet, or songs sung extolling the greatness of Krishna, are essentially devotional numbers rendered at the naam-ghar/kirtan-ghar, the prayer halls for believers of Sankardev's Neo-Vaishnavite faith. Since naam-ghars have thrived both inside and outside Vaishnava monasteries, these compositions have been sung by devotees at a shared space as well as in the privacy of their homes.

Over 500 years ago, the guru–shishya duo had enriched Assamese music—and thereby Indian sacred music—by composing around 340 such Borgeets, though several of them had vanished in the sands of time for lack of documentation. Sankardev is widely believed to have written 240 of them himself, as prayers. The story goes that the only book of those compositions were lost when the house of Kamal Gayan, one of the Guru's disciples, caught fire. 'The saint was extremely sad on account of this and urged upon his worthy disciple Madhabdev the task of composing (a) fresh set of hymns.'[3] By then, Sankardev was of ripe old age; he passed away two years later.

That was how Madhabdev began writing Borgeets too. Having taken the mantle from his Guru, he documented Sankardev's Borgeets from the oral memory of Vaishnava musicians and disciples of his times besides composing several of them himself. According to the biographical writing on Vaishnava saints, *Katha Gurucharit*, those Borgeets counted up to 191. Still, the devotees commonly refer to them as baro kuri or 240 in number, as twelve or baro is considered an auspicious number in Assamese Vaishnava culture (for instance, the concept of Baro Bhuyan, the clan Sankardev belonged to, as explained earlier in the book.)[4]

Aside from the gentle lilt and the devotional nature of the Borgeet, it needs highlighting that they were composed in a literary language, Brajawali. First used in Assam by Sankardev to produce literature, the language is a mix of an early form of Assamese and Maithili. Though the language is called Brajawali, or the language of Braja, or Vrindavan, it is unlike what we know as Braja Bhasha or Braja Boli in North India.[5] Some categorize Sankardev's Brajawali as classical Assamese too as it cemented the fount of Assamese literature and the arts, and brought about a cultural, religious, and social awakening not noted in eastern India till then.

Brajawali language had developed as a literary language and spread across eastern India, comprising Odisha, Bengal, and Assam, in the medieval era. It was called Brajabuli in Odisha and Bengal. What needs highlighting, though, is the antiquity of the Assamese version of the language. In 1935, noted Bengali linguist and historian Sukumar Sen had pointed out, 'Assamese Brajabuli seems to have developed independently through direct connexion with Mithila but in Orissa we can legitimately expect Bengali influence in the matter.'[6] Maheswar Neog had argued that Sankardev might have been the first to use it in eastern India as written records had shown Sankardev having penned his first Borgeet during his pilgrimage to Northern India between 1481 and 1494. In Raga Dhanasri, the saint sang *Mana meri, Rama-charanohi laagu; toni dekho na antaka agu* at Badrarikasrama, located 'to the extreme north at one of the many sources of the Ganges'.[7] 'As this small poem was composed during Sankardev's first pilgrimage (to North India), we can safely consider it to be the first lyric to have been written in Brajabuli (Bhajawali) in Assam, Bengal, and Orissa. The earliest Brajabuli lyric in Bengali literature is the one by Yasoraja Khan in which the poet makes a mention of Hussain Shah, the ruler of Gauda (1493–1519). The famous poem, *Pahilahi raga nayana-bhamga bhela*, by Ramananda Raya Kavi, a political agent of King Pratap Rudra—Gajapati (1504–32)—is the first such composition in Orissa.'[8]

Sankardev and Madhabdev used that literary language not only in their Borgeets, but also in Bhatima, an ode to the Lord, and in Ankiya Naat, religious dramas, an art not noticed in Odisha or Bengal at the times.

Continuing that centuries-old tradition, the daily prayer service—naam praxanga—at a Vaishnava monastery in Assam still begins with a Borgeet. In 1991, Dwijendranath Bhakat had pointed out in a book on Borgeet that the principal strand of the musical form is the Bhakti rasa.[9] 'Prior to Bhakti Movement, there was no recognition of *Bhakti* as one of the nine *rasas* in the Indian classical arts…though Sankar-Madhab didn't create a separate treatise on the *rasas* but like in their other artistic work (hinged on *Bhagavad Purana*), they also included *Bhakti* as a rasa in the Borgeets.'[10] Vaishnava scholars have, however, stated that Borgeets have six rasas or sentimentalities: leela (the divinity shown through various actions when Vishnu descends on earth as little Krishna); paramartha (the knowledge of the supreme, the Brahmin); viraha (pangs of Krishna's separation from mother Yashodha and the milkmaids of Vrindavan); virakti (indifference towards earthly objects); surr (little Krishna playing the role of a thief and stealing milk products from the milkmaids); and chatura (Krishna's cleverness and roundabout answers to his naughty acts).[11] It is because of these rasas that the Borgeets are also categorized as bhushan haranar geet (on the stealing of adornments), etc.

Since Sankardev's sect, unlike other Bhakti reformers, doesn't celebrate Radha along with Krishna, she is mentioned only in five Borgeets penned by Madhabdev which fall in the category of bhushan haranar geet. This may be because Sankardev's Neo-Vaishnavism is based on Bhagavad Gita and Bhagavad Purana which find no mention of Radha.[12]

Today, the Borgeets, when sung on stage, may be accompanied by modern musical instruments but in the days of yore, only a few were necessary for a well-rounded recital. The ensemble included the mridanga, the traditional wooden drums; khol, the clay drums; taal or kah, bell metal cymbals of varying sizes; also the one-string instruments been and tokari. In some places, there is a mention of using rabab and serengadar or sarinda with Borgeet too.[13]

Borgeets also make use of raag, though no taal or timed beat is indicated for most of them in any text. Between Sankar–Madhab, one could count the use of at least twenty-seven ragas in the Borgeets. Some of these ragas were also used by Assamese composers prior to Sankardev. Two composers senior to Sankardev—Pitambara Kavi and Durgabor Kayastha—also used ragas like Ahir, Bhairavi, Bhathiali, Dhanasri, Vasanta, Ramagiri, Suhai, and Gunjari.[14]

Since there has been a play of ragas in Borgeet and also because they are sung in praise of Lord Krishna, for a considerable period now, there has been a demand in Assam to recognize the genre as a classical form of music, like the ritualistic music extolling Lord Jagannatha in Odisha. For decades now, while some experts have equated the Borgeet to the oldest Hindustani classical form Dhrupad, some others consider it an example of Prabandha sangeet; still some see it as an altogether separate category of music. Though in the 1950s itself, the Assam chapter of the Sangeet Natak Akademi (SNA) had formed a research committee to delve into the matter, and its heads, Maheswar Neog, along with Savita Devi, the doyen of semi-classical vocal forms of Hindustani music, had co-edited a book in 1959 on the subject, years have elapsed with nothing concrete springing out of it. Among some others in Assam, Sattriya dancer Prateesha Suresh too is amplifying the Borgeet's importance. In an interview in 2019, she had celebrated the contribution of Borgeet singer Krishna Goswami, son of a former monastic head of the Samaguri monastery in Majuli, for having made notations for more than sixty Borgeet and published books about them.[15] As it is an oral tradition, Borgeets didn't have notations. Significantly, Suresh, in that interview, had also highlighted that the percussion instrument khol, used in Borgeet, and in the Sattriya dance designed by Sankardev, has not been recognized as a classical instrument by the SNA even though the dance itself had been categorized as so.

LATER VAISHNAVA GEET

After Sankar–Madhab's demise, several of their disciples continued to uphold the tradition of composing sacred songs in Brajawali. It drives home the point that a great visionary that he was, Sankardev could not only draw people to sing his compositions but also inspired several within the Vaishnava umbrella to approach that category of songwriting as a distinct genre of Assamese musical composition which they could practice. However, those later compositions were never recognized as Borgeet.

Still, it must be noted that among the four sects that had sprung out of Sankardev's teachings, Kala Samhati—the most persecuted lot by the later Ahom royals in collusion with the ritualists and Brahmin priests—had contributed the most to Vaishnava devotional music. 'Gopal Ata (the originator of the sect) himself wrote three dramas and a number of geet. Among the other three sects, while Srimanta Sarma (also known as Srirama of Ahatguri) composed 81 geets, Jadumanidev (known as Bar Ata of Bahabari or Henuliya Jadumani, 1565–1618) wrote 142, and Aniruddhadeva's (1553–1626) number came up to 182 geets.'[16] Additionally, between Srirama's son Ramananda Dvija, and Ramananda's son Ramagopala, and several successors of Jadumanideva in the Dvija Satra including Kaivalyanadeva (1715–82), there were about 161 geet which Neog could salvage through his research.[17] Several successors of Aniruddhadeva, including Nityanandadeva who is believed to have been killed at the instance of King Surampha (1649–52) during the Moamorai rebellion of the peasants led by that sub-sect, were among those who composed a rich opus of Vaishnava geet. Importantly, Gopal Ata's daughter—Padmapriya—too wrote geet on the lines of the Borgeet,[18] perhaps the first Assamese woman to do so.

Followers of yet another sect, the Nika Samhati, also composed such songs for devotional recitals.[19] Sankardev's two grandsons, and a nephew of Madhabdev, wrote such songs too.[20] A Muslim disciple of Sankardev, Chandsai or Chand-Kha, also wrote such verses.[21] Likewise, there are several anonymous geet which are commonly ascribed to Madhabdev. Apart from being an astute songwriter, Madhabdev was also a brilliant singer.

The later Vaishnava devotional songs were written either in Brajawali or in a mix of present-day Assamese and Brajawali. Neog had rightly documented, 'Gopaldev Ata, Jadumanideva and Aniruddhadeva [were] good literary successors of the two great teachers in this respect.'[22]

Between the end of the seventeenth century and mid-eighteenth century, we also find mention of songs composed by Ahom kings Rudra Singha (1695–1714) and son Siva Singha (1714–44); also by the two court poets of their times, Kaviraja Chakravartti and Gopalchandra.[23] Chakravartti had translated to Assamese the twelfth century Sanskrit poet Jaydeva's epic poem on Krishna's love for Radha, *Gita Govinda*. Though the first translation of the classic was done by Rama Saraswati, a contemporary of Sankardev, the romantic thought in devotional poetry and literature couldn't then quite outdo the thoughts promoted by Sankardev. Koch general Chilarai had penned a Sanskrit commentary on Rama Saraswati's translated verses of *Gita Govinda*. Nevertheless, it can be safely said that it was only in Rudra Singha's time, after Chakravartti had translated them into Assamese, that the verses of *Gita Govinda* had some influence in Assamese literature.

While the later devotional songs inspired by Sankar–Madhab have not quite found a wider acceptance in Assamese society yet, Borgeets have remained a key column of Assamese music. Be it Bhupen Hazarika (1926–2011), or his senior contemporaries Jyotiprasad Agarwala (1903–51) and Bishnu Prasad Rava (1909–69), or all the top singers of later generations, all have sung this genre of music, thus further consolidating its roots and reach among the masses.

JIKIR

As highlighted above, songs like 'Saheb Jai Agote' are Jikirs, compositions of the Sufi saint Ajaan Fakir who is widely believed to have trod all the way from Iran to spread Islam in medieval Assam. It is commonly said that Ajaan Fakir's compositions, to do with devotion to Allah as the supreme being, are 160 (aath kuri in Assamese) in number. However, several of them have been lost due to lack of written documentation. For a long while, Jikirs had remained alive within the Assamese Muslim community as an oral tradition. Even in the 1970s, when authors Syed Abdul Malik and Muhibul Hussain began documenting Jikirs, they faced resistance from Muslim villagers of Upper Assam because of a local belief that they should never be written down. Malik had particularly pointed this belief out in his notable book *Axomiya Jikir Aru Jaari* in 1959 as the reason why several of the compositions remained half written, forcing him to scramble for more sources to complete the couplets.[24] Still, his book, and Hussain's *Hazrat Ajaan Fakir*, turned out to be a monumental contribution to preserving the Jikir and the Jaari songs of Assam, and thereby Ajaan Fakir's legacy in the state. The Jaari songs are about the Battle of Karbala about which I shall elaborate a little later in the chapter.

Here a mention must also be made of noted Jikir singer Rekibuddin Ahmed for his pioneering role in not only popularizing the form on stage and through playback singing, but also encouraging a generation of young artists from within the community to learn and promote the form. Ahmed was backed by the likes of Bhupen Hazarika.

While Jikir recitals are conducted on stage today in a sitting position like that of the qawwali, the form had originally thrived among Assamese Muslims with a folk song-like delivery, somewhat akin to a Husori group dance during Bihu. Noted Jikir singer Samsuddin Ahmed had highlighted in his recently published book *Mur Monot Bhed Bhab Nai* (The title is taken from one of Ajaan Fakir's famous Jikirs) that Jikirs and Jaaris were as much music as they were dances. Ahmed, whose father Semiruddin Ahmed was also a Jikir singer aside from crooning Pogola Parvati songs—a kind of devotional singing in his village in Golaghat district—recalled watching such Jikir dance performances in his village during his childhood. 'The Muslim villages across Sivasagar, Nagaon, Janji, Lakhimpur, Golaghat, Kakojan, Naharoni, Batiporia, Kurighoria, Dergaon, etc. in Upper Assam sing Jikir and Jaari with a lot of devotion. Generally, they are sung after a wedding feast under the *shamiana* put up on the courtyard of the particular family.'[25] The main post of the shamiana put up for the wedding guests becomes the centre where the oja or the lead singer stands and begins a Jikir while twenty to thirty men circle him and begin a group dance by clapping hard to a particular beat. While the oja sings the primary lines, the suffix or the ghuxa (say, hoi saheb hoi) is repeated by the group that dances around him. A saucer filled with mustard oil is kept in the middle of the circle for the group to keep oiling their hands so they can continue to clap loudly late into the night. The wedding guests, men and women alike, would listen to the song and dance. 'Once the dance is over, all of them do *Munajaat* or seek blessings of Allah and thereafter bless the family. Subsequently, the host serves them curd and puff rice (akhoi) followed by areca nut and betel vines and bid them goodbye.'[26] A Bihu Husori, about which I elaborate later in the chapter, too blesses the host family and is reverentially offered areca nut and betel vines, aside from a jolpan meal comprising curd and beaten rice post performance. Ahmed had underlined that women in the villages too had traditionally sung Jikir but usually in a sitting position, unlike the men.

What is interesting is also that being an oral tradition, the manner of performance differs from one district in Upper Assam to another. 'There is no dance along a Jikir in Sivasagar district; they only dance to Jaari but don't clap, only put their hands on their chest in rhythm as they go around the Oja.'[27]

Jaaris are the morsia or songs of sadness which relate the tale of the Battle of Karbala from the seventh century between Prophet Muhammad's grandson Husayn Ibn Ali and the second Umayyad Caliph Yazid I in present-day Iraq. In that battle, both his grandsons, Husayn and Hasan, were beheaded. That battle had given birth to the observation of Muharram in Islam and the Shia Islamic sect.

Though Jaari songs of Assam are at times counted as compositions also by Ajaan Fakir, Syed Abdul Malik had underlined in his book that the form had existed much before his arrival in the state. Even though Assamese Muslims don't follow the usual division of Shia–Sunni as noticed elsewhere, that there had been a tradition of singing these Karbala songs for centuries among them do indicate that a small section of the early Muslims who had settled down in the state after multiple invasions could have belonged to the Shiite school. Ahmed had highlighted that they might have been a part of religious practice at some time, but due to their sociocultural assimilation with the local Assamese culture over the centuries, Jaari songs became inherently Assamese in nature and absorbed local dance steps from, say, the Husori or Oja Pali. It thereby fell out of the cosmos of religion to become a general custom within the community.

Even in the Jikirs, the local cultural flavour, not just in the dance but in the songs too, finds prominence. Jikir uses similes in a similar fashion as local musical forms like the Deh Bisaror geet, Tokari geet, and Naoria geet. Ahmed had underlined, 'In Tokari geet, the body is equated to a still forest or a sea or a boat or even a house. Such a simile for the body is noticed in Jikir too.'[28] Deh Bisaror geet speaks of man's desire, anger, greed, love, sorrow, etc. and have nothing to do with one's higher self like what is noticed in the Tokari geet. 'Through Deh Bisaror geet, one gets the idea to celebrate one's body.... Such bodily factors are found in Azan Fakir's Jikir too.'[29]

Assamese music also includes songs for boatmen, usually sung during Nao Khela, or the game of rowing boats. They are few in number but the way they are sung have similarities with Jikir. It must be pointed out here that several of the astute boatmen of the royal Ahom army were Assamese Muslims.

Above all, what needs to be particularly emphasized here is that, like Sankardev had employed music (Borgeet) to promote his creed, Ajaan Fakir too, after over a century in Assam, used it (Jikir) too to promote his faith. Ajaan Fakir based his compositions not on Islamic religious rigidity but, like Sankardev, stressed on devotion to the lord, on utmost bhakti, to the almighty. Significantly, several Jikirs directly refer to the Hindu faith and how a Hindu and a Muslim can co-exist with each other in harmony. The basic tenet of his creed could be gauged from his most popular Jikir still on people's lips:

Mur Monot Bhed Bhab Nai O Allah
Mur Monot Heen Por Nai O Allah
Hindu ki Mussalman, Eke Allahar Forman, Mur Monot Eketi Bhaab

(My mind doesn't discriminate one from the other O Lord; whether one is a Hindu or a Muslim, it is the wish of the same almighty, O Lord; my mind feels the same closeness with both.)

Though the language of Jikir has a good sprinkling of Persian and Urdu words and Islamic religious expressions, the compositions also use Vaishnava terms like bhokot (a religious follower) aside from reference to local rivers; customs; methods of farming; local articles like Japi (Assamese headgear), kol paat (banana leaf), dhari (mats); local dance forms like the Oja Pali, Bihu, etc. The status of Ajaan Fakir's Jikirs in Assam's cultural landscape and devotional music is high. Neog had reiterated the point, 'Like the *baro kuri* Borgeet (240 in number), *tero kuri fokora jujona* (260 Assamese aphorisms), Jikir too is a priceless treasure of Assamese community.'[30]

Post Independence, the attention given to the tradition of Jikir by the likes of Malik, Rekibuddin Ahmed, and Bhupen Hazarika, among others had helped the form attract the attention of the wider Assamese community, thus carving out a wider public forum for its performance including at the prestigious Asam Sahitya Sabha session at Sivasagar in 1993. In 1987, Shamsuddin Ahmed, under the leadership of Rekibuddin Ahmed, also sang a Jikir for Hazarika's Assamese feature film *Siraj*. Over the decades, several Jikir singers have not only participated in Jikir competitions and other public functions but also sung at the AIR and Guwahati Doordarshan programmes. One of the earliest female singers promoted by Rekibuddin

Ahmed, who spotted her at one such singing competition in 1985, was Hafeza Begum Chowdhury of Guwahati.[31]

Today, there are several popular Jikir groups comprising both young men and women. Shamsuddin Ahmed's wife Farida Ahmed is also a Jikir singer. Lilting Jikirs by young female singers like Farhaana and Nahid Afrin are particularly popular on YouTube.

BIHU AND OTHER ASSAMESE FOLK SONGS

It make sense to start talking about Bihu songs by training one's lens on what noted folk singer from Assam, Hemango Biswas, had once famously written: 'Whatever is not there in a Bihu song is not there in Assam; whatever is not there in Assam is not there in a Bihu song.'[32]

In just two sentences, Biswas, a leading light of the Assam chapter of Indian People's Theatre Association (IPTA),[33] had summed up the backbone of Bihu songs, and their place in Assamese folk culture. Biswas, who had contributed immensely to the preservation of Assamese and Bengali folk songs during the early days of Independence, had called the literary and musical components of the Bihu songs the wellspring of Assamese culture. 'It is very rare to spot within the pale of Indian folk songs an example like Assam's Bihu songs that encompasses the life of men and women lived around their hills and dales, the rivers, the birds, the flowers, the many fragrances in the air, the varied hues of nature, the paddy fields. The philosophy of Bihu is its secularism and empathy towards a life lived of hard labour.'[34]

The wide scope of these songs is testament to what Biswas had emphasized. It is in the Bihu songs that one gets the granular feel of the common Assamese man's everyday life in continuity. For instance, in a famous Bihu score, 'Sokola tengati okoloi nekhaba aama ku esokol diba', sung by the well-known Bihu musicians Khogen and Archana Mahanta, a listener navigates through multiple references to a life lived in rural Assam. There are references to the dipping water level of a tributary of the Brahmaputra triggering a concern among the local community about where to source their staple, the fish; about mundane moments like sharing a slice of a citrus fruit (sokola tenga) with someone dear to us; also a direct allusion to the custom of a young man chaperoning a girl he is in love with to Bihu toli, the open ground, to dance to a Bihu tune. In the song, the young man, in response to the girl's call to him to accompany her to the

Bihu ground, says that when he whistles in front of her house, she must come out at once. These lines only allude to the societal sanction given to young men and women to meet without inhibition and fall in love during spring, the season of bounty and fertility.

Accompanied by the dhul (the cylindrical drum), gogona (a mouth organ made of bamboo), taal (cymbals of varying sizes), been (a one-string instrument), a range of pepa (wind pipe made of buffalo horn) and clapping of hands, these songs waft in the air every spring in Assam.

Bihu songs are also a veritable record of any novelty that creeps into Assamese society. That today we find mention of mobile phones and love birds meeting in a mall in some Bihu compositions must be looked as only a continuum of a trend. Several renditions from the nineteenth century were resplendent with new phenomenons spotted in Assam, like, the whistle of a passing train; arrival of a barge on the Brahmaputra from Kolkata; owning a four wheeler; a job at a tea garden; wearing a wristwatch for the first time; the gait of Englishmen; the common man's addiction to opium; the sorrow of not being able to buy for your children a new pair of clothes for the Bihu due to a bad harvest; the prevalence of bride price in the society; etc. That there was a custom of eloping to get married from the Bihu dance ground itself can also be found in the songs. Also, in several older numbers, there is the mention of a woman, Monumati. Monumati was among several young women whisked away by the Burmese. According to Hemango Biswas, she remained in Bihu songs as a symbol of such hapless women.[35] One such song goes thus: *Ujai ahile company jahaj Oi; Prithibi tolmol dekhu; sopaide sopaide Kolikotar jahaj oi; Monumatir batori xudhu* (The East India Company's ship came upstream; it shakes the earth; let's bring it closer to the banks; the ship from Kolkata; let us ask if it has any news about Monumati). In a similar vein, some Bihu scores written during the Sepoy Mutiny and the freedom struggle speak of the supreme sacrifice made by Assamese anti-British activists of the times, Piyali Phukan and Maniram Dewan.[36]

Most old compositions have survived till date through oral traditions, though the practice of publishing booklets of Bihu songs has been picking up pace since the early 1980s, triggered by a spike in Bihu stage performances and dance competitions. With time, a considerable amount of academic research has also been done not only on the content of Bihu songs and their salience in Assamese society but also in the promotion of the form stylistically and technically. Lately, some steps have been suggested by musicians to standardize some of the instruments played with Bihu songs too. For instance, Prasanna Gogoi, an acclaimed Guwahati-based Bihu musician, has set the Juria Pepa, the single-mouthed double barrelled wind instrument used in Bihu music, on to a standard scale. In 2017, on being asked about the need for such standardization, Gogoi had told me, 'Till recently, if you go to an instrument maker, say, to buy a *Pepa* or a *Dhul* or a *Gogona*, it could be of any length or thickness or size. It would produce sound but everything was approximate, not accurate. There was no set way of tuning it to produce a certain melody. So a player (of such an instrument) had no idea what exact sound will the instrument produce, to what height or depth he can take the sound. To avoid it, I began to make my own instruments following the science of acoustics.'[37] Gogoi had started his journey by making a number of folk instruments himself including making a pepa with the wood of the commonly grown Gomari tree since finding a buffalo horn to craft a traditional Bihu pepa is not always easy these days. He had also added a string to the mono-chord been for the player to have an extra cord ready if the one being used breaks in the middle of a performance. The chord is stainless steel, unlike the traditional practice of making a string from Muga silk. With Assam receiving heavy rainfall, the been with a Muga string can only be played during spring. Gogoi is also an astute Bihu singer which is not a surprise as most Bihu musicians can not only dance or play a Bihu instrument but are usually skilled singers too.

Aside from such dedicated singers of Bihu songs, most Assamese singers have always engaged with the form. Starting from Bhupen Hazarika, several top artists of the state have taken the stage during the annual Bihu Sanmelan and the Bohagi Bidai events, held, respectively, between the first day of the Assamese month of Bohag (14 April) to its last day (14 May), to usher in the spring festival, and then to bid it adieu. Currently, among the top Bihu singers are Zubeen Garg, Papon, Zublee Baruah, Neel Akash, Manas Robin, Dimpy Sonowal, Chandan Das, and Jina Rajkumari. Some Assamese singers like Papon who reside in Mumbai, travel back to Assam particularly to take part in these soirées.

Unlike in the Bihu Sanmelan, during the Bohagi Bidai events, there has been a trend of performers belting out on stage Bollywood hits and western music alongside the Bihu scores. In my school days in Upper Assam, two popular names for the western music slot were Khasi siblings Dennis and Mala Banks. Dennis would also lend his voice to the background scores of singers like Bhupen and Shanta Ujir and Adil Ahmed as they sung in Assamese. Additionally, there has also been a long existing trend of releasing playback recordings of Bihu specials. There was a time when listeners would fervently await a new Bihu album by Bhupen Hazarika or Khogen Mahanta in the run-up to the annual festivities. The trend continues though unlike in the era of gramophone records, cassettes, and CDs, singers now can upload a single number, or release a clasp of new Bihu songs, to online platforms like YouTube and perform them in Bihu Sanmelans. Herein, a mention must also be made about the effort by some singers, particularly by Zubeen, to weave in popular expressions used by the state's tribes into Bihu songs.

It would also be appropriate to underline here that not just in Bihu songs, but in all other musical expressions of the wider Assamese community—the wedding songs (biya naam), Goalporia lokageet, Nisukoni geet (lullabies), Bongeet (songs of nature), Tokari geet (devotional songs played with the musical instrument Tokari), the Mising Oinitam, Ratkinon Alun of the Karbis—bucolic Assamese life is illustrated. Naturally then, these genres are also infused with the names of local rivers, birds, flowers, orchids, etc. For instance, noted Karbi singer Chandrakanta Terang's folk songs are a rich legacy of the tribe's life and beliefs. Some years ago, Terang's popular folk number 'Oi Ri Pajap Pajap; Karbi Purkimo; Ephan Eh Kehang', was sung accompanied by modern instruments and with a faster tempo by Assamese singer Papon along with him. More such musical partnerships of Assamese mainstream singers with musicians hailing from different ethnic groups is the call of the hour to offer a sufficient opportunity to the music lovers of the state to savour the entirety of the rich melody of the tribal tunes and lyrics. The state's Tea Tribe or the Adivasis also have a rich selection of songs including those on the sufferings of the indentured labourers lured to Assam with the promise of a better life by the colonizers and their agents. The melody of songs used in their traditional group dance Jhumur was an inspiration for Bhupen Hazarika to set to music immortal Assamese songs like 'Radhasurar phool guji'. The songs used in Lathibari, a martial dance form of Assam's Muslims of East Bengal origin, must be noted too.

As highlighted above, among the folk songs of Assam are also the soul-stirring Kamrupi lokageet and Goalparia lokageet. In the mid-1980s, the renditions of Kamrupiya lokageet by the musician couple, Rameshwar Pathak and Dhanada Pathak, had created a stir across the state. Like the Kamrupi lokageet, the Goalparia lokageet has certain masterpieces that exude the scent of the soil, also the toil of the people of that belt, their everyday emotions. The melodies on the life of the elephant herders, the mahout, are especially unique. Noted Goalparia lokageet singer Pratima Barua Pande not only elevated the form with her haunting folksy voice but also inspired a generation of young singers to follow her path. Her 'Hostir Konya' is an immortal number on mahouts living away from their families for days together typically to venture into the woods to domesticate a wild elephant. Goalpara traditionally has been home to wild elephants which were professionally domesticated and supplied even to the Mughal army, which explains the influence of the trade in the musical traditions of that area located on the cusp of Assam and greater Bengal. The songs are also representative of Koch Rajbonshi or Goalparia dialects, a shade different from the words found in Kamrupia lokageet.

JYOTI AND RAVA SANGEET, PARVATI PRASAD BARUVA

It is a given that to strengthen the roots of the musical traditions of a society, it needs the sustained effort and enterprise of a creative coterie from within a community. Without doubt, among the shining examples of that lot of trailblazers in Assamese community were Jyotiprasad Agarwala, Bishnu Prasad Rava, and Parvati Prasad Baruva. They were joined by a much younger Bhupen Hazarika. Each, in their own unique ways, assembled the bricks and bars of the community's cultural and musical identity. One must, therefore, delve a little into their individual contributions. Though the influence of these four was absolute, it would still be unfair not to mention that several others also helped fortify Assamese modern music.

A multi-talented Parvati Prasad Baruva (1904–64) was a poet, lyricist, filmmaker, and dramatist born in Sivasagar; known to the Assamese community as Geetikavi, or a lyrical poet. He was also a tea planter. Several legendary Bhupen Hazarika songs were written by Baruva. Some of my favourites from that bunch are 'Luitor saporit kore naoriya', which paints a fine picture of life around the Brahmaputra; 'Aaji phagunor puwa belate' and 'Aahin mohia xewali xorile', two songs that note the changes in one's surroundings due to transformation of seasons; also, 'Gorokhiya he ro gorokhiya ki xur bojali duporia' (O the cowherd, which tune have you played this afternoon); 'Xunor horina toi kot dekhili' (Where did you spot the golden deer); and 'Tur nai je bondhua baat' (Hey man, you don't have a fixed path in this world) from the film *Rupohi*, released in 1940 for which Baruva composed music and also acted. Since Baruva was a prolific songwriter—he could also sing about 2,000 Rabindra Sangeet[38]—it is not possible to name each song here. But it is certain that all his compositions were a documentation of Assamese life and emotion, and the fauna and flora of the region and could, therefore, easily grab listeners' attentions. No wonder then, even after nearly sixty years have passed since his demise, Baruva's songs are still on people's lips.

Prior to exploring the musical traits of his worthy contemporaries—the cultural activists Jyotiprasad and Rava—it would be helpful though to first contextualize the sociopolitical circumstances under which they composed their songs, so also the kind of musical legacy that they inherited from their immediate seniors. It would help comprehend better why the trio wrote the kinds of songs that they did.

As mentioned earlier in the book, the Burmese invasion of the early nineteenth century gave way to a turbulent period in Assam. In quick succession came the collapse of the Ahom kingdom, thus discontinuing over 600 years of considerable stability. Thereafter began a new form of governance under the British which, in course of time, paved the way for the formation of a nascent Assamese educated middle-class, and the imposition of a foreign language—Bengali—from 1836 to 1873. Because of the imposition of the new language, gradually, the hegemonic grip of Bengali and its related culture as somewhat 'superior' began to pose a threat to the Assamese sociocultural and linguistic make-up. On stage, Bengali songs ruled; Assamese culture and folk forms like Bihu began to be considered rustic, uncultured practices. Prafulla Chandra Baruah, the first Assamese singer to have a gramophone record in 1924, had once said in an interview that when he, along with Jyoti Prasad Agarwala, took up singing Assamese songs on stage in 1920s instead of Bengali, even a section of Assamese gentry, made fun of them.[39] However, in the 1924 session of the Asam Sahitya Sabha held under the presidentship of writer Lakshminath Bezbaroa, when Baruah presented two Assamese songs of Agarwala, he was applauded. 'After listening to the songs, the head of the organising committee, Lakhinath Sarma, came up to the stage, beating a fist on his heart in joy and said, I heard so many songs (in Bengali) today but these two songs touched my heart. Only today have I realised how beautiful can an Assamese song be; as an artiste it is one of my precious moments.'[40]

Gaurav Rajkhowa, in a discerning commentary on Agarwala's creative genius in 2020, had also pointed out that Lambodar Bora, in an article in

Jonaki published in 1889, had highlighted that the lack of Assamese modern songs had pushed youth from 'decent families' to turn to Bengali songs. By then though, some Assamese books on songs, their notations, etc. had been compiled, such as Lakhiram Barua's *Sangit Kos*. 'The target of this pedagogy (was) were, for the most part, youth and women. For instance, in an article in *Usha* (an Assamese magazine) in 1911, the author Padmadhar Chaliha advocated the importance of music in women's education as he wrote, "many seem to be under the misconception that there is something shameful about singing. Music is pure. Music has the power of attraction; it is a source of pleasure and cheer; it brings enjoyment to both singer and listener. Consequently, learning music is essential."'[41]

Those days, for any higher degree, an Assamese youth had to sail to Kolkata. Due to that colonial-era compulsion to depend on 'Kolikota' for most things, the city's primacy in Assamese society began to grow. The exposure to the cosmopolitan culture of Kolkata and also the subsequent Bengali rennassiance spearheaded by the likes of Rabindranath Tagore, lifted the curtain on a broader creative world for the first generation of Assamese educated youth. They were inspired to use literature and their cultural traditions and mores as tools to revive a sense of pride within the Assamese community, primarily the new middle class. They endeavoured to carve out a distinct linguistic and cultural identity, separate from that of Bengali. In the nineteenth century, Kolkata-based Assamese students led by Lakshminath Bezbaroa (1864–1938) and a few others began a literary movement to counter the Bengali linguistic hegemony over the Assamese. Music was also used to further their movement. Bezbaroa himself wrote songs to enthuse the common public towards their cause, including the popular song 'O Mur Apunar Dex' (O My Beloved Motherland). The song was soon adopted by Assam Chatra Sanmelan as the national (jatio) anthem in resistance to the primacy given in Assam to 'Vande Mataram' written by Bengali writer Bankim Chandra Chatterjee.[42]

Around the same time, Bezbaroa's able contemporaries like Ambika Raichaudhry (1885–1967) also wrote a clasp of songs documenting the colonial times including the travails of Assamese peasants at the hands of their new masters. Raichaudhry's 'Xunibi Bhai Dexor Kotha' (Come, Listen, About Your Land) was an ode to their struggle and contained this telling line: *ghor-bari tur puhor kori, xunor bhoral jole, toi tu nepao kona eta; lute dole-dole* (the fire that burns the full granary at your courtyard illuminates your house; you don't get a dime from the granary; only others come in bunches to loot it).

In 1843, much to the glee of peasants, the British administration banned slavery prevalent in the Ahom period but the system that replaced it was equally oppressive; it ultimately set off peasant revolts in Assam. In 2011, noted academic Udayon Misra in *Peasant Consciousness Reflected in the Oral Literature of Assam: A Study of Two Assamese Ballads* [43] had highlighted the effect of such uprisings on Assamese oral culture, particularly songs describing the Battle of Patharughat in 1894 and Phulaguri Dhewa in 1861, which are still imprinted in common rural folks' minds. In the early part of the twentieth century, the newly formed Congress chapter in Assam also took up the cause of the peasant exploitation, their landlessness due to heavy taxation. In 2019, Prachee Dewri, in her insightful paper 'Bishnuprasad Rava and the Rural in Assam: Inspiration and Intervention Through Music', had essayed that development, 'Congress leaders of the movement, such as Harekrishna Das, suggested that the "Assamese peasant was the basis of Assamese nationality", and that Assamese *jati* (community) and the Assamese peasant are one and the same.'[44] Songs on peasant exploitation composed by the likes of Ambikagiri Raichaudhry only indicate that in Assamese music, its shadow could be easily traced. Dewri had underlined the continuum of those influences, 'These efforts (those of Raichaudhry's generation) gained momentum in the 1920s and the 1930s, when artists like Rava, Agarwala and Parvati Prasad Baruva started to experiment with musical forms of the region. A major influence on their experimentation was the music of Rabindranath Tagore. Although they began by imitating Tagore's melodies, they gradually began to adopt his method of composition, i,e, blending of the local melodies with classical Indian and Western music.'[45]

Raichaudhry's contemporary Lakshmiram Barua (1865–1914) too made an important contribution to music but his main focus was on the Hindustani classical genre. In the preface to his play *Sonit Kuwari*, Jyotiprasad Agarwala wrote, 'No doubt his (Barua's) efforts went a long way in inaugurating a scientific music criticism; there was nevertheless little effort towards bringing Assamese music before the world.'[46]

Since the 1930s, Assamese musicians like Agarwala and Rava began using the recording facility at Kolkata, not only to produce new music but also to record existing Bihu songs. The likes of Rava and Agarwala often sailed to Kolkata with artistes, including women singers, to record songs for turntables (called pala) and also for plays penned by them. It was during one such trip in 1939 that an eleven-year-old Bhupen Hazarika was also taken. A schoolgoer Hazarika recorded a song for a woman character of Agarwala's second film *Indramalati* in that trip and also lent his voice to three songs to be sung by women characters of Agarwala's plays *Karengor Ligiri* and *Sunit Kuwori*. Those songs, recorded at Arora Studios in Kolkata, became the first gramophone recording of Hazarika's music.[47]

The likes of Arora Studios and Senola came up much later in Kolkata. Fourteen years prior to that, it was only His Master's Voice (HMV). The first recorded songs in Assamese were those of Prafulla Chandra Baruah of Sivasagar; the recordings were rolled out in 1924 by HMV. Baruah had sung four songs in that gramophone record. In October 2020, when I visited the one-room museum of gramophone records collected by Umananda Dowerah, a music teacher in Moranhat—a laudable effort driven by a personal craze for old Assamese songs—I was lucky enough to hear one of the songs from an original record. An article written in 1981 by Shekhar Jyoti Bhuyan after a conversation with Prafulla Chandra Baruah referred to some songs sung by him, and also named those who had written them: Umesh Choudhury, Radhanath Phukan, and Prasanna Lal Choudhury. Interestingly, in that interview, Baruah also mentioned that though a few years prior to him, Umesh Mukherjee, a Dibrugarh-based musician, had recorded a song at the HMV studio in Kolkata, it was never released because of incorrect Assamese pronunciations. Dewri, though, had accurately emphasized in her paper, 'The availability of recording gave further impetus to their experimentation. In the mid-1930s, many musicians of the region began to use recording technology that was available in Calcutta to record the traditional music of the region as well as the music they composed themselves. The songs written in this period came to be known as the beginning of the *adhunik sangit* (modern music) in Assam.'[48]

What comes through from the developments of the times is that young Assamese cultural activists like Agarwala and Rava utilized the recording facilities in Kolkata to reinforce the emerging anti-colonial sociopolitical thought promoted musically by their seniors like Ambikagiri Raichaudhury, and thereby helped amplify the need for musicians to celebrate folk traditions, compose new songs about its hills and dales, the people, the peasants, their everyday life, their emotions. Agarwala and Rava magnified the role art could play in a repressed society to regain pride in its culture and language. Their creative interventions, in their own ways, so also of the likes of Parvati Prasad Baruva, were, therefore, a parallel to the momentous trend set by Bezbaroa and friends in Assamese literature to help swerve it towards taking cognizance of its own cultural wealth and possibilities and thereby strengthen the concept of a jati, the community. The result of that trajectory can still be found in the society's cultural landscape.

In accomplishing the desired goal, Agarwala and Rava took inspiration from their Indian contemporaries who were then trying to retrace their roots, and also from several international artists travelling to Kolkata to collaborate with artistes like Uday Shankar in pre-independent India. Dewri had documented that on 'many occasions, Rava acknowledged that it was Anna Pavlova (the renowned Russian ballerina) who inspired him to travel the length and breadth of Assam to explore the performance forms of the region.'[49]

'According to him, the turning point in his artistic journey was his meeting with Anna Pavlova when she came to perform in Calcutta in 1929.'[50] After her performance, when Rava met her backstage and expressed his wish to learn ballet and perform with her, she advised him to return home to study the traditional music and dance forms of the region. On returning to Assam in 1930, he visited the Vaishnava monasteries and played a key role in bringing out the cloistered Sattriya dance to the proscenium stage. He collaborated with Agarwala in composing the music for the first Assamese film *Joymoti*, produced in 1935, and went on to record plays in Assamese.

Rava and Agarwala, the former seven years younger than the latter, complemented each other creatively and brought about a cultural revolution of sorts in Tezpur, their home town which had enormous influence also in Hazarika's making as a musician. Rava also went on to become an astute dancer, playwright, actor, and painter aside from being a revolutionary and a peasant rights activist. His massive cultural contribution to the community is the reason why he is called Kalaguru, the master of arts. The title was informally bestowed on him by India's first president Sarvapalli Radhakrishnan when he was the vice chancellor of the Banaras Hindu University, impressed by a Tandav performance given by Rava at the insitution.

The songs composed by Rava, or Rava Sangeet, form a wide oeuvre. Besides penning romantic and patriotic songs, Rava also wrote songs about growing landlessness and pauperism of the peasantry in Assam and in favour of social and religious equity, and helped establish a deep connect between the arts and Assam's rural life and folk traditions.

In 1947, when the Assam chapter of IPTA began, Rava became its vice president, and Agarwala its president. By then, Rava was deeply drawn to Communism. It was also the time when the Revolutionary Communist Party of India (RCPI), founded as the Communist League by Saumendranath Tagore, the grand-nephew of Rabindranath Tagore, was gaining ground in Assam. The main plank of RCPI was to mobilize the peasants based on the thought that India was essentially an agrarian economy and this must be prioritized. Several top artists had by then become associated with its study circle Radical Institute. So did Rava, in 1939. Six years later, he joined RCPI, which led an armed uprising before becoming a political party. It was during this period that Rava began to look at art as a vehicle to emancipate society. In 1999, Bhupen Hazarika, while delivering a speech at the Gauhati University, recalled an incident wherein Rava visited him at his home one day in Bharalumukh area of Guwahati as an RCPI activist to hand over two pistols for safekeeping. Hazarika's mother was a bit rattled and asked her son what the pistols were. 'I said nothing to fear *Aye* (mother), just keep them under your pillow; he will come tomorrow to pick them up.'[51] Hazarika, in that speech, also reiterated being influenced by Communism earlier in his life because of his close association with Rava, because of which he wrote his memorable songs 'Agnijugor Phiringoti Moi' (I Am the Spark of the Age of Fire) in 1944 and 'Jonotar Kulahol' (The Clamour of the Public). 'Those two songs became the property of all. They were sung by the Congress volunteers, so also by the likes of Hemango Biswas and Banamali Kakoti of the Communist Party. Some had then begun to say that Bhupen also must have become a Communist now.'[52]

In 1948, the song 'Agnijugor Phiringoti Moi' was used by Rava in *Siraj*, the film he co-directed with ace Assamese filmmaker Phani Sarma. Hazarika, a student of BHU then, was its playback singer.

In course of the decades that followed, several of Rava's songs were lost because he wrote them while in hiding as an armed RCPI activist and had to shift houses frequently. That revolutionary period of his life is well documented in a 2020 song, 'Ja Beli Ja', by talented Assamese singer Joi Barua. Its lyrics written by a brilliant songwriter, Ibson Lal Barua, highlights the sacrifice made by his aide Gajiram Rava who cut off his tongue before he was taken into custody. With a slit tongue he couldn't have divulged his co-revolutionary Rava's place of hiding to his interrogators.

Though Rava was a communist, Agarwala was not. Yet, he was labelled so by many in Assam including by members of Congress, chiefly because of his close association with IPTA. Some of his later writings were not published in local papers because of this. Ismail Hussain, in *Jyotiprasad Agarwalar Jibon Aru Dorxon* (Jyotiprasad Agarwala's Life and Philosophy), noted that Agarwala, upset by the accusations, had retorted once, 'It only means that they have accepted the power of the Communists. Today, Communism and progressive thought seem to have become alike.'[53] In that 23 May 1999 speech given at the Gauhati University, Hazarika had called Agarwala a Gandhian. 'There were several non-Communists at IPTA, such as Jyoti *kokaidew* (elder brother). He had nothing to do with the Communist party; he was a Gandhian but believed in Socialism.'[54]

Since he died early (at forty-five) in 1951, Agarwala was associated with IPTA for barely five years. However, some close watchers of Agarwala's creative writings like Hemango Biswas had often stated that what he wrote during his IPTA years was different from his earlier writings. Biswas had once written that Agarwala's later poems and songs bore the echo of the common man's footsteps and credited that transformation to his involvement with the IPTA.[55] For instance, his 'O Mur Gaon' (O My Village) emphatically encapsulates the pathetic state of Assamese peasants and rural folk. The need for the common man's welfare inherent in his cultural and creative thinking had led IPTA to bestow on him the title of Ganaxilpi, the people's artiste.[56]

Agarwala's compositions on nature are equally popular among the Assamese. Generation after generation of Assamese schoolgoers have grown up singing and dancing to two particularly unforgettable Jyoti Sangeet about the bountry of nature: '(kune) gose gose pati dile Suno re Sorai, he Ram o Ram' (O who bedecked the trees with golden Xorai, the Assamese cultural symbol); and 'Seuji Seuji Seuji O, Seuji dhoroni dhunia O' (O green, green, green is all around me, the green earth is so beautiful). He composed those songs to be a part of his two memorable plays: *Sunit Kuwori* and *Nimati Koina*. In fact, a good segment of his popular songs were from his dramas and films. His compositions were also set to traditional melodies, such as to the tune of Assamese wedding songs or lullabies.

Being a product of the pre-independent era, Agarwala's songs also had a strong patriotic tinge invoked by Gandhian principles and the resolve to fight the British regime. Such songs were often addressed to the youth—by using the term nobo juwan (new generation) in the lyrics—and prodded them to come forward in the service of Assam and the freedom movement. His 'Biswabijoe Nobo Juwan' is the most apt specimen of that thought. Decades later, in the 1980s, the song became a near anthem during the

Assamese students' movement against foreigners, and returned to the public consciousness yet again in 2019, during the vociferous protests across the Brahmaputra Valley against the central government's decision to implement the Citizenship Amendment Act (CAA) in the state in violation of the Assam Accord which had brought an end to that bloody agitation.

Thanks to his overall creative contribution to the community, Agarwala, the son of a Marwari businessman Paramananda Agarwal and an Assamese woman from Sivasagar, Kiranmoyee, is today widely addressed as Rupkonwar or the artist of Assam and every 17 January, his day of death in 1951, is observed as Silpi Divas.

BHUPENDRA SANGEET

Bhupen Hazarika not only got his first break in Kolkata through Rava but was able to see two of his first songs in print because of him as well. They were published by RCPI in *Mukti Deul* (Freedom of Temple), a dance drama. Rava had included Hazarika as a co-writer of the book because of his songs. When in 1949, Hazarika arrived in New York to study at the University of Columbia, American authorities whisked him away from the airport itself to a detention camp set up for war prisoners on an island to be interrogated for several days on suspicion of being a communist. 'I felt humiliated in America,' he had once said about his experience.[57]

Landing in that camp perhaps was providence as it was from a Black prisoner that he first heard about American artist Paul Robeson using music as a tool for political activism. Having first taken lessons from Rava about the significance of music in expressing the rights of the voiceless in his own land, Hazarika drew inspiration thereafter from Robeson's use of the medium to fight for Black rights in America. On becoming aware of protest music as a genre, and then having come in touch with Martin Luther King Jr., enabled Hazarika to add an international dimension to his music and use it as a device to express the common man's concerns. A sensitive soul, he could universalize the plight of the downtrodden through his lyrics. Be it an Assamese farmer Rongmon or Panei gripped by poverty on the banks of the Brahmaputra; a cotton farmer, John, by the Mississipi; or a peasant, Wallah, by the Nile—his songs could communicate to his listeners that their geographies could be varied but their predicaments, sufferings, and emotions were the same. He could thereby bring the world closer and also musically exhort modern-day historians to, unlike their predecessors, stop eulogizing royals and instead focus on the rights of the common people. Robeson's legendary song, 'Ole Man River', went on to become an inspiration for Hazarika to compose and sing the famous lines: *Bistirno parore axohnyo jonore hahakar xuniu nixobde nirobe burha Luit tumi bua kiyo* (O Old River Brahmaputra; why do you flow silently even when you hear the cries of helplessness of so many people). The translated version in Bengali touched the hearts of millions not just in West Bengal, his adopted home, but also in Bangladesh where too he became a celebrated name. During the Emergency, he sang its Hindi version 'Ganga Behti ho Kyun' in front of Prime Minister Indira Gandhi to register his protest against her decision to declare a state of emergency across the country.

His first trip to America in 1949 proved to be a life lesson for Hazarika, opening for him doors to an entirely new creative world. During that trip, he travelled to Colombo first, after which he sailed to Marseilles. 'Once in France, I had a strong desire to meet Picasso. An elderly guard informed me that if I managed to get up at 4 a.m., I might catch Picasso taking a walk with his friends. I did what I was told and, to my surprise, I actually saw Picasso. I went up to him and said, "Sir, this is the best day of my life." His reply was rather jocular: "Hazarika is going to America after gathering information about me!" Picasso wanted to test my knowledge and asked me which of his paintings were my favourite. I mentioned his Blue period. He was pleased and blessed me,' Hazarkia had once recalled.[58]

In 1952, on his way back from America, in the ship itself, he wrote the marvellous song 'Sagor Xongomot Kotona Xaturilu Totha Pitu Huwa Nai Klanto' (I Swam So Much on the Sea and Am Not Yet Exhausted). He went on to pen another legendary number 'Moi Eti Jajabor' (I Am a Vagabond) with which he introduced to the ordinary folk in faraway Assam not just some of the greatest names from the world of arts—Gorky, Ghalib, Mark Twain—and world cities like Ottawa, Paris, Chicago, Dushanbe, but also handpicked the everyday sights and scenes from those faraway lands to represent hope and futility, the bricks of life universal to all, thereby declaring himself a citizen of the world. In the same vein, the musician for whom the Luit or the Brahmaputra was an anchor, traversed the man-made borders to remind the people of Bangladesh (then East Pakistan) during the Liberation War that the river Padma flowing by them was his mother too. He could easily convey through his music that fondness for his mother (motherland) should never mean hating others and the message of universal brotherhood that mankind must look out for each other by crossing all barriers.

In 2020, commenting on the universality of his songs, Sankar Patowary, who had researched nationalism in Assamese lyrical poetry with special reference to Bhupen Hazarika's songs, said, 'The reason why the popularity of some of his songs have traversed beyond the map of Assam was because they talked about truth, love, right conduct, peace, non-violence.... Music is a universal language; he could address that sentiment.'[59] Patowary felt, like in William Shakespeare's *Hamlet*, one finds the expression 'What a piece of work is man!', in Hazarika's musical philosophy too one comes face to face with manuh, the man, as a complicated being. The noted researcher had also underlined an important point, 'If you see all the epics, their fundamental point is very basic, good versus evil. In Hazarika's songs too, we can spot that conflict. For instance, in his song written in 1967, *Aah aah ulai aah xojag jonota, Ram ore dexote thoka Raban bodhute jai Jodi jaak jibon tu jaak* (Come come out, you conscious citizens, in the country of Ram, if fighting Ravan you lose you life too it should be fine). It is the same conflict of Good over Evil.'[60]

Several of Hazarika's songs were also paens to Bihu, Bohag (spring), and the Brahmaputra, and included notes on contemporary history in his lyrics. The song 'Bon Jui Bonot He Jole Dekha Puwa Jai Monor Jui Monot Jole Dekha Tu Nepai' (The Forest Fire can be Seen but the One that Burns Within Is Invisible), to my mind, is the ultimate musical documentation of Assam and the Northeast caught in the theatre of World War II in a local language. His 'Zindabad Mandela', first sung in Bengali, was an ode to Nelson Mandela to commemorate the anti-Apartheid hero's famous visit to Kolkata in 1990. It was sung in his presence by Hazarika; Mandela famously danced to it. His Hindi song 'Arunachal Hamara Hai', written to mark the creation of a new entity, Arunachal Pradesh, from an arm of Assam in 1970; 'Joi Joi Nobojato Bangladesh', written to commemorate the birth of that nation in 1971; 'Koto Juwanor Mrityu Hol', a tribute to Indian soldiers fighting against Chinese aggression in 1962, etc. are musical postcards of contemporary history. His 'Mahabahu Brahmaputra' (a translation of which is provided in the epigraph to this book), is an out-and-out chronicle on the formation of the Assamese community. The songs written during the Assam agitation, like 'Juye Pura Tiraxi', are a record of 1983 when elections were held in Assam against the wishes of the electorate. 'Shillong Ore Godhule' summarizes a striking evening in that hill city, once the centre of the Northeast, and 'Gauripuria Gabharu Dekhilu' details the one-of-a-kind phenomenon of a woman mahout in Goalpara. That he could narrate a story through his songs with ample use of local expressions and exhibit the native influences in his singing is the reason he is often called the Bard of the Brahmaputra.

The songs sung by Hazarika that encompass the world of the Assamese and Bengali listeners are multi-fold but not all of them were written by him. Patowary had underlined that knowing the kind of songs that Hazarika had sung, several writers, both in Assam and Bengal, wrote scores that would fit his philosophy, the reason why one must differentiate between songs that Hazarika sang, Bhupen-dar Geet, and those which he composed and sang, Bhupendra Sangeet. Several songs that he sang in Assamese never got translated into Bengali and vise versa. Aside from Bengali and Hindi, many of his songs have been sung in other languages, particularly 'Manuhe Manuhor Ba-Be', which in 2006, was voted the second most loved song in Bangladesh after its national anthem in a poll conducted by the BBC. In 2017, during the demand for Gorkhaland in Darjeeling, protesters sang the Nepali version of Hazarika's 'Bistirno Parore'. In 1994, while attending a workshop on Bhupendra Sangeet organized by the Kamrup unit of Purbashri Kristi Bikash Samiti, Hazarika was impressed by a Bodo girl, Sumitra Boro, singing his soulful song 'Junakore Rati' in Bodo language. That famous Assamese song, recorded in the voice of Lata Mangeshkar in the 1950s, was the first of his songs sung in Bodo and he was visibly elated.

It needs a mention here that like Agarwala, Hazarika also had to face the ire of the Assamese gentry for his creative work and convictions. His music was initially barred from Bihu functions. His first Bihu song, 'Sagor Saal Selabor Dobua Kotari', written in 1953, was considered particularly offensive by the then ruling class as it spoke of poor people still suffering in independent India under the reign of 'dhuti-pindha sahab' (Sahebs who wear dhoti, meaning the local elite). His detractors spread rumours across Assam that his doctorate degree from the University of Columbia was fake. Today, the Gauhati University may have his song 'Jilikabo Luitore Paar' (They Shall Dazzle the Banks of the Brahmaputra) as its anthem, and his last remains may lie within its boundary, but there was a time in his younger years when he was pushed out of the university and from his job as a lecturer for pursuing his kind of music. Hazarika had begun teaching at the university after his return from the US. His song 'Modarore Phul Henu Kame Kaje Nelage' (It Seems the Modar Flowers Are Not for Auspicious

Occasions) is a documentation of the humiliation meted out to him by a section of Assamese intellectuals then. After this, he took to music full time—he would go on to become Assam's greatest international musical star.

While Hazarika had celebrated Assam, its culture and traditions through songs like 'Axom Amar Rupohi' in which he called it the land where the sun rises first in India, he, nonetheless, was also its critic. He composed songs like 'Aami Axomiya Nohou Dukhiya Buli Xantona Lobhile Nohobo' (We Assamese Shall Never Be Poor Is No Consolation) to remind his fellow Assamese that they must work towards taking forward the state and the community. In his book, Patowary had underlined that aside from a handful of songs expressing ultra sub-nationalism, say, 'Ranaklanta Nohou' (I Shall Never Be Weary of War), Hazarika's music had played the role of the community's unapologetic critic, expressing his disappointment through the use of terms like 'dhudor posola' (products of laziness) in songs like 'Bordoisila Ne' written in 1967.[61]

Several of his songs are also a document of tribal life and traditions. Hazarika had always admitted that he was introduced to the Assamese tribal language and customs by Rava. Once he had written, 'Tribal music made a singer of me. As a child, I grew up listening to tribal music—its rhythm saw me developing an inclination towards singing.'[62] Having begun his musical journey inspired by Sankardev, and having made his initial mark as a child artist through folk forms, he trod the path shown by Agarwala and particularly Rava, and went on to not only write thoughtful lyrics but also lent his voice to lyrics written by Parvati Prasad Baruva and several other top class writers who followed him, like Nirmal Prabha Bordoloi and Keshab Mahanta. Over time, he succeeded in going beyond the scope of his mentors by expanding the horizon of his subjects to become truly international. In his 1999 speech at Gauhati University, he had said, 'Once you made me Bhupen Hazarika, Bengal embraced me and thereafter the world.'[63] His stay in Kolkata for four decades greatly aided the growth of his musical career.

Hazarika had also always acknowledged the platform provided to him by IPTA for the opportunity to continue working closely with progressive cultural activists after returning from America. This was possible particularly because of Hemango Biswas. It was IPTA which had first published his book of songs *Jilikabo Luitore Paar*. Assam-based researcher and writer Paramananda Mazumdar had said in 2020 at a discussion that after a glance at the songs compiled in that book, it is easy to deduce that Hazarika's best songs were written during that period. It included the marvellous scores 'Dula He Dula' and 'Eti Koli Duti Paat'. Hemango Biswas, in that book of Hazarika's songs, had stated that the period of Assamese music in the 1950s–60s must be called the Bhupen Hazarika period. Significantly, when Hazarika was not allowed to sing his maiden Bihu song at a Bihu function in Guwahati, Biswas, the next day, distributed his song among the crowd as pamphlets. The duo's friendship and musical collaboration were legendary. During the Assamese language movement in the 1960s which triggered attacks on Bengalis residing in the Brahmaputra Valley, Hazarika and Biswas took a musical caravan across the violence-hit areas to bring amity. A song that sprung out of that bold artistic intervention was the immortal number 'Rongmon Haradhan'.

Over the decades, several researchers and critics have defined Hazarika and his music; Hazarika himself did it as well. Patowary had underlined that no singer in Assam till date had done that to their music. 'He didn't want his songs to be a mere source of entertainment but wanted it to convey a sense of social responsibility.'[64]

ASSAMESE FILM AND NON-FILM MODERN SONGS

Hazarika was also a trailblazer when it came to working with singers from outside Assam, particularly Bollywood playback singers, for Assamese songs. He began the trend in the 1950s with his maiden film *Era Bator Xur* (1956) with the two songs he had composed for it: 'Junakore Rati', with a solo by Lata Mangeshkar; and 'Gaum Gaum Meghe Gorojile', a duet he sang with Hemant Mukherjee. It was an important milestone in Assamese playback singing. Though Mangeshkar, then a rising star in the Hindi playback music industry, sang her first Bengali song in 1952, it was just a version of a song from a Marathi film, *Aamar Bhoopali*.[65] In Assamese though, her first song was an original number.[66] In 1956–57, Mangeshkar sang two Bengali songs, one directed by Hemant Kumar and the other by Hazarika ('Rongile Basite'). Interestingly, Hemant Kumar, impressed by the melody of 'Junakore Rati', also used it two years later in Lata's voice in a Hindi film *Sahara* (1958). Though the tune and meaning of that song, 'So Ja Dukhiya Re', was an exact copy of the Assamese score by Hazarika, only Hemant Kumar was named as the film's composer. Assamese filmmaker and critic Utpal Borpujari told me this may have been done because the duo were close friends and there was no competition between them.[67]

Since *Era Bator Xur*, the trend caught on in Assamese film songs to hire top singers of the times either from the Hindi or Bengali music industries to do the playback. It is the reason shining stars of Bombay then, be it the Mangeshkar sisters or Mohammad Rafi, Kishore Kumar, Manna Dey, or noted Bengali singers like Aarti Mukherjee, Ina Mukherjee, etc., fortified Assamese modern music with their golden hits in the 1960s and '70s. Hazarika, who brought Usha Mangeshkar to sing several iconic songs for his film *Chameli Memsahib* in 1975, bagged the national award for its music in 1976.

Several non-film songs were also sung by popular singers of the time from outside the state. The trend in Assamese film and non-film music was carried forward by other music directors for several decades; say, the 1980s album *Niribili Godhuli* saw the likes of Kavita Krishnamurthy, Udit Narayan, Kumar Sanu, and Anuradha Paudwal joining hands with Asha Bhonsle and Jitul Sonowal, a young Assamese singer who had made a mark by then. The list of such songs in Assamese music from the mid 1950s onwards till the end of 1980s is long. A well-known Assamese singer from the 1970–80s era, Sandhya Menon, had once told me, 'During that time, there were quite a few of us who were popular female singers in Assam but often the best songs of the year were given to those from Bengal or Bollywood. Unlike today's times, those songs were written by top Assamese poets and writers aside from Hazarika. But the film music directors often wanted a famous name from Bollywood or Bengal to sing and popularize those songs in Assam. We used to really grudge it.'

This is not to say that songs belted out by Menon or other Assamese singers didn't catch listeners' attention. Scores by Mohananda Majindar Boruah, Dipen Baruah, Runjun Phukan, Namita Bhattacharjee, Manisha Hazarika, Madhumati Goswami, Pradip Dohotiya, Aftab Ahmed, Anima Choudhury, Pulak Banerjee, Archana and Khogen Mahanta, ruled the lips of Assamese listeners. Kamal Hazarika's composition 'Senai Moi Jau Dei' in celebrated Assamese singer Dipali Borthakur's voice in the 1950s is still popular. Yet another song of Borthakur in a Bihu tune, 'Nahor Phul Phulibor Oi', is a golden number. Borthakur, whose musical career was cut short by a severe motor neuron disease—a rude shock to Assamese music lovers of the 1950s–60s—was widely considered Assam's Lata Mangeshkar, earning the moniker Nightingale of Assam. Aside from men, several women—Nalinibala Devi, Nirmal Prabha Bordoloi, Lakyahira Das (she sang some immortal numbers too)—also wrote modern Assamese songs.

Since a limited number of Assamese films were produced in a year anyway, the trend in Assamese modern music from the twentieth century onwards had always been to release standalone albums of non-film songs. In the non-film category of Assamese modern songs, several numbers by Bhupen Hazarika's younger brother, Jayanta Hazarika (1943–77), must be underlined here too as extraordinary. Though all the Hazarika siblings had gained varying degrees of popularity for their contributions to modern Assamese music (primarily the elder sister Sudakhina Baruah), Jayanta Hazarika's quality of voice stood out like his elder brother's and is the reason why his songs have continued to be popular decades after his death. He was the first composer to have brought in the influences of Western classical, jazz, and rock 'n' roll to modern Assamese music.

In the genre of Assamese children's music, some of the numbers that have stood the test of time are Rudra Baruah's 'Poka Dhanor Maje Maje'; Khogen Mahanta's 'Ma Aami Xodiya Loi Jam E' and Pulak Banerjee's 'Phulore Melate Pokiye Geet Gai'.

Though Vidhushi Parvin Sultana from Assam is generally noted for her calibre in mainstream Hindustani classical music, she too sang Assamese songs. Her song, 'Koto Din Aru', written by Nalinibala Devi and set to music by Bhupen Hazarika, is a notable example. The long list of golden hits in Assamese modern music only underlines that it could carve out for itself a robust foundation in the last century. The opening of the AIR station in Guwahati in 1948 (and subsequently in Dibrugarh), in which the greats like Hazarika among others were closely involved, helped open up opportunities for several local musicians. In the 1980s, Assam also had its first all-women music band in Nagaon.

Unlike before, most Assamese songs today, unfortunately, do not have the lasting impact as they did earlier due to their comparatively poor lyrics and melody. Bollywood music too has swept through Assamese society in the twenty-first century, so much so that more and more young Assamese singers are more interested in breaking into Bollywood than concentrating on working in the Assamese music industry. Among the present crop, Zubeen Garg was able to get a break by working in Mahesh Bhatt's *Gangster* (2006) but in due course of time his work has been more or less in Assamese. The change of track turned out to be beneficial for his career as he is today undoubtedly one of the top musical icons for Assamese youth.

Among the younger crop of Assamese musicians, there are a number of excellent female singers too. Tarali Sarma, Zublee Baruah, Surekha Chetri, Dimpy Sonowal, Ananya Brahma–all are impressive artists with melodious voices.

In 2017, a young singer, Nilotpal Bora, impressed the music lovers of the state with his solo 'Majuli', an emphatic rendition on life in the river island. Lately, a handful of new singers and songwriters, including Maitryee Pator and Shankuraj Konwar, have made the Assamese modern song space rather interesting by not only nurturing the quality of melody in their compositions but also with the depth of their lyrics.

In Bollywood thus far, Papon, with his unique voice quality, has been able to construct for himself a niche as a noted singer from Assam while at the same time being able to carry forward his talented parents Khogen and Archana Mahanta's musical legacy back home with Bihu songs and Tokari geet. Kalpana Patowary from Assam, aided by her powerful voice quality, is yet another name that has been able to make a mark in Bhojpuri music, aside from singing in Assamese. Though Joi Barua too sings Bollywood numbers and creates western melodies, his Assamese collection of songs is rather impressive. Written by Ibson Lal Barua, Joi's rendition of 'Teje Teje' is a notable import of the Assamese literary allegory of Tejimola to music. His 'No Jujor Ronua' is a veritable history of the Koch Rajbonshis that reminds one of what Hazarika did with his ballads.

ASSAMESE DANCES

Being a sangam of several micro cultures, it is not unusual for the Assamese community to have an eclectic posy of dances; each competing with the other in grace and vibrancy of movement, while also drawing elements from one another. While some fall in the category of folk, some others fall in the classical bucket.

In the classical lot, three Assamese dance forms are commonly cited: the Deogharar Nati Nritya, the Oja Pali, and the Sattriya. Before we delve into the folk practices, let's take a peek at the classical forms: their origins, the forces behind their survival, and expansion thus far.

DEOGHARAR NATI NITYA

Once performed at the Shaivite and Vishnu temples of Assam, Deogharar Nati Nritya is said to have been practised for a thousand years.[68] Though no temple from the ancient period has been unearthed intact thus far in the state, relics of temples made in the Gupta-era style dating back to the fifth century, and stone and terracotta sculptural remains of temples from seventh century onwards (also including dancing figures, Shiva's Nataraja avatar, and men and women playing musical instruments) bear testimony to not only the existence of exquisitely built temples in ancient Assam but also the prevalence of dance and music. Several such ancient temple sculptures preserved at the Assam State Museum in Guwahati, provide a clue that the state, like in neighbouring olden Odisha, too must have had its own Devadasi Nritya. Noted cultural commentator Maheswar Neog who had conducted extensive research on the three classical forms of Assamese dance for several decades, had highlighted in a journal of Sangeet Natak Akademi (SNA) in 1959 that the Nati dance was performed primarily at the Shaivite temples of Biswanathghat in today's Darrang district; Dergaon in present-day Golaghat district; and Dubi in Kamrup district.[69] Young girls were dedicated to Shiva and Vishnu by the devotee families, somewhat akin to young boys dedicated to the Vaishnava satras by devotee families in the later centuries in Assam. The girls would remain with their families though and were taught the ritualistic dance based on texts of songs, possibly from manuscripts; they performed twice a day at the temple in praise of the lord. A nati (dancer) would remain unmarried. On occasions like Durga Puja, Chaitra Sankranti, and Pausa Sankranti, Nati dances were performed outside of the temples too.[70]

That the centuries-old practice was in pristine form even during the Ahom era (thirteenth–nineteenth century) can be understood from a mention Neog makes about the construction of the Pariharesvara Shiva temple in Dubi under the patronage of King Shiva Singha around 1770 where three families of gayan–bayan (singers and accompanying musicians) and Nati were brought from the Negheriting Shiva temple of Dergaon to conduct the daily performance of dance and music there.[71] Neog had also referred to the prevalence of Nati dance at the revered Vishnu temple Haigrib Madhav at Hajo near Guwahati which was rebuilt by the Kamata king Raghudeva Narayan in 1583, and remarked that the dance was 'probably in conformity with the similar custom in Puri Jagannath temple.'[72] He, thus, underlined its similarities with Odisha's Mahari dance tradition from which the classical form Odissi draws features.

The Nati dance was understood to be swift and vigorous, punctuated with somersaults. 'The music in its highest tempo is known as *khatar bajana*;

the somersaults being called *khat*.[73] Such movements are not absolutely uncommon also in the Sattra school (Sattriya dance form).'[74] Local instruments like the khol (a drum) and khuti taal (small cymbals made with bell metal) were used to produce the background music. According to noted Sattriya exponent and researcher, Mallika Kandali, the term, gayan–bayan, used in Nati for the accompanying musicians, later formed a part of the Sattriya dance which had taken birth in Assam under the supervision of Vaishnava saint Sankardev.[75] Kandali has also highlighted that certain movements in Sattriya, such as the Aathu lon, Thio lon, Tomal musora, Namaskar lon, etc. have similarities with the grammar of Nati.[76] In 2019, Kandali, in an article compared other Sattriya movements, like the Thita paak, Haat xoluwa, Xoman ura, with Nati.[77]

With the destabilization of the Koch and Kamata kingdoms in western Assam due to waves of Mughal attacks from the seventeenth century onwards, and the steady weakening of the Ahom dynasty after the late eighteenth century, Nati Nritya fell into gradual decline. Some recent writings on the form claimed that several dancers had to resort to sex work thereafter,[78] attracting a ban on the dance form in the British colonial period. However, experts like Neog have blamed the British colonizers's inability to appreciate the dance form, particularly the moves evoking erotic sentiments, say, the swift trotting movement of horses, for the decline of the dance form. 'Unsavoury tales that connect themselves with such a profession led to its social strangulation, and its exit from the scene was complete under a foreign regime by the close of the 19th century. One Christian writer, Nidhi Levi Farewell (of Assamese origin), of the mid-19th century casts his caustic glances on the temple women of Hajo as he goes to describe their songs and dances in a few rough-hewn verses published in the Baptist journal *Orunudoi*. Burdened with the contempt of the age and unsupported by any royal munificence, Natis had to give up their holy duties.'[79] Assamese historian Surya Kumar Bhuyan has written about an incident where three Nati dancers were taken away 'by force' from the Biswanathghat Shiva shrine of Darrang by Satrajit Baruwa of Dacca who was a part of the Mughal force under Aurangzeb.[80]

With the passage of time, the dancers themselves forgot many of the moves. In the late 1950s, when Ratna Kanta Talukdar, a resident of Patshala town of Lower Assam, took up the cudgels to revive the dance form with Bishnu Prasad Rava, he luckily found two aged former Nati dancers, Kaushyala Devi and Royobala Devi. The dance that was reconstructed from their faint recollections could stretch only to about ten minutes. His biggest challenge, though, was to find students to learn the dance. He ultimately succeeded in convincing four families of Patshala to send their daughters to him to learn the dance which proved to be a groundbreaking moment for the form to be resurrected from its grave. In 1959, Neog, documenting the massive contribution of Talukdar in reviving the dying form, wrote, 'No song accompanying the dance (is) are today available, and nobody is definite if there was any such song at all. But the dance has come down faithfully enough to itself and can tell its own content clearly.'[81]

Thankfully, after Talukdar's demise in 1980, the brother of one of the first four students who had learnt under him, took up the baton to continue his mission. Dilip Kakati of Patshala now has a seven-member troupe and regularly performs the dance with help from his sister trained by Talukdar.[82] Aside from stage performances, there was also a recent recital at Haigrib Madhav temple in Hajo, one of its original abodes.

OJA PALI

Another Assamese classical form, the Oja Pali, is essentially choral singing with dance moves performed in a group. Oja Pali comes in three varieties: Sukananni Oja Pali, Vyah-gowa Oja Pali, and Sattriya Oja Pali. Sukananni Oja Pali is a performance in praise of the serpent goddess Manaxa (Manasa). A famous folk tale in Assam is about a couple, Beula and Lakhindar, and goddess Manaxa's revenge on Lakhindar's father, a Shaivaite merchant Chandradhar. This version of Oja Pali narrates that story, using verses extolling Manaxa or Maroi, plucked out of Padma Puran, a treatise in classical Assamese by poet Narayanadeva. A long narrative divided into three parts, such a recital can stretch to a number of days. Led by an Oja or the master narrator of the tale, the performance is aided by the members of the troupe called Pali, who repeat what the Oja had performed. The Palis manage the background music with a joi dhul (a grand drum), dhepa dhul (a conical drum), khuti taal, bor taal (the jumbo-sized bell metal cymbals), etc. The entire troupe is dressed in white, like in a monastic dance. The Oja dons a turban, a long coat, a white dhoti with ends that float in front, a sador or a cloth draped around his waist and another on his shoulders with the two ends in front. 'The Oja, as he leads the chorus, indicates the subject-matter of his song with appropriate gestures of the hand and movements of the feet.'[83] The renditions are tuned to raga patterns like Bhatiyali, Ahir, Sandhya. The performance conducted in a Shamanistic style, commences with a chanting followed by hand gestures and an invocation to deities like Shiva, Durga, Sitala, Manasa, and Dharma, to the beating of the grand drum. The Oja keeps the time beats with the mini cymbals.

An interlude to the Sukananni Oja Pali is yet another dance, Deodhani, during which a female artist performs in a frenzy with open hair. The Deodhani performance is essentially to accentuate the tension between Manaxa and Chandradhar and involves a dance by Beula to propitiate the gods. It is marked by elements like Sivar nachon (Shiva's dance); Urvasir nachon (dance of Urvasi); Kachari nachon (dance of the Kachari in praise of Manasa); Mecha nachon (Chandradhar taking to fishing after losing his wealth); and Harir nachon (dance of the man who sweeps the floor to worship Manaxa.) According to Assamese writer Nirmal Prabha Bordoloi, during Maroi Puja, the Deodhani dances in front of Goddess Kesaikhati to satisfy the all-pervading power of the universe. 'She finds herself extremely powerful, like a god, and begins to express it in a vigorous, unnatural, restless dance.'[84]

In present-day Assam, the Sukananni Oja Pali is primarily practised in Darrang, Mangaldoi, Bajali, Siphajhar, Udalguri, and Baksa districts. The popularity of the dance in this belt is perhaps because of the common belief that Darrang's king Dharmanarayan, in the seventeenth century, had been a patron of the art.[85] Significantly, this indigenous form is also a reflection of Assam's syncretic culture. King Dharmanarayan had introduced it to both his Hindu and Muslim subjects.[86] 'There are villages like Maraigaon (in Darrang) once inhabited by Muslim Sukananni-ojas, and those like Kaliyapara, inhabited by Muslim kaliya (pipe) players, and places where lived drummers of these performances.'[87]

Vyah-gowa Oja Pali are renditions from Puranas and epics like the Ramayana and Mahabharata, put to rhythm. 'The performance seems to have been connected with the Vaishnava tantric form of worship of Vasudeva, who is described as all white in colour and as possessing as many as eight arms.'[88] The songs used in this form of Oja Pali are taken from verses in classical Assamese composed by Dvija Raghunath,[89] believed to have lived in the seventeenth century around Mangaldoi area. Vasudeva is widely believed to have been worshipped by people around Mangaldoi for a few hundred years.[90]

The only musical instrument used in Vyah-gowa Oja Pali are the kar-taal, the large-sized bell metal cymbals. Like in Sukananni Oja Pali, the Oja in this form too wears ornaments and a white turban which resembles the one worn by a sutradhar or a narrator in a Sattriya performance. A Vyah-gowa Pali dresses in a similar fashion like in the Sukananni Oja Pali. This form uses about twenty-seven ragas.[91] The form varies from the Sukananni Oja Pali with more feet, hand, and body movements, and has specific gestures to represent each emotion. Vyah-gowa Oja Pali also has the chokuwa paak or reeling movement noticed in the Sattriya form.

The Sattriya form of Oja Pali, practised in the monasteries, has a host of similarities with the Vyah-gowa form. An Oja is accompanied by a group of Palis dressed in white. The mini cymbal, khuti-taal, is the only instrument used for music, and the renditions are from the Vaishnava poetical texts set to a few ragas. The Oja also has a few specific hand movements.

OPESSARI DANCE

There is a belief among a section of Assamese that praying to the Opessari (fairies) from the heavens will ward off any ill omen affecting their family. A group of women give up food and fast, then make an offering to the Opessari in the front yard of the affected family and dance while clapping their hands, their long tresses swishing as they move. This practice becomes particularly interesting when taken into note the Apsara dance performed by the Angkor Wat civilization of Cambodia in Southeast Asia.

Several such religious performances exist among tribal and non-tribal Assamese. A notable example is Sabin Alun, the performance based around the Karbi Ramayana which occupies a special place in the sociocultural life of the Karbis. According to folklorist and former president of Asam Sahitya Sabha, Birendranath Dutta, Sabin was most likely the composer or the original singer of the Ramayana ballad. The rendition stretches to several nights. Some folklorists felt that Sabin Alun might have been inspired by Madhav Kandali's Ramayana written in the fourteenth century. According to Dutta, however, it 'is so full of ethnic Karbi folk elements that it is better to regard it as an independent growth, planted and nourished in Karbi soil with only the graft taken from outside.'[92]

SATTRIYA (XATRIYA)

Though Assam has three classical dance forms, Sattriya (Xatria in Assamese) is the best known outside of the state simply because it is the one that has been performed on a variety of platforms across India and elsewhere.

The reason is, in 2000, the dance form was recognized by the SNA as a classical form. The recognition had come after a long-drawn-out struggle by people like Guru Rashewar Saikia Barbayan, Jatin Goswami, Pradeep Jyoti Mahanta, Sunil Kothari, and Himangshu Sekhar Das, among several others. The ultimate credit for the tag, though, must be bestowed on Bhupen Hazarika as the recognition finally came during his tenure as the chairman of SNA. Several mainstream dancers and critics had also highlighted the distinctive features of Sattriya around that time, which too was crucial for its acknowledgement as a classical form. Noted dancer Uday Shankar had once called the Sattriya style 'the fifth school of classical Indian dance'.[93] In 1999, after watching a dance performance by Prateesha Suresh at Delhi's Triveni Kala Sangam, top classical dance scholar Kapila Vatsayan got on to the stage to declare, 'Of course it (Sattriya) is classical.'[94]

Sattriya form is a contribution of the multifaceted Saint Sankardev (1449–1568). Though Sankardev was exposed to the Bhakti movement of mainland India during his pilgrimages to Puri and northern India, what he finally wove into the fabric of Assamese culture was an admixture of what he had experienced from his travels and what he thought would work in Assam. He thus ensured an amalgamation of folk and local lived beliefs and forms and tailored a new awakening within the community. Sattriya too reflects that abiding thought of the guru behind community construction, melding the folk with the classical. Therefore, Sattriya has elements adapted from not only the classical Nati Nritya and Oja Pali but also from several folk forms of dance from Assam.

Mallika Kandali had underlined that aside from other resemblances, Sattriya has parallels with the Vyas-gowa Oja Pali in abhinaya (use of hand and facial expressions) too. 'For instance, the Roja hasta, the Tanay hasta and Krishna Hasta used by some artistes in Oja Pali has crept into Sattriya.'[95] Some of the Deodhani features also have features that resemble Sattriya.

Sattriya also has several tribal influences. During her research, Kandali found that the dance had similarities primarily with the Bagurumba, Kherai, and Bardoisikhla dances of the Bodos; the Hamjar of the Rabhas; Bihu of the Mising and the Sonowal Kacharis; the postures and hand movements of some dances of the Tiwas; etc.[96] 'For instance, the pranam or the movement of archana done at the beginning of a Sattriya performance has a similarity with a movement of the Kherai dance of the Bodos. On the other hand, the Sereki Paak used in Sattriya can find a resemblance with a turn in the Bihu dance, so also in the Kherai.'[97] An important feature of the Sattriya dance, Haali, or the way the upper body part is swayed to a side, is also similar to the dances of the Rabhas and Deuris. 'It must be mentioned here that a Sattriya dancer follows the rules of Padakshin when she enters the stage. In Bharata's *Natyasastra*, it has been described as a main feature of the dances of the *Udra Magadhi* (eastern countries, say Assam, Odisha, Bengal, Nepal, etc). It is worthy of highlighting here that the folk dances of Assam follows this trait too.'[98] Even in the music, folk elements can be traced, leading Kandali to comment, 'The influence of the Bihu Husori of Upper Assam and the songs and music of different tribes can be found in Sattriya or can be said to have found parallel expression in them.'[99]

Though Sattriya has several things in common with the folk forms of the state, Maheswar Neog had underlined that Sattriya had been able to maintain its distinctiveness through a number of unique hastas (hand movements called haat in Sattriya), choreographic patterns, costumes, and use of masks.[100] Still, it needs pointing out that the use of masks in the dance form can also be equated with the Buddhist monastic dances ; Buddhism was once greatly influential in Assam and neighbouring Bhutan and Tibet. The bor taal used in Sattriya music is akin to the cymbals used in Bhutanese monasteries. Till date, these cymbals are called Bhutia-taal (Bhutanese cymbals) in Assam.

Over the centuries, Sattriya was nurtured by the Vaishnava monasteries, particularly those in Majuli, home to the majority of Vaishnava monasteries in Assam. The Kamalabari Monastery is especially well-known for the practice and advancement of the dance form. Taking a cue from the practice followed in monasteries like Kamalabari, Neog had classified Sattriya into three types: 'Dances included in dramatic representation; Jhumuras and Behar-Nach, originally deriving such representation; Chalis; and Oja Pali.'[101] The Oja Pali version of Sattriya has been expounded on earlier in the chapter. The Chali Nach, according to Neog, must have derived its name from the footwork (pada) noticed in the dance.[102] There are about eight variations of Sattriya Chali dance which essentially differs from each other in the use of Ramdhani that employs different talas (rhythm).[103] 'The term "natuwa" nach is sometimes applied specifically to the Chali dances. The word "natuwa" generally meant an actor in the beginning, as we have found in the biographies of the saints. It would thus indicate that this form of dance was derived from the Ankiya drama.'[104] A form of Chali dance is also called Rajagharia Nach or one devised by Maniram Bayan of Kamalbari

Satra for performance at the Ahom capital in royal presence. Then there is the Behar Nach derived from *Bhojanavyavahara*, a play that Sankardev's chief disciple Madhabdev had penned. Yet another variety is the Vara Prabesha, which is supposed to represent Krishna's dance while returning in a jovial mood from Vrindavan to Gokul at sundown. 'It is generally performed during Madhabdev's death anniversary.'[105] In another form of Sattriya dance named Manchok, the entire orchestra, the gayan-bayan, too dances.[106] In monasteries of Majuli like Auniati, certain other forms of Sattriya can be noticed which might be a later addition.[107] Variations in the dance form were also dependent on the wealth of texts that a particular monastery owned. For instance, a copy of the Subhankara Kavi's *Hasta Muktavali*, a precious text in Assamese considered to be the most elaborate in terms of hand gestures represented, was found at Auniati.[108] It is believed that Suchandra Rai Oja, who was the owner of that manuscript, resided at the Kamalabari Satra nearby. 'It is thus likely that this work was actually used by the bayans (dance gurus) in training Natuwa boys in the sattras.'[109]

The third classification of Sattriya comprises of three principal forms: the Sutradhar Nach, the Krishna Nach or Ram Nach, and Gopi Nach, the dance of the gopis of Vrindavan. The performance begins with a dance by the Sutradhar, the narrator, who is dressed in white. He dances in a slow tempo, then begins reciting slokas which are played by the orchestra. He, thereafter, expresses them in a dance. A number of dancers appear on the stage next; chief among this nritya is that of Gosain Pravesh Nach or the entry of Ram or little Krishna with cowherds; this is the Krishna Nach. Krishna dons a yellow dhoti and a black vest; the use of the colour could well be to highlight the dark colour of his skin. Then begins the entry of the gopis dressed in ghagra skirts with a black blouse (but wearing no ghungroos around their ankles) to do Gopi Pravesar Nach.[110]

An important dance within this school is also the Raas Nach. 'This dance was introduced by Sankardev through his play *Keli-Gopala* or *Rasa-krida*, and Madhabdev, through his *Rasa Jhumura*.'[111] All the top satras of Assam have their own form of Raas Nach. Raas is an important festival in all monasteries, be it in Barpeta in Lower Assam or in Majuli in Upper Assam. The one performed at the Dakhinpat monastery of Majuli has been in continuance since the mid-seventeenth century; the one presented at the neighbouring Auniati Satra was established in 1654.

The Sattriya School also has a dance called Juddhar Nach or war dance in which clubs (gada) and bows (dhanu) make an appearance.[112]

Then there is the Jhumura dance performed by young boys of Kamalabari monastery. Also, there is the Nadu-Bhangi dance generally conducted by three pairs of gopis and gopas to the tune of Borgeet, or the five songs of Rasa Jhumura.[113]

Since Sattriya is a monastic dance form, women have been conspicuous in their absence from performances of the dance. Only in the last few decades has one seen women taking to Sattriya dance on stage. Some of the leading lights of it were Indira P. P. Bora[114] and Pushpa Bhuyan.

BIHU

With the existence of a bouquet of tribes in Assam and their rich micro cultures, it is only natural to have a range of folk dances within the larger community. Each tribe has its own speciality to offer, but the mother of all folk forms of dance in Assam, or rather the meeting point of various folk strains of the state, is the Bihu.

Though Bihu is also viewed by some as a non-tribal Assamese dance, there is no denying that its many moves are in correspondence with the lilt and cadence of several tribal dances of Assam, particularly the Bagurumba dance of the Bodos. Though Bagurumba is essentially a female dance and Bihu need not be so, the footwork of the female dancer, the swaying of her body, her hand movements, the use of musical instruments made of bamboo in the performance, be it the Gongwna (Gogona in Assamese), the Sifung (Bahi in Assamese), or the Kham (Dhul in Assamese), and also the expression of desire in the dancer through lines like 'Dwi jiri jiri samo khigiri, sonani jinjiri' (in Baguruma where the female dancer pines for a gold necklace) is similar to a female Bihu dancer longing for her beau to bestow on her a precious gift.

Though some claim that the term Bihu is a corrupt (aprabhangsa) version of the Sanskrit term 'Bishuv', folklorist Nirmal Prabha Bordoloi had called it a pre-historic amalgamation of cultures brought on by recurrent waves of migrants settling by the banks of the Brahmaputra.[115] Since it is essentially a harvest festival, Bordoloi had called Bihu a pre-Aryan feature of the community and equated it to various agricultural practices prevalent among the tribes of greater Assam revolving around the fertility cult, and the worship of spring as the bringer of life and sustenance, a feature common to many early civilizations.[116] Talking about the origin of Bihu, she had underlined that it is in Rongali Bihu (in

April) that an Assamese peasant ties a tongali (a wrap around his waist) to fill up a vacant field with paddy once more. 'Does the egg-fight and the kawri-fight practiced during the Bihu festival not indicate the Austro-Asiatic belief of giving credence to life? Both the egg and the kawri are symbols of procreation. The Bihu dance is an expression of a vibrant and liberated life,' Bordoloi had written, adding that there is enough basis to deduce that the dance moves of the Bodo and Mising communities are at the root of the Assamese Bihu dance.[117]

While the non-tribal Assamese celebrate Bihu on the first day of Bohag, the month of spring (14 April), several Assamese tribes celebrate it on the first Wednesday of the month.

Though Bihu for a long period was more prevalent in Upper Assam, there is evidence of the presence of the Bhatheli dance in Lower Assam during spring with links to the fertility cult.

Since the Bodos call Bihu Bwisagu, Bordoloi had wondered if the term Bihu had sprung out of it.[118] The Rabhas call it Boikhu; Deuris call it Bisu. The festival songs of the Tangsas are called Bihouti. 'The plains tribes of Assam, say, the Mishings, sing *Oi Nitom* and dance in joy to Bihu (the Mising Bihu). The dance that the Karbi youths do with a ritual during the Bihu has its resemblance with it. The Bodo women, just prior to the start of the harvest, do a vibrant dance. In the interiors of Kamrup, there is the prevalence of a dance during the Bihu where women dress up as men in secret. These dances only highlight the man's endeavour to gratify nature to provide a bountiful harvest.'[119]

Though Bihu dances are today often performed on stage and indoors, this practice is merely a few decades old. Traditionally, the dance has belonged to the natural surroundings and was usually performed by a river, on a field, under a tree, where young and old, men and women, gathered in their woven finery to express freely their enthusiasm towards life, living, and love, with the play of suitable words picked from their surroundings and set to tune produced by instruments made with materials picked from nature. In doing so, the community reiterates its shared commitment to living a full life.

A significant segment of Bihu dance is the Husori. The Husori ritual is typically carried out by making visits to the courtyards of individual houses to bless them for a good year ahead. A group of performers begins the dance with a padakshin by forming a circle with the leader singing in praise of Krishna or Ram by clanging a bor taal. The rest follow him in a chorus before they all break into a vigorous Bihu dance with the play of instruments like dhol, pepa, gogona, khuti taal, etc.

The Rabhas, Tiwas, Bodos, and Deuris too have Husori. The Garos and the Nagas also have the tradition of performing a Husori dance in the courtyard of their clan leader or the village head. Bordoloi had stated that the custom of Husori within the non-tribal community must have spread during the Ahom period.[120] A hint of it can be found in the tradition, till date, of a Husori team first visiting the most well-known or wealthy families and higher officials of a village or a town. The Bihu, as such, had become the symbol of the greater Assamese community in Upper Assam because of royal patronage. However, during the British era, there was a concerted effort to ban Bihu by citing it as a vulgar dance, like the Nati Nritya was. The Assamese upper-caste Hindus were in support of the ban but were pushed back through the concerted efforts by lower-caste Assamese. Post Independence, Assamese cultural icons like Rava and Bhupen Hazarika promoted the folk form. In the 1950s and 1960s, the state chapter of IPTA, then under the influence of Hemanga Biswas, Hazarika, and Rava, also played a stellar role in the promotion of Bihu as the cultural pride of the community. Celebrated Bihu drummer Moghai Oja was discovered by Biswas. At the fourth session of the Assam chapter of IPTA in 1955, Oja performed on stage for the first time. After an astounding performance, IPTA members Balraj Sahni and Amar Sheikh jumped onto the stage to give him a bear hug. Oja went on to perform in several Indian cities with the support of the IPTA.[121]

The art of playing dhul (traditional drum) or the craft of the dhulia (drummer) also has a rich history in the state's Kamrup district. The Kamrupia dhulia presents an altogether different level of excellence and storytelling in a group presentation.

In the last few decades, with stage competitions of Bihu dance becoming more competitive, there are multiple Bihu gurus across the state teaching the form to young students in an organized fashion.

Nature is also a big part of the annual Bihu celebrations. Some spring-born orchids and other flowers and their leaves, say, the keteki, nahor, kopou, togor, and jetuka, take pride of place during the festivities. Two among these things are a must-have to complete the festive look of a female dancer: a kopou orchid in the hair, and a henna-like pattern on the hands drawn from jetuka leaves. Traditionally, a kopou flower is gifted to the dancer by her beau, though these days they are commonly found in the market during Bihu. A barrel-like long bloom in mauve, the kopou flower is tied around the top knot of a dancer to heighten her festive look.

The tradition of a young man gifting a kopou bloom to a young woman in Assamese culture has a similarity with a spring festival in Chinese culture; the girl would receive a flower (orchid) as a pledge from her beau to protect her.[122] Several Assamese plains tribes had migrated to the Brahmaputra Valley from China and Upper Burma at some time in the state's history. During spring, there is also a tradition in Upper Assam of wrapping a fragrant yellow keteki flower in a soft cloth and putting it into the folds of one's clothes as a potpourri of sorts. As mentioned above, yet another must for the women Bihu dancers is putting jetuka paste on their palms. Bordoloi calls this a contribution of the Assamese Muslims.[123]

Like other aspects of Assamese society, its music and dance too, as held up in this chapter, is a reflection of its past and is thereby an emblem of the cultural dynamics imbued within the wider populace due to the multiple bouts of migrations at varying times to the shores of the Brahmaputra; a result of a continuous give and take from people to people to finally result in cultural cohesion.

12

NAAT–KOTHA–BULSOBI: ASSAMESE CINEMA AND DRAMA

Amidst pin-drop silence, I heard her deliver those lines in a dark hall brimming with Assamese cinemagoers. Over three decades have passed since but those words still sit firmly in my mind.

> For eleven years of our married life, I remained in dharma and yet, one day, in front of me and my four children, you bring home a younger woman, begin to sleep with her. Why should I tolerate it? To go to heaven? What would I gain from it? I don't want to bear it quietly.
>
> To become Sita, there should be Ram too, then only (there is equality in marriage).

As celebrated Assamese actor Biju Phukan—playing Mohikanta in Bhabendranath Saikia's magnum opus *Agnisnaan* (1985)—watched a stern-faced Moloya Goswami as Menoka, his on-screen wife, in utter silence, she went on with the tirade. She eventually announced to him a decision which, to my mind, was one of the most powerful moments not just in Assamese cinema but in Indian cinema in general where a director used the medium to reflect to the masses a woman's right to demand equality in marriage. By setting the plot in pre-Independence India, the director portrayed that the demand within Assamese women for their marital rights is not recent.

Menoka went on to say:

> We have four children. The fifth one is coming; its father is you but I am not its mother; of the sixth one, I am the mother but you are not the father…we shall continue living under the same roof but I will never give you the right to ask me who is the father of the sixth one.

That striking last scene of *Agnisnaan* was a reflection of the rise in the number of quality Assamese films releasing in the 1980s. The industry was then breaking the glass ceiling by claiming not just several national awards but also by pulling in a sizeable audience to the theatre halls. In small towns, walking down to the local theatre to watch an Assamese film in a large group comprising family, friends, and neighbours had become a norm. The trend had touched villages too. A factor behind that surge was also the identity consciousness triggered by the anti-foreigner agitation. Saikia's rise as an Assamese filmmaker can also be located in that era.

Soon after watching *Agnisnaan*, I picked up *Antareep* (The Cape), Saikia's Assamese novel on which the film was based. In his writings too Saikia stood out for his astute use of the power of reason. A man of many talents, he was also the celebrated editor of *Xofura*, a popular Assamese children's magazine then. Equipped with a PhD in physics from the University of London and a diploma from the London-based Imperial College of Science and Technology, he was a professor of Physics at the Gauhati University. He had the impressive credentials to open up to young minds through *Xofura* a window to the realm of science by breaking down complex concepts into simple notions. Concurrently, Saikia also began editing *Prantik*, one of the most popular Assamese magazines to have hit the stands then, which has since continued to chronicle the sociocultural lives of the Assamese community.

What stood out in *Agnisnaan* were also its potent dialogues, delivered in the style of neo-realistic cinema that had come up in neighbouring Bengal since the 1960s. The film was conferred the central government's Rajat Kamal (silver lotus) honour for being the best regional film of that year besides Saikia picking the national award for best screenplay—the first Assamese film to have won that accolade.[1] The film did some rounds of the international festival circuit aside from being a part of Indian Panorama, the top showcase of the country's best films by the central government.

Agnisnaan gave Saikia his third taste of such national and international fame. His film *Anirban* had pocketed the national award for best regional film in 1980. In 1977, *Sandhyaraag* not only won the Rajat Kamal for the best regional film but was screened at the Cannes Film Festival in 1978. *Sandhyaraag* had also broken a record in Assamese cinema by becoming the first film made in Assamese to be part of Indian Panorama. A woman-centric film that showed its viewers the gradual mutation of Assamese society from the rural to urban, it focused on how personal dreams and desires may have to be crushed at times for modern comforts offered by the shifting times. Within that new reality, he also situated sexual harassment of women and the play of power in an inherently classist and patriarchal society that would typically fault the victim of such gender-based crimes.

Yet another important message that Saikia's cinema conveyed to his viewers was through *Abartan* (1994) where a woman was given equal licence to lead a promiscuous life and to make choices based solely on her happiness in a fashion similar to how men are often licensed by a patriarchial society. His female protagonist Jayanti, played by noted actor Mridula Baruah, refused to be the sacrificial goat for her family's selfish interests and made a choice between a lover who wouldn't promise her a dignified life and the one who would go to any length to be by her side. The film also subtly touched on the caste hierarchies present in Assamese society—Jayanti tells Parimal (played by prominent actor Tapan Das) that to be the lead actress of a well-known mobile theatre group, she had to change her screen name from Jayanti Baishya (denoting her lower caste) to Jayanti Devi (a surname commonly used by Brahmin women in Assam). In *Agnisnaan* too, the subtle play of caste and class, also addiction to opium (a bane in rural belts in colonial-era Assam), were dexterously woven into the script. Such sociocultural consciousness in Saikia's art made him a true practitioner of the cinema of neo-realism or what in common parlance is called parallel cinema. Spanning two decades, between 1977 and 1997, Saikia made only six Assamese films but each bagged at least one national award. The splash that the auteur's creations made at the national awards year after year was followed by Jahnu Barua's films making a mark even in the international arena. It was through them that a regular Assamese newspaper reader in the 1980s became familiar with names of coveted national film awards like Rajat Kamal, and world film festivals like that in Cannes, Berlin, Locarno, and Cairo.

Not that an Assamese film had not been screened at an international fest prior to Saikia and Barua's films. The first Assamese movie to feature at a global film festival was *Puberun* (1959); shown at the competition section of the Berlin International Film Festival. It had also won the President's silver medal for the best feature film at the 7th National Film Awards. The first Assamese film to have bagged the President's medal, though, was Nip Barua's *Ronga Police* (1958). By then, Phani Sharma' *Piyoli Phukan* (1955) had won the president's Certificate of Merit, a first in Assamese cinema.

While in the 1960s, Bhupen Hazarika's *Shakuntala* (1961) and *Pratidhwani* (1964), and Anwar Hussain's *Tejimola* (1963) were also conferred the President's silver medal; *Pratidhwani* made it to the Retrospective of Indian Cinema in Paris in 1967. However, a decade after these wins, the regularity with which Assamese films were able to pocket national awards provokes me to say that it was Saikia who truly was the first to make a consistent mark in quality Assamese cinema. He faced multiple odds including financial difficulties while engaging in filmmaking in an economically backward and peripheral zone of the country. Saikia's first film *Sandhyaraag* (1977) was made with a bank loan which embodies the typical struggle of an Assamese filmmaker then.

Saikia created a splash not only by making powerful films and writing/editing children's literature, but also by writing short stories and novels that bagged him the Sahitya Akademi Award in 1976. He created impressive one-act and radio plays and plays for the mobile theatre. Unfortunately, his versatility remained ensconced within Assam presumably because he didn't circulate himself in the mainstream Indian cultural and film circuit nor sought publicity for his work in the national media. Consequently, Saikia's genius and contribution to Indian cinema was never celebrated to the extent it should have been. During a conversation in 2021, veteran Assamese actor Pranjal Saikia gave a pertinent example to me on how film critics and filmmakers not knowing Saikia's genius might have affected his art. Inspite of the formidable performance as Menoka in *Agnisnaan*, the national award for best actress was not awarded to Moloya Goswami that year. 'It was most likely because several jury members might not have been familiar with Saikia's brilliance as a storyteller then. No mainstream newspaper or magazine talked about that film or his work then, unlike what we saw with films made by his contemporaries in Bengali cinema. Dozens of films come before the jury. If they know how good a filmmaker is, they are likely to give more attention to his film.' The actor had argued, 'Seven years later, Moloya Goswami got the best actress award in Jahnu Barua's *Firingoti*. She acted superbly in that role but should have got that national award for *Agnisnaan* too.'[2] The actor thought Jahnu Barua, by shifting base to Mumbai, took an appropriate career decision. 'It helped him to become visible to the rest of the world. Top jury members got acquainted to his genius, and could give attention to his films like *Firingoti* which, in turn, might have eventually helped them see the brilliance of Moloya Goswami as an actor.'

Nevertheless, for connoisseurs of good cinema, and to students of cinema particularly interested in portrayal of women in Assamese films, Saikia's oeuvre continues to stand out. Within the confines of Assamese cinema itself, his representation of women on screen stands out, particularly as a contrast to the first woman protagonist, Joymoti, in the first Assamese film by the same name.

FIRST ASSAMESE FILM

Produced by Jyoti Prasad Agarwala in 1935, *Joymoti* must be celebrated for several reasons, particularly for the perseverance of the director to make that cinematic milestone a reality despite facing a mountain of odds. The film, aside from being the first Assamese talkie, also holds the record of being the first Assamese adapted film; it was drawn from the legendary Assamese writer Lakshminath Bezbaroa's play *Joymoti Konwori* penned in 1914.[3]

Agarwala began working on *Joymoti* in 1933, just two years after the first Indian talkie *Alam Ara* was produced. From an article he wrote on the making of *Joymoti* in 1934 in *Asomiya* newspaper, what comes across is his sheer grit and tenacity to achieve that feat at a time when the genre of Indian talkie itself was just emerging from the silent era. Even though noted actor from the silent era Pramathesh Barua (1903–51) was from Assam (Goalpara), and went on to produce groundbreaking silent films like *Apradhi* (1931), the first Indian film to be shot using artificial lights, he never made an Assamese film except remaking the superhit *Devdas* in Assamese in 1937 after producing it in Bengali and Hindi.

No doubt being the son of a top businessman (Paramananda Agarwala) of Assam then, Agarwala had the financial wherewithal to make a film, an expensive affair even then, but he had no technical support within the state, unlike his contemporaries in Bengal, to produce a talkie. There were barely any cinemagoers in Assam; hardly a space to feature a film; no Assamese artist had been exposed to acting in front of the camera. Most actors that featured in *Joymoti* hadn't even watched a talkie. It must, therefore, be understood that it was his sheer personal resolve that helped to make that film a reality in a remote state like Assam at the dawn of the twentieth century.

In 1926, Agarwala had sailed to Scotland to study economics at the University of Edinburgh.[4] Before its completion though, he shifted base to London for a course on music at the Trinity College. In 1929, Agarwala sailed to Berlin with the intention of learning filmmaking, the most novel medium of storytelling then. The shift from silent films to talkies was taking place in Germany those days.[5] There, he met actor-producer Himanshu Rai, the founder of the film studio Bombay Talkies in Mumbai, and his collaborator Franz Osten. With Rai's help he enrolled himself as an intern at the famous UFA (Universum-Film-Aktein Gesellschaft) studio towards the end of 1929. Parthajit Baruah, in his excellent book on the history of Assamese cinema, *Jyotiprasad, Joymoti, Indramalati and Beyond*, holds up a fascinating sliver from that period by highlighting that Agarwala could well have been the first in India to produce a talkie if UFA had produced his play *Xonit Kuwori* that he translated into English as *The Dance of Art*. Agarwala had submitted the play to UFA as a manuscript for a talkie. Baruah reproduced in the book a letter sent by UFA in German to Agarwala on 18 June 1930, about its inability to do so as the manuscript dealt 'throughout with Indian scenes' and citing 'the difficulties for special Indian films (are) so big' that it couldn't take the 'risk of doing such a production'. Baruah commented, 'Thus Jyotiprasad missed the chance to script history by a whisker! Jyotiprasad's *The Dance of Art*, not Ardeshir Irani's *Alam Ara* (1931) would have been the first talkie in India. With the script at hand, Jyotiprasad returned to Edinburgh. Interestingly, some of the pages of the script are still preserved under his daughter's care.'[6]

Around 1932, while he was mulling over how to proceed further, Agarwala was thrown into prison in Assam for fifteen months for taking part in the Civil Disobedience Movement. He could resume work on *Joymoti* only after his release in 1933. He set up a makeshift film studio Chitraban at his family tea estate in Bholaguri, adjacent to his home town Tezpur. The tea estate's factory was used as a rehearsal space for the male actors after working hours. Agarwala soon formed his film company Chitralekha Movieton and used his family money to hire the services of the Faizi brothers of Lahore to record the film's sound.

In 1978, recounting the hurdles the filmmaker faced to produce the film, Prafulla Prasad Bora in *Cinema in Assam* wrote that for developing the film, Agarwala had to bring ice from Kolkata in a steamer to Jamugurihat in Sonitpur district and then by train to Rangapara, and thereafter had to wheel down the consignment about fifty miles in his car to his studio. One part of the studio, according to Bora, became 'a living museum where Jyotiprasad collected hundreds of traditional costumes, about 40 varieties of Assamese traditional ornaments for lady characters, *japi*, sarai (xorai), and other decoration material.'[7] With no electricity at the tea estate, the Faizi brothers had to run their sound system with the power of Agarwala's car battery.[8]

Parthajit Baruah's book recounts a major difficulty related to the film's sound. It highlights that Agarwala, accompanied by the film's assistant director Rajeen Barooah, travelled to Lahore for post production work. He was unhappy with the film's sound recording and dubbed both male and female voices wherever required. Baruah, importantly, points out that the original negatives of the first Assamese film were lost in Lahore due to an ugly legal battle that ensued between Agarwala and Faiz Mohammad who had recorded the sound of the film on behalf of the Fezi Sound Recording System. From Lahore, Agarwala returned to Kolkata only with one positive print of the film and left the negatives in Faiz Mohammad's custody. But he never returned to Lahore to reclaim them as by early 1935 he was entangled in the legal battle over his demand to re-record some sounds of the film. The case remained unresolved. 'This bitter episode with Mr. Faiz remains a dark chapter in the history of Assamese cinema.'[9]

A major challenge for Agarwala in making *Joymoti* was also to find women actors, including a fresh face to play the female protagonist, the Ahom queen Joymoti. At a time when there was barely social sanction for Assamese girls from cultured families, particularly among the village folk, to act in the traditional Assamese religious drama, Bhaona (men those days would also play the role of women), the filmmaker had to cast the net far and wide. He advertised in the newspapers *Batori* and *Tinidiniya Batori* seeking actors.[10] According to actor-director Phani Sarma who played Gathi Hazarika in *Joymoti* (he played the lead in P. C. Barua's Assamese version of *Devdas*), about a thousand applications were received but none came from a woman. Agarwala eventually took to the road on his Chevrolet car with friends Bishnu Prasad Rava and Phani Sarma and drove through Upper Assam villages in the search for possible actresses. 'Eventually, Jyotiprasad was mocked as *suwali sur* (girl thief) in the villages. Even if he would find a village girl to act in the film, he would be asked to sign a bond first by the family in the presence of the village head that if the girl lost her virginity, he would have to pay a big sum to them,' Ismail Hussain related in *Jyotiprasad Agarwalar Jibon Aru Darshan*.[11]

Agarwala ultimately found Aideu Handique in the Mohuramukh area of Golaghat to play Joymoti; also Mohini Rajkumari to become the queen mother (rajmau). The role of the Naga woman Dalimi was played by Swargajyoti Baruah. Hussain's book has a detailed list of names of the people who assisted Agarwala in the project, including that of the singers and the actors.[12]

To comprehend better the place of women in the Assamese society when Agarwala made *Joymoti*, a mention must be made here about two sets of fate that awaited the women lead actors of that film. Swargajyoti Baruah who played Dalimi could leave her husband after the film's release and remarry an already married top lawyer from an Assamese family who also accepted her children from the earlier marriage. However, Aideu Handique who played Joymoti and belonged to a village not far from where Swargajyoti had remarried was ostracized for calling actor Phunu Baruah who played her spouse on screen as bongohordeu (husband); she remained unmarried for the rest of her life. Her tragic tale was retold by talented filmmaker Arup Manna in national award winning Assamese film *Aideu* in 2007. Mohini Rajkumari once recounted, 'Even relatives ostracised us; I was offered food at their courtyard saying I had lost my *jaat* (caste). I ate that food...some people even came home with a gun to kill me for going against societal norms. If I had to attend a wedding, I had to first undergo the purity ritual (*porasit*). As if from that day onwards, my freedom was lost.'[13]

It must also be analysed why Agarwala zeroed in on the subject of Joymoti for the first Assamese film. Much before Bezbaroa created *Joymoti Kunwori*, Ratneswar Mahanta (1864–93), through his writings in *Asam Bandhu* and *Jonaki* magazines in 1892, had introduced the legend of Joymoti to the literary space in Assam. Joymati made her first appearance in Mahanta's articles 'Moamaria Bidroh' and 'Joymati Kunwari' published in *Jonaki* magazine and established the myth of the 'Sati' Joymati—the ideal Hindu woman who would give up her life for her husband but wouldn't directly participate in the political affairs of state. 'In doing so...he provided for Assam its own story of the mainstream heroine—the *patrivrata*, the self-sacrificing female icons that litter the annals of Indian myth and legend. Secondly, he provided the important linkage that included not just the husband, but also the king, and thereby the country.'[14]

This identity attributed to Joymoti in Assam towards the end of the nineteenth century, which was picked up by the likes of Kolkata-educated Bezbaroa, Rava, and Jyotiprasad, must also be juxtaposed with what was unfolding in neighbouring Bengal due to its cultural and literary renaissance. It was the time when Bankim Chandra Chatterjee (1838–1994), through literature, was moulding a new image of the Bengali woman, a mix of modernity placed in the nationalist discourse, which was added to by several other writers.[15] Such ideas were likely brought to Assam by those who had had the benefit of a Kolkata education. 'Jyoti Prasad's *Joymoti*, being the first Assamese film, necessarily required a story of "national" importance—the story that would evoke (and stoke) the collective pride of a nation—a story of heroism, a glorious national past, its cultural traditions and political–

historical heritage, its various ethnicities and the cordial relations between the indigenous people of the region.'[16]

On 10 March 1935, *Joymoti* was screened at Raunaq Theatre in Kolkata in presence of Lakshminath Bezbaroa. 'The hall was packed with famed personalities like Pramathesh Chandra Barua, Prithiviraj Kapoor, Kundanlal Saigal, Devika Kumar Basu, Dhiren Ganguli, Phani Majumdar and many others besides.'[17] Ten days later, it was screened at Kamrup Natya Mandir in Guwahati with the help of a Phillips portable projector.[18] Those days, only Guwahati had a cinema hall which Agarwala avoided, perhaps to make his film more accessible to the common man. He used the projector to take the film across Assam. While Bezbaroa and then Congress leader Gopinath Bordoloi showered praise on Agarwala for the film, there were some in Assam who outright panned it on technical grounds. Reacting to the criticism, mainly on the ground of sound, a disheartened Agarwala had stated, '*Joymoti* did have technical flaws but as the first Assamese film there were several things to be noticed.'[19] Such negative comments made the film a flop in Assam. In a letter to writer Maheswar Neog, Agarwala mentioned that Assamese people failed to particularly fathom its background music, created by using local instruments like dhol and khol as equal to western instruments. After the film's release, some also ridiculed it as 'Japimoti' or a film made only to exhibit various sizes of Japi.[20]

Bezbaroa too expressed his frustration at the rejection of the first Assamese film by a considerable section of the community. He once wrote that while he heard people in Bengal praising *Joymoti* for being much better than their first film, a section of Assamese came out determinedly to deride it.[21]

Not one to give up, Agarwala, in 1948, travelled to Kolkata inspite of his ill health, with Phani Sarma and his brother Hridayananada Agarwala, to complete the film's re-editing and added some new songs to the film. The re-edited version, released on 28 May 1949, had a fairly successful theatrical re-run in Assam. According to Hussain, though Agarwala urged the then Assam government for financial help to dub it in Hindi too, the funding never materialized. 'By then, he was associated with IPTA and was rumoured to be a Communist. So he couldn't get the state funding.'[22]

The print of the film with the total length, however, became 'decomposed and (was) lost somewhere' with only eight prints of the reprinted version found in the early 1970s at his garage.[23] On his family's request, Bhupen Hazarika made a documentary in Assamese, *Rupkonwar*

Jyotiprasad aru Joymoti, in which he used those prints, and also clips from Agarwala's second film *Indramalati* (1939). 'The documentary saved an invaluable part of the history of Assamese cinema.'[24]

TREND OF REALISM IN ASSAMESE FILMS

Agarwala, in an article published in *Jyotiprasad Rachanavali*, an anthology of his writings edited by noted Assamese writer-critic Hiren Gohain, had acknowledged that his approach to filmmaking was influenced by the realist cinema of England and Russia more than the theatrical slant spotted then in the Hindi and Bengali films. Post World War I, the creative arena in England saw a shift towards social realism including in films, which became increasingly centered on the sociopolitical realities of the working class triggered by the action of the powers that be. In Russia though, there was the rise of socialist realism emanating from the communist ideology. Social realism and socialist realism may not be the same all the time. Late Altaf Mazid, well-known film and theatre person to whom also goes the credit of retrieving some parts of the original print of *Joymoti*, had used two of Agarwala's letters to drive home the point that he was more inclined towards the socialist realism prevailing in Russia than social realism. Agarwala's letter to Kishen Deb Mehra dated 11 November 1934, had said, 'So far the actors busy in production (of *Joymoti*) are concerned, it will be quite different from other Indian films—I am employing Russian method of directing through all the pictures.'[25] In another letter to a distribution company, he said, 'The picture as contemplated will be a new move in India. No professional actors and actresses are required. All artistes are scrupulously searched and discovered and only "types" are selected following Russian method. All the girl artists are recuited from respectable families.'[26] According to Mazid, 'Inspired by socialist realism of cinema of the 1920s, expounded by Lev Kuleshov, Jyoti Prasad Agarwala crafted the first Assamese film, *Joymoti* in which he tried to achieve these endeavours. By doing so, he attempted at Assam's filmic genre "realism" (aka egalitarianism), creating an immediate connection between society and cinema which is in practice till today to a comparable extent. It is not a cinema per se but in resemblance with other cultural materials of the land, is a cinema of different manifestation compared to the rest of India. The size of the cinema is small, around 350 films in seventy six years (1935–2010). One might also like to term it as a "cottage cinema".'[27] Mazid cited several examples through the decades to highlight realism or the representation of egalitarianism in Assamese films—from Agarwala's *Indramalati* to Lakhyadhar Choudhury's *Nimila Onko* (1955); Padum Barua's *Ganga Silonir Pakhi* (1976); Bhabendranath Saikia's *Agnisnaan* (1979); Hemanta Das's *Tothapiu Nodi* (1990); Sanjiv Hazarika's *Meemanxa* (1994); etc. Barua's *Ganga Silonir Pakhi* (1976) is particularly considered by Assamese film watchers as the first to have begun the trajectory of alternative or parallel cinema in the state.[28]

To my mind, while both of Agarwala's films had elements of socialist realism, it is only through Bhabendranath Saikia's films towards the end of the 1970s and Jahnu Barua's films from the 1980s, that one may spot examples of Italian neo-realistic films in Assamese cinema where characters were located in a simple societal milieu where survival was the primary objective. We spot it in Barua's epic film *Halodhia Choraye Baodhan Khai* in 1987, based on Homen Borgohain's novel by the same name. It was the first Assamese film to corner an award at an international film festival (at Locarno in 1988).[29]

In another noted film of Barua, *Xagoroloi Bohu Dur* (1995), for which he had bagged the best regional film award, an added feature of neo-realistic films can be perceived: a child in a major role typically placed in a more observational role rather than a participatory position. Typical of that genre, Saikia also showcased the mundane life of a theatre actor in *Abartan* by showing scenes of rehearsals where the actors continued to repeat their lines. In Barua's *Aparoopa*, also judged the best regional film in 1983, the female lead Roopa (played by Suhasini Mulay) and her husband were repeatedly shown leading their routine life; finally, Roopa took a path which she thought was her best shot at survival. In Sanjiv Hazarika's *Haladhar* (1992), based on a story by Apurba Sarma, we spot the dilemma of the same working class as in Barua's *Halodhia*; the exploited peasant hoped for justice but was unsure of the power of the rich. The protagonist Balaram, towards the end of the film, was seen telling a fellow peasant Someswar that the feudal lord (mahajan) had made him a thief and one day would make him a beggar too if he failed to recognize his rights. That way, Assamese cinema had continued the spatial bond between film practice and social realism. In Jahnu Barua's *Firingoti* (1992) too, the audience could spot the protagonist Ritu (Moloya Goswami) pushing herself to the extreme to save a village school she had set up. After her husband's sudden death, the mission to set up a school in a remote village almost became a means for her survival. In the film set against the Chinese aggression of 1962, there was also a character, Lachit, painted by the government of the day as an extremist, thrown into jail for a crime he never committed. With the Indo-China War creating havoc in Assam then, Lachit succeeded in escaping from jail. On screen, he was seen asking questions fundamental to the common man's rights in a democracy: Is it fair to keep an innocent person in jail? Why don't we ask what makes an extremist? Why are innocent people exploited by the system?

Such questions invariably ran through Saikia's scripts too, subtly. Years later, in 2020, in the light of the protests against the Citizenship Amendment Act (CAA) in Assam, when I spoke at length to Jahnu Barua about his opposition to the legislation for an interview for *The Wire*,[30] I could easily pin down the fact that the director's mind had been so incessantly present in the stories of his films; his political and social messaging through cinema were primarily to build a self-dependent Assam where, akin to the Gandhian philosophy, he called for people of all shades to join hands to make the villages self-sufficient to carve out a self-dependent community. Assamese filmmaker and film critic Utpal Borpujari called the filmmaking styles of Saikia and Barua distinct from each other though, like every auteur's is, and gave a reason for saying so, 'Saikia's films have had a sense of a literary narrative and would be dialogue-based mostly; I think that came from the fact that he was a writer-playwright. His grasp on capturing minute issues on human relationships was legendary in both his writings and cinema. On the other hand, Jahnu Barua, I would say, is a more direct sociopolitical commentator, with his subjects often making a comment on the sociopolitical situation. Of course, both had exceptions to this, in the form of *Kaal Sandhya* and *Aparoopa* respectively.'[31] Made in 1997 in Hindi highlighting insurgency in Assam and its impact on common people, *Kaal Sandhya* was Saikia's last film.

While to an extent, one can agree with Borpujari on Saikia's approach in *Kaal Sandhya*, Jahnu Barua's trademark of direct social commentary, though, comes through even in *Aparoopa,* his first film. There, the hero, addressing a village panchayat meeting held to indict him for falling in love with a married woman, recounted what he had done for the welfare of the village and asked them in turn what they did for its betterment. Barua went on to direct some Hindi films including the critically-acclaimed *Maine Gandhi Ko Nahin Mara* (2005) where too we can locate his penchant for direct social commentary.

Talking of social realism, one finds it in yet another noted Assamese film from the 1990s era, *Adajya*. Based on Assamese writer Indira Goswami's *Dontal Hatir Uiye Khowa Howdah*, in *Adajya* (1996), first-time filmmaker Santwana Bordoloi poignantly held up in *Adaijya* the struggle of three widows of varying age group residing in a Vaishnava monastery in Lower Assam to lead a dignified life amidst extreme restrictions put on them by societal customs. It was also a film where the Lower Assam dialect was beautifully used. Interestingly, in 2006, exactly a decade after *Adajya* was released, we hear the voice of a woman who had not had a voice—in the talented director Manju Borah's remake of *Joymoti*. In Agarwala's version of *Joymoti*, the protagonist barely had any dialogue; she quietly did as assigned by society and tradition. Manju Borah finally put dialogues in Joymoti's mouth.

By putting a voice to the re-made Joymoti's character, Manju Borah had in a way made the protagonist a human. In December 2020, noted Assamese film critic Manoj Borpujari had pointed out that in the 1990s, he could spot similar leanings in the films of Sanjeev Hazorika, Bidyut Chakraborty, Manju Borah (*Baibhab*), Gautam Bora, etc. 'They felt the need to highlight social reality in Assamese films even while being conscious that to be commercially successful, films need to have some popular ingredients too; they wanted Assamese audience to realise that films need to portray what life really is.'[32]

In the opening scene, one finds an interesting resemblance between the films of Saikia and some of Jahnu Barua's. Like in Saikia's *Agnisnaan* and *Anirban*, the opening scene of Barua's *Aparoopa* also begins with the movement of a lead character in a vehicle and the camera panning 360 degrees to help the viewers see the environment where the story would take place. In Barua's *Halodhia* too, a young boy runs on a village path making the sound of a moving car to introduce the audience to the geography of the village. Sanjeev Hazorika's *Holodhor* too opened with one of the main characters moving on a bullock cart. Hazorika and Vidyut Chakrabarty had worked with Saikia as assistant directors. On being asked about this similarity, Hazorika, though, told me, 'I was inspired by the film *Fiddler on The Roof* where the director in the first scene itself introduced all the major characters.'[33]

Prior to Bhabendranath Saikia and Jahnu Barua, some key names of Assamese directors from the 1950s through the 1970s would have to be plucked out to understand better the trajectory of Assamese cinema. Some such noteworthy names were Phani Sarma, Nip Barua, Brajen Barua, Anwar Hussain, and of course, Bhupen Hazarika. While Agarwala made both his films in the 1930s, the 1940s saw the release of at least six Assamese films: *Manomati* (1941 by Rohini Barua), *Rupahi* (1946 by Parvati Prasad Baruva), *Badan Borphukan* (1947 by Kamal Chowdhury), *Siraj* (1948 by Bishnu Prasad Rava and Phani Sarma), *Parghat* (1948 by Pravin Phukan), and *Biplabi* (1948 by Asit Sen). *Manomati*, released at Ronghor theatre in Dibrugarh in April 1941, rung around a love story with the Burmese invasion of Assam as the backdrop.[34] *Siraj* in Assamese cinema is a significant milestone primarily for the cultural icons Bishnu Prasad Rava and Phani Sharma joining hands to produce a film in the language on Hindu–Muslim unity in response to Partition.[35]

Between 1950 and 1959, at least twenty Assamese films were produced.[36] While *Runumi* (1953 by Suresh Goswami) became the first to portray a character in a double role, Anwar Hussain's *Natun Prithibi* (1958) was the first on widow remarriage.[37] Phani Sarma's *Piyoli Phukan* (1955) stood out amongst the lot though. Reporting the news about the film winning the President's Certificate of Merit at the Third National Film Awards, *Assam Tribune* had then written, 'Rupjyoti Production's maiden venture in Assamese, *Piyoli Phukan,* is undoubtedly a milestone in Assamese films. The film possesses all the elements that can make a picture successful. Technically, *Piyoli Phukan* reaches a height. *Piyoli Phukan* not only leaves other Assamese pictures miles behind, but can rank with the better class of hindi productions.'[38] In 2014, actor Bobbeeta Sarma, in *The Moving Image and Assamese Culture–Joymoti, Jyotiprasad Agarwala and Assamese Cinema*, had noted that the Delhi-based newspaper *Hindustan Standard* had reported the film's merits in a similar vein. '*Piyoli Phukan*, a landmark in Assamese movies, marks the coming of age of the Assamese film industry. It has left its 11 predecessors leagues behind—oth in technique and in histrionics—and it can now be truly said that the Assamese movie has come past the adolescent stage and is, today, a full grown youth. Credit for the all round success of the film goes to director Phani Sarma who has also authored the story.'[39]

The 1950s was also the era when America-returned Bhupen Hazarika had entered Assamese cinema as a director. It was the period of his close involvement with IPTA. Interesingly, Hazarika, in several interviews and public lectures, had said that one of the primary reasons behind his decision to contest an assembly election in the 1960s was to ensure that Assam got a film studio to be self-sufficient which did become a reality, all thanks to him. Jyoti Chitraban, named after Jyotiprasad Agarwala's first venture, began with the state government's money at Guwahati's Kahilipara in 1961 and became fully functional in 1968, thus gradually weaning away Assamese directors from being dependent on Kolkata or Chennai for film editing. Parthajit Baruah had rightly noted, 'The 1960s were significant for Assamese cinema for two reasons—the establishment of Jyoti Chitraban in 1961 as the first government-recognised film studio and the formation of the Gauhati Cine Club in 1965.'[40] The first film shot at Jyoti Chitraban was Nip Barua's *Bhadari*.[41]

Bhupen Hazarika made his debut in Assamese cinema in 1956 with *Era Bator Sur* in which one of his mentors, Rava, also a prominent part of IPTA then, acted besides fellow IPTA member and Bollywood star Balraj Sahni appearing in a cameo. It was also the first Assamese film to have hired a Bollywood singer to croon an Assamese song, no less than the queen of the times Lata Mangeshkar ('Junakore Rati'). Hazarika had written *Era Bator Sur* around life in a tea garden, first as a one-act play before adopting it on screen.[42] According to writer Maheswar Neog, that play was never published.[43] In 2017, Utpal Borpujari had commented on the film thus, 'While one can debate the cinematic qualities of the film, it is a great document of Assam's folk art forms and as always is the case with anything made by Hazarika, has some great music.'[44]

Hazarika, in some of his later films (his last noteworthy Assamese film was *Mon Prajapati* in 1979), aside from using Bollywood and Bengali playback singers, also hired actors from outside the state to feature in his films, say, Balraj Sahni and Iva Achao. (Jahnu Barua too followed the trend to an extent in *Aparoopa* where he introduced Girish Karnad in a cameo besides Suhasini Mulay in the lead role.)

An extremely popular Assamese actress, Vidya Rao, was a Bhupen Hazarika discovery. Born in Dibrugarh to an Assamese mother and a Maharastrian father, Vidya was raised in Calcutta. In Hazarika's *Shakuntala* which won a national award in 1961, she was featured as a child artist and later played the lead in his film *Lati-Ghati* (1966); thereafter in Brajen

Barua's *Mukuta* (1970) and in Samarandra Deb's *Aranya* (1971). While *Lati-Ghati* and *Aranaya* went on to win national awards in the regional category, *Mukuta* was the first Assamese film to celebrate hundred days at a theatre hall. Her later film *Ajoli Nobou* (in 1980 by Nip Barua) created an even better cinematic history by completing twenty-five weeks of theatrical screening in a row, thus establishing her as one of the reigning queens of the 1970s–80s era in Assamese cinema.

Though Bhupen Hazarika's trajectory in Assamese cinema continued from 1959 till 1988 (his last Assamese film was the remade *Siraj*), four of the eight films that he made were produced in the 1960s. His *Chik Mik Bijuli* (1969) was shot in Mumbai, a novelty in Assamese film industry, where he vividly juxtaposed the urban chic life with that of the slums of that city. In that decade, only fourteen Assamese films were produced. What makes the 1960s important in Assamese cinema was also its first blockbuster *Dr. Bezbarua* (1969), directed by Brajen Barua. It was also the era which witnessed 'the rise of the Barua family in the realm of Assamese cinema.'[45] While Brajen Barua directed the first crime thriller in the language with *Dr. Bezbaruah* and bagged the national award for the best regional film, his two brothers—Ramen Barua as a music director and Dwipen Barua as a playback singer too—rose to prominence through that home production.[46] The film's music became a superhit collection; was owned by HMV and was available in audio tapes till 2011.[47] In Bobeeta Sharma's book, the film's male lead Nipon Goswami spoke of the director thus: 'Brojen-da can be said to have established the growth of the Assamese technicians for he did not go to Kolkata to do the shooting, and he also started the system of shooting in real locations, like actual houses instead of sets.'[48] Brojen Barua's last film was in 1972, the year he passed away. Nipon Goswami, an FTII graduate, has recently produced a remake of *Dr. Bezbarua* with noted actor from Assam, Adil Hussain, in the lead. Hussain, with Hollywood successes like *Life of Pi* (2012) under his name, is the only actor from the Assamese film industry so far who can be truly called a global face.

Dr. Bezbaruah was the second significant film to be remade in the history of Assamese cinema after Manju Borah's *Joymoti* in 2006. Earlier, there have been examples of Assamese films, say, Abdul Majid's *Chameli Memsaab*, remade in Bengali (1978) and in Hindi (1981).

Compared to the 1960s though, the 1970s registered a huge leap in the quantity of Assamese films. From fourteen in 1960s, the tally hopped to fifty-eight in the next decade. In 1972, Assamese cinema saw the first coloured production (*Bhaity* by Kamal Narayan Choudhury),[49] though it was only in the 1980s that the cinema of the state truly began to get a sizeable audience, as mentioned earlier on the chapter. In the 1980s, films like *Ajoli Nobou*, *Bowari* (1982 by Shiva Prasad Thakur), *Koka Deuta Nati Aru Hati* (1983 by Nip Barua), S*endur* (1983 by Pulok Gogoi), etc. attracted huge crowds. The 1980s saw as many as eighty-three films. Bobbeeta Sharma had rightly said in her book, 'This period can be called the golden age of Assamese cinema as films began to have a mass appeal.'[50]

Ajoli Nobou, the first to be made in Eastman colour, also gave Assamese cinema a new heartthrob, a new graduate from the National School of Drama (NSD) Pranjal Saikia. Saikia though had started acting in Assamese films prior to his enrolment in NSD (*Faguni* and *Upapath*). Songs featuring him in *Ajoli Nobou*—'Kaak buli lu kune nile' and 'Soku meli nesaba', with actress Purabi Sharma—became an instant hit. (His wife and noted Assamese actress Purnima Saikia is an NSD alumna.) In 2021, on my referring to those immortal songs to Saikia in a conversation, the actor broke into one of the songs before relating, 'Top names from Assamese literature used to regularly write songs for Assamese films then; that's why they had *sahitya*. People could hear those songs again and again unlike the film songs now.' Recalling those heydays, the actor also acknowledged, 'Those days, every film would be released with the beating of drums and conch, by planting a banana tree, considered auspicious in our society. Audience would refuse to get up from a hall even after a film would end and demand to watch it all over again. People came to nearest towns in busloads to watch us. Even though celebrated directors like Shyam Benegal had asked me to move to Mumbai then, I refused because we were given immense love by Assamese cine-goers at that time. We felt no less than Bollywood actors.'

The popularity of stars in Assamese cinema began in the 1950s and the 1960s with actors like Bijoy Shankar (*Era Bator Sur* in 1956) and Eva Asao (*Piyali Phukan* in 1955). Gradually, people began to watch a film on finding out which male/female lead featured in it, say, Biju Phukan, Nipon Goswami, Vidya Rao, Mridula Barua, Tapan Das, etc. The trend continues till date. Bobbeeta Sharma had particularly highlighted about Biju Phukan gaining stardom post *Dr. Bezbarua*, 'He (Phukan) is considered to be one of the most natural actors in Assam. His first release as a hero was Samarendra Narayan Dev's *Aranya* in 1971, which was adjudged the Best Regional Film at the National Film Awards.'[51] Though Nipon Goswami was featured in

Sangam (1968) as a hero, he too found his stardom only after the success of *Dr. Bezbarua* and never looked back since. 'Both Goswami and Phukan shared the space as undisputed heroes in the 1970s and 1980s. They graduated to character roles in later years.'[52] Significantly, till date though, no Assamese actor has bagged the national award for best male lead.

Pranjal Saikia's memorable roles include playing the lead in Bidyut Chakrabarty's *Raag Birag* (1996), for which the director had bagged the Indira Gandhi Award for best debut film. *Raag Birag* was the first Assamese film to be the opening film at the Indian Panorama.[53] Chakrabarty was the third Assamese to have received that award after Gautam Bora for *Worsobipo* (the only film he made) in 1990 in the Karbi language of Assam, and Sanjeev Hazorika for *Haladhar* (1992). Notably, Shillong-based Sher Choudhury, after a break of fifteen years years, also picked the national award for the best music director for Bora's *Wosobipo*. Choudhury was appreciated also for his music in well-known actor Dhiru Bhuyan's film *Pratham Ragini* (1987). Prior to Choudhury, Bhupen Hazarika was conferred the national award for best music in *Chameli Mehsaab* (1976). In 1992, Hazarika became the first and the only winner of the prestigious accolade, the Dadasaheb Phalke award, thus putting Assamese filmmaking on a firm footing.

NEW GENERATION OF FILMMAKERS

On a cold December night in 2016, a sprawling field packed with villagers from around Goalpara's Agia came alive as a large screen was engulfed in the light from a projector. The villagers were watching Utpal Borpujari's children's film *Ishu*.

Named after the child protagonist Ishu, the one-and-a-half-hour-long film based on Manikuntala Bhattacharjya's novel by the same name, centered around a social ill that the villagers from the Rabha community could identify with: witch hunting. Birubala Rabha, a crusader against the practice used particularly to victimize women, is from that community. Exuding immense courage, Birubala had not only saved herself from a killer mob accusing her of being a witch but would go on to rescue several such victims. In 2001, the state had successfully intervened with Project Prahari, a unique intervention at the behest of Kuladhar Saikia, then deputy inspector general of police, to counter the social evil in Kokrajhar and other affected districts. The project was a success, leading to a three-part case study named 'Being a Change Agent' at the Harvard Business Review repository.

That evening in Agia, the village crowd, children including, sat on mats and stools lugged from home in silence. They watched the film in rapt attention. A reason for screening the film for the villagers was also because several actors were from Agia and a good part of the film was shot there. Watching the film under an open night sky would remain a one-of-a-kind cinematic experience for me, primarily because this proved that it was possible to bring world-class cinema to people in remote areas where cinema halls are particularly in short supply. Prior to insurgency, Assam had around 150 cinema halls which has now dwindled to around fifty, according to Borpujari.

With a tight plot, impressive acting, and sleek direction, efforts like *Ishu* are a breath of fresh air for the rich legacy of Assamese cinema. In the first few years of the twenty-first century, only a rare few succeeded to shine at the national level, like Jahnu Barua's *Konikar Ramdhenu* (2003) and *Tora* (2003), both of which had won national awards. The 1990s saw the near death of New Wave or parallel cinema elsewhere in India. Responding to it, several Assamese directors, between the end of the 1990s and the early 2000s, looked more towards Bollywood for inspiration with the idea of producing profitable commercial hits. In 1998 came *Joubone Aamoni Kore*, packed with dance moves copying Govinda, the then reigning star of Bollywood. Even the Bihu number in that film had Bollywood moves. It introduced actress Barasha Rani Baishya and received a good response at the theatres. An out and out commercial take, Munin Boruah's *Hiya Diya Niya* hit the theatres in 2000. Zubeen Garg, a rising actor-singer then with the ability to pull in a young crowd, composed music for the first time in that film. The growing popular interest in such films firmed up the trend for commercial movies in Assamese. Munin Baruah's trajectory in commercial ventures continued. In 2010, with *Ramdhenu,* he finally did what others never could in Assamese cinema—make ₹1 crore in collection from ticket sales. It needs pointing out that these films also featured strapping heroes as in Bollywood such as Jatin Bora and Ravi Sharma.

In 2017, more good news came to this genre with Zubeen Garg's home production *Mission China* breaking *Ramdhenu*'s record by grossing ₹2.4 crore in the first week itself. Significantly, it made more business than commercial blockbusters *Baahubali* and *Bajrangi Bhaijaan* in Assam. It was fantastic news for Assamese cinema in general considering that often an Assamese film, however popular it might be, is removed from a hall in favour of the latest Bollywood blockbuster.

Interestingly, this was also the time some young independent filmmakers were quietly stepping in to create films that would break new grounds and also to, once again, take the cinema of the state to the award-winning circuit. In 2013, in came Kenny Basumatary's *Local Kung Fu*, based on a new genre—action comedy—made on a modest budget; it succeeded in receiving good audience response while also being nominated for the best feature film in Assamese in the Filmfare awards for the eastern region. Kenny, who also acted in the film, was nominated for the best director category.

At the 63rd National Film Awards, one year before Utpal Borpujari's *Ishu* was released, Bhaskar Hazarika's *Kothanodi* (2015) was picked for the best film in the Assamese language category. In October 2015, the film had a world premiere at the Busan International Film Festival. In December 2015, when I met a soft-spoken Hazarika at a Delhi restaurant for an interview on the film, I hadn't watched it yet but went to speak to him only driven by a curiosity about the subject. 'It is a night film, try not to watch it during the day,' he told me while sharing an internet link to watch it.[54] In *Kothanodi: A River of Fables*, Bhaskar Hazarika, a post-graduate on Film and Drama from England's Reading University, had strung together four popular Assamese folk takes for children, plucked out of the iconic book of grandmothers' tales in Assamese, *Burhi Air Xadhu*, complied by Lakshminath Bezbaroa. I was curious as to how he would add newness to the tales of Tejimola, Oukuwori, Champawati, and Tawoir Xadhu, stories that almost every Assamese child had grown up listening to or reading. What soon unfolded in front of me was a spellbinding drama of secrets and spectacle, magic and murder, distrust and conviction, greed and its reasons, and power and its play.[55] The play of lighting in the film also acted like a character in the dark, making me understand why he wanted me to watch it at night.

Shot in Majuli island and in the filmmaker's hometown of Dergaon in Upper Assam, the 115-minute long film had the cream of Assamese cinema in a variety of roles:—Adil Husain, Seema Biswas, and Zerifa Ahmed besides talented new actors Urmila Mahanta, Kopil Bora, and Asha Mahanta—who together fired up the screen from the word go. In 2019, Bhaskar came up with another gem, *Aamis*, which gave Assamese cinema a powerful actor in Lima Das.

By then, young director Rima Das had also created history in Assamese cinema with her low-budget *The Village Rockstars* (2017) by receiving the ultimate recognition for her work, the Swarna Kamal, at the 65th national film awards, twenty-five years after Jahnu Barua had won it for *Hkhagoroloi Bohudoor.* Rima's film also won national awards in three other categories besides breaking the glass ceiling to become the first Assamese film to be India's official nomination at the 91st Academy (Oscar) Awards. Rima Das and Bhaskar Hazarika had also succeeded in showing their films on top OTT platforms like Netflix.

Rima, who began with a short film *Pratha* in 2009, made *Kalardiya* in 2013 (with a DSLR camera) and also produced *Bulbul Can Sing* in 2018, which was conferred the national award for Assamese best film. A year before *Bulbul Can Sing*, Borpujari's *Ishu,* funded by Children's Film Society, also received the national award for the best film in Assamese.

Even as Assamese commercial cinema is beginning to do steady business, what is heartening to note is that the new crop of independent filmmakers producing award-winning films from Assam is also getting bigger with every passing year: Junmoni Khound's *Tula Aru Teja* (2012); Reema Borah's marvellous cinematic offering *Bokul* (2015); Hemanta Kumar Das's first Assamese film based on Shakespeare's *Othello* (2014); *Xoixobote Dhemalite* (2016) by Bidyut Kotoky; *Haanduk* (2016), a moving film in the Moran language of Assam by Jaicheng Jai Dohutia; *Maj Rati Keteki* (2017), Santwana Bordoloi's next after a gap of twenty-one years; Himjyoti Talukdar's *Calendar* (2018); Bobby Sarma Baruah's fantastic flick *Sonar Baran Pakhi* (2016) and *Mishing* (2018); *Jwlwi: The Seed* (2019) by Rajni Basumatary in Bodo; Monjul Baruah's *Antareen* (2017) and *Kaneen* (2019) based on Sahitya Akademi winning writer Rita Chowdhury's novel *Rajib Ishwar*; Prakash Deka's ground-breaking film *Junaki Porua* (2019); Chandra Mudoi's *Ronuwa: Who Never Surrender* (2019); Kapil Kalita's *Bridge* (2020); Himanshu Prasad Das's *Goru* (2021). Additionally, what must be noted is that the latest groundswell in Assamese cinema and cinema from Assam has also witnessed an upswing in the advent of talented women directors into the arena. The first woman filmmaker in Assam was seen only in the 1980s, Suprabha Devi, who went on to make films like *Nayanmoni* (1984) and *Sarabjan* (1985). In the 1990s, we saw Kuntala Devi (*Kanaklata* in 1990) and Santwana Bordoloi (*Adajya*, 1996) and Manju Borah (*Baibhab*, 1999). Since then, we can call Manju Borah, with over ten films spanning two decades, as the most consistent of Assamese women filmmakers. In the early 2000s, a woman filmmaker of note was Suman Haripriya whose *Kadamtole Krishna Nache* (2005) bagged the national award.

Unfortunately, while some of the award-winning Assamese films mentioned above have been able to get a breather through OTT platforms, most have not been able to garner a wider audience from their theatrical release as the commercial ventures have. The trend of Assamese commercial cinema doing good business at theatres has continued with films like Zubeen Garg's *Kanchenjungha* and Jatin Bora's *Ratnakar* reportedly doing trade of over ₹5 crore and nearly ₹9 crore respectively. Utpal Borpujari, though, gave me a reality check: 'These two films rode on star power and a publicity blitzkrieg; not every film can expect to do such kind of business. Generally speaking, Assamese mainstream films are moderately budgeted (compared to Hindi or Southern mainstream films, they would be termed low-budget), and a business upwards of ₹1 crore would be considered really good—even that doesn't happen usually.'[56] In other words, the Assamese film industry is still small in size. In 2021, during a YouTube discussion on Assamese cinema, director Bobby Sarmah Barua underlined the challenges independent filmmakers like her particularly face due to low budgets. Lack of funding often stops them from adding technical finesse or using certain dream shots. She, though, added, 'Sometimes I think perhaps it is a good thing for us; it leads us to find a solution to the problem within our limitations.'[57] Close observers of the industry like Manoj Borpujari, however, stated in that discussion that the state government could step in to provide the required backing to independent filmmakers since they are bringing international laurels to the state. Though during the tenure of the Sarbananda Sonowal government (May 2016–21), a film policy was announced, it was yet to be implemented till end-2021. 'I am also sad to underline that perhaps the worst minister who had no idea about culture would be assigned the ministry by a state government year after year. They typically would not have any vision.'[58]

Though Assamese films now have their own awards (Prag Cine Awards) and film festivals held in Guwahati (Brahmaputra International Film Festival), certainly more steps need to be adopted to expand the audience base not just for the commercial ventures but serious cinema too. During that discussion, both Manoj and Utpal also made a case for the need for educational institutions in Assam to add film studies in their curriculum as it was as important as studying literature.[59]

To my mind, yet another negative feature of Assamese cinema is the non-preservation of the prints of most old Assamese films. For instance, the only print available from Bhupen Hazarika's Assamese films is *Shakuntala*.[60] In 2013, with funds from National Film Archives of India, the ninth Assamese film *Runumi* (1953) was digitally restored after its only print, lost for about forty years, was found at a village in 2010.[61]

What can ultimately sustain the industry, though, is a ready audience bank created for quality films. 'Of course Assamese cinema has a big audience but unfortunately, there are no halls where the audiences are—the semi-urban and semi-rural locales as well as the rural parts of Assam,' Utpal Borpujari had told me. He had pointed out that the Bodo, Mising, Karbi filmmakers have overcome that gridlock by screening their films in the interior areas through mobile/travelling set-ups. Some Assamese filmmakers are now trying out that model too. 'But to make it successful and commercially sustainable, there is a need for a properly planned business model.'

ASSAMESE PLAYS

In 2021, while climbing a flight of stairs at the Seagull Theatre on Guwahati's Zoo Road to take a peek at its auditorium, I was reminded of its co-founder, the well-known Assamese actor and theatre director Baharul Islam, mentioning it to me during a chat in New Delhi some fifteen years ago. We were at the National School of Drama (NSD), Baharul's alma mater where he was also a visiting faculty then. Talking about the auditorium that he and his wife Bhagirathi Bai Kadam, also an NSD graduate, had built above their residence which also housed their theatre group, he had highlighted, 'We have to change the habit in Guwahati audience of watching a play for free. That is why we built the small auditorium in spite of financial constraints. Even though I had inherited that property from my father, I am firm that I will also charge him ten rupees to watch a play in that auditorium.'

On pushing open the door to the auditorium on that March morning in 2021, I found the stage filled with an array of props from the previous day's show. A ray of sunlight fell on the stage through a window, as if by design. Standing next to me was Bhagirathi, whom many Assamese filmgoers might also remember for a stellar role in Santwana Bordoloi's *Adajya*.

A Kannadiga by birth, Bhagirathi, before joining NSD in 1987, was exposed to theatre through Ninasam Repertory Company run by Ramon Magsaysay Award winner K.V. Subanna in Karnataka. 'I couldn't speak Hindi when I joined NSD but I knew the language of theatre much more than most of my classmates because I was already exposed to professional stage acting and that helped me immensely.'[62] The love for theatre helped her pick up Hindi in Delhi eventually, and she learnt Assamese after marrying Baharul and settling down in Guwahati.

The wooden audience gallery at Seagull's studio auditorium can accommodate a crowd of 150 people. 'For a long time, we charged ₹10 per person; it has now been hiked to ₹50. Hopefully, in coming times, if we make the auditorium air conditioned, improve the seating, we can then take up the pricing to ₹100 per ticket,' Baharul told me later. I reminded him about what he had said in New Delhi over a decade ago about the need for ticketed shows of plays in Guwahati, only to hear him respond with his inimitable toothy laugh, saying, 'Isn't it great that we stood firm and could do it? After our venture, we now have another private studio auditorium in Guwahati itself, started by Anup Hazarika. Before we set it up around 2000, Guwahati only had the Ravindra Bhawan auditorium owned by the state government for professional theatre groups which everyone could not get to hire anyway.'

Noted playwright, actor, and theatre director Anup Hazarika too is an NSD alumnus (1990), who, on returning to Assam in 1995, started the theatre group Baa. Baa has staged several notable plays within and outside Assam and has picked up awards at prestigious national theatre fests like the Mahindra Theatre Festival.

Baharul underlined that Seagull Theatre, aside from using the auditorium to stage their plays, had also been renting out the space to other theatre groups. Creation of a space for professional theatre outside of the lone notable address in Guwahati since the 1960s has been liberating, particularly when you hear from noted playwright and theatre director Sitanath Lahkar what his group, Samahar Natya Gosti, faced in the 1990s. 'Unlike now, those days, theatre groups in Guwahati were completely dependent on Ravindra Bhawan to stage their plays professionally. However, even if one would book the auditorium much in advance, the director (cultural affairs), without prior notice, could cancel a play if the government needed it for its own programme. Believe it or not, there was such a clause in the booking rules,' related Lahkar.[63] 'Though such last minute cancellations were common, no group would dare to protest, fearing blacklisting. But we did once in the 1990s.' Samahar Natya Gosti had organized a five-day show of their play *Agnigarbha* depicting 'how the political class benefitted from the Assam agitation of the 1980s while the common people didn't perhaps get what they were allured into in the name of a golden and independent Assam'. That protest led to the arrest of the entire troupe of thirty-five from the stage itself. 'We were released late in the night. The next day there were banner headlines in Assamese newspapers; Dhiren

Bezbaruah, noted journalist and then the editor of the influenctial newspaper *The Sentinel*, wrote an editorial condemning the then Hiteswar Saikia-led Congress government's actions.'

Through the decades, if you look at the trajectory of Assamese modern theatre practitioners not just in Guwahati but in the state's smaller pockets too, it comes across that the failure to generate a dedicated physical space to stage their plays with adequate ticket sales has discouraged several from pursuing their passion, with many even leaving theatre altogether to take up a permanent job, or being forced to pursue it only as a hobby through some local amateur club.

The journey of the likes of Bhagirathi and Baharul, therefore, was significant considering it was the urge to create a professional physical 'space' for theatre in the 1990s that led them towards their fairly successful journey. The car shed in the front yard at Baharul's father's house in Guwahati was pulled down to create an open space; two of his father's rented houses adjacent to their residence were vacated where Baharul and Bhagirathi opened a theatre school to train Assamese youth in the art of acting. In the first year itself, twenty students joined their training workshops, several of them from villages. Some from that batch could enrol themselves at the NSD which Bhagirathi said further firmed their resolve.

A young batch of actors that Bhagirathi and Baharul worked with in the early 1990s became noted names in the field of acting and theatre direction, like Jaya Seal, Prabin Saikia, and Rabhijita Gogoi. Jaya went on to focus more on acting and dancing (Bharatanatyam) and moved to Mumbai to work on tele-soaps and thereafter to Kolkata. Rabhijita, acted in one of Seagull's productions after undertaking a short course with Assam Abhinaya Pratisthan led by noted actor-theatreperson Indra Bania and now is a noted play director. Prabin ushered in the one-of-a-kind theatre festival in 2016 called Aranya, organized in a jungle under the banner of his theatre company Baat. Unfortunately, the talented theatre veteran passed away in 2022, leaving a vacuum not just in his hometown Gohpur but in Assamese theatre in general. Interestingly, Guwahati-based Rabhijita who has been acting and directing plays under the banner of her group Jirsong Theatre, has also been making good use of her NSD training by running a formal theatre acting training programme for youth for over two decades now. Though she started Jirsong in 2017, much before it, between 1999 and 2008, she conducted theatre workshops and created productions across the Northeast.

In mid-2021, when I caught up with Rabhijita in Guwahati, she also pointed out, 'Not just in Assam and the Northeast but elsewhere in the country too, you will not find too many examples of a professional drama schools run only by women and producing students eligible for NSD admission. It is not easy for a woman director to also survive doing only theatre but I have been able to, till now, and that makes me immensely happy.' It reminded me of one of her mentors, Baharul, telling me that on returning from NSD he had resolved not to be associated any more with an amateur theatre club that performed plays merely as a hobby. For some years, Baharul's academy received a modest grant from the Union Ministry of Culture. Once it dried up, they had to bank only on staging plays. 'Anyway, how much does a play in Assam get typically, maybe ₹20,000–30,000 which is not enough if we have a play that needs a large crew or some senior actors to play a serious role,' highlighted Baharul. This is the reason why, he emphasized, most independent theatre groups, including Seagull, have begun doing plays that have only three or four characters. 'There is more chance of a play with a small crew getting sponsorship not just in Assam but also outside it. However, this trend is hugely affecting Indian theatre. Masters like Ratan Thiyam of Manipur, the pride of the Northeast, a pillar of Indian theatre, are hardly doing plays any more because their plays are usually grand presentations; typically have a large crew. They no more find sponsors.'

Baharul further spoke to me about the role his schoolteacher Karuna Deka played in his choosing theatre as a profession. 'In 1979, Karuna Deka attended the first intensive theatre workshop conducted by NSD in Guwahati for about three months which had also the likes of noted Assamese actors Seema Biswas, Tapan Das, Chetana Das among others as participants. Then NSD director B. V. Karanth along with some other faculty from the institution had visited Guwahati to conduct that workshop at Rabindra Bhawan.' Seema Biswas, later admitted that the exposure made her take up acting seriously.

In Baharul's journey in theatre, one also comes across Surjya, a well known theatre group in Guwahati then. That group, formed in the style of a club to stage plays, gave the initial platform to a number of Assam's top actors and film and theatre directors. Senior actor-theatre director Sattyakee D'com Bhuyan, son of late Dhiru Bhuyan, a noted actor, theatre director, filmmaker, and former announcer at the All India Radio, Guwahati, too had begun with Surjya. While his father and his seniors like playwright and former Asam Sahitya Sabha president Lakhyadhar Choudhury congregated at the legendary Bhaskar Natya Mandir in Guwahati's Uzan Bazar, and thereafter at the Pragati Silpi Sangha to perform plays, the younger lot in the city organized themselves under Surjya. 'Not just Baharul da, some other top Assamese actors and film directors like Sanjeev Hazorika, Bidyut Chakraborty, Nayan Prasad, Tapan Das, etc. were also from Surjya,' D'com, a member of the theatre group, reminded me in April 2021 when we had a conversation on the multiple threads that make up the trajectory of modern theatre in Assam.[64] Hazorika later added, 'Surjya began in 1984. There is a story behind it. While several of us were associated with our local drama groups in Guwahati, Bidyut Chakraborty had assembled all of us at Pragati Silpi Sangha to do a play under its banner. After that, we began to visit the Pragati Silpa Sangha office for an adda or two. It was around that time Bidyut wanted to direct the next play from Pragati which was, however, an Assamese translation of a Hindi play by Nirmal Verma. The Sangha seniors didn't permit it citing a pre-existing resolution that it would stage only original plays. The play eventually didn't take place but the younger lot led by Bidyut soon left Sangha to form Surjya. The first office of Surjya was set up in Bidyut's house in Uzan Bazaar.' Hazorika also recalled that the prize money from a government theatre competition in 1985 helped Surjya fund its initial plays. 'We had picked Arun Sarma's play *Kukurnesia Manuh* for that competition and assigned well-known director Nilu Chakraborty to direct it. Tapan Das played the lead role.'

Around 2003, Surjya shifted to its present premise on Guwahati's C. K. Agarwala Road. Hazorika related, "Theatre veterans like Amarjyoti Choudhury, Kamal Rana Sarma, etc. had a drama group, Samalay. They had managed to get a plot of land on long lease from the railways to set up an office. However, all the members, due to their work compulsions, had to leave Guwahati. On their suggestion, we moved in there. Gradually, we built on it. Today, we have a rehearsal space and an auditorium of sorts which can accommodate an audience of fifty. We lend the space to other groups too.' Though actor-directors like Santwana Bordoloi took part in Surjya's productions, it never had women members.

D'Com recalled that Surjya was the first group in Guwahati to use the technique of intimate theatre to help build a tension within the audience. Hazorika too shared his memories of Bidyut Chakraborty and Nayan Prasad staging such intimate plays at Gauri Sadan in Guwahati and also at the union hall of the Cotton College around 1989.

What needs discussion here is also the effort of a singular force, Moinul Haque, in 1970, to popularize miming in Assam. Guwahati-based Haque began with the mono-act and specialized in sound effects. On realizing that he enjoyed doing comedy more, he began specializing in that genre. Interestingly, with no praticioners to learn the art from in Assam, he learnt the tricks of the trade from a book on the famous mime artiste Jogen Dutta of West Bengal. Some years later, in 1992, he founded the Mime Academy, the first of its kind in the Northeast, to popularize the form amongst the youth.[65]

ASSAMESE MODERN DRAMA

D'com had often felt that what lured him to theatre since his childhood was not only because much of his paternal family, starting from grandfather Mudkhoda Bhuyan, were theatre actors but also because of Uzan Bazaar, the colony by the Brahmaputra in Guwahati where he was born and raised. Right opposite their house stood the fabled Bhaskar Natya Mandir with which his family's male members were intimately associated. Lakhyadhar Choudhury, in a write-up in memory of his father Dhiru Bhuyan in 1999, had particularly termed the Latasil colony (or Uzan Bazaar) of the city as an illustrious landmark of Assamese history where, within the limits of four landmarks—the Latasil primary school, Latasil grounds (khelpothar or playground), Manik Chandra Baruah M. I. School, and Kumar Bhaskar Mandir—sprouted a number of eminent Assamese personalities who went on to contribute to the state in various fields through the decades. One such family was that of filmmaker Brajen Barua mentioned earlier in the chapter.

Bhaskar Natya Mandir was initially known as Kamrup Natya Mandir, formed in 1915. It was Jyotiprasad Agarwala who had named the proscenium stage Bhaskar Natya Mandir;[66] it was also the first venue where his film *Joymoti* was screened in Assam in 1935.[67] In that write-up, Lakyadhar Choudhury had recalled that as a Bhaskar Natya Mandir actor, Premada Kanta Bhuyan (from Mukhoda Bhuyan's family) created a sensation not just in Guwahati but in other parts of Assam by playing Sakuni (from *The Mahabharata*) in the 1920–30. Choudhury who too was closely associated with Bhaskar Natya Mandir, recalled how the entire colony was involved in the rehearsals for plays every evening through the decades. While seniors like him practised their role, the younger ones watched them in rapt attention. 'Aside from our plays, the space was also used by members of Guwahati Sandhiya Sanmilani, Kamrup Kala Sangha, Abhinay Sangha, etc. In other words, the rehearsals at Bhaskar Natya Mandir never ceased,' Choudhury wrote.[68]

While Bhaskar Natya Mandir played a crucial role in strengthening the course of Assamese modern drama from the second decade of the twentieth century, by 1875, the first modern theatre hall was constructed in Guwahati. 'In 1879, Arya Natya Hall came up in Sukreswar Ghat on the banks of the Brahmaputra and it was a joint venture of both Bengali and Assamese drama activists.'[69] While the Jorhat Theatre began at the behest of writer Chandradhar Baruah more or less around the time Bhaskar Natya Mandir was born in Guwahati, the Sibasagar Natya Samaj opened doors in 1899. Golaghat got its first stage in 1885. 'The foundation of a permanent theatre hall and the stage was laid down at Nagaon in 1902. Permanent theatre halls were also established in Mangaldoi (1904), Patshala (1912), Nalbari (1927), Nazira (1928) and at the Biswanath Chariali (1934). By 1920, almost all the district and sub-divisional towns including some progressive villages of Assam could boast of having a semi-modern type of proscenium-arch stage and theatre halls.'[70]

While the mushrooming of these venues was an indication that the trend of Assamese modern theatre had spread across all nooks and crannies by the 1930s, an important milestone was the establishment of Baan theatre in Tezpur, in 1907–1908 with writer Padmanath Gohainbaruah (1871–1946) as its secretary. The theatre came up adjacent to a naam-ghar constructed in 1897 by the Tezpur unit of the Assamese Language Improvement Society (Asam Bhasha Sadhini Samiti). The Samiti, at a cost of ₹522, added the stage and bought musical instruments. The theatre was later named after the kirata king Baan (Bana) who ruled Tezpur. While some say the first play staged at the Baan Theatre was *Baan Roja* by Gohain Baruah, it might have taken place later as that play was written only in 1932. Baan Theatre came up as a separate linguistic entity from the Bengali theatre prevalent in the early part of the twentieth century in Assam. The space was patronized by Assamese cultural luminaries like Agarwala, Phani Sarma, Bishnu Prasad Rava, and Bhupen Hazarika. Since 1971, in memory of Phani Sarma, Baan Theatre has been hosting the annual Natasurya drama festival. Between 1997 and 2003, with state funds, this cradle of Assamese performing arts was renovated; it now has the capacity to seat an audience of around 900.[71]

An astute playwright, Gohain Baruah's oeuvre of historical plays began with *Joymoti*. Written in 1900, it became the first Assamese historical play. A noted writer who trod the path of playwriting immediately after him was Laksminath Bezbaroa, with three plays in 1915—*Joymoti Kunwari*; *Cakradhvaja Simha* (on the Ahom and Mughal clashes during the reign of that Ahom king); and *Belimar* (on the repeated Burmese incursions on Assam and its loss of independence).[72] Much later, in 1933, Dandinath Kalita (1890–1955) also wrote a play on Joymoti which highlights the importance that character had in the Assamese creative world in the first half of the twentieth century. Two more plays written on the Burmese invasion of Assam after Bezbaroa's *Belimar* were by Nakulchandra Bhuyan (1895–1968): *Badan Barphukan* (1927) and *Candrakanta Simha* (1931). 'Like Bezbaroa, he (Nakulchandra Bhuyan) also takes liberty only in the creation of minor characters (referring to imagined characters like Dalimi in *Joymoti Kunwari*).'[73]

Two more historical plays that must find mention here are *Bamuni Konwar* (1929) by playwright Daiba Chandra Talukdar, based on the Ahom–Sutiya tensions hinged on the theme of revenge; and *Naga Konwar* (1935) by Kamalananda Bhattacharya depicting the heroism of a prince born to an exiled Ahom princess. Also significant was Prasannalal Choudhury's *Nilambara* in 1933, on the fall of the Kamata kingdom. 'Some of those who had looked beyond the frontiers of Assam history and collected materials from the other sources are Paziruddin Ahmed, Bipin Barua and Atul Chandra Hazarika.'[74] While Ahmed wrote *Gulenar*, a tragic love story between Mughal prince Salim and an Iranian girl Gulenar during the reign of Akbar, in 1924, Hazarika wrote *Chatrapati Shivaji* in 1927 and *Kannauj Kuwari* in 1933. Bipin Barua penned *Mevar Sandhya* in 1937 based on Queen Padmini.

Before the lure of the historicals hit Assamese modern playwriting, Gunabhiram Barua (1837–95) wrote *Ram-Navami* in 1857, a social tragedy. Barua, noted actress Sharmila Tagore's grandfather, centred the narrative on widow remarriage. A member of the Brahmo Samaj, he was influenced by Ishwar Chandra Vidyasagar's writings. Pranati Sharma Goswami, who studied modern Assamese drama under the supervision of noted theatre scholar, writer, and educator Sailen Bharali, had pointed out in the book *Female Characters in Modern Assamese Drama* that Gunabhiram Barua's play, though largely modelled on western dramaturgy (used soliloquys like in a Shakespearean play), gave away the influence of both Sanskrit dramas (there was an influence of Kalidasa's *Abhijnana Sakuntalam*) and the Ankiya Naat of Assam. It could be because during that time Ankiya Bhaonas were still a popular medium of theatre in Assam[75] and the modern Assamese drama, written and presented on the lines of western plays, might not have set roots in the society yet. We have no information about where the play was staged in Assam or if at all. Much later in 1926, yet another play written on the lines of *Ram-Navami* was *Nirmala* by Lakhmidhar Sarma.

Though modern Assamese drama began with social plays, not too many were written on the topic. *Seuti-Kiran* by Benudhar Rajkhowa (1872–1955) was one such play from 1894. There were also some plays with a comic strain during the end of the nineteenth and the early twentieth centuries before the craze for mythological and historical plays took over. Take for example, Hemchandra Barua's *Kaniyar Kirtan* in 1861, dealing the issue of widespread opium addiction which had punched irreparable holes into Assamese rural life then; Rudraram Bordoloi's *Bangal-Bangalani* grounded on the influx of migrants into Assam and a secret illicit relationship of an Assamese woman with a migrant; Padmannath Gohain Barua's *Gaonbura* in 1877 on the despondent state of a village headman after the arrival of the British; Durga Prasad Mazindar Barua's *Mahari* in 1883 on the exploitation of tea garden clerks; and the renowned comedy *Litikai* in 1890 by Lakshminath Bezbaroa.[76] 'Besides them, those who made significant contribution to the development of this genre of play (light comedies and farces) are Mitradev Mahanta (1894–1985), Padmadhar Chaliha (1890–1969), Surendranath Saikia, Binanda Chandra Barua (1905), among others. These plays were written not with an eye on the stage but to bring out some reforms in the society. In other words, they were the results not of dramatic movement but of social consciousness.'[77] Assam saw more of mythological and historical plays than social dramas unlike in Bengal perhaps because unlike the urbanization seen taking root in Bengal, there was no difference between the rural and urban societies in Assam till the twentieth century which also meant the problems of the modern society didn't exist. Additionally, what worked in favour of mythological and historical plays in Assam was that there were already enough subjects for playwrights to work with. Most Assamese writers of the times romanticized and looked at their past with a tinge of glory, pride, and also nationalistic emotion for being in a colonized condition. Though the series of Ankiya Naat of Sankardev were also allegorical, the human element in them was somewhat passive to focus more on the need for faith, thus making the new mythological dramas somewhat different from the traditional ones.

Towards the end of the nineteenth century, Ramakanta Choudhury (1846–89) wrote an Assamese mythological play, *Sita Harana*, though there exists no copy of it for any evaluation. In 1893 came *Harischandra* and *Haradhanubhanga* by Purnakanta Deva Sarma (1856–1920), followed by *Brsaketu* in 1899 and *Guru Dakshina* in 1901 by Durga Prasad Mazindar Barua; *Baidehi-Bicched* in 1901 by Deva Nath Bordoloi (1873–1916); *Durjyudhonor Urubhongo* in 1901 and *Dakshya Yajna* in 1908 by Benudhar Rajkhowa (1872–1955); also Chandradhar Barua's (1874–1961); *Meghnad-Vadha* in 1904. 'Among all the mythological plays (of that era), *Meghnada-Vadha* is the most significant one. The drama, however, is based not directly on the original story of Ramayana, but on Bengali Kavya of the same theme written by Michael Madhusudhan Dutta (1824–1873).'[78]

Several mythological plays were written in the first part of the twentieth century by Assamese writers in blank verse, like *Meghnad-Vadha* was. However, the most significant ones came from Agarwala starting with *Sonit Kuwari* in 1925. 'Although the story is taken from mythology, the focus of the play is on the romantic episode. The hero and the heroine, Aniruddha and Usha, are the legendary lovers, but the playwright has succeeded in depicting them as young lovers of all ages. Moreover, it is in *Sonit Kuwari* alone, that indigenous Assamese songs were used for the first time as a dramatic device. The detailed stage directions and the lyrical quality are two more attractions of the play.'[79] Sonit Kuwari is special also since 'the experiments [Agarwala] tried in this play to assimilate the traditional elements did catch the imagination of the theatre critics of Delhi and this play was adjudged the best one of this type at the All India Drama Festival organised by the Sangeet Natak Akademi as early as 1956.'[80]

In all, between 1925 and 1951, Agarwala wrote six plays: *Sonit Kuwari*, *Karengar Ligiri*, *Lobhita*, *Rupalim*, *Nimati Kanya*, and *Khanikar*. Barring the last one, the protagonist of the rest were women. *Karengar Ligiri* was written in Europe and tried presenting to viewers a new way of looking at love and marriage other than the traditional way in a conservative society. 'The successful portrayal of self-conflict in a character can be for the first time seen in Assamese drama in Jyotiprasad's *Karenagar Ligiri*. In this drama, the playwright in the manner of western dramatists like Galsworthy, Ibsen, etc. has made his move through complicated dramatic situations.'[81] But unlike Ibsen who too highlighted women characters in his plays and assertive ones at that, Agarwala's female characters had the sacrificial zeal and were subdued by male authority, perhaps in keeping with the social mores of the time of his writing. Nevertheless, he will always stand out in Assamese drama for crafting an array of female characters. A play he left half-written in 1951 was also on a woman character, a historical drama titled *Kanaklata* on the renowned Assamese freedom fighter.[82]

Agarwala had also introduced to stage a significant change in the sitting arrangement of the orchestra at a play, shifting the musicians from either side of the stage to its front. The trend continues till date in the mobile theatre of Assam.[83] Aside from introducing generators for the first time in Assamese plays to light the stage, he also used scenes made by Assamese Paat painters, breaking away from the then prevailing trend of importing Bengali paintings to present the landscape scenes from a play.[84]

Bezbaroa had created the tribal character Dalimi in *Joymoti Kunwari* who gives shelter to Ahom king Dadapani and thereby saves his life. The character was essentially created with the aim of forging a mutually co-dependent wider Assamese society. In *Rupalim*, we see a similar move by Agarwala, showing the female character as the loving daughter of an imaginary Rukmi tribe. Though Agarwala's contemporaries like Phani Sarma wrote plays too, after him though, it is rare to name a playwright who consistently gave Assamese modern drama original work that created a sensation. 'It is not that there were none after Agarwala, but yes, none so great to have left a mark like he did. To my mind, Agarwala took Assamese playwriting to such a summit that it might have been difficult for the future writers to match his genius and they preferred to rather do something else. That is why we find a wide gap in quality Assamese playwriting. After Agarwala, we have to come straight to a playwright like Arun Sarma (1931–2017),' remarked director Sanjeev Hazorika.

Immediately after Independence, the fascination for historical plays continued with plays on freedom fighters like *Maniram Dewan* (by Prabin Phukan in 1948), *Piyoli Phukan* (in 1948 by Prafulla Barua and Nagaon Natya Samiti), *Kanaklata* and *Kushal Konwar* (by Suren Saikia in 1949), etc. The version of *Piyoli Phukan* staged by Nowgaon Natya Samiti created quite a ripple.[85] In the 1950s, thus, modern Assamese drama didn't see any experimentation, though in the 1960s and the 1970s, some things began to change. 'The playwrights who contributed towards it are Arun Sarma, Arup Chakrabarty, Ratna Oja, Himendra Barthakur and others. The three plays written by Arun Sarma are worth mentioning—Sri *Nibaran Bhattacharje* (1967), *Purus* (1964), and *Ahar* (1971). Two of them—*Sri Nirbaran Bhattacharjee* and *Ahar*—were written with familiar themes in an unconventional dramatic form. *Ahar* marks the influence of the theatre of absurd, a dramatic movement that developed in the West after the Second World War.'[86] There remains no doubt in an observer of Assamese theatre that it was Arun Sarma who played a considerable role in ushering in newer trends of world theatre into modern Assamese drama. Sarma, who worked in the drama department of AIR Guwahati for a long while, wrote over forty plays which also included radio plays. His plays like *Nibaran Bhattacharjee*; Satya Prasad Barua's *Mahi*; Mahendra Barthakur's *Janma*; etc. were presented as radio plays.[87] Radio plays broadcasted from AIR Guwahati, since its inception in 1948, and broadcasted from AIR Dibrugarh too later succeeded in developing a dedicated listener base for Assamese drama. Noted theatrepersons who also worked at the drama section of AIR Guwahati, Kulada Bhattacharjee—said to be the first from Assam to take professional training in theatre and stage technique at an international institution (University of Leeds and thereafter a course in production design at the British Drama League)—also contributed immensely towards radio plays through programmes like *Naat Chora* in the 1960s.

Since the 1940s, several new theatre groups popped up across Assam, say, Pragati Silpi Sangha (1940), Sivasagar Seujiya Samaj (1941), Jorhat Milit Natya Samaj (1951), New Art Players (1954), Nagaon Natya Samiti, Rangghar in Barpeta, Golaghat Amateur Society, etc.[88] There was also a rise in staging of one-act plays in modern Assamese theatre from late 1950s onwards. In 1959, Bishnu Prasad Rava and Tafazzul Ali organized a state-wide competition of one-act plays under the banner of Sadou Asam Ekanka Nat Sanmelan. The central government did that too where a young Bhupen Hazarika also participated. This period gave to Assamese theatre some notable plays, like Birinchi Kumar Bhattacharjee's *Newton*; Lakhyadhar Choudhury's *Enisar Atithi*; Arun Goswami's *Aaji*; Nirmal Prabha Bordoloi's *Tritiya Prahar*; Satya Prasad Barua's surrealistic play *Bhasawati*; Bhabendranath Saikia's *Putala Nach* and *Bawona*; Himendra Borthakur's *Dwip* and *Siralu*; etc.[89]

Since the 1970s, Assamese theatre also saw translated plays, particularly from English and Hindi, being staged increasingly. The man at the forefront of that paradigm shift was one of the first NSD graduates from Assam, Dulal Roy. He returned to Guwahati with the degree in 1963.[90]

Roy, who also had a degree from FTII in 1970, joined the state cultural affairs department (he went on to head the department) at a time when the city got its first professional stage and auditorium Rabindra Bhawan, set up by Assam government as part of the Tagore Centenary Celebrations in

1962. Roy made good use of that space to introduce to modern Assamese drama a swarm of plays by great masters from across the world through translation. Those plays directed by him were also staged in various towns, presented mostly with Assamese titles, thus opening a window to world theatre for audiences in remote areas. The astute actor and director also did original plays written by Assamese playwrights, say, Sarada Bordoloi's *Bhutai Deka*; Prabin Phukan's *Over Bridge*; *Aahar* by Arun Sarma, etc.

Bina Baruwoti who had acted in plays directed by Roy, in a recent book on the theatreperson, wrote, 'In my opinion, it is far more difficult to direct a translated play than an (Assamese) original one invariably written keeping the place in mind. While directing a translated play, one has to keep in mind the lifestyle, social and cultural ethos of a different society.'[91]

Another of Roy's substantial contributions to Assamese theatre and films (he acts in films too; directed an Assamese film too) is producing a number of top actors. 'I am not saying only because Dulal da had picked me and my wife to be, Purnima Pathak (Saikia), to be a part of the first team for the drama section of the cultural affairs and also advised me to go to NSD after watching me act, which I did. It is acknowledged by many in Assam that he contributed hugely to modern Assamese drama also by producing several good actors,' said Pranjal Saikia. Saikia's wife Purnima Pathak was exposed to Roy's sharpness as a theatre director during her days at Guwahati's Santipur area where he as a resident of the colony directed plays at the local drama club during the 1970s. Top actors from the 1980s like Tapan Das and Runu Devi, among several others worked with Roy. Recalling her experience of taking part in the 1979 workshop by NSD at Guwahati mentioned above, Seema Biswas had once recalled that Roy was assigned to direct Gohain Baruah's *Gaonbura* with the workshop participants as actors. The play, with her as the female lead, was also staged at NSD in New Delhi. 'For the first time, I acted at the NSD premises…it was then that I resolved to study there and fulfil my dream. I was always reminded by Dulal da about the need to look at theatre and learn to do it scientifically. Perhaps it was because of Dulal da that I got a chance to get admission at the NSD.'[92]

While there is no denying the greatness of his contribution to modern theatre in Assam, it needs underlining that he didn't quite tread the path to craft a local vocabulary of theatre by going back to the community's roots, the way his contemporary like Ratan Thiyam did in neighbouring Manipur. Thiyam ensured that Theatre of Roots, which had enriched modern regional drama, reached Manipur. But the movement largely skipped Assam which is tragic considering the state had a rich theatrical culture in the likes of Oja Pali, Ankiya Naat, Yatra, mask-making, and puppetry. Still, certain plays using the state's folk elements can be named here, like, Ali Haider's *Dhumuha Paakhir Neer, Juga Sandhikhonor Kabya*, Akhil Chakraverty's *Ajaan Raja Achi*, Ananda Bhagawati's *Jatugriha*, and Gunakar Deva Goswami's *Veerangana and Jerengar Sati*, which drew from Sattriya dance. Satish Bhattacherya's *Maharaja*, Arun Sarma's *Buranjir Paath*, Karuna Deka's *Suna Suna Sabha Sada* and *Luit Kanya*, and Rafiqul Hussain's *Kourav*, all utilized Oja Pali elements. While Paramananda Rajbanshi's *Mati Aru Manuh* had Khuliya Bhawna elements, *Tejimola* drew from the Assamese folk tale and features from Kushan Gaan and Nagara naam, Biya naam, and Diha naam were used in *Kamala Kuwarir Sadhu*. Pankaj Jyoti Bhuyan's *Guti Phulor Gamusa* had Bihu elements woven in.

MOBILE THEATRE OF ASSAM

In the early 1980s, a major outlet for entertainment in the small towns of Assam every winter would be a series of mobile plays or Bhraymaman Natak, staged under a huge tent late into the night. A series of trucks carting tents, music systems, bamboo poles, drama props, chairs, etc. would herald the arrival of the plays. Locals would gather to watch the tent being readied. Huge billboards of the actors in the plays painted by local artists would be put up at strategic points to attract an audience.

Soon a crowd of men, women, and children would show up to watch the plays, taking with them roasted peanuts to munch; extra shawls for cover in case the temperature dipped at night; torches, even sticks to ward off barking stray dogs while returning home at midnight.

Some years later, the single stage set under the tent became dual; with the arrival of better technology came the trend of revolving stages, adding excitement to the performances.

Typically, Nritya Natika or a dance drama would open such a play An orchestra placed in front of the stage would play music as and when the scenes required that effect.

This pop or mass culture phenomenon began in the early 1960s in Assam due to the singular effort of a small town resident, ushering in, gradually, a revolution of sorts to modern Assamese drama. In 1963, in a small town called Patshala in Lower Assam, Achyut Lahkar began Bhraymaman theatre under the banner of Natraj Theatre. 'Combining the basics of dramatic art—dance, music, acting, stagecraft with most modern technology, Natraj Theatre (it began on 2 October 1963) stood as an institution. It moved through the length and breadth of Assam, entertaining people, urban as well as rural, for forty long years. The process enriched the cultural heritage of Assam with a unique dramatic tradition, which ensured a strong foundation for mobile theatre in the national cultural scenario.'[93]

Lahkar was barely thirty-one when he began the drama movement. His father Gaurikanta Lahkar was the owner of a well-known shop of musical instruments, drama costumes, and make-up in Patshala, then a nerve centre of the mobile dance drama called Yatra, a nineteenth century cultural import to that belt from neighbouring Bengal. After Lahkar lost his father, he returned home from Kolkata without finishing his studies to join the family business. His younger brother Sadananda Lahkar had already started the Natraj Opera, a mobile Yatra company, seemingly to also act as a profit-making subsidiary to the family's allied business. Several notable actors of the region joined Natraj Opera and toured Lower Assam and also the tea gardens of Upper Assam with Assamese plays. 'This theatre group also initiated the tradition of performing dance-dramas before the play. Some prominent artists of the genre were Robin Das, Jatin Das, Kalawanta Sing, Surya Baishya, Sanamal Das, etc. One of the most prominent and famous dance artists of Assam, Khagen Barman, also made his first appearance in this Nataraj Opera.'[94]

Natraj Opera was a step ahead of the typical Yatras that would tour Assam then. Here a brief trajectory of the Yatra in Assam would be helpful to get an idea of the times that were. Taking advantage of the introduction of Bengali as an official language of Assam by the British, Bengali Yatra parties began touring parts of Assam. Their stories would typically stretch from mythological to historical dramas. In 1860, sensing a market for such plays, Tithiram Bayan from Barpeta started a Yatra troupe, thus becoming the first Assamese to do so. Still, the plays had to be in Bengali. He began with two Bengali plays—*Ram Banabas* and *Radhikar Manbhanjan*—written by Govinda Ram Choudhury, the grandfather of former Asam Sahitya Sabha president Prasanna Lal Choudhury. For about eight years, Bayan's Yatra party travelled by boat on the rivers with the necessary equipment to present the dramas in several parts of Assam. Gradually, a number of Yatra parties emerged but they still had to present plays in Bengali even though the artists hired by the owners were Assamese. That compulsion to present plays in Bengali probably also delayed the writing of original plays in Assamese for Yatras for a long period. It was only in 1921 after Brajanath Sarma of Shila village in Barpeta started a drama group named Xila Kalika Opera Party that Assamese plays began to be staged. Sarma, who fought in World War I as part of the imperial army, staged *Rana Pratap* and *Bajirao* after translating them into Assamese from Bengali. Actors like Phani Sarma joined the initiative when he formed Assam Kohinoor Opera. Brajanath Sarma also started the practice of giving a monthly remuneration to every actor who performed in his opera and introduced the system of selling tickets of varying prices to audience members ranging from four annas to two rupees. Among the novelties he is credited with introducing to Assamese theatre was the inclusion of female actors (in 1933) on stage. In coming times, several such Assamese Yatra parties popped up across Assam. They were much more popular in Lower Assam than in Upper Assam where the art of Bhaona, about which I elaborate later in the chapter, was still a lot more prevalent. The tradition of opening a drama performance with a Nritya Natika in the mobile theatre of Assam in the 1960s was most likely drawn from the Yatra where the musical component was an integral part. The Yatras also had a sutradhar (narrator) called bibek (conscience) which would reappear during a performance.

When we cut to the starting of Natraj Opera at Patshala by Sadananda Lahkar in 1959, it comes across as only a continuation of a tradition already prevalent in the town and the rest of Lower Assam. His elder brother Achyut Lahkar, having noted the success that the mobile theatres of Bengal and Maharashtra had gained by then, was hoping to replicate the model in Assam.[95] It was that thought at the back of his mind that eventually pushed him to 'infuse technology, science' and play with 'lights, orchestra etc. mesmerising the audience.'[96] He set up huge tents which could accommodate an audience of around 2,000 where they were exposed to 'two stages to give cinema-like continuity to the drama performances' and 'pioneered the projection of pre-shot films on stage giving a cinematic feel'.[97] 'The idea of the Mobile Theatre espoused by Achyut Lahkar was similar to the Western Proscenium stage theatre complete with an auditorium; the only difference imagined by him was that it would be mobile—transportable from one place to another—just like the Yatras.'[98]

The first show at Natraj Theatre was on a makeshift stage erected at the premises of Hari Mandir in Patshala in October 1963. It was after watching a performance by Natraj Theatre at the Judge's Fields in Guwahati in 1963 that the founder of The Assam Tribune Group Radha Govinda Barua named it Bhramyaman, and the name has stuck.

The theatre group began with four dramas in its initial years—*Jerengar Sati* (written by Uttam Barua), *Bhogjara* (by Phani Sarma; it was the first play to be staged by Natraj Theatre), *Tikendrajit* (by Atul Chandra Hazarika), and *Haidar Ali* (a translated play). Cultural icons like Bishnu Rabha became its patrons. Soon, a number of other mobile theatre groups sprung up. The first to follow suit was Kohinoor Theatre by Ratan Lahkar in 1976. To it goes the credit of not only adding more technology to amaze audiences but also for adding glamour to the mobile theatre in general by hiring actors from Assamese cinema. Kohinoor Theatre also managed to bag a loan from the Central Bank of India to start the business, an anomaly then. In coming decades, it went on to replicate on stage films like James Cameron's *Titanic*.

After Kohinoor entered the arena, some other players joined in; dramas began to be specially written for mobile theatres. From the Lahkar family came another mobile theatre company, Aradhana Theatre, started by Achyut Lahkar's brother Sadananda Lahkar in 1978. Prior to Kohinoor and Aradhana, came Purbojyoti Theatre and Suradevi Theatre, around 1966–67. Suradevi was started by Dharani Barman with Bishnu Prasad Rava directing his plays initially and noted music composer and filmmaker Brajen Barua making the music; no wonder then Suradevi with such a grand beginning tasted immense success and remained in operation for about thirty-one years. Dharani Barman's wife Abala Barman had also begun Moon Theatre in 1977, the first women-centric mobile theatre. A popular theatre company Bhagyadevi, began in 1968. Krishna Roy, who had collaborated with Ratan Lahkar to start Kohinoor Theatre, parted ways with Lahkar in 1980 to start yet another popular banner Awahan Theatre. Roy succeeded in creating waves in the field by roping in two major playwrights of the times: Bhabendranath Saikia and Mahendra Barthakur. 'Bringing Dr. Bhabendra Nath Saikia to mobile theatre is reason enough to make Krishna Roy immortal in the history of mobile theatre.'[99] By then, Saikia's one-act play broadcast on AIR Guwahati—*Xanta Xista, Hrista Pusta, Maha Dusta*—had created ripples among the audience. 'His dramas like *Ramdhenu, Bandixal, Andhakup, Nilakantha, Aranyat Godhuli, Samudra Manthan, Ramyabhumi, Satabdi, Dinabandhu,* etc. had eventually created a new class of audience.'[100]

In Upper Assam, the most well-known mobile theatre group was Hengul Theatre which began in Jorhat in 1986; it was in operation as of 2023. Sadly, the curtains came down on the Nataraj Theatre in 2003 after forty glorious years due to Achyut Lakhkar's inability to keep it commercially viable. He eventually had to sell his company's gadgets and other belongings in the local bazaar to meet the pending salaries of the actors and to pay the debtors. With no one coming to his aid, Assamese mobile theatre industry lost forever the option of preserving the very items that had given it the seed. Achyut Lahkar died in abject penury in 2016.

The Kohinoor Theatre also folded up in 2017. Today, though some companies continue the practice with popular faces from Assamese cinema still featuring in them, the quality of the plays and the razzmatazz around them has lost the earlier grace and charm.

ANKIYA NAAT

Having come under the shadow of British colonization, modern Assamese drama drew its life breath from Western dramas, and from Bengal in the nineteenth century. However, the tradition of writing a play in prose in Assam is one of the oldest in India. Sankardev, as early as 1468 CE, wrote *Chinna Jatra*. Hiren Gohain had termed him the first in India to have written a play in a regional language in prose.[101]

In Assam, prior to Sankardev, scholars like Madhav Kandali, Haribor Bipra, Hema Saraswati, Rudra Kandali, and Kabiratna Saraswati wrote in verse which would make Sankardev also the first Assamese playwright.[102] One certainly can't call it an Indian import as Sankardev wrote *Chinna Jatra* prior to his first pilgrimage to the mainland. *Chinna Jatra* is essentially a painted spectacle of the seven heavens of Hindu mythology (Baikuntha). After illustrating them for his disciples, Sankardev directed them to play-act the scenes; the painted scenes were a backdrop to the play. Thereafter, Sankardev wrote six more plays: *Patni Prasada*, *Rukmini Harana*, *Keli Gopal*, *Kaliya Damana*, *Parijat Harana*, and *Rama Vijaya*. *Rukmini Harana*, *Parijat Harana*, and *Rama Vijaya* have more dialogues than the other plays, and can be called full-fledged dramas with 'definable plots, characters, and dialogues'.[103] The early Vaishnava writings, however, didn't call those plays Ankiya Naat and Bhaona; Sankardev referred to his dramatic creations as nata, nataka, or yatra and also nritya.[104] He called the actors natuwa or nartkaka. Vaishnava plays written by Sankardev and Madhabdev, also those by their disciples later began to be known as Ankiya Naat, and Bhaona. According to Maheswar Neog, the term Bhaona, meaning the representation of a drama, has the same roots as the Sanskrit word bhavana—'producing, displaying, manifesting, imagining' etc.[105] He had, however, underlined that in Assam, the term Bhaona is applied exclusively to the Vaishnava religious dramas and not to any other form of dramatic performance practised in the state.

About Ankiya Naat or a play in a single act, Neog had said, 'It is quite likely that the Assamese drama as an one-act piece came to be called *anka*, in imitation of a Sanskrit terminology in spite of the fact that Sankardeva's or Madhabdeva's dramas do not conform to all the requirements of the definition *anka* or *ursrstikanka*. On the other hand, it also cannot be dismissed as improbable that the Assamese variety of drama was called *anka* just because it contained a single act.'[106] Madhabdev's shorter plays are, however, referred to as Jhumura in which songs are an integral part; at times even dialogues are delivered in song.

Typically, Bhaonas are of two types: Ankiya Bhaona or plays by Sankardev and Madhabdev; and Bhaona or the plays penned by Vaishnava monastic heads who followed the two gurus. While the language of the Ankiya Bhaona is invariably in Brajawali dialect, the rest may either be in Brajawali or in pure Assamese. Neog had pointed out that akin to seventeenth–eighteenth century Kerala when one had to write a Kathakali play in order to be known as a poet, in post-Sankardev Assam too, it became imperative for the abbots (satradhikars) of the monasteries to also produce a religious play to be recognized as worthy of their position. That practice gave birth to a number of plays.[107]

Assam also has a fascinating tradition of presenting Hejaria or Barechahariya Bhaona, and Dhura Bhaona.[108] Practised in Nagaon district and Jamuguri area of Tezpur, the Hejaria (a thousand) version had been named so just because more than one performance would take place simultaneously. Such Bhaona were typically held during the dry season when the paddy fields (pothar) would lay bare after the harvest. 'A part of an extensive field is cleared of the paddy stumps and made even by the collective labour of a number of villages agreeing to organise the show. If twelve plays are to be produced, a large *pandal* (platform) is built to consist of a central circular or twelve-faceted ground plan covered by a wood and bamboo three-terraced structure at the centre, and twelve constituent pandala, all raditating out from that central structure.'[109] The community worked together to decorate the central structure where the Vaishnava holy book, the Bhagavad Purana, would be placed on a pedestal.

Dhura Bhaona grew in popularity primarily in Upper Assam during the British era presumably to thwart the impact of Bengali Yatra plays on the local populace.[110] This form of Bhaona has nearly disappeared now. Harichandra Bhattacharyya has also mentioned another later variety influenced by Bengali plays named Bangali Bhaona.[111]

Traditionally, an Ankiya Naat or Bhaona would be staged at the naam-ghar, or at times under a robha (temporary shed). Madhabdev presented his *Govardhana-yatra* for the first time under a robha. At Barpeta, he also built a separate house, Bor-ghar, to stage his plays *Bhojana-Vyavahara* and *Dadhi-Mathana.*[112] Sankardev's dramas were said to have been screened at the royal court of the Koch kingdom too; Koch general Chilarai patronized the first staging of Sankardev's *Ram Vijaya*. Later, the Ahom kings did it too. 'In March 1906, Sankardev's *Rukmini-Harana* was enacted on four consecutive days at the Ahom capital under the aegis of the Mahanta of Bareghar sattra.'[113]

Bhaonas also have the concept of the green room, called cho, to carry out the make-up of the actors and also to stock the accessories and props required in a play.[114]

Of the six plays of Sankardev, only *Ram Vijaya* was based on the Ramayana, the rest on Krishna. While *Chinna Jatra* uses a backdrop of painted scenes, the rest of the saint's plays didn't have any such backgrounds. Instead, 'the *Sutradhar* appears on the stage as soon as the preliminary music items known as *Dhemali* (literal meaning in Assamese is playful) are over, announces the subject of the drama, and conducts the whole show with dances, songs and explanatory commentary.'[115] Apart from the plays mentioned above, Madhabdev also wrote notable plays alike *Chor-dhara Pimpara-guchara* and *Arjuna-Bhanjana.*

Following the fall of the Ahom kingdom due to the Burmese invasion which generated a huge disruption in everyday life in Assam, the practice of staging the religious drama form began to wane progressively. After the British colonial rule began, there was the advent of Bengali Yatra plays in Assam. The bhaona 'came to be much maligned as a form of rustic amusement in spite of its classic qualities', thus pushing it to remain confined to the Vaishnava monasteries and in some rural belts.[116]

OPEN-AIR THEATRE

In the last few years, a significant trend noted in Assamese theatre is the birth of open air drama festivals. That there was already a practice of Barechahariya Bhaona in parts of Assam may nudge someone to reflect on this fairly new phenomenon in Assamese theatre only as a natural progression, especially the kind held in a paddy field (pothar theatre). Still, in the arena of open-air theatre, one can't overlook the role played by the annual Under the Sal Tree festival since 2008 to popularize the trend, a significant development that occurred at a nondescript village in Assam's Goalpara district in 2008. The force behind Under the Sal Tree was theatre actor/director Sukracharjya Rabha and his group Badungduppa Kala Kendra. Sukra started the theatre group, named after a bamboo musical instrument used by the Rabhas, in his family's paddy field way back in 1998. Since 2008, the three-day soiree of plays began taking place every December under a grove of Sal trees, considerd sacred by his community, the Rabhas.

I came across Sukracharjya in 2016, the year the festival went international with a play each from Brazil, Bangladesh, South Korea, and Sri Lanka. Sukra passed away from a heart attack in 2018 but by then he had shaped a model of rural theatre that had not only gone on to enrich modern drama in Assam but Indian theatre in general. In 2008, the festival took off with his mentor and noted Manipuri theatre director Heisnam Kanhailal not only providing him the adequate training needed to direct a play but also the seed money for it. He had come across Kanhailal at a drama workshop held at the Kalakshetra in Guwahati in 2003.[117] During a conversation in 2016, Sukra had related to me some of the reasons that brought him to theatre. In the 1990s, Assam was limping back from insurgency; he being a local student leader was aware of youth from his community needing a way to express themselves creatively. Additionally, Sal trees, the sacred groove of the Rabhas traditionally used to bury their dead, were being chopped by villagers due to the lure of the crash crop rubber. On sharing his worries with Kanhailal, he came up with the idea of an open-air theatre under a Sal grove. A clearing under a Sal groove in his village was readied as an experiment. 'I was firm that if we are using a natural space as a stage for the plays, we should not use any mic or lights, no artificial effects. Theatre anyway teaches us how to throw our voice at the audience. We decided to host the festival of plays only at day time under the sunlight. Kanhailal sir was very pleased with me for going ahead with the idea and gave me ₹70,000 to do the festival.'[118] Not just Assamese plays but drama in his Rabha language too began to be staged. Readying the stage and the audience gallery made of bamboos under the Sal grove and temporary quarters for the participants became a community effort. Over the years, the audience swelled from local villagers to theatregoers travelling down from Guwahati and the neighbouring towns. Noted Kannada playwright H. S. Shivaprakash who has also been closely associated with Under the Sal Tree, told me in 2016 that looking at the success of the festival it gave him hope for theatre in India. 'It is the closest you can bring theatre to people; no grand auditorium, no mics, no lights, just the actors, the play and people.'[119]

Since 2012, another talented Rabha youth, Pabitra Rabha, has been getting national attention for setting up a theatre village in Tangla, about 90 kilometres from Guwahati. There, he teaches drama to a group of people with dwarfism and thereby gives them not just a means of livelihood but also a purpose in life. Their first play *Kinu Kou* was a super hit.

Theatre director Rabhijita counted for me as many as twenty theatre festivals that take place today across Assam by drawing from the Under the Sal Tree model. 'The credit must go to Sukra for creating that consciousness among young theatre practitioners on how to take drama to the people truly,' she said.

Rabhijita also pointed out to me a key element of this new revolution of rural theatre in Assam, particularly in the tribal areas, 'I also look at this development as part of an ethnic assertion of some communites through drama. We can't overlook that element. Sukra had directed plays in the Rabha language. Somewhere [in] the backdrop, there is also the question of mainstream Assamese exploitation of the tribes.'

Having grown up in Diphu (Karbi Anglong), when Rabhijita started her theatre group in 1994, she called it Jirsong, a Karbi term for a bachelor's pad. Her first play *Rangpharpi Rangbe* was in Karbi. Yet she added, 'However much I try, I am not an insider to the community. I, therefore, encourage youngsters from different tribes across Northeast to form their own groups because they must also tell their stories the way they see it. I see Sukra's journey in theatre in that light too.'

Such recent examples of the blooming of modern theatre within the ethnic tribes of Assam has not only helped add freshness to the firmament of Assamese theatre in terms of new stories, new actors, and directors but has also gone some ways in making the space more inclusive.

13

SANCHIPAAT–TULAPAAT, CHITRAKALA–BHASKARJYA: ASSAMESE VISUAL ART

Along national highway 37, in Puranigudam town in Middle Assam, stood Kolong Kala Kendra. While I waited for Chittaranjan Bora, its founder, to join me in a conversation on the art he practises, the modest building of the Kendra shook periodically, as if a mild earthquake had hit the area. The unsettling sensation was due to heavy digging of earth to widen the highway.

On being asked about this, Chittaranjan seemed resigned to the reality.[1] To me though, that experience was a metaphor for the ground-shifting work that the young artist, through the Kendra, has done in the realm of traditional Assamese visual art.

For over a decade now, Chittaranjan has been on a single-minded endeavour to revive Assam's ancient tradition of art sketched on sanchipat—the treated leaves of the agaru or agarwood/eaglewood tree. The primary colours used in that art form are extracted from hengul and haital, a range of hand-prepared pigments. Chittaranjan's dogged effort has now given more than a ray of hope to the survival of the near extinct practice.

The seed was sowed when back in the late 1980s, Chittaranjan, then a student of noted Assamese artist Pranab Baruah, heard his teacher rue about the rich past of the visual art form of Assam which was then on the path of death. In 1990, Chittaranjan, with help from Baruah (Assam's first graduate from Mumbai's J. J. School of Art) approached Naren Kalita, a noted historian, art critic, and an ardent researcher of that visual art form, to gather more information. By then, he had come across an article on the subject by Kalita in an Assamese magazine in his college library. Kalita was a resident of Nagaon, not far from Chittaranjan's home in Puranigudam, which helped matters. 'That year, I accosted Kalita sir, then a lecturer of Assamese literature at Nagaon's Anandaram Dhekial Phukan College, several times, both at the institution and at his home, to know more about *Sanchipat* paintings,' he told me. The thought that spun in his head then was: what would it be like for a community to lose a tradition which had been practised for 300 years in the Sankari jug (Sankardev's era)? Being a student of art, he felt a pull within to try preserving whatever might be left of that chitrakala (visual art form).

On Kalita's advice, Chittaranjan visited the Vaishnava monasteries in Majuli Island to locate a Sanchipat khanikar, a traditional practitioner. He was not only looking for someone who would know how to draw on the barks but also how to season the barks for the art and the know-how to create the pigment. But his efforts were in vain.

On returning home, Chittaranjan did what he could—he planted a row of agarwood trees in the backyard of his house which now houses the Kendra. 'I thought at least I could start experimenting on my own on how to make agarwood barks from those trees,' he told me. The year was 1992.

For a tree to yield bark, it has to develop a girth of a certain size which takes at least fifteen years. 'Still, I went ahead. It was some kind of madness that had gripped me. While most plants died in course of time either due to the dampness of the soil or from pest attacks, a few survived,' he related. Simultaneously, he started Kolong Kala Kendra to offer lessons on terracotta art, wood cutting and Assam's mask-making art besides setting up a museum of traditional items that he would collect from places in and around Nagaon.

In 1994, Chittaranjan came across yet another article on Sanchipat chitrakala in the Assamese magazine *Prantik* by Lohit Bora. The search for more information on the art form continued. Two years later came Kalita's notable book *Asamar Puthichitra* (Assam's Books of Paintings), published by the state-owned Assam Prakashan Parishad. Picking up that book, he admitted, helped him further steel his resolve. 'It was a vast reservoir of knowledge on the art form. I could also get an idea from it about how the traditional pigments were created from hengul-haital by the Khanikars in the olden times. I became restless to start experimenting,' he told me. While hengul is traditionally prepared by mixing mercury, sulphur, and lead in equal proportion to help produce the basic colour red (by grinding it continuously with fresh water on stone), the dye haital is a product of an orpiment, or an orange-yellow arsenic sulphide mineral found in hot springs. It too needs rigorous grinding on stone with fresh rainwater or a spot of morning dew to produce another basic colour, yellow.

HENGULIA BISONI: TRADITIONAL HAND FANS

Chittaranjan's numerous attempts to find hengul-haital in the bazaars of Assam met with despair. A breakthrough came when around 1997, he learnt from an acquaintance that the practice of using hengul-haital existed in the Auniati monastery in Majuli but only to paint the bamboo handles of the traditional cane hand fans, the bisoni. Though in olden times, the practice of producing hengulia bisoni, a rich craft of Assam, was the forte of the Auniati and Kamalabari Vaishnava monasteries, their use and status in Assamese society began to diminish with the arrival of motor-driven fans. 'It is worth a mention that in *Gurucharit*, during the conduct of the death rituals of Sankardev (in 1568), Koch general Chilarai, among other things, also offered a hand fan,' Naren Kalita had pointed out its pride of place in a chapter in *Hengul Haital*, an informative book published in Assamese by Chittaranjan's Kendra in 2019.[2]

To craft a hengulia bisoni, the khanikar, using the hengul-haital pigments, embellishes the chiselled bamboo handle attached to the woven fan with floral motifs while its border is dressed in cloth trimmings. One such khanikar of hengulia bisoni at Auniati, Budhindra Nath Barpathak, turned out to be a lucky charm for Chittaranjan. He met Barpathak by chance at an event in Guwahati's Kalakshetra in 2001. He found Barpathak writing on a bark and embellishing its borders with lota, creepers—a traditional practice on such texts called lota-kota—by using hengul-haital. Some amount of pestering of the artisan helped him get the address of a shop in the city's Fancy Bazaar to procure hengul.

Chittaranjan later placed a small piece of hengul at the feet of Barpathak and called him his guru, who then set aside his initial reluctance to share any information with him on the art form. 'I understood his reluctance to share information about the art with someone not from within the monastery. Various practices were taken out of the monasteries only to be misused and he wouldn't like to see the art form meet the same fate,' related Chittaranjan.

On returning home, Chittaranjan began preparing the pigments following the verbal instructions of Barpathak. Though Barpathak could only draw creepers along the borders of the Sanchipat texts prepared for the monastery and didn't draw figures, like the art was practised in the olden times, Chittranjan said, 'Still, we must consider him to be the last of the practising khanikars at a Vaishnava monastery who practised the art.'

Budhindra Nath Barpathak passed away in 2013. By then though, a lot had taken place in the field of reviving the art form at Chittaranjan's end. He not only learnt how to treat the agarwood barks to prepare the Sanchipat canvases but was also successful in his experiment to produce not just the colours red from hengul, and yellow from haital, but white too from khorimati (chalk); blue from guta neel (indigo); black from xilikha seed, nol-khagori, the dried exterior of lau—a local variety of gourd—and engaar or ash; and also how to extract an adhesive from bael fruit to help the colours stick permanently on the canvas. Some colours also needed the blood of earthworms to make them glow at night.

The process of creating mohi, the ink, to write on the agarwood barks was arduous too; it needed the dried bark of certain trees, fruits like gooseberry; seeds of elephant fruit, local herbs like Kehraj, etc. He had to wait for the rains to collect the freshest of the water or painstakingly gather the morning dew, drop by drop, to be able to add while grinding the colours.

Chittaranjan recalled that in the process of chasing the nitty-gritties of the Sanchipat chitrakala, he also learnt how to treat cotton buds to create a canvas of pressed tulapaat to write on and create visual art—yet another medium used by Saint Sankardev but today, a dying form in Assam.

Chittaranjan's first work on sanchipat by using the handmade colours was a replication of Sankardev's *Gunamala*, created overnight by the saint at the request of his patron, the Koch king Naranarayan. Chittaranjan confessed he too was initially reluctant to teach the art form to others after having worked so hard to acquire the knowledge but eventually did take in students on the advice of Kalita for the sake of preserving the form. Since then, he has been holding periodic workshops at the Kendra, producing several worthy young practitioners. They, in turn, are also holding workshops and passing on the art form.

About a hundred kilometres from Chittaranjan's Kendra, at a monastery in Jorhat district, yet another try at promoting the art form has ensued. Around 2002–2003, Jadav Chandra Mahanta, a retired teacher and practitioner of the traditional mukha (mask) art at Bor Elengi Bogi-aai monastery, began creating the traditional ink to apply it on the motifs painted on Guru Aaxon, the pyramidal wooden tiered platform placed at a naam/kirtan ghar on which the holy book Bhagawat is placed. During Mahanta's childhood, he had seen an old monk of the monastery using hengul-haital to paint the Guru Aaxon. The monastic head (now deceased) Satradhikar Nabin Chandra Goswami took up the responsibility after the monk's death. Mahanta, though, learnt how to prepare the colours from the subsequent monastic head Indrakanta Mahanta. 'He didn't demonstrate it to me, just orally shared the process. I began experimenting and was successful around 2003,' Jadav Mahanta said in an interview published in the book *Hengul Haital.*[3] By 2005, Mahanta was also deep into drawing on Sanchipat. Today, while he is promoting the replication of sketches from the Vaishnava texts, a practice long prevalent in the monasteries, Chittaranjan has used the traditional art form to also express contemporary realities. In other words, he has drawn from the roots to not only replicate religious motifs and texts but also draw secular art and thereby make it relevant within contemporary Assamese art. An example of it is his art work *Nari* in Sanchipat where one spots even a woman dressed in salwar kameez, a current reality in the small towns of Assam. An art work on agarwood bark features Assamese cultural icon Jyotiprasad Agarwala and another shows the Covid-19 pandemic that had gripped the world in 2020.

Chittaranjan may have contributed in reviving the art form but is quick to add, 'One doesn't need to take this art form all over again to the world stage. [With the] number of notable books, mainly in English, published since the times of Pandit Hemchandra Goswami (on Assamese manuscripts in general titled *Descriptive Catalogue of Assamese Manuscripts* in 1930) till Naren Kalita's work, the task has been completed. Noted art historian Kapila Vatsayan, by terming it as the Assam School of Painting, has already categorized it as an exclusive form of Indian traditional painting.'[4]

THE GLORIOUS PAST

The oldest mention of Assam's Sanchipat puthi (Sanchipat books) can be found in the seventh century in Bana's *Harshacharita* where the court poet of Magadha king Harshvardhan recorded the king being gifted 'volumes of five writings with leaves made from aloe bark and of the hue of the ripe pink cucumber' by then Kamrup king Bhaskarvarman.[5] The oldest representation of the art form on Sanchipat is the illustrated tenth book of the Bhagawat, retrieved from Nagaon's Bali monastery, in the early twentieth century. The illustrated colourful paintings from that text were published for the first time in partly multicoloured hues in 1949 by Harinarayan Duttabaruah as *Chitra Bhagawat*; the chitra refers to the illustrations.[6]

Even though the year 1461 saka (1539 CE) was found scribbled on the back of that precious Sanchipat treatise, which would mean it was created during the lifetime of Sankardev (several also claim on that basis that it was written by the saint himself), Maheswar Neog (1915–95) has stated that Dr Moti Chandra, the legendary curator of the Prince of

Wales Museum (Chattrapati Shivaji Maharaj Vastu Sangrahalaya), had dated it between the end seventeenth and early eighteenth century.[7] The reason behind such a placement in time is because of the strong Rajput–Mughal artistic properties in some of the illustrations in those folios. In Chandra's words, 'The costume of men usually consists of *dhoti*, *dupatta* and turban (popularly called *mughlai tupi or Aurangebor tupi* in Assam) and in some cases *jamah* and women wear sari and bodice. The pattern of their texture throws light on the textile patterns in (of) the 17th century Assam. The turban bound with sash became common (in Assam) by the middle of the 18th century.'[8] What gives weight to Chandra's contention is also a comment by Kesavananada Devagoswami from Bali Satra who had carried out substantial research on that illustrated manuscript from his monastery. Devagoswami had mentioned in a chapter in *Hengul Haital* that though followers of the monastery still believe that it was a work done during Sankardev's lifetime, he would call it a work by Ramchandra Ata based on his study done in close consultation with California-based Dr Dilip Basu.[9] Ramchandra Ata was the grandson of noted artist of the monastery, Damodar Ata. Significantly, Devagoswami had also stated during a discussion held on the topic at the Kalakshetra in 2013 that the year 1461 was scribbled on the copy of the illustrated Bhagawat Book X much later by his grandfather Dhaneswar Ata, which should clear the air once and for all.[10]

In August 2021, during a discussion on Assam's illustrated manuscripts hosted by Guwahati-based magazine *Nezine*, Naren Kalita also categorically stated that there has thus far been no empirical evidence to claim that the art form had been practised in the Vaishnava monasteries since the time of Sankardev. Sankardev had, however, painted the seven vaikunthas (heavens) to form the backdrop for his first dance-drama *Cihna Jatra* on tulapaat. Also, there is a popular belief that Sankardev, before engaging weavers to weave the story of the Bhagavad on cloth—the Brindabani Bastra—also drew the episodes for King Naranarayan.

Whether illustrations of texts on barks were a practice at the monasteries since Sankardev's era is a subject of debate. What cannot be refuted, however, is the continuance of the robust practice of writing texts on agarwood barks during the saint's lifetime, a couple of which he wrote himself. Anyway, the tradition of writing on tree barks was an ancient practice across civilizations—Indonesia's Batak manuscripts, written on the strips of bark of the alim tree, are rather well-known; in northern India, there was a custom of writing on birch bark.

Maheswar Neog and Moti Chandra seemed willing to stretch the time period of the creation of the illustrated Bhagawat only till the early eighteenth century on the grounds that it was during king Rudra Singha's era (1696–1714) that the Ahom monarchy had officially introduced the Mughal turbans spotted in those paintings, and also clothing like the jamah coat, to the royals and the ministers. But Naren Kalita had positioned the illustrations strictly between 1661 and 1683.[11] He had offered a rather interesting point of view to argue his case. Though Rudra Singha might have formally introduced such trends in royal attire in the later Ahom period, there existed no reason to also not accept that such components were brought to Assam prior to his era by the artists among the migrants from Kannauj in the medieval era. Sankardev's ancestors were also from Kannauj.

'It could be that because of such migration, some influences from the Mughal School of painting practiced in Northern India crept into Assamese art,' argued Kalita. He pointed out that in the first part of the seventeenth century, certain features of the Mughal paintings had slipped out of the royal confines to enter the Rajput School of painting and the Rajasthani Ragamala miniature paintings. 'It was during that time Mughal art had come out of the royal bounds and became popular as Mughal School of painting. One sees the *Mughlai pag* (turban) and *jamah* in the Rajput paintings from the first half of the 17th century and also in the Ragamala paintings. It could be that certain influences from the Rajput paintings of that period had tiptoed into Assamese visual art.'[12] The noted art historian also underlined, 'Significantly, according to Jugal Das, the Assamese artists had collected hengul and haital from Gujarati and the Rajasthani traders operating in the region. These factors could be why one spots the *Mughlai pag* and jamah in the Satriya paintings too.'[13]

Kalita further reasoned:

> An indirect connection between Assam and the *Mughlai pag-jamah* could probably be during the Mughal attack led by Mir Jumla in 1661. After that event, we find in history about Emperor Aurangzeb gifting *Surpau pag* to Ahom king Chakradhaj Singha (1663–70). That Rudra Singha in 1704 decided to adopt the attire of the Mughal badshah could also be from the memory left behind by Mir Jumla. What must be mentioned is, in the *Chitra Bhagavad*, the *asura* and *danava* were

> dressed in *pag-jamah* with beard and moustache. This could give a hint of a memory of invaders from those times. The use of *pag-jamah* in *Chitra Bhagavad*, therefore, indicates that it must be after 1661.[14]

Eminent art critic and historian Ananda K. Coomaraswamy had stated that the Rajput pag or turban had crept into Mughal court during Akbar's era. 'According to him, the *jamah* too was a pre-Mughal Indian outfit. It later became popular once again among the Rajputs due to the Mughal influence.'[15]

Somiran Boruah, as the curator at the Assam State Museum in 2005, carried out research on the subject and had also stated that the illustrated Bhagavad of Bali Satra was structurally closer to those of the fifteenth century manuscript of *Laur Chandra* and the sixteenth century manuscript of *Mrigavat* preserved at the Bharat Kala Bhawan in Varanasi. Both these works belong to the western Indian tradition.[16] Though the illustrated Bhagawat, considered the oldest surviving specimen of the art form in Assam, was discovered in Bali monastery, Kalita believess that at least the illustrations in it might have been created in Majuli. That contention was because of a peculiar practice adopted while creating such illustrated books in Assam. Often two artists—one to draw, and the other to paint alongside the text—were used to complete the folios which would then be wrapped in cloth, or in a wooden box or in leaves to be kept in the temples and naam-ghars. According to Surya Kumar Bhuyan, 'The skill of a painter was generally requisitioned to decorate the labourers of penmanship. The scribe was sometimes a painter himself; and if not, a regular painter supplemented the work of the transcriber by sketching appropriate pictures on spaces left blank for the purpose.'[17] Maheswar Neog also wrote, 'It was generally considered to be an act of piety to copy out old religious works on *sanchipat* or *tulapaat*. If the pious copyist had the knack, he would insert miniature paintings from page to page illustrative of the text or, if he could afford, would utilise the services of a *khanikar*. The rich Satras had their own *khanikars*. A religious school of painting thus grew up in Assam.'[18]

Keshabananda Devagoswami of Bali monastery had already made a significant observation. On looking closely the paintings of the monastery's copy of the Bhagawat, it showed that the aa-kar (to denote the sound aa) added to a word at times in the treatise was written at a distance from the mother word, seemingly due to lack of space for it. He deduced from such occurrences on the folios of that Bhagawat that the paintings must have been done prior to writing the text.[19]

Kalita's contention that the illustrations were concluded in Majuli is based on another argument. While some Vaishnava monasteries were set up outside of the river island too, the practice thrived mostly in Majuli since the seventeenth century and the several Satriya style illustrated books, including the two oldest copies of *Bhakti Ratnavali*, still preserved at the Majuli monasteries, give us a hint that the area was truly the hub of the art form.

THREE STYLES OF ASSAMESE ILLUSTRATED ART FORMS

Cultural experts have divided the Assamese illustrated art form into three styles: the Sattriya style or the method used in the Vaishnava monasteries to illustrate the texts on Sanchipat; the Tai-Ahom style or the method which is akin to the Burmese Buddhist approach; and the royal style, or the method that is noted to have moved from the monasteries to the Ahom royal realm. Kalita, who had brought out a precious collection in 2008—*An Alphabetical Index of Illustrated Manuscripts of Assam*—listed an illustrated *Bhakti Ratnavali* housed at the old Kamalabari monastery of Majuli dating back to 1683 as the oldest specimen of the art form to be found so far in the river island. In all, he had mentioned six such illustrated works present in the island currently where the date of their creation was duly mentioned by the creator. According to Kalita, the next oldest such text is the eleventh book of the *Bhagawat*, preserved at Dakshinpat monastery in Majuli from 1697 onwards; followed by *Sundarakand Ramayan* at Bengenaati monastery from 1715; *Bhakti Ratnavali* at Karatipar Satra from 1732 and *Aadi Daxam* at Bengenaati monastery from 1804. The last illustrated work he could spot with a date was completed in 2013, *Chachitra Ankavali*, at Natun Kamalabari Satra in Majuli. Among other listings in that valuable book, he also catalogued seven important works representing the art form where the illustrations were most likely carried out at Majuli but are today preserved outside of the island. Among them was the *Chitra Bhagawat* found in Bali Satra. The others were the first book of Bhagavad Purana, presently lodged at the ghoruwa guxain-ghar (a prayer room in the house) of Sarada Prasad Borbora of Baruahgaon in Golaghat district; the eighth book of the *Bhagavad Purana* where the illustrations might be between 1683 and 1732, preserved at the Assam State Museum in Guwahati; and *Ananda Lahari*, preserved at the library of Kamrup Anusandhan Samiti in Guwahati. The paintings of *Ananda Lahari* are stated to be from around

1720–22. Chronologically placed after *Ananda Lahari* is a copy of *Gita Govinda*, also stocked in the Samiti's library. Kalita had deduced that its illustrations were created around 1713.[20]

The next important work is the *Bor Kirtan*, preserved at the Kathbapu monastery in Jorhat district. Also, the copy of *Bhakti Ratnavali*, currently at the Ratnavali Than of Kampur in Nagaon district.[21]

INFLUENCE OF JAIN SCHOOL OF ART

Moti Chandra, commenting on the illustrations of the Bali monastery's copy of the illustrated Bhagawat, had stated, 'The comparatively late date of the manuscript, however, does not detract the artistic and aesthetic merits of the illustrations.'[22] Painted in arched or zigzag panels against monochromed red or at times in blue, grey, or brown, the figures in the illustrations are somewhat angular; the eyes are usually fish-shaped, the eyebrows arched, the nose pointed, and the forehead sloping and wide while the waist is narrow. 'These conventions speak of ancient traditions…the dancing and the music scenes are full of charm and have been beautifully handled by the artist. In short, the lyrical draughtsmanship, simple composition, dramatic narration, and splendid colours give the Bhagavad illustrations a charm which distinguishes them from similar Bhagavad paintings from Udaipur and elsewhere.'[23]

Kalita had added that not just the fish-shaped eyes but also several other artistic components noted in not only the Bhagawat of Bali monastery but other illustrated texts of Assam too have Jain elements. Say, in the naked torso of men; the figures of men and women are drawn the same way and can be differentiated only by their attires. The Jain school of painting had influenced a large swathe of Indian paintings before the rise of the Mughal school anyway. The Jain era elements can be spotted in the Lodi era paintings too. 'Either directly or indirectly, the artistes of Vaishnava Satras did adopt the Jain elements. However, the Sattriya style illustrations were far more secular than the Jain style, though in Assam, they were also used for religious purpose.'[24]

Somiran Boruah, pointing particularly at the abstract illustrations of *Anadi Patan*, an eighteenth-century work preserved at Kuji Satra, had also underlined, 'This is quite unique in the sense that nowhere in India similar abstract visualisation is found except in the illustration of the Jain manuscript *Trailokya Dipika*, with which it shares some remote connection. Both these manuscripts deal with cosmology. But the illustrations of *Trailokya Dipika* are mostly mathematical drawings lacking any organic and visual quality. In contrast, the illustrations of *Anadi Patan* are quite organic and exceptionally rich in pictorial quality enabling them to stand independently without the aid of their intended signification.'[25] In the 1930s, Hemchandra Goswami had described *Anadi Patan* as a representation of the theory of creation as given in the Bhagavad Purana Book III and Baman Purana.[26] Though he mentioned that the original version was by Sankardev, Kalita has emphatically stated that so far there is no proof to claim it as so. It must be pointed out that the copy of *Anandi Patan* catalogued by Goswami in 1930 was created in 1686, over a century after the saint's demise. Kalita had also argued that since the Sattriya style of the art form was nurtured primarily at the monasteries through which the community's sense of aesthetics was imagined, that particular style should be recognized as the Assamese collective (jatio) art form.[27] Assam's royal/court style of the art form, according to Kalita, most likely moved away from the monasteries to add more regal ornamentation into it.

The Tai-Ahom style of illustration, mentioned above, is also essentially religious, practised by the Ahom Mohon, Deodhai, Bailung priests. Akin to the Sattriya style, the Tai-Ahom style, over time, too had fallen into dereliction. According to Pushpa Gogoi, a noted researcher on such illustrations, the art of writing and illustrating these treatises is currently prevalent only among the Buddhist monks. 'The tradition is still alive among the Tai language speaking Khamti, Aiton, Khamyong, Turung, Phake people. It is essentially centred around the Buddha vihars. Those practicing it presently buy paper from the market to scribble and draw on. The custom is more prevalent among the Khamtis of Arunachal Pradesh.'[28] He was of the view that the tradition had survived only because of the practice among the Theravadi Buddhists to create copies of religious texts and gift them to the Buddha vihars.

On looking closely at the Tai-Ahom style, it can be safely said that it is best represented by *Phung-chin*, an illustrated book written with round shaped letters similar to the letters of the Burmese script. Gogoi had pointed out that since the original text of that book was copied several times, it would not be easy to pinpoint which among the existing ones is the oldest specimen. 'The illustrations in it may go back to 14th–15th centuries. The name of the original scribe is not mentioned in any version; one comes across only the names of the copier. In reality, this book is the Tai translation of Theravadi Buddhist text written in Pali language or inspired by it.'[29]

In the later Ahom period, under royal patronage, books like the *Hasti-Vidarnava*, an illustrated text on types of elephants and their uses; *Ghora Nidhan*, a text on horses; and *Xenor Biyadhi*, a book on training hawks; were produced. Gogoi underlined, 'Those were not the only ones that the Ahom kings patronised. They patronised the Vaishnava monasteries in this regard too though arranging an accurate index of such books is difficult now.'[30]

If you go by Gogoi, there is not much difference between the Sattriya and the Tai-Ahom styles of illustrated books. 'The body of the human figures, the shape of their eyes and hands, the way the landscape was painted or the use of the lines is similar. Only the painter kept in mind certain religious norms.'[31] In the Tai-Ahom illustrations too, hand-made colours from local organic sources were used. The canvases were either treated tree barks, barks of roots, pressed cotton, palm leaves, etc.

While *Hasti-Vidarnava*, created at the behest of Siva Singha (1713–44), could be called the most remarkable example of secular illustrations of the Assamese school of painting patronized by Ahom kings, Maheswar Neog had also highlighted the extraordinary illustrations in the eighteenth century work *Darang Raja Vamsavali*, sponsored by the Darangi chief who ruled the area around present-day Mangaldoi.[32]

The folios of *Hasti-Vidarnava*, drawn by artists Dilbar and Dosai brought from North India by king Siva Singha, were also a documentation of how the Ahom kings held their royal court; the formation of the royal procession with elephants; the practice of falconry. 'The pictures were in water colours and a large number of them were gold-plated; they have beautifully preserved their colours and the lustre of the gold in spite of age and rough handling.'[33] Interestingly, *Hasti-Vidarnava* not only had portraits of Siva Singha, his wife Ambikadevi and the nobility of the times, but also that of the scribes Sukumar Barkath and Dilbar and Dosai, besides the portraits of eight rulers spread over eight quarters to convey that they too had heard the glory of the Ahom king. 'One of these rulers looks like a European. A Burmese king (Mantara) is also portrayed.'[34]

SAMADHANBAD: SOLVISM

Utilizing the play of elementary colours that have featured on the folios of old Assamese illustrated manuscripts, a clasp of artists and creative thinkers have organized themselves in Assam since 2016 to structure a rather novel train of thought and imagination. They have named their endeavour Samadhanbad (Solvism).

A conversation with the upholders of that stream of thought shows that they prefer looking at all things creative in ancient Kamrup solely based on the topography and immediate environment of Assam. It comes across that their primary aim is to break out of the colonial mindset in the Assamese creative space and view ancient practices and customs still extant within the larger community through a new lens. Guwahati-based writer Ashok Sarma, a promoter of Solvism, defined it for me in April 2021, 'As the name suggests, we, as creative people, make an effort to find an answer (samadhan or somidhan) to a mystery. We try to look for an answer or truth behind those mysteries within Assam's ecosystem, its topography and nature, in its ancient philosophy and beliefs, its understanding of astrology and science, in its creative work. That is our basis.'[35]

The father of Solvism was the late Tezpur-based artist and sculptor Lambodar Hazarika and his now deceased son and noted artist Anup Hazarika. Sarma, a friend of Anup, believes that the father–son duo had silently created a 'renaissance' of sorts by showing several people like him the path to look at things anew in Assam. He particularly mentioned to me one folio each from *Anadi Patan* and *Chitra Bhagawat* to present how Lambodar Hazarika tried to solve 'certain mysteries'. The followers of Solvism go by the belief that the illustrations of both *Anadi Patan* and the *Chitra Bhagawat* of Bali Satra were creations of Sankardev. 'In *Chitra Bhagawat*, there is a painting where the sun was coloured in black. We usually see sun in red, orange, or dark yellow. But Sankardev knowingly made it black because he drew the idea from source light. When the sun doesn't emit its reflection, it is black in colour. When the energy grows, the vacuum helps it to emanate colours. That's how we get the basic colour particles like red, blue, and white. Because of this colour separation we have concepts like some colours situated within some other colours, say, yellow is hidden in green,' said Sarma. The painting from a folio of *Anadi Patan* that he had pointed out was the *Xikha Danda Parbat* which featured eight figures, four drawn above and four below a line.

Offering an example of 'how it has always been possible to think things differently in Assam', Sarma spoke to me about a lamp designed by Lambodar Hazarika which could be lit in such a way that the flame didn't go upwards but towards the gravitational force. 'We tend to believe that the flame of the fire always goes up because the force of the buoyancy is far more than that of the gravitational force. But Hazarika, by designing that lamp, had proven to us that maintaining a certain balance in the universe can allow us to do things differently. He told us that in Kamrup, such things are possible, have always been practised by the people of the land by going against the tide and, therefore, it could give a lot to the world civilisation at one point in history.' At present, at least fifteen artists and writers are involved in promoting the new way of looking at the old, established by Lambodar Hazarika. 'Several paintings are also being drawn based on such ideas.'

While a range of Anup Hazarika's work can be spotted at Tholgiri, the Guwahati-based endeavour of entrepreneur Manorom Gogoi that aims to promote local goods and culture, a quick idea of the artistic acumen of the unsung artist Lambodar Hazarika can be had from an exquisite painting of a village scene in Assam preserved at the State Museum.

ASSAMESE MODERN ART

In early 2021, around the time Sarma had proffered the possibility of viewing Assamese art and aesthetic sensibilities from a fresh lens through Solvism, art critic and academic Moushumi Kandali was adding the finishing touches to a one-of-a-kind institutional endeavour in the field of modern art in Assam. An alumna of the fine arts department of M. S. University of Baroda and a faculty at the Department of Cultural Studies of Tezpur University, Kandali, aided by her able collaborators from the institution, was setting up within its premises a museum of the notable works of Assamese contemporary artist Neelpawan Baruah.

Named the Neelpawan Baruah Museum of Modern Art, it was being readied under the Centre with Potential for Excellence in Particular Area (2016–21), a special scheme awarded to the central university in 2016 with Kandali's department as the nodal agency to work on the theme 'Cultural Memory in North East India: A Research and Documentation Programme of Textual and Visual Narratives'. In all, the museum would permanently display fifty-six of Baruah's works. The endeavour was to hold up to the viewer a fair impression of the variety of the artist's oeuvre in terms of canvas, medium, and subjects.

Son of noted Assamese writer and poet Binanda Chandra Barua, Neelpawan's training in painting and glazed pottery began in Shantiniketan in 1966. That was also the era in Indian modern art where students at Shantiniketan's Kala Bhawan soaked in the creative vibe of the greats like Nandalal Bose; witnessed the work of key figures in contemporary modern painting and sculpture like Ramkinkar Baij. On returning to Assam in the late 1960s, Baruah, though, couldn't find the right environment to practice art. In 1968, he began teaching art at the Guwahati Art School, a private endeavour by self-taught artist Jibeswar Baruah started in 1947 which later became the Government College of Art and Craft. Kandali's curatorial note on Baruah described him as 'a romantic in search of a significant form' and part of the 'Early Moderns' of the Progressive Artists' Group of Bombay (PAG) even though his ideological and conceptual groundings had differed a lot from them. '[Baruah] seems to inherit the similar legacy, an urgent need to liberate oneself from the prevailing confusion and conformity of the local scenario. Of course, unlike the Early Moderns, Neelpawan Baruah would never reject the Indian aesthetical orientations, or his innate yearning to locate himself [in] his ethno-cultural environ, or his rootedness to the tradition, even if the tradition is imagined or constructed at times.'[36] Making his presence felt in Assam's contemporary art scenario since the 1970s, Baruah, hence, relentlessly engaged in conceptualizing, experimenting, and executing ways for blending the traditional/folk/indigenous elements with those of modern Western idioms and lingual expressions. An article published in the Guwahati-based magazine *Thumbprint* encapsulated him as an artist who 'explored many avenues, from poetry, painting, pottery, mask making (paper machie) etc., without getting stuck to any.... His bohemian approach helped him explore the if's and but's of Modernity, in a way that few in Assam had ever explored before.'[37]

Among several of Baruah's works that stood out were his artistic expressions through rarely used mediums like matchbox covers, cards, cigarette packets, and newspaper strips. It echoed his impulse to create art even within tiny spaces. He produced about 2,000 calligraphic figurations on old news prints reminiscent of Franz Klive, published in a book named *Basundhara*. 'Although one doubts if these have any politically reflexive agenda a la Hussein's *Splash Front Page* (1991) but this experiment is immensely significant in itself. These innovative attempts in the matchboxes, cigarette packets and newspapers speak about his fervent search for the endless possibilities of forms and designs, speaks in volume about an endeavour surcharged with a continual inquisitiveness for something novel and to transform anything, any everyday mundane object to an object d'art,' wrote

Kandali.[38] Guwahati-based Baruah who passed away in 2022, had once said, 'These messages are always around us; I have only added my colours to make them more apparent.'[39]

Eminent Assamese artist Noni Borpujari who had watched Baruah's artistic trajectory closely, told me in 2021, 'The sad part about Neel da was he remained confined to Assam; his works never got the recognition they deserved in mainstream Indian art world. Among his early works, what made me stop and stare was his series of sketches on Nepali paper (rice paper). I am not sure if they have been preserved. Several of his works have got lost due to lack of storage space and proper care.'[40]

Like Baruah, a handful of Assamese artists contemporary to him, and also trained at some of the top art schools of the country, began working in modern art in the 1960s–70s Assam, thereby succeeding, gradually, in formulating a small but striking fraternity within the state. That trend of learning art formally in institutions outside of the state was only an extension of what their seniors did in the colonial era. Akin to Bengal, the advent of the British in Assam also gave wind to Western cultural influences which triggered the replacement of old traditional artistic pursuits with an interest in the modern, including in art. The new colonial power established art schools in some parts of India to promote Western art but in eastern India, it didn't look beyond Kolkata. This forced a section of artistically inclined Assamese youth to sail to Kolkata around the second decade of the twentieth century to enrol in an art school for formal training. The first lot included Assamese youth Muktanath Bordoloi, Jagat Singh Kachari, Suren Bordoloi, and Pratap Baruah.[41] Though the exact years of their training in Kolkata is not known, veteran Assamese writer-poet and critic Nilomani Phookan once said that Suren Bordoloi was a contemporary of noted sculptor Devi Prasad Roy Choudhury (1899–1975), a student of Abanindranath Tagore who went on to become the founding chairman of Lalit Kala Akademi.[42]

Prior to that batch of formally trained Assamese artists, there was also Lakhiram Boruah from Mangaldoi in the then Darrang district, believed to be the first from the Northeast to have acquired a diploma in fine arts from the Government School of Art in Kolkata between 1914 and 1919. In 2019, forty-three of his paintings were exhibited for the first time at a private art gallery in Jorhat. One of the organizers of the show, artist and assistant professor of visual arts at Assam University (Silchar), Raj Kumar Mazinder, had then said that it is likely that greats of the times in Kolkata, like Abanindranath Tagore, Jamini Prakash, Lala Ishwari Prakash, and the school's principal Percy Brown, were Boruah's art teachers. 'He had lived at a time when the appreciation and value of art was wanting, especially in India. However, several of his earlier works have been bought by British and American people.' The paintings exhibited in 2019 were his work from the 1950s, '60s, and '70s and were 'an amalgam of Christian gospel and social values.'[43]

Those early Kolkata-trained artists can be termed the first practitioners of modern art in Assam. Since most began to paint from the 1930s onwards, one could safely assert that the era of modern art in Assam began in that period. Simultaneously, Assamese magazine *Abahan,* published in 1929, introduced Assamese readers to not just modern Indian art, its technique and philosophy but also the works of Assamese artists. It helped create an atmosphere, albeit limited, for modern art appreciation. In 2011, Kandali, in her enlightening book on Assamese modern art and its practitioners, *Axomor Adhunik Silpa Kala,* wrote, 'In that magazine, Sarbeswar Kataki wrote an article on Assamese old paintings and paved the way for research on art history. Aside from him, yet another art aficionado of the times was Jyoti Prasad Agarwala. In real terms, the publication of *Abahan* helped usher in the era of Assamese modern art.'[44]

Through the 1930s, '40s, and '50s, a posy of self-taught artists joined forces with those formally trained artists which included Jibeswar Baruah, the founder of the Guwahati Art School. Baruah later became the secretary of the Assam chapter of the Lalit Kala Akademi. Some other artists from those decades were Citrasen Barua, Ratneswar Barua, Tarini, Pragya Das, Hem Mahanta, Hemchandra Barua, Piyari Mohan Chaudhari, Chittaranjan Barua, Prakash Barua, Tarun Duwara, Sashisdar Saikia, Bishnu Prasad Rabha, Gajen Barua, Robin Bhattacharjee, Ashu Deb, and Hemanta Misra.[45] Amidst that lot were also some youth who had to leave their course midway in Kolkata due to their families' poor financial conditions.[46]

Though utterly limited and poorly preserved, some of the work of Assamese artists from the early period are on permanent display at the Assam State Museum in Guwahati. Works that can be viewed include Mukta Bordoloi's *Jakoi Suwali, Joymoti Sati,* and *Opium Eater*; Tarun Duwara's work on oil *Assamese Weavers*; *An Evening in a Mising Village* by Tarini; and Hemanta Misra's two works in oil. That not even a single painting of Bishnu Prasad Rava, otherwise celebrated as Kala-guru in Assam, has been preserved at the government-run museum may suggest a lack of commitment towards preserving Assamese modern art.

On looking at the subjects of the early practitioners of modern art in Assam, one can state that they tried replicating their immediate surroundings and realities. In an article written in 2015 for *Nezine*, Kandali had remarked, 'The artists of this early modernist phase were obsessed with certain definite range of thematic explorations, like that of scenes from the rural life of Assam—its collective social occasions, the scenic landscape of the lush green Brahmaputra Valley, and certain mythological (*Buddha and Sujata* by Citrasen Barua) and historical (*Sati Joymoti* by Muktanath Bordoloi) themes taken from literature. The language or artistic idioms could not go further than the limitations of academic realism or Renaissance like depictions with an underlying mood for a lyrical romanticism.'[47] She also pointed out something significant in that article—though the first batch of artists were trained in Bengal at a time when Bengal School of Art was at its peak, its influence could be traced only in one (Pratap Baruah) of them. 'In few works of Pratap Barua such as *In the Hat* (open bazaar) or *Joymotir Xasti* (Punishment of Sati Joimoti), the typical Ajantasque figure types of "Bengal School"—the slender–elongated–elegant bodies with dreamy eyes and the typical hazy landscape or the mysterious setting can be witnessed.'[48]

Barua's *Apples*, painted in 1930, was the first recorded example of still life in Assam's modern art. Muktanath Bordoloi was the first Assamese artist to absorb and assimilate the medium of oil with a Western perspective, utilizing chiaroscuro and creating an illusionistic rendering. 'It was in his (Bordoloi's) art that the element of social reflexivity and critical self-consciousness as modernist manifestation was evident for the first time. In his painting *Opium Eater* (1926), the modernist socialist concern is manifested through the depiction of the horrific reality of a social evil. Tarun Duwara's *Assamese Weaver*, a lyrical rendering capturing the mundane yet creative moments in the everyday life of Assamese women seemed to weave up the identity narrative in a very subtle manner.'[49] An artist who dabbled with art the way Duwara did was Kandarpa Sarma.[50]

In 1947 when Guwahati resident Jibeswar Barua decided to set up the Guwahati Art School in the Panbazar area of the city, it provided a much needed avenue for local art practitioners. Nine years later, in 1958, the convention of the Fourth Arts and Crafts Exhibition by Lalit Kala Akademi and the National Art and Craft Exhibition organized by the Art and Craft School of Assam in 1960 helped inspire a generation to look at art seriously.[51] Noted artist, the late Ashu Deb (1917–83), considered the first to have practised Western modern art in its true form, had taught at the Guwahati Art School.[52] Deb, born in Dhubri, would remain in Assam modern art chronicles as a distinguished name for being successful in expressing a new idiom through pointilism.[53]

'The artist was a realist. To pursue his path, he, instead of taking the romantic route, chose to chase the contours of *bindu* (dot or point). Through such a path, he was successful in creating an aerial view of an image. In an interview to noted Assamese writer Navakanta Barua, Deb had said, "There are no lines in nature, only shapes and that is why I break up outlines into dots."'[54] Be it his *The Wave, Portrait of a Tree, Santhal Virgin, The Harijan, The Contender, In the Cornfield, Harvesting, Looking for Fish, Stone Breaker, Crucial Month*, Deb's subjects were taken from nature and rural life. Commenting on his art, Kandali had remarked, 'The tonal quality of colours in his paintings is yet another speciality of the artist.'[55] According to her, the female images that featured in several of his paintings are an important visual documentation of local women's exquisiteness. His self-portrait too, unlike the usual variety, featured a woman. Deb also produced sculptures.

Born in the same year as Deb in Assam (in Sivasagar) was another trailblazer of Indian modern art: Hemanta Misra (1917–2009). Misra, who had moved to Kolkata to pursue art, was truly the first Assamese artist to have created a splash in the national arena. Significantly, he was invited to be a member of the exclusive Kolkata Group in the 1940s for his exceptional work along with top names of the times like Ramkinkar Baij, Abani Sen, Govardhan S., and Sunil Madhav Sen.[56] Misra's work was featured in India's first international Triennale on Contemporary World Art held in New Delhi in 1968.[57] Kandali who had travelled to Jadavpur in 2003 to meet the artist, wrote in an article on him in the Assamese magazine *Satsori* in 2009, 'Misra was not only the first Assamese artist to feature in a national exhibition organised by Lalit Kala Akademi but also the first among artists whose paintings got published in the Akademi's magazine. He was the first Assamese artist to exhibit his work outside of India. He was also the first from Assam whose work had found place in the permanent collection of the National Gallery of Modern Art, National Academy of Art, so also at Russia's Museum of Oriental Culture. His work and life has found a place in the *Dictionary of International Biography* (published by the International Biographical Centre in the UK)'[58]

In 1973, Kolkata's Birla Academy of Art and Culture, in a brochure published to coincide with its exhibition of his work, presented Misra's work thus: 'Misra's drawings showed the stamp of his uneasy and restless mind trying to force a way of expression which can be termed as violent. On the extraordinary strength of his drawings alone Misra was elected as a member of the Calcutta Group. The gleam of the promise in him justified this election.'[59] Kandali rightly pointed out that Misra's canvases ushered in a wave of anti-rationalism not just to the world of Assamese modern art but to Indian art in general.[60] 'His flights of fantasy are boundless. Yet the juxtaposed objects painted in luminous colours are placed in the atmosphere always carry with them a pictorial meaning of their own which is image-bound and poetry-oriented. Misra's application of colours for creating such an expression of surrealism is unique. His colours merge into the atmosphere without crying out for separate existence of their own. This abstracted harmony of colour plus the inner content of a mystic message build up his paintings to a fruitful meaning,' summed up the brochure.[61]

From the 1950s onwards, quite a few young Assamese men and women earned their degrees from Shantiniketan, J. J. School of Arts, Mumbai, M. S. University, Baroda, and the Lucknow Art College. 'Among them (from the 1950 through the 1990s), the names that come to my mind first are Ramesh Ghosh, Madan Lahkar, Shobha Brahma, Padum Borgohain, Neelpawan Baruah, Madhav Baishya, Pranab Baruah, Bhaskar Atul Baruah, Pranbendu Bikash Dhar, Saleha Ahmed, Sonaram Nath, Dilip Tamuly, Ajit Seel, Durlabh Bhattacharjee, the writer of this article (referring to himself), Rajen Hazarika, Paresh Saikia, Raj Kumar Mazindar,' noted Assamese artist from the 1970s Benu Misra wrote.[62]

A well-known name from this ilk from Assam, Shobha Brahma, not only painted but also made sculptures in mediums like wood. Brahma, after graduating from Cotton College in Guwahati in 1948, joined the fine arts department of Shantiniketan under its two leading lights, Nandalal Bose and Ramkinkar Baij. On returning home, he began searching for his own artistic vocabulary; researched the life of the state's plains tribes including his own, the Bodos; and succeeded in being inventive in his expressions. He began to be known for his stress on iconic and monumental figures. The images that he portrayed on the canvas were bigger in more ways than one, conveying something larger to the viewer, not just in shape and body but in concept too. To throw more light on Brahma's work, Kandali, in an essay had recounted the following incident during a discussion on his artistic trajectory held in 2002. A youth, pointing at a painting featuring a voluptuous woman, had asked Brahma if it was not a voyeuristic representation of the female figure. Kandali wrote, 'The bodily aspect of an image is the prime trait in Brahma's creations. He makes use of it to create his own idiom, to convey a certain thought. But in the first glance itself, like that youth did, it would be wrong to deduce it only as voyeurism.'[63] Calling for decontextualizing such an image, she said, 'In my opinion, the root of the bodily thrust in Brahma's art lies in the Indian visual art history. More than a western voyeuristic expression, it was hinged on Indian philosophy to which Brahma could amalgamate a flash of tribal beliefs and the ancient practice of fertility cult. In actuality, that image of the woman was that of an archetypal mother figure.'[64]

While several works of Brahma are worthy of a detailed account, Kandali, in that essay, had particularly focused on a painting he created in 1989 to drive home the point of how throughout his artistic course Brahma remained true to documenting tribal life, the land he was born in, the times, and his political convictions. Named after his village, *Bhumka* portrayed his artistic dissent against incidents of rape of Bodo women by the armed forces during the thick of insurgency then. Against the women's maimed and marred bodies, he placed a military boot. A little distance away sat huddled a group of people, still, voiceless. Referring to it, and to two other paintings of his, *Target* and *Gaze*, Kandali had stated that Brahma, through the images of the human body, had portrayed a political anatomy or tried to show them as a representation of a political battlefield. 'We can pluck more such examples from his works. But these three paintings themselves are a significant reference to his strident political conviction.'[65]

All the three paintings of Brahma preserved at the State Museum—*Bagurumba*, *Women Dancing*, and *Dakhana*—are fascinating too. The panel *Bagurumba* stands out for the typical play of colours we note in his canvases. Brahma's teaching tenure at the Government College of Art and Craft in Guwahati influenced a swathe of young artistic minds to walk on his path.

A worthy contemporary of Brahma was Benu Misra (1939–2009) who too went to Shantiniketan in the late 1950s; earned his stripes under the watch of Baij, and after a brief stint at Sir Jacob Sasoon School in Mumbai as an art teacher headed back to Assam after finding a job as an artist at the state government's directorate of Information and Public Relations (Janasanjog). Like Brahma, Misra too was a follower of the figurative strain of Indian modern art. On his canvas, one notices a glorious harmony of form and colour. The only painting of Misra preserved at the State Museum, *Bodo Weavers*, catches a visitor's eye not only for being a visual documentation of the entire process of weaving in a single canvas but also because of a bevy of beautifully drawn female figures whose expressive eyes give one a realistic experience of watching them at work. 'On his canvases, one finds a synthesis of the traditions of Indian visual art to the folk tenets of tribal life to western expressionist and surrealistic tones. Be it the thermocol (kuhila) craft of Assam's Gauripur area or Michelangelo's artistically playful style, Van Gogh's surrealism or J. W. M. Turner's picturesque and sublime depiction of colours, one finds Misra drawing his inspiration from all.'[66] Misra is also known to have contributed particularly to the aesthetics of designing the covers (betupat) of Assamese books.

Yet another of the pioneers that helped erect a firm foundation of Assamese modern art was Nagaon-based Pranab Baruah (1835–2002). He injected a modern outlook into traditional Indian art forms. His immortal painting, *Tejore Kamalapati*, little Krishna in deep slumber on the lines of Sankardev's Borgeet by the same title, reflects the influence of Indian miniature painting. Kandali had placed another one of his noteworthy paintings, *Bonxibadan Krishna*, in this category besides pointing out that he had incorporated aspects of miniature paintings in them, such as drawing the protagonist Krishna in a monumental form and stressing on sketching a profile figure and a flat surface.[67]

In the mid-twentieth century, the Mumbai-based Progressive Artists Group had famously brought to their canvases an eclectic set of styles which drew from Indian folk tradition as well as from Western Modernist practices.[68] In the paintings of M. F. Husain, F. N. Souza, S. K. Bakre, S. H. Raza, K. H. Ara, an amalgam of east and west could be spotted. Baruah, being a student of Mumbai's J. J. School of Arts in the 1960s, had adopted such a stimulus which reflected in his work.[69] Sadly, no work of this eminent artist can be found in the State Museum though his family is currently building a gallery in Nagaon to celebrate his artistic journey. Some other families of Assam's top artists have also preserved their work privately since the state's effort at doing so has been dismal.

Among the group of noted Assamese artists was also Gauri Barman (1936–2020). His sole painting at the State Museum, *Kaziranga*, is a window to his engagement with local subjects. While he did dip, and remarkably so, into such local themes, he was particularly known for his series on birds and boats. Interestingly, going against the tide, Barman's boats were motionless, often tied to the shore with ropes. 'One may wonder why his boats don't sail on the sea, don't ride on a wave. The artist himself had given an answer to it in his book *Subhaxit Sandhya* brought out in 2000. He said that at some point, those boats turn into birds.'[70] In other words, his Bird and Sail series fused to become an unbroken artistic mien. His last completed work in 2016, after his return from a trip to Dubai, also featured a boat.

Barman's images often show Expressionist and Cubist influence. 'We also spot Impressionist and Geometric effects on his canvases. He had drawn a painting of a woman or a hill which had turned into a woman with geometric lines. A brown hill with blue-green plains by it in symmetrical lines can remind a viewer about paintings of J. Swaminathan (1928–94).'[71]

Another name that can't be missed from the Assamese modern art scape is Pulak Gogoi. If Barman had his weakness for birds and boats, Gogoi's canvases had the quintessential horse, akin to that of Husain. Gogoi was manifestly inclined towards Formalism of which Husain was one of the topmost practitioners from the Bombay Progressive Group. Since Husain was influenced by Picasso, one could perhaps also say that Gogoi was too. 'I get a feeling that such an influence flowed on to him through Husain's work because Husain's adaptation of Picasso's artistic grammar was quite similar to that of Gogoi's. Though in the subsequent time, he moved beyond it to develop his own idiom.... The motifs in some of his paintings have bearings in Assam's illustrated paintings, ancient sculptures, Sattriya traditions or tribal life,' notes Kandali.[72] Gogoi's brush also documented the uncertain life lived in the state's char-chapori areas (sand bars) of the Brahmaputra, prone to the annual floods. Notably, Gogoi also gave a chromatic face to some notable songs of Bhupen Hazarika, say, 'Bimurto Mur Nixati' or 'Xagar Xongomot'. He was also one of Assam's top cartoonists and had started dabbling in video art later in life.[73]

Yet another artist whose work can be spotted at the State Museum is Prasenjit Duwara (1930–2003). The self-taught artist who promoted the concept of solo exhibitions in the state, was instrumental in the opening of the Assam State Art Gallery in 1976 at the Asam Sahitya Sabha complex in Guwahati.

Assam may have more painters than sculptors but some did make a mark in the field. One such name is Padum Gogoi. Sculptor Biren Singha must particularly be acknowledged for promoting public art by creating no less than 200 life-size sculptures that adorn Guwahati city and various parts of Assam and Arunachal Pradesh, including the sculpture of Ahom general Lachit Borphukan in the Brahmaputra waters by Guwahati and also the sculptures of singer Pratima Barua Pande in Chandmari and Bhupen Hazarika by the Dighalipukhuri lake in the capital city. The latter, a fibreglass sculpture, was inaugurated by Hazarika in 2009, making it perhaps the first statue to be inaugurated by the subject himself. That same year, Sinha also made a memorial in Chandmari for the 855 youth who had lost their lives during the Assam agitation. Born in 1951, Guwahati-based Singha is particularly known for his decades-long study and visual documentation of the state's Karbi and Dimasa communities. His statues of Rongpharpi Ringve, a woman Karbi warrior, and Chongbodhan Phanglosa, a Dimasa freedom fighter tortured by the British, are worthy of mention here. In the last few decades, there have also been quite a few sculptors in Assam showing promise through their work.

Noni Borpujari is another important Assamese artist who has made a significant mark in the state's modern art scene without any formal training. Having started in the 1970s with etched work in oil, he was in his seventies at the time of writing, and still going strong. He has experimented with printmaking, graphic art, video art, acrylic, on all sizes of canvases, rice paper, and much more. In early 2020, when I met up with him at his Guwahati home, he was still excitedly relating to me his experiment with new colours extracted from tea and betel vine.

Borpujari can be called the noted Assam-born artist B. C. Sanyal's discovery. In that conversation at his house, Borpujari had related to me his first meeting with Sanyal in Guwahati in 1979.

> Bhabesh da (Sanyal) had then come to visit his birth place. The Guwahati Artists Guild held an event to felicitate him. He was then not only the vice chairman of Lalit Kala Akademi in New Delhi but a very big name in Indian art. During that visit, he noticed my work on display at the Government-run art gallery, the only one then, at the Asam Sahitya Sabha building. He told me that I should exhibit in Delhi. I took his words very seriously and began working day and night. Within three months, I landed up at his office in Delhi with a couple of my paintings, little realising that one needs to finalise a space first for an exhibition in a big city like Delhi. Bhabesh da was surprised to see me; he wanted to help but there was no free gallery to exhibit my work. He then called up the owner of Little Theatre for help who turned the balcony of the auditorium into a gallery where I displayed my paintings. Bhabesh da and then Congress stalwart from Assam Devkant Barooah inaugurated the exhibition. I stayed on in Delhi because Bhabesh da asked me to.

After that exhibition, Sanyal enrolled him in the Akademi's Garhi Studio to work on printmaking. 'I had no formal training in it; didn't know how to take out prints. The top Delhi artists then held sway over Garhi Studio; I was a nobody. I was not even allowed to work in the shared space during daytime, pushing me to ask R.L. Barthelomow, the then secretary of the Akademi, to allow me to work at night. Reluctantly, he did. On those nights, I learnt how to make prints from a studio assistant named Puran, who was not an artist but had learnt after closely watching the printmakers. I call him my guru too.'

For about a year, he worked hard at Garhi. 'In 1981, when the Akademi had to choose work of artists for its annual national exhibition, none from Garhi got selected except three works of mine. Artists like Manjit Bawa's works were not selected. I was immediately noticed by all; fellow artistes on seeing my prints, asked when did I do my work; by then I had over 100 frames ready.'

In 1985, commenting on one of those print works from 1981—a close-up of a face in black with a pair of stark eyes, the eyeballs placed against the white sockets, looking sideways—Nilomani Phookan had expressed surprise that a group of printmakers, of which Borpujari was the leading light and untrained, came out of 'a place where till the other day there was no graphic machine, in a state where there is not yet a full-fledged art college, from within such a socio-cultural milieu.'[74] Borpujari had taken fifty prints of that image, some of which are in the permanent collections of museums worldwide.

Borpujari got his first lessons in art from Pranab Baruah in Nagaon. Baruah's contribution to art in Assam was also through a well-known art school, Kallol, in Nagaon. Borpujari related, 'In the initial period, I never used a brush to paint; I didn't have any. Baruah had taught me how to paint in oil without it. He had learnt the technique of etching with scalpel at J. J. School. Since he couldn't afford scalpels later, he began using a shaving blade. He taught me how to draw images in oil with blade. That is why, like Baruah, my early oil paintings were a bit raised from the canvas.' The artist called himself lucky to have been in Delhi during the early 1980s. 'That decade was the golden period of Indian art. All top practitioners were in Delhi. I not only got to see closely the work of Himmat Shah, Manjit Bawa, Kishen Khanna, etc. but also developed a friendship with them. I remember Shah inviting me and photographer Raghu Rai almost every day to share his *khichri* at his private studio at Garhi, which was then inside the National School of Drama on Copernicus Marg. I slept less, had little money but was having the best time creatively.'

Among Borpurjari's notable creations are his works in graphics, the Scarecrow series, and the Bandage series. 'While his Bandage series deals with the overwhelming universal theme of human suffering and misery, the other (Scarecrow series) stands out as remarkable due to its style of presentation of thoughts relating to human helplessness and dependence on nature,' wrote writer Tapati Baruah Kashyap.[75] In an interview published in Assamese newspaper *Ajir Asom* in January 2003, Borpujari said that when he as a young man was combating life without a steady income, he often drew death on his canvases; it was the reason behind the creation of the Death series. 'Then I began drawing scarecrows as a children's series as the mind began to settle down a bit. But when I saw starvation death in neighbouring Bangladesh and death of children in war-torn Africa, I returned to the *Death* series. During the students' agitation in Assam, I drew the *Bandage* series because several people didn't see what they should as if they have a bandage wrapped over their eyes. These days, I feel as if our base as a community is slipping away, so I am drawing anti-gravitational series.'[76]

Borpujari was also the first in Assam to use acrylic paints. 'I had gone to the US in 1983 to participate in an art workshop; saw artists there using acrylic. It came to India in 1984 but I brought it with me in 1983 and began working on it as it was so much easier than oil; it gave that sense of transparency, it was like using watercolours,' he related to me. The artist, however, prefers using only a few colours on his canvas; black being one (seen on many faces); shades of brown and red. 'Red is a colour I have weakness for,' he admitted. On the wall of his drawing room is hung a large canvas in acrylic off which a red face stares ahead. 'This was one of the paintings I did during the Assam agitation days,' he said.

WOMEN IN ASSAMESE MODERN ART

While sketching a pen picture of the foundation of Assamese modern art, the role of women artists must find place. Particularly so because in a patriarchal society like that of the Assamese, there was (is) certainly no level playing field. Several serious jabs at creativity were (are) often shrouded in personal struggle. Women who could overcome such barriers to pursue a career in art attracted less public attention for their work and thereby less opportunities than their male counterparts. For instance, Pushpa Das, whom

Nilomani Phookan had named the first Assamese woman artist, never got a chance to learn art professionally like her brother Pratap Baruah did.[77] Baruah was the first among the Assamese artists to have trained in Kolkata in the 1940s. All we have today from Pushpa Das's works is a painting preserved at the Tezpur Chitrakala Parishad.

There were rare exceptions though. In 1959, Pratap Baruah's contemporary and artist Suren Bordoloi's daughter Hemangini Bordoloi (1925–2007) was sent to Shantiniketan to train in fine arts. She returned home in 1963. Three of her contemporaries who too went to Kolkata for formal training in art were Morjina Begum, Sapala Baruah Bhuyan, and Malati Barua. Only Hemangini Bordoloi continued to pursue art on returning home. According to Kandali, 'Looking at the continuity of her trajectory, the quality and quantity of her work, the maturity of her thoughts and the deep sensibilities, one can call Hemangini Bordoloi truly the first Assamese woman artist.'[78]

Like Pushpa Das, Hemangini too was married off at an early age and went to Shantiniketan long after her marriage. That her father was a noted artist himself may have helped her case. After returning to Assam, she joined North Guwahati Government Girls' School as an art teacher and continued to teach there till her retirement in 1983. Post retirement, she opened an art school at her residence in North Guwahati and ran it till she passed away in 2007.[79]

Hemangini was also a noted practitioner of puppet craft. Because of her initiation at Kala Bhawan in Shantiniketan, she largely followed the Bengal School of art. What comes across strongly in her images is an attempt at visual documentation of historical events, say, her painting on Chinese traveller Hiuen Tsang engaged in a meeting with Kamrup king Bhaskarvarman; also paintings from her growing up days in Upper Assam. A series of her watercolour paintings had the reflection of North Guwahati by the Brahmaputra, a trend also spotted in the artworks of young artist Utpal Baruah. Her *Upagupta Aru Basabadatta*, painted in 1961, was inspired by Tagore's poem 'Obisar' from *Geetanjali*, suggesting a typical bent towards the Bengal School while choosing subjects.[80]

Through the 1960s one doesn't come across any important women artists in Assam, making one wonder what obstacles must have come in the way of budding female artists at the time. In the 1970s though, the tide turned and a clasp of women artists, trained at Shantiniketan, and in Mumbai, Baroda, etc., entered the art scene professionally in Assam. Among them were two women sculptors too: Hela Das (from M. S. University, Baroda) and Saleha Ahmed (from Shantiniketan). Ahmed trained under the likes of Ramkinkar Baij and Sarbari Raichoudhury, and their influence can be seen in her sculptures.[81] Hela Das (1944–2019) primarily worked on wood. *Immaculate Embrace* in mahogany, *Purity* and *Tea Lady* in sal, and *Saraswati* in teak are some of her most impressive works. Though Das's subjects often embraced women, towards the end though, she sculpted a figure showing men's relationship with fellow men.

Das, along with two other women artists—Parinita Bujarbaruah, trained in Shantiniketan, and Deepali Mahanta Kayal, a doctor by profession and an artist by passion—had formed a group to hold exhibitions of their work. The trio's last exhibition was *Manjari*, held in Nagaon in April 2019.

The 1970s onwards saw a great number of female artists engaging in a wide span of mediums, looking at a variety of subjects through a woman's gaze. That list includes Lungfa Akhtar, Zebin Rahman, Poonam Kalita, Meenakshi Borgohain, Monica Devi, Nibha Devi, Aditi Chakravarty, Syamoli Chaliha, Paranwanti Devi, Ripanjali Barua, Jaya Boro, Dipali Medhi, Dharamani Sarma, Arundhuti Goswami, Wahiha Ahmed, Tulirekha Debdhar, Rubi Bhuyan, Manisha Bora, and Upasana Bora.[82] Quantitatively and qualitatively, several women artists in Assam have continued to show promise since and have created impressive pieces of art. But there are still miles to go when it comes to showcasing novelty of artistic manifestation through newer mediums and the tenacity to cross more fences like some of their counterparts in other parts of the country have.

14

JATIOTABADI–RAJNITI: ASSAMESE POLITICS

On the morning of 15 August 1985, the common Assamese woke up to breaking news delivered by Prime Minister Rajiv Gandhi in his Independence Day speech from the Red Fort, broadcast by the All India Radio. Gandhi said that before the sun had risen that day, past midnight, in faraway New Delhi, his government had signed the Assam Accord with the representatives of the All Assam Students' Union (AASU) and All Assam Gana Sangram Parishad, a conglomeration of various civil society and political groups. Signing of the Accord meant curtains down on the six-year-long anti-foreigner agitation in the northeastern state and expectantly the prevailing volatile situation on the ground too.

The Accord signed by Assamese student and civil society leaders at the Prime Minister's official residence also meant the triumph of Assamese jatiotabad, or sub-nationalism, which had bound the community to the common cause of expelling all outsiders, rather all 'illegal immigrants', from their homeland. 'Foreigner Go Back!' was the slogan that had rung through every nook and cranny of Assam as part of that agitation led by AASU. People were asked to march on the streets with the call of 'Aah Oi Aah, Ulai Aah' (Come, Come Out). Thousands hit the road with raised fists. Over 800 youth who lost their lives in the agitation were declared 'sohid', martyrs, by the AASU in the fight to be recognized as first in the pecking order in the state by dint of being 'khilonjia' or the indigenous offsprings of the soil. Across Assam, sohid bedi or martyrs' columns, were erected with public money as a reminder of that combat with New Delhi.

Since before Independence, Assamese jatiotabad has been the crux of the community's politics, registering its first coup in 1947 when Assamese Congress stalwarts like Gopinath Bordoloi succeeded in thwarting the Muslim League leaders' plan to include Assam in East Pakistan during Partition. Only the jurisdiction of three and a half police stations of the Sylhet division of East Pakistan remained attached to Assam post Partition.

After Independence, from time to time, the dominant sub-nationalist strain surfaced to unite people as a common entity when it came to posing certain demands on New Delhi, say, to set up a university; create plants to refine the crude oil produced by the state and offer employment in the refineries to be delivered to the local population in the oil-rich state; express frustration at the Centre's 'stepmotherly' attitude during the Chinese aggression, etc. However, it reached the peak of its success only on 15 August 1985, with the signing of the Assam Accord. The Accord paved the way for not only the formation of a political entity hinged on jatiotabad—the Asom Gana Parishad (AGP)—but the Centre also facilitated it to grab the reins of the state. For the first time in Assam's political history, a regional entity sat on the saddle in 1985 by holding high the flag of jatiotabad. The victory chant of 'Joi Aai Axom' (Hail Mother Assam) rang through the skies of the northeastern state.

ASSAMESE JATIOTABAD: ITS FIRST SEEDS

To comprehend better Assamese jatiotabad and its trajectory as the primary political vein of the community, we must look at the first seeds of that sense of 'jati', or nationality formation, sowed in the Ahom and the Koch eras. The Ahoms ruled the wider Assamese community for the longest epoch in their political history. Chaolung Sukapha founded the Ahom kingdom in a part of Upper Assam in the thirteenth century which, in course of a few hundred years, brought under its sway several smaller principalities across the Brahmaputra Valley, as elaborated earlier in the book. Bringing under its governance a contiguous stretch of land also meant bringing under the Ahom administration a wide assortment of people. Gradually, the Ahoms succeeded in instilling the sense of a common nation on those people with the kings showing a tolerant path themselves by, say, entering into inter-marriages, and inducting people from all ethnic groups into vital social and political roles and in warfare. The titles handed out to people were as per the job assigned to them by the Ahom administration and never on caste, a norm prevalent in mainland India then. By and by, through such public outreach, the Ahoms could inculcate a sentiment for a common jati within the wider Assamese community. The prevailing Assamese language, a lingua franca of the region, was also adopted by the rulers without imposing their own, thereby helping in sowing the first seeds of linguistic commonality and affinity as the harbinger of a common nationality. In *India's North East: Identity Movements, State, and Civil Society*, academic Udayon Misra concluded 'that the idea of a composite Assamese *jati* or nationality took shape during the later part of the Ahom rule. This process which started during the reign of the Ahom king Suhungmung (1497–1539), when the Kachari and the Chutiya (Sutia) kingdoms were occupied, was further consolidated during the Muslim invasions from neighbouring Bengal in the first half of the sixteenth century (1532–33) when the people were brought under an Ahom or Assamese banner against the common enemy.'[1] During later Ahom king Pratap Singha's rule (1603–41), a further consolidation had taken place, again due to the subsequent Muslim incursions.

Alongside, Saint Sankardev, in the fifteenth–sixteenth centuries, attracted people from different ethnic groups to envelop them under the common umbrella of his Ek Sarana Nama Dharma, essentially laying for them an egalitarian path to reach the almighty by circumventing the rigidity and exclusionary tenets of Brahmanical Hinduism. This also aided in cloaking the sense of jati in the community with a tolerant and inclusive approach. Sankardev's dharma could charm not just the tribes but Assamese Muslims too. 'The neo-Vaishnava movement was largely responsible for bringing within the broader Assamese fold many of the tribal nationalities. The democratic content of the movement which popularised a monotheistic cult of bhakti and a congregational form of worship devoid of expensive rituals and which stressed the salvation of all, irrespective of birth, attracted large segments of tribal population to its fold.'[2] Though eminent writer on Assam, Amalendu Guha, had called Sankardev's Neo-Vaishnavism 'essentially a feudal ideology that was helping to detribalise a society in transition',[3] his contemporary and noted public intellectual Hiren Gohain suggested that by attracting these communities to be part of the wider Assamese fold, Sankardev had truly laid 'the foundation of the modern Assamese nationality'.[4]

In Assamese, Gohain had written somewhat to this effect, 'although the Mahapurusiya religious movement was indebted in some form or the other to the tribal, Ahom, Koch, Brahmin, and other communities, yet there is no doubt that its contribution to the process of the growth of Assamese life and culture was both original and great. By contributing to the material, intellectual, and emotional this movement helped in the growth of intimate bonds between the different segments of Assamese society. Hence, even those who are not Mahapurisia by faith do feel that in the context of their Assamese identity as revealed by their speech, behaviour, thought-pattern, and values, there is a very great influence of the Mahapurisia movement.'[5]

Gohain's observation helps us recognize the fact that the Assamese community is a unique composition of tribal and non-tribal folds, unlike most Indian communities today. Here, is it worth noting that when the Ahoms went after Sankardev, it was Koch king Naranarayan who along with his brother Cilarai gave him shelter in Cooch Behar, and thereby helped him continue his work. The duo, through their conquest, also consolidated the Koch kingdom, thereby also giving a large swathe of people the idea of one composition, a jati.

ASSAMESE JATIOTABAD IN BRITISH ERA

While these historical strains have had their pull on the community, the binding force of jati, principally Assamese jatiotabad, further developed its firm contours during the British colonial era, in the early-twentieth century. While the sense of jati in the Assamese prior to the colonial control of Assam was founded from a position of power, the consolidation of the community's jatiotabad during the British era stemmed from a sense of loss—of native culture, language, territory, identity, and opportunities—in their homeland.

The English sahibs began administrating the Assamese by imposing on them the Bengali language, which made the community outrightly view the language also as a tool of their subjugation. What contributed to the dissonance was also that the colonial masters brought in English-educated Bengali babus to run the administration. Most such officials came with an air of superiority, backed by a renewed pride in their community triggered by the Bengal Renaissance. The educated Bengalis were keen to preserve their language which became an official language in the Bengal Province after 200 years of the hegemony of Persian imposed on them by the Muslim rulers. The British continued with Persian for a long while before replacing it with the tongue of the commoners, Bengali, in the early nineteenth century.

In Assam, the imposition of the Bengali language for thirty-six years (1836–72) wasn't restricted only to its official use and usage in school education. Bengali culture and literature began to take over the native culture, as described earlier in the book. While the Assamese were learning Bengali and English to corner a government job in their own state, such a necessity also created considerable resentment in a large swathe of people not just against the British but also towards the Brown sahibs brought from Kolkata who were controlling the administration of the state. Those days, Assamese youth had to travel to Calcutta (Kolkata) on steamers for days together to receive higher education. The newly educated Assamese youth, between the late nineteenth and early twentieth centuries, had to eventually fight not just to reclaim and re-establish their language in their homeland but also demand their political rights as separate people through the platform of a nascent Congress, set up in the state in 1921. By 1872, they succeeded in removing Bengali as the official language of the Brahmaputra Valley in British-held India. A few decades thereafter were needed to publish enough reading material in Assamese to completely remove Bengali from schools. The division of Bengal in 1905 led Assam to be attached to Bengali-dominated Dacca as its capital but this didn't quite take away the influence of the language on the Assamese. Thereafter, with the Bengali-dominated Sylhet division remaining an arm of Assam Province till 1947, the Bengali community continued to corner government jobs, and the fear of the community's hegemony over the Assamese remained.

After Independence, the see-saw of power shifted between the two communities intermittently; both using their respective languages as their battle tool. Unlike in the colonial era, post 1947, the reins of the state were truly handed to the Assamese community after over a hundred years; Assamese Congress leaders became the state's chief ministers one after the other. The tables had clearly turned. Assamese political leaders, fenced by the old fear of losing their hegemony in the state, went ahead and declared Assamese the state language while the states were being divided across India in terms of language from the late 1950s onwards. In the early 1960s, that move led to a watershed moment in Assam, with the Bengali dominated Barak Valley hitting the streets demanding that Bengali be made the official language in that portion of the state. Tensions between the two communities rose to a fever pitch with lives lost on both sides. While a Partition-bruised Bengali community of the Barak Valley fought hard to keep their language in that area as a mark of their identity and as a reminder of the loss of a large swathe of their homeland to East Pakistan, the Assamese, equally bruised by the hegemony of the Bengali community and their language over them during the colonial era, stood up to the challenge, this time from a position of power. Both the communities became prisoners of history and tailored mass agitations with differing demands, putting pressure on their respective political leaderships to give in. While the ruling Congress leadership in Assam was all for Assamese, the Barak-based Bengalis took the help of West Bengal Congress leaders and those from the community at the helm of affairs in New Delhi to ensure that their demand was not overlooked. Ultimately, both the communities prevailed. While Assamese became the official language of the Brahmaputra Valley, Bengali was declared the language of the Barak Valley bordering what is now Bangladesh. Since then though, a disquiet has existed between the two communities dominant in the two valleys of Assam and has manifested itself in their politics. This includes opposition to the Assam agitation of the 1980s hinged on linguistic identity by the Bengalis of Barak; so also to the Accord which stated that those who had entered Assam between 1 January 1961 to 25 March 1971 would lose their right to vote for ten years before they became regularized citizens. An exclusive clause was inserted into the Citizenship Act by the Centre to reflect that change. The ugliness of the festering linguistic fight between the two communities raised its head as recently as during the Narendra Modi government's move to include Assam within the purview of the Citizenship Amendment Act (CAA) in December 2019, whereby Bengali Hindus who had moved through the open international border into Assam after the formation of Bangladesh in 1971 were to be granted Indian citizenship. Once again, the 'fear' of the Assamese language losing its primacy in Assam due to a surge in the population of Bengali speakers, facilitated by the CAA, began to grip the Assamese community, kicking in a strong sense of jatiotabad, leading many to raise slogans, triggering violence, state action, and loss of life. Though the Centre formed a committee to grant the Assamese community some rights over their land and language to appease them and get them to agree to the CAA, not much had moved at the time of writing this book.

However, prior to such developments occurring in the twenty-first century, much had happened in the last half of the twentieth century, particularly during the two AGP regimes (1985–90 and 1996–2001) which made Assamese jatiotabad a hegemonic force over other ethnic languages prevalent in the state, so much so that today each ethnic tribe is stressing their political identity through their language. The Bodos were the first to raise the flag, ultimately leading the Bodo language to be listed as a recognized regional language in the Constitution in 2003. Today, it is an official language in the Bodo Territorial Council areas in western Assam and also given the status of an associate language by the state government. What is noteworthy here is also the domino effect seen in the assertion of one community's identity through language on another throughout eastern India. Aided by the invention of the printing press in the colonial era, the creation of linguistic identities could be seen unfolding in West

Bengal first which cascaded into the Assamese psyche as Bengali linguistic hegemony. Educated Assamese youth opposed that hegemony by using the same tools of the printing press and the Assamese language as a medium to establish a distinct identity for the community. It was also the result of self-realization of the community politically.

In the years post Independence, the Assamese linguistic hegemony over other smaller ethnic communities of the state also ignited their own identity movements with their respective languages as the primary apparatus. Political awareness within these groups also played a role in that assertion. Today, though most ethnic tribes culturally come together as a wider Assamese community, politically they tend to assert their rights as distinct from the non-tribal Assamese. The driving force behind such a political assertion is seen in most social groups across the Northeast, also because of the fear of the other, the 'outsider', the one outside the immediate pale of their community. This fear is hinged on a singular factor—their smaller number in terms of population, and thereby the possibility of losing political heft in their own homeland. Even though a certain community may be termed a 'majority' in a northeastern state, that 'majority' community also has a smaller population when compared to the 'majority' communities in other Indian states, and thereby a strong insecurity festers in them which finds expression from time to time as the fear of the 'other' who is set to seize their land and opportunities, and thereby their distinctive identities and cultures and precipitating an erasure of their histories. The anti-foreigner agitation led by the Assamese community is an acute example of this phenomenon.

ASSAMESE INSURGENCY

A dark chapter in the political history of the Assamese community is also an armed struggle by a large section of youth to secede from the Indian Union in the 1990s, a move that too was fuelled by jatiotabad. The insurgent outfit leading that struggle, the United Liberation Front of Asom (ULFA), was born of a decades-long sentiment within the majority community that their rights as the sons of the soil were being ignored by New Delhi in the interest of the 'outsiders'. Here, a little explaining of the concept of jatiotabad would help. While seen from the lens of Indian nationalism, Assamese jatiotabad can be termed sub-nationalism, like it exists in several communities across the country in some form or the other but when seen independently of it, Assamese jatiotabad can also mean somewhat of a nation-state. While one section looks at it as self-rule within the Indian state, thereby handing over the larger subjects like defence, foreign affairs, currency, etc. to New Delhi, the outfits like ULFA also included in the concept of jatiotabad the idea of sovereignty, and thereby a free nation-state. The sovereignty issue was hinged on the argument that since the British took control of Ahom-ruled Assam from the Burmese in 1826 through the Treaty of Yandaboo, on their leaving the state, it must first then be returned to the rightful owners, thereby negating the role of the new country born of Independence, India.

The tipping point for a section of this group was the signing of the Assam Accord. That lot felt the Centre handed down to the AASU a watered-down version of a peace agreement, particularly for putting in place in the agreement an exclusive cut-off date for citizenship in Assam—25 March 1971—unlike other states even in the Northeast. The cut-off date for citizenship in the rest of India was 1949, as per Article 6 of the Constitution. Such a step by the central government in Assam was certainly to accommodate refugees, mostly Bengali Hindus who fled East Pakistan during the movement for creation of Bangladesh. That 'foreigners' were given a better deal at the cost of the 'Khilonjia' population pushed a set of people within the community to jump into an armed struggle to set things right. Young boys from both rural and urban areas, from well-to-do and poor families, joined the underground movement. Batches after batches of youth took to an arduous path to reach Kachin in Myanmar for arms training to be able to take on the Indian security forces. In some time, ULFA became a force to be feared.

The advent of insurgency in Assam in the 1990s also meant the arrival of the military. The Centre felt that the home minister of the first AGP government, Bhrigu Kumar Phukan, was supportive of the armed struggle and so the Chandra Shekhar government decided to dismiss the state government months before its term ended; President's Rule was imposed on Assam. Immense power was granted to the security forces operating in the state under the draconian Armed Forces (Special Powers) Act (AFSPA) to fight the ULFA leadership. Several cases of human rights violations against common people by the army were documented by civil society groups from Assam like Manab Adhikar Sangram Samiti (MASS) and those from outside the state like the Committee for Protection of Demorcatic Rights even as the security forces carried out operations (Bajrang and Rhino) to flush out militants.[6] Several were killed, arrested; many fled to neighbouring Bhutan and Bangladesh. While some leaders were later nabbed with help from Bangladeshi authorities, the ULFA camps set up in Bhutan not far from the Assam border were also subsequently levelled by the Bhutanese authorities, thus pushing the outfit to move base to Bangladesh. The military action under operations Bajrang and Rhino also steered several cadres and their unit commanders towards surrendering their arms militancy; that lot began to be locally known as SULFA (Surrendered ULFA). Since 2008, a section of the ULFA leaders have been roped in for talks with the central government to arrive at a peace accord, while one faction led by Paresh Baruah has refused to join the parleys since the Centre has not given a nod to a discussion on Assam's 'sovereignty'.[7] The formal talks with the pro-talks faction of the ULFA began in 2011.[8]

The firm stance taken by the Baruah faction (ULFA-Independent) on the need to discuss sovereignty is hinged on the outfit's original argument that the British usurped Assam not from the Assamese but from the invading Burmese forces as part of the Treaty of Yandabo of 1826 and therefore, once the British had left Assam, India should have returned Assam to the Assamese and negotiated the terms for political co-living. In other words, that faction also looks at India as a colonizing force intent on exploiting only its valuable resources like tea, timber, coal, and oil without taking the welfare and interests of the native population into cognizance. That the native Assamese couldn't generate within itself a thriving business community after 1947, and the Marwari traders brought by the colonial rule continued their stranglehold on the state's economy, also helped aggravate matters. Marwari traders and businesspeople were targeted by the ULFA; several lost their lives at the hands of the militants, forcing many among them to shift base outside of the state in the 1990s.

SHIFTING PARADIGM OF ASSAMESE JATIOTABAD

The ugly face-off between the state and the non-state actors in Assam during the 1990s continued even though AGP seized power once again in May 1996, from Congress. Extra-judicial killings of ULFA cadres and their family members, termed 'secret killings' in Assam—allegedly at the behest of the state government—were noted during the five-year-term of the Prafulla Kumar Mahanta government.[9] With ULFA cadres also unleashing violence on common citizens, more and more Assamese began to feel not just disenchanted with the outfit and the insurgency but also with the jatiotabadi political forces like the AGP for failing in governance and indulging in alleged corruption. There came a time when a common Assamese began fearing both the state and non-state actors. The late 1990s were the dark days when none would venture out of their homes post sundown.

In the 2001 assembly polls, people's sentiments against the AGP government came to the fore. In came Congress under the leadership of Tarun Gogoi. Gogoi, an astute politician, knew that to perpetuate his rule in the state, he would have to accommodate Assamese jatiotabad in his politics even as a Congress leader. Steering that strategy forward to keep his government intact, he tied up with a regional party of the Bodos, the Bodo People's Front (BPF), instead of seeking support to form his government from the All India United Democratic Front (AIUDF), formed by an Assam-based Islamic preacher Maulana Badaruddin Ajmal. AIUDF, the first political party in the country to be backed by the Jamaat-e-Islami, is essentially a formation set up in 2005 backed by the Muslims of East Bengal origin to augment their voice in the fragmented political space of the state. The community had borne the brunt of the horrific Nellie riots of February 1983, administered by the agitation supporters on 'illegal immigrants' for their refusal to boycott the 1983 parliamentary elections called by the Indira Gandhi government.[10] That election was boycotted by the AASU demanding that the state's electoral rolls be revised and names of 'illegal immigrants' be weeded out before the voting took place. The demand was not entertained, unleashing violence across the state; the first 'sohid' of the anti-foreigner agitation, Khorgeswar Talukdar, lost his life during that election.

Going back to the question of Muslims of East Bengal origin, it needs a mention here that in the run-up to Independence, a majority of them who settled in British Assam were mobilized by Muslim League leaders to back the idea of Assam joining East Pakistan. After 1947 though, to avoid migration once again, and instead to assimilate themselves into the dominant Assamese society, the community discarded the Bengali language officially and declared Assamese as their language in the Census. This resulted in a sudden surge in the percentage of Assamese speakers in the state. That tactical move led by the community's leaders helped Assamese remain the most spoken language in the state as per Census data. Immediately after Emergency, with the rise of the Janata Party and Jan Sangh in Assam, many within the opposition began slotting the community, though, only as a 'vote bank' of the Congress. The idea was also to weaken the roots of the otherwise well-entrenched Congress within the majority Assamese community. The idea caught on which gradually led to the birth of the anti-foreigner agitation in Assam between end-1979 and mid-1985. The first Janata Party chief minister in Assam, Golap Borbora (1978–79) whose government helped fuel the agitation[11] riding on the local sentiments of the Assamese being swamped by 'outsiders', however, included not just the Muslims and Hindus of East Bengal/Bangladesh origin in that bracket but also the Nepalis residing in the state. Several Nepalis had entered the North East Frontier Province (NEFA) attached to Assam, now the state of Arunachal Pradesh, mostly to work as labourers in the construction of roads after the Chinese debacle in the 1960s. Since NEFA was a protected area and Inner Line Permit was in force, many Nepali labourers later settled down in Assam. In the 1980s, some crossed the border from Bhutan too when the community was persecuted in that country that borders Assam.

If we cut to the time of Tarun Gogoi's chief ministership, by the time his three terms ended in 2016, Assamese jatiotabad had taken another leap. A considerable part of jatiotabadi civil society forces, with tacit support from the AGP, now long out of power, and also the BJP, which has been trying to topple the Congress from power across the country, began pushing the bogey of the need to update the National Register of Citizens (NRC) put together in 1951 by the central government. The demand was raised to be able to officially identify 'illegal immigrants' residing in the state and thereby remove their names from the state's electoral rolls. In 1951, the NRC was created with the aim of thwarting any possible attempts by Pakistani forces infiltrating into Assam through an open border. An outcome of that move was also the creation of a border police unit in Assam to identify infiltrators. In the subsequent times, that line of thinking also led to the formation of foreigners' tribunals in the border state to stem the flow of people coming in from across the international border without documents.

The demand of the jatiotabadi forces to update the NRC in Assam was put before the Supreme Court which agreed to monitor the process. Looking at that development as an opportune time, the BJP and the AGP began flogging the 1970s narrative about Congress that if it returned to power it would likely back only the 'outsiders' as they had been its vote bank in the state. By the mid-2000s, factors like the formation of the AIUDF as a political force of the 'Miyas', the local pejorative used for Muslims of East Bengal/Bangladeshi origin; rise of Islamic fundamentalist forces in neighbouring Bangladesh; a spurt in Muslim population in some districts of Assam; etc., helped create the image of an 'illegal immigrant' in the Assamese as a skull-cap wearing, lungi-clad Bengali-speaking Muslim set to outnumber the majority community as part of a conspiracy to grab political power in the state. This also helped the BJP to push the bogey of religion into the sphere of Assamese jatiotabad as a popular consciousness. Former AASU president Sarbananda Sonowal who had defected from the AGP to the BJP some years ago, was projected as the BJP's chief ministerial candidate in the 2016 assembly elections to counter Tarun Gogoi and Congress. Sonowal, for successfully challenging the Indira Gandhi regime's Illegal Immigrant (Determination) Act, 1983 in the Supreme Court as an AASU leader, was termed by the community as 'Jatiyo Nayak', a hero. IMDT Act had put the onus on the complainant to prove that a person had illegally entered Assam from Bangladesh. That Sonowal was handpicked by the BJP to open its account in Assam was to make sure that Assamese jatiotabad must be roped in to command an electoral victory. The BJP promised to the community to protect their 'Jati Mati Bheti' (Community, Land, and Identity).[12] The result was an astounding success.

CONCLUSION

What has been decribed above happened in the 2022 assembly elections as well. Through political manoeuvring, Assamese jatiotabad has been suspended on hope, anyway, since 2014 onwards when the BJP first tried to oust the Congress at the Centre. The party's prime ministerial candidate, Narendra Modi, had promised during his campaign that once he sat on the saddle, the 'illegal Bangladeshis' would have to leave Assam 'bags and baggage'.[13] That hope about the Centre packing off the 'illegal' immigrants to Bangladesh endured when in 2016 the BJP came to power in the state.

In 2019, though the NRC was updated when the central and state governments were led by the BJP, that only 19 lakh people were kept out of it for want of proper documents made the AASU doubt the process. Since most among those left out of the updated NRC belonged to the Bengali Hindu community, it helped the ruling party, though, to successfully push a narrative that the updated NRC was faulty only because most Muslims of East Bengal origin found place in it, allegedly through forged documents.[14] Though massive protests were seen across Assam against the Citizenship Amendment Bill (CAB), which, in violation of the Assam Accord, would grant Indian citizenship to Hindu Bangladeshis residing in the state, the Centre was quick to form a committee to implement the principal clause of the Assam Accord by involving the AASU. In other words, it helped the government find a handle to be able to pass in Parliament the bill in December 2019.

What needs underlining here is that positioning by political forces on religious lines clearly feeds on not just the fear of the Assamese losing their primacy in their own state politically but also steer jatiotabad away from being a secular entity to a religious one, or rather anti-Muslim. The political benefit of such a veering has since been reaped by the BJP and the AGP in Assam including in the 2022 assembly elections. Prior to that state election, two political entities that hinged on jatiotabad without a religious tinge were formed: Asom Jatiyo Parishad (AJP) and Raijor Dal (People's Party). These parties were clearly born of the anti-CAB (CAA) movement in Assam. Though they fought the elections, only Raijor Dal was able to send an MLA to the state assembly.

At the same time, there has been a simultaneous growth in influence of the AIUDF within the Muslim community of East Bengal origin, particularly in the course of the 2022 assembly polls. Post polls, as many as thirty-one Muslim MLAs entered the state assembly, a fact that had not gone unnoticed by the majority Assamese community in a politically divided environment. Most of those MLAs are of East Bengali origin. In that election, the Congress, for the first time, merged its secular space with a party like AIUDF which occupies the communal arena. While it benefitted the AIUDF by transferring all Muslim votes to it because of its seat sharing arrangement with the Congress, the biggest loser in terms of political optics in Assam became the Congress. The majority Assamese community saw the Congress as a 'pro-Miya' party during the assembly polls, unlike during the times of Tarun Gogoi. That Congress gave the licence to the Jamaat-backed AIUDF to merge the secular and the communal political spaces in the state, in turn, helped the BJP and the AGP to extend its footprint in Assam.

With the communal divide widening in Assam, it is imperative perhaps that more and more common people in the state realize that these are concerted attempts by communal forces on both sides to manipulate the trajectory of the ethos of all stakeholders. The Assamese community, particularly, will have to ask itself if it can allow any political/communal entity to decide the definition of who is an Assamese and what should the complexion of their sub-nationalism be. Since history can also teach us lessons, it is time that the stakeholders flip through the pages of the past to take back the reins. Today, the challenge before all in Assam is to protect their secular and egalitarian heritage which the torchbearers of the community had, through various epochs, done, both culturally and politically. The hope lies in more and more people realizing that communal forces on both sides of the divide are pummelling the very core of the wider Assamese community—its assimilative and absorptive nature, of which the Bard of the Brahmaputra, Bhupen Hazarika, had reminded the common Assamese through his memorable song 'Mahabahu Brahmaputra' with which I begin this portrait of the community.

Perhaps it would then be appropriate to end this book with what yet another hero of the community, Rupkonwar Jyoti Prasad Agarwala had documented in his legendary poem 'Asamiya Dekar Ukti' (Response of an Assamese Youth). Though written much before four states were carved out of Assam, this creation of Agarwala, nevertheless, sprung out of the Assamese community's egalitarian ethos that encompasses one and all without taking religious beliefs into cognizance:

I am Khasi
I am Jaintia, the Dophola, Abor, Aka
I am the Singpho, the Miri (Mising) of the plains,
The youth of the Subansiri
I will be the victor; I am of the Kachari,
The Koch, Mech, the Rajbonshi, the Rabha,
I am the Lalung (Tiwa), Sutia, Lushai (Mizo), Mikhir (Karbi), Garo,
Mishimi, Khamti, the Angami hero
I fight for equality and friendship
I am the one who labours in the tea garden
The Na-Asamiya, the new Assamese
The Mymensinghia
The village of Nepali
The skilled dancer of the Manipuri
Of so many hills and plains,
Of the waters of a hundred streams
I flow, taking all in my path
To be one with the Brahmaputra.[15]

APPENDIX

MOTAMOT: VOICES

Assam is rare for being a state in India where a central government instituted a 'high powered committee' in 2019 to define who the 'Assamese people' are.* Hardly any other community in independent India's history has undergone a similar intervention at a governmental level. It is worth repeating here then that the government-driven endeavour has also suggested that the Assamese identity construct is yet to seal its confines, officially.

That would mean the question—who is an Axomiya or Assamese, or, who is a khilonjia, indigenous, in Assam—has remained relevant to the state's sociopolitical milieu. Several Assamese intellectuals over time have also dealt with the subject. This is because, aside from the recent government exercise, what is key is also the thinking and understanding of the stakeholders—the residents of Assam—on these enquiries. It is still relevant to ask then, what is the impression one acquires from the wider Assamese society on the prickly matter?

In this appendix to the book, I have, therefore, trussed up a posy of voices, a multiplicity of opinions, from an array of people hailing from various ethnic groups that reside in Assam and who also consider the state as their home, to deal with the question that weighs heavy with the load of Assam's complicated history. Most of the interviewees are associated with public life in some form, and have either already engaged with that question or have shown their willingness to do so and this is why they have been picked for this space. The names are in no way exhaustive but only a sample to get an impression of what is the common understanding of the Assamese identity within the wider society that exists in the state today.

The latitude of this chapter also covers a stretch where several of them examine their own placement within the expanse of the identity question which has been so raw, palpable, and, at times, limiting and discordant in the state. While unpacking their response to who they define as an Assamese, each comes across as a distinctive voice responding in their own way and

---

*'Home Ministry Constitutes a "High Level" Committee on Clause 6 of Assam accord', *The Wire*, 18 July 2019.

manner of understanding of the society they are a part of. It is not to offend one section or the other.

The aim of this exercise is not just to give a fair idea to the reader about the general taxonomy of 'Assamese people' from a collective point of view but also a tapestry of life lived in Assam, then and now.

HOMEN BORGOHAIN†

Prominent Assamese intellectual, Sahitya Akademi Awarded writer, editor-columnist

Who, according to you, is an Assamese?

Who is an Assamese is a question I have asked myself too. Engaging with the question may not have been necessitated so much at a personal level but because I have been in the public arena for a long time, and also served once as the president of Asam Sahitya Sabha—the fulcrum of Assamese language, literature, and therefore the identity—I couldn't have afforded not to.

To contextualize what I want to say, I would like to relate here a speech I had delivered in 2002. It has been a tradition of the Sahitya Sabha for the outgoing president to hoist the organization's flag at its annual session and deliver a speech to the august gathering. In 2002, the annual session was in Lakhimpur and I was the outgoing president. It was the time when the question...was beginning to raise head in the state once again. So, I chose to speak about it to the congregation.

In that speech, I gave the example of several Indian and Pakistani origin persons occupying important positions, as Americans or British today. ... Do those people identify themselves only as Indians and Pakistanis, or as Americans and British citizens, which is their adopted country and national identity? I underlined that people of such origin have continued to hold prominent positions in those countries. Just to give a few recent examples, the former London mayor Sadiq Khan is of Pakistani origin but is British. The United Kingdom's home secretary Priti Patel is of Indian origin but very much British....

Once, I interviewed in my Assamese TV chat show *Kotha Barta* a person who was born in a well-known Assamese family but became an American

†The interview with Homen Borgohain was recorded at the office of the Assamese daily, *Niyomia Barta*, in Guwahati, on 25 January 2020.

citizen. Throughout the conversation, my guest kept referring to herself as 'We Americans'. I liked hearing that. She is a permanent resident of that country…for all practical purposes, she was an American even though she was born in Assam and had her family roots in the state. What she said only held up the fact that people from 180 nations reside in that country and they came together to become Americans. This also underlines that it is a system for nation or nationality-building and by doing so, the Americans have built themselves as a huge jati or a community. I pointed that out in my 2002 speech to drive home the argument that various people can come together to formulate a common identity and we Assamese can do so too.

So, if I were to repeat the question, who is an Assamese, who would you put in the category?

Those who have been calling themselves Assamese in the last 600–1000 years are anyway Assamese. But, the Tea Tribe or the Sah Janajati (brought to the state by the British in the early twentieth century) is Assamese too.

Though lately, there has been a clever effort to turn the Na Axamiya Musalman who also came to Assam during the British period from East Bengal as Bengali, but they too are Assamese. I have a strong belief that 90 per cent of them will continue to call or declare themselves in future population censuses as Assamese.

Aside from those whose mother tongue is Assamese, the plains tribes whose first language is not Assamese but Assamese is their cultural and social language, are also Assamese. They also identify themselves as so. My larger point is, if a Mising, a Tiwa, a Rabha, can speak their own language at home and call themselves Assamese, why can't a Marwari who speaks her language at home, a Na Axomiya Musalman who speaks her duwan (dialect) at home, be Assamese? Many Biharis have become Assamese too in their daily life. Several have married into families whose first language is Assamese. Those who have scattered in different parts of the state are intermingling with the rest of the society and assimilating into the larger Assamese society. But the problem arises mainly in those areas where there is a strong concentration of one community or the other and there is an increased assertion of their non-Assamese identity, often leading to confrontation.

So for me, the khilonjia or tholuwa Assamese…, the plains tribes, and those who speak a duwan at home but are culturally and socially Assamese, are Assamese people. Even the Bengalis who are scattered in the Brahmaputra Valley and are not politically asserting themselves as Bengalis, are Assamese too.

However, it is important to highlight here that even in the Assam Accord, the identity of the 'Assamese people' remained undefined. That's the reason the Clause 6 of the Accord has not been able to be implemented since 1985. Also, whatever I have been suggesting (the definition of Assamese) has also not been accepted by everyone. Now, a committee has been formed by the central government. Let's see where we reach, what they suggest, what is the outcome.

HIREN GOHAIN[‡]

Prominent Assamese intellectual, author, political commentator

In mid-2019, the central government formed a committee to decide the definition of 'Assamese people' under the Assam Accord. So, will we now finally have an official definition of who is an Assamese?

Defining 'Assamese people' was a part of the pact between the anti-foreigner movement leaders and Assam and central governments in the 1980s. It should have been done long ago. New Delhi didn't do it and I think knowingly so. The Bodos, the Misings, all have gone away since. I dare say, the Indian deep state had injected this separatist feeling in them. It has always been the Centre's policy to divide Assam into smaller states. That way, it would help the Centre administer better its borderland. It will never show any interest in slicing out a huge state like Uttar Pradesh into smaller states for better administration. But it will do it in Assam, which is comparatively much smaller in size and population.

I was asked twice through letters from the state government to advise the Clause 6 committee set up by Ministry of Home Affairs; I refused it because I am convinced that it is a false promise to the people; will roil things up further unnecessarily. It will create more misunderstanding between communities, more mistrust, conflict; it will benefit none eventually. This is something that Lenin had called a 'rotten compromise'.

In your book, Struggling in a Time Warp, you have expounded on nationality construction in the light of Assamese identity construction. Will you elaborate it for readers to understand your point better?

Nationality construction is a very dynamic thing. In that book I proffer the example of the British society of which the Scots were once an integral part.

[‡]The interview with Hiren Gohain was recorded at his house in Guwahati on 26 January 2020.

There were many Scots among the British officers posted in pre-independent India too. But they later drifted away. After political fragmentation, the Scots also moved away culturally from the British identity. This happened after three centuries of being together. So, nationality construction can go either way—can evolve into one entity, or can disintegrate too.

The Assamese nationality, since the 1930s and the 40s, has also been in an evolving state. I sense primarily two thought processes among the Assamese. One is aimed at the dominance of the caste Hindus, what is referred to as pravutta (dominance) of tholuwa or indigenous people, which All Assam Students Union leaders like Sammujjal Bhattacharjee represent. However, when you say tholuwa, many get pushed out of that umbrella. Following Independence, the dominance (of caste Hindus) was taken for granted, and the basic ingredient of integration and democratic equality was ignored, to the chagrin of the marginalized groups.

The roadblock to Assamese nationality building has been a two-pronged attack. On one hand, it is a fight against more powerful nationalities, including Hindi-Hindu. On the other, there is ethnic separatism. On one hand, we want to assert that this is our identity, our culture, and it includes the tribals too, but then the tribals say, we will not accept it. They ask, if Bihu, Naam Kirtan, are the only elements of Assamese culture, then where are we? The Assamese society has not wrestled with this problem fully... because for a long time, those whose mother tongue is Assamese could hold on to power...they could afford to ignore these rumblings. Also, from time to time, they could unite all indigenous groups against outsiders.

However, what has happened is that the outside groups have figured it out and have helped promote ethnic separatism among the tribal groups, which have been inundated with cash. Look at how the Centre handled the anti-Citizenship Amendment Act protests (in end 2019-early 2020) in Assam. It clearly tried to separate the tribals and non-tribals of the state. But in districts like Karbi Anglong, some Karbi leaders with foresight, like Jayanti Rongpi and Holiram Terang, have been able to see through the game, and are opposing the Act....

I would like to bring you to the question of the Muslims of East Bengal origin. Where do they stand in this shifting identity politics in Assam?

Since the British period, while the elite Muslims were with the Muslim League across India, the common people mostly backed Jamiat-Ulema-e-Hind which was resolutely nationalistic.

In case of pre-Partition Assam though, the vast majority with the recent Muslim immigrants were led by a fiery Maulana named Abdul Hamid Khan or Maulana Bhasani who gave a ringing call for Pakistan. It was only after Partition that the nationalist Jamiat-Ulema-e-Hind gathered their flock together in Assam and negotiated with Congress leaders to build a modus vivendi together with the Assamese. But its drawback was that despite a liberal outlook in religion, Jamiat, over the decades, grew increasingly more orthodox under Arab influence and patronage under a vast global plan by the CIA to block the advance of communist influence. That stood in the way of spread of liberal ideas and attitudes among the unlettered immigrant Muslim masses across the country, though the well-off among them acquired such liberal values with ease.

Post-Independence, people from the community also became ministers and MLAs, judges and bureaucrats in Assam. However, while the educated few did rise in life, nothing fundamental changed for the common people from the community. In the unscrupulous times, it became a tinderbox for competitive communalism.

The spread of Salafism in neighbouring Bangladesh was also a reason for it. It penetrated into Assam. At one time, people from the border areas of the state, such as Goalpara, Dhubri, Barpeta, would tune in only to Bangladesh radio. This was because they didn't find anything about them in Assam's radio, while the same language, culture, religion, etc. with Bangladesh helped develop a sense of belonging and bonding. But nobody in Assam bothered about the growing closeness and the sociopolitical complications it can lead to in a state with strong identity consciousness. Banning the radio waves would not have worked.

Visionaries like Jyotiprasad Agarwala had coined the term 'Na Axamiya' (neo-Assamese) for the community. The lead of Jyoti Prasad and Bishnu Rava was followed in right earnest by Bhupen Hazarika in his appeals to embrace immigrant Muslims into the Assamese fold, only to regret later that the latter had loved his music but dismissed the words.

Side by side, what we have seen is that there has been an attempt by the Hindu right-wing forces to infiltrate the tribal societies and make them good Hindus. I see that even in my own community, the Ahoms. Such absurd thinking is being promoted by some leader centric groups; there is no modern thinking. The semi political leaders of these cliques have been able to absorb a lot of people though. ...These organizations are brought out with a downpour of money; their headquarters are in plush buildings.

If this is happening to a large community like the Ahoms, think what it can do to smaller groups like the Misings. This kind of politics is rife in Assam presently.

What, according to you, should the Assamese community do at the moment to remain a robust, integrated society?

We, as a community, are always swayed easily by emotions. But we need to be practical. What we need today is to assimilate people to create a democratic, liberal society. If we continue to say to various sets of people, no, you are not an Assamese, it will never work.

It is not that we can't have a democratic, liberal society. My perennial disagreement with my eminent contemporary Amalendu Guha has been on this issue. While he has dismissed the Assamese middle class as petty bourgeois, I have always held on to the hope that it may carve out a path for itself, based on democratic liberal ideals.

Though, I have now developed a doubt about it!

NAGEN SAIKIA[§]

Noted Assamese writer, former Rajya Sabha member

Who would you define as an Assamese?

The definition of Assamese is not as difficult as envisaged by many. People, irrespective of their caste, creed, and religion, who speak the Assamese language, even with local variations, at home, are Assamese.

Secondly, people who look at themselves as Assamese, and also declare (officially) themselves as Assamese, are Assamese too.

Some people, without knowing much or with some vested interest, do count all the tribal people of Assam as non-Assamese. The tribals of Assam, be it the Bodos, the Rabhas, the Misings, the Tiwas, the Deuri, the Karbis, the Dimasas, and the Tai group, except the Ahoms, have two sections of people in each group. One that speaks her own language at home as her mother tongue, and the other that speaks Assamese as her mother tongue. Moreover, most of these groups use Assamese as their social medium of communication and as the medium of instruction in educational institutions, etc. In the broader sense, they are also Assamese.

John McCosh, a British officer from the first half of the nineteenth

---

[§]The interview with Nagen Saikia was conducted on email on 27 May 2020.

century, in his book *Topography of Assam*, had observed that even some of the people of hill tribes came down and mixed with the people of the plains and after some time became Assamese. This is similar to the tea garden people of Assam. They have become an important part of the larger Assamese community. Though they came from other parts of India during the British colonial period, they mixed with the local Assamese people, both in blood and in culture, including the language. It is also to be noted that during the Ahom regime, the people of the sovereign country in those days, irrespective of caste, creed, or religion, were taken to be subjects of the Ahom king and thereby they naturally became Assamese.

KULADHAR SAIKIA[¶]

Prominent Assamese writer and President, Asam Sahitya Sabha

As the present president of Asam Sahitya Sabha, a pillar and protector of Assamese language and identity, who would you define as Assamese?

It is seen that the Asam Sahitya Sabha had a series of deliberations and discussions within the Sabha and with other stakeholders to arrive at an acceptable solution to the question so as to evolve a prescription for the connected questions in regard to providing different safeguards and measures to such people. On the basis of these deliberations, a note on the core outline of the definition was submitted to the high-powered committee constituted by the government on the implementation of Clause 6 of the Assam Accord in 2019.

It was stated in the note that the term 'Assamese people' incorporated in the Accord should mean Assamese and indigenous people of Assam. This should include any Indian citizen irrespective of caste, creed, race, religion, language, and ethnic origin who permanently resides in the state of Assam and uses and speaks the Assamese language or any indigenous tribal language of the state as his or her first language, second language, or third language.

The Sabha has also noted that the term 'tribal' should include all those communities which have been placed in the list of Scheduled Tribes (Hills and Plains) of Assam. Moreover, the term 'indigenous' people would refer to the communities/tribes included in the list of Scheduled Tribe (ST) plains, including the More Other Backward Classes.

[¶]The interview with Kuladhar Saikia was conducted via email on 23 May 2020 when he was the President of Asam Sahitya Sabha.

Over and above this, the Sabha feels that communities which are Assamese but are not included in the above categories, are required to be decided upon by a high-powered committee as 'other indigenous' communities.

KANAKSEN DEKA**

Prominent Assamese writer, editor, intellectual

What would be your definition of Assamese people?

I don't want to go back too much in time to define who are Assamese people. For me, whoever speaks the language, loves and promotes Assamese literature, culture, and its heritage are Assamese people. But yes, there is one condition there: the person has to be an Indian citizen.

SANJOY HAZARIKA

Writer, commentator on the Northeast

Who, according to you, is an Assamese? You grew up in Shillong when it was a part of Assam. It later became the capital of Meghalaya, which is still your home. Where do you locate yourself as an Assamese, someone whose home is in Meghalaya?

We can't give an answer strictly on the basis of a geographical and physical identity. These have a role in the shaping of an identity but are not the only markers. Thus, an Axomiya can be anybody who is from the area of Assam, and where they have their roots, where their forefathers come from. Though the cultural definition of who is an Assamese is a bit more complicated.

...An Assamese may live anywhere in the world but if they recognize that their roots are in the state, they speak Axomiya, they are Assamese. The acceptance of the language is, in my view, one of the key markers of Assamese identity. You may be born anywhere in the world of Assamese parents. I have my home in Shillong which is today in another state but my father was from Sivasagar and my mother from Nowgong in Assam. To give another instance here, my uncle, the illustrious historian of contemporary Assam, Dr Nirode Barooah, lives in Europe but is very much an Assamese. So, if you ask me, I am as much an Axomiya citizen as I am an Indian citizen, a Shillongian, and also a citizen of the world.

...I want to say that any person who resides within the physical bounds

**The interview was conducted on telephone on 29 May 2020.

of Assam, irrespective of whichever culture or language group they belong to, while retaining their independent identity, may recognize that being part of a larger whole opens up a pathway, a gateway to greater economic and social mobility. But there is an important IF, a caveat here—they should not feel pressured or subsumed by that whole. The Axomiyas should not insist on assimilation or domination as that has produced counter-currents and was counter-productive in the past. Co-existence and respect for each other, especially smaller ethnic groups who may even prefer not to speak Axomiya, and an approach based on equity, equality, and inclusiveness are the factors which would help us live in greater peace.

JAHNU BARUA[††]

Eminent filmmaker

What would be your definition of an Assamese?

I will have to say here that the first Ahom king Chaolung Sukapha, and saint Sri Sri Sankardev helped define for us long ago who is an Assamese. It is a language-centric identity; has nothing to do with religion, caste, or creed.

Before Sukapha, all our tribes and sub-tribes were scattered. He brought them together, also made people understand that if there is an attack from outside, the collective unity is vital to resist it, to protect all. That is how the people of Assam could defeat the Mughals at their peak for sixty-eight years (1614–82).

...Sankardev brought in a beautiful social system whereby tribals, non-tribals, even Muslims, could come under one umbrella identity. So, both had already fixed for us who is an Assamese.

Though lately, I have observed some divisive tendencies.... Some would say, but Sukapha was only an Ahom Swargadeo (king) and I am, but, a Kalita, a Sutiya, or a Bamun, etc. I insist that it is important to see him only as an Assamese king. This sense of divisiveness will only weaken us as a community.... We are anyway just a few in number.

Look at the Assamese surnames. You will find a Phukan or a Baruah who may be an Ahom, Kalita, Brahmin, or even a Muslim. What does it signify? The kings gave the surnames as per their duties. Importantly, it shows that we are bound in oneness by the language and not by religion or communities. We all must remember it in order to be able to safeguard

[††]The interview was conducted on telephone on 24 June 2020.

our Assamese identity from any future threat, including the one posed recently by the Citizenship Amendment Act (CAA).

I also feel it is time we should work towards widening the span of the Assamese identity. The people of East Bengal origin who settled in Assam prior to 1971 in various bouts of migration are part of Assam. I often say this when I visit Assam's Bengali-dominated Barak Valley. I urge them to come, join us, to form that composite identity as one. I always say, the land is yours, protect this land and we live together as one. We can't afford to settle any Bangladeshi in Assam any more. Let's protect all of us.

I often say, land will never forget you but you may forget the land. The moment you do it, your sense of belonging goes away and it is the beginning of the end.

VICTOR BANERJEE[‡‡]

Noted actor

You are born in a Bengali family but have grown up in Assam, have featured in Assamese films, have been involved in promoting the state's culture. In a state where identity consciousness is so tangible, where do you place yourself in that spectrum?

I feel lost when I am asked such a question. …I just enjoy being part of Assam. It is too close to my heart in so many ways. Besides having worked in Assamese films (four until 2020), I also run a Residential Charitable School for the visually handicapped (Moran Blind School) in Moran, near Dibrugarh, in Upper Assam. It was started by my father (Major S. N. 'Bruno' Banerjee, who spent thirty years as a tea planter in the Assam Valley) in 1971. The school was primarily set up for the children of tea garden labourers.

These workers, ostensibly labelled 'Adivasis', were…brought to Assam as bonded labourers from Chotanagpur and today's Jharkhand when the East India Company by special dispensation of the British Parliament were allowed to continue with their disgraceful form of 'Slave Trade' (after officially abolishing slavery in 1833) while setting up tea gardens in Assam and the plantations of the Malaysian Peninsula and East Africa. To this day, these 'labourers' in the Assam gardens still represent the most ill-treated and inhumanely subjugated workers in India. …I have been raising the demand to grant ownership rights to the houses they have been living in

[‡‡]The interview was conducted on email on 4 May 2020.

for generations in the labour 'lines' that demarcated and segregated them from the owners' representatives. That's how they remain. They are graciously permitted to occupy a house, often in shameful disrepair, for thirty to fifty years, own nothing, and can be asked to vacate the premises at short notice. I grew up with them and their children and at the fag end of my life have a moral duty to do what I can to alleviate their suffering....

But if you ask me where I belong...I have always proudly and happily said—my heart lies in Assam, embracing all the northeastern states that were once one union in my childhood, and my soul rests in the Garhwal Himalaya, Uttarakhand.

I am one of the few people who wear the gamosa everywhere, whether I am in New York or Paris or in Guwahati. I wear it every day; it is not for fashion but because I honestly identify with it and dip it in the waters of the Hudson or the Seine or Siang, and use it to wipe my face and hands and during the sad Covid-19 days I had used it as a mask.

We have a naamghar (Vaishnava prayer house) in our school in Moran. The satradhikar of the Sri Sri Auniati Xatra, Chief Monk Parbhu Dr Pitambardeb Goswami, came specially from the riverine island of Majuli to sacredly establish and inaugurate our naamghar. As you may know, the cover over the monikut (sanctum sanctorum) is typically a gamosa. Ours is being handcrafted with motifs and colours of several tribes who inhabit the valley, not just the typical red and white gamosa. Our visually impaired children sing kirtans and are taught to do Bhaona wearing traditional masks and the costumes.

I also promote the egalitarian teachings of our saint Sankardev, outside the state and have been the government's Goodwill Ambassador for many years now. In the sixteenth century, Srimanta Sankardev brought together people from various communities and tribes under a simple religion, Ek Sarana Dharma. This predated Guru Nanak and Sri Chaitanya Mahaprabhu. The controversial caste system has, therefore, never been a dominant part of Assamese culture and life and explains why they never mastered the skills of blacksmiths, potters or carpenters, cobblers and sanitary workers. Weavers they were, with a loom in almost every village home.

I am also the 'Goodwill Ambassador' of the Dimasa tribe of Assam, who live in the Dima Hasao district of Haflong. A small tribe of Vaishnavs struggling to survive in the Northeast; the rest were converted to Christianity in British India. The Dimasas have a rich culture with dance and music that is unique and their language is as rich as any other in India. Haflong is world famous amongst ornithologists, for the village called Jatinga where hundreds of birds mysteriously fly into the lights on dark nights during the fall every year and perish. It's called their 'Valley of Death'.

Assam is where I played football with urchins, used bows and arrows to learn to hunt, rode outboard motors across its rivers, learned from my Nepali batman to eat the flesh of snakes and big cats, reared leopards that we donated to the Calcutta Zoo, captured wild elephants in dense jungles beyond Doomdooma, and went to the most exciting migratory duck, red jungle fowl and green pigeon shoots in the world. 'Civilization' has destroyed it all. Now one sees few cobras, no mongoose, and the jungle fowl and jackals no longer howl into the night.

If you look at the sociopolitical history of Assam, the Assamese and Bengalis have had a love–hate relationship. Has it ever bothered you? The vociferous protests in Assam in late 2019 and early 2020 was against granting citizenship to Hindu Bengalis.

...Assam made me—a Bengali—Sankardev's ambassador to the world. Anywhere I go in Assam or Meghalaya, from Kaziranga to Barapani, me and my family are invited in as guests to live for free for as long as we want without ever being made to feel beholden to anyone. Asam Sahitya Sabha had invited me to launch the English translation of noted Assamese writer Birinchi Kumar Baruahh's classic *Jibonor Batot* (On the Road of Life).

Assam loves me and I love her and the Northeast. I used to joke that if I were captured and held hostage by rebels anywhere in the hills and valleys of the Northeast, I'd be dined and given a great time and dropped back into the world of hatred I had been picked up from, once they knew who I was, a true son of their soil.

I have willed that, after I die, a small matchbox containing my ashes should be strewn on the jheels (waterbodies) of Kaziranga so that my spirit can roam there in peace and ecstasy, forever.

ARUPA KALITA PATANGIA[§§]

Well-known Assamese writer, Sahitya Akademi winner

Who would you call Assamese? Also, what do you think the Assamese community should do to keep its roots strong?

[§§]Arupa Kalita Patangia's response to the question in Assam was received via Whatsapp message on 9 September 2020 and was thereafter translated by the author into English with her permission. It was shared with Patangia for approval.

To offer a definition of who is an Assamese is a tough ask. The Assamese community or Axomiya jati is the sum total of a set of migrants...a variety of people from a variety of regions began to reside in what is Assam today. It resulted in a jati, a community, born of amalgamation; it ensued creation of a variegated culture. Social ills like feudalism could never find fruition in this land. The tribal influence helped shape a social practice hinged on tolerance and liberalism.

Like the common goal behind the movement against anti-colonialism brought Assam closer to the rest of India in the early twentieth century, the relations between different communities also developed in a similar manner, towards a common goal. The idea of the seven sisters, of collective unity, also sprouted from it.

However, the ultra-sub-nationalists of Assam, at various points in time, had hammered on that unity and brought the process to a halt. The Assam Agitation of the 1980s adopted a big brother attitude and further broke the course of that community formation. The Assamese jati went helter skelter and fell into the lap of militant extremism. This development is a proof that a community is formed not by domination of one over the other(s) but by following democratic norms among the stakeholders.

As I mentioned earlier, migration has put a strong stamp on the formation of Assamese community. However, if people from only one religion, language group or community continue to migrate to a place, the social fabric of that place is bound to change. This tendency, if it continues in Assam, can pose a threat to the wider Assamese community. Therefore, rampant migration (from neighbouring Bangladesh) must end in Assam. But oppression of the residents of Assam in the name of suspected (illegal) migrants will harm the state ultimately.

Today, I ponder, who is an Assamese? What should be the definition of an Assamese? According to me, whoever speaks the Assamese language is an Assamese. Nobody can deny that Assamese is a community dependent on the language.

However, when the Asam Sahitya Sabha had declared that the tribal groups are Assamese, several of them opposed that identity. Even many among the Ahoms, there is lately a lot of interests directed towards the promotion of the Tai language, which their ancestors once spoke. Several have begun seeking its roots. The Bodo-Kacharis can be called to have discarded their Assamese identity altogether.

Therefore, it is good to keep in mind that Assam is also an abode of multiple languages and a rainbow of cultures. Those who speak Assamese as their first language are a part of it. There was a time when a thought existed to call all those residing in Assam as Assamese. However, many don't want to accept this identity any more because of the ultra-sub-nationalists backing the imposition of Assamese language on them....

Let me point out that even those who have been accepted as Assamese don't have a homogenous culture. Let's say, we have to describe an Assamese wedding here. Which one will I do? Even funerals have different rituals. I am not even talking about religion here. I am not talking about an Assamese of Islam faith or an Assamese of Sikh faith....

On the other hand, those who entered the Assamese fold a bit late, say the Nepalis or the Muslims of East Bengal origin, are often not recognized as so by the ultra-sub-nationalist fold. The consequence of it is, this process too is coming to a halt, if not completely reached a full stop yet.

I think Assamese language speakers will have to adopt a democratic process of community formation. That is how the Assamese community would be strengthened and can come together to work for the welfare of the state. To my mind, this is crucial because in order to claim its share in Indian federalism, Assam too would have to adopt a federal political structure.

MOUSHUMI KANDALI¶

Well-known Assamese fiction writer, art historian, academic

Who, according to you, is an Assamese?

This question is extremely interesting. If you see it from one angle, the question should never be asked. However, for some time lately, we have been seeing it popping up in Assam, say, over who is an Axomiya or a pure Assamese, or who are Assamese people.
Of course, the question has resurfaced because it has a political backdrop too but if we see it historically, who is an Assamese has already been decided. We have our own language, culture, a distinct cuisine, textiles, traditions, history, and a particular way of life. Like any community that takes shape in any part of India or the world, the Assamese community too has taken that trajectory. If we go by Raymond William's second definition of culture, we know we have a distinct culture and that very well will define our distinct identity.

¶The interview with Moushumi Kandali was conducted on telephone and email on 7 May 2020.

Even then, we have been asking this question...from one angle, I feel it is pointless. And then at another moment, I feel it is a significant question because it also presents us an opportunity to delve within.

If we see this question even if only historically, it is true that some of the historical claims are common between the Assamese, Bengalis, and Odias. Say the Dakor Boson, or the list of truisms in Assamese society. But if you take note of the genealogy of the regional literary history, the literary compositions of Srimanta Sankardev, Shri Madhabdev, and all other Vaishnavite composers, or say, for instance, Madhab Kandali's Ramayana, the way these were written with ample geo-cultural contexts and contents, they set strong links to Assamese identity both in terms of the language and the culture. Also, the references made to ancient Assam (or Kamarupa as it was called,) in the Kalika Purana, tantra literature such as *Yogini Tantra*, in Kalidasa's Raghuvamgsa or Mahabharat, in the historical accounts and inscriptions, such as the Allahabad Pillar inscription of Samudragupta, Nidhanpur inscription, the Chinese traveller Hiuen Tsang's account of his visit to Kamarupa, there is enough proof of a different foundation archaeologically, in art history. These references and accounts had highlighted that a cultural foundation existed in ancient or medieval Assam. ...So culturally too, we should be rest assured that there is a separate strain called Assamese. Like I mentioned before, it has of course evolved over the centuries like any other community of the world through a process and has manifested now in what we term as 'Assamese'.

Apart from that, what needs to be highlighted is that when we say Assamese, it speaks of a unique identity. Yes, this identity kicks up its own problems but the solutions lie within it too. I am referring to the admixture of caste Hindu, Muslim and 'tribal' elements entwined into what, or whom, we call Assamese. The Assamese identity has an assimilative definition. Multiple strains are assimilated so closely and for so long that it is now difficult to separate them. And, this assimilative definition would constitute not only the intra-cultural pollination amongst multiple ethnic groups within the geo-cultural space but also assimilation of multiple trans-cultural elements across [India]....The set of illustrative manuscript paintings on Jayadeva's Geet Govinda is one such example. The brilliant artworks of the seventeenth century manuscript painting folio, *Hasti-Vidarnava* (A Treatise on the Elephants), were done by two Mughal painters named Dilvar and Doshai from the royal Mughal Court who settled in Assam permanently. So I would equate it to Indian identity. When we say, Indian identity, the

Assamese identity too comes under that canopy. But within the Indian canopy, the Assamese identity is a separate identity. Similarly, who is an Assamese also comes with its diversity within a unity....

This identity formation also gives the hint of nation building, culturally speaking. Like I said, as everyone contributes to the identity that is Indian, same is with the Assamese identity. The so-called Assamese whose first language is Assamese, are Assamese, but so are the others, the tribes, with their own languages, cultural practices, cuisine, textiles. We have co-existed like that. British colonialism brought in certain changes and repercussions. Post-Independence, say particularly post 1980s, each group within the Assamese canopy became conscious of their ethnic identity and have begun asserting it. I don't term it as an unwelcome development. I don't want the tribes to be only Assamese at the cost of sacrificing their own micro identity. It is a matter of choice and agency. If the Bodos today have called themselves only Bodos, they have a right to do it. But at the subconscious level, the oneness, the assimilative nature of the society, exists. I have felt it on many occasions. I have seen my Bodo or Karbi friends expressing anger and grievances against the Borkokaidew (big brother) kind of hegemonic tendencies of the mainstream Assamese at one level and on the other showing indissoluble unity in terms of cultural expressions, be it food, textile, music and other aspects. Going deeper, whenever you study the most important cultural signifiers of Assamese identity, say for example, the Sattriya classical dance or music, or the Bihu festival, all you see is syncretism and complete cultural assimilation of multiple ethnic groups. Even the religious manifestations are by nature syncretic. Just listen to a Jikir or Jaari sung by our indigenous Axomiya Muslims, you will feel and realize this.

You belong to a caste Hindu Assamese family but grew up in Karbi Anglong. How do you see your identity?

Yes, I was raised in Karbi Anglong. So, today, I am more comfortable in a Karbi wrapper than in a mekhela sador. My identity includes that strain too. There is no one singular identity here, its plural or at least dual inside, externally, there could be one identity, but at the subconscious level, in the psychological or existential sense of the selfhood, I feel it is multiple.

When someone asks me, what is Assamese identity, I think of the DNA structure. While one part of it is linked to mainland India—the Sankritized culture, the other is the Asian culture and influences. The Ahoms who came in the twelfth century, all the branches of the Tai people, the Singphos and others represent that vibrant strand from Asian culture. Assam is a melting pot of all these strains from both the sides and we are a living example of it. None of it can be removed from my or our collective Assamese identity.

MAYUR BORA***

Prominent Assamese social commentator/writer

As a close watcher of Assamese society, who would you define as Assamese?

...I think, the first Assamese are those who settled in Assam first: the Karbi, the Dimasa, the Bodo, the Tiwa, the Rabha, the Mising, etc. Today, some of them may not be comfortable with the nomenclature 'Assamese', but I think they are the first claimants to the title, even if their mother tongue is not the Assamese language. These tribal groups are deeply inspired by their rich and wonderful legacy and tradition.

The second lot is the people whose mother tongue is Assamese.

The third group comprises of those who migrated from different parts of India, like Rupkonwar Jyotiprasad Agarwala, whose ancestors came from Rajasthan. We all know that Sankardev's and Madhabdev's ancestors came from Kannauj and Bengal respectively. Lakshminath Bezbaroa's family is said to have migrated from Bengal. But they all adopted the language, showed their undying love and unflinching commitment to it, and helped create a unique Assamese identity. I have taken the names of only famous people here but there are many common people who did the same. They looked at themselves as Assamese and used the language to a large extent in their daily life. Those are the Assamese people.

Fourthly, many who have come from other side of the border—East Pakistan before 1971—and adopted Assamese culture, embraced the language, are Assamese too.

But I would have reservations about accepting someone as Assamese who may have come from some other parts of India and stayed for years together in the state and yet never engaged with the language, its culture. I hold no grudge against them because they are also fellow Indian citizens but to what extent they could be called Assamese can be debated.

***The interview with Mayur Bora was recorded in Guwahati on 26 January 2020.

NAHENDRA PADUN†††

Assamese writer, academic

What would be your definition of the Assamese?

...I would say, all those people who have been residing in Assam are Assamese. This is because the word 'Assamese' itself has sprung out of the word 'Assam'. However, a section of people would like to proffer that only those who speak the Assamese language as their mother tongue are Assamese. But that would be further from the truth.

I want to point out that the word 'Axomiya' or Assamese came into being only from the second edition of the first Assamese newspaper *Orunudoi*, published in 1846. Prior to that, there is no proof of the wide use of the term 'Axomiya'. So, if you take that into consideration, then whoever has been residing in Assam prior to Independence is an Axomiya.

Secondly, since there is also a language called Assamese or Axomiya which has got the status of one of the regional languages, those who speak it as their first language are Assamese. However, the tribes and adivasis who have been residing in Assam have their own languages, which had led to the birth of a dual linguistic identity among many in Assam. So, in my case, I am first a Mising and then an Assamese. I can't set aside my Assamese identity to become only a Mising. Since Assamese is a state language, it has widely been accepted by one and all. Having said that, I also can't deny that I have my own Mising language, a separate culture, which I have imbibed too and is an inseparable part of my identity.

As I mentioned, prior to the circulation of the term 'Axomiya' in *Orunudoi*, the language used by say, Sankardev, Madhabdev, Madhab Kandali, to write literature, were termed desi bhasha or prantiya bhasha, not as Assamese language or what we know of it as so today. People wrote in dialects that were commonly in use in their areas. So those strains have been there in the state's linguistic history. Therefore, I would say those who have been residing in Assam prior to Independence are Assamese, not just those who speak what we know as the Assamese language now as their first language.

It is like, if you are outside of India, you identity yourself as Indian. When asked where in India are you from, we would say, Assam, and then

†††The interview with Nahendra Padun was conducted on telephone on 6 April 2020 in Assamese. It was translated into English by the author and shared with Padun for approval.

would come our respective identities as Mising, Rabha, Karbi, Bodo, Tiwa, etc.

You were one of the founding forces behind the highest Mising literary body Mising Agom Kebang. You are also an Assamese writer. Where do you personally locate yourself in this entire stretch?

We would like to claim ourselves as Assamese but it is the fault of those whose first language is Assamese for not being able to accept us as one, as we are. For instance, in some literary or poetry events and meetings, I am introduced as a Mising writer or poet. I take objection to it. I ask them in return: have I done my literary work in Mising language? Since I have written in Assamese, I should be introduced as an Assamese writer in a literary event. Such things make it difficult to locate oneself confidently within this dual identity and that must end.

HAFIZ AHMED[‡‡‡]

Assamese writer and founder, Char Chapori Sahitya Parishad

Who, according to you, is an Assamese?

To give you the definition of an Assamese is easy for me because I follow what was articulated long ago by Kalaguru Bishnu Rava and Rupkonwar Jyotiprasad Agarwala. What Agarwala said in his powerful poem 'Axomiya dekar ukti' (The Response of an Assamese Youth) firmly defines what comprises the Assamese society.

Unfortunately, after these luminaries have passed away, Assamese thinkers didn't quite follow up on it; they allowed it to wane, get enfeebled, till we became a divided society. When revered Bodo leader Kalicharan Brahma had an audience with the Simon Commission visiting Assam in 1935, he said, 'We are nothing but Assamese'. Today, Bodo brothers have drifted away. When we visit Bodo-dominated Kokrajhar town today, it is not strange to hear people asking us to speak in Hindi instead of Assamese. Isn't it unfortunate?

What I have now increasingly noticed is the growing militant tendency among the ultra jatiotabad forces of Assam to not count the marginalized groups of Assamese society, such as the Tea Tribes and the Na Axamiya Mussalman (People of East Bengal origin), as Assamese. People came under

[‡‡‡]The interview with Hafiz Ahmed was conducted on phone on 8 March 2020 in Assamese and translated into English by the author and shared via email with him for approval.

the umbrella of an Assamese identity not because of religion but because of linguistic reasons, for the love and celebration of the language. So, language is our defining identity. I am from the Na Axamiya Mussalman community but my literary moorings are within the Assamese literary realm. I am Assamese.

I also want to point out a grave danger that is staring at us, the Assamese society. As per 2011 Census, Assamese speakers are 48 per cent of the state's total population. There are about 60–65 lakh people in the sand bars of Assam who identify themselves as Assamese in every population census enumeration. This means a good 16–17 per cent of the 48 per cent Assamese speakers come from these areas. If you alienate these people, the number of Assamese speakers will slide down further and that of Bengali speakers will escalate.

Bengali speakers in Assam, as per 2011 census, is 28.91 per cent. Imagine 16–17 per cent of these people identifying themselves as Bengali in the next Census? What would be left of us, the people who identify ourselves as Assamese, in Assam itself?

I see this development as a huge failure on the part of Asam Sahitya Sabha. In 2003, during the presidentship of Homen Borgohain, a serious attempt was made to strengthen the bond between the mainstream Assamese society and the Na Axamiya Mussalman community. But after his term ended, no follow up was done.

UPEN RABHA HAKASHAM[§§§]

Assamese writer, academic, Sahitya Akademi winner

What would be your definition of Assamese people?

When one asks around who are Assamese people, many whose first language is Assamese would try to proffer in a very narrow sense that only they are the Assamese people.

Suppose I say, I am Indian, or say, this is Indian literature, it would mean being Assamese also means being Indian, or Assamese literature also means Indian literature. These greater identities—Indian or Indian literature—envelope all regional identities and literature. But if you say, Assamese literature, will it also mean literature written in, say, Bodo, Mising, Karbi,

[§§§]The interview with Upen Rabha Hakasham was recorded on telephone from Delhi on 10 April 2020.

Rabha, Tiwa languages of Assam? For instance, the Assam government in January 2020 sanctioned a sum of ₹1 crore to Asam Sahitya Sabha for the promotion of Assamese literature. Will that fund be also utilized to promote writings in the other indigenous languages spoken in Assam, or only in Assamese language?

I sometimes feel that it is a misfortune for all of us in Assam that there is also a language called Assamese and it is spoken as a first language by a section of people. Even in description of Bihu as Assam's main festival, it is often not mentioned that not all communities who celebrate Bihu, do it on the first day of Bohag. Communities like Deuri, Moran, etc, celebrate Bihu on the first Wednesday of Bohag. Many make merry by eating pork, drinking local brews. Why can't these be included also as cultural practices of Assam when we talk of celebrating Bihu in our school books? When it comes to explaining the dress of Assamese women, why is it only riha mekhela sador but also not dokhona, risa, kambang, etc.? This narrow definition of Assamese over the years has proven to be a barrier for other indigenous people to identify themselves as Assamese too.

To return to your question about who is an Assamese, I would say, those communities who have no other homeland but only Assam are the Assamese in the true sense. Most communities of Assam have migrated from some other place to Assam during different periods of history. They have adopted the local culture, language, way of life, to become Assamese. But lately, there has been a strong attempt in several communities to revive or keep alive a bond with their original homeland or original culture. So does that make them Assamese?

For instance, Assamese don't pray to Brahmaputra but we did see Namami Brahmaputra, a signifier of mainland caste Hindu practice, in Assam in 2017. Lately, there seemed to be an attempt to revive the Hindu culture of the original Hindu homeland. The Sikhs of Borhola area of Assam were practically Assamese. Lately, they have developed a bond with the original land of Sikhism, Punjab, and have begun marrying from there, adopting the Punjabi language, etc. Jyoti Prasad Agarwala was Assamese but many Marwaris maintain a strong bond with their original homeland, Rajasthan, and marry only from there. Agarwala's great grandfather married an Assamese woman.

Many Bengalis may have been residing in Assam for a long time but they have an original homeland, West Bengal, with which the bond is strong. Many East Bengal original Muslims too assert their Muslim identity more than their Assamese identity. That is why I state, those communities which have no other place to call their homeland but only Assam should be called Assamese in the true sense.

PADMA PATOR¶¶¶

Noted Assamese writer

Who would you term as Assamese?

All those people who have migrated to Assam in various centuries and have resided in the state since are Assamese. It must be highlighted that the jati janagusthis (the tribes) comprise the spine of the Assamese identity, the kernel of Assamese-ness. Karbis were the first among us to migrate to this land. Then entered the Bodos, the Dimasas, the Rabhas, the Tiwas, the Misings, the Ahoms, et al. They began to spread themselves to reside along the Brahmaputra. Their culture, traditions, language, customs, way of life were drawn to craft what is Assamese culture today. The caste Hindus entered Assam much later.

I have dwelt on these influences that form the crux of the Assamese culture in my book *Janajatiya Samaj Sankskriti*.

Like most people in Assam, you too have a dual or a hyphenated identity. You belong to the Tiwa community, and are also a member of the wider Assamese society. You are a prominent Assamese writer. Have the two folds of your identity ever clashed your everyday or professional life?

We, the tribes, want to remain together with the non-tribal part of the Assamese society. But it must be mentioned that the role of Asam Sahitya Sabha, the primary literary body to keep all of us together, has been deplorable in this regard. It has failed to keep the bond strong. Some of the noted non-tribal Assamese writers served as presidents of the Sabha and had used the platform to express in derogatory terms the tribal way of living and worked in a divisive manner. It was extremely unfortunate, and detrimental to the well-being of the composite Assamese culture and society. I had raised this particular issue at the Sabha when I was a member of the executive in mid-2000. However, it was not given much attention, which led me to resign from it. Lately, worse has happened; the Sabha has become more of a political than linguistic platform.

¶¶¶The interview with Padma Pator was conducted on phone from Delhi on 11 April 2020.

It must be remembered that the unity of the tribal and non-tribal sections of Assamese society is primary to protect the Assamese language and culture.

SAMEER TANTI****

Assamese poet, Sahitya Akademi Awardee

Who would you call an Assamese?

Many people have come to reside in Assam in different periods of history. They settled down on Assam's soil, got used to its land, the air, the way of life; adopted local culture, the language; had begun contributing to the state's welfare—politically, economically, socially, culturally. I consider all such people, those who have contributed to the state and love it, as Assamese.

Most people in Assam have at least two identities when it comes to identifying themselves ethnically or linguistically. Being from the Tea Tribe or adivasi community and being part of the Assamese society, you too have a dual identity. Has one identity clashed with the other?

This clash of one's dual identity has come to exist in our society lately but I have never suffered from it. This is because I grew up in a tea garden where the babus (the officials) were willing to give people like me the space within the greater Assamese community. They helped lift up the people belonging to the lower strata from where I came from. They set up night schools in the tea garden areas; those youth who never could go to school because of day work could study in those facilities; they exposed us to local arts like the Bhaona. My community had its own forms of arts too, which it practised alongside. So, I never suffered from the confusion of having two identities; it became one for me; those around me helped me achieve it. So, with their help, I trod off to a different life.

However, at times, I do think of what Paul Robeson wrote: Sometimes, I feel like a motherless child. Particularly so when I return to the tea garden life; when I listen to their songs, the dialects. I feel a sense of longing which is beyond words.

Though I have not faced this dual identity crisis, I do notice it among the next generation of my community. Sometime ago, my son

****The interview with Sameer Tanti was conducted on phone on 6 April 2020 in Assamese and translated into English and shared with him on email for approval.

asked me at the dinner table: *Deuta (father in Assamese)*, do you think you are a complete Assamese? I asked him in return: How did that question come to your mind? He lives in Bangalore, and replied that when he introduces himself with his surname to others in Bangalore, he is often told, mainly by those from Odisha, that he is not from Assam but an Odia. My son then told me: Now I often say, I have half Odia and half Assamese blood in me.

I told him that it is not what blood you have in your veins; it is where your heart feels you belong to; to a place you think of dearly; the land where you stand is your first identity. Never think of anything else. I am glad that it set my son thinking about the gravity of what I told him that night.

I feel I am an Assamese also because of what my father told me once. He said I came to Assam because your grandfather came to the state. And therefore, you are also in the state. However, unlike us, you have started going to school; are studying the Assamese language. I don't know what you are studying but I hope someday you will marry an Assamese woman and will contribute something worthwhile to the state. If you can achieve that, I will be very happy.

This is the message I have always tried to pass on to my three children. They have studied outside of Assam. But I told them, wherever you may be, but you are an Assamese till your bones. You are not Odia.

In 2012, when I visited Puri to take part in a literary event during the Rath Yatra at the Jagannath Temple, some journalists did ask me, while having Odia origin, why do I identify myself as an Assamese. I asked them to look at the history of people like me who had to travel to Assam about 200 years ago and then ask the question: did anyone in Odisha ever think of us? Have you written anything about my community in your literature?

PULAK BANERJEE[††††]

Well-known Assamese singer

Who, according to you, is an Assamese?

...I have always loved to call myself an Assamese first. This is because I love the language, its sweetness, the soft words. I feel whoever loves this

[††††]The interview with Pulak Banerjee was recorded on phone on 9 April 2020.

language is an Assamese. One will have to love the land, the air, the water, of Assam. Somebody may not like you but you have to ask yourself, what do you like?

I love the soil of Assam, its air, the water, the culture. It could be that your mother tongue is not Assamese, like my parents were Bengali. But I don't count it as more significant than what I have grown with, what I hold as important to me. By birth I am a Bengali, but in deeds, in my way of life, in imbibing a culture, being surrounded by friends and acquaintances, I am an Assamese. They are what that makes me.

...I had worked in the All India Radio and was posted in Kolkata for some time. One day, a colleague was interrupting me while I was busy, to which I responded: Please digdari korben na. He was baffled and asked me, what is digdari? I said, not to disturb me. He asked me, in which language? I said, in Bengali. He then replied, in Bengali we don't have that word. For the first time, I thought of it; was made to realise that I was using an Assamese word. Then, often, there, I was pointed out that I used the word, aar (and in English), even if it was not required in a Bengali sentence. It is we, the Assamese, who often add, aru, to our sentences, which I unconsciously was using in my Bengali too.

Has this twin linguistic and cultural identity of yours ever come in the way of each other?

My father was born in Barpeta town of Assam. My grandfather came to Barpeta as a police officer and later built his house in Ulubari area of Guwahati. Though I was born and brought up in Guwahati, my closeness to Barpeta has remained because it was my father's birthplace. Though I studied in a Bengali medium school in Guwahati, we developed strong social links with Assamese neighbours. Gradually, we imbibed the Assamese culture, almost unintentionally. It grew on us. I got exposed to music because of Dilip Sarma, the music teacher in my school. He taught me Assamese songs, Assamese tunes. Along with a few other Assamese teachers, he ensured that I got an environment to learn music. I also learnt to read and write Assamese in the high school.

When I studied at the B. Barooah College in Guwahati, there too I was encouraged to take up music. Top Assamese poets like Nirmal Prabha Bordoloi were my professors who encouraged me immensely, wrote songs which I sang. They created for me an environment where I could take up singing in Assamese, be it in folk or in modern music. Alongside listening to Bengali hits, I was also exposed to Assamese songs at music functions, on the radio. Then, there was an environment at home for music because of my elder sister and my parents. It all helped me to become a professional singer.

Senior artistes like Bhupen Hazarika, Keshab Mahanta, Khagen Mahanta, encouraged me immensely. I sang in Bhupen da's films. I never felt that I was born in a Bengali household. I became one of them, became an Assamese singer. But then, in any society, there are people of diverse views, different mentality. So in my long journey in the field of music, I have also met people of all shades. Some had embraced me as their own, some others didn't. I did hear on some occasions, rarely though, that I shouldn't be given a particular song to sing or be invited to a particular event because I am not one of 'them'. Those words did hurt me. But I was never cold-shouldered by Assamese people in general, particularly the music lovers. I have received immense love.

I believe we, as members of Assamese society, will have to rise above those narrow thoughts; will have to look at the other as a human being first. Then only can we help spread the Assamese culture far and wide.

MONISHA BEHAL[‡‡‡‡]

Noted social activist, Founder of the North East Network

Who, according to you, is an Assamese?

...For me, I am definitely an Assamese but my identity construction was influenced by two major factors. One, I belonged to a very liberal family. Nobody told me not to do anything. My parents have been always involved in activities that were connected to social issues. People from different walks of life visited my home. I first met Bhupen Hazarika in my house in 1957...I was exposed to social issues, Assamese songs, cultural traditions early on. I grew up in a world where there was rational discourse. Then, I was sent to a boarding school in Darjeeling and thereafter to Delhi for my college in the 1970s. It was the high period of Naxalism then, and many were deep into 'revolutionary' discussions. College life encompassed an important part of my commitment to future work.

The second factor is, I read a lot about Assamese literature, in English of course. Say, Birinchi Kumar Baruahh's *History of Assamese Literature*, books

[‡‡‡‡]The interview with Monisha Behal was recorded on phone on 12 April 2020.

on the history of cultural Assam by Prafulla Dutta Goswami, etc. It helped me to launch myself into village work.

I would also like to point out that there are three [reasons] why our Assamese society will remain protected from many ills. One is the Ahom period of history. Because of the 600 years of uninterrupted rule, we were saved of many evils. For instance, we don't have the rigid purdah system like in several parts of India. There was no occasion for women to be kept within the four walls of the house, like in many other parts of India, say in Rajasthan, where my family roots are from (Behal belongs to the family of Assamese cultural icon Jyoti Prasad Agarwala). Since the external forces were kept under check, it kept our women in a less oppressive position than in many other areas.

The second factor is the strong presence of tribal elements within our society. There is a high level of assimilation of the tribal and non-tribal elements within the Assamese society which added a blanket of liberalism over our society in general, and provided mobility to most of our women. This is reflective in our collective work participation, characteristic of tribal norms such as weaving, running of grain banks, and so on.

The third factor is, the Namghoria system instilled into Assamese society by Vaishnavism in the sixteenth century. Sankardev brought to our communal consciousness that be it a Brahmin or of a lower caste or a tribal, everyone is equal in the eyes of God. I used to go to naamghar as a youngster with my mother, particularly during the Hindu month of Bhado, as it was the birth month of Sankardev. The experience remained etched in my kind. My mother always wore a simple mekhela sador to go to the naamghar. Everyone was same there, rich or poor. These teachings gradually got embedded in our value system. Vaishnavism gave us the value of simplicity. That is why, when I went to work in the villages, I never felt any class difference.

Under these influences, my identity was formed and so were many others.

I would also like to add that our society still has a very strong relationship with the greenery around us, the foliage, the flora, in our everyday life. For instance, however educated or high society you may be, if you feel a little under the weather, it is not uncommon to hear suggestions to have some rice with local herbs like, say, manimuni, bhedailota, etc. All these herbs are still so easily available and are a part of the way of life in Assam.

For me, all of these comprise to define who is an Assamese, or what my identity is.

Lately though, we are noticing the strain of religious division gaining prominence in Assam.

Yes. But again, I would like to say that it is not as black and white as we notice in several other parts of India. For instance, within the Assamese Muslim community, the level of assimilation with the other groups of Assamese community is very strong. I will give you two recent examples to drive home my point. When during the Covid-19 scare, some positive cases were registered in Assam which had links to the religious group Tabliqi Jamaat's congregation in Delhi, I overheard a conversation among a [group] of three women, accusing 'these Muslims' of bringing the virus to the state. This was, while all of them were themselves Assamese Muslims.

Then, in March 2020, I attended an event in Guwahati on the identity of Muslim women in Assam. A male participant from Upper Assam said when he saw his daughter doing hijab for the first time, he was happy that she was following the norms of his religion, and took her to the 'goxai ghar' (Assamese for prayer house) to bless her. In the subconscious, the assimilation of the composite Assamese society and culture exists. But yes, there is no denying that the society is also getting increasingly polarized on religious lines. I don't feel the same as what I felt as a child. But I think that our historical and cultural narratives will check its proliferation.

AJIT BHUYAN[§§§§]

Senior journalist, Rajya Sabha member

As a close observer of Assamese society, who would you define as Assamese?

As far as the definition of 'Assamese' is concerned, I would like to quote a portion of the recommendations submitted to the Clause Six Committee, set up by the Ministry of Home Affairs, by the Axom Nagarik Samaj because I was also a party to it (as its executive president). To the question: Who are the indigenous Assamese, the Samaj said:

a) All the communities which were included as indigenous communities in the census of 1891;

[§§§§]Ajit Bhuyan said this in an email interview with the writer, published in *The Wire* on 3 April 2020.

b) All the communities enlisted by the Census Commissioner in the census report of 1951;
c) The people who identified themselves as one of the indigenous communities of Assam in the 1971 census and pledged to do so in future.
d) The Tea Tribe communities who were brought to Assam in the British colonial period. Again, all the communities who were considered Original Inhabitants (OI) at the time of the preparation of the updated National Register of Citizens.

HOLIRAM TERANG[¶¶¶¶]

Noted Karbi leader, former legislator

What would be your definition of an Assamese? Since most people in Assam have a dual identity, where do you locate yourself in Assam's identity movement as a Karbi?

I do not have the authority to define who is an Assamese. However, I do have some opinion about it. I would like to put it in this way. Different ethno-linguistic groups or communities migrated to the geographical area which in a particular period of time came to be identified as Assam, and settled down permanently. These groups of people are the natives of Assam.

Many of these communities have their own distinct language, culture, and social systems. Those whose mother tongue is Assamese language can be called or identified as Assamese people. Then there are also some whose mother tongue may not be Assamese but in course of time identified themselves as Assamese, who can also be termed as Assamese.

As to your second question, a person may have multiple identities. A person who primarily identifies oneself as Assamese but settled permanently in a state outside Assam or in a different country would have other identities as well. Similarly, I am a Karbi and a native of Assam. I, being a Karbi, would have another identity as a Meghalayan if I had permanently settled in that state.

SASHADHAR CHOUDHURY[*****]

Leader, pro-talks United Liberation Front of Asom (ULFA)

[¶¶¶¶]Holiram Terang responded to the questions in English via a WhatsApp message on 7 August 2020.

[*****]Sasadhar Choushury responded to the questions in Assamese via telephone on 21 April 2020. The English translation by the author was shared with him on WhatsApp for approval on 22 April 2020.

Who, according to you, is an Assamese?

...My view on this is very personal. Basically, you can't define the Assamese nation or identity from the format of the Indian context. The formation of this nation is very different in respect to the others. There is no ambiguity from my end that the Ahoms had settled the issue of Assamese nationality. The process was completed during the Ahom rule itself. The concept of Assamese nationality or identity has been fixed since.

There is no agency to provide a certificate of Assamese-ness to anybody. But the burden of proving oneself to be Assamese or not is on the person who claims himself or herself to be an Assamese. You can be a resident of Assam but that doesn't make you Assamese. What had made Jyoti Prasad Agarwala an Assamese inspite of his Marwari roots is because he and his family became culturally Assamese. It is not enough to contribute to the economy of the state but also important to the culture of the state.

He who speaks and communicates within his family in Assamese is, of course, Assamese. There could well be distinguished forms of Assamese, say Kamrupia, Nalbariya, Uzoni, etc. The second point is, he or she must adhere to or perform the cultural aspects of being Assamese, what is being fixed and prescribed by our ancestors during the Ahom period itself to be an Assamese.

Also, all cultural aspects have the essence of the Neo-Vaishnavite religion, Ek Sarana Dharma, propagated by Sankardev. Take for instance, the Kati Bihu, the Bohag Bihu, they have the essence of Sankardev's dharma. One will have to feel comfortable with it, no matter which religion one belongs to. The Vaishnavite essence exists in our culture but it is not what one understands typically of belonging to one religion only. For instance, when we perform Husori during Bohag Bihu, we refer to Krishna, Govinda, Ram, etc, but it is not in the typical religious sense. It is not ritualistic, but completely cultural. For instance, the food habits can make one an Assamese but never religion. Those who propagate religion more than the cultural aspects of Assamese identity are not Assamese.

I will give you another example. Take gamosa, an important marker of Assamese identity. It is not enough to just hang it by your neck. That piece of cloth has much more cultural significance than that. We put it around the womb of an expectant mother; we place it on the most revered place, the Thapona or the sanctum sanctorum of our naamghar.

The Miya Mussalmans have been identifying themselves as Assamese in population census. Together, they contribute to make Assamese language speakers the majority community in Assam. Yet, the matter is still not settled about their Assamese identity. What do you have to say to that?

I have come across some families of East Bengal origin who have adopted the cultural part of Assamese society. That makes them Assamese. They perform Bihu, speak the language at home, have contributed to Assamese literature, etc. Since they perform all aspects of Assamese cultural ethics, they are Assamese.

But we can't say all the people residing in the char chapori areas (sand bars of the rivers) are Assamese because they reside within the geographical bounds of the state. Yes, many of them want to be Assamese. So, it is our responsibility to give them the scope, the chance, to become one. We have to show them how can they be so. They will have to adopt the Assamese way of life, culturally.

Just because many from the community declare themselves as Assamese linguistically in Census doesn't make them one. The political forces do support it for reasons of vote but culturally, they will have to accept the Assamese way of life to become one. ...My point is, if anyone wants to become Assamese, the Assamese people must welcome them and it is their duty to show them the way to be one.

For instance, the rights of the Assamese women can't be compromised by practising polygamy, which is prevalent within the community. Monogamy is in our cultural ethics. It has to be practised. The women have to be allowed their rights and equal space within the community to be counted as Assamese.

If you tread back to, say, 1979, when the Assam's anti-foreigner agitation started, most people in Lower Assam where I come from, didn't celebrate Bihu in a big way, like it was in Upper Assam. However, I have noticed that more and more people began to realize that Bihu is a binding force of Assamese identity and it had to be adopted. Today, every colony in my district, Nalbari, has huge celebrations of Bihu.

In the char chapori areas, this duty of instilling the cultural practices of Assamese society should have been carried out by Asam Sahitya Sabha and the All Assam Students Union (AASU), which are considered to be principal organizations that uphold and protect Assamese identity. Unfortunately, they have failed to do so. So far, we are using the community to fulfil only our political needs.

UPAMANYU HAZARIKA[†††††]

Supreme Court lawyer and activist for protection of indigenous communities

Who would you call an Assamese and where would you locate yourself in the state's sensitive identity spectrum?

I am of the opinion that identity formation is an evolving facet of an individual. ...I was born and brought up in Assam, in a family where the first language was Assamese. On growing up, I moved to Delhi for work, where I also tried to establish my identity as a lawyer. But having lived in Assam during my formative years, and having witnessed the students' agitation which was launched to protect our collective identity in the context of migrants outnumbering us in what we call our homeland, our primary identity, it became the overriding backdrop for my identity formation as an Assamese first. That I returned to Assam with the thought that I would fight for the rights of the indigenous people of Assam has a lot to do with that consciousness.

So, if you ask me where I locate myself in terms of the identity question, in the context of the nation, I would begin by saying that I am an Indian first, and then an Assamese. But when I narrow it down in the context of my region and my state, I see my identity as part of the mosaic of the indigenous communities of the region and doing something to strengthen the roots of the multiple ethnic groups that are also a part of the nation. It is in this you will have to locate my fight against the Bangladeshi migrant community in Assam. There are about 115 ethnic groups in my state alone, out of 525 in India and all comprising a total population of two crores. The sizes of such communities are very small, ranging from 5,000 for Tai Phake and Tai Khamyam to 60 lakhs for the Tea Tribes and Koch Rajbonshis. The smaller size of their population leaves them extremely vulnerable to mass infiltration from Bangladesh. The protection of their identity is important to me. Unlike in many states where there is some amount of homogeneity in terms of population composition, Assam is much more complex.

In the last forty years or so, various ethnic communities which had earlier identified themselves as Assamese with Assamese as the link language, have begun to assert their individual identity. A factor for it is also because

[†††††]The interview was recorded on phone on 7 April 2020.

the Assamese identity began to comprise only the more advanced (in terms of education, sociopolitical position, etc.) communities. Along with the caste Hindus, the Ahoms, Morans, Motok, etc. too were there. But several plains tribes and other ethnic groups with socio-economic advancement began to assert their individual ethnic identity which was over and above the Assamese identity. However, since these communities have lived side by side for centuries with the other ethnic groups which have remained Assamese, a large number of customs, traditions, food habits, etc. remained common, aside from the fact that Assamese remained the link language between the communities. These commonalities, alongside accentuating the difference, in turn, have contributed to make Assamese society multifaceted. The acceptability of each other is through the assertion of their identity being part of a larger whole, rather than one identity. This, I feel, has helped the communities to feel themselves as a part of a larger identity which some would like to call Bor Axom or greater Assam.

TERESA RAHMAN[‡‡‡‡‡]

Award-winning journalist, writer

Who would you define as an Assamese, and where do you locate yourself in the identity spectrum?

I have never really tried to define the term 'Assamese'. But certain traits in me are very Assamese. For instance, I don't even know how to drape a sari. I have always worn the mekhela sador. I would gorge on pitha any day. I would prefer pitha to any other Indian sweet. I speak in Assamese at home. I celebrate Bihu. I would gift a gamosa or Assamese tea leaves to my friends from other parts of India. I always wore this identity on my sleeves, unknowingly. Being Assamese came naturally to me. If I am not one now, what am I then?

Have you noted any change/s in your lived experiences in Assamese society, particularly because of your Muslim identity, even though Assamese identity is hinged more on language than religion?

I have always grown up in a cosmopolitan atmosphere, with my non-Muslim friends and family friends. However, I have now noticed how changes have crept into our social fabric and the divisions are stark among acquaintances

[‡‡‡‡‡]The interview with Teresa Rahman was recorded on phone on 9 June 2020.

and friends. I suppose social media has amplified these differences. Somehow, the online world has taken over the real world by storm. I dare say that I don't think we can ever go back to the good old days.

RASHMI NARZARY[§§§§§]

Writer and winner of Sahitya Akademi Bal Puraskar (2016)

Who would you call an Assamese?

We're all parts of the whole. Neither the head, nor the heart can say it is the complete being. Yet, without any one part, the being isn't whole. Precisely that is the current equilibrium of the Assamese society.

You are born a Bodo and have always lived in Guwahati. You speak both Bodo and Assamese languages. How do you negotiate these twin identities in your daily life?

Being a Bodo living mostly in Guwahati, surrounded by a host of wonderful, non-Bodo people, negotiating these two identities has not really been a big issue, at least not till now. That probably is because of my ease with speaking Assamese and wearing the mekhela sador. However, the dilemma does not come from me but comes to me, when I am associated with Bodo literature or referred to as a writer of Bodo fiction, and not as a writer from Assam associated with English literature/fiction. I am then compulsively made to think of my identity. I have never written in Bodo, though yes, I have definitely projected Bodo society in the global platform, in English. Come to think of it, an Assamese writing in English, however, is not associated with Assamese literature.

So one identity has come in the way of the other? How do you negotiate it?
Sometimes, yes. So in those moments, I am a Bodo...from Assam!

SANDHYA MENON[¶¶¶¶¶]

Assamese singer

You had a Malayali father and a mother who belonged to a Marwari family. You are a popular Assamese singer. How do you see your identity?

[§§§§§]The interview with Rashmi Narzary was conducted via email on 17 March 2020.

[¶¶¶¶¶]The interview with Sandhya Menon was conducted at her home in Guwahati on 21 March 2021.

My father, K. Madhava Menon, was an engineering graduate from Kerala's Trichur Engineering College. He had come to Assam at the invitation of the state government in 1954 to work on the development projects and was posted in various parts of the state, including the North Eastern Frontier Agency (Arunachal Pradesh) which was within Assam then. When he was posted in Lakhimpur, he met my mother, Kumudini Agarwala, whom many also remembered there as Konmoina. She was from the extended family of Assamese cultural icon Jyoti Prasad Agarwala. They were cousins. Her father was a builder; he built the Lakhimpur airport. My mother had said that theirs was the first poki ghor (cemented construction) of Lakhimpur. Though my mother wrote the Agarwala surname, some from the family also wrote Maheswari. Later though, her father changed the family surname to Dutta.

My father fell in love with Assam and with my mother and settled down in the state. He, however, died in Kerala during a visit to his family in 1995.

My mother had four sisters; all were married to Assamese families. Some years ago, while in Lakhimpur for a stage show, I happened to mention that my mother's youngest sister was married to the local mouzadar (landlord)'s family there; it turned out that one of the organizers was her son.

When you ask me, how do I see my identity, I must say I am a human being first. When I meet someone, I don't look at the person's features first, but treat her as a person. The Assam my father saw treated people as so, the reason why he settled down and loved it so much. There was acceptance; one was welcomed to be part of the greater Assamese society. However, it did happen that some people looked at me only as a 'madrassi' in Assam and when we went to Kerala, only as an Assamese. But I got immense love and blessings from the people of Assam through my music. After my son was born, I took a break from stage shows for about three–four years. When I went back, there was a standing ovation and I cried in public.

Also, I am married to a person (Swapan Nath) who is half Bengali and half Assamese. Together, we have raised our children in Guwahati. So, you can say, my family represents what Assamese society truly is: a product of assimilation of various sets of people.

KAMAL TANTI******

Poet, critic, writer, translator, Sahiya Akademi Yuva Puraskar winner (2012)

Who, according to you, is an Assamese?

Although we believe that Assamese is a sociolinguistic community, but there are more meanings and essences to be added to this identity. The Assamese/Axomiya, being used as a generic name, is an umbrella term for the people of entire Brahmaputra and Barak valleys, including the surrounding hills and landscapes. In the past and in the present too, it has been as per their languages, culture, society; even ethnicity of various groups of people inhabiting in this part of Northeast India. Since the pre-historic period, many ethnic groups, like Austric, Dravidian, Mongoloid, and Aryan people came to this region along with their languages, heterogeneous cultures, variations of social systems and multi-identities, and as such, they had constructed their common language, culture, and identity, even losing some of the original part of their identity, culture and languages. As it is a common identity now in various sectors and fields, it should be preserved and developed for future.

Identities have been a very important part of sociocultural and political life of Assam. Where do you locate yourself in it and why?

Indeed. Accordingly, the common generic and umbrella-like identity of the people of present political and geographical Assam is to be developed democratically amongst them along with all the sociocultural aspects of the people of Assam for making it their common identity. Democratic thoughts and policy in the sociopolitical arena should be constructed, that includes all the ethnic groups of people of Assam in order to make it a wider nationality in this part of the country.

As a young representative of the Adivasis of Assam, I always felt that we need to understand the basic meaning and essence of the current struggle and crisis of identities among the Adivasis of the state. It is my humble attempt to signify the importance and at the same time, differentiate, the current political movements from the past movements in the community. It is important to relate this current struggle for making of a new identity with the much-hyped formation of greater Assamese identity, as that will

******The interview with Kamal Tanti was conducted through email on 1 April 2020.

help us delineate the complexity and compositeness of the new identity of Adivasis.

At the very onset, I would like to clear a perception in terms of the current situation. I disagree with the naming of my community as 'Tea-garden labourer community/ex-tea garden labourer community/Tea-tribe'. Is there any community in this world named after a commodity? It is the best example of the colonial domination of British, and later the internal colonialism taken over by the State. What I believe is that we have a duality regarding the nature of identity. I understand that we are an integral part of the greater Adivasi nationality of India and at the same time, we are also actively taking part in the formation of the greater Assamese identity. People who are progressive, liberal in thought, democratic in attitude, and put a firm stand against communalism, have recognized the Tea Tribes or the Adivasis as one of the most important communities contributing to the formation of the greater Assamese society.

So, I prefer to be called an Adivasi. I also prefer to put a duality into the identity of 'Tea-tribes and Adivasis of Assam'—first, we should be called as (only) 'Adivasi' and second, an 'Assamese'—rather 'Adivasi Assamese'. Further on this, I would identify all the ethnic groups who were brought to Assam primarily as indentured labourers to work in the tea plantations from various parts of India during the colonial period as 'Adivasi Assamese'.

PARVIN SULTANA[††††††]

Academic and social/political commentator

Who would you call an Assamese?

I understand the Assamese community as a linguistic community. While there is still a disagreement amongst the various groups of stakeholders about who is an Assamese, it remains a fact that language will be one of the deciding factors. This again boils down to the question: which Assamese speakers should be included in this category? Should it be only those whose first and primary language is Assamese or those who can speak the language along with other languages? What about those people who consciously chose Assamese as their language? Should their sacrifice be overlooked? I believe that people who can speak the language, who vouches allegiance to the Assamese culture and who wants to be a part

[††††††]The interview with Parvin Sultana was conducted via email on 12 March 2020.

of the greater Assamese society should be incorporated because these are people who believe that Assamese is a nationality in the making and they want to contribute to this process.

Where do you locate yourself within this identity consciousness?

Coming to the question of where do I situate myself on the plank of identity, I have to start with stating that I hail from Dhubri and I belong to the Deshi Muslims community. While my primary language or mother tongue is Deshi, I am equally comfortable with Assamese. On the question of whether I consider myself an Assamese, I do because I believe that diverse communities cutting across religion, ethnicity, and even language enriches Assamese as a community. But at the same time the tendency to keep certain communities outside this identity makes me wary. This tendency has more to do with a very narrow understanding of who is an Assamese and runs the risk of creating new fissures amongst the people. I believe that my identity as a Deshi Muslim woman is not in contradiction to the greater Assamese society which has benefitted from being inclusive and historically faced setback every time it tried to draw restrictive lines of divisiveness. So, I consider myself an Assamese but I also bring my own language, culture, and history to this identity.

UTTAM BATHARI[‡‡‡‡‡‡]

Associate professor, Department of History, Gauhati University

Who, according to you, is an Assamese? Since most people in Assam have a dual identity, as a Dimasa, where do you locate yourself in the state's long-drawn-out identity movement?

Assam, since the prehistoric times, has witnessed migration and settlement of disparate racial, linguistic groups over the millennia as the corridor of human migration. It continued through the colonial and post-colonial period, adding new dimensions to the identity issues. Leveraged by the colonial governmentality, hitherto fluid identities began to ossify with far reaching implications. Thus, defining Assamese is the most daunting task, given this historically bequeathed complex inter-ethnic relations that is played out in the realm of politics and quotidian details.

Since its inception, articulation of the Assamese nationalism/identity

[‡‡‡‡‡‡]The interview was Uttam Bathari was conducted via email on 16 August 2020.

is premised on language. The early Assamese nationalist leaders fervently exhorted immigrant population to adopt Assamese language. The historical link of the Assamese to the Sanskrit also elicited a sense of superiority among its practitioners thereby 'othering' the non-Aryan local indigenes as inferior/primitive. This, together with preferential treatment accorded to the Assamese language over other languages in the state, alienated the other ethnic groups, over time, leading to redrawing of the political map in the region. Articulation of separate political homeland, however, did not end there. Various communities like the Bodos, Karbis, and Dimasas are the prominent ones, at this moment.

However, it would be wrong to read the relationship of the Assamese with other marginal groups in ever antagonistic lens. There are occasions of cooperation too. An example of it is the anti-CAA movement. Even though the Sixth Schedule areas have been exempted from the proposed Act's operation, the hills of Assam did protest in solidarity with their plains counterpart. It may be noted here that Dimasa is one of the communities worst affected by immigration, and identifies itself with the anti-foreigners' movement of Assam. Thus, the relationship of the Assamese and other ethnic groups is rather a contextual flux between competition, cooperation, and negotiation.

Given this, 'tribal' or the non-Assamese speaking identities are layered. Thus, the idea of dual identity may further be illustrated as 'hyphenated identity' as argued elsewhere by Subir Bhowmik drawing analogies from Italian–American, Japanese–American, etc. Similar practice is witnessed in the neighbouring state of Nagaland, where all the ethnic groups come under an embracing terminology of Naga prefixed by sub group such as Ao Naga, Lotha Naga, Sema Naga, etc. However, actualization of such 'hyphenated identity' in Assam can be achieved only through an inclusive political action.

KAUSTUBH DEKA[§§§§§§]

Academic and sociopolitical commentator

What it means to be an Assamese or 'Axomiya' to you?

The question took me into a deep personal journey. In this quest within, I had to negotiate with quite a few inverted commas and quotation marks....

[§§§§§§]The interview with Kaustubh Deka was conducted via email on 24 July 2020.

Looking back, I became more aware of my 'Axomiya' identity when I moved to Delhi for my college studies, thus confirming the theory that one's sense of identity is shaped more by the 'non/mis-recognition' from others. I can also say now that one's sense of self-identity goes through a shift. To the question about my sense of identity, I would perhaps give different answers at different junctures of life. Depending on my location my sense of my 'Assamese-ness' kept changing. But does it mean that there is nothing essential or indispensable about being an Assamese? Let me try to define few 'core' aspects, the frontiers of which are in a permanent flux.

The immediate connection to my sense of 'Axomiya-ness' is of course the 'Axomiya' language itself. To be able to communicate, read, and write, in that order. For, languages are central to life-worlds. Having studied in 'vernacular' Axomiya medium school, the flare to read and write the language came much easily. But which 'Axomiya' is 'Axomiya' enough? That the Assamese language itself is fraught with contestation came out sharply once I came down from Dibrugarh town to study at the Cotton College in Guwahati and got exposed to the subtle but inexorable frictions around the Lower and Upper Assam dialects, coming out specially in the shared hostel spaces. The Cotton College days were also a window to the multi-ethnic character of the land. Difference seemed 'different' for the first time. The inherited 'set definition' of Assam constructed around 'Bihu-Sankardeva-Bhupen Hazarika' got problematized to some extent.

To be Assamese then was to connect to the land and to its myriad identities. This sense of 'belonging' got enhanced once I shifted to Delhi, the 'nobodies city' with the notorious reputation of othering the Northeastern people. Yes, that's the category where one 'belonged to'. Delhi breaks you and then finds you 'homes' too. Spaces that young migrants from Northeast India collectively build. This then became another essential aspect of me understanding my own Assamese-ness, as part of a shared imagination. An identity that is part of a larger collective negotiating with the 'othering' pushed down on it by the 'centre' that holds power. At that point, the best way I could make sense of my Assamese identity was as a peripheralized one that finds its voice only through its assertion of cultural and political rights.

Identities also materialize through our lived memories, episodes that leave a lingering impact on our subconscious. Stories about 'army operations' back in the ancestral village, families being subjected to fatal torture resurfaced in a new light. Lived and inherited trauma is what bound us, the 'northeasterners' together. My Assamese-ness became an undeniable part of this thread of sorrow, camaraderie, and resistance. The thread, however, followed me 'home', and soon after moving back to Assam, one got to witness the 'intertwined' moments of National Register of Citizenship (NRC) build-up and the passing of the Citizenship Amendment Act (CAA). The intense debates that surrounded these episodes helped one define one's own sense of 'Axomiya-ness', crafted around assertions as against denials.

...Once I moved back to Assam, the frames of identity shifted yet again and I began to find my sense of 'Assamese' self-identification inadequate on many counts. Agreed that Assamese and other 'indigenous' languages of the land were a good place to begin the identification with. But what about those speakers who do not speak one of these languages but remain 'attached' to the land? Could one not share a normative vision about a place despite not sharing a linguistic bond? It began to feel that the distinction between 'Axomiya' (Assamese speakers) and 'Axom baxi' (resident of Assam) did not add much in getting a grip over one's sense of 'Axomiya' identity. After all, an identity cannot and should not be built on negations alone. Although in the name of 'affirmations' one should guard against imposing 'Axomiya' identity on those who do not wish to identify as one.

Finally, an organic identity, one that commits to a judicious existence with the ecological habitat began to make more sense to me as a defining parameter of 'Assamese-ness'. In this understanding, an aspect of ecological responsibility that makes one look at the resources and the landscape with accountability and wisdom becomes almost a foundational trope to the one's sense of identity. To be an Assamese thus is to show respect and commitment to the natural habitat in which one lives. This is what perhaps is at the core of 'indigeneity', a certain organic attachment to the land, where the ideas of sustainability come naturally. Thus, I put one's 'Assamese-ness' to an ecological litmus test, with only those that show commitment to the resources and habitats deserving to qualify. Does it mean that I am denying any importance to the elements of language and culture while defining 'Assamese-ness?' No. But I am definitely trying to define it beyond these. Do I prioritize one over the other? Is there a hierarchy into this 'structure of experience'? To this, I do not have a fixed answer. 'To be an Axomiya' is to constantly negotiate between these experiences and critically engage with the categorizations in which one finds oneself.

SUREKHA CHHETRI[¶¶¶¶¶¶]

Popular Assamese and Nepali singer

Who do you consider as Assamese?

For me, all those people who live in Assam and speak Assamese, can read and write it, love, practice and promote Assamese culture and language, are Assamese. I may be born Gorkhali, may speak Nepali at home but I am also Assamese because I also speak Assamese and promote Assamese culture. If I can sing Dohori well, so can I do Bihu songs. If I am invited to Gorkha functions, I am invited to Bihu functions too to sing both in Assamese, Nepali, and also Hindi languages. Every Rongali Bihu in April, like other singers of Assam, my schedule is also packed because of the invites to sing at Bihu functions. It is the beauty of a multi-ethnic state like Assam that I get invitations to Bodo, Karbi, Mising, Adivasi, and other tribes' and community functions too.

You have two linguistic identities. Has it ever happened that one has come in the way of the other?

Never. As I said, I have been able to promote both my identities equally well. I am born in Assam, live in the state, so I can't be not Assamese. Gorkha, the community I belong, speaks Nepali as its common tongue which is recognized in the 8th Schedule of the Constitution. At the same time, I also want to promote my language, which is Nepali. In my most popular song, I have said as much: 'Nepali jodiu Axomiya moi' (Even if I am born a Nepali, I am Assamese too).

Long ago in India, Nepali was used as synonymous term for Gorkhas, like Mikir for Karbis, Kachari for Bodos, Miri for Misings, and Lalung for Tiwas in context of Assam, so the lyrics read so. Today, Gorkhas in Assam is a sub-community within the composite Assamese society and it is the only community in my knowledge demanding Assamese identity via Gazette Notification for itself to integrate while disintegration is taking place rampantly with twenty-nine-plus community organizations clubbed together to be Assamese.

In 2018, I took part in Voice of Nepal, the popular singing contest in that country, in lines of the international singing reality show The Voice.

[¶¶¶¶¶¶]The interview with Sureka Chetri was recorded on telephone on 14 March 2020.

There, I also mixed both Assamese and Nepali songs, wore Assamese mekhela sador, presented Axomiya phoolam gamoocha on stage to the coaches and celebrity guests. People appreciated those gestures a lot. Now, because of me, many people in Nepal listen to not just my Assamese songs but others' as well even if they don't understand the language. They love our pahari tunes. It gives me immense pleasure that I have been able to promote both my linguistic identities equally.

VIKAS TRIPATHY[*******]

Assistant professor, Department of Political Science, Gauhati University

Identity consciousness has been a salient feature of Assamese society or in Assam in entirety. Your native language is not Assamese but you speak it; live and work in Assam; are married to an Assamese. Where do you locate yourself in this identity spectrum? Have you ever found it difficult to negotiate through your dual linguistic identity in the state or because you are primarily Hindi speaking?

I agree with your assertion that identity consciousness has been a salient feature of Assamese society. I consider myself partly Assamese based on the kind of relationships that I have in this state and also because of the nature of my job. I teach Assamese students and seldom do we come across any difficulty in the process of teaching and learning in the classroom. The medium of instruction being English makes it more convenient.

However, apart from teaching, I have to involve myself in various corporate activities of the University and I feel language has never been much of a problem since the beginning. In part, because I could pick up the language, and adapt to the ethos of the society but more importantly, because people, in general, are not much resistant to communicate in Hindi with a person whom they consider to have come from outside or who doesn't know Assamese. People can understand Hindi. They may not be able to speak though. It makes communication easier and I did not face much problem interacting with people in everyday life....

I feel the language is the central marker of Assamese society but from my experience, I think the society is very open-minded and liberal in terms of accepting the 'other' in its fold through marriages. I have come across many families in the state that have matrimonial relations with non-Assamese families. I personally know Assamese persons married to persons

[*******]The interview with Vikas Tripathy was conducted via email on 13 May 2020.

from Tamil Nadu, Kerala, Uttar Pradesh, Bihar, Bengali (both Bengali from Assam and Bengali from West Bengal), and Kashmir. So marital and personal ties transcending linguistic divide is quite common though the language remains the most pertinent marker of political mobilization. The openness of society is apparent in the manner in which I see people celebrating diverse festivals. Though, festivals are mostly community specific, the access to space to diverse linguistic communities to celebrate its festivals indeed speaks volume about the flexibility of the larger Assamese society. Mostly, people are for a language and not against any language as such.

Politically, communities may be more divided on the basis of language. Yet, there is a profound exchange among communities despite ethnic and linguistic divide.

NOTES

PROLOGUE

1 These paragraphs are excerpted from Nagen Saikia's book, *Axomiya Manuhor Itihaax* (The History of the Assamese People), Katha Publications, Guwahati, p. 52. The excerpt has been translated into English by the author with the permission of the author.
2 Here, Nagen Saikia refers to the Assamese historian Rajmohan Nath (1899–1964) who wrote important books on the Northeast including *The Background of Assamese Culture*, published in 1948 in Shillong.

CHAPTER 1: THOLUA–KHILONJIA–NA AXOMIYA: THE ASSAMESE

1 Nina Simon, 'Introduction', *The Art of Relevance*, Museum 2.0, 2016.
2 Tony Joseph, *Early Indians: The Story of Our Ancestors and Where We Came From*, New Delhi: Juggernaut, 2018, p. 23.
3 Ibid., p. 5.
4 Ibid., p. 25.
5 Richard Cordaux and others, 'The Northeast Indian Passageway: A Barrier or Corridor for Human Migrations?', *Molecular Biology and Evolution*, Vol. 21, No. 8, August 2004, pp. 1525–33.
6 Ibid.
7 P. C. Choudhury, *The History of the Civilisation of the People of Assam to the Twelfth Century AD*, Guwahati: Department of Historical And Antiquarian Studies in Assam, 1966 (second edition), p. 75.
8 Ibid., p. 75.
9 B. C. Barua, *A Cultural History of Assam (Early Period)*, Guwahati: Lawyer's Book Stall, 1969, p. 67.
10 Ibid.
11 Ibid.
12 Ibid., p. 109.
13 Ibid., p. 109.
14 Ibid., p. 68.
15 Ibid., p. 109.
16 Ibid., p. 110.
17 Ibid.
18 P. C. Bagchi, *India and China: A Thousand Years of Cultural Relations*, Bombay: Hind Kitab, 1950, cited in Barua, *A Cultural History of Assam (Early Period)*, p. 110.
19 Ibid., p. 110.
20 Sir Arthur p. Phayre, *History of Burma Including Burma Proper, Pegu, Tuangu, Tenasserim and Arakan*, Truber and Co., Ludgate Hall, 1883, p. 15.
21 Ibid., p. 15.
22 Choudhury, *The History of the Civilisation*, p. 77.
23 Barua, *A Cultural History of Assam*, p. 112.
24 Ibid., p. 112.
25 *Indian Historical Quarterly*, Volume VIII, pp. 683–701, cited in Barua, *A Cultural History of Assam*, p. 111
26 Barua, *A Cultural History of Assam*, p. 111.
27 Nagen Saikia, *Asomiya Manuhar Itihaas*, Guwahati: Katha Publications, 2013, p. 52.
28 Barua, *A Cultural History of Assam*, p. 112.
29 Saikia, *Asomiya Manuhar Itihaas*, p. 52.
30 Barua, *A Cultural History of Assam*, p. 113.
31 Choudhury, *The History of the Civilisation*, p. 75.

32 Ibid., p. 75.
33 Ibid., p. 79.
34 Edward Gait, *A History of Assam*, Guwahati: Spectrum Publications, 2014 (1905), p. 4.
35 Ibid., p. 4.
36 Choudhury, *The History of the Civilisation*, p. 76.
37 Ibid., p. 76.
38 Ibid., p. 82.
39 Ibid.
40 Ibid.
41 Ibid.
42 Ibid., p. 83.
43 Ibid., p. 87
44 Gait, *A History of Assam*, p. 7.
45 Barua, *A Cultural History of Assam*, pp. 5–6.
46 Ibid., p. 6.
47 Choudhury, *The History of the Civilisation*, p. 98.
48 Ibid.
49 Ibid., p. 96.
50 Ibid., p. 95.
51 Ibid., p. 100.
52 Ibid.
53 Gait, *A History of Assam*, p. 6.
54 Choudhury, *The History of the Civilisation*, p. 101.
55 Gait, *A History of Assam*, p. 8.
56 Ibid., p. 38.
57 Choudhury, *The History of the Civilisation*, p. 104.
58 Ibid.
59 Ibid., p. 79.
60 Satyakam Phukan, available at drsatyakamphukan.files.wordpress.com/2011/10/asm-uni.pdf.

CHAPTER 2: PRAGJYOTISA–KAMRUP, ASHAM–AXOM–ASSAM: WHAT'S IN A NAME?

1 Gait, *History of Assam*, p. 74.
2 Ibid., p. 74.
3 Ibid., p. 245
4 Ibid.
5 Ibid., p. 246.
6 Ibid.
7 M. S. Prabhakara, 'In the name of changing names', *The Frontline*, 16 June 2006.
8 B. Bhattacharya quoted in Choudhury, *History of Civilisation of Assam*, p. 26.
9 Ibid., p. 26.
10 Ibid.
11 Saikia, *Asomiya Manuhar Itihaas*, p. 23. All Nagen Saikia quotes are translated by the author.
12 Ibid.
13 Ibid., p. 23.
14 Ibid., p. 24.
15 Ibid., p. 25.
16 Ibid.
17 Banikanta Kakati, *Assamese: Its Formation and Development*, Department of Historical and Antiquarian Studies, Narayani Handique Historical Institute, Gauhati: G. S. Press, Madras, 1941, p. 1.
18 Rajen Barua, *Asom, Oxom Aaru Ahom Namor Utpatti, Prantik*, Guwahati, 1–15 July edition, 2009.
19 Ibid.
20 Ibid.

21 Ibid.
22 Banikanta Kakati, *Mother Goddess Kamakhya*, p. 6, quoted in Choudhury, *The History of the Civilisation of Assam*, p. 27.
23 R. M. Nath, *The Background of Assamese Culture*, Shillong: A. K. Nath, 1948, pp. 4–5.
24 Ibid., p. 27.
25 Gait, *A History of Assam*, p. 15.
26 Choudhury, *The History of the Civilisation of Assam*, p. 27.
27 Ibid., p. 27.
28 Ibid., p. 36.
29 Barua, *A Cultural History of Assam*, p. 13.
30 Choudhury, *The History of the Civilisation of Assam*, p. 37.
31 Saikia, *Axomiya Manuhor Itihaax*, p. 29.
32 Choudhury, *The History of the Civilisation of Assam*, p. 37.
33 Ibid., p. 38.
34 Ibid., p. 29.
35 Ibid., p. 40.
36 Ibid., p. 35.
37 Saikia, *Axomiya Manuhor Itihaax*, p. 27.
38 Choudhury, *The History of the Civilisation of Assam*, p. 42.
39 Ibid.

CHAPTER 3: AXUR-DANAB-MLECHHA, ROJA-MOHAROJA-SWARGADEO: THE RULERS OF ASSAM

1 Kanak Lal Barua, *Early History of Kamarupa*, Guwahati: LBS Publications, 2020, first edition 1933, p. 25.
2 Nath, *The Background of Assamese Culture*, p. 26.
3 Gait, *A History of Assam*, p. 17.
4 Ibid.
5 Gait, *A History of Assam*, p. 12.
6 Choudhury, *The History of Civilisation of the People of Assam*, p. 108.
7 Ibid., p. 109
8 Lal Barua, *Early History of Kamarupa*, p. 42.
9 Choudhury, *The History of Civilisation of the People of Assam*, p. 109.
10 Nath, *The Background of Assamese Culture*, p. 26.
Choudhury, *The History of Civilisation of the People of Assam*, p. 108.
11 Ibid., p. 26.
12 Ibid.
13 Ibid., p. 27.
14 Nath, *The Background of Assamese Culture*, p. 27.
15 Ibid.
16 Choudhury, *The History of Civilisation of the People of Assam*, p. 113.
17 Ibid., p. 112.
18 Ibid.
19 Ibid., p. 111.
20 Ibid., p. 112.
21 Ibid., pp. 111–12.
22 Ibid., p. 114.
23 Nath, *The Background of Assamese Culture*, p. 28.
24 Ibid.
25 Ibid., p. 29.
26 Gait, *A History of Assam*, p. 14.
27 Ibid.
28 Ibid., p. 15.
29 Barua, *Early History of Kamarupa*, p. 36.

30 Gait, *A History of Assam*, p. 14.
31 Ibid., p. 15.
32 Choudhury, *The History of Civilisation of the People of Assam*, p. 126.
33 Nath, *The Background of Assamese Culture*, p. 31.
34 Ibid., pp. 32–33.
35 Ibid., p. 133.
36 Ibid., p. 33.
37 Choudhury, *The History of Civilisation of the People of Assam*, p. 153.
38 P. C. Sarma, *Architecture of Assam*, Delhi: Agam Kala Prakashan, 1988, p. 13.
39 Ibid., p. 141.
40 Choudhury, *The History of Civilisation of the People of Assam*, p. 140.
41 Ibid., p. 141.
42 Ibid., p. 145–153.
43 Ibid., p. 154.
44 Ibid., p. 164.
45 Ibid., p. 170.
46 Ibid., p. 179.
47 Ibid.
48 Ibid.
49 Gait, *A History of Assam*, p. 29.
50 Ibid., p. 30.
51 Ibid.
52 Barua, *Early History of Kamarupa*, p. 103.
53 Ibid., p. 201.
54 Ibid., p. 109.
55 Ibid., p. 225.
56 Ibid.
57 Gait, *A History of Assam*, p. 34.
58 Ibid., p. 236.
59 Ibid.
60 Choudhury, *The History of Civilisation of the People of Assam*, p. 238.
61 Ibid., p. 254.
62 Ibid., p. 256.
63 Ibid.
64 Nath, *The Background of Assamese Culture*, p. 50.
65 Barua, *Early History of Kamarupa*, p. 240.
66 Ibid., p. 45.
67 Ibid.
68 Ibid., p. 242.
69 Ibid., p. 251.
70 Gait, *A History of Assam*, p. 39.
71 Barua, *Early History of Kamarupa*, p. 257.
72 Ibid., p. 260.
73 Gait, *A History of Assam*, p. 49.
74 Barua, *Early History of Kamarupa*, p. 260.
75 Gait, *A History of Assam*, p. 49.
76 Ibid., p. 52.
77 Ibid., p. 55.
78 Barua, *Early History of Kamarupa*, p. 268.
79 Ibid., pp. 268–69.
80 Ibid., p. 270.
81 Gait, *A History of Assam*, p. 56.
82 Ibid., p. 62.
83 Sarma, *Architecture of Assam*, p. 161.
84 Ibid., p. 71.

85 Ibid., p. 161.
86 Ibid., p. 275.
87 Ibid., p. 161.
88 Ibid.
89 Ibid., p. 164.
90 Ibid., p. 248.
91 Ibid., p. 252.
92 Nath, *The Background of Assamese Culture*, p. 71.
93 Ibid., p. 71.
94 Ibid.
95 Ibid.
96 Ibid.
97 Gait, *A History of Assam*, p. 247.
98 Ibid.
99 Ibid., p. 250.
100 Nath, *The Background of Assamese Culture*, p. 72.
101 Gait, *A History of Assam*, p. 249.
102 Ibid., p. 251.
103 Ibid., p. 256.
104 Nath, *The Background of Assamese Culture*, p. 68.
105 Ibid., p. 70.
106 Ibid., p. 61.
107 Ibid., p. 63.
108 Ibid., p. 64.
109 Ibid., p. 60.
110 Ibid.
111 Gait, *A History of Assam*, p. 78.
112 Ibid., p. 74.
113 Ibid., p. 75.
114 Ibid., p. 76.
115 Ibid., p. 77.
116 Nath, *The Background of Assamese Culture*, p. 125.
117 Ibid., p. 125.
118 Gait, *A History of Assam*, p. 80.
119 Ibid., p. 83.
120 Ibid., p. 84.
121 Ibid., p. 94.
122 Ibid.
123 Ibid., p. 101.
124 Ibid., p. 106.
125 Nath, *The Background of Assamese Culture*, p. 108.
126 Ibid., p. 109.
127 Gait, *A History of Assam*, p. 128.
128 Ibid., p. 137.
129 Ibid., p. 138.
130 Ibid., p. 154.
131 Ibid.
132 Ibid., p. 159.
133 S. K. Bhuyan, *Tungkhungia Buranji or A History of Assam (1681–1826 AD)*, London: Oxford University Press, 1933, p. 20.
134 Ibid.
135 Ibid.
136 Gait, *A History of Assam*, p. 184.
137 Ibid., p. 185.
138 Ibid., p. 188.

139 Ibid., p. 189.
140 Bhuyan, *Tungkhungia Buranji*, p. 60.
141 Ibid., p. 116. This is Bhuyan's translation of the *Tungkhungia Buranji* by Ahom official Srinath Duara Barbarua.
142 Gait, *A History of Assam*, p. 214.
143 Bhuyan, *Tungkhungia Buranji*, p. 204
144 Ibid.
145 Gait, *A History of Assam*, p. 289.
146 Ibid.
147 Ibid.
148 The telephonic conversation with Jishnu Barua was recorded on 7 February 2021.
149 Bhuyan, *Tungkhungia Buranji*, p. 216.
150 Ibid.
151 Ibid., p. 218.

CHAPTER 4: 'SILY SIKEN' AND THE 'X' FACTOR: THE HISTORY OF ASSAMESE LANGUAGE

1 Kaliram Medhi, *Asamiya Byakaran Aru Bhashatatva*, Guwahati: Lawyers Book Stall, 2019 (1936), p. 19.
2 Ibid.
3 Ibid.
4 Debananada Bharali, *Asamiya Bhasar Moulik Bisar*, Guwahati: Lawyers Book Stall, 2016 (1912), p. 10.
5 Ibid.
6 Ibid., p. 11.
7 Ibid., p. 12.
8 Bani Kanta Kakoti, *Assamese, Its Formation and Development*, Gauhati: Department of Historical and Antiquarian Studies, Government of Assam, 1941, p. 7.
9 Bharali, *Asamiya Bhasar Moulik Bisar*, p. 12.
10 Ibid., p. 12.
11 Kakoti, *Assamese, Its Formation and Development*, p. 10.
12 Bharali, *Asamiya Bhasar Moulik Bisar*, p. 49.
13 The interview with Nagen Saikia was conducted on email over email on 25 May 2020.
14 E. J. Rapson, *Ancient India: From the Earliest Times to the First Century AD*, Cambridge University Press, 1914, p. 10.
15 Medhi, *Asamiya Byakaran Aru Bhashatatva*, p. 21.
16 Ibid., p. 22.
17 Ibid.
18 Ibid., p. 31.
19 Saikia, *Asomiya Manuhar Itihaas*, p. 256.
20 Ibid., p. 256.
21 Bharali, *Asamiya Bhasar Moulik Bisar*, p. 20.
22 Saikia, *Asomiya Manuhar Itihaas*, p. 255.
23 Bharali, *Asamiya Bhasar Moulik Bisar*, p. 21.
24 Kakoti, *Assamese, Its Formation and Development*, p. 16.
25 Bharali, *Asamiya Bhasar Moulik Bisar*, p. 22.
26 Saikia, *Asomiya Manuhar Itihaas*, p. 256.
27 Kakoti, *Assamese, Its Formation and Development*, p. 9.
28 Ibid., p. 10.
29 Bharali, *Asamiya Bhasar Moulik Bisar*, p. 17.
30 Ibid., p. 18.
31 Ibid., p. 12.
32 James M'Cosh, *Topography of Assam*, 1975, Delhi: Sanskaran Prakashn, p. 5.
33 Ibid., p. 14.

34 Kakoti, *Assamese, Its Formation and Development*, p. 7.
35 Ibid., p. 8.
36 Ibid., p. 12.
37 Saikia, *Asamiya Manuhar Itihaas*, p. 257.
38 The telephonic interview with Upen Rabha Hakasam was recorded on 10 April 2020.
39 Kakoti, *Assamese, Its Formation and Development*, p. 52.
40 Upendranath Goswami, *Asamiya Lipi*, Guwahati: Assam Prakashan Parishad, 2016 (1989), p. 3.
41 Ibid.
42 Ibid., p. 4.
43 Ibid.
44 Choudhury, *The History of the Civilisation*, p. 364.
45 Ibid.
46 Ibid.
47 Ibid.
48 Goswami, *Asamiya Lipi*, pp. 6–7.
49 Ibid., p. 10.
50 Ibid.

CHAPTER 5: PUJA–PATOL, NAAM–PROXONGO: ASSAMESE FOLK AND RELIGIOUS BELIEFS

1 Nirmal Prabha Bordoloi, *Asamar Loka Sanskriti*, Calcutta: Nabajiban Press, 1972, p. 102.
2 Sukumar Sen, *History of Bengali Literature*, New Delhi: Sahitya Akademi, 1960, p. 159.
3 Bordoloi, *Asamar Loka Sanskriti*, p. 102.
4 The interview with Padmeswar Gogoi was recorded at his residence in Golaghat on 24 November 2020.
5 Nath, *The Background of Assamese Culture*, p. 50.
6 Baruah, *A Cultural History of Assam*, p. 187.
7 Choudhury, *The History of Civilisation of the People of Assam*, p. 394.
8 Ibid., pp. 413–14.
9 N. N. Bhattacharyya, *Religious Culture of North-eastern India*, Daryaganj: Manohar Publishers, 1995, p. 88.
10 Ibid.
11 Ibid., p. 89.
12 Ibid., p. 98.
13 Choudhury, *The History of Civilisation of the People of Assam*, pp. 413–14.
14 Ibid., p. 414.
15 Bhattacharyya, *Religious Culture of North-eastern India*, Manohar Publishers, Daryaganj, 1995, p. 99.
16 Maheswar Neog, *Sankardev: The Great Integrator*, New Delhi: Omsons Publications, 2011, p. 11.
17 Ibid., p. 107.
18 B. C. Allen, E. A. Gait, C. G. H. Allen, H. F. Howard, *The Gazetteer of Bengal and North East India*, Delhi: Mittal Publishers, 1979, p. 53.
19 Esther Bloch, Marianne Keppens, and Rajaram Hedge (eds.), *Rethinking Religion in India: The Colonial Construction of Hinduism*, Routledge, 2011, p. 51.
20 Satyendranath Sarma, *A Socio-Economic & Cultural History of Medieval Assam* (1200 AD – 1800 AD), Guwahati: Arunodoy Press, 1989, p. 266.
21 Ibid., p. 267.
22 Bordoloi, *Asamar Loka Sanskriti*, p. 97.
23 Choudhury, *The History of Civilisation of the People of Assam*, p. 392.
24 Ibid., p. 206.
25 Ibid., p. 392.
26 Arpita Sarkar and Tapas Mistri, 'A Discourse on the Religious Practices of Rabha Community of West Bengal', *International Journal of Research in Social Sciences*, Vol. 8, Issue 7, 2018.
27 Bordoloi, *Asamar Loka Sanskriti*, p. 93.
28 Nabin Chandra Sarma and Prabin Chandra Das, *A Handbook of Folklore material of North-East*

India, Birendranath Datta (ed.), Assam: Anundoram Barooah Institute of Language, Art & Culture, 1994, p. 161.
29 Bordoloi, *Asamar Loka Sanskriti*, p. 91.
30 Choudhury, *The History of Civilisation of the People of Assam*, p. 406.
31 Ibid., p. 407.
32 Bordoloi, *Asamar Loka Sanskriti*, p. 100.
33 Choudhury, *The History of Civilisation of the People of Assam*, p. 408.
34 Sarma and Das, *A Handbook of Folklore material of North-East India*, p. 155.
35 Ibid.
36 Prafulla Datta Goswami, *Bohagor Bihur Bareboronia Sobi*, Guwahati: Chandra Prakash, 1975, p. 3.
37 Ibid., p. 4.
38 Ibid.
39 Ibid.
40 Ibid.
41 Choudhury, *The History of Civilisation of the People of Assam*, p. 392.
42 Barua, *A Cultural History of Assam*, p. 115.
43 Ibid.
44 Ibid.
45 Ibid., p. 119.
46 Choudhury, *The History of Civilisation of the People of Assam*, p. 314.
47 Ibid.
48 Ibid.
49 Barua, *A Cultural History of Assam*, p. 128.
50 Choudhury, *The History of Civilisation of the People of Assam*, p. 318.
51 Ibid.
52 Barua, *A Cultural History of Assam*, p. 127.
53 Soumyadeep Datta, *Asomot Boudha Dharma Aru Boudha Sanskriti*, Guwahati: Banalalta, 2015, second edition, p. 13.
54 Ibid., p. 31. However, Birinchi Kumar Baruah in *A Cultural History of Assam* said the king was a Vaishnavite (p. 169).
55 Datta, *Asomot Boudha Dharma Aru Boudha Sanskriti*, p. 13.
56 Barua, *A Cultural History of Assam*, p. 182.
57 Choudhury, *The History of Civilisation of the People of Assam*, p. 400.
58 Ibid., p. 401.
59 Ibid., p. 402.
60 Datta, *Asomot Boudha Dharma Aru Boudha Sanskriti*, p. 15.
61 Choudhury, *The History of Civilisation of the People of Assam*, p. 402.
62 Datta, *Asomot Boudha Dharma Aru Boudha Sanskriti*, p. 187.
63 Ibid., p. 267.
64 Ibid., p. 242.
65 Ibid., p. 227.
66 Ibid., p. 16.
67 Barua, *A Cultural History of Assam*, p. 169.
68 Ibid., p. 409.
69 Choudhury, *The History of Civilisation of the People of Assam*, p. 409.
70 Barua, *A Cultural History of Assam*, p. 169.
71 Ibid., p. 172.
72 Choudhury, *The History of Civilisation of the People of Assam*, p. 413.
73 Barua, *Early History Of Kamrup*, p. 272.
74 Ibid.
75 Ibid., p. 273.
76 Choudhury, *The History of Civilisation of the People of Assam*, p. 413.
77 Barua, *Early History Of Kamrup*, p. 276.
78 Swadesh Ranjan Ghosh, *Teachings of Sri Sankardeva*, R. Malakar (ed.), Chandigarh: Sankar Jyoti Association, 1977, p. 149.

79 Barua, *Early History of Kamrup*, p. 276.
80 Ibid., p. 84 (The essay was by Satyendra Nath Sharma).
81 Neog, *Sankardev*, p. 5.
82 Ghosh, *Teachings of Sri Sankardeva*, p. 145.
83 Barua, *Early History of Kamrup*, p. 275.
84 Neog, *Sankardev*, p. 6.
85 Kirpal Singh Narang, *Teachings of Sri Sankardeva*, p. 68.
86 Satyendra Nath Sharma, *Teachings of Sri Sankardeva*, p. 81.
87 Sangeeta Barooah Pisharoty, '"Unless Assam is allowed to Develop on its Own Resources, Unrest Will Always Be There": Hiren Gohain', *The Wire*, 9 December 2017.
88 Neog, *Sankardev*, p. 7.
89 Barua, *Early History of Kamrup*, p. 282.

CHAPTER 6: TI–LAO–AANOI–ABUNG–BULUNG BUTUR, LAUHITYA–LUIT–BRAHMAPUTRA: THE RED RIVER IN ASSAMESE LIFE

1 Arup Jyoti Saikia, *The Unquiet River*, Delhi: Oxford University Press, 2019, p. 238.
2 Birinchi Kumar Baruahh, *Asomiya Sanskriti*, Hariprasad Neog and Lila Gogoi (eds.), Asam Sahitya Sabha, 1975, p. 316.
3 The conversation with Nahendra Padun was recorded on 2 March 2021.
4 Choudhury, *The History of Civilisation of the People of Assam*, p. 36.
5 Banikanta Kakati, *Assamese: Its Formation and Development*, Gauhati: Department of Historical and Antiquarian Studies in Assam, 1941, p. 55.
6 Choudhury, *The History of Civilisation of the People of Assam*, p. 46.
7 Saikia, *The Unquiet River*, p. 92.
8 Ibid., p. 94.
9 Ibid., p. 98.
10 Ibid., p. 81.
11 Sangeeta Barooah Pisharoty, 'Modi In Majuli: In Assam's Riverine Island, BJP Hopes to Trump its Rivals', *The Wire*, 29 March 2016.
12 Ibid., p. 484.
13 Ranjita Biswas, *Brahmaputra and the Assam Valley*, Niyogi Books, 2013, p. 9.
14 Saikia, *The Unquiet River*, p. 216.
15 Biswas, *Brahmaputra and the Assam Valley*, p. 9.
16 Ibid., p. 10.
17 Ibid.
18 Saikia, *The Unquiet River*, p. 210.
19 Ibid., p. 265.
20 Saikia, *The Unquiet River*, p. 484.
21 Ibid., p. 487.
22 Ibid., p. 479.
23 'Nitin Gadkari announces Rs. 40,000 expressway project in Northeast', *Economic Times*, 4 April 2017.
24 'No Proposal for building highway along Brahmaputra, says Nitin Gadkari', *The Sentinel*, 8 February 2021.
25 Rajiv Konwar, 'Dredging Along the Brahmaputra not feasible: Panel', *The Telegraph*, 4 February 2020.
26 'No Proposal for building highway along Brahmaputra, says Nitin Gadkari'.
27 Saikia, *The Unquiet River*, p. 103.

CHAPTER 7: KHAAR–KHORISA, LAI–LOPHA, MAAS–KASO, HAAH–PARO: ASSAMESE CUISINE

1 Sarbeswar Rajguru, *Medieval Assamese Society* (1228–1826 CE), Nagaon: Asami, 1988, p. 168.
2 Saikia, *Axomiya Manuhor Itihaax*, p. 193.
3 Rajguru, *Medieval Assamese Society*, p. 161.
4 Saikia, *Axomiya Manuhor Itihaax*, p. 195.
5 Barua, *A Cultural History of Assam*, p. 138.
6 Choudhury, *The History of Civilisation of Assam*, p. 338.
7 Saikia, *Axomiya Manuhor Itihaax*, p. 182.
8 Moushumi Bordoloi Hazarika, *Karbi Anglong Zilar Pahariya Tiwaxokolor Xomaj Aaru Xonsoskriti*, Guwahati: Jagaran Sahitya Prakashan, 2019, p. 79.
9 'Bridging The Gap: A discussion in Assamese on food culture in Assam enriched with ethnic food heritage', 9 January 2021.
10 Rajguru, *Medieval Assamese Society*, p. 162.
11 Ibid., p. 166.
12 Satyendra Sarma, *A Socio-Economic and Cultural History of Medieval Assam*, Guwahati Arunudoy Press, 1989, p. 250.
13 Saikia, *Axomiya Manuhor Itihaax*, p. 182.
14 Utpal Parashar, 'Assam's biggest religious body "expels" family for rearing pigs', *Hindustan Times*, 18 May 2019.
15 This was related to me by journalist Prasanta Bora during an interview conducted on 10 January 2021.
16 The interview with Shabnam Bora was conducted on 15 January 2021.
17 This was related to the author by Nanda Kirati Dewan in an interview for the chapter conducted on 16 January 2021.
18 Saikia, *Axomiya Manuhor Itihaax*, p. 195.
19 The telephonic interview with Sanjay Kumar Tanti was recorded on 6 December 2020.
20 Choudhury, *The History of Civilisation of Assam*, p. 327.
21 Ibid., p. 336.
22 This information was shared by Nanda Kirati Dewan with the author.
23 Choudhury, *The History of Civilisation of Assam*, p. 328.
24 Ibid.
25 Saikia, *Axomiya Manuhor Itihaax*, p. 196.
26 Ibid.
27 Jawahar Jyoti Kuli, *Mising Sanaskriti*, Dibrugarh: Kaustubh Prakashana, p. 68.
28 Saikia, *Axomiya Manuhor Itihaax*, p. 193.
29 Vijaita Singh, 'North East Citizens Faced Racial Discrimination amid Covid-19 Outbreak, Says Govt Study', *The Hindu*, 12 April 2021.
30 Dina Fine Maron, 'Wet Markets launched the Coronavirus: Here's What You Need to Know', National Geographic, 15 April 2020.
31 Physche Williams-Forson, *More than Just the 'Big Piece of Chicken': The Power of Race, Class and Food in American Consciousness*, Carole Counihan and Penny Van Esterik (eds.), Routledge, 2013, p. 117.
32 Zilkia Janer, 'Assamese Food and the Politics of Taste', *Seminar*, No. 640, 2012.
33 Ibid.
34 J. B. Tavernier, *Travels in India*, Vol. 11, second edition, p. 222, quoted in Barua, *A Cultural History of Assam*, p. 96.
35 Barua, *A Cultural History of Assam*, p. 96.
36 Mangalsingh Ronghphar, 'Traditional Cuisine of the Karbis', *Nezine*, 16 February 2016.
37 Saikia, *Axomiya Manuhor Itihaax*, p. 175.
38 Sarma, *A Socio-Economic and Cultural History of Medieval Assam*, p. 250.
39 This information was shared with the author by Sanjay Kumar Tanti.
40 Choudhury, *The History of Civilisation of Assam*, p. 335.
41 Saikia, *Axomiya Manuhor Itihaax*, p. 194.
42 Sarma, *A Socio-Economic and Cultural History of Medieval Assam*, p. 249.
43 This information was shared with the author by Sanjay Kumar Tanti.
44 The interview with Padmeswar Gogoi was conducted in November 2019 at his house in Golaghat, Assam.

45 Surja Das, *Mass Aaru Masmoria*, self-published, Kamrup: Palashbari, 1989, p. 7.
46 Ibid.
47 Ibid.
48 Nahendra Padun, *Axomiya Xongostitiloi Janajatio Borongoni*, Siwasagara, 1988, p. 22.
49 Saikia, *Axomiya Manuhor Itihaax*, p. 196.
50 Ibid.
51 The interview with Hussain Ahmad Madani was conducted on 19 January 2021.
52 Saikia, *Axomiya Manuhor Itihaax*, p. 175.
53 Sarma, *A Socio-Economic and Cultural History of Medieval Assam*, p. 247.
54 Saikia, *Axomiya Manuhor Itihaax*, p. 194.
55 Rajguru, *Medieval Assamese Society*, p. 165.
56 Choudhury, *The History of Civilisation of Assam*, p. 335.
57 Saikia, *Axomiya Manuhor Itihaax*, p. 194.
58 Ronghphar, 'Traditional Cuisine of the Karbis'.
59 Ajit Patowary, 'Neolithic Age Site Discovered in Assam', *Assam Tribune*, 15 September 2010.
60 Barua, *A Cultural History of Assam*, p. 95.
61 The interview with Girin Phukan was conducted on 10 August 2021.
62 Chandrika Das, 'From being a small town boy to an acclaimed chef – Journey of Atul Lahkar, *Guwahati Plus*, 22 December 2017.
63 The interview with Snehalata Saikia was conducted on 20 December 2019.
64 Rajguru, *Medieval Assamese Society*, p. 169.

CHAPTER 8: KAAH–PITOL, DA–KUTHAR, DOLA–KHORAHI: ASSAMESE CRAFTS

1 The interview with Maheswar and Tapan Neog was recorded at his residence on 29 December 2020.
2 Saikia, *Axomiya Manuhor Itihaax*, p. 230.
3 Rajguru, *Medieval Assamese Society*, p. 331.
4 Ibid., p. 330.
5 The interview with Manoj Bhuyan and Dinabandhu Deka was recorded at the Assam Samabai Kahar Sangha Limited, Sarthebari, on 29 December 2020.
6 Rajguru, *Medieval Assamese Society*, p. 331.
7 Sarma, *A Socio-Economic and Cultural History of Medieval Assam*.
8 Allen, Gait, Allen, and Howard, *The Gazetteer of Bengal and North East India*, p. 83.
9 Saikia, *Axomiya Manuhor Itihaax*, p. 228.
10 Ibid., p. 229.
11 Ibid., p. 228.
12 Rajguru, *Medieval Assamese Society*, p. 330.
13 Saikia, *Axomiya Manuhor Itihaax*, p. 229.
14 Ibid., p. 227.
15 Sarma, *A Socio-Economic and Cultural History of Medieval Assam*, p. 312.
16 Ibid., p. 312.
17 Allen, Gait, Allen, and Howard, *The Gazetteer of Bengal and North East India*, p. 83.
18 Ibid., p. 84.
19 Rajguru, *Medieval Assamese Society*, p. 335.
20 Ibid., p. 336.
21 Ibid., p. 349.
22 Ibid.
23 Sarma, *A Socio-Economic and Cultural History of Medieval Assam*, p. 314.
24 Rajguru, *Medieval Assamese Society*, p. 319.
25 Sarma, *A Socio-Economic and Cultural History of Medieval Assam*, p. 313.
26 Arupjyoti Saikia, *The Unquiet River*, Kolkata: Oxford University Press, 2019, p. 104.
27 Ibid., p. 107.
28 Ibid., p. 113.
29 Ibid., p 112.

30 The interview with Uttam Somua was recorded at the construction site in Majuli on 26 December 2020.
31 'This man from Assam is making eco-firendly bamboo water bottles to reduce plastic use', *YourStory*, 9 August 2019.
32 Ibid., p. 316.
33 Ibid., p. 317.
34 Ibid., p. 309.
35 Saikia, *Axomiya Manuhor Itihaax*, p. 222.
36 Sarma, *A Socio-Economic and Cultural History of Medieval Assam*, p. 309.
37 Saikia, *Axomiya Manuhor Itihaax*, p. 222.
38 Brojen Chandra Neog, 'Majuli artisans keep ancient handmade pottery and centuries old barter trade system alive', *Nezine*, 23 June 2016.
39 Sangeeta Barooah Pisharoty, 'Of Theatre, Masks and Traditions', *The Wire*, 15 February 2017.
40 Ibid.
41 Ibid.
42 Sangeeta Barooah Pisharoty, 'The Sorrow of Majuli', *The Hindu*, 24 December 2011.

CHAPTER 9: ERI–MUGA–PAAT–KOPAHI–KERU MONI: ASSAMESE WEAVE AND JEWELLERY

1 The conversation with Dakhinpat Satradhikar Nani Gopal Devagoswami was recorded in the Satra on 23 December 2020.
2 Utpal Parashar, 'Attempt to recreate 16th century sacred cloth divide Assam's Vaishnava monasteries', *Hindustan Times*, 14 July 2019.
3 Richard Burton, 'Krishna in the Garden of Assam – The cultural context to an Indian textile', The British Museum, YouTube, 2016, available at www.youtube.com/watch?v=S8c5ZarOmvY.
4 Ibid.
5 Rosemary Crill's write-up as part of the exhibition at the Victoria and Albert Museum can be accessed at www.atributetosankaradeva.org/vastra.pdf.
6 The interview with Sanjiv Borkakoty was recorded on 4 April 2021.
7 Ibid.
8 Rosemary Crill's write-up as part of the exhibition at the Victoria and Albert Museum.
9 Roopa Sharma quoted in 'Vrindavani Vastra – A Kohinoor From The North-East India', *The Kootneeti*, 28 October 2017.
10 'Hidden in the Lining - Krishna in the Garden of Assam': Inside an Eighteenth-Century Banyan', *The Costume Society*, 26 November 2017.
11 Ibid.
12 Ibid.
13 The interview with Kanaksen Deka was recorded on 29 May 2020.
14 Utpal Parashar, 'Attempt to recreate 16th century sacred cloth divides Assam's Vaishnavite monasteries', *Hindustan Times*, 14 July 2019.
15 Ibid.
16 The interview with Pranjal Saikia was recorded on 31 March 2020 in Guwahati.
17 Ibid., p. 71.
18 Ibid., p. 69.
19 Saikia, *Axomiya Manuhor Itihaax*, p. 210.
20 Ibid., p. 58.
21 Ibid., p. 155.
22 Ibid., p. 47.
23 Labanya Mazumdar, *Textile Tradition of Assam – An Empirical Study*, Bhabani Books, 2013, p. 87.
24 Gargee Bhattacharjee, 'Dimasa Textiles: Weaving Texhniques and Processes, Terminology and History', *Sahapedia*, 28 September 2018.
25 Ibid., pp. 118–19.
26 Ibid., p. 121.
27 Ibid., p. 125.

28 Ibid., p. 129.
29 Ibid., p. 138.
30 Ibid.
31 Ibid., pp. 139–41.
32 Mazumdar, *Textile Tradition of Assam*, p. 141.
33 Ibid., p. 142.
34 Ibid., p. 98.
35 Ibid., p. 105.
36 Ibid.
37 'Design and Development of a semi-automatic handloom', Indian Institute of Technology (IIT), Guwahati, 12 April 2014, available at http://gyan.iitg.ernet.in/bitstream/handle/123456789/2351/TH-3028_166105007.pdf?sequence=2&isAllowed=y.
38 Ibid., p. 23.
39 Manimala Saikia, *Mugar Itu-Xitu Kotha*, Jorhat: Sanskriti Prakashan, 2019, p. 25.
40 Ibid., p. 23.
41 Ibid.
42 The interview with Bipul Saharia was recorded on 29 December 2020.
43 Ibid.
44 Samudra Gupta Kashyap, 'When Looms Burned', *Indian Express*, 7 April 2013.
45 The interview with Naren Barman was recorded on 29 December 2020.
46 Tora Agarwala, 'How the Weavers of Sualkuchi Finally Earned Official Recognition for Their Products', *Indian Express*, 31 May 2018.
47 The interview with Punnu Mahajan was recorded at his house in Sualkuchi on 29 December 2020.
48 The interview with Haren das was recorded on 29 December 2020.
49 Ibid., p. 21.
50 Ibid., p. 20.
51 Ibid., p. 64.
52 The interview with Ajoy Doley was recorded in Majuli on 24 December 2020.
53 Ibid., p. 41.
54 Ibid., p. 80.
55 Ibid., p. 75.
56 Ibid., p. 83.
57 Ibid., p. 172.
58 Rajguru, *Medieval Assamese Society*, p. 172.
59 Ibid., p. 178.
60 Mazumdar, *Textile Tradition of Assam*, p. 29.
61 The interview with Lakhimi Baruah Bhuyan and her daughter Ananya Baruah was recorded at Zangphai in Guwahati on 29 December 2020.
62 F. C. Henniker, *The Gold and Silver Wares of Assam – A Monograph*, Assam Secretariat Printing Office, 1905, p. 6.
63 William Robinson, *Descriptive Account of Assam*, 1841, p. 35.
64 Henniker, *The Gold and Silver Wares of Assam*, p. 7.
65 Allen, Gait, Allen, and Howard, *The Gazetteer of Bengal and North East India*, p. 83.
66 P. Ramirez, 'The Lac in Assam and Meghalaya', 14 December 2009, Brahmaputra Studies Database, available at http://brahmaputra.ceh.vjf.cnrs.fr/bdd/spip.php?article68.
67 Henniker, *The Gold and Silver Wares of Assam*, p. 23
68 Ibid.
69 Saikia, *Axomiya Manuhor Itihaax*, p. 218.
70 Ibid., p. 219.
71 Thunu Saikia, 'Cosmetic Tradition, Hair-dos and Jewellery', *Costumes, Cosmetics and Ornaments of the Tiwa tribe of Assam*, Department of Folklore, Gauhati University, 2015.
72 Saikia, *Axomiya Manuhor Itihaax*, p. 216.
73 Saikia, 'Cosmetic Tradition, Hair-dos and Jewellery'.
74 Henniker, *The Gold and Silver Wares of Assam*, p. 35.

75 Saikia, *Axomiya Manuhor Itihaax*, p. 219.
76 Ibid., p. 218.
77 Rajguru, *Medieval Assamese Society*, p. 184.
78 Saikia, *Axomiya Manuhor Itihaax*, p. 218.
79 Ibid., p. 217.
80 Ibid., p. 218.
81 Henniker, *The Gold and Silver Wares of Assam*, p. 27.
82 Ibid., p. 23.
83 Choudhury, *The History of Civilisation of Assam*, p. 331.
84 Saikia, *Axomiya Manuhor Itihaax*, p. 219.
85 Rajguru, *Medieval Assamese Society*, p.184.
86 Choudhury, *The History of Civilisation of Assam*, p. 331.
87 Saikia, *Axomiya Manuhor Itihaax*, p. 219.
88 Ibid., p. 215.
89 Barua, *A Cultural History of Assam*, p. 146.
90 The interview with Rini Barman was conducted via email on 2 December 2020.
91 Saikia, *Axomiya Manuhor Itihaax*, p. 217.
92 Saikia, *Axomiya Manuhor Itihaax*, p. 12.
93 Ibid.
94 Kache Teronpi, 'A Living Tradition – A peek at the customary ornaments that Karbis wear', *Nezine*, 31 August 2015.
95 The interview with Naba Bordoloi took place at his residence in Sonarigaon, Jorhat on 25 November 2020.
96 Henniker, *The Gold and Silver Wares of Assam*, p. 6.
97 Ibid., p. 13.

CHAPTER 10: GADYA–PADYA–SUTIGOLPO: MODERN ASSAMESE LITERATURE

1 Nilakshi Phukan Borgohain, *Studies on Modern Assamese Writers – Homen Borgohain*, Guwahati: Purbanchal Prakash, 2016, p. 77.
2 Ibid., p. 75.
3 Anindita Kar, 'Homen Borgohain – the Workhorse of the Assamese Literary Scene', *The Hindu*, 28 May 2021.
4 Sangeeta Barooah Pisharoty, '"I Draw all my characters from the real world": How Homen Borgohain Dominates Assamese Life', *The Wire*, 21 October 2017.
5 Borgohain, *Studies on Modern Assamese Writers*, p. 19.
6 Ibid., p. 11.
7 The interview with Areendom Borkataki was recorded on 8 June 2021.
8 Bikash Dewri, 'Contribution of Ramdhenu magazine to Assamese literature', *Pal. Arch Journal*, 1 November 2020.
9 Mayur Bora, 'Kal Bolukat Roi Jabo Aru Bohukeita Khuj,' *Niyomia Barta*, Guwahati, 4 June.
10 Bhaben Barua, *The Assam Quarterly: Lakshminath Bezbaroa Birth-Centenary Issue*, Vol. 4, No. 4, 1969–70, p. 224.
11 Ibid.
12 Sailen Bharali, *Modern Indian Literature, an Anthology: Surveys and Poems*, Vol. 1, K. M. George (ed.), Sahitya Akademi, 1992, p. 66.
13 Ibid., p. 67.
14 Ibid., p. 66.
15 Ibid.
16 Ibid.
17 Dhurrjyoti Sarma, 'Syed Abdul Malik's readers have trapped his intellectual vision within his religious identity', *The Wire*, 14 May 2020.
18 Ibid.
19 Ibid.
20 Debendranath Acharya, *Jangam: A Forgotten Exodus in which Thousands Died*, tr. Amit R Baishya, New Delhi: Vitasta, 2018, back leaf.

21 Ibid., 'Preface'.
22 Ibid., p. 252.
23 *Chandradhar Barua Rachanavali*, Asam Sahitya Sabha, 1975, p. 577.
24 Sangeeta Barooah Pisharoty, *Assam: The Accord, the Discord*, Gurgaon: Penguin Random House, 2019, p. 242.
25 Saikia, *Background of Modern Assamese Literature*, pp. 14–15.
26 Ibid., p. 147.
27 Ibid., p. 147–48.
28 Ibid., p. 148.
29 Ibid.
30 Ibid., p. 163.
31 Ibid., p. 225.
32 Ibid., p. 188.
33 Pisharoty, *Assam: The Accord, The Discord*, p. 247.
34 Saikia, *Background of Modern Assamese Literature*, p. 193.
35 Ibid., p. 194.
36 Ibid.
37 Ibid., p. 283.
38 Ibid., p. 298.
39 Ibid., p. 291.
40 Ibid., p. 293.
41 Ibid., p. 301.
42 Bharali, *Modern Indian Literature*, p. 62.
43 Ibid., pp. 16–17.
44 Ibid., p. 17.
45 Ibid.
46 Ibid., p. 63.
47 Maheshwar Kalita, *Poetry of Navakanta Barua and Sitakant Mahapatra*, Bhabani Books, 2014, p. 23.
48 Ibid., p. 34.
49 Bharali, *Modern Indian Literature*, p. 65.
50 Ibid.
51 Ibid.
52 Prahlad Kumar Baruah, *Asamiya Suti Galpar Adhyan*, Guwahati: Banalata, 1995, p. 251.
53 Ibid.
54 Arup Kumar Dutta, 'Foreword', *Barcarolle And Other Stories*, tr. Jiban Goswami, Guwahati: Purbanchal Prakash, 2021.
55 Baruah, *Asamiya Suti Galpar Adhyan*, p. 258.
56 Ibid., p. 263.
57 Ananda Bormudoi, *Sahitya Samalochana Tatwar Somu Buranji*, Publication Board, Assam, 2008, p. 15.
58 Ibid.
59 Ibid.
60 Sangeeta Barooah Pisharoty, 'There Is a Conspiracy to show Bengal-origin Muslims as anti-Assamese: Hafiz Ahmed', *The Wire*, 23 July 2019.
61 Pori Hiloidhari (ed.), *Female Author-ity*, Guwahati: Papyrus, 2021, p. 12.
62 Nandana Dutta (ed.), *Communities of Women in Assam*, New Delhi: Routledge, 2016, p. 23.
63 Ibid., p. 21.
64 Ibid.
65 'Arupa Kalita Patangia: In Conversation with Aruni Kashyap', *Muse India*, Issue 20, July–August 2008.
66 Hiloidhari (ed.), *Female Author-ity*, p. 54.
67 Ibid., p. 77.
68 The interview with Ratna Bharali Talukdar was recorded on 5 June 2021.
69 Sangeeta Barooah Pisharoty, 'The Art of Being', *The Hindu*, 14 August 2013.

70 Hiren Gohain's blurb on the back of Moushumi Kandali's short collection of stories *Tritiottor Galpa*, Guwahati: Lawyers' Book Stall, 2007.

CHAPTER 11: XUR–TAAL, NAAS–GAAN: ASSAMESE MUSIC AND DANCE

1 Syed Abdul Malik and S. M. Hussain, *Asomiya Jikir-jari Saar*, Guwahati: Jyoti Prakashan, pp. 147–48.
2 Neog, *Cultural Heritage of Assam*, p. 196.
3 Ibid., p. 163.
4 Ibid., p. 164.
5 Ibid., p. 164.
6 Ibid.
7 Ibid., p. 165.
8 Ibid., p. 166.
9 Dwijendra Nath Bhakat, *Sri Sri Sankardev-Madhabdev Birosito Borgeet*, Guwahati: Chandra Prakash, 1992, p. 59. Bhakat served as a lecturer in Chiralai College in Dhubri district.
10 Ibid., p. 68.
11 Neog, *Cultural Heritage of Assam*, p. 169.
12 Ibid., p. 327.
13 Ibid., p. 188.
14 Ibid., p. 173.
15 Anjana Rajan, 'Should Borgeet be recognised as a classical art form?', *The Hindu*, 4 July 2019.
16 Neog, *Cultural Heritage of Assam*, p. 176.
17 Ibid., p. 177.
18 Ibid.
19 Ibid.
20 Ibid.
21 Ibid.
22 Ibid.
23 Ibid.
24 Samsuddin Ahmed, *Mur Monot Bhed Bhab Nai*, Guwahati: R. R. Graphics, 2020, p. 19.
25 Ibid., p. 31. The translation of these sentences, like all Assamese quotes across the chapters, have been translated by the author of this book.
26 Ibid.
27 Ibid.
28 Ibid., p. 41.
29 Ibid.
30 Maheswar Neog, *Asamiya Sahityar Ruprekha*, Guwahati: Chandra Prakashan, p. 29.
31 Tapati B. Kashyap, 'On a musical journey', Deccan Herald, 18 December 2010.
32 Hemango Biswas, *Lokasangeet Sameeksha*, Nalbari: Journal Emporium, 1990, p. 1.
33 IPTA played a stellar role in promoting cultural awakening among common people in India since 1943 through the early days of Independence.
34 Biswas, *Lokasangeet Sameeksha*, p. 1.
35 Biswas, *Lokasangeet Sameeksha*, p. 4.
36 Ibid., p. 5.
37 Sangeeta Barooah Pisharoty, 'Folk artiste Prasanna Gogoi on his relationship with Bihu dance', *The Wire*, 27 August 2017.
38 'Parvati Prasad Baruva – an iconic voice of Assam', *Ok! Northeast*, September 2019.
39 Shekhar Jyoti Bhuyan, Flashback, February 1981, from the news clipping collection of Umananda Dowerah of Moranhat.
40 Ibid.
41 Gaurav Goswami, 'A song of our own: Jyotiprasad, music and Assamese national identity', *Sahapedia*, 16 April 2020.
42 Debabrat Sarma, 'Asomiya Jatigathan Prokriya Aru Jatio Janagusthigata Anusthansamuh', Jorhat: Ekalavya Prakashan, 2006, p. 336.
43 Udayon Misra, *The Oxford Anthology of Writings from North-east India: Poetry and Essays*, New Delhi: Oxford University Press, 2010, pp. 146–185.

44 Prachee Dewri, 'Bishnuprasad Rava and the Rural in Assam: Inspiration and Intervention Through Music', *Journal Review of Agrarian Studies*, Vol. 9 (1), pp. 76–98, January 2019.
45 Ibid.
46 Goswami, 'A song of our own'.
47 Samiran Kalita, *Aamar Bhupen Hazarika*, Guwahati: Student Stores, 2012, p. 14.
48 Dewri, 'Bishnuprasad Rava and the Rural in Assam'.
49 Ibid.
50 Ibid.
51 Surya Hazarika, *Dr. Bhupen Hazarikar Bhashan Samagra*, Guwahati: Bani Mandir, 2011, p. 148.
52 Ibid.
53 Ismail Hussain, *Jytoiprasad Agarwalar Jibon Aru Darshan*, Guwahati: Jyoti Prakashan, 2001, p. 44.
54 Hazarika, *Dr. Bhupen Hazarikar Bhashan Samagra*, p. 148. Like quotes plucked out of all books written in Assamese cited throughout this book, this quote is also translated into English by the author.
55 Hussain, *Jytoiprasad Agarwalar Jibon Aru Darshan*, p. 47.
56 Ibid., p. 46.
57 Kalita, *Aamar Bhupen Hazarika*, p. 139.
58 Ibid., pp. 138–39.
59 'A discussion in Assamese on literature and universalism in Bhupen Hazarika's songs', *Nezine*, 27 July 2020.
60 Ibid.
61 Dr. Sankar Patowary, *Bhupendra Sinta Aru Ananya*, Dhemaji: Kiran Prakashan, 2015, p. 27.
62 Kamal Kakati and Devajit Bhuyan, *Bhupenda: Bard of the Brahmaputra*, Guwahati: Spectrum Publications, 2012, p. 137.
63 Hazarika, *Dr. Bhupen Hazarikar Bhashan Samagra*, p. 148.
64 Dr. Sankar Patowary in 'A discussion in Assamese on literature and universalism in Bhupen Hazarika's songs'.
65 Shamik Bag, 'Banga Bibhushan award celebrates Lata Mangeshkar's glorious links with Bengal', *Mint*, 21 September 2016.
66 Sangeeta Barooah Pisharoty, 'How Lata Mangeshkar Helped Strengthen the Assamese Playback Singing Industry', *The Wire*, 6 February 2022.
67 Ibid.
68 'Revival of a Glorious Tradition', *The Hindu*, 4 August 2016.
69 Maheswar Neog, *Aesthetic Continuum: Essays on Assamese Music, Drama, Dance and Paintings*, New Delhi: Omsons Publications, 2008, p. 312.
70 Ibid., p. 313.
71 Ibid.
72 Ibid., p. 312.
73 Ibid., p. 314.
74 Ibid., p. 313.
75 Naren Kalita (ed.), *Hengul Haital*, Kolong Kala Kendra, Puranigudam, p. 144.
76 Ibid., p. 146.
77 Ibid., p. 145.
78 'Revival of a glorious tradition'.
79 Neog, *Aesthetic Continuum*, pp. 312–13.
80 Ibid., p. 312.
81 Ibid., p. 314.
82 'Revival of a glorious tradition'.
83 Neog, *Aesthetic Continuum*, p. 317.
84 Nirmal Prabha Bordoloi, *Asomor Loka-Sanskriti*, Guwahati: Lawyers Book Stall, 1972, p. 137.
85 Neog, *Aesthetic Continuum*, p. 315.
86 Ibid.
87 Ibid.
88 Ibid., p. 318.
89 Ibid.

90 Ibid.
91 Ibid., p. 319.
92 Birendranath Dutta, *Cultural Contours of North-east India*, Delhi: Oxford University Press, 2012, p. 164.
93 Neog, *Aesthetic Continuum*, p. 320.
94 Anjana Rajan, 'Should Borgeet be recognised as a classical art form?', *The Hindu*, 4 July 2019.
95 Kalita (ed.), *Hengul Haital*, p. 147.
96 Ibid., p. 148.
97 Ibid., pp. 147–48.
98 Ibid., p. 149.
99 Ibid.
100 Neog, *Aesthetic Continuum*, p. 320.
101 Ibid., p. 331.
102 Ibid., p. 330.
103 Ibid.
104 Ibid., p. 331.
105 Ibid., p. 332.
106 Ibid.
107 Ibid.
108 Ibid., p. 333.
109 Ibid.
110 Ibid., p. 326.
111 Ibid., p. 327.
112 Ibid., p. 328.
113 Ibid., p. 329.
114 Indira P. P. Bora and Subhalakhsmi Boruah Khan were two of the first disciples from Assam of Bharatanatyam legend Rukmini Arunadale in Kalakshetra, Chennai.
115 Bordoloi, *Asomor Loka-Sanskriti*, p. 146.
116 Ibid., p. 149.
117 Ibid., p. 150.
118 Ibid., p. 152.
119 Ibid., p. 136.
120 Ibid., p. 153.
121 Paramananda Majumdar (ed.), *Ganasilpi Moghai Oja*, Nalbari: Samannay Granthalay, 1988, p. 10.
122 Bordoloi, *Asomor Loka-Sanskriti*, pp. 211–12.
123 Ibid., p. 215.

CHAPTER 12: NAAT–KOTHA–BULSOBI: ASSAMESE CINEMA AND DRAMA

1 Parthajit Baruah, *Jyotiprasad Joymoti Indramalati and Beyond: History of Assamese Cinema*, Krantikaal Prakashan, 2021, p. 282.
2 The interview with Pranjal Saikia was recorded on 31 March 2021.
3 Ibid., p. 281.
4 Anirban Kapil Baishya, 'Understanding Jyotiprasad Agarwala's Cinematic Vision', *Sahapedia*, 16 April 2020.
5 Baruah, *Jyotiprasad Joymoti Indramalati and Beyond*, p. 52.
6 Ibid., pp. 53–54.
7 Prafulla Prasad Bora, *Cinema in Assam*, Guwahati: Performing Arts Centre, 1978, p. 11.
8 Ismail Hussain, *Jyotiprasad Agarawalar Jibon aru Darshan*, Guwahati: Jyoti Prakashan, 2001, p. 66.
9 Baruah, *Jyotiprasad Joymoti Indramalati and Beyond*, p. 105.
10 Hussain, *Jyotiprasad Agarawalar Jibon aru Darshan*, p. 66.
11 Ibid.
12 Ibid., p. 68.
13 Hussain, *Jyotiprasad Agarawalar Jibon aru Darshan*, p. 68.
14 Asha Kuthari Chaudhuri, 'Rewriting Women – Revisiting Women's Narratives in Film: Adajya and Joymoti', *Margins: A Journal of Literature & Culture*, No. 4, pp. 100–115, 2014.

15 Ibid.
16 Ibid.
17 Baruah, *Jyotiprasad Joymoti Indramalati and Beyond*, p. 96.
18 Hussain, *Jyotiprasad Agarawalar Jibon aru Darshan*, p. 65.
19 Ibid., p. 70.
20 Ibid., p. 71.
21 Ibid.
22 Hussain, *Jyotiprasad Agarawalar Jibon aru Darshan*, p. 70.
23 Baruah, *Jyotiprasad Joymoti Indramalati and Beyond*, p. 120.
24 Ibid., p. 120.
25 Altaf Mazid, 'Filming the Egalitarianism – Notes for a film theory about Assamese Cinema', *Northeast Films*, available at northeastfilms.wordpress.com/category/film.
26 Ibid. The letters were taken from Geetasri Tamuly and Akhil Gogoi, *Uribo Parahole Akou Jujiluheten*, Banalata, 2002, p. 71.
27 Ibid.
28 Baruah, *Jyotiprasad Joymoti Indramalati and Beyond*, p. 282.
29 Ibid., p. 283.
30 Sangeeta Barooah Pisharoty, 'As a Humanist, I am not happy with what's happening in the country: Filmmaker Jahnu Barua', *The Wire*, 25 July 2020.
31 The interview with Utpal Borpujari was conducted on 7 March 2021.
32 'Discussion on Assamese Cinema in 21st century', *Nezine*, 7 December 2020.
33 The interview with Sanjeev Hazorika was conducted on 4 June 2021.
34 Baruah, *Jyotiprasad Joymoti Indramalati and Beyond*, p. 145.
35 Ibid., p. 148.
36 Bobbeeta Sharma, 'How Assamese Film Found Its Mojo', *Scroll.in*, 30 August 2014.
37 Baruah, *Jyotiprasad Joymoti Indramalati and Beyond*, p. 281.
38 Sharma, 'How Assamese Film Found Its Mojo'.
39 Ibid.
40 Baruah, *Jyotiprasad Joymoti Indramalati and Beyond*, p. 156.
41 Ibid.
42 Neog, *Aesthetic Continuum*, p. 154.
43 Ibid.
44 Utpal Borpujari, 'Cinema of the Northeast: From Joymoti to Era Bator Sur, 13 must-watch films from the region', *Firstpost*, 15 October 2017.
45 Baruah, *Jyotiprasad Joymoti Indramalati and Beyond*, p. 159.
46 Ibid.
47 Sharma, 'How Assamese Film Found Its Mojo'.
48 Ibid.
49 Baruah, *Jyotiprasad Joymoti Indramalati and Beyond*, p. 283.
50 Sharma, 'How Assamese Film Found Its Mojo'.
51 Ibid.
52 Ibid.
53 Baruah, *Jyotiprasad Joymoti Indramalati and Beyond*, p. 283.
54 Sangeeta Barooah Pisharoty, 'Reinterpreting folk tales', *The Tribune*, 11 December 2015.
55 Ibid.
56 The interview with Utpal Borpujari was conducted on 7 March 2021.
57 'Discussion on Assamese Cinema in 21st century', *Nezine*, 7 December 2020.
58 Ibid.
59 Ibid.
60 Sharma, 'How Assamese Film Found Its Mojo'.
61 'NFAI restores 9th Assamese film Runumi', *Assam Times*, 8 January 2013.
62 The interview with Bhagirathi Bai Kadam and Baharul Islam was conducted in Guwahati on 30 March 2021.
63 The interview with Sitanath Lahkar was conducted on 1 June 2021.
64 The interview with D'com Bhuyan was conducted on 12 April 2021.

65 'Moinul Haque: The pioneer of mime in Northeast India who turns silence into a powerful mode of communication', *Nezine*, 5 June 2020.
66 Jayanta Kumar Sarma and Kishore Kumar Kalita, *Theatre on Wheels – A Brief History of Mobile Theatre in Assam*, Guwahati: Blue Sparrow Books, 2020, p. 60.
67 Ibid.
68 Lakhyadhar Choudhury, *Ei Jibon Aparajeo – Dhiru Bhuyanr Smaraniyo Kisu Kotha*, Guwahati:s Pragati Silpi Sangha, 1999, p. 2.
69 Sarma and Kalita, *Theatre on Wheels*, p. 60.
70 Ibid., p. 61.
71 Ibid., p. 60.
72 Pranati Sharma Goswami, *Female Characters in Modern Assamese Drama*, Delhi: B R Publishing Corporation, 2004, p. 54.
73 Ibid., p. 55.
74 Ibid., p. 56.
75 Ibid., p. 48.
76 Ibid., p. 49.
77 Ibid., p. 48.
78 Ibid., p. 51.
79 Ibid., p. 52.
80 Sarma and Kalita, *Theatre on Wheels*, p. 62.
81 Goswami, *Female Characters in Modern Assamese Drama*, p. 100.
82 Ibid., p. 118.
83 Sarma and Kalita, *Theatre on Wheels*, p. 63.
84 Ibid.
85 Goswami, *Female Characters in Modern Assamese Drama*, p. 124.
86 Ibid., pp. 126–27.
87 Sarma and Kalita, *Theatre on Wheels*, p. 72.
88 Ibid., p. 61.
89 Ibid., p. 73.
90 Utpal Dutta and Nayan Prasad (eds.), *Pratyay Aru Annexon – Dulal Royor Sadhonar Sobi*, Publisher Santisaya Roy, 2016, p. 193.
91 Ibid., p. 82.
92 Ibid., p. 76.
93 Sarma and Kalita, *Theatre on Wheels*, p. 91.
94 Ibid., pp. 92–93.
95 Ibid., p. 94.
96 Ibid.
97 Ibid.
98 Ibid., p. 91.
99 Ibid., p. 214.
100 Ibid., p. 215.
101 Hiren Gohain, 'Positions on Assam History', *Economic and Political Weekly*, Vol. 45, No. 8, pp. 37–42, 2010.
102 Sarma and Kalita, *Theatre on Wheels*, pp. 49–50.
103 Ibid., p. 50.
104 Neog, *Aesthetic Continuum*, p. 122.
105 Ibid., p. 164.
106 Ibid., p. 122.
107 Ibid., p. 208.
108 Ibid., p. 211–13.
109 Ibid., p. 212.
110 Ibid., p. 213.
111 Harichandra Bhattacharyya, *Origin and Development of the Assamese Drama and the Stage (From the Earliest Times up to 1940)*, Guwahati: Barua Agency, 1964, p. 51.
112 Ibid., p. 123.

113 Neog, *Aesthetic Continuum*, p. 124.
114 Ibid., p. 125.
115 Ibid., p. 113.
116 Ibid., p. 136.
117 Sangeeta Barooah Pisharoty, 'Under The Sal Tree, a unique theatre festival that unites the villages of Assam', *The Wire*, 10 January 2017.
118 Ibid.
119 Ibid.

CHAPTER 13: SANCHIPAAT–TULAPAAT, CHITRAKALA–BHASKARJYA: ASSAMESE VISUAL ART

1 The interview with Chittaranjan Bora was recorded at the Kolong Kala Kendra on 7 March 2021.
2 Kalita (ed.), *Hengul Haital*, p. 75.
3 Ibid., p. 275.
4 Ibid., p. 337.
5 S. K. Bhuyan, *Note on Assamese Manuscripts in Hemchandra Goswami's Descriptive Catalogue of Assamese Manuscripts,* University of Calcutta, 1930.
6 'Discussion in Assamese on illustrated manuscripts of Assam', *Nezine*, 10 August 2020.
7 Neog, *Cultural Heritage of Assam*, p. 1.
8 Ibid., p. 8.
9 Kalita, *Hengul Haital*, p. 21.
10 'Discussion in Assamese on illustrated manuscripts of Assam'.
11 Kalita (ed.), *Hengul Haital*, p. 48.
12 Ibid., p. 47.
13 Ibid.
14 Ibid., p. 49.
15 Ibid., p. 45.
16 Sushanta Talukdar, 'A Treasure Trove from Assam', *The Frontline*, 20 July 2005.
17 Bhuyan, 'Note on Assamese Manuscripts in Hemchandra Goswami's Descriptive Catalogue of Assamese Manuscripts', p. XIII.
18 Neog, *Cultural Heritage of Assam*, p. 9.
19 Kalita (ed.), *Hengul Haital*, p. 21.
20 Ibid., p. 38.
21 Ibid.
22 Neog, *Cultural Heritage of Assam*, p. 8.
23 Ibid., pp. 8–9.
24 Kalita (ed.), *Hengul Haital*, p. 46.
25 Talukdar, 'A Treasure Trove from Assam'.
26 Goswami, *Descriptive Catalogue of Assamese Manuscripts*, p. 4.
27 Kalita (ed.), *Hengul Haital*, p. 44.
28 Ibid., p. 33.
29 Ibid., p. 34.
30 Ibid.
31 Ibid.
32 Neog, *Cultural Heritage of Assam*, p. 10.
33 Ibid.
34 Ibid., p. 11.
35 The interview with Ashok Sarma was recorded on 24 May 2021.
36 Moushumi Kandali's note on Neelapawan Baruah at the Museum of Modern Art of Neelapawan Baruah, Tezpur University, Assam.
37 Bistirna Barua, 'When a brush holds a voice', *The Thumbprint*, 10 April 2015.
38 Moushumi Kandali's note on Neelapawan Baruah at the Museum of Modern Art of Neelapawan Baruah, Tezpur University, Assam.

39 Rupanjali Baruah, 'Blue wind of the soul', available at www.wordsmithpublishers.com.
40 The interview with Noni Borpujari was recorded in Guwahati on 27 December 2020.
41 Moushumi Kandali, *Asomor Adhunik Silpa-Kala*, Gujarat: Black and White, 2011, p. 7.
42 Moushumi Kandali, 'The Early Moderns', *Nezine*, 8 July 2015.
43 Smita Bhattacharyya, 'Lakhi Ram Boruah: Shedding light on an unknown Assam artiste', *Northeast Now*, 26 June 2019.
44 Kandali, *Asomor Adhunik Silpa-Kala*, p. 6.
45 Kandali, 'The Early Moderns'.
46 Kandali, *Asomor Adhunik Silpa-Kala*, p. 7.
47 Kandali, 'The Early Moderns'.
48 Ibid.
49 Ibid.
50 Kandali, *Asomor Adhunik Silpa-Kala*, p. 12.
51 Kandali, 'The Early Moderns'.
52 Kalita (ed.), *Hengul Haital*, p. 198.
53 Kandali, *Asomor Adhunik Silpa-Kala*, p. 106.
54 Ibid., p. 107.
55 Ibid.
56 Ibid., p. 108.
57 Ibid., p. 101.
58 Ibid.
59 Available at https://hemantamisra.com/downloads/7th.pdf.
60 Kandali, *Asomor Adhunik Silpa-Kala*, p. 100.
61 Avialable at https://hemantamisra.com/downloads/7th.pdf.
62 Kalita (ed.), *Hengul Haital*, p. 198.
63 Kandali, *Asomor Adhunik Silpa-Kala*, p. 110.
64 Ibid.
65 Ibid., p. 114.
66 Ibid., p. 117.
67 Ibid., p. 128.
68 Tausif Amin Noor, 'The Legacy of the Progressive Artists Group', *Sothebys*, 7 June 2019.
69 Kandali, *Asomor Adhunik Silpa-Kala*, p. 128.
70 Ibid., p. 136.
71 Ibid., p. 137.
72 Ibid., p. 140.
73 Ibid.
74 Chandan Goswami (ed.), *Noni Borpujari*, Saraighat Offset Press, 2019, p. 21.
75 Ibid., p. 202.
76 Ibid., p. 120.
77 Kandali, *Asomor Adhunik Silpa-Kala*, p. 58.
78 Ibid.
79 Ibid.
80 Ibid., p. 131.
81 Ibid., p. 61
82 Ibid., pp. 67–70.

CHAPTER 14: JATIOTABADI–RAJNITI: ASSAMESE POLITICS

1 Udayon Misra, *India's North East, Identity Movements, State, and Civil Society*, Delhi: Oxford University Press, 2014, pp. 163–64.
2 Ibid., p. 165.
3 Ibid.
4 Ibid., p. 166.
5 Ibid. Translation by Udayon Misra.
6 Sangeeta Barooah Pisharoty, *Assam: The Accord, The Discord*, Gurgaon: Penguin Random House, p. 137.

7 K. Anurag, 'Ulfa rules out unconditional talks with Centre', *Rediff*, 7 August 2008.

8 Jaideep Saikia, 'What Centre should do to re-engage dialogue with ULFA', *The Federal*, 3 March 2022.

9 Mrinal Talukdar, Utpal Borpujari, and Kaushik Deka, *Secret Killings of Assam*, Guwahati: Bhabani Books, 2008, p. 4.

10 Pisharoty, *Assam*, p. 90.

11 Ibid., pp. 25–26.

12 Sangeeta Barooah Pisharoty, 'How the BJP set the agenda for its ambitious "Look Northeast" policy', *The Wire*, 31 December 2016.

13 PTI, 'Modi threatens to deport Bangladeshis after May 14', *India Today*, 29 April 2014.

14 Shoaib Daniyal, 'Why the Assam BJP is now against the NRC: Explaining the politics behind the exercise', *Scroll.in*, 1 September 2019.

15 The English translation of this poem is courtesy *The Telegraph*. Arunabh Saikia, 'The Art of Resistance: "Asomiya Dekar Ukti" by Kyoti Prasad Agarwala is about Assam Then and Now', *Scroll.in*, 1 January 2020.

INDEX